MARGARET THATCHER

Margaret Thatcher

Power and Personality

Jonathan Aitken

BLOOMSBURY

NEW YORK · LONDON · NEW DELHI · SYDNEY

Published by Bloomsbury USA, New York

All papers used by Bloomsbury USA are natural, recyclable products made from wood grown in well-managed forests. The manufacturing processes conform to the environmental regulations of the country of origin.

LIBRARY OF CONGRESS CATALOGING-IN-PUBLICATION DATA HAS BEEN APPLIED FOR

ISBN: 978-1-62040-342-6

First U.S. Edition 2013

1 3 5 7 9 10 8 6 4 2

Typeset by Graphicraft Limited, Hong Kong
Printed and bound in the U.S.A. by Thomson-Shore Inc., Dexter, Michigan

To Elizabeth

Contents

List of illustrations

Acknowledgements

I gratefully acknowledge all those who have helped me in the research, preparation and production of this biography of Margaret Thatcher.

There are two treasure troves of Thatcher papers to which I owe an immeasurable debt of gratitude. One is the Thatcher Archive at Churchill College, University of Cambridge. I particularly thank Dr Allen Packwood the director of the Churchill Archives Centre and the Thatcher Archivist Andrew Riley. The other and closely linked main source of papers is the Margaret Thatcher Foundation and its website. Its editor Christopher Collins and its head Julian Seymour deserve the highest praise for their vision and their industry in making such huge resources of historical material on Margaret Thatcher so easily available to scholars, students, historians and biographers.

I have trawled through several other collections of source material and would like to thank the staff of the British Library, the British Library Newspapers, the Churchill Archives Centre, the Templeman Library at the Univeristy of Kent, the Boris Johnson newspaper cuttings archive and the Hans Tasiemka Archives.

The old agricultural saying 'There's no manure like the farmer's foot' applies to political biography. So I am immensely grateful to the many helpful guides and welcomers who showed me around places and institutions which were part of Margaret Thatcher's life story.

At Grantham I would like to thank Michael and Diana Honeybone, former teacher at KGGS, who escorted me around the locations in the town, the schools and the churches which the young Margaret and the Roberts family attended. In particular I am grateful to local historian Malcolm G. Knapp and Denys Lambley of the Finkin Street Methodist Church. My thanks also go to Ian Todd, Assistant Head Teacher of Kesteven and Grantham Girls' School, Mrs Janet Thompson, the Archivist, and Diane Barrett, Office Manager at the school; also to Mark Anderson, Head Teacher of Huntingtower Community Primary

Academy, Grantham, and Margaret Lockwood, Office Manager. Sandra Good, the proprietor of Living Health on North Parade, kindly showed me around what used to be Roberts Food Stores on the ground floor and the flat above where the family lived, including the room where Margaret Thatcher was born.

At the University of Oxford I appreciated visiting Margaret Thatcher's old room at Somerville and touring the college with the distinguished historian Dr Franklyn Prochaska, husband of the Principal Dr Alice Prochaska.

At the Royal Hospital Chelsea I was most grateful to be shown around and briefed by the Lieutenant Governor, Major General Peter Currie, and the Chaplain the Revd Dick Whittington.

The most enjoyable sources were the living witnesses to Margaret Thatcher's career in public life, some ninety of whom gave me interviews. Their names are listed, with gratitude, at the end of the book.

Lastly, I must thank the many previous authors who have written books on Margaret Thatcher. Most biographers assimilate fragments, large or small, from their predecessors' writings. I am no exception to this practice and I would particularly like to thank the earliest Thatcher biographers, Patricia Murray, Ernle Money, George Gardiner, Russell Lewis and Penny Junor. I also much appreciated Hugo Young's portrait *One of Us*, the two-volume biography by John Campbell and the first volume of the official biography by Charles Moore published earlier this year.

Finally, the greatest thanks of all go to my own home team of researchers and secretarial helpers.

The chief researcher on my two-year biographer's journey was Jacqueline Williams, whose diligence and dedication in unearthing the raw material of history was magnificent. She was ably assisted by two talented interns from Oxford University, Mark Holmes and Tom Perrin, whose enthusiasm was infectious as we read through the first draft of the manuscript and made many changes. I am also grateful to my daughter Victoria Aitken for her encouragement and occasional research.

The brunt of the typing of the manuscript was borne by the excellent Prue Fox. She was supported by Helen Kirkpatrick and Rosemary Gooding, while the onerous task of scheduling interviews and collating the draft chapters was superbly executed by Susanna Jennens.

I would also like to thank everyone concerned with this book at my publishers Bloomsbury, particularly my editor, Robin Baird-Smith, and his assistant editor, Joel Simons.

The last but really the first helper, encourager and sharer of my workload has been my beloved wife Elizabeth. She walked every step of the road of my author's journey, and the book is lovingly dedicated to her.

Jonathan Aitken
July 2013

Prologue

After the applause comes the appraisal.

The applause created the most moving moment at Margaret Thatcher's funeral. As her coffin was carried out of St Paul's Cathedral on the shoulders of military pallbearers while the choir sang *Nunc Dimittis* to the hauntingly beautiful setting of Stanford in G, the first sight of her cortège by the crowds spontaneously produced a swelling wave of sound.

It was so unexpected that those of us still seated beneath the great dome of Christopher Wren's ecclesiastical masterpiece were startled. For days the London media had been predicting hostile protests. So at this fleeting instant I and many others in the congregation wondered whether we were hearing the ultimate anti-Thatcher demonstration.

Far from it. For it quickly became clear that the great roar rolling up from Ludgate Hill and other streets near St Paul's bore the unmistakable resonance of massive cheering.

What were those crowds cheering her for? Some were too young to have known the age of Thatcher. Many more were likely to have disagreed with the values and the policies she championed. But on the day of her obsequies the overwhelming majority seemed ready to salute her life's journey for its achievements, breakthroughs and for its footprints on the sands of time.

Applause is usually thought inappropriate at a funeral, but Margaret Thatcher broke so many conventions and ceilings in her life that the shattering of one more establishment custom in death seemed right. She would have enjoyed those cheers. Not only did they symbolise the affection of her fans; they also marked one last victory over her foes.

Because she was such a political polariser, it was anticipated that her adversaries from the militant left would turn out to give their old enemy a farewell booing. I encountered some of them on my walk towards St Paul's. These would-be troublemakers were hostile enough to give me and others attired in our tailcoats a few jeers. But a friendly apple-cheeked woman in the same part of the crowd had a different message. 'Don't you worry about them lot,' she said in her West Country burr. 'We'll drown them out.' And they did.

The subtleties that were important elements in the make-up of Margaret Thatcher were often drowned out. She herself concealed many of them. She could be politically cautious while preferring to sound proudly radical. She had an overdeveloped sense of privacy. Throughout her life she suppressed personal information, insecurities, emotions and inconvenient truths behind a façade of carefully projected self-certainty. She became the most famous woman in the world on account of her highly visible political directness. Yet on the less visible sides of her character she could be more difficult and complicated than most people guessed.

The paradoxes in Margaret Thatcher have long intrigued me. Ever since I first met her nearly fifty years ago, it was clear that her most important feature was the strength of her personality. This was the force that drove her forward, conquered the obstacles in her path, shaped her vision for Britain and won three successive general elections. Her successes in domestic and international politics never softened her argumentative nature or smoothed her sharp edges. She irritated many of her colleagues, infuriated most of her opponents and challenged the comfortable consensus of the status quo at every opportunity. She was much easier to admire from afar than to work with at close quarters. She could be personally kind to her staff but impersonally unpleasant towards those whose views or misfortunes lay outside her field of empathy. She was never an easy person.

Because of these and many other complexities, I hope that a biographical portrait of Margaret Thatcher that focuses on her personality may make a contribution to her historical appraisal. But it would amount to pointless psy-chobabble if the portrait was not grounded in the narrative of how she sought, won, wielded and lost power. For this was the context in which she lived her life.

As her journey progressed her personality changed. There was a metamor-phosis from Grantham to grandeur; from humility to hubris; from a realistic courageousness in fighting her corner to a reckless Ride of the Valkyries.

The Shakespearean nemesis of the coup against her was an agony, as were her outpourings of bitterness that followed it. The personality shifts that accompanied these dramas deserve interpretation, sometimes critically, some-times sympathetically.

In the latter category, it needs to be said that some of the grandeur and the hubris were not of her own making. It was twentieth-century history that cast her as a figure on the world stage. She became an icon of freedom to the peoples of Eastern Europe. Women across global and political boundaries admired her for breaking the highest barriers of male-dominated leadership. She liberated millions of her aspiring fellow countrymen in areas such as home ownership, class barriers and economic opportunity. She was ahead of her time, but right, in challenging the pressures from the UK's foreign-policy and financial estab-lishments towards joining the single currency and the Eurozone. She restored national pride and economic strength to Britain. These were such momentous achievements that she would have been inhuman not to have been tempted towards some feelings of vaulting self-aggrandisement.

The changes in her personality carried a price tag. It was paid in the currency of hurt feelings by those damaged in her personal and political battles. They included bullied colleagues, derided officials, ignored communities and neglected family members. Ultimately she herself joined the ranks of the wounded, for her ousting from power was calculated, craven and cruel. She never recovered her equilibrium after her fall.

I had a ringside seat at many private and public spectacles in the Margaret Thatcher saga. Before I met her she was a name to conjure with in our home. My father was present in the House of Commons to hear her maiden speech. He repeatedly told my mother how impressed he had been by the young Member for Finchley. After a conversation with her in the tea room three days later he was so taken with her intensity and beauty that he frequently compared her to the film star Virginia McKenna.*

When I first met Margaret Thatcher during the 1966 general election, she was the junior opposition spokesman for housing and land and I was the youngest Conservative parliamentary candidate in the country. She reminded me that she had been in the same position as candidate for Dartford in 1950. On that occasion and on some subsequent encounters when I was a candidate,† I did

---

*   See Chapter 6
†   See Chapter 7

not share my father's enthusiasm for her. The feeling was mutual. 'That young man needs his wings clipped,' I heard her say in a piercing voice at a Young Conservative conference we had both been addressing in 1972.

Entering the House of Commons in February 1974, I started out as a Ted Heath admirer, unsurprisingly since his home town of Broadstairs was in my constituency and I was a frequent guest at the home of his father. But Ted's weaknesses grew all too apparent at first-hand observation.* Also at first hand I witnessed the earliest stirrings of the Thatcher bandwagon in the form of Peter Morrison's manoeuvres with the upper-class splinter group called 'toffs for Thatcher'.† I also followed the more solid support she received from members of the Economic Dining Club and a group of Treasury Committee specialists headed by my friends Peter Rees and Norman Lamont. Amidst the extraordinary turbulence of the 1975 Tory leadership election I reckoned, after numerous conversations with players like Hugh Fraser, Airey Neave, Edward du Cann and Ted Heath himself, that I had a well-informed insider's view‡ of how Margaret Thatcher won the crown, even though I was not a cheering member of her coronation party.

Her opposition years were the most fragile period of her career. It was the time when I came to know her well. She was a warmer and more interesting character than I had expected. Although she was struggling in the House of Commons at the gladiatorial battles of Prime Minister's Questions (which she usually lost), she came across as a strong and attractive leader to many backbenchers and to the party in the country. I saw her interest in new ideas at meetings of the Conservative Philosophy Group# in my home, and in House of Commons discussions on Home Office policy after being made a junior front-bench spokesman on police matters.

At this same time I began to understand the private side of her personality because for three years I dated her daughter Carol. She was one of the great loves of my life, but I handled our romance badly. Nevertheless, while the relationship

---

* See Chapter 9
† See Chapter 10
‡ See Chapter 10
# See Chapter 11

was in full swing I caught many glimpses of a little-known Margaret Thatcher. She was hospitable, feminine, confiding, dysfunctional within her family, direct with her daughter's boyfriend and much more vulnerable than I had realised. One night I found her in tears in her Flood Street home because some back-bench critic had told her she was 'wrecking the party'. I told her to ignore it but she left the room in emotional distress saying: 'I hurt too, you know.'*

The 'winter of discontent' was the turning point for Margaret Thatcher as Leader of the Opposition and she seized her opportunities brilliantly. I think I was the second person (ironically the first was Jim Callaghan) to tell her, in Westminster Abbey after a memorial service, that her party political broadcast of 17 January 1979 had started a sea change in public opinion.†

Soon after Margaret Thatcher won the general election and became Prime Minister, my romance with Carol ended. 'You have brought great personal distress to the Queen's First Minister,' said her Parliamentary Private Secretary (PPS) Ian Gow. I understood his message. It was conveyed in other ways, not least in leaks to journalists. Although this was painful, I thought it was reasonable that I should have been sent to Siberia. What mother does not feel angry if she thinks her daughter's happiness has been destroyed by a young man? Margaret Thatcher's human instincts were entirely understandable.

Siberia was not outer darkness. I continued to stay in touch with the Prime Minister vicariously. Ian Gow was one of my best friends and late-night drinking companions. So was his successor as her PPS, Michael Alison (but with less drinking!). So were numerous senior and junior ministers and whips. The parliamentary club is a small one and a good vantage point for watching a new prime minister.

Like many others I grew into becoming a great admirer of Margaret Thatcher because of her courage. The Falklands War, the 1981 Budget and the victory over Arthur Scargill in the 1984 miners' strike were shining examples of this cardinal virtue. The stories of her personality during these epic battles soon filtered through from insiders of whom the most indiscreet was Willie Whitelaw and the most extraordinary David Hart.‡

---

* See Chapter 11
† See Chapter 12
‡ See Chapter 26

In addition to the wealth of material available in archives and collections of papers, I kept my own diaries and other records throughout my twenty-three years in Parliament alongside Margaret Thatcher. From these and from many contemporary sources I hope it has been possible to portray her with some fresh brush strokes on my biographer's canvas.

It has to be said that I occasionally saw her, and have painted parts of her personality, in unattractive colours. For example, I remember growing angry at her outrageous behaviour towards my friend Bernard 'Jack' Weatherill* before and after he became Speaker of the House of Commons. Her constant bullying of Geoffrey Howe[†] was worse. She could be nastily unpleasant to a minister or an official against whom she had formed an instant, and sometimes inexplicable, dislike. She was cruel in her constant disparagement of her chosen successor as Prime Minister, John Major.[‡] She had little empathy or sympathy for those members of society who were too different or too disadvantaged to appreciate her self-help philosophy.

On the other side of the coin her virtues far outweighed her occasional streaks of viciousness. Great men and women often have their Achilles heels. Margaret Thatcher's failures of behaviour were painful to those on the receiving end of them. But on the big picture of politics it was the strength of her personality that made it possible to achieve what was thought almost impossible.

While her second and third terms as Prime Minister continued, I was no longer exiled to Siberia. As a back-bencher I saw her quite often, occasionally in one-to-one conversations whose subjects ranged from problems with an RAF base in my constituency, to the obduracy of the Kent miners,[#] to conversations about the King of Saudi Arabia and former US President Richard Nixon.** At one point she sent me a message through her PPS Michael Alison saying that I would not have to wait long before being brought into the government. This never happened, not I think because of lingering feelings about Carol but because I came to be regarded by the whips as an intolerable nuisance over Europe.

---

* See Chapter 23
[†] See Chapter 33
[‡] See Chapter 38
[#] See Chapter 26
** See Chapters 25, 27, 29 and 37

This was ironic because the Prime Minister was becoming far from un-sympathetic to the rebellions against European legislation organised by the Conservative European Reform Group (CERG)* of which I was chairman. Indeed, when she got into trouble over her own galloping Euroscepticism it was CERG's supporters in the House of Commons who became her most vociferous backers.

The fall of Margaret Thatcher had three ingredients. Her personality went off the rails because of an excess of hubris and a want of listening. Her party went off the rails because of a surfeit of fear and a shortage of loyalty. A pincer movement of two plotters and the collapse of her support in cabinet dealt her the killer blows.

Watching this tragedy unfold was the saddest spectacle I ever witnessed in politics. My blood still boils when I watch, in television replays, my grimaces of anger immediately behind Geoffrey Howe as he delivered his resignation statement in which I was 'doughnutted' by the cameras.[†]

In the parliamentary arena spectators are often participants, never more so than in the public execution of Margaret Thatcher. I have made no attempt to tell this part of the story even-handedly. For all their good years of service to the state, Geoffrey Howe and Michael Heseltine will always to me be the villains of the piece for the parts they played in the downfall of a prime minister whose term of office should only have been ended by the votes of the electorate.

My angles of observation on Margaret Thatcher grew closer again during her unhappy years of enforced retirement and decline. In the immediate aftermath of her overthrow her agony was unbearable. I often saw this and felt for her at close quarters.

Although the pain dulled, it always troubled her. My penultimate chapters 'The agony after the fall' and 'Snapshots of her retirement years' are full of poignant glimpses of the wounded lioness caged into inactivity.

In spite of having had some unique insights on Margaret Thatcher, it will be clear from my narrative that politically I was an unimportant spear carrier on her back benches – although I hope an observant one. Many of my Westminster and Whitehall friends were much closer and more important figures in her

---

* See Chapters 32 and 36
[†] See Chapter 36

world. Over ninety of them have been generous with the time they gave me in their interviews for this book. So have many other witnesses to her years in power including some who have never talked about her to an author before. Heading this latter category I am particularly grateful to Mikhail Gorbachev for giving me his first ever account of his Chequers talks with Margaret Thatcher in 1984.*

Although this book covers virtually all the important milestones and episodes in Margaret Thatcher's career, I end this prologue with two caveats.

First, I have written a biographical portrait rather than a definitive biography. I tell her story, but with the freedom to capture its light and shade with reflective criticisms at the end of every chapter.

Finally, I should say that at the end of my biographer's journey, even more so than when I started it, I admired Margaret Thatcher enormously.

This is a portrait that attempts to combine both the applause and the appraisal.

---

* See Chapter 28

1

The early years

THE BIRTHPLACE

In the beginning was the discipline: one of six characteristics ingrained in the life of Margaret Roberts the child that shaped the career of Margaret Thatcher the Prime Minister. The other five were a mixture of positives and negatives.

In the first category came her determination of character, forthrightness of expression and certainty of belief. The two negatives were less visible because she tried to cover them up. They were her personal insecurity and her lack of empathy towards those, particularly her mother, with whom she had sharp disagreements.

If this looks a strange and narrow list, lacking in the more natural features of childhood such as enjoyment, laughter, relaxation, family tactility and parental love, it is because Margaret's upbringing was an unnaturally restricted one, shaped by straitened circumstances and strait-laced parents.

She was born on 13 October 1925, in an upstairs room above her father's corner shop at No. 1 North Parade, Grantham in Lincolnshire. From the outside it looked a substantial three-storey building but the living accommodation was cramped and the facilities basic.

The shop took up most of the property. The family sitting room was on the first floor, and could only be accessed by a staircase behind the counter, which led to it through the main bedroom. Margaret and her older sister, Muriel, born 24 May 1921, each had their own small room at the top of the house. There was no running water or central heating. The most awkward missing amenity was the lack of a bathroom. The family took their baths in an unplumbed iron tub. It was in the same ground-floor room as the outside lavatory, located across the backyard of the shop. There was no garden or indoor toilet.

Even by the standards of the 1920s, the house in which Margaret grew up was Spartan. Yet the austerity was not caused by poverty. Her father, Alfred Roberts, owned two grocery stores in Grantham, and could easily have afforded to install what estate agents of the time called, 'modern conveniences'. But for reasons of principle, he decided that his family should live frugally. He believed in saving, not spending, money. He told his daughter that he had kept this rule ever since his first job as a shop assistant. In those days, he earned fourteen shillings a week, of which twelve shillings paid for his board and lodging. After that, 'For every one shilling saved there was one shilling to spend'.[1] Her father's financial priorities resulted in the purse strings being held so tight that he would not even pay for running water in the family home.

'Alderman Roberts would become prosperous because he wouldn't worry about things like plumbing,' explained Marjorie Lee, one of Margaret's classmates.[2]

Margaret herself did worry about them. In a revealing interview given after she had been Prime Minister for six years, she told Miriam Stoppard: 'Home was really very small, and we had no mod cons, and I remember having a dream that the one thing I really wanted was to live in a nice house, you know, a house with more things than we had.'[3]

Uncertainty was another cause of Alfred Roberts' reluctance to find the money for basic home improvements. 'Grantham people were having a hard time in Margaret's childhood,' recalled her contemporary Malcolm Knapp, a local historian still living in the town. 'We had 40 per cent unemployment here in 1930 and soup kitchens, visited by the Duke of Kent, no less, in 1933. Mr Roberts must often have worried whether his customers had the money in their pockets to pay for their groceries.'[4]

The austerity of the Depression years required a regime of relentless hard work for the family living above the shop.

'You are always on duty,'[5] recalled Margaret in a phrase that applies to politicians as well as shopkeepers. For even though Alfred Roberts employed three assistants at his two grocery stores, it was still very much a family business. He was the hands-on proprietor, usually behind the counter operating the bacon slicer. His wife and mother-in-law served the customers. His daughters were also expected to help out, particularly in the school holidays. Margaret's earliest memories included weighing the sugar, which had been delivered in large wholesale sacks, into 1lb and 2lb bags.

When she was Prime Minister, Margaret Thatcher liked to describe her father as 'a specialist grocer'.[6] The words were a gilding of the lily, perhaps derived from the same heightened filial pride that led Ted Heath to call his father 'a master builder'.[7]

In fact both Prime Ministerial patriarchs were ordinary tradesmen. The Roberts' store on North Parade was a basic corner shop selling sweets, cigarettes, bread, pet food, fruit and vegetables. It was also a sub-post office where local residents bought their stamps, collected their pensions and cashed their postal orders. Although Alfred Roberts had a reputation for stocking quality produce that was superior to its nearby rival, the Co-op, his establishment was a general store of a type that was commonplace across small-town provincial England in the 1930s. The tight budgets of its customers were typical too. But the characters of the family who ran the shop and moulded Margaret's upbringing were far from typical.

FAMILY TENSIONS

Alfred Roberts was a shopkeeper, a lay preacher and a local politician. He had hidden depths of faith and wide reading. His greatest achievement was that he groomed his youngest daughter Margaret for stardom on a stage far greater than Grantham – even though he had no clear idea where that stage might be.

Born in 1892, Alfred was a handsome young man, 6 feet 2 inches tall, with a strong head of blond hair and piercing blue eyes. His weakness was that he was seriously short sighted, a problem that caused him to wear bi-focal spectacles from his early years.

When he volunteered for military service on the outbreak of war in 1914, he was rejected on grounds of defective eyesight. He made five further attempts to join the army. One of them succeeded but only for two days. After 48 hours in uniform in Lincoln barracks he was invalided out following an eye test. For the same reason he failed his medical each time he tried to enlist.[8]

Frustrated in his attempts to join the colours, Alfred did not follow his Northamptonshire father into shoemaking, but learned the retail trade at various establishments including the Oundle School tuck shop. At the age of twenty-one he was appointed assistant manager of Cliffords' grocery store in Grantham. He was an omnivorous borrower of books from the town library. Its librarian was so impressed by Alfred's thirst for knowledge that he described him as 'the best-read man in Grantham'.[9]

In May 1917, Alfred married Beatrice Ethel Stephenson, who he met at the Methodist church. Four years older than her bridegroom, she was Grantham born and bred; the daughter of a cloakroom attendant at the railway station and a factory worker. Photographs of her as a young woman make it easy to understand why Alfred felt attracted. For Beatie (as he called her) was something of a beauty. She had high cheekbones, shining dark hair tied back in a bun, sparkling blue eyes, sensual lips and a curvaceous if slightly overweight figure. The firmness of her features hint at firmness in her character.

Some Grantham contemporaries say that Beatie was far stronger than Alfred when it came to imposing parental discipline on the girls. A close friend of Muriel Roberts was Betty Morley who from her visits to the shop during their school-days remembers Beatrice as 'especially severe . . . she was not much fun at all'.[10]

Beatie's severity as a mother was complemented by her practicality as a homemaker. She was house proud, almost obsessive about cleaning and tidiness. She had run a small dressmaking business before becoming engaged to Alfred. She was an accomplished seamstress, who made all her daughters' clothes, including their school uniforms. She was also a good cook and a thrifty saver.

By 1919 the couple had saved enough money with the help of a mortgage to buy the shop at No. 1 North Parade. In the bedroom above the shop Muriel was born in 1921 and Margaret in 1925.

Margaret's arrival in the world was marked by a notice in the births, marriages and deaths column of the *Grantham Journal*.[11] No such announcement accompanied the birth of Muriel – perhaps a subtle indication that the status of the Roberts family had risen during the four years separating the two daughters.

From an early age it was clear that Margaret was much closer to her father than to her mother. On the maternal side there are indications that the younger daughter had many battles with Beatie. 'I used to feel, just occasionally, that she rather despised her mother and adored her father,' recalled Margaret Goodrich, a schoolgirl contemporary of the future Prime Minister.[12] This negative impression was reinforced by Muriel in a comment she made to her sister's official biographer, Charles Moore: 'Mother didn't exist in Margaret's mind.'[13]

The daughter–mother *froideur* seems to have prevailed long after Margaret left Grantham for Oxford, marriage and politics. In a number of interviews during her public career Mrs Thatcher seems to have had difficulty in finding the words or the tone to say anything favourable about Beatie aside from praising her domestic skills. 'She was very much the Martha* rather than the Mary' was one revealing filial description.[14] Another came in 1961, eighteen years before becoming Prime Minister when, as a new Member of Parliament, Mrs Thatcher was asked about her mother by Godfrey Winn of the *Daily Express*. She answered, 'I loved my mother dearly, but after I was 15 we had nothing more to say to each other. It wasn't her fault. She was weighed down by the home, always being in the home'.[15]

The implication from such comments is that Margaret did not think much of her mother. However, there are suggestions that the real trouble was not indifference but a clash of temperaments between these two strong-willed women. Beatie was not a submissive housewife confined to her cooking and her dressmaking. Some Grantham contemporaries refer to her as 'a right old battleaxe' who clearly had a mind and a voice of her own.[16] It would hardly be surprising that disagreements took place between such a mother and her opinionated daughter.

Two other family members lived in the home above the shop at North Parade. One was Margaret's elder sister Muriel, who chose to stay in the shadows of the media attention that can engulf the close relatives of a prime minister. She died in 2004, rarely giving interviews throughout her life. Four years older than her famous sibling, Muriel was an easygoing character with less drive but more likeability. One of her closest friends and later golfing partner, Betty Morley, remembers Muriel as 'a pleasant and bright girl, but not nearly as serious or studious as Margaret. The four years between them meant they were not particularly close as sisters. But they got on during their childhood, particularly when they were both resisting their mother's pressures for discipline and strictness'.[17]

That discipline was in the genes. Some of it came from the fifth member of the household, Beatrice's mother, Phoebe Stephenson. She was a formidable old lady who wore long black dresses buttoned down to her ankles. She was much given to repeating clichés such as 'Cleanliness is next to Godliness' and 'if a

---

* Martha is described in the King James Bible as 'cumbered about with much serving . . .' (Luke 10:40).

thing's worth doing it's worth doing well'. Margaret described her grandmother as 'very, very Victorian and very, very strict'.[18]

FUN (OR LACK OF IT)

Thanks to this strictness there was precious little fun in the childhood of Margaret Roberts. 'For us, it was rather a sin to enjoy yourself by entertainment,' she said. 'Life was not to enjoy yourself. Life was to work and do things.'[19]

In this prohibitive atmosphere, many innocent pastimes and pleasures were banned. Children's parties, dancing, cycling, card games, board games (even Snakes and Ladders), walks in the countryside and visits to the theatre were off limits. On Sundays the rules were even stricter. Reading a newspaper, having tea with friends, and even sewing or knitting was forbidden on the Lord's Day. Some of these restrictions were relaxed after the death of Grandmother Phoebe Stephenson in 1934. Until then the family rarely travelled outside Grantham. Margaret's longest journey as a child was a fifty-two-mile bus ride to the seaside town of Skegness where she, Muriel and Beatrice had a bucket and spade holiday in a self-catering flat while Alfred stayed at home minding the store.

At Skegness, Margaret saw her first live show of variety music and light-comedy sketches. 'We would never have gone to the variety while Grandmother Stephenson, who lived with us until I was ten, was still alive,' she recalled.[20]

Another prohibition, also lifted after Grandmother's death, forbade having a wireless set in the house. In the autumn of 1935, to Margaret's great excitement, a radio was installed in the sitting room above the shop at North Parade. But there were rules about which broadcasts the girls could listen to. Talks and news bulletins were permitted. Musical entertainment programmes were not. In a rare interview given by Muriel Cullen (née Roberts) to author Ernle Money in 1975, she explained that she and her ten-year-old sister Margaret had to wait until their parents went out before they could tune in to dance bands and light orchestras.[21]

Alfred Roberts was too intelligent to be a wholehearted supporter of such narrow restrictions. He gradually relaxed them once the hard line puritanism of his wife and mother-in-law began to crumble after Phoebe's death. Away from his public and preaching duties he sometimes displayed a light-hearted side to his nature.

'Alfred had a sense of humour and could let his hair down,' recalled a family friend, Betty Morley. 'I remember how he and my father went to an amusement park after playing bowls. Alfred really enjoyed himself. He even had a modest gamble at one or two of the fairground stalls.'[22]

Betting would never have been allowed under the eagle eye of Beatie. She ruled the roost on behavioural issues and also kept a tight grip on her side of the family purse strings. 'Many, many is the time I can remember [my mother] saying, when I said: "Oh my friends have got more", "Well we are not situated like that!",' recalled Margaret.[23]

Although the financial situation of the Roberts parents, who drew their income from two shops, was not particularly tight, Beatrice turned prudence into parsimony. In an interview when Margaret Thatcher was Prime Minister, she let slip a poignant glimpse of shopping with her mother when she had to suppress her own yearnings for materials that were more colourful but more costly.

'Or when you went out to buy something and you were going to actually have new covers for the settee. That was . . . a great expenditure and a great event, so you went out to choose them, and you chose something that looked really rather lovely, something light with flowers on. My mother: "That's not serviceable!" And how I longed for the time when I could buy things that were not serviceable!'[24]

There were upsides as well as downsides to this frugality. Margaret was always well dressed as a little girl, thanks to Beatrice's skill in making clothes at home. She grew up with a keen understanding of getting value for money. She respected her mother's ability to make the housekeeping budget go far. 'Nothing in our house was wasted, and we always lived within our means,' she recalled. 'The worst you could say about another family was that "they lived up to the hilt".'[25]

Living up to the hilt just once or twice might have seemed an attractive prospect for Margaret, but it was not permissible under the regime at North Parade. Yet this stringency had its advantages too. For Margaret Roberts soon learned how to make her own entertainment, and how to explore, with her father's encouragement, the pleasures of reading by borrowing many books from the library.

Music was another outlet for her creative energy. Margaret was a good child pianist, winning prizes at local music festivals. She had a clear alto voice and became a member of the Methodist church choir. She sang in its performances of oratorios, including Handel's *Messiah*, Haydn's *Creation* and Mendelssohn's

Elijah. In her enjoyment of music she was following the example of her father who had been a chorister and was a member of the Grantham Philharmonic Society.

Margaret's early years were notable for their lack of *joie de vivre.* Later in life she became rather defensive about such suggestions. Her memoirs have some purple patches about her enthusiasm for watching Hollywood movies in the Grantham cinema. She waxed lyrical to one of her first biographers, Tricia Murray, about her love of big-band music and the compositions of Jerome Kern, Cole Porter, Irving Berlin, Richard Rogers and Lorenz Hart. These tastes may have been acquired later in her teenage years or they may have a touch of revisionism about them. For the adult Margaret Thatcher never seems to have had much time or inclination for going to the cinema or listening to music.

In youth, relaxation rarely formed part of her routine and the disciplines, which were first set in her childhood, stayed with her throughout her life. 'In my family we were never idle,' she recalled. 'Idleness was a sin.'[26]

There was, however, one glorious episode of escapism, relaxation and idleness. It was hardly a sin because it took place under the supervision of a Methodist minister, the Reverend Ronald N. Skinner. He invited the eleven-year-old Margaret to come, without her parents, to visit his family in Hampstead. 'I stayed for a whole week,' she told Tricia Murray, 'and was given a life of enjoyment and entertainment I had never seen!'[27]

For a provincial schoolgirl who had never travelled further from Grantham than the journey to the seaside at Skegness, London was a thrilling eye opener. Margaret saw sights like the Changing of the Guard, the Tower of London, St Paul's Cathedral and the Zoo. 'We were actually taken to the theatre – to a musical called *The Desert Song.* We saw the crowd, and the bright lights, and I was so excited.'[28]

Nearly half a century later, when ex-Prime Minister Margaret Thatcher wrote the first volume of her memoirs, she relived this highlight of her childhood with the same gushing enthusiasm. 'I could hardly drag myself away from London or from the Skinners, who had been such indulgent hosts. Their kindness had given me a glimpse of, in Talleyrand's words, '*la douceur de la vie*' – how sweet life could be.'[29]

There was a wistful contrast between this enchanting *douceur* of the London visit and the workaholic *froideur* of her life in Grantham. The penny-pinching restrictions of her mother's discipline were beginning to grate. They were not ameliorated by expressions of loving maternal tactility. Hugs, kisses and cuddles for her children were as rare if not alien to Beatrice as they were to be for Margaret herself when she became the mother of twins.* She had a strangely joyless childhood. Yet, all work and no play made Margaret not a dull girl but a different one. The difference was that she became motivated by her education – which came from her Grantham schooling and from her father.

FIRST SCHOOL

On 3 September 1930, six weeks before her fifth birthday, Margaret Roberts enrolled for her first term at Huntingtower Road Council School. It was thought to be the best elementary school in Grantham, with modern classrooms built sixteen years earlier. It was non-denominational, which was one of the main reasons why Alfred Roberts chose it. He had a progressive outlook when planning the education of his daughters.

Margaret made an odd first impression on her form mistress Mrs Grimwood when she refused to use the school lavatories. According to her school contemporary Joan Bridgman, the girls' 'office', as their lavatory block was coyly called, was often smelly and dirty because some of the pupils, coming from homes without water closets, did not know how to pull the chain. Too fastidious to go to these lavatories, Margaret trained herself to control her bladder until the lunch break. Then she walked one mile back to her home, repeating the process again in the afternoon. This meant four miles of walking each day – a considerable distance for a young child, particularly if nature is calling.[30]

A more elevated example of Margaret's determination came when Mrs Grimwood told her class about a handwriting competition which was being organised for all the schoolchildren in the town. She emphasised how carefully and neatly the entries had to be submitted. 'I'll enter, and I'll win it,' said Margaret.[31] And she did.

Another memory of Margaret Roberts in her elementary school days is that she was good at reciting poetry with a 'posh accent' from which all traces of

---

* 'Mum was not the slightest bit tactile,' Mark Thatcher told me in 2005 (Jonathan Aitken, *Heroes and Contemporaries*, Continuum, 2006, p. 135).

her early Lincolnshire twang had been eliminated. Private elocution lessons arranged by her father altered her tone of voice. It became more refined than the homespun dialect used by most pupils at this council school.

In one heated moment at Prime Minister's Question Time some five decades after her first elocution training, she slipped back into an idiom of the broad Granthamese she once spoke. Shouting across the despatch box in April 1983, she accused Denis Healey of being scared of an election. 'The right hon. Gentleman is afraid of an election, is he? Afraid? Frightened? Frit? Frit, Frit!' [32]*

There were few such linguistic lapses as the education of Margaret Roberts progressed. When she was nine years old her clear diction helped her to win first prize in a poetry recital competition at a local festival in 1934. When her headmistress Miss Margaret Glenn congratulated her, saying, 'You were lucky Margaret,' Margaret retorted: 'I wasn't lucky, I deserved it.' [33]

The principal target of Margaret Roberts' efforts to deserve success was winning a scholarship to the local grammar school. She studied for this exam with noticeable intensity. She was always a hard worker. Before she arrived at Huntingtower Road Council School, she could read and write well. During her first term she was moved up into a form for children a year older than herself. From then on she consistently came top or near the top of her class. She was exceptionally diligent at her homework. Her fellow pupils remembered how she used to arrive each day weighed down with a satchel so full of books that she had difficulty in undoing its straps.

Aside from her studies, Margaret Roberts is recorded as having participated in some royal events while at the school.

On 6 May 1935 King George V and Queen Mary celebrated their Silver Jubilee. The school took part in a pageant whose highlight was the display of the word Grantham by the town's children in Wyndham Park. Half a century later, when Prime Minister, Margaret Thatcher was sent some commemorative mementos of the celebrations by a Grantham resident Gerald Tuppin. She replied to him from Downing Street, adding in her handwriting: 'It was a wonderful

---

* The official Report of this exchange in the House of Commons records Margaret Thatcher as saying 'Frit' only once. But I, and many others present, heard her using the word with high excitement three times. Even great Hansard nods.

occasion, quite the most exciting day of my young life. I seem to remember we formed the "M" in Grantham.'[34]

A more solemn occasion was the announcement to the school of the death of King George V on 21 January 1936. The following day Margaret was one of a group of pupils who went down to the Guildhall to hear the proclamation of the new King, Edward VIII.

The school Log Book also provides a portrait of the local events that affected the lives of its 291 children in Margaret Roberts' last year. Epidemics of flu, measles and whooping cough disrupted school attendances, which at one stage fell to eighty-two. An accident on the railway killed the father of two of her contemporaries. Her class performed an Empire Day play for the whole school 'and patriotic songs were sung'.[35] A second-hand wireless set was brought for £2 and adjustments were made to its volume so that all pupils could listen to it.

School milk became available for sale in one third of a pint sealed bottles. The cost was a halfpenny per bottle. On Monday mornings pupils were asked to bring 'tuppence ha'penny' to pay for their week's supply of milk. This was a memory that resonated with Margaret when as Secretary of State for Education she became embroiled in the 'Milk Snatcher Thatcher' furore after cancelling free milk for schoolchildren.*

The most important event in the life of the young Margaret came on 13 July 1936. On that day, the school Log Book recorded: 'A scholarship has been granted to Margaret Roberts, as although she is very young (10 years 6 months) her work was exceptionally good.'[36]

It meant that she could go to the best grammar school in the town, Kesteven and Grantham Girls' School (KGGS). Her achievement was expected, but when the results came through she recalled feeling 'pretty elated'.[37]

This success was the turning point in the early life of Margaret Roberts.

FATHERLY INSPIRATION

When she entered No. 10 Downing Street for the first time as Prime Minister, Margaret Thatcher paused on the doorstep to respond to a reporter's question about her father Alfred Roberts. 'Well, of course, I just owe almost everything

---

* See Chapter 6.

to my own father,' she said, 'I really do. He brought me up to believe all the things I do believe and they're just the values on which I've fought the election . . .'[38]

In a moment of supreme elation, this filial piety was as touching as it was justified. For any study of Margaret Roberts' early years confirms that her relationship with her father was the force that shaped her character and inspired her ambition. There were at least four areas where his example made a profound impact – on her education at home; on her spiritual values learned at the Methodist Church; on her first experiences of politics; and on the development of her personality that was greatly influenced by his principles.

Alfred Roberts started life wanting to be a teacher. This career was denied him by financial difficulties in his family. He had to leave school at thirteen in order to earn a living. But he made up for the education he missed by forming a lifelong habit of wide reading.

One of the passions of Alfred's life was to make sure that his daughters were better educated than himself. In this endeavour Margaret became the proverbial apple of her father's eye. Maybe she filled the place of the son he was thought to have longed for. Or perhaps her bookish, argumentative temperament appealed to Alfred's own penchant for reading and politics. Having been denied his vocation to be a teacher, he found it in his tutoring of Margaret.

A shared love of poetry was an important ingredient in their father–daughter relationship. Alfred had a well-tuned ear for the rhythms and cadences of the English language. He venerated the *Oxford Book of English Verse*. Margaret was made to learn many of its poems by heart. When she won first prize at a local festival in 1934 it was for declaiming Walter de la Mare's 'The Listeners', after much paternal coaching. Her father also taught her to recite many lines from Victorian poets, which conveyed a moral message.

Two stanzas Margaret learned in childhood and often quoted in adulthood were:

Does the road wind up-hill all the way?
Yes, to the very end.
Will the day's journey take the whole long day?
From morn to night, my friend.

(Christina Georgina Rossetti, 'Up-Hill')

The heights by great men reached and kept
Were not attained by sudden flight,
But they, while their companions slept,
Were toiling upwards through the night.

(Henry Wadsworth Longfellow, 'The Ladder of St. Augustine')

There was plenty of 'toiling upwards through the night' in Margaret's child-hood, which at times seemed hard, even to her. She was not allowed to go out and play with other children. Her nose was kept to the grindstone of extra studying, reading or poetry learning. On one occasion she wanted to go for a walk with friends. Her father refused his permission, telling her 'Never do things just because other people do them'.[39]

These words may have upset Margaret on the occasions they were first said to her, but later in life she praised her father for his stern remonstrance. 'In fact, this was one of his favourite expressions,' she recalled, 'used when I wanted to learn dancing, or sometimes when I wanted to go to the cinema, or out for the day somewhere. Whatever I felt at the time, the sentiment stood me in good stead.'[40]

The example and teachings of Alfred Roberts were the stars his younger daughter steered by. Some commentators, notably the biographer John Camp-bell, have argued that this paternal contribution to her upbringing has grown in the telling. As Campbell puts it, 'Margaret was very much less devoted to her wonderful father while he was alive than she became to his sanctified image after he was dead.'[41]

This view might be sustainable if it was applied only to the political career of the future Prime Minister. That was nurtured by other father figures to whom she was grateful. But Alfred Roberts alone was responsible for her spiritual upbringing and her moral compass. As a father, lay preacher and mentor he was by far the greatest influence in laying the foundations on which she built her life. As she put it: 'We were taught what was right and what was wrong in very considerable detail. There were certain things you just didn't do, and that was that. Duty was very, very strongly engrained into us. Duties to the church, duties to your neighbour and conscientiousness were continually emphasised.'[42]

Duties to the church had a high priority. Alfred and Beatrice were devout Methodists. They had met at the Bridgend Road Mission Chapel in one of the most deprived areas of Grantham. By the time Margaret was born they had become regular attendees at the more socially elevated Finkin Street Church close to the centre of the town. This was a citadel of Wesleyan Methodism in the 1930s, for it had refused to join the Methodist Union of 1932. The outstanding feature of the church was that it was said to be 'a powerhouse of good preaching . . . you had really arrived as a preacher when you were asked to give a sermon at Finkin Street'.[43]*

Alfred Roberts had undoubtedly arrived, for he was not just a respected deliverer of good sermons; he was the senior lay preacher of the area. His official title was Circuit Steward, which meant that he was responsible for organising preachers for the thirty-two Methodist chapels and churches on the Grantham circuit. He gave many sermons in them himself, travelling around the towns and villages of Lincolnshire in a church car known as 'the circuit taxi'. Margaret sometimes accompanied him. On one occasion she criticised him for putting on his 'sermon voice'. But she became an admirer of his preaching, later praising his sermons for having 'intellectual substance'.[44]

A small number of Alfred Roberts' sermons have survived in his old notebooks.[45] They justify his daughter's comment. Despite some misspellings ('beleif'; 'desease'),[46] which were understandable in a man who left school at thirteen, they display a theological understanding that was broadminded and original. He was liberal in his doctrine, claiming no monopoly of wisdom for Methodism, and quoting from a wide range of secular writers.

Listening to a father's sermons, however worthy, might seem heavy weather for a young girl. But even at an early age, Margaret Roberts was *a femme sérieuse*, particularly in her religious observance. Every Sunday she attended four events at the church, sitting in the family pew four rows down in the centre left aisle. Her day started with morning Sunday school at 10.30, followed by the morning service at 11 o'clock. Alfred Roberts called this 'The Sandwich Service' because it had three layers of spiritual nourishment: hymn, prayer, hymn; Bible reading, hymn, Bible reading; and sermon, Bible reading, hymn.[47]

Just in case this might not be enough religion for one day, Margaret went back to Finkin Street at 3 o'clock for afternoon Sunday school where she often

---

* On a visit to Grantham, I met Denhys Lambley, Senior Lay Preacher at the Wesleyan Methodist Finkin Street Church. This is the church that the Roberts family attended when Margaret was growing up.

played the piano. Sometimes she went back again for the Evening Service at 6.30 or she went out with her father to hear one of his sermons on the circuit. Not surprisingly, Margaret sometimes found this Sunday routine 'too much of a good thing', and on a few occasions I remember trying to get out of going'.[48] But her flashes of youthful rebellion were balanced by a genuine commitment to the teachings of her church, even if not to its repetitive services.

Spiritual values, as proclaimed by Methodism, were important in Margaret Thatcher's childhood. She knew her Bible. She loved singing Charles Wesley's hymns; particularly 'Lo, He Comes with Clouds Descending'; and 'And Can It Be That I Should Gain'.[49] She learned the Methodist Catechism by heart. Her signed copy of this sixteen-page document, price 'Threepence Net', has survived complete with interesting underlinings on repentance. She could quote, in later life, texts and sayings from the sermons of her father, her headmistress Miss Gladys Williams and a leading Grantham Congregationalist Minister, Reverend Henry Childe. All this activity may not have turned her into John Wesley's ideal of 'a soul on fire', but it suggests an inquiring and energetic mind which took spiritual values and teachings seriously.

Alfred Roberts was a political, as well as a spiritual, leader of his community. Two years after Margaret was born, he was elected to the Grantham Town Council, on which he served for the next quarter of a century. Although he stood as an Independent Ratepayer candidate, according to his daughter Muriel, 'He was always a Liberal at heart'.[50] But by the 1930s he had become a staunch Conservative. In the general election of 1935, he gave ten-year-old Margaret her first experience of politics, using her as a runner who carried voting slips from the Tory tellers outside the polling station to the nearest committee room. She also folded leaflets for the Conservative candidate Sir Victor Warrender who held the seat by a reduced majority. He made a good impression on his young election helper. 'He was rather a handsome man. When he spoke, you listened . . . He understood that personality attracts votes,' she recalled in old age.[51]

Aside from the excitement of electioneering, Margaret took a keen interest in her father's life as a Councillor and Town Mayor and also in the wider responsibilities he undertook. At various times in her early years he was President of Rotary, President of the Chamber of Trade, Chairman of the Workers' Educational Association and Chairman of the National Savings Movement.

Alfred's leadership of these local voluntary organisations must have given Margaret a sense of the value of community and public service.

Having the right values was as important to Alfred Roberts as holding public office. He mingled his Methodism with his politics. 'Individual responsibility was his watchword, and sound finance his passion' was Margaret's summary of his philosophy, as she recalled how often her mother would tell her: 'Your father always sticks to his principles.'[52]

One unusual principle Alfred Roberts passed on to his second daughter was the importance of being certain. Like him, she was determined to stick to what she was sure was right. Unlike him, she could become abrasive and angry in support of her opinions. By all accounts he was a gentle, tolerant figure. Although he could sometimes be stubborn, in general he was consensual as a councillor and non-judgemental as a man. There are no stories of him having aggressive arguments let alone blazing rows with anyone in Grantham. But in this area of life, even in her schooldays, Margaret was noticeably different from the father she revered as a role model.

REFLECTION

Something is missing from the accepted and official accounts of the early life of Margaret Roberts. This is because they emanate largely from herself.

By the time journalists began to track down details of her upbringing – from 1975 onwards, when she became Leader of the Opposition – she was able to airbrush from the record most of the sharp edges in her childhood she presented in her own writings and interviews. The Iron Lady liked to control the narrative of her early life with an iron grip. She had an over-developed desire for privacy on family matters, discouraging her elder sister and other relatives from discussing them. Even her children were kept poorly informed about her growing up years in Grantham.

As a result, the authorised version of Margaret Roberts' youth has a sanitised feel to it particularly as recorded in the opening chapter of her memoirs *A Provincial Childhood*. At first reading this is a stilted account of the upbringing of a mild child. There are a few hints of the electrifying qualities, positive and negative, which were to make her such a polarising figure in British politics and on the world stage.

Also edited out of the authorised version were the social and economic insecurities that troubled the young Margaret. In class-conscious Grantham the Roberts family were tradesmen. This put them well down the ladder from the better-off county and commercial families in and around the town. Margaret was never regarded as 'one of us' by the posher customers she served from behind the counter in the North Parade shop. Her frugal upbringing, her home-made clothes and her social status as the daughter of a shopkeeper were likely to have made her feel inadequate when visiting the homes of her school contemporaries who came from these higher echelons of Lincolnshire life.

As for the local grandee, Lord Brownlow, Margaret went on annual school picnics in the grounds of Belton, his stately home on the edge of Grantham. She was noticed by him and by other members of the Cust family* for her personality, intelligence and good service in the shop. But, being 'in trade', she was not invited to a meal at Belton until becoming Prime Minister nearly half a century later.[†]

The social boundaries of Grantham in the 1930s, together with the exclusions, tensions and feelings of insecurity they must have produced, are not mentioned in Margaret Thatcher's account of her childhood in her memoirs or in later interviews. Without them, the picture of her early years is incomplete. So is her self-portrait of her youthful personality. These omissions raise interesting questions.

At the height of her powers, her critics thought that Prime Minister Margaret Thatcher showed flaws in her character. She sometimes displayed a belligerent temperament that could explode into anger. She was a bully towards some of

---

* An exotic rumour, much discussed by Tory MPs in the aftermath of the 1975 leadership election, suggested that Margaret Thatcher might be the daughter of the Hon. Harry Cust. He was a scion of Belton, the younger brother of Lord Brownlow, and a notorious womaniser. Cust was widely believed to be the father of Lady Diana Cooper, who had allegedly inherited his piercing blue eyes. She enjoyed fanning the speculation that the Prime Minister might be her half-sister. However, since Harry Cust died eight years before Margaret Thatcher was born, the rumour was demonstrably nonsense.

[†] Soon after her election as Prime Minister, Margaret Thatcher was the guest of honour at a private lunch at Belton House. Lord Brownlow, following an approach from Lincolnshire MP Marcus Kimball, loaned her his magnificent collection of table silver for use at No. 10 Downing Street for several years.

her senior colleagues. She bore grudges. She gave an impression of lacking compassion for the poorer members of society. She took instant likes and dislikes, which rarely altered. She could be gratuitously rude to ministers and civil servants who she thought were flannelling. She was indifferent, often to the point of rank discourtesy, towards other women – including ministerial wives she found uninteresting. Some thought these flashes of offensiveness and over-assertiveness stemmed from insecurities buried deep within her. Even if this charge sheet seems exaggerated, it would be strange if none of the failings that gave rise to it ever surfaced during her youth.

The paradox is that it was the clash of good and bad forces in her nature that gave the future Prime Minister such a formidable personality. It was unfortunate that the grit in the oyster of her inner feelings should have been carefully suppressed by the time she came to write and speak publicly of her formative years.

Answering an interviewer's question during the 1983 general election about what she had learned in her childhood, she replied:

> We were taught to work jolly hard. We were taught to prove ourselves; we were taught self-reliance; we were taught to live within our income. You were taught that cleanliness is next to godliness. You were taught self-respect. You were taught always to give a hand to your neighbour. You were taught tremendous pride in your country.[53]

Even though this is the authorised version, it is true. But it may not be the whole truth. The suspicion remains that the young Margaret Roberts was more rebellious, more argumentative, more insecure and more disagreeable than her self-portrait as a dutiful daughter suggests. Her sharpest clashes came with her strong-willed mother. They also came when she fought her grammar school headmistress. What seems likely is that scenes of angry confrontation must have been part of her personality when a child, just as they were part of her personality as Prime Minister.

That said, the positives of her upbringing far outweighed the negatives. Thanks to the extraordinary discipline and determination she showed in her early years, she was destined to climb far above the horizons of Grantham, a town which was itself rising in importance because of the war.

2

The war, grammar school and fighting her headmistress

GRANTHAM AT WAR

The Second World War, and the events in Germany leading up to it, made a seminal impact on the life of the young Margaret Roberts. In this period the seeds of her strongest instincts were sown, which later influenced her decisions and attitudes as Prime Minister. Her passionate patriotism; her admiration for the armed forces; her affection for the Jews; her suspicions of Germany; and her reverence for the Anglo-American alliance are all traceable to her formative experiences as a Grantham teenager.

Although she was only a thirteen-year-old schoolgirl when war was declared, eighteen months earlier she had come into face to face contact with Hitler's persecution of the Jews when the Roberts family welcomed into their home a young refugee from Austria. From her conversations with this Viennese student, Edith Mühlbauer, and from the internationalist outlook of her father, Margaret became well informed about the Nazi domination of Europe, and held strong views on it.

There is a story from a Grantham fish and chip shop on Margaret's pre-war hostility to Hitler. She was queuing on a Friday evening in 1938 to buy a cod and chips supper for the family, when a discussion started about the German Führer. One of the customers said that at least Hitler had given his country some self-respect. The twelve-year-old Miss Roberts vigorously disagreed. The forcefulness of her argument caused irritation among others in the queue. With tension rising, the manageress defused the situation by saying with a laugh, 'Oh, she's always debating.'[1]

Margaret was able to debate in a well-informed way because she had been listening to her family's Jewish guest. Edith Mühlbauer was the seventeen-year-old daughter of a Viennese banker. When Hitler annexed Austria on 13 March 1938, and the first of Vienna's 170,000 Jews were being rounded up by the SS, Edith wrote to her English pen friend, Muriel Roberts, asking if she could come and stay, to escape from the Nazi persecution.

This was followed by a letter making the same request from Edith's father to Alfred Roberts, who read it to the next meeting of the Grantham Rotary Club. The Rotarians responded generously.

They organised a group of Grantham hosts who each agreed to open their doors to the young refugee for a month or so. They also paid for Edith's travel and provided her with a guinea a week in pocket money. The first English home she stayed in was above the shop at North Parade with the Roberts family.

Edith's stay was not an unqualified success. Grantham gossip had it that Alfred Roberts became concerned that his sophisticated Viennese guest, who wore lipstick, smoked cigarettes and flirted with boys, might be exerting a bad influence on his strictly brought up daughters. For her part, the seventeen-year-old Edith found life with the Roberts family somewhat awkward and uncomfortable. 'We didn't have a proper bathroom in those days. She was used to better things,' recalled Margaret.[2]

Although Edith Mühlbauer stayed only for a few weeks at North Parade (she moved around eighteen Rotarian families before joining relatives in Brazil in 1940), her plight made a considerable impression on Margaret.[3] She heard about the *Anschluss*, *Kristallnacht* and other episodes of Jewish persecution, learning that some of Edith's relatives were made to sweep the streets before being taken away to Auschwitz. One result of these conversations was that Margaret borrowed from the library an important new book, published in June 1938, *Insanity Fair* by Douglas Reed. It was a powerful indictment of German anti-Semitism.

As the Edith Mühlbauer episode shows, Alfred Roberts had a compassionate and international outlook. His Methodism and his chairmanship of Grantham's Rotary's international service committee gave him knowledgeable insights into the growing menace of Nazi aggression in Europe. However, he was an early supporter of Neville Chamberlain and the 1938 Munich Agreement, a political position he abandoned after Germany's invasion of Czechoslovakia.

The outbreak of war in September 1939 made some immediate effects on Margaret's life at the age of thirteen. Her school had anti-blast sandbag walls built around its classrooms. Trenches were dug on one side of the playing fields, and daily drills were held to practise evacuation and air raid shelter procedures. The teachers were trained in extinguishing incendiary bombs.[4]

Soon the practices became the real thing. Grantham was literally in the firing line, partly because two major munitions factories were located in the town, and partly because so many RAF personnel were billeted there.

In the first three years of the war Grantham was hit by twenty-one Luftwaffe bombing raids, which destroyed eighty homes and killed seventy people. One of Alfred's civilian roles was to be Chief Welfare Officer in charge of civil defence, which meant he was the town's organiser of Air Raid Precautions, or ARP. He found himself doing so much night duty as a warden that he joked the initials stood for Alfred Roberts Purgatory.

He was not alone in his discomforts. Because the house at North Parade did not have a garden, no underground shelter could be dug there. On evenings when the air raid sirens sounded their alert, Margaret with her mother and father had to huddle under the kitchen table until the sirens gave the all clear. Muriel was away, first in Birmingham and then in Blackpool, working as a physiotherapist.[5]

The separation of the two sisters resulted in a considerable correspondence between them during the war years. Their letters, according to Margaret Thatcher's official biographer, Charles Moore, told him 'much more about her private life than had previously been revealed by all the other sources put together'.[6]

The sisterly correspondence did not contain much in the way of revealing insights during the 1939–1943 period while Margaret remained at Grantham as a schoolgirl. Her letters are mainly about the 'terrific amount of swotting' she was doing for her School Certificate; the detailed results of that examination (distinctions in chemistry, arithmetic and algebra); and descriptions of her birthday presents and her visits to the Grantham cinema.[7] The most surprising omission from these communications to Muriel was the war, which is barely mentioned.

In fact, the war loomed large in the teenage life of Margaret Roberts. The heavy bombing of the town's homes and factories; the disruption to the timetables of KGGS; the extra pressures of her father's work as a councillor; and the military presence of the Royal Air Force in the streets and skies of Grantham all made a considerable impact on her.

Lincolnshire was known as 'Bomber County', because forty-nine RAF airfields were located there with No. 1 and No. 5 Bomber Command groups operating from bases such as RAF Scampton, Coningsby, Cranwell, East Kirkby and Digby. So the young Margaret became familiar with hearing the overhead roar of the Lancaster heavy bombers, and seeing their aircrews in and around the town. Her father had at least one encounter with Wing Commander Guy Gibson VC, DSO, DFC, who led the 'Dam Busters' raid. She herself caught several glimpses in Grantham of the Air Officer Commanding No. 5 Group Bomber Command, Air Vice-Marshal Arthur 'Bomber' Harris, in the town. He was a controversial figure to many, but a hero to Margaret Roberts.

Fifty years after her schoolgirl sightings of the wartime commander, a statue of 'Bomber' Harris was unveiled by Queen Elizabeth the Queen Mother, patron of the Bomber Command Association, outside the Church of St Clement Danes in London, in May 1992. Ex-Prime Minister Margaret Thatcher attended. Knowing of this Grantham connection I had asked the RAF to send her an invitation.

As a newly appointed Defence Minister, I was concerned that more senior figures in the government were unwilling, because of the anticipated protests, to come to the ceremony; so I telephoned Margaret Thatcher.

'Of course I'll come,' she said. 'I remember seeing him in my Grantham days. He was a most remarkable leader of Bomber Command. We wouldn't have won the war without them. I'll be there.' And she was.

The atmosphere and emotions of Grantham in those times left an indelible mark on Margaret Roberts. 'Our thoughts were at the front,'[8] she recalled, speaking in later life of huddling round the family's wireless set to hear the six o'clock news read by Alvar Lidell, or listening to the wartime broadcasts of Prime Minister Winston Churchill.

The fervent atmosphere of English patriotism in the family was reinforced by the books that Margaret and her father took out from the library and discussed together. Two that made a particular impact on her were *Ronald Cartland*, Barbara Cartland's biography of her brother who was killed at Dunkirk, and Richard Hillary's *The Last Enemy*, a classic portrait of the lives and losses of RAF pilots in the early years of the war.

Later in her teenage years Margaret worked as a WVS* volunteer in Service canteens, where she met young RAF pilots from Bomber Command, many of whom never came back to their Lincolnshire bases. Towards the end of the war,

---

* Women's Voluntary Service, later the Women's Royal Voluntary Service.

when she returned to Grantham during her Oxford vacations, she found the town full of American servicemen.

In late 1943, the RAF allocated twelve of its airfields in the Grantham area to the 82nd Troop Carrier Group of the US 9th Air Force, who were preparing to move large numbers of soldiers to France for the liberation of Europe. The reassuring presence of the American military may have contributed to Margaret's lifelong enthusiasm for good UK–US relations.

The mosaic of Margaret Roberts' wartime memories created an influential background to her formative years. Even though her experiences of the conflict were tangential, they played their part in creating her values and shaping her personality. But the foreground of her life was her progress at school towards her dream of winning a scholarship to Oxford.

KGGS

The most important part of Margaret Roberts' schooldays took place at Kesteven and Grantham Girls' School, locally known as KGGS. The 350 pupils were drawn from all levels of society and were a meritocracy. Their parents were means-tested, and as a result about two-thirds of the pupils were charged fees of three pounds and ten shillings a term. Alfred Roberts had to pay these fees for Margaret, even though she had won a scholarship place. He also paid two guineas a term for her piano lessons.

KGGS girls were a mixed bunch, socially and economically. They included the daughters of some of the poorest families in the town. There were also girls from farming, business and upper-middle-class backgrounds.

Margaret Roberts was always something of a loner among her contemporaries. But it was noticed that her closest acquaintances came not from Grantham, but from the higher social strata of families who lived in the Lincolnshire countryside. This may have been the origin of her school nickname, 'Snobby Roberts'. One of these friends was Margaret Goodrich, whose father, Canon Harold Goodrich, was the incumbent of Corby Glen, a nearby village said to contain the finest vicarage in the county. A second was Betty Morley, whose father created a successful tyre-making company in Great Ponton. A third was Catherine Barford, the daughter of a prominent industrialist who founded the Aveling Barford group of companies. Catherine arrived as a new girl at KGGS on the same day as Margaret Roberts, in September 1936. 'Margaret became a friend,' she recalled. 'The first thing I noticed about her was how hard she worked. The second was her closeness to her father.'[9]

Margaret made several visits to the Barford country house for tea. This was a mark of her friendship with Catherine, but the invitations also came because their fathers had business to discuss. The Barford companies were expanding and needed to find council houses for the workers they recruited. Alfred Roberts, a member of the Housing Committee, was helpful. His career in local government was on the rise. One headline in the local paper dubbed him 'Grantham's Chancellor of the Exchequer' on account of his chairmanship of the Finance Committee.[10]

He was well known for his interest in national and international affairs, and respected for his integrity. His political activities soon rubbed off on his daughter. As a new girl at KGGS, Margaret Roberts came top of her class in her first year. What she was best remembered for was her prominence, and her air of superiority when putting questions to visiting speakers.

'I can first remember her at a lecture we had . . . The well-known author and lecturer Bernard Newman came to talk about spies,' recalled Margaret Goodrich.

> At the end, he asked for questions in the usual way and instead of a sixth-former standing up, this young, bright-eyed, fair haired girl from the fourth year stood up and asked him a question. But the thing that rather annoyed her contemporaries was that she asked him these questions in almost parliamentary language: 'Does the speaker think so and so?'[11]

Another contemporary who found herself irritated by the inquisitorial style of Margaret Roberts at lectures was her classmate Madeline Edwards. 'Margaret could be guaranteed to get up on her hind legs and ask penetrating questions,' she recalled. 'The rest of us sort of looked at each other – with our eyes rolling as if to say, "Oh, she's at it again".'[12]

The questions were well rehearsed. What her classmates did not know was that Alfred Roberts was training his daughter in the art of public speaking. 'Have something to say. Say it clearly. That is the only secret of style,' he told her.[13] He often took her on Thursday evenings to University of Nottingham Extension Lectures held in Grantham, where he encouraged Margaret to put her points to the lecturers.[14]

Another source of her confidence was her participation in the group discussions, usually led by her father, among the community of Methodists who
attended the Finkin Street Church. It was a feature of their fellowship that after
the Sunday evening service, her father's friends took it in turns to have supper
together. Even though she was the youngest present, Margaret liked to take part
in these conversations, which she remembered 'ranged far wider than religion
or happenings in Grantham to include national and international politics'.[15]

Alfred Roberts' role in his daughter's education expanded further when it
looked as though wartime pressures at KGGS were having an adverse effect
on Margaret's academic performance. In her lower sixth year of 1940–41 her
average marks slipped below 70 per cent for the first time. In her favourite
subjects of chemistry, biology, zoology and geography she continued to achieve
the highest grades. But her weakest subjects of French and English dragged her
down, as she scored only F grades ('fair to weak') in them.

Her father took a keen interest in these results. Extra hours of tuition at
home were deemed necessary, partly to improve Margaret's low marks, and
partly because KGGS became overcrowded when the Camden School for Girls
was evacuated from London in 1939 to share its buildings for five terms. This
resulted in 'Operation Double Shift', which meant that KGGS used the school
in the mornings and Camden in the afternoons. Both sets of pupils spent fewer
hours in the classroom.[16]

Alfred rose to the challenge of home-schooling Margaret in the afternoons
and at weekends. He was out of his depth in science, but this did not matter as
KGGS had an outstanding chemistry teacher in Miss Kay, who Margaret found
inspirational. But on other subjects, his self-educated mind was better stocked
than several of the KGGS staff. Alfred was certainly an improvement on Miss
Ophelia Harding, the history mistress. 'Very disappointing. She is quite middle-
aged and dowdy in dress,' was Margaret's tart comment. Another bad review
came from Muriel's friend Betty Morley, who described the history teacher as
'a bit of a dud . . . She was always going off into long silences and trances.'[17]

Silences and trances were not a feature of Margaret Roberts' upbringing. She
liked to argue, often with the fervour of moral certainty she absorbed from her
father's teachings and from the Methodist Church. These arguments were often
conducted with older people, particularly with her father and his Sunday night
supper group.

To most of her contemporaries at school she was not a particularly memorable or congenial figure. She sang in the choir, looked rather plump and was thought of as a swot. She had a minor speech defect, an inability to pronounce her Rs. Another course of elocution lessons eliminated the problem. They may also have given her the famously precise and slightly precious diction that grated on the ears of her political critics some forty years later. At the time, this made her seem out of the ordinary.

'The best description of Margaret is that she was always ladylike, sensible and serious,' said her classmate Gladys Foster. 'She worked very hard, and spent a lot of time reading and studying at home.'[18]

The perception that Margaret Roberts was an industrious but unmemorable pupil at KGGS changed during her last two years. Her carefully polished questions (she invariably asked the first one) to visiting school speakers continued to irritate one or two of her contemporaries. But what really brought her to the attention of her teachers were the blazing rows she had with the headmistress of KGGS, Miss Dorothy Gillies. The issue at stake was that Margaret Roberts was determined to get her own way.

GETTING HER OWN WAY

There were two remarkable headmistresses of KGGS during Margaret Roberts' time there. She revered one and despised the other. The difference had to do with a clash of wills provoked by Margaret's dislike of being patronised, a feature of her personality which lasted long into her political career.

When Margaret entered KGGS in 1936, the headmistress was Miss Gladys Williams, a petite, energetic Mancunian who had been in her post ever since the school opened its doors in 1910. Her vision, spelt out in a speech-day address in the 1920s and often quoted to subsequent generations of her girls, was: 'It is not our business to turn out teachers or typists, or even housewives, but to try to send out girls capable and desirous of doing some part of the world's work well.'[19]

This was a purpose that would have appealed to Alfred Roberts, who became a governor of the school in 1941, and also to his ambitious younger daughter. Margaret was inspired by the scholarship, the infectious enthusiasm and the sermons of Gladys Williams; one of which she quoted some forty-seven years after it was preached.

Coming out of a Sunday service in Kent in 1976 with Margaret Thatcher, she remarked to me that the vicar's sermon, which had featured a Roman centurion, was 'very ordinary'.* She then continued, 'Very ordinary indeed – at least when I think of the greatest sermon I ever heard.'

'What was that?' I asked.

'It was the sermon preached at the service to mark the retirement of my old headmistress,' declared the Leader of the Opposition, 'and it was about a centurion, too. My headmistress took as her text the words: "For I also am a man under authority."[20] She explained in the most inspired terms how the centurion who said that was absolutely confident of his own authority, but he also had absolute trust in his higher authority.'[21]

A few months after hearing this sermon, Margaret Roberts was in angry conflict with the senior authority of KGGS, her new headmistress, Miss Dorothy Gillies.

Miss Gillies was a classicist from Edinburgh, described by one former pupil as being 'rather fierce . . . with a Morningside accent just like Maggie Smith in *The Prime of Miss Jean Brodie*'.[22] According to the official history of KGGS Miss Gillies was 'a perfectionist and a disciplinarian'.[23] These qualities should have given her a natural rapport with the disciplined perfectionist who was destined to become her most famous pupil. Not so. Their clashes became a school legend.

The problem was that Miss Gillies' career guidance and Miss Roberts' career ambition came into headlong collision. Their first disagreement came when Margaret informed her headmistress that she intended to get to the top of a career stream in the British Empire that was notoriously difficult for women to succeed in. 'She told me that she wanted to enter the Indian Civil Service,' recalled Dorothy Gillies. 'I expressed surprise and pointed out that, like almost every other walk of life at that time, it was male-dominated. Margaret replied: "All the better for it. If I succeed, my success will be all the more creditable".'[24]

Entering the Indian Civil Service was a high hurdle for academic as well as gender reasons. The ICS examination was fiercely competitive. Passing out near the top of the list opened a golden road to the glittering prizes of the Raj. It was a first-class ticket to the realm of viceroys, governors, judges, administrators and

---

* Throughout her life Margaret Thatcher was often critical of preachers. Delayed for lunch one Sunday at Chequers because the sermon had been too long, she told her guests: 'That's one vicar who will never be a bishop' (AC: Interview with Lord Bell).

district officers on the sub-continent. But Miss Gillies was right to warn that no woman had ever climbed near the top of this imperial ladder. Although Margaret Roberts was to be admired for disregarding the warning of sex discrimination difficulties, she showed little political discernment in her desire to proceed down the Indian Civil Service route. It took the paternal guidance of her father to point out, with the perspective of the 1940s, that India was unlikely to go on being governed by a British civil service. Eventually, after a family argument, Margaret dropped the idea.

The flame of her ambition also burned in the direction of winning a scholarship to Oxford. Only nine KGGS girls had achieved this in the thirty-two-year history of the school, but one candidate in the year above her, Margaret Goodrich, had recently secured a scholarship at Lady Margaret Hall. Margaret Roberts wanted to emulate her friend's success. But Miss Gillies rather patronisingly thought she would not be up to it. When the headmistress tried to discourage her pupil from making the attempt, a furious row took place: 'She's trying to thwart my ambition,' complained Margaret.[25]

The thwarting nevertheless continued. The Somerville examination required Latin as a compulsory paper. The headmistress firmly pointed out that although KGGS taught *First Steps in Latin* (the basic textbook) to its junior forms, advanced lessons in this subject were not part of its sixth-form curriculum. Margaret no less firmly replied that the problem could be overcome by taking private lessons in Latin. These had been organised for Margaret Goodrich. Miss Gillies refused the same arrangements for Margaret Roberts on the grounds that she would be studying advanced Latin over a year too late, so could not possibly achieve the standards required by the Somerville College examiners in two terms. This led to another argument that ended in defeat for Miss Gillies. Margaret was allowed to attempt the impossible, but only if private lessons could be arranged for her outside school hours. Even this concession was said to have been reluctantly granted to the daughter of Alfred Roberts solely because he was about to become Chairman of the Board of Governors of KGGS.*

According to her Grantham contemporary Malcolm Knapp, Margaret herself organised her extra-curricula Latin lessons by knocking on the door of

---

* Alfred Roberts was Chairman of the Board of Governors of KGGS from 1943 to 1969.

a neighbour at No. 55 North Parade. He was V.R.W. Waterhouse, a schoolmaster with a big nose, which brought him the nickname of 'Beaky' at King's School in Grantham.

'Beaky' Waterhouse was not a classics master, but he knew his Latin. So, when Margaret Roberts asked him, 'Can you teach me enough Latin to get me into Oxford?', he responded positively, striking a deal for tuition payments with her father.[26] As a private tutor, 'Beaky' did a good job. For after some twenty weeks of his intensive coaching, Margaret was judged to have reached a sufficiently high standard of Latin to be capable of passing an Oxford paper in the subject. One up to Miss Roberts, and one down to Miss Gillies.

The battle of wills between the headmistress and her combative sixth-former gave some interesting signposts to the latter's personality. They showed that Margaret could be fearless in argument and dedicated in application. These qualities gave her confidence that 'doing the impossible' was not necessarily as hard as the conventional wisdom suggested. Yet these positive aspects were balanced by one negative side of her personality. For the episode later revealed that Margaret could bear grudges.

In the Thatcher archives at Churchill College, Cambridge there exists an undated speaking note about her education at KGGS. It consists of bullet points in her adult handwriting under the heading 'Fortunate School'. The purpose of the bullet points is to draw a comparison between her two headmistresses. The subheading 'Miss Williams' is followed by favourable points such as 'set out to achieve the highest values'. In stark contrast, the name 'Miss Gillies' is accompanied by just two words; 'obstacles overcome'.[27]

These back of the envelope jottings may have been used as speech notes for Margaret Thatcher's return visit, as Prime Minister, to KGGS in 1982. On this occasion she poured praise on the virtues of Miss Williams, but conspicuously failed to make any mention of Miss Gillies. At least this was an improvement on Margaret Thatcher's behaviour towards her second headmistress when she first came back to the school as a newly elected MP in 1960. In the view of other old girls present, she caused extreme offence by snubbing Miss Gillies and gratuitously correcting her former headmistress's rendering of the Latin grace.[28] Margaret Goodrich, who also attended the evening, commented on her friend's rudeness: 'That very small thing turned the entire dinner party away from her. It was a very silly thing to do.'[29]

For her part, Miss Dorothy Gillies bore these demonstrations of resentment with dignity. However, in her retirement she gave a glimpse of her feelings when she told one former pupil: 'I believe I had an influence on all my girls – but not on Margaret Roberts.'[30]

The battles with Miss Gillies may well have acted as a spur to the seventeen-year-old Margaret. She spent the last five months of 1942 studying intensively for the Somerville examination, which she sat in December. The result seemed to her 'something of a blow'[31] because she was not awarded a scholarship. But as a consolation prize she was offered a place at Oxford for the academic year commencing in Michaelmas term, October 1944.

The consolation prize was a huge achievement. However, it had disadvantages in comparison to a scholarship. Fees would have to be paid by her father; her entrance to the university would be postponed for a year; and under wartime regulations she would only be permitted to take a two-year Oxford degree before being called up to do her military service at the age of twenty. These constraints were a disappointment but, as she put it, 'there was nothing I could do about it'.[32]

Margaret Roberts somewhat reluctantly enrolled for another year at KGGS. She was appointed joint head girl in the third-year sixth form. 'I hope that she will show wisdom in the allotting of both time and energy to her work during the coming months, in order that she may do herself full justice,'[33] wrote Miss Gillies in a disparaging comment on a pupil who had just won a place at Oxford.

Luck came to the rescue. Six weeks after the term started, a telegram arrived from Somerville. One of the new entries of arriving undergraduates had dropped out, so an unexpected place at the college was on offer. It was accepted with alacrity. In the first week of October 1943, a few days short of her eighteenth birthday, Margaret Roberts left home in Grantham and headed for Oxford University.

REFLECTION

'I would not have been in No. 10 but for this school,'[34] declared Prime Minister Margaret Thatcher when she came back to KGGS in 1986 to open Roberts Hall, named after her father in recognition of his long service as Chairman of the Governors. In 1992, she paid her *alma mater* an even greater tribute when she took her title, Baroness Thatcher of Kesteven, from her school rather from her home town and birthplace.

Despite these retrospective compliments, Margaret Roberts did not have a smooth ride throughout her five years as a KGGS pupil. The change of headmistress upset her, so much so that she developed an angry and confrontational attitude towards Miss Gillies. The disruption to school classes caused by 'Operation Double Shift' reduced Margaret's access to good teaching. There must have been times when the bleak war news and the bombing raids on Grantham unsettled her.

Against this background, her achievement in winning a place at Oxford looks all the more outstanding. She had shown a remarkable capacity for hard work and a granite determination to overcome the obstacles put in her way. Her success was well deserved.

There were, however, two lingering doubts that hovered over her grammar school years. One concerned her relationships with other girls. Although the evidence is mixed, there were signs that she found it difficult to develop a good rapport with many of her KGGS contemporaries; to some she seemed dismissive towards them. In later life this characteristic was to cause similar problems with her female contemporaries in politics. In both settings Margaret was a loner with no apparent inclination to become 'one of the girls'.

A second area of concern was that as a schoolgirl she tried to cram in too much, too fast. This was partly a product of the wartime regulations governing education and the call-up dates for military service. For Margaret Roberts these pressures resulted in her applying to Oxford when she was sixteen. She arrived there as an undergraduate when she was seventeen. This was probably too early, but she was never one to let the grass grow under her feet when it came to seizing the moment.

3

Oxford, boyfriends and political ambition

EARLY UNHAPPINESS AT OXFORD

Margaret Roberts had an unhappy start to her life as an Oxford under-graduate. That was surprising. To the majority of its students, the university is a welcoming and exciting place, especially for those who have fought as hard as she did to get there. From the outset she found Oxford 'cold and strangely forbidding'.[1] Her disenchantment did not lift until she was well into her second year.

There was no single reason why she should have felt disillusioned with her early time as an Oxonian. Perhaps she went up too young. She was lonely, homesick and hard up. Also, she had chosen to read chemistry – a subject which did not capture her imagination, and required long hours of isolation in the lab. But the strongest negatives related to the insecurities of her personality. She was overawed by the atmosphere of Oxford. She was patronised by the dons and smarter students at Somerville. She was unlucky in her first love.

These negative sources of her unhappiness were balanced by interesting positives, although they took time to develop. She became a successful student politician, grinding tenaciously through the tedium of college membership administration of the Conservative Party, until in her fourth year she was elected President of the Oxford University Conservative Association (OUCA).

In addition to politics, she participated in extra-curricular activities that ranged from choral singing to Methodist preaching. In her second year she had a serious relationship with one boyfriend, and was admired by others. She went down with a good second into an immediate job. Yet, for all these accomplishments, the impression remains that she was out of sorts with Oxford, and that her personality jarred with it. This was an antipathy that later became mutual when, in 1985, Oxford refused her an honorary degree. Her relationship with her university was never an easy one.

It did not help her early days at Oxford that the city was lacking in its usual *joie de vivre* because of the dislocations of war. Many young men had deferred their studies to join up. The era of blackouts in the quadrangle and boarded-up stained-glass windows in the college chapels may have made the wartime intake of undergraduates feel more fearful than joyful. But the major problem for Margaret Roberts as an undergraduate was her loneliness.

There was no obvious explanation for why she should have felt lonely. She had a room in Somerville, and took her meals with other students in college hall. But she was slow to make friends, privately troubled by suppressed feelings of insecurity. These came out in a revealing conversation with the one familiar face to her at Oxford, Margaret Goodrich. She recalled Margaret Roberts asking her 'Don't you wish you could say you had been to Cheltenham or somewhere, instead of KGGS?'[2]

Another contemporary and fellow chemist who noticed these insecurities was Pauline Cowan. 'Margaret and I were known to be among the poorer members of the college. We came from a similar sort of state education background, in my case Glasgow School for Girls, and it was easy to feel patronised by the better off students. I think we both felt the Cheltenham clique looked down a bit on us.'[3]

Margaret's insecurities were compounded by a growing sense of isolation. Early in her time at Oxford, the Goodrich parents, visiting their daughter, made an impromptu call on the fellow Grantham girl who a few months earlier had seemed such a gregarious visitor to their home. They found Margaret Roberts alone in her room,* despondently toasting a crumpet and manifestly unhappy. Late in life she admitted her feelings in this period, telling the author Tricia Murray: 'I was always rather homesick. I think there would be something very wrong with your home life if you weren't just a little.'[4]

The homesickness and the insecurity made her first year fairly miserable. For the first and last time in her life she did a great deal of walking. This was

---

* Her room at Somerville was Penrose 5 on the ground floor. It was darker and smaller (12 ft × 10 ft) than her bedroom in Grantham, looking out on a gloomy backyard. Perhaps its atmosphere contributed to her low spirits.

a solitary activity, taking her on lonely perambulations along the banks of the Cherwell, or around the parks. She later claimed that on these walks she was 'enjoying my own company and thoughts'.[5]

This seems improbable, given her lifelong aversion to fresh air and exercise. Also her weight was going up, perhaps another indication of unhappiness. The combination of a sweet tooth and easy access to the confectionery in her father's shop had made her a noticeably plump schoolgirl. As an undergraduate, she became even plumper. In her second year at Oxford she tipped the scales at 150 lb, which is overweight for a young woman student only 5 feet 5 inches tall.

Another problem was money. Alfred Roberts' finances were stretched by having to pay the full Oxford fees for his daughter's tuition, board and lodging. So Margaret had precious little cash to spare for luxuries or student frivolities. When her chemistry tutor, Dorothy Hodgkin, discovered how difficult it was for her pupil to make ends meet, a modest bursary from Somerville was quietly arranged. This was supplemented by further grants from an education trust and by occasional earnings from work in vacations. After a stint as a temporary science teacher in the long vacation of 1944, she saved up enough money to buy her first bicycle – a near necessity for getting to labs and lectures on time in Oxford.

Hard work always came first in the life of Margaret Roberts, but it is not clear how much she enjoyed her studies. She read chemistry with her usual diligence. But her tutor Dorothy Hodgkin detected that 'she was not absolutely devoted to it',[6] adding: 'I came to rate her as good. One could always rely on her producing a sensible, well-read essay and yet there was something that some people had that she hadn't quite got.'[7]

The Principal of Somerville, Dame Janet Vaughan, was more dismissive of Margaret Roberts' academic abilities. 'I mean nobody thought anything of her. She was a perfectly good second-class chemist, a beta chemist.'[8]

Dame Janet's condescension extended from science to the social and political inadequacies of her college's most celebrated graduate:

> She wasn't an interesting person, except as a Conservative. I used to entertain the young a great deal, and if I had amusing, interesting people staying with me, I would never have thought really of asking Margaret Roberts because she wasn't very interesting to talk to, except as a Conservative.[9]

The damning with faint praise tone of these retrospective assessments, recorded by the BBC forty years after Margaret Roberts left Oxford, were clearly affected by donnish distaste for her politics as a Tory prime minister. She was better and more fairly judged at the time. She worked hard enough to achieve a decent second, even though she was sick with flu during her finals and had to take some of her most important papers in bed rather than in the examination schools. Her academic record qualified her to spend a fourth year at Oxford doing the research that upgraded her BA into a BSc.[10]

Like many undergraduates, her wider interests took her to horizons beyond her academic subject. She may have moped during the early stages of her Oxford life, but she soon picked herself up, and developed interests that took her away from her solitude and those long melancholy walks. Music was one antidote to loneliness. She joined the Oxford Bach choir, conducted by Thomas Armstrong.*

As an alto in this choir, she sang in performances of the *St Matthew Passion* at the Sheldonian Theatre, and also in *Prince Igor* by Borodin, *Rio Grande* by Constant Lambert and *Hymn of Jesus* by Holst.

Religion was important to her. She was much influenced by *Mere Christianity* by C.S. Lewis, which she first heard in a series of radio talks with the title *Christian Behaviour*. She was a regular worshipper at the Wesley Memorial Church and an active member of the John Wesley Society. This was an evangelical arm of the Methodist movement. It sent its members out in pairs to preach the gospel in churches and chapels across Oxfordshire. Margaret Roberts was one of those preachers.

Jean Southerst, also a Methodist and Somerville undergraduate, remembers a sermon on the text, 'Seek ye first the kingdom of God, and his righteousness; and all these things shall be added unto you',[11] being delivered by Margaret Roberts. It was 'outstanding', according to Southerst.[12] Like father, like daughter. It was interesting that the future prime minister was preaching sermons before she was making political speeches.

---

* Sir Thomas Armstrong (1898–1994), organist and conductor, Principal of the Royal Academy of Music, 1955–68. His son Robert (Lord Armstrong of Ilminster) was Margaret Thatcher's Cabinet Secretary, 1979–1987.

STIRRINGS OF ROMANCE

So far as is known, Margaret Roberts had no boyfriends during her growing-up years at Grantham. This changed at Oxford. Although her romantic life began with a painful rejection (heavily influenced by the boyfriend's mother), she recovered from it and was later well admired, particularly by one serious suitor who she met in Michaelmas term 1944.

In her first year, Margaret was an ingénue about her love life, talking candidly about her feelings for various young men she found attractive. Over dinners in Hall at Somerville, 'She would blush from the neck upwards'[13] when teased by her contemporary, Betty Spice, and others, about possible boyfriends. Another Somerville undergraduate who shared these confidences was Pauline Cowan. 'We all knew that Margaret had set her cap at a young man with money and a title', she recalled. 'It went well for a while until he took her home for the weekend and found his mother couldn't stand her.'[14]

Other versions of this romance circulated among several of Margaret Roberts' Oxford contemporaries. They were summarised by one of her earliest biographers, Penny Junor, who after stating that the men Margaret sought out were in OUCA, continued:

> She fell quite soundly for the son of an earl, who went on to become something of a luminary in the Tory Party. She made no secret of her feelings, and talked about him quite gushingly, unaware that by so doing she was laying herself open to more teasing from the other girls in Hall, who by this time were growing increasingly disillusioned by her blatant use of people. They felt that if she caught herself a lord, it would be the last straw. But Margaret failed to net her lord. The relationship came to an end soon after she had met his mother.[15]

The aristocratic boyfriend whose mother took against Margaret Roberts was Lord Craigmyle. In the summer of 1944, he was a twenty-year-old undergraduate reading Modern History at Corpus Christi College. He knew Margaret quite well because they were both active Conservative students. He makes his appearance, somewhat incongruously, in the first volume of her memoirs, named in a photograph of three young men in dinner jackets, captioned 'OUCA Party in Oxford'. Besides being a handsome, clean-cut man of the type for whom Prime Minister Margaret Thatcher later showed an occasional weakness (such as Cecil Parkinson, Humphrey Atkins, Alan Clark and John Moore), 'Craigie' Craigmyle had other qualities she mentioned to the Somerville gossips.

Craigie had inherited his father's title. He was heir to an enormous ship-owning fortune, which was known to be coming to him from his grandfather, the Earl of Inchcape. He was committed to his Christian faith, keenly interested in the social and political issues of the day. Besides being a great catch, he was regarded as a leading undergraduate character, showing a gregarious warmth of hospitality to his friends. But he could also be an acutely shy young man. He was exceptionally close to his mother, Lord Inchcape's eldest daughter, who often visited him in his rooms at Corpus. If Lady Craigmyle formed the view that the provincial Miss Roberts was not a suitable girlfriend for her son that would have been an obstacle, if not a veto to their romance. Did Craigie, acting under the influence of his mother, break the young Margaret's heart?

It seems likely. As her Somerville contemporaries knew, Margaret's relationship with Craigie was serious enough for him to invite her to stay for the weekend at the family's London house in the Boltons. But the meeting with Lady Craigmyle was not a success. As another Inchcape grandson, Lord Tanlaw, explained: 'My Aunt Margaret was a formidable character, bearing more than a passing resemblance to Lady Bracknell. When she met my cousin Craigie's new Oxford girlfriend, her comment was: "In trade and in science! We know nobody who is in either!"'[16]

Poor Margaret Roberts! But if her hopes of catching a titled husband* were dashed by this maternal snobbery, her slimmed down figure, elegant legs and sparkling eyes were soon catching the eye of other admirers. She began to take much more interest in clothes, make-up and feminine colours. From 1944 onwards, her Oxford letters to her sister Muriel are full of reference to frocks, shoes, silk stockings and the problems of affording them. In one of these letters she described her first visit to Bond Street, where she bought brown Debutante Lanette shoes to match her brown Marshall and Snelgrove handbag. 'Also, I had

---

* Lord Craigmyle (1923–1998) might not have been a good match for her on other grounds. He was an eccentric: he delivered his maiden speech in the House of Lords wearing the bell-bottomed uniform of an Ordinary Seaman in the RNVR. He was a passionately devout Catholic, which would not have pleased Alfred and Beatrice Roberts. He also suffered from alcoholism.

in mind to get a nigger brown* fairly brown frock in order to have a completely brown-faun rig out.'[17]

All this effort to buy attractive 'rig-outs' was not unconnected with Margaret's interest in the opposite sex. She had several flirtations in her latter Oxford years, with men who included Roger Gray (later a Queen's Counsel (QC) and Crown Court Recorder), Neil Findlay and John Stebbings, a handsome swimming Blue from Kent who later became President of the Law Society. However, none of them were serious, at least in comparison to her relationship with Tony Bray, who came up to Oxford in October 1944 as an army cadet on a six-month military training course.

Initially attracted by their shared interest in OUCA politics, Margaret and Tony were going out together on a regular basis by the summer of 1945. They went to several college dances and to one particularly special ball at the Randolph Hotel. Margaret's ecstatic description of the evening in a letter to Muriel conveys the impression of a young woman falling in love:

> I managed to borrow a glorious royal blue velvet cloak which match [sic] the blue frock perfectly . . . I felt on top of the world . . . The ballroom was marvellously decorated . . . The refreshments were lovely. Altogether, it was the best and biggest ball I've ever been to.[18]

Tony, who had begun the events by presenting her with a Moyses Stevens spray of carnations, took her up to London for lunch at the Dorchester, a tea dance at the Piccadilly Hotel and a performance of Strauss's *A Night in Venice* at the Cambridge Theatre. Soon afterwards, she invited him to stay the weekend with her parents in Grantham. Although it was a somewhat strained and awkward visit, the fact that it happened was a sure sign that she was seriously interested in him.

However, her seriousness does not seem to have been fully reciprocated, perhaps understandably since Tony was nearly two years younger than she was and not ready to settle down, at the age of eighteen, with such an intense girlfriend.

Charles Moore tracked Tony Bray down in old age, and with the omniscience of an official biographer reached the conclusion that the couple 'never slept together',

---

* Nigger brown was not regarded as a racist term in those days. It was a standard colour description used in shoe shops, dress shops and outfitters.

although Margaret 'showed a delight in physical intimacy'.[19] Although they drifted apart when Tony's short army course ended, they had something of a reunion three years later in 1948, but the old fires were not rekindled. Nevertheless, in that glorious Oxford summer of 1945, against the historical background of the D-Day landings and the expectation of an Allied victory, nineteen-year-old Margaret Roberts enjoyed her first serious experience of romantic love.

SUCCESS IN OUCA POLITICS

However important Tony Bray may have been to Margaret Roberts, politics were more important. To her Somerville contemporaries, she was seen as a rather boring oddball because of her political enthusiasm for the Conservatives. Pauline Cowan recalled:

> She amazed me by her persistence in trying to persuade me to join OUCA, She kept on and on at me, even after I had told her that I wasn't interested because my loyalties were in the opposite direction. She was quite insensitive, as though it was the only thing that really mattered to her . . . She wasn't the confiding or pally type. I often thought of her as a rather unhappy person, who had no close friends in the college. Of course we talked over coffee in our digs every morning, but usually about our work, or our shared dislike of one of our landlady's frequent breakfast dishes – hot pilchards with mashed potatoes. I don't think Margaret and I have ever been able to look at a pilchard ever since.[20]

Pilchards and Conservatives ranked about equal in the popularity stakes at traditionally left-wing Somerville. One college contemporary who tried to dislodge Margaret Roberts from her Tory loyalties was Nina Bawden.* The two undergraduates were doing fire-watching duty together in the summer of 1944. Nina, an active Labour supporter, argued that all the people who joined OUCA 'were dull as ditch water'. According to Bawden's account:

> Margaret smiled her pretty china doll's smile. Of course, she admitted, the Labour Club was, just at that moment, more *fashionable* . . . but that, in a way, unintentionally suited her purposes. She meant to get into Parliament and there was more chance of being 'noticed' in the Conservative Club just because some of the members were a bit stodgy.[21]

---

* Nina Bawden (1925–2012), novelist and writer of children's stories. She read PPE at Somerville College, Oxford.

Margaret's passive acceptance of OUCA's stodginess suggests that, like most Tories of the time, she had little awareness of the coming sea change in British politics. In the mid-1940s, the leading Conservative undergraduates of Oxford tended to be hereditary aristocrats or members of upper-class families with double-barrelled names. M. Roberts (as she was listed on the Association's term card) came to their attention because she worked so hard at the thankless task of OUCA College Rep for Somerville. She managed to recruit such an impressive number of those extremely reluctant Conservatives in her own college that she was considered for the role of being in charge of all the College Reps in the university, as the General Agent. This was a tedious job, which most undergraduate politicians sought to avoid because it required so much work. On the other hand, the post had status because it was the Association's fourth highest elected office after the President, Treasurer and Secretary. At the end of her second year at Oxford Margaret Roberts was elected General Agent of OUCA.

Ever since she had helped with committee-room duties in Grantham during the 1935 general election, when she was nine, Margaret had taken an interest in the mechanics of Conservative Party electioneering. She had polished these skills at a wartime by-election in the town in February 1942 when, to the consternation of local Tories, their candidate lost the seat by 367 votes to a colourful local Independent. Although Margaret was little more than a leaflet deliverer, she was shocked by the result and criticised the party's administrative weaknesses in failing to get its voters to the polls. 'Then and later the Conservative Party was inclined to complacency', she concluded.[22]

No such complacency was allowed while Margaret Roberts was General Agent of OUCA. Under her 'queenly sway', reported *Isis*, its membership climbed to over a thousand for the first time since the 1920s.[23]

In the general election campaign of summer 1945, she recruited a regiment of student canvassers, who helped Oxford's Conservative Parliamentary Candidate Quintin Hogg* to hold on to the seat, narrowly defeating the Labour challenger Frank Pakenham, later Lord Longford.

Later in the 1945 election, Margaret Roberts went back to Grantham, where she delivered her first political speech to be reported. She made her debut on

---

* Quintin Hogg, Baron Hailsham of St Marylebone (1907–2001), barrister, Conservative politician, Lord Chancellor in Margaret Thatcher's cabinet, 1979–1987.

the hustings supporting the Conservative candidate Squadron Leader G.A. Worth. The *Grantham Journal* reported that she had inherited 'her father's gift for oratory', and commented that 'the presence of a young woman of the age of nineteen with such decided convictions has been no small factor in influencing the women's vote in the division'.[24]

Her convictions were reported in greater detail in another local newspaper, the *Sleaford Gazette*. According to its two-column account, the nineteen-year old alderman's daughter voiced two strands of opinion that came to prominence again four decades later, when she was prime minister. The first, predictable in 1945, was her antagonism towards Germany: 'Germany had plunged the world into war. Germany must be disarmed and brought to justice . . . just punishment must be meted out.' Her second and more unexpected theme was her advocacy for developing Britain's relationship with the Soviet Union. She heaped praise on Churchill and Eden for having 'worked unsparingly for cooperation with Russia'.[25]

These early views of the nineteen-year old warm-up speaker destined to become Britain's first woman prime minister were submerged in the great Labour landslide victory of 1945. Margaret attended the Grantham constituency count, which ended in the defeat of Squadron Leader Worth. Then she went to watch the national results in the Grantham Picture House where, like most Tory activists, she was utterly astounded by the outcome. She could not understand how the electorate could have ousted Winston Churchill from No. 10 Downing Street.

Returning to Oxford after the long vacation, Margaret Roberts, as General Agent of OUCA, did not appear to have been subdued by her party's crushing defeat. One of her first actions was to co-author and chair an OUCA policy report on how to revive Tory fortunes in the university. Her own unmistakable tones are to be found in several passages of the report which, in somewhat hectoring style, told OUCA that it 'can no longer drift in its present aloofness' and must become 'an active proselytising body, and should have an active propaganda policy'.[26] The responsibility for implementing these initiatives was given to the General Agent.

Taking charge of proselytising and propaganda did no harm to the student political career of Margaret Roberts. She became Treasurer and then President of OUCA in the elections of March and October 1946. One of the reasons for her success was her increasingly confident speaking ability. It was transformed by Mrs S.M. Gatehouse, who had her own niche in the history of twentieth-century OUCA as its public-speaking tutor.

Stella Gatehouse was an Oxfordshire vicar's wife who was recruited in the 1930s by Conservative Central Office to give weekly speech-making lessons to undergraduate members of OUCA. She was a formidable character with a touch of Joyce Grenfell in her own diction. Gentle with stumbling novices, but fierce with youthful arrogance, her classes were lively affairs, which knocked several generations of aspiring parliamentarians into better oratorical shape. Between 1938 and 1970 at least twenty future Tory ministers were cajoled and charmed by 'Mrs G' into improving their public speaking.

Mrs G was a good talent spotter. In 1961, she was asked to predict which of her former pupils would have most success in politics. She replied, 'No 1, Michael Heseltine. No 2, Margaret Thatcher.'[27] Since the former was not even an MP at that time and the latter was a little-known back-bencher that was quite a forecast.

Once or twice during Margaret Thatcher's early days as Leader of the Opposition I thought I could hear echoes in her parliamentary speeches of Mrs Gatehouse's recommended techniques. These included rubrics such as: 'Summarise your argument with a good strong boom at the end of your last paragraph'; and 'Have a crescendo, but keep it short and sharp, with no more than six words'. At the end of a 1976 debate in the division lobbies of the House of Commons, I wondered in a conversation with Margaret Thatcher if her speech earlier in the day could have been influenced by Mrs Gatehouse's lessons. 'Yes, Mrs G transformed my speaking' was the response.[28]*

One of the principal duties of the President of OUCA is to organise 'the term card', the published list of visiting speakers. This task requires a great deal of correspondence and persistence. President-elect Margaret Roberts was remarkably prescient in attracting both famous and interesting guests. They included two future prime ministers, Anthony Eden and Alec Douglas-Home; a future Lord Chancellor, Lord Kilmuir, who had achieved fame as a prosecutor at the Nuremberg trials; and a future Chancellor of the Exchequer, Peter Thorneycroft.

---

* Margaret Thatcher paid tribute to Mrs Gatehouse in the first volume of her memoirs, *The Path to Power*, page 45.

Wining and dining such guests at the Randolph Hotel before and after the public meetings gave Margaret Roberts new social and networking skills. Her experiences at OUCA focused her thoughts on becoming a Member of Parliament.

There are several versions of how and when the first stirrings of Parliamentary ambition manifested themselves in Margaret's life story. Her own accounts (retold on different occasions to several interviewers) suggest that an almost Damascene flash of light on the road to Westminster hit her at a Lincolnshire dance, or during a midnight argument with 'one of the boys' after a village hop at which young RAF pilots were present. All these conversion experiences are dated post-1945, and involve a surprise declaration of intent followed by a solemn commitment in words such as 'Suddenly it was crystallised for me. I knew.'[29]

Perhaps the discrepancies between these various descriptions can be rationalised by the formula used in the Scottish Psalter, 'Another version of the same'. That said, the most authentic of the versions to judge by its simplicity and its source is given by Margaret Goodrich.

In her account there are no pilots, no dancing and no theatrical pronouncements. The scene was the vicarage at Corby Glen near Grantham, where Canon and Mrs Goodrich hosted 'a very unsophisticated party' for their daughter's twenty-first birthday in December 1944. No alcohol was served, and there was no dancing or music. Towards midnight the festivities had dwindled to a handful of girls sitting round the kitchen table drinking cocoa. During the conversation Mrs Goodrich asked Margaret Roberts what she wished to do in life. The reply was memorably forthright: 'I am going to be an MP. I want to be an MP.'[30]

The didactic certainty of these words left quite an impression. They had the ring of the increasingly confident nineteen-year-old General Agent of OUCA, who had put herself in charge of 'propaganda'. Perhaps she felt she could show her hand this early in a private setting, for the Goodrich vicarage was safe territory. Some two and half years later, Margaret Goodrich was again the recipient of another surprising confidence about her friend's political ambition, at the end of term at Oxford. The two Margarets were walking down South Parks Road near Rhodes House, when Margaret Roberts declared: 'Of course this degree is not much use to me as an MP. I must now try to read Law.'[31]

The remark was further confirmation that by the time she left Oxford she had found her vocation.

REFLECTION

Oxford confirmed rather than changed the personality of Margaret Roberts. She arrived from Grantham with a mind-set of certainties and ambitions. Her university years sharpened these qualities but did not visibly deepen them. Unlike most undergraduates, she knew from the start her direction of travel.

Her journey was not easy, for she had to overcome many overt and covert barriers of prejudice. Male chauvinism was still a surprisingly strong obstacle. Margaret would have enjoyed honing her debating skills at the Oxford Union, but it did not admit female members until 1963. The same was true of many other clubs, from the Oxford University Dramatic Society to the Alembic Society. The latter was the meeting ground of all science students, unless they happened to be women – so she was excluded from it.

A more subtle form of prejudice was social snobbery. Margaret Roberts felt it from the Cheltenham old girls at Somerville, from the mother of the first young man she fell for and probably in many other settings. Oxford in those days was described as a university of seven thousand experts on class. In such an environment a grocer's daughter would have had to endure an unfair share of slights and snubs. But her insecurity may well have been the spur to her ambition.

The main purposes of her Oxford life were political. Yet in those days she focused not on ideas but on the mechanics of elections and membership drives. She did read Hayek's *Road to Serfdom* in 1944, but its impact on her was minimal until she re-read it on the recommendation of Sir Keith Joseph, thirty years later. OUCA was her vehicle for career advancement, not intellectual curiosity.

OUCA was also the arena where she met interesting young men. All her boyfriends came from the Tory stable. Her wider circle of male acquaintances, such as Sir Edward Boyle, Maurice Chandler and Johnny Dalkeith (later the Duke of Buccleuch), were also active in OUCA. Finding a husband may have been subliminally on her agenda, but once her relationship with Tony Bray cooled, she made no discernible progress towards it.

The *joie de vivre* that manifests itself in the journeys of many Oxford undergraduates seems to have been largely missing from the life of Margaret Roberts. She may have had some happy moments, but on the whole she was too intense and competitive. After four years spent mainly in the science labs and at OUCA meetings, she had never warmed to Oxford.

In later life her relationship with her *alma mater* became even colder when Congregation, its governing assembly, voted to refuse her an honorary degree. This was an unprecedented snub to a serving prime minister. Despite this hurtful insult from the university, Margaret Thatcher retained a genuine affection for her old college. She gave generously to its various appeals and supported the creation of an auditorium centre named after her in the main quadrangle.

Another strange indication of the bond she felt for her college came on the day in October 1984 when Prime Minister Indira Gandhi was assassinated in New Delhi. It was just two weeks after the Brighton bombing. On hearing of the Indian Prime Minister's death from her Political Secretary Stephen Sherbourne, Margaret Thatcher clasped his arm saying: 'What terrible news! First they tried to get me. Now they get her. And we were both at Somerville.'[32]

These events involving Somerville's two prime ministers lay far ahead in the future. At the time when she went down from Oxford in 1947, Margaret Roberts had to deal with her immediate concerns of the present – how to get her first job and how to continue her interest in Conservative politics.

4

First steps in politics

YOUNG CONSERVATIVE

By the time she left Oxford, twenty-one-year old Margaret Roberts had firmly decided that her future career lay in politics. But there were practical hurdles that had to be overcome on the road to this objective. They included getting her first job; securing a place on Conservative Central Office's general list of approved candidates; and winning the nomination for a constituency. It says much for her energy and determination that she achieved these goals within the next two years.

It was not all plain sailing, for some aspects of her personality could rub other people up the wrong way. As she travelled around the country meeting prospective employers she had several disappointments. One of them came at a factory in Billingham, North Yorkshire, owned by Imperial Chemical Industries. The manager who turned her down wrote in his report, 'This young woman has much too strong a personality to work here'.[1]

The strength of her personality continued to make both positive and negative impressions. When she did find a job in September 1947, working as a researcher for British Xylonite Plastics at Manningtree in Essex, she was unhappy during her first few months with the company.

Some of her fellow researchers thought she put on airs and graces, because she spoke with a posh accent and seemed overdressed as she travelled to work on the company bus wearing a Burberry coat and gloves. The unfriendly nicknames 'Duchess' and 'Auntie Margaret' were applied to her at this time.[2]

At BX she was never bashful in expressing her political opinions, not always to the approval of her colleagues. One of them, Joyce Duggan, used to tease Margaret Roberts by joking to her, 'There goes the future Prime Minister'.[3] These catcalls from the clerical department were taken in good part. But Joyce Duggan also remembered that Margaret could become aggressive in her politics, turning red in the face when she argued over issues of the day.

Her boss, Stanley Booth, was also underwhelmed by his researcher's political certitudes. 'Her views seemed rather simplistic', he recalled. 'She believed . . . that people should stand on their own two feet. I'd come up the hard way and didn't quite see things quite like that.'[4]

However people saw her at work, Margaret Roberts was not letting the political grass grow under her feet. She was a hyperactive Young Conservative, becoming Secretary of the Colchester branch in 1948, entering the national speaking competition and attending regional Young Conservative conferences all over the home counties and South East England. At one of these conferences in Kent in the summer of 1948, a speech she delivered on the economy mightily impressed the Chairman of the county's Conservative Associations. He was Alfred Bossom, Member of Parliament for Maidstone.* 'Miss Roberts, yours was the best speech I have ever heard from a Young Conservative', declared Alfred Bossom. 'May I have the honour of recommending your name for the candidates' list?'[5]

MENTORED BY ALFRED BOSSOM MP

Alfred Bossom was one of the minor characters of British politics, but he became a major influence on the life and career of Margaret Roberts. He was a rich but obscure Tory back-bencher. His greatest claim to fame prior to meeting her was that he had once been the subject of a much-quoted Churchillian wisecrack. Soon after his election as the Conservative MP for Maidstone in 1931, Alfred Bossom was introduced to Winston Churchill, evidently in a convivial mood, on the terrace of the House of Commons. 'Bossom, Bossom; that's a funny name', observed Churchill. 'Neither one thing nor t'other.'[6]

In 1932, tragedy struck the Bossom family when Alfred's wife and eldest son were killed in a flying accident. In what may have been a reaction to his loss, the Member for Maidstone redoubled his commitment to his political activities,

---

* Alfred Charles Bossom (1881–1965), MP for Maidstone 1931–1959. He was created a baronet in 1953 and a life peer in 1960. His son, Sir Clive Bossom Bt, also a Conservative MP, became Margaret Thatcher's first Parliamentary Private Secretary in 1957.

with emphasis on two unusual angles. 'My father carved out an odd political niche for himself', said Alfred's son, Sir Clive Bossom. 'He specialised in giving parties and bringing on protégées. Margaret Roberts was his star young guest and pupil on both fronts.'[7]

Alfred Bossom made his fortune in the early years of the twentieth century, building skyscrapers in New York, Dallas and Houston. He was a British-born and trained architect. When he returned to his native London in 1926, he was a star of his profession, designing the landmark Dorchester Hotel on Park Lane. His success enabled him to enter politics and to buy a grand home at No. 5 Carlton Gardens overlooking The Mall.

From this house he entertained lavishly, so much so that he was regarded as a successor to the legendary pre-war hostess Lady Londonderry because of his generosity in holding glittering political soirées. His annual white-tie dinner on the eve of the new parliamentary session became a fixture for the Tory elite, and was attended by the cabinet and every Conservative prime minister, from Stanley Baldwin to Anthony Eden. Margaret Roberts was invited for the first time in November 1948.

In addition to being a good host, Alfred Bossom was regarded as having a keen eye for talent among aspiring Tory candidates. He was a diligent attender of Conservative Party meetings in Kent, often driving down from London to their functions three or four times a week in his yellow Rolls-Royce. Several of the Young Conservatives he picked out owed their eventual ascent to Westminster to the encouragement they received from the MP for Maidstone. He was, unusually for the time, helpful to aspiring women candidates.

The Americanised Bossom believed that the country needed more women MPs. 'We've got to find successors to Lady Astor', he used to say.[8]

In the post-war years he helped to groom two young protégées for this role. The first was Patricia Hornsby-Smith,* a flame-haired Young Conservative branch secretary who became MP for Chislehurst. The second was Margaret Roberts.

---

* Patricia Hornsby-Smith (1914–1985), only daughter of a saddle dealer and master umbrella maker. MP for Chislehurst for twenty years, she was Margaret Thatcher's immediate predecessor as Parliamentary Under Secretary at the Ministry of Pensions and National Insurance. She became a life peeress in 1974.

Alfred Bossom was the first national political figure to see the potential of Margaret Roberts. In the most practical and effective of ways he became her mentor, patron and introducer to the upper echelons of the Tory hierarchy. His many kindnesses to her included helping her with political and travelling expenses; supporting her application for the candidates list; entertaining her at his lunches and dinner parties; advising on her speeches; guiding her on constituency selection meetings; urging her to get married; hosting her wedding reception at 5 Carlton Gardens; and trying unsuccessfully to get her chosen as his successor as the Member for Maidstone.

Aspiring politicians are lucky if they have a good mentor and patron to help them along their road. Margaret Roberts needed Bossom's early encouragement because, for all her ambition, she was full of insecurities both financial and political. In 1949 she was not even trying to get on the Conservative Party's approved list of candidates because, as she put it, 'With no private income of my own there was no way I could have afforded to be an MP on the salary then available'.*[9] She also had serious doubts about her short-term prospects for winning a nomination for a constituency. When an Oxford friend, John Grant, asked her if she hoped to be an MP one day, she replied: 'Well, yes, but there's not much hope of that. The chances of my being selected are just nil at the moment.'[10]

These odds changed when, with Alfred Bossom's help, she attended the Conservative Party Conference in Llandudno in 1948.

YOUNG CANDIDATE

Margaret Roberts had not been planning to go to the 1948 Party Conference until Alfred Bossom began championing her cause. He tried to get her included in the delegation of Kent Young Conservatives to Llandudno, but when this did not work out she managed to wangle a conference pass as a representative from the undersubscribed Oxford University Graduate Conservative Association (OUGCA).[11]

Bossom helped her with her travelling and accommodation expenses, and took her under his wing by inviting her to the parties he was hosting for the

---

* The annual salary of an MP in 1949 was £1,000; expenses averaged £716. Current equivalents: £29,938 and £21,436 (www.thismoney.co.uk).

Maidstone and Kent Area delegates. But she was disappointed at not being called to speak on a motion deploring the Labour government's abolition of university seats. She nearly went back from North Wales in a mood of frustration, but her spirits were lifted by an unexpected invitation to a lunch on Llandudno pier.

The invitation came from John Miller, the Chairman of Dartford Conservative Association. He was under some pressure from Conservative Central Office to pick a candidate for this safe Labour seat in North Kent. A friend at the conference urged him to consider Margaret Roberts.

'Oh, but Dartford is a real industrial stronghold. I don't think a woman would do at all',[12] was Miller's immediate reaction. But he reconsidered it. He made contact with Miss Roberts, inviting her to lunch with the key members of the Dartford delegation at a restaurant at the end of the pier, on the last Saturday of the conference, just before the final address of the leader of the party, Winston Churchill.

Margaret Roberts presented herself well at this lunch. Several of the Dartford delegates were impressed with the forceful opinions of the young woman they were meeting for the first time. But some of them had reservations on the question of whether she would be the right choice as the Conservative standard bearer in an industrial seat. Their doubts seem to have been more about the sex than the strength of the potential candidate for in the 1940s Conservative women MPs were a rarity. John Miller himself felt that the vigorous Miss Roberts might have just the right fighting spirit to bring down the large Labour majority and to breathe life into his somewhat moribund Association.

Although the early signals from Dartford seemed to have been positive, there followed a disconcerting three months of silence. John Miller used the time to assemble a list of twenty-six candidates, even though he already had expressed his own preference for Miss Roberts. He still wanted a strong slate to choose from. Among those he approached was a local businessman, Denis Thatcher, who had stood in a council election as the representative of the Ratepayers' Association. 'I said no without hesitating', was Thatcher's response to the suggestion that he should put his hat into the ring for the nomination.[13]

Dartford Conservatives followed the traditional pattern of constituency association selection procedures. They interviewed the long list of Miller's twenty-six hopefuls in two rounds, reducing them down to a short list of five. The final selection of the Parliamentary Candidate was made from this quintet at a meeting of the fifty strong Executive Committee of the Association, held on 31 January 1949 at the Bull Hotel in Dartford.

Margaret Roberts went into this final run-off as the favourite with the backing of the Chairman. The Central Office Deputy Area Agent, who attended all the interviews, described her speaking ability and political knowledge as 'far above those of the other candidates'.[14]

If that was the way the betting was moving before the run-off, Margaret Roberts turned it into a certainty. In her fifteen-minute speech and in her answer to questions she gave a fiery performance. Not only was it in harmony with the views of her audience, it was streets ahead of her competitors. The best of these was the runner-up Anthony Kershaw, an Old Etonian barrister with a fruity voice and a less than stellar intellect. A gregarious, clubbable figure who later became a Gloucestershire MP and a junior minister in the Heath government of 1970–74, he was no match for Margaret Roberts on the night of 31 January 1949. She won the nomination by a clear majority on the first ballot.

The next milestone in the developing love affair between the Dartford Tories and their new candidate was her adoption meeting. This is a formal event, which by Conservative tradition has something of the feel of a coronation ceremony, as the victor of the selection process is presented to and acclaimed by the full membership of the association. Her adoption had two ingredients that were unusual. The first was an unprecedentedly high turnout at the meeting. The second was the presence of her father and her future husband.

Despite a cold, frosty night on 28 February 1949, 380 Dartford Conservatives turned out to inspect and approve the Executive Committee's choice of candidate. They were not disappointed. As the Central Office Area Agent reported to headquarters: 'It was a first class show; quite the best meeting of any type that the Dartford constituency has held for many a long day. Miss Roberts made a brilliant speech, and the decision to adopt her was unanimous.'[15]

The brilliance may have owed some of its sparkle to being the equivalent of 'preaching to the choir'. It consisted mainly of a trenchant attack on the Labour government's economic policies expressed in language that was both simple and super-patriotic: 'The Government should do what any good house-wife would do if money was short – look at their accounts and see what was wrong', declared the candidate. Furthermore, 'If the Socialists continued with their disastrous policy, unemployment and other evils would result and the working people would suffer'. [16]

This message of thrift and anti-socialism must have gone down well with the person in the audience whose presence meant most to the candidate – Alfred Roberts. It was the first time father and daughter had spoken from the same platform. Their dynastic duet was emotionally moving and politically astute. At a time when the party leader, Winston Churchill, was wooing the Liberal vote, Alfred testified that his family had always been Liberal but it was now the Conservatives who stood for the old Liberalism. [17]

One other listener in the hall destined to become a dynastic pillar in the family life of Margaret Roberts was Denis Thatcher. He warmly applauded the new candidate's anti-socialist rhetoric, and congratulated her on it after the meeting. They had an opportunity to talk at a supper party after the adoption given by staunch Tory supporters Mr and Mrs Stanley Soward. He worked in the constituency for the Atlas Preservative Company of Erith and had invited along his managing director, Denis Thatcher.

Denis was well liked by the staff of his family business. They called him 'The Major' on account of his war record. But he was a shy man, particularly in the company of women. So it was a surprise when towards the end of the evening Denis asked the candidate, 'Miss Roberts, how are you going to get home?' [18]

The offer of a lift was useful because the newly adopted candidate could not afford a car. In those days, there was no Dartford Tunnel connecting Kent and Essex. The only way she could cross the Thames and get back to her flat in Colchester was by returning to central London, then taking a train on the north side of the river. So when Denis Thatcher said he would be glad to drive her to Liverpool Street Station, he solved her difficult late-night transport problem.

The solution took longer than either of them expected, because by the time they reached Liverpool Street Station, all the trains to Colchester had gone. She had to wait for the early morning milk train, which departed at 3.40 a.m. Denis gallantly kept her company until this hour. He may have been personally interested in her, since he had been invited to the adoption meeting by his friend, Stanley Soward, with the words: 'Come to dinner: I want you to meet a very pretty girl.' [19] Unfortunately for him, the pretty girl, now revealed as the new candidate, did not reciprocate Denis Thatcher's stirrings of interest. As she described the scene in a letter to Muriel: 'A Major Thatcher, who has a flat in London (age about 36, plenty of money), was also dining with them, and he drove me back to town at midnight. Not a very attractive creature – very reserved but quite nice.'[20]

Denis took a more favourable view of his passenger. Years afterwards, he was asked by the wife of a rugby-playing friend what he had first found attractive about Margaret. He replied, 'Several things; she's got a good pair of legs'.[21]

THREE MEN ON A STRING

Her good legs became energetic legs as Margaret Roberts buckled down to the task of nursing the Dartford constituency. But away from her public duties of canvassing and addressing meetings she was also showing her paces in a private life of some complexity. During the period 1949–51 she dated three different men at the same time, carefully considering marriage to each one of them. This trio of potential bridegrooms were a Scottish farmer, a distinguished surgeon and Denis Thatcher. The way Margaret Roberts handled them showed that she could be both manipulative and mixed up in her relationships.

The Scottish farmer was Willie Cullen. He met and fancied Margaret but ended up marrying her sister Muriel. The manoeuvring and matchmaking behind the plot of this Roberts girls' operetta was complicated.

Willie Cullen was a thirty-four-year-old Scotsman who had come south to buy a farm in Essex, Foulton Hall. He met Margaret at a Conservative event in Colchester, fell for her and pursued her with dinner invitations, visits to the theatre and presents such as chocolates and nylons, some of which he delivered in person to her office at BX Plastics. Soon after she had been his date and dancing partner at the Colchester Caledonian Ball in the town hall, Margaret wrote to Muriel: 'He [Willie] is awfully sweet; I am getting quite fond of him, and a very welcome relaxation.'[22]

The fondness ripened into many more dates, dinners, movies, gifts of perfume and visits to the races. Margaret took him seriously but not seriously enough to make him her husband. After she had stayed at Willie's farm near Foulton, she came to the conclusion that he would make a better match for her sister than for herself.

Muriel had recently broken up with her boyfriend, and this was the catalyst for Margaret to start playing Cupid. She did it with considerable skill. Muriel was invited down to Essex. Meetings with Willie Cullen were subtly engineered.

He was encouraged to, and did, like the older of the two Miss Robertses. His preference stayed firmly for Margaret, but it gradually became clear that she was transferring his affection away from herself. 'Though very fond of him, I am not in love with him,' she wrote to Muriel, 'and a marriage between us would falter after 2 or 3 months. We have completely different outlooks, and quite different sorts of friends. While I get on all right with his, he would feel out of water with mine.'[23]

This was Margaret's way of leaving the water clear for Muriel. Willie Cullen jumped, or was pushed, into it. He married Muriel in April 1950, and they lived happily ever after. The tale may well have been more tangled than either privacy-loving sister let on. Throughout it, Margaret called the shots. She probably knew in her heart of hearts that she could not settle down as a farmer's wife, so she created a clever vacuum in order to do her sister a good turn. This was partly because Margaret had bigger and better fish to fry.

The surgeon, a big fish in his profession, was Robert Henderson, a forty-seven-year-old bachelor who had invented the iron lung for polio patients, and been awarded a CBE for services to medicine. He met Margaret towards the end of 1949 when he was medical superintendent of the 1700-bed Southern Hospital in Dartford. Despite the twenty-four-year age gap between them, the doctor and the candidate hit it off romantically. Robert took her to parties, dinners, drives around the Weald of Kent and to Eastbourne for the weekend. There are several clues in Margaret's letters from this period that his courtship was making him her favourite suitor.

Denis Thatcher, however, had not faded out of her life. After their drive on the night of her adoption to Liverpool Street Station, the 'perfect gentleman' who she had not found very attractive continued to keep in touch. He took her on a series of dates to the Royal Tournament, the Festival of Britain, the National Paint Federation dinner and to a West End play *His Excellency*. At first Margaret pretended that she was not giving him much encouragement. 'I can't say I really ever enjoy going out for the evening with him', she wrote to Muriel, after the play. 'He has not got a very prepossessing personality.'[24]

Either she was dissembling about her feelings, or somewhere along the line she changed her mind. For in early 1950, one of Denis's close friends, David Roe, unexpectedly dropped into the Thatcher bachelor flat in Chelsea. 'I was very surprised to find that we were greeted by a lovely smiley girl', recalled Roe.

'Denis introduced us, and she soon disappeared into the kitchen while he and I sat talking for a few minutes. When she came back she brought some tea and sat on the floor, joining in the conversation . . . Her name was Margaret Roberts'.[25]

The impression created by this story is that Margaret and Denis were behaving, if not living together, as a couple. Yet this was at the same time when she was also going out with Robert Henderson, apparently with rather more enthusiasm. Some might call it playing the field, hedging her bets or even two-timing. There was certainly rather more to the private life of the demure Miss Roberts than met the eye. But public life was always her first priority.

THE GENERAL ELECTION OF 1950

For an ambitious newcomer to politics, a first election campaign can be as passionate an affair as a first love. Margaret Roberts launched her campaign in the general election with two fiery slogans: 'Vote Right to Keep What's Left' and 'Stop the Rot: Sack the Lot'. She had no truck with the message transmitted by many Tory candidates, including Edward Heath in Bexley, that some of Labour's reforms such as nationalisation and heavy public spending on welfare were there to stay as part of the new post-war consensus.

In her opening campaign speech at the meeting on 3 February to adopt her as the Conservative parliamentary candidate, Margaret Roberts described the election as 'a battle between two ways of life, one which led inevitably to slavery and the other to freedom'.[26]

Her three-week campaign proved an exhilarating but exhausting experience. Like many a new candidate she had not learned to pace herself, but her youth, her passion and her adrenalin kept her going. In those pre-television days, an energetic candidate was expected to speak at two or three public meetings every night. Hers were astonishingly well attended, with the doors sometimes having to be closed a quarter of an hour before the start time because the hall was full. The atmosphere could be electric, with noisy clashes between supporters and opponents. At one early meeting in Crayford, a Labour heckler shouted: 'What have you got that we haven't?' A Tory yelled back, 'Brains!'[27]

The retort was appropriate because the intellectual and physical qualities of Margaret Roberts were getting noticed. The national press – the *Daily Mail*, the

Daily Graphic, the *Evening Standard* and the *Illustrated London News* – gave her favourable coverage as the youngest woman Conservative candidate in the country with well-planned photo opportunities. The *Daily Mail* ran a picture of her behind the bar pulling pints in a Dartford working men's club.[28] The *Sunday People* gave her the tabloid treatment, headlining her as the 'Election Glamour Girl', and declaring: 'She is young – only 24 – and she is beautiful. Lovely fair hair and beautiful blue eyes . . . By the way she's got brains as well.'[29]

Although Margaret Roberts had a showman's touch when it came to attracting column inches in the newspapers, her self-presentation to the electorate was serious. For daytime campaigning she dressed in a tailored dark suit and a feathery black hat trimmed with blue ribbon. For evening events she wore a black velvet dress. Many of her policy warnings from the platform were sombre. Her recurrent theme was that Britain was losing its influence in the world and its economic strength at home because of socialist failures. At the start of her campaign she wrote a 1,500-word article for the *Gravesend and Dartford Reporter* in which she set out her stall in a series of rhetorical questions followed by the line, '*YOU will decide*'.[30]

One of her strongest demands, to be repeated with similar consistency when she became Prime Minister in 1979, was for sound public finances. As she put it in her 1950 article:

> Are YOU going to let this proud island race, who at one time would never accept charity, drift on from crisis to crisis under a further spell of shaky Socialist finance? Or do you believe in sound finance and economical spending of public money, such as the Conservatives will adopt? YOU will decide.[31]

As the campaign reached its third week, the *Dartford Chronicle* thought they could scent a surprise upset in the constituency. Margaret Roberts herself entered the familiar fantasy land of young candidates fighting hopeless seats, and began to believe that she might actually win. 'We really thought that we might conceivably do it', she told one of her earliest biographers, Tricia Murray.[32]

Older heads at Conservative Central Office had no such illusions, but were impressed by the campaigning efforts of the Dartford candidate.

'I do not think there is a hundredth chance of winning the seat,' wrote Beryl Cook, Conservative Central Office Agent, Home Counties South East, 'but I am quite sure the majority will be down with a bump. This will be an entirely personal triumph for Miss Roberts.'[33] It was. She reduced the Labour majority by a third, cutting the majority of Norman Dodds MP from 19,714 to 13,638.*

Although this was an excellent result, there was a downside to it. Because both the Dartford and the national swing to the Conservatives had been so strong, and because the overall result of the general election was so close, it soon dawned on Margaret Roberts that it would be difficult for her to move on to a better constituency from what remained an unwinnable seat.

FRUSTRATION, CONSOLIDATION AND ENGAGEMENT

With a second general election expected within a year, Margaret Roberts had little alternative but to stick with Dartford. Politically this was frustrating, but emotionally the warmth of her party workers uplifted her. She felt a moral obligation not to abandon them, so she consented to early re-adoption in March 1950. At an enthusiastic special meeting of the Association, she was presented with a Marcasite brooch and a scroll signed by 991 supporters. Some of them had become real friends, including her chairman, John Miller, and her landlords, Raymond and Lucy Woollcott.

Margaret had fought a good election in 1950. Even her opponent, Norman Dodds, praised her campaigning skills and invited her to lunch in the House of Commons. On another occasion they were photographed dancing together at the Mayor's Charity Ball. He insisted that she should choose the dance and the music. She picked a fast-paced tango, which she said was 'her favourite dance', and a tune with political overtones – 'Jealousy'.[34]

In fact there was not a trace of such negativity in their roles as political opponents. Norman Dodds was a chivalrous Old Labour stalwart who came to admire his young challenger. They campaigned against each other fairly and with mutual respect.

Respect was also growing for Margaret Roberts within the Conservative party. In election post-mortems she was credited not only for having fought exception-ally well in her constituency, but for having played a significant role in helping

---

* Election results: Norman Dodds (Labour), 38,128; Margaret Roberts (Conservative), 24,490; Anthony Giles (Liberal), 5,011. Labour majority, 13,638.

Ted Heath to squeak home by 133 votes in his next-door constituency of Bexley. The Central Office view was that the vigour of her battle had dissuaded many Labour Party workers in Dartford from coming over to Bexley to help with the vital polling day drive of getting their supporters out to vote. Heath showed no particular appreciation for this assistance. There was already a chill in the atmosphere between the two neighbouring candidates. She found him 'somewhat aloof and alone', even when he was 'at his most affable'.[35]

Margaret Roberts gained confidence from the success of her first campaign in Dartford. Her share price rose on the invisible stock market of young polit-ical comers. She became prominent in attending meetings of the Conservative Candidates' Association. She gave up her holidays to study policy courses at the party's staff college at Swinton Castle in Yorkshire. She stood out as a rare woman candidate at these predominantly male gatherings. Some of the men with whom she would soon be competing for nominations in winnable seats were ambivalent in their attitudes towards her.

As one of them, twenty-five-year old Edward du Cann,* the candidate for Walthamstow West, recalled:

> She was strikingly attractive, obviously intelligent, a goer. But she didn't do herself any favours or win any friends. She tried too hard, in a slightly overbearing sort of way. She was invariably the first one of us in all the sessions to get to her feet and ask the opening question. Most of her fellow candidates found this habit off-putting: they thought her too keen by far, too pushy.[36]

Grumbles about her pushiness among contemporaries were balanced by golden opinions from party elders. Alfred Bossom continued to champion her cause. He invited her to grand political soirées in his London home, and arranged speaking invitations for her in Kent.

She was becoming in demand on national platforms, too. Her most exciting opportunity came when she was invited to second the vote of thanks to Winston Churchill at a Conservative Women's rally at the Royal Albert Hall on 7 June

---

* Sir Edward du Cann KBE (1924–), MP for Taunton, 1956–1987; Chairman of the Con-servative Party, 1965–1967; Chairman of the 1922 Committee, 1972–1984. In the general election of 1951, Edward du Cann contested his first seat in Walthamstow West as the Conservative candidate. His opponent was the Labour Prime Minister Clement Attlee.

1950. This was the first time she had met the great man whose wartime broadcasts had inspired her during her teenage years in Grantham. Alas, there is no record of the conversation between the past and future prime minister at this encounter.[37]

The lame duck Labour government of 1950–51 took eighteen months to expire. It was a time of political career frustration for Margaret Roberts, but her ambition to find a husband was gathering momentum.

Early in 1951, Alfred Bossom took her out to lunch together with his son Clive, who had recently been adopted as Prospective Conservative Parliamentary Candidate for Faversham. Clive Bossom recalled:

> Father banged on to both of us with a list of dos and don'ts for young politicians. And at the end he became rather serious, saying to us, 'Politics can be a very lonely life, so to both of you I say, find. the right partner to marry, to relax with and to share your life with'. I noticed that Margaret kept nodding when he said that.[38]

Who she had in mind when she nodded was a mystery that she had not yet solved for herself. She was still hesitating between two suitors. Robert Henderson remained her no. 1 choice. The weekend after the count, he took her dining and dancing at the Berkeley Hotel where she wore a new white frock. 'I go out with him most weekends and one night during the week,' she wrote to Muriel in the spring of 1950, 'but whether it will ever come to anything I very much doubt, for he thinks the difference between our ages is very great.'[39]

A stomach operation for Robert in June, followed by a long convalescence, slowed their courtship down. Margaret found herself a new job working as a research chemist for the food manufacturer J. Lyons in Hammersmith. She also rented a flat in Pimlico. One of the reasons for her move was that her Dartford landlady, Mrs Woollcott, was taking too much interest in her private life. 'You know how I hate everyone knowing my own affairs', she wrote to Muriel. 'Robert refuses to come in now, and as often as not I go to the end of the road and meet him at the traffic lights.'[40]

Welcoming him to her new flat in London was a much more comfortable experience than waiting for him at traffic lights in Dartford. She entertained Robert there royally. 'Last time he came I cooked a slap-up dinner, four courses, just to show him!' she told Muriel.[41] Yet for some reason, the romance she had

nurtured so hopefully broke up some time in the summer of 1951. Its ending
was evidently painful to her. As Alfred Roberts described it in a letter of 25
September 1951 to Muriel: 'The Robert business upset Margaret very much, but
that will pass.'[42]

What happened can only be guesswork. With the caution of a much older
bachelor, well set in his ways at the age of forty-eight, Robert Henderson continued to dither over becoming engaged to a fiancée of twenty-five. Perhaps
he was put on the spot by her about his hesitation, for they seem to have split
distressingly rather than drifting apart gently. Her father's words, 'The Robert
business upset Margaret very much', suggest an abrupt ending.

At the time when Robert Henderson was finding it difficult to make up his
mind about proposing to Margaret, Denis Thatcher moved into matrimonial
decision-making mode. Ever since the 1950 election he had continued to see
her for dinners at smart London restaurants such as The Ivy, The White Tower
and L'Ecu de France. She invited him at least once for a drink in her Pimlico
flat, and she sometimes cooked dinner for him at his flat in Chelsea. This was
not the same level of romantic treatment as she gave to Robert Henderson, but
Denis Thatcher was nevertheless being encouraged by her to stay in the game.
Yet this encouragement was deceptive, for she kept him in the dark about her
secret and deeper relationship with Robert.

The decision to propose to Margaret was taken by Denis not when he was in
her company but when he was driving around France in August 1951 with an
old school friend, Kent Green, in a car he described as 'a tart trap'.

As he later told his daughter Carol, the moment of revelation struck him on
these motoring travels. 'During the tour I suddenly thought to myself, "That's
the girl".'[43]

Margaret did not say 'yes' at once when Denis proposed to her over dinner
in his flat. She needed time to think it over. She also wanted her prospective
husband to meet her parents. She thought they might be worried, as she was
worried, about her becoming the second Mrs Thatcher.

Denis had been more emotionally bruised than he let on by the break-up of
his first marriage. This had taken place in a moment of wartime passion when,
as a young army officer, he fell madly in love with a glamorous girl he met at a
tea dance at the Grosvenor House Hotel in Park Lane. She was Margot Kempson,
a horse-riding beauty from Hertfordshire serving in the WRAF as a transport
driver. In March 1942 they married. Soon afterwards Denis was posted overseas.

He had a good war as a staff officer in the Royal Artillery in Sicily, Italy and France. He was twice mentioned in dispatches, and awarded a military MBE. In 1946 he was demobbed with the rank of major. When he arrived home he discovered his marriage was over. As one of his close friends described the impact on him: 'He came out as a sort of gallant, elegant Major – the breakdown of his marriage shattered him totally, and he seemed rudderless.'[44]

All his life, Denis Thatcher kept his emotions well hidden beneath a mask of geniality. It is unlikely that he allowed Margaret to catch any glimpses of the pain that he was still feeling three years after his divorce from Margot Kempson. He was wary of making any new commitment. Perhaps that was the reason why he moved so cautiously and patiently before proposing marriage to a second prospective wife. However, he was growing increasingly attracted by her combination of beauty, brains and fighting spirit.

Denis's proposal was unexpected to Margaret. Receiving it swung her emotions his way. She may have already been on the rebound from the indecisive Robert. Any further doubts were swept away by the reaction of her parents in Grantham. Alfred Roberts reported on this to Muriel, making it clear that Denis's first marriage was no obstacle, in his eyes: 'I told Margaret she could disregard this as he was in no way at fault and actually he is an exceedingly nice fellow. Also, of course, very comfortably situated financially.'[45] Later in the letter, Alderman Roberts approvingly noted that Denis owned both a Triumph sports car and a 1948 Jaguar, intending to buy the latest Jaguar model, a Mark V. The only tricky incident in the prospective son-in-law's reception in Grantham came when Margaret told her parents that Denis liked to drink. 'I swear her father had to blow the dust off the sherry bottle', was her fiancé's recollection of this moment.[46]

Although Denis's proposal was accepted by Margaret with the full consent of her parents, the engagement was kept secret for another five weeks for political reasons. By October 1951, the Labour government was on the verge of collapse, so Prime Minister Clement Attlee called a general election, with polling day set for 25 October.

Margaret took the view that announcing her engagement to a divorced man might not go down well with the Dartford electorate. So she went through the campaign with Denis much in evidence as a loyal election helper, but not avowed as her future husband. Then, twenty-four hours before the poll, the news of the engagement was leaked to the London evening papers by Conservative Central

Office. Margaret was furious, fearing the gimmick might backfire. It made a good story, but had no discernible effect on the voters.

In the election, Margaret Roberts again fought a thoroughly professional and energetic campaign. One of its brighter moments came when the *Daily Graphic* photographed her canvassing in Attlee Drive. But generally her 1951 election-eering was quieter and duller than her first battle the previous year. She felt a dispiriting sense of déjà vu as the earlier fires of excitement and dreams of victory failed to re-ignite.

Even so, the result in Dartford was a creditable one as the Labour majority was reduced by a further 1,304 votes. But as she made her concession speech at the declaration of the poll, Margaret Roberts must have known that she would not be fighting a third election campaign in the constituency. It was time to move on.

REFLECTION

By the time she was twenty-six, Margaret Roberts had fought two general election campaigns and had become engaged to an eligible constituent. Dartford was good to her. But she was already much more than a capable local candidate. In the wider world of political recognition, she was being seen as a young woman with a national future.

Not everyone liked her. Inside the jealous club of Conservative candidates, she ruffled feathers. But even there she was respected for her abilities, as she was by more seasoned political observers.

'An excellent candidate in every way', was the view of Beryl Cook, the influential Area Agent for South East England. Writing her valedictory report on the candidate for Dartford, Ms Cook continued:

> I gather she intends to drop out of politics for a time, but to return later. As she is still only 26, she can well afford to do this. She should not be lost sight of, because she is quite outstanding in ability and has, in addition, a most attractive personality and appearance.[47]

This was an alpha plus rating by Conservative Central Office. But it ignored the negative factor that in the 1950s women candidates faced a serious bias in many Conservative constituencies. This was to be the next big hurdle for the new Mrs Margaret Thatcher to overcome.

5

Marriage, motherhood and Finchley

MARRIAGE

Margaret Roberts became Margaret Thatcher when she married Denis at Wesley's Chapel, City Road on 13 December 1951. It was a cold and foggy day, brightened by the radiant smile of the bride. She was given away by her father, who thought the ceremony 'halfway to Rome',[1] despite being held at the most famous Methodist church in London. Perhaps this was because Denis, chose traditional Church of England hymns. The words of the second hymn – 'Lead us, heavenly Father, lead us O'er the world's tempestuous sea' – were to prove highly appropriate, as the Thatchers' life story later demonstrated.

Because Denis had been married before, Margaret chose not to wear a traditional white dress. Nevertheless, she was arrayed, literally, like a duchess. For her outfit was a replica of the dress immortalised by Georgiana, Duchess of Devonshire, in the renowned Chatsworth portrait by Thomas Gainsborough. It was made of sapphire-blue velvet with a matching hat crested on the right-hand side by a spectacular plumage of ostrich feathers.

The reception had originally been planned to take place in the Bull Hotel, Dartford. But when Sir Alfred Bossom was told of the engagement, he had a better idea. 'We had a jolly good wedding reception recently for my son Clive and his bride at my home in Carlton Gardens', said the hospitable MP for Maidstone. 'Would you like to have your reception there?'

'You bet we would', said Margaret, who had often been a guest at parties in his magnificent house overlooking The Mall.[2] Even so, being a practical fiancée, she asked if she could come and see the kitchen before accepting Alfred Bossom's offer.

The first night of the marriage was spent in the Savoy Hotel. The newly-weds then set off for their honeymoon, by flying boat, to Madeira. It was the first time Margaret had been abroad, but the travel arrangements were not to her liking. A bumpy seaplane landing shook the new Mrs Thatcher so badly that she resolved never to use that form of air transport again. So the homeward journey was by ship. However, the three-day crossing to Portugal made her so seasick that it gave Margaret a lifelong aversion to boats.[3]

Arriving back in London in the New Year, the couple moved into Denis's flat at 112 Swan Court in Chelsea. Two sentences describing their early life together in Margaret Thatcher's memoirs are positively elegiac in their Jane Austen-like echoes of marital bliss: 'To be a young married woman in comfortable circumstances must always be a delight if the marriage is a happy one, as mine was. But to be a young married woman in the 1950s was very heaven.'[4]

The heavenly circumstances of Margaret Thatcher's first years of marriage were not unconnected with money. In the early 1950s the continuing growth of Atlas meant that Denis was taking home around £100 a week or over £5,000 a year in salary and dividends – an equivalent of over £150,000 in 2013 money. He was paying £7 a week for his rent-controlled flat in Swan Court. So there was plenty of surplus income for re-decorating, entertaining and even buying two of the best seats in the covered stands opposite Westminster Abbey for the Queen's Coronation on 2 June 1953.

These comfortable circumstances meant that there was no need for Mrs Thatcher to work, but a life of ease would have been alien to her nature. So she concentrated her energies full time on reading for the bar and attending lectures at the Council for Legal Education. She ate her dinners at the Inner Temple, and passed part I of the bar exams in July 1953.

Meanwhile, a political career was still firmly in her sights. Her reputation as a successful candidate in Dartford resulted in a steady trickle of speaking invitations and also occasional media opportunities. The most interesting of these was a commission from the *Sunday Graphic* to write an article about the role of women 'at the dawn of the new Elizabethan era'. Queen Elizabeth II had succeeded to the throne on 6 February 1952. Eleven days later, the newspaper wanted a female contemporary of the monarch to comment on the opportunities for women that might open up in the new reign. With foresight, the paper selected Mrs Thatcher (just six months older than the Queen) for this task. She rose to it with enthusiasm.

Under the headline 'Wake Up, Women', Margaret Thatcher sounded a trumpet call to the regiment of ambitious female careerists. She dismissed the notion that women should have to sacrifice their professional lives for their husbands and families. Taking a viewpoint that was advanced, almost revolutionary, for the 1950s, she championed the cause that came to be known as 'Having it all', and specifically applied it to her own field of politics. Not only did she want more women in the House of Commons; she had a vision of them rising to the highest offices of state: 'Should a woman arise equal to the task, I say let her have an equal chance with the men for the leading Cabinet posts. Why not a woman Chancellor – or Foreign Secretary?'[5]

No one else in politics was voicing such thoughts in 1952. At the time when this article was published there had only ever been two women cabinet ministers – Margaret Bondfield, Minister of Labour, and Ellen Wilkinson, Minister of Education. Both were Labour politicians, unmarried and with low-ranking posts in the cabinet's pecking order. Margaret Thatcher was setting her sights higher, although not yet as high as becoming prime minister.

Throughout 1952 she continued to manoeuvre towards her goal of a seat in Parliament. Although just before her marriage she told Conservative Central Office that she would put her political ambitions 'on ice for some time to come', she reversed this stance a few months later.

In June 1952, She went to see 'Auntie Beryl', as she had come to call her Conservative Central Office friend, Beryl Cook, and told her: 'It's no use; I must face it: I don't like being left out of the political stream!'[6] Beryl Cook arranged for her to see John Hare MP, the Party Vice Chairman of candidates. After hearing that her husband was supporting her re-entry into the fiercely competitive arena of constituency selection races, John Hare fought her corner and managed to get her on the short-list for the inner London marginal seat of Holborn and St Pancras.

To his surprise Margaret Thatcher withdrew her name, ostensibly on the grounds that, 'I would rather not tackle an area so close to Central London, as it has no community life of its own'.[7]

This was a disingenuous explanation. The real reason she pulled out was that she thought she deserved a better constituency than a Labour marginal with a majority of 2,000.

In search of a safe seat, she put herself forward for Canterbury. She was interviewed but not even short-listed. This was a disappointment and also a reminder that her speeches could polarise her listeners. Sometimes she did worse than merely polarise them.

There are embarrassing accounts of how she positively affronted a gaudy of Somerville alumnae in the summer of 1952. Instead of delivering the light-hearted fare of after-dinner witticisms expected on these occasions, Margaret Thatcher gave a ponderous presentation about marriage and home life.

'That was *dreadful*. I'll *never* invite her to speak again', spluttered the college Principal, Dame Janet Vaughan. She was agreeing with another Thatcher critic in the audience, Ann Dally, who had found the guest of honour's cut-glass accent embarrassing, and her content 'alien and uncongenial' because of her 'sanctimonious platitudes'.[8]

Whether Margaret Thatcher's speeches were being met with favourable or unfavourable reactions, her attempts to find a constituency came to a temporary halt in early 1953 when she discovered she was pregnant. Politics had to be eclipsed by motherhood. Contrary to her intentions, the eclipse created a five-year gap in her political career.

MOTHERHOOD

Margaret Thatcher had a difficult pregnancy. She suffered from unusually heavy morning sickness and from long periods of feeling unwell. The reason, unknown to her at the time, was that she was carrying twins. The gynaecologist decided that an urgent Caesarean operation was required so, six weeks ahead of schedule, Mark and Carol Thatcher arrived in the world on the afternoon of Saturday 15 August 1953, at Queen Charlotte's Hospital in Hammersmith.

Their father, unaware of these medical dramas, had 'very sensibly', in the view of his wife,[9] gone to the England *v*. Australia Test Match. He returned from the Oval to find himself the head of a family of four. It was the first of many great surprises that his marriage to Margaret would give him.

She handled the challenges of maternity with impatient efficiency. In those days, it was standard practice for nursing mothers to stay in hospital for three weeks of recovery after the birth. She persuaded her doctors to discharge her after a fortnight. Even so, she chafed at finding herself with time on her hands.

Unaccustomed as she was to relaxation, she spent some of this spare time filling in the application for her bar finals, sending off a cheque to pay the examination fees in advance. She explained: 'This little psychological trick I was playing on myself would ensure that I plunged into legal studies on my return to Swan Court with the twins.'[10] She also recalled thinking: 'If I fill in the entrance form now, pride will not let me fail.'[11]

Having psyched herself up to combine her new life of motherhood with bar exams, Margaret Thatcher set about achieving the difficult target of passing her bar finals four months after giving birth to Mark and Carol.[12]

As a young mother, Margaret was both dutiful and bountiful. She gave her children everything they wanted and more. But it was motherly love by over-compensation. She was no more tactile or intimate with Mark and Carol than Alfred and Beatrice Roberts had been with her and Muriel. Even though Margaret's maternal instincts were to be less strict with rules and more liberal with home comforts, she found it difficult to be generous with her time. She seemed to think that everything could be fitted into her schedule with good planning and organisation.

She did not like to delegate the tasks of motherhood. 'She was a "superwoman" long before Shirley Conran ever invented the phenomenon', observed Carol Thatcher, relating how her mother even took up knitting to make her children royal-blue jackets for birthday presents. She became proficient at home knitwear out of a wish to compete with their nanny, Barbara, who was an accomplished knitter.[13]

Another treat for the twins came on their fourth birthday. Their mother turned herself into a pastry cook for the event. She spent a couple of days baking and icing two huge cakes. One was in the shape of a car for Carol; the other was a marzipan fort for Mark.[14]

Such special manifestations of maternal affection were impressive. But it was the nanny who carried most of the daily workload in looking after the children.

Even during her earliest years of motherhood, law and politics took up most of Margaret Thatcher's time. She paid a price of high pressure for the pride that had driven her to attempt her bar finals before the end of the year.

December 1953 saw three important milestones in her life: celebrating her second wedding anniversary, christening the twins at the City Road Methodist church, and passing all nine of the papers in Part II of her bar exams.

After being called to the bar in January 1954, she had to do her pupillage, as barristers call apprenticeship. Her first pupil master was Fred Lawton,* later acclaimed as a giant of bar and bench, to whom she paid £50 for six months training, plus five guineas to his clerk. 'As I am costing Denis that much,' she wrote to Muriel, 'I shall just have to go about in rags when my present clothes drop off me.'[15]

Lawton rated Margaret Thatcher as the best pupil he ever had, and retrospectively thought that if she had stayed in the law, she would have been a highly successful QC. But he also told Charles Moore: 'I don't think she would have been the first woman Law Lord, because she hadn't got that depth of mental capacity you have to have if you're a Law Lord.'[16]

Nevertheless, it was during her pupillage that Margaret Thatcher began forming the belief, reiterated many times when she was prime minister, that the rule of law and what she called 'Law-based liberty' were the foundations of a free society.

After some minor disappointments in finding the right niche for herself in the law, Margaret Thatcher decided to go to the Revenue Bar and was offered a seat in the tax chambers of C.A.J. Bonner QC.

Her decision to specialise in taxation law caused a temporary flare-up with Denis, which was one of the only times he interfered directly with her career. He came home to their flat one evening in early 1955 to find his wife poring over the application forms for the Institute of Chartered Accountants.

'What on earth is all this?' he asked.

'I want to study accountancy.'

'In God's name why?'

'Well, they told me that if I want to be a tax lawyer I have to know something about accountancy.'

'Forget it', said Denis.[17]

The thought of another four years of professional studies and examinations appalled him. He put his foot down so firmly that his veto had to be accepted. He was right. As his wife soon discovered, it was perfectly possible to work as a tax barrister without an accountancy qualification.

---

* Sir Frederick Lawton (1911–2001), QC 1957; High Court Judge 1961; Lord Justice of Appeal 1972; knighted 1961.

It is likely that Margaret Thatcher's decision to specialise in taxation law was made with an eye to her parliamentary prospects. At this time she was an active member of the Inns of Court Conservative Association. Its members included several politically ambitious young barristers, such as Geoffrey Howe, Patrick Jenkin, Anthony Barber, Michael Havers and Airey Neave. All of them became important parliamentarians. In such circles she would have become aware that a well-trodden road to ministerial promotion was to shine as a back-bencher in House of Commons debates on the annual Finance Bill – the legislation that turns the Chancellor's Budget into law.

For career reasons, Margaret Thatcher may well have been planning ahead politically when she opted to do taxation law professionally. Her strategy was right, because some twenty years later it was her speeches on the Finance Bills of 1974–5 that played a vital role in winning the leadership of the Conservative Party.

THE BUMPY ROAD TO FINCHLEY

Although happy in her marriage, the mid-1950s were a frustrating period for Margaret Thatcher in her career. She did not shine at the law, and her quest for a seat in Parliament was faltering. The problem in both fields was the prejudice of that era against ambitious women.

Neither the bar nor the Conservative Party would ever have admitted to any such prejudice. Yet it was a reality Margaret Thatcher had to face. Her difficulties in finding chambers and being given good briefs seem to have been affected by the undercurrent of male chauvinism that then prevailed in the bar's world of clerks, silks, juniors, pupils and Inns of Court. It was still a Dickensian milieu, at best only half open to women of talent.

There was plenty of male chauvinism in the Conservative Party too, although paradoxically much of it came from women activists in constituency associations. They had a large say on candidate selection committees. Their voices were often hostile to women contenders in general, and Margaret Thatcher in particular.

After her rejection at Canterbury, she had a succession of disappointments. Although Conservative Central Office supported her strongly, she lost out in the final rounds at Orpington, Beckenham, Hemel Hempstead and Maidstone. In Orpington, she was pipped at the post by a local resident, Donald Sumner, whose pitch to the selectors was that what the constituency needed was 'someone in Parliament who knows the state of the roads in Locks Bottom'.[18] Margaret Thatcher managed to laugh at her rival's winning line, but the next three defeats left her feeling 'hurt and disappointed'.[19]

Her difficulty was that a worrying pattern seemed to be emerging in these rejections. Unlike the short-listed male contenders she was pointedly asked questions suggesting that she might have problems balancing the demands of being a wife and mother with the demands of being an MP.

These tensions came to a head at Maidstone where she started the race as favourite, partly because of some keen lobbying on her behalf by the retiring Member Sir Alfred Bossom. In the final round she was up against two agreeable lightweights, Captain John Litchfield and John Wells. Neither of them could hold a candle to her in terms of speaking ability and political knowledge.

At the end of the speeches on the set topic 'My policy if I was adopted as the Candidate for Maidstone', she was 'miles ahead', according to one of the selectors, Bill Henderson. But in the end, he and evidently others thought that she 'completely ballsed it up' when answering questions.[20] The report by the Deputy Central Office Area agent, John Entwistle, explained the problem:

> She was asked about her ability to cope as a Member, having in mind the fact that she had a husband and a small family, and I do not think her reply did a lot of good. She spoke of having an excellent nanny, and said that as a Member she would have the mornings free (quite ignoring that fact that Members have committees in the mornings). She also spoke of having the weekends free, and made no reference to spending time in Maidstone at the weekends. She did say she would have to give up the Bar.[21]

Reading between the lines, it was her response to the loaded question 'about her ability to cope' that cost her the seat. Afterwards, she fumed to Denis that no similar questions had been asked to John Wells, who had four children under ten, or to Captain Litchfield, who had two. Selection committee life seemed unfair.

John Wells, who won the nomination on the final vote by forty votes to Margaret Thatcher's twenty-seven votes, was an affable, nonchalant Old Etonian fruit farmer who represented Maidstone for twenty-eight years. He was one of nature's backwoodsmen, more noted for his absences than his contributions to the House, which were usually confined to the subjects of local roads and apple orchards. On the night of his selection there was a vocal minority who thought Margaret Thatcher had been treated unfairly. Twelve of them took the unusual step of refusing to make the choice of Wells formally unanimous by the customary show of hands at the end of the meeting. This feeling that the runner-up had been hard done by was also reflected in a note to Central Office by the President of the Maidstone Conservative Association, who went out of his way to sing her praises:

> Mrs Thatcher: Very pleasant personality – good speaker – calm yet forceful delivery and very much to the point – Has a thorough grasp of politics – tendency to the right of centre – A fine brain – great 'appeal'. This lady should surely be in Parliament soon.[22]

The lady herself was despondent after Maidstone turned her down. Her spirits might have fallen further had she been aware at the time how strongly the initial tides of prejudice were running against her in Finchley, the next seat she decided to try for.

When he heard that Margaret Thatcher had put her hat into the ring to be his successor, the sitting Member, Sir John Crowder, expostulated to the Party Chairman, Lord Hailsham, that Conservative Central Office was trying to rig the selection in order to give Finchley a choice between 'a bloody Jew and a bloody woman'.*[23]

These prejudices sound inconceivable today but they were not uncommon in the Tory Party of the 1950s.

In fact, the view from headquarters was discouraging to all female contenders. The Deputy Central Office Area agent for North London (herself a woman) had already reported: 'For your information, I gather that Finchley are determined to see some women so that they may be seen to have gone through the motions, but I should be very surprised indeed if they selected one.'[24]

Finchley was a North London constituency. It was regarded as a safe Conservative seat because of its prosperous commuter districts like Totteridge,

---

* 'The bloody Jew' in this story was Peter Goldman, head of the Conservative Research Department, who did put his name forward for Finchley, but withdrew it. He later had the misfortune to be selected as the Tory candidate in the Orpington by-election on 15 March 1962, which was lost to the Liberals.

Whetstone, Hampstead Garden Suburb and Friern Barnet. It had a large Jewish community making up about 20 per cent of the electorate.

The Conservative Association was thought to be dysfunctional and disenchanted with its MP, Sir John Crowder. A loud and overbearing figure, he was a landowner, an Old Etonian and a senior officer of the powerful 1922 Committee of Conservative backbenchers. It was believed that the Finchley selectors wanted a fresh face who was as different as possible from their sitting Member. Margaret Thatcher at least fitted this bill. From a field of 150 entrants, she was shortlisted as one of three candidates for the final run-off, which was to be decided on 14 July 1958.

Good luck and bad luck then intervened. Margaret Thatcher's good fortune came when one of the last three, Christopher Montague 'Monty' Woodhouse, withdrew because he had been selected as the candidate for Oxford. In front of the ninety members making the final choice, he might well have been her most formidable competitor for he was a war hero of the Greek resistance, a scholar and a former Director of the Royal Institute of Foreign Affairs at Chatham House.

After the exit of Monty Woodhouse, the Executive Committee would not accept a run-off between the two remaining candidates, Thomas Langton and Margaret Thatcher. So the final round was enlarged to a four-sided competition by bringing in the two next placed runners-up from the interview stage, Ian Fraser and Francis Richardson.

The other three finalists were all married men. They brought their wives. Mrs Thatcher was unable to be accompanied by her husband. Denis was away on a business trip to South Africa, 'going out after orders', as she told the meeting.[25] She felt his absence was an unlucky blow to her chances, but there was nothing she could do about it. Communications with that part of the world were so slow in the 1950s that Denis had no idea his wife had reached the last round. Her letter giving him this news had failed to catch up with him.

The fight for the Finchley nomination was tantalisingly close. On the first ballot Margaret Thatcher squeezed ahead by a single vote. She scored thirty-five votes to the thirty-four votes cast for Thomas Langton. As a Brigadier who had lost a leg but won a Military Cross in the Second World War, he was a popular but inexperienced local candidate. The remaining two runners were eliminated after collecting only twenty-two votes between them.

On the second ballot Mrs Thatcher made it to the winning post by a nose.*
She had forty-six votes to Langton's forty-three. It was not the most decisive of
triumphs. However, it is custom and practice at Conservative Party selection
meetings for even the narrowest victories to be confirmed as unanimous by a
subsequent show of hands.

Unfortunately, a determined minority of the Finchley Conservative Executive
committee refused to go along with the tradition of unanimity. A small but vocal
group of Association members, relentlessly opposed to the idea of a woman MP,
tried to deny Margaret Thatcher the nomination. Their attempt to re-open the
voting got nowhere. She was declared to be the selected candidate, and the date
for her formal adoption meeting was set for the end of the month.[26]

The press gave her selection a gushing welcome. 'Tories Choose Beauty', ran
the headline in the London *Evening Standard*. 'The woman many Tories reckon
their most beautiful member has been chosen as candidate for Finchley.'[27]

Two days later a discarded copy of this newspaper was picked up by a
passenger nursing a hangover on the Johannesburg–Lagos leg of a homeward-
bound flight to Heathrow. He was Denis Thatcher. After a hard drinking
night with his business friends, he had 'staggered aboard the plane' when his
eye caught the *Evening Standard* report of his wife's selection in Finchley.
He was proud and delighted, but reacted with typically self-deprecating
humour. 'It was bloody lucky that I was away because it was a close-run thing',
he recalled. 'If they'd taken one look at me, they would have said, "We don't
want this pair".'[28]

Constituency adoption meetings to confirm a selection committee's choice
of a candidate are usually harmonious events, but occasionally they run into

---

* In his official biography, Charles Moore recounts a story that Margaret Thatcher won
the Finchley nomination through a fraud perpetrated by the Chairman of the Conservative
Association, Bertie Blatch. He allegedly told his son: 'She didn't actually win. The man
[Thomas Langton] did, but I thought: "He's got a silver spoon in his mouth. He'll get another seat. So I lost two of his votes, and gave them to her".' (in Moore, *Margaret Thatcher*,
Vol. 1, p. 135). This is an improbable tale. Conservative Central Office officials carry out
the count at constituency selection meetings, and always insist on scrutineers of the ballot.
It is unlikely that any chairman could withdraw two votes from one candidate and real-
locate them to another. In a tight final round which was bound to be a photo finish, as the
previous round had been, the scrutineering would or should have been intense.

turbulence. Conservative Central Office was anticipating trouble at Finchley on the night of 31 July because the rump of objectors at the executive committee was expected to remain vocal.

Despite these inauspicious signs, Margaret Thatcher's adoption meeting on 31 July 1958 was a personal triumph. By all accounts she made an outstanding speech and routed her critics. Reports on her adoption to Conservative Central Office by the area agent confirmed that the audience had contained a clique known to be opposed to a woman candidate but continued: 'Mrs Thatcher gave a most excellent speech and altogether went down splendidly.'[29]

When the resolution proposing her adoption was put, it was carried according to the local paper, 'with about five descensions [sic] who looked extremely red-faced and stupid'.[30] The Finchley Press waxed even more lyrical in its account of the proceedings:

> The Conservatives came to see – and went away conquered. If any had come to oppose – they went away converted . . . Speaking without notes, stabbing home points with expressive hands, Mrs Thatcher launched fluently into a clear-cut appraisal of the Middle East situation, weighed up Russia's propagandist mores with the skill of a housewife measuring the ingredients in a familiar recipe, pinpointed Nasser as the fly in the mixing bowl, switched swiftly to Britain's domestic problems (showing a keen grasp of wage and Trade Union issues), then swept her breathless audience into a confident preview of Conservatism's dazzling future . . . Willy-nilly, her spellbound audience felt the exhilaration of Conservatism planing through the spray of a lifting wave.[31]

Margaret Thatcher remained far more down to earth than the journalist who concocted this rhapsodic mixture of culinary and aquatic metaphors. But she was disappointed not to have won over her doubters. Unsettled by the absence of this reassuring word at the end of the meeting, the new candidate bleakly noted that some Conservatives 'were still determined to make life as difficult as possible' for her.[32]

A few days after her adoption, she wrote to the new Vice Chairman in charge of candidates at Central Office, Donald Kaberry MP: 'I am learning the hard way that an anti-women prejudice among certain Association members can persist even after a successful adoption meeting, but I hope it will subside when I have done more work in the division.'[33]

Margaret Thatcher's idea of hard work was to 'campaign as if Finchley was a marginal seat'.[34] She started to hold meetings, functions and canvassing sessions on three evenings each week.

Although she was right to take no chances against a background of disagreements within the Association about her selection, there was little doubt that Finchley was safe Conservative territory. The constituency was a prosperous swathe of North London with a strong preponderance of owner-occupiers, managers and commuters. There were only two potential obstacles. The first was the lethargy and disunity of the Tory workers. The second was an attempt by an opportunistic Liberal candidate to woo the large Jewish vote on the grounds that some Conservative activists had displayed anti-Semitism by blackballing Jews for membership of the Finchley Golf Club.

Margaret Thatcher briskly sorted out both difficulties. She went to see the Chief Whip, Ted Heath, to brief him on her constituency problems. He responded helpfully, arranging for a succession of past, present and future cabinet ministers to come and speak in Finchley. They included Iain Macleod, Peter Thorneycroft, John Boyd-Carpenter and Sir Keith Joseph.* The latter, although oddly described by the *Finchley Press* as 'a cricketer', was a leading figure in the national Jewish community.[35] His support was helpful in putting an end to the rumours that Margaret Thatcher condoned anti-Semitism in the local golf club or anywhere else. In fact, she had a lifelong affinity for Jews, as her later career was to show.

ELECTED

By the time the general election was called in September 1959, the Finchley Conservative Association was in much better and more united shape than it

---

* Sir Keith Joseph (1918–1994), hereditary Baronet; Fellow All Souls College, Oxford; Conservative MP for Leeds North East, 1956–1987; first met Margaret Thatcher in 1959 when as Parliamentary Secretary for Housing and Local Government he helped her to steer her Private Member's Bill into law; Secretary of State for Social Services, 1970–1974; Secretary of State for Industry, 1979–1981; Secretary of State for Education and Science, 1981–1986. As founder and Chairman of the Centre for Policy Studies, 1974–1979, he was the strongest intellectual and policy-making influence on Margaret Thatcher in her years as Leader of the Opposition. Created Lord Joseph, 1987.

was at the time of Margaret Thatcher's selection fourteen months earlier. She campaigned as a loyal mainstream Conservative, supporting the government's record over Suez, rent decontrol and accelerated independence for African colonies. 'Life is better with the Conservatives, don't let Labour ruin it', was the slogan of the Tory manifesto and she backed it with fervour. Although she claimed in her memoirs to have felt 'uneasy'[36] over Harold Macmillan's non-chalance about what he called 'the little local difficulty' of a £50 million increase in public expenditure, which caused his entire Treasury team of ministers to resign in January 1958, there is no evidence that such doubts were ever expressed during Margaret Thatcher's campaign in Finchley. Her election address gave the clear impression that she was a wholehearted supporter of Macmillan's expansionism.

She had an easy ride in her constituency. The tide was flowing the Tory way in 1959, and in Finchley the anti-Conservative vote was evenly divided between the Liberals and Labour, allowing neither party to mount a serious challenge.

The Labour candidate was Eric Deakins, who later became a junior minister in James Callaghan's government. He found Margaret Thatcher a punctiliously correct opponent, full of strongly expressed convictions. However, at a personal level he assessed her as 'one of the few people I've ever met in life who seemed to lack a single ounce of human warmth'.[37]

During the campaign, there were four well-attended public meetings at which all three candidates shared the platform. Eric Deakins remembers one of them for the lesson Margaret Thatcher taught him about political preparation. The Bishop of London chaired the meeting. An emotive and topical issue was the atrocities that had been committed at Hola camp in the British colony of Kenya. The Liberal and Labour candidates were critical of the colonial authorities.

In response, Margaret Thatcher produced from her handbag a copy of the committee of inquiry's report. 'My Lord Bishop, I seem to be the only one of the candidates who has read this document from cover to cover',[38] she began. Then she took the audience through carefully underlined passages from the two-inch thick report, reading aloud detailed extracts, which effectively neutral-ised her opponents' broad-brush attacks. 'It was game, set and match to Mrs Thatcher that night', recalled Deakins.[39]

As a well-briefed debater, Margaret Thatcher was formidable. But she could also be overbearing. Eric Deakins remembers an incident at one of the meetings when a Tory lady in the front row made so many repetitive interjections that he finally snapped at her: 'Why don't you shut up?' This brought out the schoolmarm in the Conservative candidate. 'Mr Deakins, that's not the way to behave at a public meeting!'[40] was how Margaret Thatcher loudly rebuked him. She seemed to have forgotten that it was the chair's job to keep the candidates in order.

There were some frictions in the Conservative camp during the election. It was recorded in a Central Office report that the hard core of those who originally opposed Margaret Thatcher's adoption maintained their hostile stance. It was also noted that the Conservative constituency agent had been 'treated pretty roughly' by the candidate. Whatever she said or did to him, the agent was magnanimous, for the report ended by saying that he had 'nothing but praise for her campaign'.[41]

The praise was justified by the figures declared at the Finchley count at 12.30 a.m. on Friday 9 October 1959. They were better than expected.*

This was an excellent result. She had increased the Finchley majority by almost 3,500 votes, riding high on the Tory tide which had re-elected Harold Macmillan's government with an overall majority of 100 seats.

Margaret Thatcher, at the age of thirty-four, had arrived at Westminster as one of the youngest members of the new House of Commons.

REFLECTION

Margaret Thatcher was elected to her safe seat some two weeks before her thirty-fifth birthday. So she had followed the traditional advice, 'Get into Parliament young'.[†] This was no small achievement, especially for a woman.

After a successful debut as a candidate in Dartford, her path to Westminster did not run smoothly. Constituency selections of candidates are often a lottery, but why did she lose five of them in succession? It was surely not on grounds of ability, since the men who defeated her – Donald Sumner, John Baker White, Philip Goodhart, James Allason and John Wells (becoming respectively the MPs for Orpington, Canterbury, Beckenham, Hemel Hempstead and Maidstone)

---

* General election results 1959: Finchley: Mrs Margaret Thatcher (Conservative), 29,697; Mr Eric Deakins (Labour), 13,437; Ivan Spence (Liberal), 12,260. Conservative majority: 16,260.

† H.A.L. Fisher is the first to have written this pearl of parliamentary wisdom, but others alleged to have said it range from Pitt the Younger to F.E. Smith and Winston Churchill.

– were all poor speakers who achieved little of distinction in their parliamentary careers.

The built-in bias against women candidates was one explanation for this string of defeats. Another less obvious cause was that Margaret Thatcher failed to understand that a winning speech at a constituency selection contest could depend more on likeability than knowledgeability. The key factor is establishing a personal chemistry between the candidate and the selectors. A cricketing phrase more meaningful to Denis than to Margaret, 'Knowing the pitch of the wicket', is one way of summarising the art of wooing a local association.

It is easy to see why the young Margaret Thatcher might have lost support in a selection process by trying to hit every ball for six. She appeared more forthright than friendly, combative rather than charming, and better at generating political heat than human warmth. Even so, it is still hard to understand why such a first-rate woman should have been beaten by a series of second-division men.

Whatever the temporary disappointments, she achieved her goal. Yet there was a price to be paid for it, which she denied at the time: her family life suffered.

In several conversations with friends during her retirement years, Margaret Thatcher lamented that she had not devoted more of her time and energy to the upbringing of Mark and Carol. In 1995 she even went so far as to say to Sir Michael Spicer: 'If I had my time again, I wouldn't go into politics because of what it does to your family.'[42] These misgivings, however sincerely expressed in her eighties, do not represent the true feelings she had in her thirties, forties and fifties. Her retrospective regrets should not be taken too seriously.

Margaret Thatcher was always driven by ambition. She put her career first, and her role as a wife and mother second. She put country before family: that was the way she was made. The public should not complain about it, particularly since Denis, Mark and Carol have never openly done so.

Although her shortcomings as a matriarchal figure were real and sometimes painful, she was far too intelligent not to have chosen her priorities with some deliberation. She gave the primacy of purpose to her life in politics. Her nearest and dearest may have suffered, but in 1959 Finchley gained an outstanding Member of Parliament, and in 1979 Britain began being governed by an extraordinary prime minister. From the outset, she knew the cost of a career in public life.

6

First years in Parliament 1959–1964

THE LUCKY LEGISLATOR

Margaret Thatcher's early days as a Member of Parliament were shaped by a remarkable stroke of good luck. Within two weeks of arriving at Westminster she came second in the ballot for Private Members' Bills. This was the equivalent of winning (at odds of approximately 300–1) the second prize in the annual House of Commons lottery that decides which back-benchers will be allocated time on the floor of the House to propose the bill of their choice with good prospects of it becoming law. She seized her chance with skill and bravado, although she had to swallow her pride and make several U-turns during the bill's progress.

At the time of winning this ballot, Margaret Thatcher was completely unknown to most of her colleagues. She had not opened her mouth in the chamber. She was having more than her fair share of beginner's difficulties in mastering the arcane procedures, obscure practices and labyrinthine geography of the House of Commons. This task, which has been compared to learning the ropes at a traditional boys' school, was problematic for a new arrival who was manifestly not 'one of the boys'.

The House of Commons in 1959 was a male-dominated and male chauvinistic place. Only twenty-five of its 630 MPs were women, twelve of them Conservatives. They tended to be marginalised, often rather badly treated in terms of facilities and fellowship. Most of them had to do their constituency work in the communal 'Lady Members' Room'. That was where Margaret Thatcher sorted out her daily post, dictating replies to her secretary, Paddi Victor Smith. If the Lady Members' Room was crowded, as it often was, the alternative was to perch on a bench in the corridors.

The House of Commons in the 1950s took a cheeseparing attitude towards newly-elected back-benchers. They were allocated a locker, a space for their secretaries in the typing room, a filing cabinet – and that was it. Parliamentary expenses were minimal. The only perks were free parking and free calls, which had to be made from a semi-public line of telephone booths.

Margaret Thatcher made no complaint about these inadequate facilities. But she must have found the prevailing culture of condescension towards women MPs difficult to endure. Her parliamentary contemporary Pat Hornsby Smith once yelled at a male colleague for telling her that she should not 'worry her pretty little head' about the technical wording of a motion on the order paper.[1] Although no comparable insult is remembered in the early career of Margaret Thatcher, as the youngest new woman back-bencher it is unlikely that she would never have encountered occasional slights, sexist remarks and suppressed misogyny.

In the era of her arrival at Westminster, there was an atmosphere of snobbish male supremacy on the Tory benches, heightened by the commonly shared experiences of war and National Service. This quasi-regimental attitude had many unattractive features such as heavy drinking in the smoking room, a Tory-dominated bar which the younger and older Margaret Thatcher generally avoided. But for all these enclaves and examples of bad behaviour, there was one parliamentary arena where equality ruled. This was the chamber of the House of Commons, in which every new member is judged by the quality of their speeches.

A maiden speech is the first hurdle of a parliamentary career, and long-established conventions apply to it. By tradition, a maiden should be non-controversial, contain a brief description of the new member's constituency (often boring, but occasionally amusing) and a complimentary reference to the previous MP. It may not be interrupted, although the maiden speaker's *quid pro quo* for this calm passage is to ensure that the content is uncontroversial.

Margaret Thatcher broke all these rules in her first speech. Her reason for ignoring the conventions was that she decided to make her parliamentary debut a combination of delivering a maiden speech and moving the Private Member's Bill she had won in the ballot. This was a bold and unprecedented start to her career.

Before tabling her bill she had to engage in a week of frantic activity to choose its subject, negotiate its passage with government whips, ministers and civil servants, and to prepare its detailed clauses with the help of a parliamentary draftsman. All this was new territory. How she handled it revealed several interesting dimensions of her personality and character.

Any winner or runner-up in the Private Members' ballot is immediately inundated with suggestions. Margaret Thatcher decided to follow her instincts and to introduce a bill to weaken the power of the closed shop. She had developed an interest in this subject as a result of following the case of *Rookes* v. *Barnard*, which centred on the dismissal of an airline employee for refusing to join a trade union. She had also been influenced by an Inns of Court Conservative Society pamphlet on the same subject, *A Giant's Strength*, which had been largely written by an unknown young barrister, Geoffrey Howe.[2]

Restricting the power of the trade unions was becoming a popular cause with some sections of the Tory Party. But it was too controversial a step for the 'middle way' approach of Harold Macmillan's government. Margaret Thatcher was firmly told by the whips' office that a Private Member's Bill on the closed shop would not get government backing. This would have killed her chances of getting the bill through the House, so she made her first U-turn and abandoned it.

Her next proposal was a bill to tidy up certain aspects of the law of contempt of court, which had caused clashes between the press and the government's law officers over the reporting of a prominent murder case. Margaret Thatcher was on the side of making life easier for the press, but the law officers were not on the side of her bill. The Attorney General, Sir Reginald Manningham-Buller,* whose nickname in the House was 'Bullying Manner', took a condescending approach to the proposals of the Member for Finchley. His line was that changing the contempt of court law was 'too complicated a task for a back-bench member who was not even a Silk'.†

The task of breaking this bad news to Margaret Thatcher fell to the Chief Whip, Martin Redmayne. They had a vigorous argument at which neither of

---

* Reginald Manningham-Buller (1903–1980), Northamptonshire MP, 1943–1962; Attorney General, 1954–1962; Lord Chancellor, 1962–1964, as Viscount Dilhorne; Father of Baroness Eliza Manningham-Buller DBE, first woman Director General of MI5, 2002–2005.
† 'Silk' is a colloquial term for a senior barrister who has achieved the rank of QC and is entitled to wear a gown made of silk.

them minced words.[3] She failed to persuade the Chief Whip, so a second U-turn was necessary.

Her third attempt at producing a bill did find favour with the government. Showing a good eye for catching the attention of the press gallery, she took up a cause that was being championed by the Guild of Newspaper Editors. This was the right of admission for journalists and other members of the public to attend meetings and committee meetings of the local councils.

It was a topical subject because a year earlier a number of Labour-controlled councils in big cities denied normal reporting facilities to journalists working for a chain of provincial newspapers involved in an industrial dispute with the printing unions. This apparent abuse of union power caused so much national concern that the Conservative Party in its 1959 election manifesto had promised 'to make quite sure that the Press have proper facilities for reporting the proceedings of local authorities'.[4]

However, when Margaret Thatcher made her next visit to the whips' office, she was disappointed to discover that the manifesto promise was not quite what it seemed to be. She was told that the government's remedy for the problem was a code of practice rather than an Act of Parliament. Describing this attitude as 'extremely feeble',[5] she went to see the cabinet minister responsible for local government, Henry Brooke.

He was sympathetic but ambivalent. Mindful of the manifesto commitment, he offered her what in effect was half a loaf. To slice her down to size, he delegated the reduction in her expectations to his officials. These negotiations almost came to a stalemate because of what Mrs Thatcher later described as 'peppery exchanges'[6] with civil servants.

Most of the pepper seems to have been provided not by the Member for Finchley but by another formidable lady, Dame Evelyn Sharp,* the Permanent Secretary of the Ministry of Housing and Local Government. The Dame, as she was labelled in the diaries of Richard Crossman,† wanted

---

* Evelyn Sharp (1903–1985), Permanent Secretary, Ministry of Housing and Local Government, 1955–1966; the first woman to reach this position in the civil service; DBE, 1961; created Baroness Sharp of Hornsey, 1966.

† Richard Crossman (1907–1974), author and cabinet minister, MP (Lab) for Coventry East, 1945–1974; Editor, *New Statesman*, 1970–1972.

a minimalist bill that imposed only limited restrictions on councils' rights
to exclude reporters from some local authority meetings. Margaret Thatcher
proposed a far wider and tougher measure. There was a headlong collision
of views, apparent even in the officialese of the civil service minutes of their
meetings.

'I warned her flatly', recorded Dame Evelyn Sharp, 'that if she did go ahead
with her Bill in its present form, I thought the Government would be bound to
advise the House to vote against it'.[7]

The Dame also reported an 'extremely unsatisfactory discussion' at which
Mrs Thatcher seemed to be reneging 'on the clear understanding which I thought
I had reached with her, and on the undertaking which she gave to the Minister
in response to his letter'.[8]

In the end there was another U-turn. Faced with the reality that only with
the department's full support would her bill have a chance of reaching the statute book, Margaret Thatcher backed down and accepted the minimalist version.
It was progress, but watered down progress.

Margaret Thatcher introduced the second reading of her diluted Public
Bodies (Admission of the Press to Meetings) Bill on Friday 5 February 1960. In
that era, Fridays were known as 'dead days' in the House of Commons, often
attracting only single-figure attendances in the chamber for non-contentious
business such as Adjournment Debates or Private Members' Motions. The
danger of such doldrums was that some ill-wisher of the subject under discussion might call for 'a count'. If the number of MPs fell below the required
quorum of forty, the motion was automatically postponed – a delay usually
disastrous to a bill's chances of becoming law.

To avoid such a fate for her bill, Margaret Thatcher sent handwritten letters
to 250 Conservative back-benchers, requesting their presence and support. It
was quite a favour to ask, for most MPs were committed to constituency engagements on a Friday. But her assiduous correspondence achieved a good turnout
of over a hundred Tory MPs.

Margaret Thatcher was understandably nervous, but she did not look or
sound it as she rose to introduce her bill. Wearing a coat dress of bronze and
black brocade buttoned down the front with a black velvet collar, she opened
with a brisk self-dispensation from the conventional maiden speech tributes to
her constituency and her predecessor.

The Official Report of Parliamentary Debates in *Hansard* can be a cold leveller and deceiver. Read half a century after the event, Margaret Thatcher's maiden speech seems a rather clinical if competent performance, with little sparkle. But at the time it was seen as a brilliant debut that immediately established her as a parliamentarian to watch. What dazzled her colleagues in the House and the reporters in the press gallery was that she spoke without referring to notes. She was master of her subject, with a delivery that was both impassioned and *ex tempore*. A combination of these abilities is a sure-fire winner when it comes to building a parliamentary reputation, as was apparent on the day. Even allowing for the convention that compliments to a maiden speaker are expected to be gracious, the tributes to Mrs Thatcher from all parts of the House were exceptionally fulsome.

From the Labour benches Barbara Castle* recognised 'her outstanding maiden speech'. The future Foreign Secretary Michael Stewart praised 'a most striking, impressive and skilful performance'.

Charles Pannell, who had admired Margaret Roberts from his then position as Labour leader of Erith Council when she was adopted to fight Dartford in 1949, offered flowery congratulations on 'rather a beautiful maiden speech', describing it as 'almost a model to the occupants of the Government Front Bench on how to deliver a speech in favour of a Bill, instead of having a dreary essay read to us in a turgid monotone'.

From the government front bench, the minister winding up the second reading debate, Henry Brooke, was almost equally flowery in his congratulations:

> No words of mine can be too high praise for the brilliance with which my hon. Friend the Member for Finchley opened the debate. She spoke with charm, as we all expected, she spoke with a fluency which most of us would envy, and she achieved the rare feat of making a Parliamentary reputation on a Friday.[9]

It might have been expected after these felicitous tributes that the bill would get an easy passage. Not so. Henry Brooke was only at the last minute persuaded (by the size of the 152 to thirty-nine majority at the second reading vote) to

---

* Barbara Castle (1910–2002), Labour cabinet minister; MP for Blackburn, 1945–1979; MEP Greater Manchester West 1984–1989; author, *The Castle Diaries*; created Baroness Castle of Ibstone, 1990.

allow the long title to be extended to include members of the public as well as journalists. This could only be done on a government motion, and was a vital step in order to avoid a procedural quagmire at the committee stage.

Steering a bill through a standing committee is a challenge to a well-briefed minister. For an inexperienced back-bencher it is a mountain to climb. It was hardly surprising that Margaret Thatcher lost her footing several times during its passage. Away from the committee debates, she managed to give offence to the departmental officials whose help she most needed – the parliamentary draftsmen. One of them advised against arranging a meeting between the appropriate clerks of the House of Commons and Mrs Thatcher, and wrote a minute warning about her abrasiveness: 'If she treats them as she has treated us, she may well put their backs up.'[10]

She also lost supporters within the standing committee by being aggressive rather than conciliatory in debate. She annoyed some Tory MPs so much that they voted against a crucial clause to give public access to all local authority committees, which exercised delegated functions. After this defeat she had to settle for access to be granted only to committees of the full council. A leader in *The Times* reported that this reduced the bill to a 'half measure'.[11]

To those who were not following these manoeuvres in standing committee, the half measure still looked like a full-scale success for the Member for Finchley. Although weakened, the bill went through all its stages in both Houses and received the royal assent in October. The end result may have underwhelmed a handful of Whitehall and Westminster insiders, but most outsiders regarded the passing of the bill into law as a considerable achievement and triumph for Margaret Thatcher. Because her Private Member's Bill directly affected the interests of the press, the reporting of its progress was extensive and favourable.

After the second reading debate the *Daily Express*, then selling over four million copies a day, proclaimed, 'A new star was born in Parliament'.[12] The *Sunday Dispatch* declared 'Fame and Margaret Thatcher made friends yesterday'.[13] The Peterborough column in the *Daily Telegraph*, almost certainly written by William Deedes MP,* a golfing friend of Denis Thatcher, forecasted

---

* William Deedes (1913–2007), cabinet minister, journalist and author; Conservative MP for Ashford, 1950–1974; Editor, *Daily Telegraph*, 1974–1986; created Baron Deedes of Aldington, 1986. He was the inspiration for the 'Dear Bill' column in *Private Eye*, a series of satirical letters purportedly written by Denis Thatcher to Bill Deedes.

that her maiden speech 'is unlikely to be excelled by any of her contemporaries'. In the same panegyric style, the column continued: 'To her intellectual and forensic abilities she added yesterday a new frock and not merely charm, but an uncanny instinct for the mood of the House.'[14]

MAKING HER WAY IN THE HOUSE

The success of her maiden speech enabled Margaret Thatcher's parliamentary career to get off to a flying start. She impressed the House not only by her performance but also by her good manners afterwards.

Having written to 250 of her colleagues asking them to stay at Westminster on a Friday to support her bill, she sent a second handwritten letter expressing her gratitude to more than a hundred of them who responded to her request and voted for it. She also thanked many of them personally.

One recipient of this gratitude was my father, William Aitken, the Conservative MP for Bury St Edmunds. He enjoyed telling the story of how he 'didn't know Margaret Thatcher from Adam', when he received her first letter.[15] It persuaded him to cancel his constituency engagement, on that Friday. He was even more impressed the following week when the Member for Finchley sat down beside him in the tea room, thanked him for supporting her bill, and began questioning him about his time in the RAF.

She wanted to know if he was the same William Aitken (he was) who featured in Richard Hillary's classic memoir of fighter pilot life, *The Last Enemy*. She said it was her favourite wartime book. She also asked about his injuries, which were visible as he walked with a stick and had been badly burned in a Spitfire crash.

Naturally, my father was charmed by her attentiveness. He told his wife, 'This Mrs Thatcher will go places. She is bright and a good looker. She seems to have a thing about the RAF.'

In later years, my mother claimed that her husband had a thing about the Member for Finchley. 'Your father kept going on about her blue eyes and blonde curls. He compared her to the actress Virginia McKenna', she said.[16]

The anecdote confirms what other MPs were saying at the time: the young Margaret Thatcher had sex appeal. Yet, even at this early stage in her career, she also polarised opinions among her colleagues.

There were early signs of the formation of a Margaret Thatcher fan club in the House. Denis's friend Bill Deedes was a founder member of this group of admirers. His backing, as a columnist and future editor of the *Daily Telegraph*, was to prove of considerable importance to her career. Other Tory MPs who heard her maiden speech and who later became overt or covert Thatcherites included Humphrey Atkins, Clive Bossom, Robert Grant-Ferris, Patricia Hornsby-Smith, Billy Rees-Davies and Nicholas Ridley. Some were stars, others were merely spear-carriers in the Thatcher story, but all played a part in it.

The most important of them was Sir Keith Joseph. He was the Parliamentary Under Secretary at the Ministry of Housing and Local Government, who became extremely helpful to Margaret Thatcher in steering her bill through its standing committee. They may have looked an odd couple. He was a sensitive, deep and intellectually brilliant Fellow of All Souls, Oxford. She was pugnacious, full of simple certainties and shallow in her knowledge of the legislative process. But they bonded. Their political relationship was later to change British politics.

After her bill, with considerable support from Keith Joseph, became an Act of Parliament, Margaret Thatcher did not settle easily into the collegiate House of Commons groove where back-bench friendships are made. Her early success caused occasional jealousies. She affronted some of her contemporaries at the peak of her maiden speech acclaim by telling a newspaper reporter, 'I couldn't even consider a Cabinet post until my twins are older'.[17]

Aside from this particular immodesty, there was a brassy, humourless presumption to her that grated with some normally affable colleagues. One who quickly decided he could not stand her was Peter Rawlinson, the MP for Epsom, a talented barrister who was later appointed Attorney General. Because of his rudeness to her, the aversion became mutual and later cost him the summit of his ambition, which was to become Britain's first Catholic Lord Chancellor.

Another early critic was David Walder, the Member for High Peak in Derbyshire. She joined him and Julian Critchley at lunch one afternoon in the Members' Dining Room. After she had left the table Walter declared: 'My God! She is like the chairman of my women's committee in High Peak – but writ hideously large.'[18]

The only identifiable example of Margaret Thatcher holding populist views writ large during her first years in Parliament came when she rebelled in a vote on the 1960 Criminal Justice Bill. She supported a right-wing amendment to restore birching for young offenders convicted of second or subsequent crimes of violence. This brought her more headlines, of which the most colourful was to be dubbed 'the most beautiful of the Tory floggers' by the *Sunday Pictorial*.[19]

Alfred Roberts wrote rather gloomily to his elder daughter Muriel that he didn't suppose that Margaret's rebellion 'will help her much in the party'.[20] This paternal pessimism was misplaced. Defying the liberal-minded Home Secretary, R.A. Butler, on corporal punishment was a popular cause with the Tory right. In any case, she did not make a habit of being a rebel. This was the one and only time when she voted against the requirement of the whips during her thirty-one years in the House of Commons.

Margaret Thatcher waited for more than a year after her Private Member's Bill debut before making her second speech on the floor of the House. She chose an important occasion – the Budget debate of 1961. She used her speech to put down a marker that she wanted to be recognised as a specialist in tax and Treasury matters. The Chancellor of the Exchequer, Selwyn Lloyd, was impressed by the technical points she made about the Inland Revenue's powers to tax short-term speculators. He was also surprised when she wished him well 'throughout the many battles that he will have in the process with his Treasury advisers'.[21] The abrasive young MP apparently took a more negative view than the emollient Chancellor about the need for ministers to fight battles against their civil servants.

Margaret Thatcher's speech in the Budget debate revealed one weakness – her inability to make a joke. Knowing that a light touch can be appreciated in the House of Commons, she attempted a humorous reference to the preceding speaker, Hervey Rhodes, the Labour MP for Ashton-under-Lyne. He had made a passing but entirely proper mention of a friend who was a gamekeeper. She unwisely tried to make a link from this to the topical subject of the trial of D.H. Lawrence's *Lady Chatterley's Lover* for obscenity. With ponderous joviality, she observed that she was being asked to follow 'a man who has described his friendship with his gamekeeper, particularly as he described it in such graphic terms, using four and five letter words'.[22] As Hervey Rhodes had not used any of the four and five letter words made famous in *Lady Chatterley's Lover*, he and others present were baffled by her incomprehensible effort to amuse the House. It was an early indication that a sense of humour was not one of her strengths.

During the summer of 1961 there was speculation that Margaret Thatcher might be promoted in an impending government reshuffle. Her Private Member's Bill and her speech in the Budget debate had caught the eye of influential figures in the party. The Chief Whip thought well of her despite their early arguments about the subject matter of her Bill. Selwyn Lloyd believed she might be 'not un-promising material' for a future junior minister in his team at the Treasury.[23]

What counted most in her favour was that one of only three women in the government, Patricia Hornsby-Smith, had signalled a wish to resign from her post as Joint Parliamentary Secretary to the Ministry of Pensions and National Insurance in order to pursue her business interests. She also told the whips' office that Margaret Thatcher would be the best choice as her replacement. The Alfred Bossom connection was responsible for this recommendation. Clive Bossom recalled:

> Pat and Margaret were both young protégées of my father back in the late 1940s. He brought them together and nurtured their friendship. When Pat said she wanted to leave the government, the whips asked her if she had any ideas about who should be her successor. Pat urged them to take Margaret, partly because she knew she would be damn good at the job, and partly because Pat felt strongly that we needed more women as ministers. Pat tipped off Margaret that she was likely to be chosen.[24]

As a result of this advance intelligence, Margaret Thatcher admitted 'I even had more than an inkling of what my future post might be' when, in the middle of a lunch date with her sister Muriel on 9 October 1961, she was summoned to see the Prime Minister.[25] She had been told in advance about the likelihood of being sent for, so she wore her best sapphire blue suit for the anticipated appointment with her boss.

Harold Macmillan was in a languid mood when he invited Margaret Thatcher to join his government. He told her that she would only have to come into the Ministry of Pensions at around eleven each morning and 'sign a few letters'.[26]

This affected casualness was part of Macmillan's style when appointing ministers. In 1962 he told another Parliamentary Under-Secretary, James Ramsden, who was Master of the West of Ure Fox Hounds in North Yorkshire: 'Of course there's no need for you to be in your department on Mondays and Fridays. You must take off all the time you need to continue as an MFH.'[27]

Although Margaret Thatcher enjoyed telling the 'just a few letters' story in later years, it is unlikely that either she or Macmillan believed a word of this charade. The Prime Minister had taken some trouble over her appointment, discussing it in advance with Selwyn Lloyd and Martin Redmayne. He had also cleared it with the Minister of Pensions, John Boyd-Carpenter, who professed himself 'delighted', although privately he was doubtful:

> I thought, frankly, when Harold Macmillan appointed her that it was just a little bit of a gimmick on his part. Here was a good-looking young woman and he was obviously, I thought, trying to brighten up the image of his government.[28]

In image terms, the appointment went down well, although *The Times*, having praised the new minister's charm, youth and debating ability, struck a prescient note in its profile: 'Those who know her well detect a strong will, some might say almost a ruthlessness, behind her smiling appearance.'[29]

Whether it was her talent or the government's need to fill its complement of women ministers, or any one of the factors that make faces fit in reshuffles, Margaret Thatcher now had her foot on the ladder of government. She was the youngest woman ever appointed to ministerial office. She was the first MP in the 1959 intake to be promoted. She had arrived on the front bench where she was to stay for her next twenty-nine years in the House of Commons.

JUNIOR MINISTER

Life as a junior minister started well for Margaret Thatcher. It began with an elegant gesture of politeness from her boss. On her first day in the job, she turned up at 9.30 a.m. – an hour and a half earlier than the time suggested by Harold Macmillan. She was delighted to be met at the front door by the minister himself, a courtesy she never forgot. She emulated him by greeting all her junior ministers in the same way when she became Secretary of State for Education.[30]

Her minister was John Boyd-Carpenter,* nicknamed 'spring heeled Jack' by his colleagues because of his habit of rocking from his heels to his toes when

---

* John Boyd-Carpenter (1908–1998), Conservative MP, 1945–1972; Minister of Pensions and National Insurance, 1955–1962; created Baron Boyd-Carpenter of Crux Easton, 1972.

addressing the House of Commons. He was an adroit debater and a capable administrator of his department. He made some early misjudgements of Margaret Thatcher. 'She's trouble', was his initial comment to his senior civil servant, Sir Eric Bowyer, after his first meeting with the new Joint Parliamentary Secretary.[31]

Boyd-Carpenter also underestimated her capacity for hard work. 'Knowing that she had two young children, a husband in Burmah Oil, a house in Kent and like the rest of us a constituency to look after, I must admit that I wondered whether I or the Department would get much help out of her.'[32]

He did not have to wonder long. The Ministry of Pensions and National Insurance* (MPNI) was known as 'the salt mines' because of its exceptionally heavy workload in one of the most subterranean areas of government. The junior minister had to bear the brunt of the large volume of correspondence with Members of Parliament about the cases they raised on behalf of constituents on pension claims, national assistance entitlements and national insurance contributions. This could be grindingly dull work, requiring the minister's approval and signature of over a hundred letters a day.

Margaret Thatcher increased her pressures by her own diligence. She frequently corrected or redrafted the correspondence submitted to her. Sometimes she became irritable in this process, occasionally even tearing up letters she considered to have been badly drafted. This earned her sometimes the resentment and sometimes the grudging admiration of MPNI officials.

One friend who witnessed her bad temper with letters she considered to have been badly drafted was her Parliamentary Private Secretary, Clive Bossom.

She used to get in a terrible tiz, crossing out paragraphs and writing things like 'Rot!', 'Bad Grammar' or 'Double Dutch' in the margins. Once or twice I saw her tear up letters. Needless to say, this did not make her loved by the civil servants who wrote them. I remember one angry mandarin complaining to me, 'That bloody woman. Her job is to sign letters, not to read them'.[33]

---

* In 1966 the Ministry of Pensions and National Insurance was renamed the Ministry of Social Security. In 1968 it merged with the Ministry of Health to become the Department of Health and Social Security.

Even if she sometimes upset her officials, her mastery of her brief impressed them. Another tongue-in-cheek complaint to Bossom was, 'This Minister seems to know the Beveridge Report* by heart'.[34]

She showed that she had a heart for matters more human than the small print of Beveridge, by trying to change the law in order to give more help to widows. She attempted to persuade her minister, and on one occasion the prime minister, to relax the earnings rule for widowed mothers: 'I thought that if a woman who had lost her husband, but still had children to support, decided to try to earn a little more through going out to work, she should not lose pension for doing so. Perhaps as a woman I had a clearer view of what problems widows faced.'[35]

Margaret Thatcher was frustrated in her efforts to relax the earnings rule by one of the time-honoured arguments of the civil service. Her officials repeatedly claimed there would be 'repercussions' in other parts of the benefit system if the rules were changed. She came to hate the Whitehall word 'repercussions', as it compelled her to defend the indefensible in adjournment debates and Parliamentary Questions on the earnings rule. When she was out of office, following the general election of 1964, she was amazed when the incoming Labour government decided to ignore the so-called repercussions and to change the earnings rule in the way she had been arguing. 'The moral was clear to me: bureaucratic logic is no substitute for ministerial judgment', she commented.[36] It was a lesson she took to heart. It stood her in good stead in her frequent clashes with the civil service after she became prime minister.

During her stint at MPNI, the judgement of her minister on the abilities of Margaret Thatcher steadily improved. John Boyd-Carpenter, who had initially treated his new junior colleague with condescension on the grounds that 'To the male eye, she always looked as though she had spent the morning with the coiffeur and the afternoon with the couturier', soon revised his opinion upwards. He came to feel that she showed 'such spirit, competence and courage as a newly appointed Parliamentary Secretary . . . that I came to the conclusion that she would go very high in public life'.[37]

She in turn came to respect him for being 'a real Tory', with deep roots in a private hinterland that ranged from a passion for vegetable gardening to serving as a church warden for forty years. She learned much from her minister, not

---

* The Beveridge Report (1942) established the basis for Britain's welfare state.

least from his mastery of the House of Commons. One anecdote of her apprenticeship, which she told at John Boyd-Carpenter's memorial service in 1998, involved him cooling her down on the front bench during a parliamentary confrontation by whispering, 'Margaret, I know that you are enjoying yourself, but do remember our object is to get the Bill through!'[38]

Her best moment of enjoyment in the House came after the 'Night of the Long Knives'. This was Fleet Street's headline for a badly mishandled reshuffle in which Macmillan sacked seven cabinet ministers including his Chancellor, Selwyn Lloyd, on 13 July 1962. The Tory back-benchers were shocked and sullen over this bloodletting. The Labour Party was jubilant.

In the middle of this debacle, Margaret Thatcher seized her moment. It could have been one of discomfort, for she had suddenly been deprived of a minister by the promotion of John Boyd-Carpenter to the cabinet. In the chaos of the cull of ministers below the cabinet (where the reshuffle was wider and even more botched), no successor to him was chosen for several days. This left an awkward vacuum.

The Monday after the Night of the Long Knives, 16 July, Parliamentary Questions to the non-existent Minister for Pensions and National Insurance were first business in the House of Commons. So, Margaret Thatcher had to fulfil the unusual task of answering fourteen questions single-handed. She rose to the challenge with gusto. At the peak of Labour knockabout on the issue of when Macmillan would be drawing his own pension, the Parliamentary Secretary demurely promised to pass on the opposition's comments to 'my new chief'. Then she added *sotto voce* after a well-timed pause, 'when I have one'.[39]

Laughter in the House. She had even learned how to make a joke.

IN THE CONSTITUENCY

Like most new Members of Parliament, Margaret Thatcher took great pains to carry out her constituency duties. Every Friday afternoon she held a 'surgery' to which local residents came with their problems. Before the age of emails, the phrase 'I'll go and see my MP about it' symbolised a well-used channel of communication between the elected and the electorate. Upholding this tradition, the Member for Finchley soon made an impact by both her availability and her

ability in the service of her constituents. One of her party workers, Derek
Owens, recalled:

> My word, she worked hard for us. She was a real hands-on lady when she was doing
> case work. In her early days, I remember taking her to see how the other half lived in
> Lodge Lane, North Finchley, which is one of our poorest areas. When we got to a really
> run-down property with holes in the ceiling and no bathroom it turned out that she
> knew all about the problems of the old lady who lived there because she had visited her
> twice before. 'Hello, Mrs Smith. How is your acne treatment going? Has it cleared up
> yet?' was Margaret's greeting. I was most impressed that she knew even the back streets
> of her constituency so well.[40]

On a more cerebral level of communication, Margaret Thatcher was
approached at one of her surgeries in 1963 by a clever fifth-former from Christ's
College, Finchley. He was doing his A-level coursework on the British constitution, and wanted to ask his MP some detailed questions about whether the
voting system should be reformed by introducing proportional representation.
'You're not a Liberal, are you?' was Margaret Thatcher's opening question to
her young constituent. Fortunately for him, the answer was no, so the sixteen-
year-old was given the full benefit of her views on this subject. 'She obviously
loved teaching', recalled the boy. 'She made a big impression on me by being
wonderfully frank and vigorous in her arguments.'[41]

The impressed schoolboy was Jonathan Sacks, who in later life became the
Chief Rabbi of Britain's Orthodox Jews. As a teenager he formed a relationship
with Margaret Thatcher, returning to her office to get more help with his weekly
essays, and persuading her to speak at Christ's College Debating Society. In the
vote of thanks at the end of the evening, another pupil described her as 'Queen
Boadicea, equipped with Hansard and hatpin'.[42] It was not a bad description of
her fierce and forensic style as a debater.

Margaret Thatcher was regularly in Finchley, but never quite *of* Finchley.
She chose neither to live in her constituency, nor to have any kind of *pied à
terre* there. In her thirty-three years as Member for the borough she never spent
a single night in it.

An interesting aspect of her electorate was its unusually high concentration
of Jewish voters, who constituted about 20 per cent of the population. Margaret
Thatcher felt a particular affection and affinity for this community. 'She was an

outsider herself; she had a true sense of religion, and she admired many Jewish values', recalled Lord Sacks. 'In particular, she liked the Jewish emphasis on accountability and responsibility, on entrepreneurial ambition mixed with compassion and on the priority Jews accord to giving back to their community.'[43]

What Jonathan Sacks spotted in the 1960s about Margaret Thatcher's rapport with Jews seemed to be confirmed during her Downing Street years. She appointed more Jews as cabinet ministers than any previous prime minister in British history. Harold Macmillan was reported to have quipped that her government contained more Estonians than Etonians. If this was the Finchley factor it was much in the public interest, for the names of her Jewish ministers and No. 10 advisers give their own testimony to the Prime Minister's sharp eye for talent.*

Meanwhile, from the other side of the Middle East, it was a source of amusement that the biggest donor to the Finchley Conservative Association in the early 1960s was Prince Naif bin Abdulaziz Al Saud of Saudi Arabia. He owned two houses in Totteridge Lane, the most expensive residential area of the constituency. In the 1964 general election, Margaret Thatcher canvassed Totteridge Lane and found the Prince in residence at Loxwood House. He was unfamiliar with the processes of democracy and the existence of women legislators. Nevertheless, he received the candidate with courtesy. After establishing in an interpreted conversation with her that his MP was both a Conservative and a monarchist, he sent a £1,000 cheque to her fighting fund.[44]

Margaret Thatcher's diligence as a constituency MP did not diminish as she climbed to the highest rank in politics. As Prime Minister she carried out surgeries and public appearances in Finchley two or three times each month. It was geographically helpful that Chequers was only forty-five minutes away, but even so her assiduity to her constituents' problems was outstanding. In return, Finchley provided her with a rock sold base in nine general elections.

FAMILY LIFE

Like many a hardworking young minister and Member of Parliament, Margaret Thatcher found that her family life suffered from her workload.

---

* The cabinet ministers were Keith Joseph, Nigel Lawson, Leon Brittan, Malcolm Rifkind, David Young and Michael Howard. Her Jewish advisers included David Wolfson, Norman Strauss, Alfred Sherman, David Hart and Stephen Sherbourne.

One sadness was that the gulf between Grantham and Westminster weakened her already fragile links with her parents. Beatrice Roberts died on 7 December 1960. For some years, the communication between mother and daughter had been almost non-existent. As Margaret put it in an unusually candid 1961 comment to Godfrey Winn of the *Daily Express*: 'I loved my mother dearly, but after 15 we had nothing more to say to each other. It wasn't her fault. She was weighed down by the home, always being in the home.'[45]

The widowed Alfred Roberts came to stay with Margaret and Denis for the first Christmas after his wife's death. He was not an easy guest, outlasting his welcome. 'Re Pop – he is determined to stay with us both as long as possible', wrote Margaret to Muriel. 'He dreads the thought of going home. At the moment, it is most difficult here.' In the same letter, she told her elder sister; 'I shall have to shunt Pop off on Saturday 14th Jan . . . Will this be all right with you?' She advised Muriel to set a definite date for their father's return to Grantham. 'Otherwise he will just hang on and on and not take any hints.'[46]

For his part, Alfred Roberts gave signs of resentment that his younger daughter was too busy to answer his letters promptly. One year she forgot his birthday. She was not unduly neglectful of her father, but he became a low priority in her life. She was too preoccupied with her career to give him much of her attention.

The same complaint could have been levelled at her by any other member of her family. In 1960, the *Evening News* published an interview with Margaret Thatcher that read like a caricature, as she explained the compatibility of her daily routine with motherhood and marriage. 'However busy I am, I always manage to phone the twins shortly before 6 pm', she said, adding rather defensively on the subject of Denis: 'You will be wondering what happens to my husband in the evenings when the House is in session and I am not at home. He is every bit as busy as I am, if not more so . . . it is rare for him to be at home for more than one evening a week.'[47]

This was true, but it was not quite the whole truth. Denis also worked hard. But his wife's obsession with her duties was becoming more than he had bargained for. He stayed in the pub after leaving his office until closing time. He spent more and more evenings with his mother and sister Joy, who lived together in Notting Hill Gate. It was one of the sadnesses of Denis's life that his wife never got on well with his mother. Mrs Thatcher senior was an exuberant, joke-cracking lady who loved having her son to dinner, and enjoyed entertaining her grandchildren amidst gales of laughter and funny stories. By contrast, the humourless Margaret never had a single meal in her mother-in-law's house. It was an unexplained and unattractive example of her tendency to bear grudges over some earlier contretemps between the two Thatcher women.

A further erosion of harmony in the marriage was caused by Margaret's enthusiasm for accepting weekend speaking engagements, not just in her own constituency but all over the country. As a junior minister, she exceeded the call of duty in her willingness to address audiences on a Saturday.

One weekend in the summer of 1963, she made a tour of old age pensioner associations in the West Country. The last stop on her travels was at The Walnut Tree Centre in Taunton. The local MP, Edward du Cann, recalled:

> She went down extremely well with the pensioners, but when she came over to my house for tea afterwards, she did not go down so well with the Chancellor of the Exchequer, Reggie Maudling. He was staying with us. He, like me, had spent the day watching a cricket match between our village and a team of City editors that included Fred Ellis, Patrick Sergeant and other great names from national newspapers. Reggie was quite a laid back character. So he found it difficult to relate to this eager beaver of a junior minister, who wanted to explain the details of how she had answered questions from OAPs about their pensions on a Saturday. He found her not at all relaxed or sociable. I remember him saying, 'She's far too over-keen'.[48]

Her over-keenness to be away on official engagements had an impact at home. Denis gradually found that he preferred to go sailing on a yacht named *Winnie* with his rugby-club friends at weekends. The alternative was to come back to an empty house or to a wife overwhelmed with ministerial papers from her red boxes.

Their children felt the weight of her workload too. She was often an absent mother. Even when she was with them at home, she could be completely obsessed by her job.

An example of her ability to cut herself off from the family life around her came one Saturday when *Top of the Pops* was blaring from the TV to the delight of Mark and Carol. When a particularly noisy number raised the decibel level, Carol asked her mother, sitting beside her on the sofa: 'Is the television disturbing you, Mum?'

No reply. Carol repeated the question.

'Pardon, dear? The TV?' answered a surprised Margaret. 'Oh, I didn't realise it was on.'[49]

Carol was later to write: 'When I look back, I have no doubt that my mother's political ambitions – and the single-mindedness with which she pursued them – eclipsed our family and social life.'[50]

Denis was another side of the eclipse. He was away a great deal on overseas business trips and at weekend sporting events. The absences of their parents led to a certain dysfunctionality in the upbringing of the twins. But they were not the complaining types. Somehow the family stuck together, although a lot of the glue had to be provided by outsiders, particularly by a hardworking nanny called Abby.

In 1964, Denis nearly became unstuck when he went through a particularly bad patch of business worries. He had a form of nervous breakdown. In his account of this episode:

> My doctor said that I was making myself ill working at that pace and if I carried on then I was endangering my health. And then he handed me an ultimatum. 'There's nothing wrong with you physically but if you don't stop working so hard, you are going to be very ill indeed. You've simply got to take some time off.' I got myself on a boat – it shook Margaret – and took myself off to South Africa.'[51]

His sabbatical may well have shaken his wife, but it avoided the breakdown of his health and the break-up of their marriage. How close did he come to these disasters? According to an old friend, unnamed but quoted in Carol Thatcher's biography of her father:

> He was terribly depressed and decided to go to South Africa to sort himself out. I knew he was unhappy because he discussed it with me. He had his mother and Joy, who doted on him, and a wife who was totally absorbed in her political career.[52]

Denis enjoyed an idyllic few months off in a country he loved. He saw old friends and relatives, and became absorbed in learning the art of photography. He found the long sea voyages to and from the Cape particularly relaxing. Above all, he did a great deal of thinking about how to resolve the problems that had grown into his mid-life crisis.

The biggest strategic decision he took was to sell his business. The Atlas Preservative Company was profitable but under-capitalised. Denis decided to lift the load off his shareholders and make an approach to Castrol Oil. An agreed takeover was completed within six months. The deal put the equivalent of over a million pounds into his bank account. Denis went on running Atlas, but with the backing of a powerful parent company behind him. He also secured a seat on Castrol's main board, with a package that included a company car, share options, plus a good salary and pension. From then on, the financial stability of the Thatcher family was assured.

Margaret steered her way through the rough passages that preceded this success with outward calm, although she must have had inner worries.

In the constituency, she was unsettled by the brash claims of her Liberal challenger John Pardoe who predicted victory for himself. This was hot air. The Finchley result in the general election of October 1964 was better than expected. Margaret Thatcher was re-elected with a majority of 8,802.

The national result was also better than expected for the Conservatives. Sir Alec Douglas-Home, the most mocked and satirised Prime Minister in history, made a startling comeback in the campaign and was only just pipped at the winning post. The new Labour government, after cliffhanging recounts in a handful of marginals, particularly Meriden, eventually had a majority of just four in the new House of Commons. But a defeat is a defeat, and its consequences sent Margaret Thatcher's spirits plummeting.

Denis, who missed the whole of the election campaign, remained in South Africa until late December. She could not turn to him when she lost her ministerial post and perks. Nor was he around when she suffered the disappointment of being kept in place as an opposition spokesman at the same level for the same department. She deserved better than being asked to soldier on as shadow junior minister for Pensions and National Insurance. Her career appeared to have hit a roadblock.

Compounding these reverses, and her concerns for Denis, were some unexpected health problems of her own. Margaret may have been depressed. She was certainly at a low ebb emotionally, politically and physically. As 1964 ended, a chest infection turned into a severe bout of pneumonia. She was too ill to rise from her sick bed to attend the lying in state at Westminster Hall of her hero Sir Winston Churchill, who died on 24 January 1965. The combination of loss of office, an absent husband and pneumonia made this the winter of her discontent. It was the lowest moment in her life – until she was ousted from 10 Downing Street twenty-six years later.

REFLECTION

During her first five years in Parliament, Margaret Thatcher's career in public life advanced, but her family relationships deteriorated. She did not seem to be unduly bothered by this imbalance. Perhaps it left scars on Mark, Carol and Denis, but at the time they took it as a *fait accompli*. Collectively, they kept their heads down and got on with their somewhat dysfunctional lives.

By the end of 1964, Margaret Thatcher's career seemed to be stalling. She had proved herself a most capable parliamentary junior secretary at MPNI, far outshining the two senior ministers in her department who followed John Boyd-Carpenter – Niall Macpherson and Richard Wood. Yet she could not climb her way out of the salt mines. She missed two good opportunities for promotion. The first came in October 1963, when Harold Macmillan resigned for health reasons. His unexpected successor was Sir Alec Douglas-Home. She backed him in the 'customary processes of consultation', which was the mysterious and undemocratic procedure by which the Tories chose their new leader. Unfortunately, Sir Alec did not return the favour. So Margaret Thatcher remained marooned as a junior pensions minister. The same fate befell her after the Conservatives lost the 1964 election. The opposition front bench was reshuffled, but she stayed where she was. Rumour had it that she was out of favour with the whips' office. She must have felt frustrated by her lack of upward mobility at a time of opportunity within the party.

> It's easy to be a starter,
>   But are you a sticker, too?

The lines she had learned in her Grantham childhood had a negative resonance after five years at Westminster. She had made a promising start. But now she was stuck.

7

Front-bench opposition

ENTERING OPPOSITION

The health and husband worries that were making Margaret Thatcher so miserable at the turn of the year soon lifted. She recovered from her pneumonia. Denis recovered his equilibrium. The marriage and the family finances regained strength. Soon she was fighting fit to do battle in a surprisingly wide spread of portfolios as an opposition front-bencher.

There is an old parliamentary saying: 'Opposition creates opportunities.' Margaret Thatcher seized hers with gusto mingled with good luck. In the six years while the Conservatives were out of office between 1964 and 1970 she was appointed to be an opposition front-bencher, covering six separate portfolios – pensions, housing, economic policy, power, transport and education. The last three posts brought her into the shadow cabinet, and in 1970 she was appointed Secretary of State for Education in the new government. She had a good run. Her major benefactor, despite a relationship of mutual uneasiness, was Ted Heath.

Alec Douglas-Home never looked likely to stay long as leader of the opposition. He resigned, after some none-too-gentle pushing by Heath supporters, in July 1965. Margaret Thatcher was 'stunned and upset' by her leader's departure, rightly blaming 'mysterious cabals' which had clearly not tried to recruit her support.[1]

A new system of election for the leadership of the Conservative Party had been established. The leading contenders were Edward Heath and Reginald Maudling. Margaret Thatcher was initially inclined to support Maudling but Keith Joseph persuaded her to change her mind. She was not close to either candidate. If Maudling had reached out to her he would probably have secured her vote, for she preferred both his personality and his policies. But Maudling was too complacent to canvass his supporters.

By contrast the Heath campaign, well organised by Peter Walker, had a sophisticated system of approaching every MP through a close colleague, most likely to influence his or her vote. Walker won over Joseph, who in turn won over Thatcher. What seems to have swung her round was less a dissection of Maudling's weaknesses by Keith Joseph, but more his advocacy of Heath's strengths. 'Ted has a passion to get Britain right' was the line that finally convinced her.[2] She always put passionate professionalism well ahead of laid-back detachment when making her choices.

Ted Heath, even though she had never warmed to him, received her backing. He won the election with 150 votes to Maudling's 133. Enoch Powell, regarded as a maverick candidate, received fifteen votes.

As the new leader of the opposition, Heath reshuffled his pack of frontbenchers, making Margaret Thatcher the subordinate Shadow Minister for Housing and Land under her former boss John Boyd-Carpenter. She had a juicy target to attack in the Labour government's proposal for a Land Commission, an ill-conceived quango designed to control the price of housing development. She did an effective demolition job on the legislation and its hapless minister Fred Willey in several speeches and articles, but long before the Commission could be established Harold Wilson called an early election in March 1966.

The contest was a lacklustre event for the Conservative Party. Margaret Thatcher, like many others, was privately critical of its manifesto, *Action not Words*,[3] which seemed arid and unconvincing. The same adjectives could also be applied to the new leader, Ted Heath. In the polls he trailed badly behind Harold Wilson, who had shown some deft foreign-policy skills in his handling of the Rhodesia crisis, and was far more effective as a television performer.

At the ripe old age of twenty-three, I was fighting my first election in 1966 as the Conservative Parliamentary Candidate for Meriden, one of the most marginal seats in the country. The campaign brought about my first meeting with Margaret Thatcher – fleeting but interesting.

The background was that although the national polls were predicting a Labour landslide, some regional polls suggested that because of a special 'West Midlands Factor' the trend might be reversed in the Birmingham area, with the Tories picking up some marginal seats. One of the constituencies forecast to produce an upset was Meriden, where I was battling to overturn a slender Labour majority of 364.

Once the 'West Midlands Factor' became a talking point in the general election, Conservative Central Office sent its biggest guns down to Meriden. In ten days, nine front-bench spokesmen passed though my patch on their whistle-stop tours of the area. These eminent visitors included the three past, present and future Tory leaders – Sir Alec Douglas-Home, Ted Heath and Margaret Thatcher – although no one in those days entertained the remotest thought that the junior opposition spokeswoman for Housing and Land might be a future prime minister.

Central Office gave her a walk-on part in Meriden. I met her at a shopping centre in Coleshill, where her minders said she could spend just fifteen minutes. We used it in accosting pedestrians, handing out leaflets and asking the shadow minister to say a few words into a battery-powered megaphone.

My first impressions of Margaret Thatcher were positive. She went out of her way to be agreeable to a neophyte politician. She mentioned that she too had once been the youngest Conservative Parliamentary Candidate in the country when fighting Dartford in 1950. 'You learn a lot quickly, don't you?' she said. I was pleased to be bracketed together with her in this way.[4] Given the frantic pace of her visitation, I thought she would barely know my name. But she was gracious. 'I've seen you listening to debates in the House from the gallery', she said. I explained that this was part of my job as a part-time private secretary to Selwyn Lloyd. 'Doing your homework – quite right!' she commented.[5]

Unfortunately, the Meriden megaphone went quite wrong and sounded dreadfully screechy. My agent, Gill Rogers, apparently offended by the peremptory way her hand had been shaken, or rather yanked, by our latest visitor offered the unhelpful view, 'It's her voice that's the trouble'. I did not pass on this observation. Margaret Thatcher was rather shrill, but the erratic amplification made things worse. Unfazed by the technical malfunctions, she pressed on with a vigorous denunciation of 'this socialist land grab, which will take away our basic individual freedom'.

Her words did not make as much impression on the passers-by as her millinery did on the gaggle of Tory women in the greeting party. Her hat was a creation shaped like a tea cosy, topped with a flamboyant blue bow. 'Very stylish, but not right for Coleshill', was the verdict of Alderman Mrs Marjorie Leech MBE, the Chair of the Meriden Women's Advisory Committee.[6]

Before either fashion or politics could be discussed further, Margaret Thatcher declared, 'Time's up! I have to be on my way to Coventry!'[7] So she bustled away from the shopping centre in a high-speed, jerky walk, which could have been a parody of the wound-up clockwork dolls of that era. Apart from some mild amusement caused by the briskly rolling gait of her receding rear view, her visit to Meriden in 1966 was not a memorable one.

Even less memorable, from a Tory point of view, was the final result of the general election. In Meriden, and almost everywhere else, Conservative candidates were crushed by swings to Labour of between 4 and 7 per cent. Harold Wilson returned to Downing Street with a handsome majority of ninety-seven seats. A rare exception to this trend was in Finchley. Thanks to a fall in the Liberal vote, Margaret Thatcher increased her majority to 9,464. She was one of only three Conservatives in the country to achieve an improved result.

There was press speculation after the election that Margaret Thatcher would be promoted into the shadow cabinet. She disbelieved the reports, knowing that her leader had no great liking for her. 'My acquaintanceship with Ted', as she archly put it, 'had never risked developing into friendship.'[8] However, he did briefly consider her elevation as 'the statutory woman' in his front-line team. Equally briefly, he rejected the idea, which came from Jim Prior, his Parliamentary Private Secretary.

As Prior described the scene in the Leader of the Opposition's office after putting Mrs Thatcher's name forward, 'There was a long silence. "Yes," Ted Heath said, "Willie [Whitelaw, the Chief Whip] agrees she's much the most able, but he says once she's there we'll never be able to get rid of her. So we both think it's got to be Mervyn Pike."'[9]

Being passed over for the mild-mannered Mervyn Pike was only a temporary disappointment to Margaret Thatcher. She had two consolation prizes. Denis gave her a beautiful eternity ring.* Iain Macleod, the Shadow Chancellor of the

---

* The ring was bought for £220 from William Mullins, proprietor of J. McCarthy (established 1798), an antique jewellery shop in Artillery Row, Victoria. Both Thatchers were his regular customers for over forty-five years. Mr Mullins, a shopkeeper of considerable character, received an invitation to attend Lady Thatcher's funeral at St Paul's Cathedral in 2013.

Exchequer, asked to have her in a key role for his opposition Treasury team. Heath consented, appointing her as the no. 2 Opposition Treasury and Economic Affairs spokeswoman. She shone far more in this understudy position than she would have done if she had been appointed to the shadow cabinet with her own portfolio.

IAIN MACLEOD'S NO. 2

A lucky break combined with prodigious hard work was the formula that propelled Margaret Thatcher's career forward during her eighteen-month stint as a member of Iain Macleod's Treasury team in opposition.

The luck came in the form of a new tax proposal from the Labour government, called Selective Employment Tax (SET). Introduced in the 1966 Budget of Chancellor James Callaghan, it was perhaps the silliest, most complicated and least successful tax innovation of any post-war government. The hard work lay in the diligence with which Margaret Thatcher prepared and executed her attack on SET.

SET had been prepared in great haste to raise essential tax revenue without appearing to break Labour's election pledge that there would be no severe increase in taxation. It was meant to shift resources from service industries into manufacturing by making employers pay SET of 25s (£1.25) a week on all male employees. Employers in manufacturing industries could reclaim the SET six months later and receive a bonus of 7s 6d (£0.37) per employee on top. Service industries got nothing back. There was a whole range of variables for women employees, part timers and different classifications of industry. The scheme was riddled with anomalies. It proved to be a political goldmine for the new opposition spokeswoman for Treasury and Economic Affairs.

Making her debut in this role in the third day of the Budget debate on 5 May 1966, Margaret Thatcher was on devastating form. She turned the SET proposals and Jack Diamond, the hapless Chief Secretary of the Treasury who had to defend them, into a laughing stock. She compared the administrative absurdities of the tax to a Gilbert and Sullivan opera, lampooning the concept of the Chancellor taking 25s a week off manufacturing employers and then repaying them 32s 6d six months later. Why not, she demanded, just pay them the 7s 6d and have done with it.

This is absolute nonsense . . . I really think the right hon. Gentleman needs a woman at the Treasury . . . If my chief had come to me and put up a cock-eyed scheme like that, I should have asked him if he was feeling all right.[10]

Jack Diamond must have felt even worse when she crushed one of his interventions. She had been lambasting him for failing to understand the impact on working women who paid for childcare. 'The hon. Lady has overlooked', he complained, 'that this is a tax on employers.'

'Precisely', she retorted. 'I do not think the right hon. Gentleman has been listening. In this case the married woman and the widow is the employer.'[11]

Margaret Thatcher sat down to resounding Tory cheers and even some admiration from her opponents.

Her boss, Iain Macleod was fulsome in his congratulations. Over a drink in the smoking room after the debate he confided to Angus Maude, 'After listening to Margaret's speech tonight, it no longer seems absurd to think that there might one day be a woman Prime Minister'.[12]

A few days later, Macleod poured public praise over his No. 2. 'I have heard many excellent speeches from women Ministers and Members from the front and back benches', he wrote in the *Daily Mail*, 'but cannot recall another in a major debate that was described as a triumph.'[13]

Iain Macleod took over where John Boyd-Carpenter left off as a mentor in parliamentary debating to Margaret Thatcher. She sat beside her new boss on the front bench for hundreds of hours of late-night sittings. They were a fine partnership. She had the stamina and the application to detail. Macleod was weak in both. But he had a master's touch at high scorn and trumpet-blasting invective when it came to attacking his opponents. It became clear later in the year that his pupil had absorbed several of the same oratorical techniques of the Shadow Chancellor.

In October, Margaret Thatcher wound up a debate on taxation at the Tory Conference in Blackpool. For the second time in six months, she achieved a triumphant *tour de force* with her fiery denunciations of SET.

Having been a parliamentary candidate in the March 1966 general election, I was a West Midlands delegate sitting in the conference hall and retained three memories of her speech, which won a standing ovation – a rarity in those days.

My first memory was that she teetered on the brink of over-the-top crowd pleasing. Some winced, though the ultra-faithful applauded when she declared that SET was 'a step not merely towards Socialism but towards Communism'.[14] This synthetic start was replaced by real substance.

My second memory was of listening with close and increasingly admiring concentration to her detailed dissection of the technical flaws and anomalies of SET. She concluded with a firework display of rocket attacks on Callaghan's record of tax increases, culminating in the final salvo, 'This chap Callaghan must go!'[15]

The words look mundane, but in the fevered atmosphere of the hall they brought the cheering delegates to their feet. Seen in retrospect, this speech was one of the early turning points in her career, for it established her as a new and rising star with the party faithful.

My third memory is of discussing Margaret Thatcher's success in the bar afterwards with a group of West Midlands candidates and MPs. The most interesting line of comment was that she had clearly studied and imitated the conference oratory of Iain Macleod. He was an expert in turning a banal line such as 'on the higher ground of character and principle – there I take my stand' into a clarion call that could make the welkin ring. Someone in our group imitated Macleod's compelling counter tenor delivery of those last five words in an earlier speech, and compared them to Margaret Thatcher's rhythmic and rising five-word crescendo, 'This chap Callaghan must go'. I was reminded of Mrs Gatehouse, the OUCA speaking tutor, telling Margaret Roberts and successive generations of students, 'End with a good strong boom of not more than five or six words!'[16] She was always a good learner.

Macleod linked the Thatcher conference speech to her Budget-debate speech, describing them in his *Daily Mail* column as 'a magnificent double'.[17] It was one of many good reviews in the press.

A Fiery Blonde Warns of the Road to Ruin was the headline in the *Sun*, which saluted her for delivering 'one of those magnificent fire-in-the-belly speeches which are heard too seldom'.[18]

From the vantage point of both the tabloids and the Tory conference goers, Margaret Thatcher was becoming a woman to watch.

JOINING THE SHADOW CABINET

After the acclaim for Margaret Thatcher's conference and parliamentary performances, Ted Heath was urged by Iain Macleod to promote her into the shadow
cabinet. He did so, but waited for almost a year until the existing 'statutory
woman', Mervyn Pike, retired on grounds of ill health. Margaret Thatcher
had now arrived at the top table of the Conservative hierarchy, but she did not
make a favourable impression there.

Although she soon mastered her new portfolio as Shadow Minister for Fuel
and Power, speaking with passion and compassion in the House on the report
into the Aberfan Disaster,* her relations with Ted Heath remained cool.

One problem was that she could *'never* stop arguing', according to the
Crossbencher column in the *Sunday Express*.[19] The Shadow Attorney General,
Peter Rawlinson, who was often in attendance at the shadow cabinet, reflected
the murmurings of complaint that she was too loquacious. 'How she talked . . .
I believe that she honestly did not realise how irritating she was.'[20]

By contrast, other colleagues were surprised by her reticence at their early
meetings. 'I don't think she was much noticed at Ted's shadow cabinet', recalled
Lord Carrington. 'She made no mark at all.'[21]

For her part, Margaret Thatcher found discussions at the Heath shadow
cabinet 'not very stimulating'.[22] She put this down to the simmering tensions
between her senior colleagues. It was an ill-kept secret that some of the key
men at the top, notably Ted Heath, Reggie Maudling, Iain Macleod and Enoch
Powell, did not get on well with each other. They could agree on what they
opposed, but there was little unity on what they supported as policy for an
alternative government.

There is little evidence to suggest that Margaret Thatcher played a significant
part in the philosophical debate that was starting to divide the Conservative
Party between Heath's ideas and Powell's ideas. Enoch Powell believed, as
Margaret Thatcher came to believe, that inflation should be kept low by tight
control of the money supply; that market forces should determine the exchange

---

* The collapse of the colliery spoil tip at the village of Aberfan on the 21 October 1966
killing 116 children and twenty-eight adults. The National Coal Board was heavily criticised
for their failings in the aftermath of the disaster.

rate; and that state intervention in almost everything from wage bargaining to incomes policy should be diminished. He was also outspokenly hostile to the growing encroachments on British national sovereignty of the European Economic Community (EEC).

These ideas were anathema to Ted Heath. He feared Powell's intellect and disagreed with his rival's philosophy. Heath believed in building a consensus between what he called 'the great interests of the state', i.e. big business and powerful trade unions. He was a government interventionist who wanted to consolidate the corporate state by making it more efficient. He had no desire to reform it, let alone to dismantle it or to encourage free-market forces. Securing Britain's entry to the EEC was at the heart of his political beliefs.

Margaret Thatcher eventually became much more of a Powellite than a Heathite. But in the shadow cabinet of the late 1960s she was notable for her invisibility on policy issues. She handled her portfolio well, but as an attacking debater rather than as a thoughtful contributor to policy. She sent in no policy papers to the shadow cabinet, unlike most of her colleagues, during the two and a half years she was a member of it.

There were, however, one or two interesting clues that she was more sympathetic to Powell and his ideas than she was letting on. On 20 April 1968, Enoch Powell made his explosive speech on immigration, quoting in Latin a line from Virgil's *Aeneid*: 'I am filled with foreboding. Like the Roman, I seem to see the River Tiber foaming with much blood.' The next day Ted Heath telephoned her and all his shadow cabinet ministers to say, 'I have come to the conclusion that Enoch must go'. Alone among her colleagues, Margaret Thatcher tried to resist Powell's instant dismissal, telling her leader that she thought it would be 'better to let things cool down for the present than to heighten the crisis'.[23]

She agreed with the thrust of Powell's views about the spate of new Commonwealth immigration. She felt that the selective quotations from his speech had been taken out of context, and was confident that he was no racist. Heath was in no mood to listen to such excuses. 'No, no. He absolutely must go', he retorted.[24]

Powell went from the shadow cabinet. But he did not depart from the scene of influencing either Conservative policy or the mind of Margaret Thatcher.

As Shadow Minister for Fuel and Power, she tried to find a way for privatising electricity generation. That would have been a radical exercise in rolling back the frontiers of the corporate state in 1968. But despite her many visits to power stations and conversations with business contacts, her research turned out to be 'a fruitless exercise'.[25]

She was, however, quickly gathering fruit from other research into the benefits of free-market economics. She regularly attended meetings of the Institute of Economic Affairs (IEA), a crusading free-enterprise think-tank run by Ralph Harris, which counted her as a supporter of some of its own and Enoch Powell's ideas. She was far too savvy a political operator to praise Powell at a time when Heath was trying to bury him. Nevertheless, when Margaret Thatcher was invited to give the important Conservative Policy Centre (CPC) lecture at the Party Conference in 1968, she covertly revealed her sympathy for Powellite monetarism.

Taking as her subject the rhetorical question 'What's wrong with politics?', the main theme of her complaint focused on the growing power of the state over the individual, particularly as exercised by the incomes policy of the Labour government. In a later passage of her speech she said:

> We now put so much emphasis on the control of incomes that we have too little regard for the essential role of Government, which is the control of the money supply . . . For a number of years some expenditure has been financed by what amounts to printing money.[26]

Her flirtation with Powell's theories on controlling the money supply passed almost unnoticed at the time. More prominence was given to her attack on consensus politics that she dismissed as 'an attempt to satisfy people holding no particular views about anything'. Instead, she wanted 'a philosophy and policy which, because they are good, appeal to sufficient people to secure a majority'.[27] This was an early glimpse of Thatcher's future 'conviction politics'. They were deepened by two interesting overseas visits.

WOOED BY THE AMERICANS, DISMAYED BY THE SOVIETS

The first voices seriously to predict that Margaret Thatcher might one day become Britain's first woman prime minister were American. One of them was Dean Mahin, Director of the Governmental Affairs Institute in Washington, DC. He ran a State Department International Visitor programme designed to bring future foreign leaders and rising parliamentarians to the USA.

On the basis of reports from William J. Galloway, First Secretary and Political Officer at the US Embassy in London, Margaret Thatcher was invited to make a six-week tour of America. Her schedule was much more prestigious than those arranged for other British MPs of the period. 'The Embassy clearly indicated that it was possible that she would become the first female PM of Britain', recalled Dean Mahin. 'Most of her high level appointments were possible only because Mrs T was billed as a future Prime Minister.'[28]

The prescience of the US Embassy in making such a forecast in 1966 was remarkable at a time when virtually no British observers were predicting such a future for Margaret Thatcher. The result was that she came, saw and was conquered by her first visit to the United States.

She travelled on 20 February 1967 to Washington, DC, where she had twenty-eight appointments in five days. They included meetings at the Federal Reserve Board, the Department of Defense, the State Department, the Brookings Institution, the Supreme Court, the IMF, and the National Security Council. On Capitol Hill she saw several members of Congress, including two prominent Senators, Margaret Chase Smith and Joseph Clark. Later, in New York, she met Governor Nelson Rockefeller, a future Vice President of the United States under Gerald Ford.

Her six-week trip went far wider than politics. It took in visits to DuPont's headquarters in Delaware; NASA in Houston; Strategic Air Command in Omaha, Nebraska; the grain trading market in Chicago; the University of California in Berkeley; NBC's first colour television studios in Los Angeles; and the Harvard Business School. Her journey was a mixture of fact-finding, meeting interesting people and sight-seeing. Her favourite city was San Francisco; 'the most beautiful of them all',[29] she wrote on a postcard to her sister, Muriel.

The totality of these experiences filled her with grateful enthusiasm for American friendliness, hospitality and free enterprise. Her immediate reactions were more superficial than substantive. Yet, in a more lasting way, the tour affirmed her commitment to the Anglo-American alliance and impressed her with the management of the US economy. On returning to Westminster, it did not take long for her favourable view of America to be reflected in her speeches and writings. She particularly emphasised the virtues of free markets and low tax rates in the US, pointing out that the highest level of tax paid by a top American earner was 60 per cent, compare to the British equivalent of 91.25 per cent.

Her love affair with the United States strengthened with a second visit to New York and other cities, organised by the English Speaking Union in 1968. One of the topics for her speeches was 'Preparing for the future: Britain and America'. This was her first attempt at expounding the virtues of the 'special relationship', to which she would contribute much in the 1980s.

In 1969, she had an opportunity to examine the vices of Communism. Having become the opposition spokeswoman on Transport, she was invited by the Soviet government to come and admire their transport projects, such as the new Moscow Metro. Insisting on paying her own travel expenses to avoid any suspicion of being in the pocket of her hosts, she had meetings at the Kremlin, Moscow University and in Leningrad. Her observations of ordinary people and her exposure to a relentless barrage of Soviet propaganda from her guides confirmed her hostility to the moral bankruptcy of the Communist system.

Occasionally, she managed to score a keen debating point over her hosts. Outside one art gallery, she was invited to admire a sculpture of a blacksmith hammering a sword. When the guide announced, 'That represents Communism', Margaret Thatcher retorted: 'Actually, it doesn't. It's from the Old Testament. "And they shall beat their swords into ploughshares, and their spears into pruning-hooks." '[30] Trust the Methodist preacher's daughter to know Isaiah 42:3 by heart!

Whatever those egalitarian optimists at the US State Department might be forecasting, no British political prophets at this stage in her career would have dared to predict that Margaret Thatcher might one day climb to the top of the greasy pole. She herself told friends that the 'ultimate horizon' of her ambition was to be Chancellor of the Exchequer.[31]

Throughout the 1960s, the prospect of a woman prime minister was unthinkable. The *Sunday Times*, shouting the odds in 1967 for the runners in a future Tory leadership stakes, put Margaret Thatcher in the field at 1000–1 against.[32] She was not even a dark horse.

PREPARING FOR GOVERNMENT

She was, however, quietly moving up on the rails within the shadow cabinet. In 1969, her old OUCA contemporary Sir Edward Boyle resigned from politics to become Vice-Chancellor of Leeds University. His departure left a vacancy in the Education portfolio. Ted Heath initially wanted Keith Joseph to fill the post, but Maudling refused to co-operate in the reshuffle plan and replace Joseph. So, as his second choice, Heath appointed Margaret Thatcher to be the opposition spokeswoman for Education.

She made an uncertain start. The issue that was troubling the Conservative Party on education was an argument about comprehensive schools versus selective or grammar schools. As a former grammar-school pupil herself, Margaret Thatcher was instinctively in favour of the selective examinations and traditional teaching methods. But by late 1969 most local education authorities (LEAs) had followed the Labour government's national directive to turn all secondary schools into comprehensive schools.

Believing that she had no mandate for reversing the consensus in favour of comprehensivisation, Margaret Thatcher concentrated on keeping herself busy as a national political figure. She spoke all over the country on subjects well outside her shadow responsibilities. One such address was to a club of East Midlands businessmen in late 1969. Unfortunately, her words of political wisdom on the taxation of small companies were subsumed by a slapstick comedy involving the chairman of the meeting.

The chairman was Maurice Chandler, who had been her contemporary at Oxford and a fellow officer of the OUCA. He persuaded her to visit the Millbank Club in Uppingham, where she drew a capacity crowd. Half way through her speech, Chandler needed to go to the bathroom. But instead of departing through the body of the jam-packed room, he decided to climb out of a ground-floor window behind the platform on which Margaret Thatcher was speaking. This attempt at a discreet exit failed because Chandler, a burly figure, got stuck in the window frame. The meeting soon became distracted by his cries for help forwards into the courtyard and by his ample posterior wriggling backwards into the audience. Margaret Thatcher, however, ploughed on regardless of these noises and movements behind her. She kept going without varying her tone of voice, even when the marooned chairman had to be levered to safety by a rescue party of local worthies from the platform.

'It was a scene worthy of Feydeau,' recalled Michael Palmer, a solicitor who drove the speaker to and from London in his Morris 1100, 'in which she played the straight-woman, completely ignoring the commotion and the laughter. On the drive back to Finchley she never mentioned the incident. I don't think she saw the funny side of it at all.'[33]

Slapstick humour had no appeal to Margaret Thatcher. Soon into her eight-month spell as Shadow Education Secretary, the political scene became tense because an early election was on the cards. Ted Heath summoned his shadow cabinet for a weekend conference at the Selsdon Park Hotel in Surrey to plan the Conservative manifesto. This gathering was lampooned by Labour as a lurch to the right by 'Selsdon Man'.[34] It was no such thing for the only woman present.

The leader of the party allowed surprisingly little discussion on Margaret Thatcher's area of responsibility, observing curtly at the start of the session that the party had 'got our education policy'.[35] This meant that there was tacit acceptance of the status quo of leaving schools policy in the hands of the LEAs. The only higher education issue to come up was the question of whether to say anything in the manifesto about the proposed new independent University of Buckingham. Margaret Thatcher was all for it and supported the vice-chancellor designate, Professor Max Beloff, in his aspirations for Buckingham to be granted a royal charter. According to the record, Heath cut her off with the dismissive comment: 'Not committing myself to Royal Charter. Wouldn't trust Max Beloff for a minute. Already got too many universities.'[36]

This churlish view, apparently based on Heath's mistaken impression that Professor Beloff was still the left-wing socialist he had been in his pre-war days at Oxford, bemused Margaret Thatcher. She was underwhelmed by the Selsdon deliberations. On the Saturday night of the conference, she left the hotel to attend part of her constituency annual dinner in Finchley. The guest of honour was Enoch Powell. It was just as well that her absence for this purpose was never noticed by her leader.

Ten days after the Selsdon meeting, when Margaret Thatcher was preparing for a major House of Commons speech opposing a government bill to speed up comprehensivisation, she received the news that her father, Alfred Roberts, had died. His end was not unexpected. She had been to see him in Grantham a few days earlier. He was terminally ill with severe emphysema, and had oxygen beside his bed to help him keep breathing. One of his last conscious acts had been listening to his daughter's voice on a BBC radio women's discussion programme, *Petticoat Lane*. He passed away soon afterwards on the afternoon of 10 February 1970.

Father and daughter had drifted apart during Margaret Thatcher's six years as an opposition front-bencher. She only took Mark and Carol to visit him twice throughout this period. She communicated with him infrequently. 'I never hear anything from Margaret either by letter or by phone',[37] he complained in a letter to Muriel, nine weeks before his death.

Some of this coolness may have arisen from his younger daughter's reaction to his re-marriage. After her mother Beatrice died in 1960, Alfred married a Lincolnshire farmer's widow, Cissie Hubbard. 'I suppose that's a good thing', Margaret Thatcher unenthusiastically observed. 'She's a nice, homely little woman.'[38] She was more gracious about Cissie's nursing care of her father in his final days.

In May 1970, Harold Wilson called a general election, apparently buoyed up by a sudden surge for Labour in the opinion polls. Most Tories, including Margaret Thatcher, were privately pessimistic about their chances of winning. But to his credit, Ted Heath never wavered in his self-belief, and delivered an impressive final party election broadcast. Mrs Thatcher thought his presentation 'showed him as an honest patriot who cared deeply about his country and wanted to serve it'.[39] This was a widely shared view at the time, and may well have been the factor that unexpectedly turned the tide towards the Conservatives on polling day.

On election night, there was a swing of between 3 and 6 per cent to the Tories. Listening to one of the early victories, announced on the car radio, a surprised Margaret Thatcher said to her husband, 'If that result is right, we've won'.[40] Denis turned the car round and they went to the *Daily Telegraph* party at the Savoy. By the end of the night it was clear that Ted Heath would form the next government with an overall majority of about thirty. When the seats that were counted the next day, among them Finchley, had all declared, the final result was indeed a Conservative overall majority of thirty, a lead over Labour of forty-three seats. Margaret Thatcher increased her majority to 11,185. She was not among the top tier of cabinet ministers whose appointments were announced on Friday 19 June. She waited, on tenterhooks, for the summons to 10 Downing Street. It came the following morning.

REFLECTION

The wait could not have been unduly tense for her place in the cabinet was a certainty. She had grown in stature during her six years in opposition, climbing from the anonymous shallows of junior front-benchers to the senior ranks of recognised party figures. As an attacker of Labour government policies in the debating chamber, she was second in effectiveness only to Iain Macleod. But her relationships with her colleagues were less assured. Life in the shadow cabinet and cabinet requires team players. She was a loner, strangely angular and intense in her non-collegiate approach.

Ted Heath was not so much hostile as indifferent towards her. His admiration for her competence was diminished by his irritation over her talkativeness. He was bored listening to her opinions on subjects about which he thought she knew nothing. He wanted to keep her firmly in her place as 'the statutory woman' of his administration, a concept that she found insufferably condescending.

She was wise enough to suffer in silence. She knew that his view of her reflected a widespread attitude amongst male members of the parliamentary club. It held that women MPs, even women in the cabinet, could only be Second XI players. This was pure prejudice, but it was a prejudice shared by the new prime minister.

Perhaps with more graciousness from him and less pushiness from her they might have built a better relationship. They were never likely to become kindred spirits, yet they shared obvious areas of kinship because they were fellow outsiders and pioneers. They had both broken new ground in the old hierarchical power structure of the Tory party by rising from their similar backgrounds of tradesmen fathers, strait-laced provincialism, grammar-school education and a socially uncertain start at Oxford.

One difference between them, which became much noticed by the time they contested the Tory leadership in 1975, was that Margaret Thatcher had good manners, whereas Ted Heath could be brusque to the point of rudeness. She had been well trained at home and in the shop to be polite. He brought to mind Talleyrand's observation on Napoleon: 'What a pity that such a great man should be so badly brought up.'[41]

This divergence between their styles of behaviour was displayed on the morning of Saturday 20 June 1970 at 10 Downing Street. At her first meeting with the new Prime Minister, Margaret Thatcher was all smiles and congratulations. Ted Heath was abrupt. As she described this contrast later, 'not much time was spent on pleasantries. He was, as ever, brusque and businesslike'.[42] His curt manner was surprising but nothing personal. Other cabinet appointees on the same day were astonished by his coldness on what is normally an occasion for warmth between colleagues.

Whatever the atmosphere, Margaret Thatcher got the job she had expected. She was appointed Secretary of State for Education and a Privy Councillor. Her career as a cabinet minister had begun.

8

Secretary of State for Education

FIRST MOVES

The flaw in Margaret as Education Secretary was the same flaw that became apparent in her as Prime Minister. Everything had to begin, continue and end with a vigorous argument. It is not always the best way of getting things done.[1]

This comment of Norman St John-Stevas, Junior Minister at the Department of Education and Science (DES) under Margaret Thatcher, would have been agreed with by her departmental officials.

Arriving as the new Secretary of State at her department's Curzon Street office on Monday 22 June 1970, she presented her Permanent Secretary with a page torn from a school exercise book listing eighteen actions she wanted taken that day. William Pile* was also a newcomer, having just been promoted to the top rung of the Whitehall ladder at the young age of fifty. From day one they were at loggerheads on many issues.

Top of Margaret Thatcher's action list was an instruction to local education authorities telling them that they could disregard the previous Labour government's directives on the compulsory comprehensivisation of secondary schools. This was not unexpected since it had been promised in the Conservative manifesto. Pile put the draft circular on her desk by the end of the day. It led to the first of many clashes between them.

What Margaret Thatcher wanted was the swift and simple withdrawal of Labour's directives on comprehensives. She was advised that to remove one

---

* William Pile (1919–1997), Deputy Under-Secretary of State, Home Office, 1967–1970; Director-General, Prison Service, 1969–1970; Permanent Under-Secretary of State DES, 1970–1976; Chairman, Board of the Inland Revenue, 1976–1979; KCB 1971.

circular she had to issue a replacement. The draft replacement circular was a long and circumlocutory paper setting out the department's view on the future shape of secondary education across the country. It was not to the taste of the new Secretary of State. She rejected it and produced a much shorter draft in her own handwriting, which became known as Circular 10/70. It withdrew the existing Labour directives making comprehensivisation compulsory and contained the sentence, 'The Secretary of State will expect educational considerations in general, local needs and wishes in particular and the wise use of resources to be the main principles determining the local pattern.'[2]

Although the new circular produced a noisy debate in Parliament, it was hardly a counter-revolutionary call to arms. The power to decide the future of local schools remained firmly with the LEAs, of which 70 per cent had already gone comprehensive. So, despite being accused of 'sheer high-handed ideological arrogance',[3] and described as 'the feminine version of Selsdon Man operating in education',[4] Margaret Thatcher was right to retort that she was not stopping anyone from doing anything, nor was she changing the law. She was merely removing the compulsion from Labour's policy and restoring the right of LEAs to make their own decisions. When existing schemes were working well there would be no change. 'I fail to see what is reactionary or extreme about that', she told the House.[5] She won the argument but she made some enemies.

The charge of arrogance against Margaret Thatcher in her early days as a Secretary of State had justification both politically and personally. She took no notice of the Prime Minister's warning to all his colleagues at the first meeting of his cabinet on 23 June: 'Don't be rushed into hasty decisions of policy.'[6] Against official advice, she ploughed her own policy furrows with more haste than speed.

On the personal front, there was a revealing incident at her father's memorial service on 18 October 1970, at the Finkin Street Church in Grantham. Margaret Thatcher complained to her elder sister, 'They don't know how to treat a Cabinet Minister, do they?' Muriel's tart response was, 'This service isn't for you'.[7]

Her self-importance and self-certainty could be assets in confronting senior colleagues. One of her boldest challenges was mounted against the Treasury, which had decided to cut £300 million from the DES budget. Margaret Thatcher, after some vigorous arguments with the diffident Chief Secretary Maurice Macmillan, fought and won her corner. Her budget remained virtually unscathed and she managed to avoid the Treasury's axe falling on its two priority targets: Raising of the School Leaving Age (ROSLA) and the Open University (OU).

Raising of the school leaving age to sixteen had been delayed by the Labour government, and the Treasury made the case for a further postponement. But Margaret Thatcher firmly reminded her colleagues that ROSLA had been a manifesto promise. The Prime Minister supported her. So this big spending policy commitment was given the green light.

The preservation of the Open University (OU) was a more remarkable feat, although the way it was saved raised hackles among senior colleagues. In his quest for savings, Iain Macleod was determined to abolish the OU, which he saw as a dubious conjuring trick of Harold Wilson's. The outgoing Labour Prime Minister loved telling the story of how the idea of a university of the airwaves, open to all, had floated into his mind when walking round St Agnes in the Isles of Scilly. Macleod, who described Harold Wilson as 'an illusionist without ideals',[8] took the cynical view that the project should follow its originator into oblivion.[9]

Margaret Thatcher was convinced of the Open University's potential to offer graduation opportunities to mature students at low cost. She outflanked the Prime Minister and the Chancellor by boldly announcing her support for the Open University at a press conference two days after taking office. Macleod, from his hospital bed, was upset, and Heath was furious.[10] The Open University's future might have been brought back to full cabinet for further review had not Iain Macleod* suddenly died of a heart attack, aged only fifty-six, at the end of July 1970.

At the DES, Margaret Thatcher's highest priority, after defending her department's budget, was fighting a rearguard action to save good grammar schools. There was a power, under Section 13 of the 1944 Education Act, for the Secretary of State to give or withhold approval for reorganisation schemes

---

* Iain Macleod (1913–1970), MP for Enfield West 1950–1970; Minister of Labour and National Service 1957–1959; Secretary of State for the Colonies 1959–1961; Chairman of Conservative Party and Leader of House of Commons 1961–1963; Shadow Chancellor 1967–1970; Chancellor of the Exchequer 1970; died in No. 11 Downing Street after thirty-nine days in office as Chancellor.

– but the grounds for withholding were strictly limited. Unlike her Conservative and Labour predecessors, who had regarded Section 13 as giving only 'reserve powers' to the minister, Margaret Thatcher personally examined nearly 3,500 school reorganisation schemes. This required a massive increase in her workload. To her chagrin, she found that over 90 per cent of the schemes submitted by LEAs were correct and locally approved reorganisations. Even in her hometown of Grantham she had to accept that her *alma mater* KGGS had to merge on the practical grounds of needing to create larger sixth forms to cope with the raised school-leaving age.

Margaret Thatcher did however intervene in 326, or in 9 per cent of the comprehensivisation schemes submitted to her. She claimed in her speech to the Conservative Party Conference in June 1972 that she had saved ninety-four 'famous grammar schools with supreme reputations'.[11] Some of those reprieves were only temporary. Even in her constituency's local authority of Barnet, where she preserved Christ's College and Woodhouse Grammar, both of them were merged with comprehensives or sixth-form colleges three years later.

The outcome of her largely unsuccessful efforts to preserve selective education was that while she was Secretary of State, comprehensivisation advanced on a wider and faster scale than ever before. She preserved only a handful of grammar schools in Conservative controlled areas such as Surrey, Harrow, Walsall and Birmingham. But her rearguard action was not a complete failure. She kept alive the flame of choice in education. It was to burn more brightly again under subsequent governments, including her own.

The warfare over comprehensivisation brought Margaret Thatcher into a feeling of growing animosity towards her Permanent Secretary, Bill Pile. He was a smart and stubborn Sir Humphrey when it came to confrontations. Sparks flew between him and Margaret Thatcher, particularly when he advised her that she had no powers to dismiss officials whom she felt had let her down, or to intervene in disputes which were beyond her legal powers.

In the middle of one of her rows with Pile she went to see the Minister for the Civil Service, Lord Jellicoe, and made a tearful appeal for her Permanent Secretary to be transferred to another department. She did not help her case by suggesting that Pile's Russian wife made him a security risk. Ted Heath, on the advice of the Head of the Civil Service, Sir William Armstrong, rejected Margaret Thatcher's request. Pile stayed in his post.[12]

Norman St John-Stevas recalled:

Margaret's rows with Bill Pile could be dreadful. They would go at each other hammer and tongs, neither of them would concede anything and the meetings ended with them both stalking out of the room at opposite exits. But for all the explosions, most of the time they both got on with the department's agenda with icy co-operation. The main thing they fell out about was her fierce criticism of individual officials who she wanted sacked and Pile wouldn't have it.[13]

The Secretary of State could be equally abrasive with her junior ministers. One she disliked for his 'wetness'[14] (an early use of a term she made famous as Prime Minister) was Lord Sandford. He was a well-off Anglican clergyman who had inherited a peerage and assimilated a liberal viewpoint on comprehensives. 'She kept bashing him up one day, and then sending him to Siberia the next', was how Norman St John-Stevas remembered their relationship.

I used to think she was so silly with him and some of the top civil servants. If only she'd occasionally let them win a point or two! But no, she just had to crush them into the ground and grind them into little pieces.[15]

This style of aggressive arguing and personal bullying was reserved for just a handful of ministers and decision-making officials at DES. Below this level, most of the middle-ranking and junior civil servants who engaged with their Secretary of State liked her. She was courteous, solicitous and at times rather motherly towards them. When they worked late with her she would rustle up snacks, pour them out mugs of coffee laced with a splash of whisky and thank them warmly for their extra effort.

Her flashes of bad temper were reserved for the high fliers. She saw many of them as ideologically obstructive. They saw her as a confrontational Home Counties lady who wanted to impose Tory radicalism on an area of national life that they thought was already well run by the prevailing educational consensus. Both perspectives had rights and wrongs in them. If the two camps had managed to find a better working relationship as a team, they might have avoided the nastiest and most artificial row during her three years and eight months as Secretary of State, when she was labelled 'Thatcher, the Milk Snatcher'.[16]

MILK SNATCHER

The row about free milk and schoolchildren was artificial in its political substance but it had a devastating impact on Margaret Thatcher's reputation at the time. To this day, the phrase, which originated from a floor speaker at the Labour Party Conference of 1971, is remembered as the most pejorative and personalised negative campaigning slogan of the early 1970s.

The row did not surface when the Secretary of State for Education conceded the £8 million cut in free school milk during her public expenditure round of negotiations with the Treasury in the autumn of 1970. The press commented favourably on her defence of her department's programme. The *Guardian*, mentioning the milk cut, praised Margaret Thatcher for her victories over the Treasury, and thought she had done well to escape with 'a remarkably light raid on the education budget'.[17]

The *Guardian*, the rest of the press and the Labour Party changed their tune by the time Margaret Thatcher came to introduce the legislation ending free school milk. The *Sun* voted her 'The Most Unpopular Woman in Britain', and asked its readers, 'Is Mrs Thatcher human?'[18] The *Guardian* described the Education (Milk) Bill as 'a vindictive measure that should never have been laid before Parliament'.[19] During debates in the House of Commons she was variously described by Labour MPs as 'the most mean and vicious member of a thoroughly discredited Government',[20] 'Mrs Scrooge with the painted face' and as 'a reactionary cavewoman',[21] while Gerald Kaufman opined that she was to British education 'what Attila the Hun was to Western Civilisation'.[22]

These over the top exaggerations were mild compared to some of the unrecorded taunts shouted from a sedentary position during the later stages of the debate. I was listening in the gallery to the wind-up speeches, having been tipped off by the Speaker (my godfather) that it would be a noisy occasion. It certainly was. Hansard edited out the epithets of uproar, mentioning them only by the neutral word 'Interruption'. In fact, the decibel levels were stratospheric on the opposition benches, where the tauntings of the Secretary of State ranged from the offensive to the obscene. 'Ditch the bitch!' was one of many insults. The repetition of the chant 'Thatcher, milk snatcher' was the main noise of the night. Some ministers feel exhilarated when at the receiving end of alcohol-fuelled rowdy scenes during the wind-up speeches in a House of

Commons debate of that era. Margaret Thatcher, at this moment in her career, was unnerved, particularly as the abusive taunts continued at public events for some months.

It was the personalised tone of the attacks that got to her. Logically she considered the arguments unfair. Labour had withdrawn free milk from secondary schools two years earlier with no fuss and no ill effects on the health of the nation's children. Many of the archaic one third-of-a-pint glass milk bottles went unopened by primary school pupils in the 1970s, often because their tastes had changed since the scheme was introduced in the 1940s. Free milk was no longer a priority or a need – although Margaret Thatcher had preserved the concession for children who were medically prescribed it. She saw the campaign as a synthetic row. Nevertheless, she was severely thrown by the obloquy that poured down on her.

One of her senior civil servants, Toby Weaver, recalled that the firestorm of anger 'shook her to the core' and 'temporarily unhorsed her'.[23] Norman St John-Stevas also noticed that she was 'terribly upset, but at the same time terribly careful not to let her distress show. In those days she was not the Iron Lady but the Lady in the Iron Mask'.[24]

The most hurtful aspect of the furore was that it was directed against her feminine role as a wife and mother. To be caricatured as a wicked witch who snatched milk bottles from the lips of young, thirsty innocents was absurd. But by failing to spot the potential of the issue for personal denigration she had given her opponents a target.

Flailing out in the aftermath of the parliamentary rumpus she criticised her officials for not warning her of the backlash. This part of her blame-game was unfair. She was the decider of political risks. In any case, she was offered at least one piece of advice on the issue, which she chose to ignore. In an early meeting at the DES, her civil servants expressed concern that some children would not drink milk at all if they did not get it at school. 'Gentlemen, none of you is a mother', she replied. 'No mother ever neglects her child.'[25] But she did neglect the potential for negative campaigning that the school-milk issue offered her adversaries.

Some months later, when the 'milk snatcher' vilification seemed to be running out of steam, Margaret Thatcher needlessly opened up a second front of personal controversy. She had developed strong views about the tendency of student unions to spend their funds on left-wing political causes. It was a problem but a small one. She proposed to curb the alleged excesses of political spending by creating a registrar of student unions with supervisory powers. When she presented her plan to the cabinet committee for Home and Social Affairs, it was rejected. Her colleagues felt that legislation to correct these comparatively minor abuses at a time when student militancy was at its zenith might be a hostage to fortune.

Against the advice of her officials, Margaret Thatcher came back to the cabinet committee with a second attempt at dealing with the problem. Instead of legislation, she proposed a new set of rules that would make student-union subscriptions voluntary. She published a confusing consultation document on the issue, which put her on a collision course with the National Union of Students (NUS). Its President in 1971 was Jack Straw.* The NUS counter-argument was that the facilities it provided for its members such as travel concessions depended on compulsory subscriptions.

This difference of opinion erupted into widespread student demonstrations. Effigies of Margaret Thatcher were burned on campuses around the country. During visits to universities (Liverpool, Leeds and the London School of Economics) and polytechnics she was mobbed by noisy students and required police protection. The worst of these upheavals came when over 2,000 scream-ing NUS members tried to prevent her from presenting the designation document of the South Bank Polytechnic at the Queen Elizabeth Hall.

These troubles caused her to worry about her teenage daughter Carol, who had just started to read Law at University College London. Carol was given a hard time, writing later: 'To my student friends and contemporaries, the Minister of Education was public enemy number one, and I was her daughter . . . It meant that I never brought student friends home to the townhouse we'd bought in Flood Street Chelsea.'[26]

Family pressures were always the stresses Margaret Thatcher found hardest to bear. But although she was rattled by the degree of public hostility she faced, leaving the battlefield was never an option for her.

---

* Jack Straw (1946–), Labour politician and minister. As Home Secretary, Foreign Secretary and Leader of the House of Commons, he served continuously in the Blair and Brown cabinets from 1997 to 2010. MP for Blackburn since 1979.

According to one of her earliest biographers, George Gardiner, there was a moment when on top of the student demonstrations and the 'milk snatcher' chants, a group of Tory MPs from the 1970 intake started a whispering campaign against her with the message, 'Shift Thatcher'. Denis reacted to these mutterings by asking his wife, 'To hell with all this, why not pack it up?'

'Not likely' came the immediate retort.[27]

Although this story may be apocryphal, it is clear that Margaret Thatcher was sufficiently upset by the turbulence to make her first U-turn as a cabinet minister. She dropped her proposals for changes in student-union funding. This retreat was forced on her when university vice-chancellors, including her old friend Edward Boyle, as Vice-Chancellor of Leeds, backed the case put forward by Jack Straw and the NUS.

Margaret Thatcher had no one but herself to blame for this fiasco. She had needlessly stirred up a hornet's nest of student unrest on a minor issue. Taken in conjunction with the other avoidable rows she had been responsible for over school milk and her circular on comprehensives, she was beginning to look like a minister who was causing more trouble than she was worth.

Ted Heath heard these complaints, many of them from Tory MPs, and briefly considered sacking his accident-prone Secretary of State for Education. In his later years of acrid hostility towards her, he grumbled: 'She was no good. Should have got rid of her when she was causing us all that trouble.'[28] This was the revisionism of personal resentment. At the time, Prime Minister Heath had more protective instincts. He disliked being told what to do by back-benchers and newspapers. He thought the 'milk snatcher' label unfair. So he battened down the hatches and helped Margaret Thatcher steer her way out of the storms.

SAVED BY THE PRIME MINISTER

On 12 January 1972 Margaret Thatcher and her senior officials at DES were invited to Chequers to discuss education strategy with the Prime Minister. It was a turning point in her career. She went to the meeting as a beleaguered minister. She returned from it as a cabinet colleague who knew she had the full confidence of her leader.

This transformation took place because Ted Heath decided she needed his support. She might have made herself unpopular but she was an asset to his government. Although he often found her annoying, he also saw qualities in her that appealed to his managerial instincts. Unlike several other members of his cabinet, she was a team player; she did not leak stories to journalists; and she loyally accepted her collective responsibility for bearing a share of the Treasury's expenditure cuts. This was the reason she had come under such hard pounding. As Heath knew, it was Treasury policy not Thatcher policy that had caused most of the hysteria against her.

There may have been other factors working for her survival. The government needed a woman in the cabinet and there was no credible alternative. More importantly, the Prime Minister liked the future educational plans she rolled out before him at Chequers. He was willing to support her vision for expanding nursery education, teacher recruitment and a larger number of higher education places. He also appreciated the thoroughness of her briefing on the school-milk, student-union and grammar-school controversies. With better political skill than she had displayed in these areas, Heath spotted some new presentational angles, which could be used in the House of Commons to defend the government's record on education.

On 3 February, three weeks after the Chequers briefing, Ted Heath faced a Prime Minister's Questions that were focused mainly on educational issues. Like a batsman on top form, he hit ball after ball to the boundary. It was a splendid innings by the Prime Minister but the real match winner was Margaret Thatcher.

The opposition bowling was opened by Gerald Kaufman. He wanted Margaret Thatcher dismissed for her 'petty-minded and vindictive interference with Manchester Corporation', because she would not provide free hot drinks (instead of milk) to children who received school dinners. Harold Wilson followed up by asking that if the Secretary of State for Education could introduce a bill to stop free milk, 'one of the filthiest Bills we have ever had in this House', she could easily introduce legislation to allow LEAs to provide free hot drinks. Having been warned of a concerted Labour attack on the most unpopular member of his cabinet, Heath was ready to defend her. He dismissed the opposition leader's call for a new law on free school drinks, reminding him that Labour had cut free milk in all secondary schools without any exemptions. When Ted Short, the former Education Secretary, condemned Margaret Thatcher for her 'constant, monotonous decisions . . . to reject local authority reorganisation schemes' for comprehensivisation, the Prime Minister retorted that it was her statutory duty to judge every scheme on its merits, and added, 'At least she has not tried to bully local authorities to accept one scheme'.[29]

After this knockabout, some slow bowlers came on from the Tory benches. Invited by a well-primed Conservative to congratulate Mrs Thatcher on her achievements, Heath scored a flurry of runs on her behalf. He thanked her for increasing the primary-school building programme, expanding the poly-technics, raising the school-leaving age, saving the grammar schools of Surrey and recruiting more teachers. As he left the chamber to cheers from his own back-benchers, it was clear that Ted Heath had changed the game for Margaret Thatcher.

The government's most derided minister had escaped the brickbats and been festooned with bouquets. From the Labour front bench to the press gallery to the Tory MPs who had been encouraging the 'sack Thatcher' rumours, it was apparent that there was no longer any mileage in attacking an Education Secretary so strongly supported by the Prime Minister.

The tide was turning for her in other ways too. She won an unexpected ovation at the annual conference of the National Union of Teachers in April 1972. Although the hard-left section of her audience walked out before she started, the moderate majority of teachers who had the courtesy to stay and listen began to like her for raising the school-leaving age, expanding their profession and for championing the cause of smaller comprehensive schools.

One newspaper reported her NUT speech as 'The Making of Margaret Thatcher'.[30] The newspaper that had created the headline in January, 'The Lady Nobody Loves', was by May writing about 'the Mellowing of Margaret'.[31] In June, *The Times* published a profile praising her 'remarkable political rebirth'.[32]

These positive articles may have owed something to the arrival at the DES of a new press secretary, Terry Perks. He got on well with his Secretary of State, who seven years later brought him into 10 Downing Street as deputy to her Press Secretary, Bernard Ingham.

The high peak of favourable media coverage was reached in December 1972 when she published a White Paper, *Education: A Framework for Expansion*. This confirmed Margaret Thatcher's journey on the high spending path she had agreed with Ted Heath at Chequers. School building, teacher staff levels and higher education institutions were all increased. The most important announcement was a major expansion of nursery education, which she said would be provided for 90 per cent of four-year-olds and 50 per cent of three-year-olds. It was a first attempt at early interventionism, which is now being championed by Iain Duncan Smith in David Cameron's cabinet.

The White Paper received what Margaret Thatcher later called 'a disconcertingly rapturous reception'.[33] Improbable enthusiasts for her handiwork included the Labour back-bencher Renee Short – hitherto an implacable adversary – and the *Guardian,* which praised her 'progressive programme' and added the backhanded compliment, 'Mrs Thatcher is more than half way towards a respectably socialist education policy'.[34]

Margaret Thatcher's political fame in the 1970s could be compared to a tennis match in which the play becomes exciting because the ball is being struck so hard on both sides of the net. She achieved her stardom by going from wicked witch to heroine of the education world in less than eighteen months. She did not deserve either status. When she was riding high, her success was more apparent than real. Many of the expansionary plans she announced, particularly in nursery education, were never delivered due to a sudden deterioration in the public finances. But the combination of negative and positive media coverage made her one of the most recognisable politicians in Britain. In a monochrome Tory cabinet she stood out as one of its most colourful characters. In terms of public awareness she ranked fourth in the government behind Heath, Maudling and Douglas-Home. But few, if any, saw her as a dark horse moving up on the rails in a future leadership race.

WIDER THAN EDUCATION

One outsider who took an interest in Margaret Thatcher's future potential was Dr Henry Kissinger. He did this vicariously through his wife, Nancy. She had been involved in an Anglo-American educational project that brought her into contact with Britain's Education Minister. 'Nancy was so impressed by her meetings with Margaret Thatcher that she kept telling me I needed to see her',[35] recalled Kissinger. He tried to arrange this on two of his visits to the United Kingdom as National Security Advisor to President Nixon. But the Cabinet Office in London was unhelpful and did not facilitate the appointment. Their encounter was delayed until 18 February 1975, when Kissinger became the first international statesman to meet Britain's new opposition Leader.

The US Embassy, whose officials had continued to monitor Margaret Thatcher's progress since sponsoring her first tour of America in 1969, kept in touch with her. Over lunch with First Secretary Dirk Gleysteen at the Connaught Hotel on 25 June 1973, she made a number of indiscreet comments on her ministerial colleagues. 'Michael Heseltine', she said, 'had everything it took in politics except brains.' 'Peter Walker', she observed, 'doesn't have the kind of first-class mind needed at the top.' She thought Geoffrey Howe 'too willing to compromise', and wondered if he would 'get over this weakness'.[36]

Her own weakness at this time was that she was a marginalised member of the cabinet, exercising little or no influence on national issues outside her own education brief.

By the middle of 1972, the Heath government was losing control of the national agenda. It reversed its previous policies of not bailing out 'lame ducks' such as the commercially doomed Upper Clyde Shipbuilders. The public spending spree of industrial subsidies was designed to halt unemployment, but it unleashed the forces of inflation and union militancy.

Another U-turn took place when the government backed down from its stand against prices and incomes policies. Looming over all other considerations was the threat and then the certainty of a strike by the National Union of Mineworkers (NUM). The Industrial Relations Act, which had come into law in 1971, was being openly defied. It collapsed in a black pantomime of dock strikes, newspaper strikes, interventions by the Official Solicitor and confusing rulings by the new National Industrial Relations Court. The last straws were a ballot by the NUM showing an 81 per cent majority for a strike; the establishing of a three-day week to conserve fuel supplies; and the calling of a general election on 28 February 1974.

In later years, Margaret Thatcher did her best to distance herself from the mistakes of the Heath government, which preceded this chaos. At the time, not a squeak of protest emanated from her in cabinet or in discussions with her colleagues on economic policy. She was a loyal Heathite.

So subservient was she to the views of the Prime Minister that in December 1973 he considered promoting her to the post of Minister for Europe.[37] Her only reported speeches on this issue, delivered in her constituency, never mentioned the arguments about loss of British sovereignty that were causing concern to Conservative opponents of entry such as Enoch Powell, Hugh Fraser, John Biffen or Teddy Taylor. By contrast, the Margaret Thatcher of the 1970s displayed some insouciance about the consequences of joining the EEC. 'I think we have a tendency in this country to be slightly isolationist', she told a Finchley audience. 'France is no less French or Holland less Dutch for joining. We have a great deal to contribute.'[38]

Even when the march of international and domestic events were giving the government a rough time, Margaret Thatcher was not a significant contributor to general policy discussions. In the autumn spending round of 1973, when all ministers were asked to cut their budgets in the prevailing economic crisis, she fought hard to preserve education spending. She could not negotiate a settlement with the Chief Secretary of the Treasury, so took her argument to the Chancellor, Anthony Barber, and then to the Prime Minister. She emerged from these battles with one of the smallest expenditure reductions of any spending minister – a trim of £157 million out of a total departmental budget of £3.5 billion.[39] The later champion of cutting public spending was not keen to wield the axe in her own backyard in 1973.

When Ted Heath's confrontation with the miners came to a head in 1974, Margaret Thatcher was more gung-ho than her Prime Minister. She defended the three-day week on the grounds that it would 'conserve stocks and use them prudently like a frugal housewife'.[40]

More controversially, she argued that the three-day week was doing its job so well that the NUM feared a long stalemate. 'In my opinion, the miners' leaders are now trying to force their members to strike because our steps have succeeded and theirs have not', she optimistically claimed.[41]

In the same mindset, she wanted Heath to call an election several weeks earlier than the polling date he eventually chose, fighting it 'unashamedly', as she put it, 'on the issue of "Who governs Britain?"'[42]

Amidst mounting chaos, the date of the general election was announced for 28 February. While Parliament was going through the final stages of business before dissolution, an incident took place, which illustrated that Margaret Thatcher, whatever else she might have gained as a cabinet minister, had not acquired an ear for humour.

She was standing behind the Speaker's Chair in the House of Commons with a group of Tory MPs, when they were joined by her Parliamentary Private Secretary, Fergus Montgomery. An elegant but somewhat effete figure, he had just had his election photographs taken. He was was looking so well groomed that she complimented him. 'You do look smart today, Fergus.' Montgomery was gratified. Preening himself, he replied, 'Well I've just been to the hairdresser.' With a straight face, Margaret Thatcher responded, 'I expect you've had a blow job'.[43] The laughter was so loud that the Speaker turned round in his chair to find out the cause of the mirth. Margaret Thatcher had no idea why she had caused so much amusement.

There were not many jokes for Tory politicians in the next four weeks. The election was blown badly off course. Instead of answering the question 'Who governs Britain?' the voters elected a hung Parliament. Margaret Thatcher was returned with a significantly reduced majority (down to a still-comfortable 5,978) but the Conservatives lost thirty-three constituencies. They held 297 seats in the House of Commons compared to Labour's 301. Heath made abortive efforts to negotiate a coalition with the Liberal Party, but this attempt foundered because its leader, Jeremy Thorpe, failed to win the support of his colleagues. In her memoirs, Thatcher later wrote, 'This horse-trading was making us look ridiculous'.[44] Heath, also retrospectively, retorted, 'She certainly did not say that at the time'.[45]

Heath was right on this one. Margaret Thatcher not only kept silent about any criticisms she may have had about the Prime Minister's handling of his final months and days in office: at his last cabinet meeting on Monday 4 March she was fulsome in her praise for him.[46] Alone of the ministers present, she spoke in glowing terms of the privilege it had been to serve under the Prime Minister in such a united and harmonious team. Was this hypocrisy? Or was she overcome by the valedictory emotions of the moment? Perhaps it merely showed that she could hit the wrong note at the wrong time.

REFLECTION

Wrong notes loomed large during Margaret Thatcher's time as Secretary of State for Education. She was unfairly attacked, but she did herself few favours.

She had too many unnecessary personality clashes with her officials. She had an unsure touch when it came to the presentation of herself and her policies. Through inexperience, she allowed herself to become caricatured as a right-wing hate figure.

Not all of this was her fault, but she made bad mistakes. Within a month of her appointment, she allowed herself to be filmed in a cringe-making *Panorama* programme. It was hard to decide which sequence made her look more absurd. Maniacally pruning roses, while Denis no less maniacally roared up and down the two-acre lawn of their country house, stamped her with the image of suburban privilege. Rather more insensitive was her visit to a London comprehensive school. In a precocious voice, she advised science pupils on camera about what spoons they should use in their experiments with sulphur: 'Breakfast spoons, you know, the spoons you use for boiled eggs. You dip in and, if they're silver, they go brown and Mother has to clean them. So these days we tend to use stainless steel, don't we.'[47]

'Carry on Lady Bountiful', Labour's spin doctors might have said to the voters not born with silver spoons.

Even when she was doing well, she received limited plaudits because her style tended to alienate. Her forcefulness was her albatross. To many of her colleagues she was lacking in charm. She had much to learn from the Dale Carnegie school of *How to Win Friends and Influence People*. She could offend even those whose support she wanted to reciprocate. Norman St John-Stevas, a genuine fan of his Secretary of State, told a bizarre anecdote about the time he mentioned to her that his mother was Irish. 'I thought most Irish people over here were descended from navvies', responded Margaret Thatcher. St John-Stevas thought she must be making a joke. She was not.[48]

Despite her sharp elbows and wrong notes as a new cabinet minister, Margaret Thatcher was appreciated where it mattered most – inside 10 Downing Street. Ted Heath had many failings, but he was loyal to his colleagues. When she was in trouble, he gave her steadfast support. She forgot this episode too quickly. He remembered it too vividly. This was to be a cause of future tension between them as their relationship moved to centre stage in the passion play of Tory politics.

9

Heath on the ropes

THE TWILIGHT OF A TORY LEADER

The inconclusive result of the February 1974 general election left the Tory Party in disarray. Margaret Thatcher's standing improved among her demoralised colleagues, but mainly because she was not Ted Heath. He was blamed for the hung Parliament, the minority Labour government and the return of Harold Wilson to 10 Downing Street. As the political world waited for a second election later in the year, the strongest force inside the Conservative Parliamentary Party was the surging tide of negativity against the incumbent leader. This was far more important than the tiny ripples of early support for Margaret Thatcher. She was not in consideration as a possible contender for the leadership until the autumn.

The gradual emergence of a Heath–Thatcher power struggle was all about him and hardly anything to do with her. This inconvenient truth could only be grasped by understanding the intensity of the discontent that was simmering within the narrow leadership electorate – the 297 Tory MPs elected to the House of Commons in February 1974.

As one of those MPs, arriving at Westminster for the first time, I was astonished by the strength of hostility against Ted Heath personally. As his hometown of Broadstairs was in the heart of my new constituency of Thanet East, I had come to know his father and stepmother quite well. I had met Ted Heath on many occasions in their home on Dumpton Park Drive. Although my respect for the visiting Prime Minister was great, I had detected in his wooden aloofness a curious dissonance between his character and his circle of friends.

A revealing incident one Sunday morning in Broadstairs highlighted the problem. Sitting in Will and Mary Heath's garden, Ted was reading the *Sunday*

Times when he suddenly flew into a rage. What had caused his anger was one particular sentence in a serialised extract from a biography of him by Margaret Laing. The sentence read, 'Ted Heath has no close friends'.[1]

Expostulating over what he kept calling 'this bloody lie', Heath turned to a Broadstairs neighbour, Edward 'Teddy' Denman. He was an insurance broker with Lloyds who had known the family for some years. Ted Heath thrust the offending copy of the *Sunday Times* under the nose of Mr Denman.

'Look at this, Teddy! No close friends! How can they print this lie? They don't know about you and me, do they?' Soon after this outburst Teddy Denman murmured *sotto voce* to me: 'You heard what Ted just said? Well, until this moment I didn't have the faintest idea he considered me as a close friend.'[2]

On 5 March 1974, the day I entered the House of Commons as an elected MP, I remembered this Broadstairs conversation all too well for I was having my first ever drink in the smoking room with several of Ted Heath's 'friends'. We had just come from a meeting of the back-benchers' 1922 Committee. The public expressions of support and sympathy for the defeated Prime Minister from his colleagues sounded sincere. Robin Maxwell-Hyslop, the Member for Tiverton, alone raised the question of whether Heath should remain our leader. But this appeared to be a maverick viewpoint which elicited chilly murmurs of disagreement, in sharp contrast to the warm thumping of desks and 'hear, hears' which greeted Heath.

Yet, as the Scotch flowed in the smoking room, it was clear that the applause at the 1922 Committee had in many cases been as phoney as Margaret Thatcher's encomium of Ted Heath at his final cabinet meeting. The resentments that emerged in the conversation ran deep. They were more about the leader's behaviour than his judgement. Apparently he had inflicted all manner of slights on his back-benchers in recent years, from refusing to listen to their views to snubbing their wives. I was amazed, having experienced nothing but courtesy from Ted Heath as a young candidate from 1966 to 1974. But the personal criticism of him by these colleagues was so bitter that I immediately sensed that his hold on the leadership was far less secure than it looked from the outside. The smoking-room conversation broke up with someone saying, 'But we're stuck with him for the time being'. To which another voice retorted, 'Until he's lost the next election – which must come within six months'. It was an accurate prediction.[3]

Margaret Thatcher would have been aware of the strong currents of anti-Heath opinion on the back benches, but she did nothing to exploit them. She remained a hard working member of the shadow cabinet. She was pleased to be given the Environment portfolio, which included the responsibility for working out new policies on mortgages, housing and rates. Since there was a general expectation that Harold Wilson would call an autumn general election, the opposition had to race against time to produce a manifesto that would contain novel ideas without repudiating the record of the Conservative government. Squaring this circle was difficult.

Margaret Thatcher did her best to make the manifesto pledges politically attractive and fiscally responsible. She was more cautious than Heath, reluctantly agreeing only after heavy pressure from him to announce two major promises. One was to abolish the rating system. The other was to peg mortgages at a maximum interest rate of 9.5 per cent. A third pledge was to offer council-house tenants who had lived in their homes for over three years the right to buy them at one-third below market value. However, this 'right to buy' (an idea which had originated from Peter Walker) was hedged around by so many qualifications and caveats that Margaret Thatcher herself later came to see her own restrictions as 'narrow and unimaginative'.[4] She would not make the same mistake again as Prime Minister.

Her contribution to the draft election manifesto was well received by the press at the time of its announcement in late August. 'It went down with hardened reporters almost as well as the sherry', said the *Evening Standard*.[5] However, at the highest levels of the party Margaret Thatcher was more noted for her caution than for her creative thinking. Retrospectively, she claimed that during this period she was busy re-examining the party's values. 'After the defeat of 1974 Keith Joseph, and I asked how did it happen? We went back over the fundamental philosophy', she told an interviewer in 1990.[6]

This was an exaggeration. Sir Keith Joseph was starting to re-examine his own and his party's principles in a series of intellectually challenging speeches. But Margaret Thatcher was either too busy or too careful to give him public support. The Editor of the *Sunday Express*, John Junor, tried to persuade her in the summer of 1974 to emulate Joseph and make a speech on Conservative philosophy. Her reaction was to ask which Oxford dons might help her with

such a project, mentioning Robert Blake* and Hugh Trevor-Roper.[†7] A stirring
of interest perhaps, but a long way from putting her head above the parapet as
a Tory champion of new philosophical thinking.

Another sign of both her caution and her interest in reappraising the Conservative record came when she accepted Keith Joseph's invitation to become
Deputy Chairman of the Centre for Policy Studies (CPS). This was a think-
tank set up under Joseph's chairmanship (with Heath's reluctant approval),
supposedly to study what Britain could learn from the social market economies
of EEC countries. In reality, the CPS soon emerged as a powerhouse of fresh
ideas, most of them opposed to the inflationary interventionism of the previous
Conservative government.

At first Margaret Thatcher kept her distance from the controversial work
of the CPS. When Keith Joseph presented its paper on inflation to the shadow
cabinet in May 1974, she remained uncharacteristically quiet. As Peter Walker
recalled, 'Margaret did not side openly with Keith except to say that we should
pay careful attention to what he was saying'.[8]

By August, as Deputy Chairman of the CPS, she was becoming more
involved in its work, privately helping Keith Joseph to prepare his speeches.
Yet publicly she remained loyal to Heath even when she resented the pressure
he was putting on her to devise policies on rates and mortgages, which she
thought would increase public spending and inflation.

Ted Heath was having an unhappy summer. Because he had no home of
his own apart from a Pimlico flat borrowed from his Parliamentary Private
Secretary, Timothy Kitson, he often stayed at his father's house in Broadstairs.
The polls and the press gave him a difficult time. To help him through the
August doldrums, my constituents in the Thanet East Conservative Association
organised a series of somewhat artificial events, at which his speeches could be
filmed by television cameras.

---

* Professor Robert Blake (1916–2003), Provost, The Queen's College, Oxford University,
1968–1987; created Baron Blake of Braydeston, 1971.

† Professor Hugh Trevor-Roper (1914–2003), Regius Professor of Modern History and
Fellow of Oriel College, Oxford University, 1957–1980; Master of Peterhouse, Cambridge,
1980–1987; created Baron Dacre of Glanton, 1979.

A typically downbeat occasion was the renaming of our constituency office in Ramsgate as Heath House. As guest of honour, Ted Heath gave a defensive address, mainly in praise of his government's record. He seemed to be put off his stride by the mild booing he received in the street by a group of Kent miners. Inside Heath House, some of my leading supporters had been his contemporaries at the local grammar school, Chatham House, so they were ready for their old school chum with lines like, 'Hello Ted, do you remember the time when we were in the choir together?' Astonishingly, despite some advance prompting from the Member of Parliament at his elbow, Ted did not remember. He blanked the men who said they had grown up with him. In an attempt to soothe their umbrage after the event, I fell back on the suggestion that the former Prime Minister could have been feeling unwell. This excuse may have been more accurate than I could have guessed, for a year later he was diagnosed as suffering from a thyroid illness that had been sapping his energies for months.[9]

In early September, with election fever rampant, Keith Joseph was preparing to deliver his major CPS address on economic policy. Fearing that this would be a rethinking exercise that could only give rise to headlines about Tory rifts and splits, Ted Heath attempted to use Margaret Thatcher as an intermediary who might persuade Joseph not to deliver his speech. This was mission imposs-ible. She had already seen the text, describing it as, 'one of the most powerful and persuasive analyses I have ever read'.[10] However, she responded to Heath via Jim Prior by saying that she did not have much influence over Keith Joseph. This was an economy with the truth.

Joseph's speech at Preston on 5 September did indeed rock the boat. It was an appeal for the defeat of inflation by tight control of the money supply. It was the opposite of Heath's policy in government of increasing public spending in order to save jobs. Labour seized on the speech as evidence that a future Tory government would deliberately increase unemployment by monetarism. The press gave the controversy huge coverage. The ideological split within the Conservative leadership was headline news.[11] Ted Heath was incandescent.

Like Brer Rabbit, Margaret Thatcher 'lay low and said nothing'. As the election got under way, she avoided the furore over economic policy and stuck rigidly to her shadow-cabinet responsibilities. As she was the only member of

Heath's team with something new to announce, she played a prominent part in the campaign. Despite her reluctance a few weeks earlier to give firm public-spending commitments on housing and rates, she did exactly that during a morning press conference on 27 September. She made a clear pledge that mortgages would be cut to 9.5 per cent by Christmas.[12] 'Santa Thatcher', the press dubbed her.[13]

It was a popular policy, which gave the Tories a temporary lift in the polls. It also lifted Margaret Thatcher's profile. She appeared on television in three of the party's political broadcasts allocated to the Conservatives. She performed so well in the first of these that she was promoted to introduce the second. She was coached for her appearances by a young television producer, Gordon Reece, with whom she established a rapport. He was to become a key player in the remodelling of her television image over the next few years.

The presentations by 'Santa Thatcher' of the giveaway mortgages and rates abolition policies caused qualms among the economic purists of the Conservative right, who feared the consequences for inflation. Margaret Thatcher shared their anxieties, but consoled herself with her private opinion that the pledges would never have to be delivered anyway. She did not believe that the Conservatives were going to win the election. This was the loud and clear message from the polls and from the canvassers in the constituencies. Heath was fighting such a lacklustre campaign with muddled promises about forming a government of national unity that he looked a beaten man by the last week.

Morale was far higher in the Labour camp with optimistic talk of a landslide. There were even signs that Finchley might be one of their surprise gains. Harold Wilson took the trouble to visit the constituency, boosting the Labour candidate's hopes by telling him, 'I gather you have dear Margaret on the run'.[14]

At the count on 10 October, 'dear Margaret' did appear to be highly nervous, with a voice that was 'cracked and strained'.[15] But she got back safely, although for the first time her majority fell below 4,000, to 3,911. This was her lowest margin of victory in thirty-three years as a Member of Parliament. Her result was in line with the drift away from the Tories all over the country. Yet it was a reverse not a rout.

The Conservatives lost twenty constituencies, leaving them with 276 seats in the Commons. Labour scraped home with an overall majority of three, but had forty-three more seats than the Tories. This parliamentary arithmetic gave the

Conservative Party a strong base from which to recover. The same could not be said of its leader, who was now encumbered with the dismal record of having lost three out of the last four elections.

THE PHONEY WAR IN THE PARTY

The most obvious and most honourable course of action for Heath to take in the aftermath of the election would have been to resign, or at least to offer himself immediately for re-election. But it was not in the nature of the man to listen to his friends who were giving him such advice. Instead he wanted to tough it out, calling on his immediate circle of loyalists to back him in this endeavour. With varying degrees of enthusiasm, the centrists in the cabinet closed ranks around their leader. At his insistence they made determined efforts to block both a vote of confidence and a leadership election.

This stubbornness by Heath and his immediate circle turned the rumblings of discontent within the parliamentary party into the beginnings of a rebellion. But there were no obvious organisers of the 'Heath must go' movement. Still less was there any consensus about who could replace him as leader. So what descended on the Conservative Party was a twilight phoney war of pretending, plotting, muttering and muddle. Heath's cabal of loyalists pretended they could maintain the status quo. The plotters were determined to get rid of Heath, but could not begin to unite behind a candidate who might replace him. The mutterers, probably the largest group among the Tory MPs who remained in Parliament, went round in circles as ideas, rumours, people and votes were endlessly discussed but with no conclusions being reached. We were a tribe that had lost its head.

Having a ringside seat at this spectacle of chaotic events made me, and most other backbenchers, less rather than more knowledgeable about what the outcome would be. Yet gradually, out of these mists of confusion, a challenger emerged. How Margaret Thatcher moved into this role is a fascinating saga. If one was looking for a catchy headline to describe how she did it, the battle-cry of the US Marine Corps would do:

Hey diddle diddle,
Straight up the middle!

There was no movement for Margaret Thatcher as a leading candidate during the weeks after the second 1974 election. On 31 October, most of the 276 surviving Tory MPs crammed into Committee Room 14 for the first full 192 Committee meeting of the new Parliament. Margaret Thatcher was present, sitting a few feet away from me. She frowned at many of the interventions, perhaps more to conceal her feelings than to indicate disagreement at what was being said.

The early contributions reminded me of a much-quoted line from David Walder MP: 'The first three speakers at the "22" are usually mad.' Sir John Rodgers, the Member for Sevenoaks, opened the discussion by saying with heavy pomposity that we should all be steady on parade and stay loyal to the leader. 'All right, John, he's already given you your K', someone heckled. Next on his feet was the venerable but obscure Member for Rutland, Kenneth Lewis, who after a cloud of platitudes coined a telling phrase. He said that the leadership of our party was 'a leasehold not a freehold'. There were murmurs of suppressed assent. Hugh Fraser was then called. 'I could not agree more with Mr Harris', he began, misnaming the previous speaker. 'Get your islands right, Hugh', cried out Marcus Kimball. His sally produced laughter, more frowning from Margaret Thatcher and a sudden loss of temper by Hugh Fraser. 'This is serious!' he shouted. 'This is the most important meeting in the history of this committee. We have to make a change.'

His anger altered the mood. Twenty more speakers were called. Eighteen of them were critical of Ted Heath. Only one followed the line of Sir John Rodgers. By the time the meeting ended an hour later, the leader's fate appeared to be sealed. But nothing happened. The word was put out: 'Ted's not budging. He regards the 1922 as just an expression of opinion.'[16]

Many plots and cabals took place over the next few weeks with the objective of budging Ted Heath. One of them stands out in my memory. It was a dinner party hosted by Hugh Fraser at his home in Campden Hill Square. Airey Neave, Nicholas Ridley, Nicholas Fairbairn, Winston Churchill and myself were among the dozen or so guests – all of us Tory MPs. The discussion went round and round in ever decreasing and depressing circles. The general tone was that we could not carry on any longer with Heath at the helm. But from then on, there was total disagreement. One potential candidate after another was named but rejected. 'Keith Joseph – mad as a hatter'; 'Edward du Cann – not quite a hundred annas to the rupee'; 'Robert Carr – so wet, you could shoot snipe off him'; 'Richard Wood – decent but not clever enough'. Eventually, someone said, 'You'll have to do it, Hugh'. 'I am ready to unsheathe my sword', declared Fraser, reaching for his imaginary scabbard. We all laughed, but our host was semi-serious.[17] Nobody mentioned the name of Margaret Thatcher.

The problem, which this and a hundred other conversations diagnosed, was that in October 1974 the Conservative Parliamentary Party was desperately short of talent at the top. It had no leaders in waiting who were obviously *papabile*. The strongest runner in the field should have been William Whitelaw. He was a likeable Wykehamist of shrewd political judgement, supported by a clever mind, which he did his best to conceal by genial bluster. He had the experience for the leadership, having served well in various crises as Chief Whip, Northern Ireland Secretary and Minister of Labour. But there were three obstacles in his path. The first was Ted Heath, to whom Whitelaw was impeccably, perhaps excessively loyal. As long as the leader wanted to stay, his number two stayed quiet.

Second, Whitelaw was endearingly modest about his ability to be a future prime minister. He was not hungry with ambition for the top job. Deep down, he instinctively felt that he lacked the toughness and the talent to be *capax imperii*. This self-doubt was his greatest disqualification and it immobilised him at the time of his greatest opportunity.

The third obstacle was that Whitelaw had the wrong image to be leader of the Conservative Party in the last quarter of the twentieth century. He was a throwback to a different era of country squires, grouse shooting, gentlemen's clubs, vintage port and over-ripe pheasant. To these symbols of his lifestyle he added a *bonhomme* of manner which was all too easy to caricature. As Bernard Levin put it in *The Times*, 'Mr Whitelaw . . . only needs a sprig of holly in his hair to be mistaken for a Christmas pudding'.[18]

The same article contained a more positive assessment of Margaret Thatcher's prospects, but concluded that she could not win because in a nation of male chauvinists her sex was too great a handicap. Another disadvantage was that she was even colder than Ted Heath. In the opinion of Levin, 'There is no point in the party jumping out of the igloo and onto the glacier.'[19]

Although she would not have been amused by these objections, Margaret Thatcher accepted that her hour had not yet come. She said as much on *Any*

Questions, with an answer that sounded forthright but left an intriguing sliver of wriggle room:

> I wouldn't be overjoyed at the prospect of being the Leader of the Party at the moment . . . Nor do I think somehow that the country is ready to have a woman leader . . . unless there clearly is no alternative man available. Now, I just don't see that there will therefore be a woman Prime Minister in the next ten years. Now let's not think beyond that.[20]

Having stated her position with becoming, if qualified, modesty, Margaret Thatcher concentrated her energies on supporting the best alternative man available. In her view, this was her intellectual mentor, Sir Keith Joseph. With her encouragement, he now moved into the spotlight as the leading contender for Heath's crown.

THE RISE AND FALL OF SIR KEITH JOSEPH

Seen from a distance, Keith Joseph looked a strong right of centre candidate to lead the Conservative Party. He had served in the cabinets of Macmillan and Heath as Minister for Housing, and as Secretary of State for Social Services. He was a second-generation baronet with inherited wealth. He had a successful track record in business as Chairman of Bovis, the family building company. Although Harold Macmillan condescendingly described him as 'the only dull Jew I know',[21] Joseph had a brilliant intellect. His academic distinctions included a First in Law, and a fellowship at All Souls, Oxford.

Yet these glittering prizes had not given him the self-confidence that is an essential part of the armour for political battle. He was a troubled and at times tormented soul. His intellectual wrestling with ideas left him plagued with self-doubt and political guilt. These drawbacks, already known to some of his colleagues, became increasingly apparent as he set off on a one-man voyage of political exploration in search of new policy ideas for a different Conservative Party.

Companions on this voyage were few and far between at first. In the aftermath of the February 1974 election defeat, Margaret Thatcher was more of a sympathiser than a fellow traveller. She was loyal to him personally, but she kept her distance politically. She was not among the small group of MPs who overtly supported what was becoming known as the monetarist approach to the public finances. Those pioneers included Nicholas Ridley, Jock Bruce-Gardyne, Ian Gow and, below the radar, Geoffrey Howe. The last two urged Joseph to stand against Heath, in the spring of 1974. But Sir Keith was far more interested in political ideas then self-promotion. He turned down their approaches, at least for the time being. Instead, he concentrated on loading up the good ship Joseph, and set sail under the flag of the CPS, with intellectual fire-power.

He recruited as his master gunner, officially called Director of Studies at the CPS, a mercurial hard-pounder turned speech-writer, Alfred Sherman. A former communist, who fought in the Spanish Civil War, Sherman had undergone a spectacular ideological conversion from extreme left to radical right. By 1974, his passion for free markets, monetarist economies and the ideas of Friedrich Hayek were equalled only by his contempt for the policies of Edward Heath.

Joseph and Sherman were an odd couple, and at the newly established CPS they mixed a heady brew of new ideas. Margaret Thatcher joined in as the CPS Deputy Chairman. This was partly out of affection for her old friend Joseph, partly out of infatuation for Sherman, who she briefly described as 'a genius',[22] and partly because she was setting out on her own intellectual quest for a new philosophical framework for her political position. She had never shown interest in such searchings before. Alfred Sherman rightly described her as a politician 'of beliefs not of ideas'.[23] But she was changing. Encouraged first by Ralph Harris at the Institute of Economic Affairs and then by the two founding fathers of the CPS, Margaret Thatcher was moving from old certainty to new questioning. She was on a mission to understand the free-market philosophy that Keith Joseph was staring to proclaim in his public speeches.

In one of his first proclamations he announced a shattering discovery. 'It was only in April 1974 that I was converted to Conservatism', he wrote. 'I had thought I was a Conservative, but now I see I was not really one at all.'[24]

Margaret Thatcher, much though she admired Joseph, had no time for such theoretical musings. She was an intensely practical Conservative, secure in her certainties even when they turned out to be wrong. The theology of repentance, applied to contemporary politics, was *terra incognita* for her. So, although she encouraged Joseph privately, she stayed detached from him publicly until the October 1974 election ended in the expected defeat. Then she came out of the closet and became a supporter of the leadership bid that Joseph was expected to make. However, her role was neither as prominent nor as active as she later claimed. In her memoirs she wrote that by the weekend after the election 'I had virtually become Keith's informal campaign manager'.[25]

This virtual appointment was largely in her own mind. The job of being campaign manager for a leadership candidate requires visibility, organisational know-how and energetic activity at a number of menial but essential tasks such as intelligence gathering, canvassing, keeping reliable lists and horse trading for votes. There is no evidence that Margaret Thatcher began doing any of this work. The new Parliament did not assemble for several days, and then only briefly for the election of a Speaker and the swearing in of new members. Before even these introductory formalities were completed, Keith Joseph's hopes of becoming leader imploded. He pressed the self-destruct button with a speech in Edgbaston, Birmingham, on Saturday 19 October.

Margaret Thatcher played no part in this fateful speech. She was not even aware of its subject matter. It was not part of the series of addresses Joseph had been delivering in the months before the election designed to redirect Conservative philosophy. Usually she was sent first drafts of Keith Joseph's speeches. But this time she was not in the loop.

The first she knew of Joseph's speech was when she picked up a copy of the *Evening Standard* at Waterloo Station on Friday 18 October. The paper had broken the embargo and splashed the text on its front page. 'My heart sank',[26] was her immediate reaction as she read the lurid headline: '"STOP BABIES FOR LOWER CLASSES" – SIR KEITH.'[27]

As the first blasts of media notoriety suggested, Joseph had strayed from economics to eugenics. He unwisely opined that 'Our human stock' was threatened by the birth of too many children from teenage mothers 'in social classes four and five'.[28]

The hysteria these remarks created was worse than anything Margaret Thatcher had to endure at the height of her 'milk snatcher' notoriety. She was strong enough to bear the slings and arrows of outrageous vilification, but Keith Joseph was far more sensitive. He crumbled under the weight of condemnation and caricature. One nickname, 'Sir Sheath', exposed him to national ridicule. Another, 'Mad Monk', struck a deeper chord at Westminster, causing a sharp decline in the number of his parliamentary supporters.

The real trouble was that his own writhing, convoluted explanations about what he had meant to say made him look all the more like a doubting and tormented novice from some closed monastic order. He was unlucky, particularly as his original words were much distorted. Politics is a rough trade. Heath's supporters made it rougher. With the paparazzi camped on his doorstep and the parliamentary party chanting like a Greek chorus that he showed 'lack of judgement',[29] Sir Keith Joseph decided to throw in the towel. There now seemed to be no potential challenger to Heath in sight. But Margaret Thatcher was watching and waiting.

REFLECTION

The year of 1974 was a decisive turning point in the life of Margaret Thatcher. It was the period when, most unexpectedly, opportunity knocked with a chance for her to become the leader of the Conservative Party.

Much less noticed at the time, 1974 was the year when she sowed one of the seeds that brought about her destruction as Prime Minister. For it was during her few months as Ted Heath's Shadow Environment Secretary that she became convinced of the unfairness of the rating system. So she made a public commitment to abolish the rates, and to replace it with a fairer method of taxation to finance local government. This was the genesis of the Community Charge (or 'poll tax') that she so unwisely turned into her 'flagship' policy in 1988–1990.

Both the move to abolish the rates and the move towards competing for the party leadership revealed an interesting dimension in the political character of Margaret Thatcher – her pragmatic opportunism.

Viewed in historical perspective, she is rightly seen as a principled politician. But her election promise to abolish the rates in October 1974, coupled with her simultaneous pledge to peg mortgage interest rates at 9.5 per cent, were unprincipled decisions. They were crowd-pleasing and leader-pleasing initiatives which, had they been implemented, would have sent inflation and public expenditure soaring. She knew this perfectly well. Her only excuse was that she thought that the price of her promises would never have to be paid, since the Conservatives were bound to lose the election anyway.

Although she was flaky about the inflationary consequences, she was firm about the moral reasons for abolishing the rates. Time and again in her 1974 speeches as Shadow Environment Minister, Margaret Thatcher highlighted the unfairness of a widow living alone in a big house who had to pay her rates out of her fixed income pension, when in the same street a family of wage-earners paid the same rating bill out of their much larger collective earnings. This was a moral issue. Margaret Thatcher, whose longstanding sympathy for widows dated back to her days as Joint Parliamentary Secretary at the Ministry of Pensions and National Insurance, felt passionately about it. This passion for rating reform ended up as the poll tax, and hastened her demise as Prime Minister. It all started in 1974.

More importantly, this was the year in which the green shoots of Margaret Thatcher's leadership ambitions began to emerge. At first, she kept them well under wraps. She knew Keith Joseph too well to believe that he would ever run the full distance as a leadership challenger himself. He was a good man, and a clever man. But even if he had never made his fateful eugenics speech, his handwringing temperament and his intellectual propensity to see merit in all sides of all questions made him quite unfit to give the strong leadership the Conservatives needed. The same could well be said, for different reasons, of all the other potential candidates from the shadow cabinet. It was a weak field in which a strong woman might just beat the bookies' forecasts. Her logical mind must surely have led her to dream this unthinkable dream long before she put her hat into the ring.

Whatever went on in her head during the first ten months of 1974, her political positioning was impeccable. She was both constitutionally loyal to Ted Heath, while politically supportive of Keith Joseph. She gave no clues that she had aspirations of her own. Yet while all the other horses in the race were faltering, she was gaining ground. This did not happen by chance. The Iron Lady was preceded by the Iron Candidate.

10

Winning the leadership

DECIDING TO RUN

Margaret Thatcher bided her time while the media row about Keith Joseph smouldered on for a month's worth of bad headlines. His embarrassment emboldened Ted Heath to reshuffle the shadow cabinet. But the Leader's confidence that his position had been strengthened was undermined by the parliamentary reaction to his new appointments.

If Heath had brought in some fresh faces from the right of the party, or promoted Margaret Thatcher, he might have calmed the murmurings against him at least for a while. But Edward du Cann, who was exercising an increasing influence as Chairman of the 1922 Committee, refused to serve in the shadow cabinet. The only two newcomers invited to join it were Nick Scott and Tim Raison, both regarded as left of centre Heathites. Their appointments increased the grumblings from the right.

Before the reshuffle, Margaret Thatcher was tipped in the press to become Shadow Chancellor of the Exchequer. Heath did not want to put her in such an important role. In an attempt to take her down a peg, he did not assign a departmental portfolio to her. Instead, he made her the number two spokesman under Robert Carr. He was a colourless figure, who had served as Home Secretary with decency but without distinction. Unlike his new deputy, he was no match as a debater for the Labour Chancellor, Denis Healey. This gave Margaret Thatcher her opportunity to shine.

Her first outing at the despatch box in her new role for the opposition was in the Budget debate, exactly as it had been after her appointment as number two to Iain Macleod eight years earlier. She won cheers from the Conservative back-benchers for her entertaining digs at Labour's Treasury ministers. After being congratulated on her appointment by Labour's Chief Secretary to the Treasury, the multi-millionaire Harold Lever, she got a good laugh (not least from him) by responding that she could never hope to rival his expertise on 'the four ways of acquiring money, to make it, to earn it, to marry it, and to borrow it. He seems to have experience of all four'.[1]

Later in her speech she had a lively clash with Denis Healey, who she taunted with a newspaper clipping about his new house in Sussex. This reported him as saying 'I never save. If I get any money I go out and buy something for the house'.[2] He not only protested too much at this slur on his reputation for prudence, and noticeably omitted to mention his country-house purchase. To which she retorted: 'I am delighted that we have got on record the fact that the Chancellor is a jolly good saver. I know that he believes in buying houses in good Tory areas.'[3]

Winning an exchange with Healey, the Labour government's most flamboyant debater, was a good start for Margaret Thatcher in the high profile Budget debate. At a time of low morale for the Conservative Party she raised the spirits of her back-benchers with her attacking speech. Some of them started muttering about the need to take her more seriously as a leadership candidate. Once again, she had seized her moment as an effective parliamentary debater. She backed this up with some impressive performances on the early stages of the Committee on the Finance Bill.

A few days later she seized a far more important moment. On 21 November she was working in her room at the House on the Finance Bill when the beleaguered Keith Joseph came in to see her. 'I am sorry, I just can't run', he told her. 'Ever since I made that speech the press have been outside the house. They have been merciless. Helen [his wife] can't take it, and I have decided that I just can't stand.'[4]

Margaret Thatcher responded, 'If you're not going to stand, I will, because someone who represents our viewpoint *has* to stand'.[5] Later that evening, she returned to Flood Street and told her husband she had decided to run for the leadership. 'You must be out of your mind', she claimed he replied. 'You haven't a hope.'[6] Denis's account of his response was, 'Heath will murder you'.[7]

These versions are suspect. Both Thatchers were viewing the rising tide of party support for her more positively than their later stories suggest. Speculation among Tory MPs that she could be a serious and credible leadership candidate had been around for several weeks. It rose sharply with the fall in Keith Joseph's stock among his colleagues, climbing even higher in the aftermath of her Budget debate speech. Margaret Thatcher was well aware of the growing buzz of interest in her favour. She also knew that support for her was gathering momentum in some unexpected quarters.

TOFFS FOR THATCHER AND OTHER SURPRISES

Margaret Thatcher's earliest encouragement to run for the leadership did not come, as was erroneously claimed at the time, from a 'peasants' revolt'* within the party. Her first supporters were toffs, country gents and Treasury specialists.

The first time I heard Margaret Thatcher's name mooted as a leadership candidate was in July 1974. I had just played a game of squash on the House of Commons court with Peter Morrison, the twenty-nine-year-old Member for Chester. We were good friends.

On this particular morning he was rather full of himself. 'I've been seeing Margaret Thatcher', he confided. 'I told her that she must stand and that I could organise quite a few votes for her.'

I expressed amazement, and asked what her response had been.

'She said I was the first Member of the 1974 intake to say this to her', replied Peter Morrison. 'Then she said she had no chance. But in the next breath she asked me how much support I thought she had. I replied, "Well you've got the Fonthill vote. My father's been saying he's certain you'll be our next leader." '8

This information was intriguing. Peter's father, Lord Margadale, was a legendary figure of influence in the Tory Party. As Major Sir John Morrison MP, he had been Chairman of the 1922 Committee for many years. He was one of the last of a vanishing breed of back-bench heavyweights known as 'Knights of the Shires'. He was widely credited with delivering the emergence of Sir Alec Douglas-Home as leader in 1963 and the election of Ted Heath in 1965. 'Major Shrewd' was his nickname. He was the father of two current MPs, Peter and his elder brother Charlie, the Member for Devizes.

---

* 'Peasants' revolt' was the label given to the 1975 leadership election by Julian Critchley, Conservative MP for Aldershot 1970–1997. Journalist, wit and *bon viveur*, Julian was not a man to let historical accuracy stand in the way of an amusing phrase.

Another source of Lord Margadale's continuing influence was that he held court at Fonthill, his country estate in Wiltshire, where weekend house parties for political guests were a regular fixture. If the 'Fonthill vote' was really moving Margaret Thatcher's way, it was an intriguing development. On the other hand, Peter Morrison might be getting the wrong end of the stick – which was the view I expressed.

'Well, watch this space!' was his cheery response. 'Of course it's early days, but some wise money's going on La Thatcher.'

The summer recess and the October election filled the space for both of us in the next three months. But back in the squash court again at the start of the new parliamentary session, we returned to the subject of Margaret Thatcher. By this time she was being talked about, but only as a long-odds runner, in the leadership stakes.

'I've become the sort of White's Club whip for her', confided Peter. The title had a meaning in high Tory circles. In the 1970s, there were still about forty old-guard MPs who belonged to clubs in St James's Street like White's, Boodle's, Brooks's, Pratt's and the Carlton. One of the better-connected Conservative whips (at the time, Spencer le Marchant) was tasked with digging these club members out of their dining rooms in time to vote in nocturnal divisions. So I understood the role Peter Morrison was describing, but thought it would be an impossible job to find supporters for Margaret Thatcher in these circles.

'Difficult territory for you', I said.

'Oh, you're out of touch, old boy', he responded. 'Quite a few of my chums are talking of coming into Margaret's camp.'

'Like who?' I asked.

'Like Robin Cooke, Alan Clark, Bill Benyon, Michael Ancram, Marcus Kimball, Julian Amery, Maurice Macmillan and Stephen Hastings. My father's putting in a word for her with some of them, too.'[9]

My amazement increased. None of these names were from Margaret Thatcher's natural constituency. She was a lady of the suburbs, not the shires. These alleged supporters were men of old money, old regiments and old school ties.

'Shurely shome mistake', I responded, using a *Private Eye* catchphrase. 'No way!' insisted Peter. He knew his fellow-grandees and club members. As we towelled down in the squash-court dressing room, he managed to convince me that owners of great estates like Athelhampton (Robin Cooke), Highgrove

(Maurice Macmillan), Englefield (Bill Beynon), Saltwood (Alan Clark), Lothian (Michael Ancram), Milton (Stephen Hastings) and Fonthill (Morrison family) were swinging Thatcher's way.

'But why?'

'Because we think she's the only one with balls, even though she's a filly. Brains, too', he replied. 'And she is running well enough to end up the winner.'

Peter Morrison in those days was lean, energetic and enthusiastic, with considerable gifts of persuasion. He quietly conjured at least thirty or more improbable votes out of the upper social echelons of the parliamentary party. While later backers of Thatcher (including Airey Neave) were dithering, Peter was working flat out for her. His role was underestimated at the time, but not by Margaret Thatcher, or by one or two of her below-the-radar confidants, such as Gordon Reece[10] and the theoretically neutral Chief Whip, Humphrey Atkins.

One effect of the early dedication of Peter Morrison was that it won him the enduring loyalty of the candidate. When she became Prime Minister in 1979, she appointed him Minister of State for Employment, and to a succession of further posts during the next eleven years of which the last, and most disastrous, was to be her Parliamentary Private Secretary at the time of the fateful leadership election in 1990. But the failure of his final service to her has obscured the success of his original initiative on her behalf. Peter's progress started with 'toffs for Thatcher', sixteen years earlier. He was her first unequivocal backer, and she never forgot it.

The toffs were joined by a more cerebral strand of support from a clever group of Tory MPs who specialised in Treasury matters. Their leader was John Nott, who just after the February 1974 election defeat met Denis Thatcher at a Burmah Oil board meeting. 'Your wife could be Ted Heath's successor', said Nott. 'My God, I hope you're wrong', replied Denis.[11]

John Nott was one of the founder members of the Economic Dining Club, a group of Conservative MPs interested in Treasury issues who dined together every month in one another's London homes. The other members included Nicholas Ridley, Jock Bruce-Gardyne, Enoch Powell, Peter Hordern and John Biffen. After being invited to some of these evenings as a guest, Margaret Thatcher was put up for membership in the early 1970s. 'But she was blackballed on the grounds she talked for too long', recalled Nott.[12]

The blackballs were lifted in March 1974, so the future leader of the party became a regular attendee at the Economic Dining Club. She was ideologically sympathetic to the group's enthusiasm for free markets, floating exchange rates, and the theories of monetarism. So, when her bandwagon started to inch forward, it was no surprise that the members of the club put their shoulders to its wheels.

They were joined by a second wave of Tory Treasury specialists who participated alongside her on the 1974 Finance Bill Committee. Many of its stages took place on the floor of the House where Margaret Thatcher's professionalism as a debunker and destroyer of government amendments was winning golden opinions, not least from the brightest new stars in the Finance Bill firmament. They included two future Chancellors, Norman Lamont and Nigel Lawson.

Rave reviews for her leadership of the front-bench team also came from the newly elected Member for Croydon, John Moore, a future Treasury minister, who volunteered to be one of the first Thatcher canvassers. Another fan, playing a key role on the Finance Bill was my next-door parliamentary neighbour Peter Rees, the Member for Dover and Deal. He was a tax QC and a future Chief Secretary to the Treasury. He advised me and other members of the East Kent group of MPs that we should all back Margaret Thatcher for the leadership because 'She is performing brilliantly, even on the most complicated and technical amendments'.[13]

Since the Finance Bill was the centrepiece of parliamentary life in the opening weeks of the new House of Commons, the praise for Margaret Thatcher from its ablest debaters on the Tory team had a ripple effect throughout the entire party. Yet most of its backbenchers, including myself, still had no clear idea as to who they might vote for in a leadership election, if there was going to be one. However, the combination of toffs, Treasury specialists and Ted Heath haters was creating a degree of momentum for Margaret Thatcher, even if it was not yet strong enough to propel her to the front of the pack.

A DEAL WITH EDWARD DU CANN

Although Margaret Thatcher told Ted Heath that she intended to stand against him, her position was not a strong one. In the autumn of 1974 there were only a handful of believers, like Peter Morrison, who thought she could win the crown. Most Tory MPs were hedging their bets, half-heartedly paying lip service to the status quo while they waited for the emergence of a stronger challenger. But who would this be?

With Willie Whitelaw refusing to enter the lists, and Keith Joseph withdrawing from them, a number of unlikely names were fleetingly mentioned as possible contenders. Most of them were slightly dated establishment grandees, such as Christopher Soames, Richard Wood, Hugh Fraser and Julian Amery. Heath was supremely confident of seeing off all of them, and Margaret Thatcher too. But one potential candidate worried the Leader's praetorian guard. It was that of Edward du Cann, Chairman of the 1922 Committee, former Chairman of the Conservative Party and former Economic Secretary to the Treasury. His strongest qualification was that he was implacably opposed to Ted Heath and determined to put an end to his leadership of the party.

In early November, Edward du Cann and all seventeen members of the Executive of the 1922 Committee were re-elected. This was a blow to Heath, who had been trying to engineer their defeat. For the first of many great divides between the leader and the 1922 Executive was that Heath did not want any kind of vote on his position, whereas the 1922 were determined to have a leadership election as soon as possible.

Just how fraught this tension had become was clear at a meeting held in the leader of the opposition's room on 12 November 1974. The Chief Whip, Humphrey Atkins, invited six of his senior colleagues to discuss the problem they knew would arise at the next full gathering of the 1922 Committee, on the following Thursday. These colleagues were Willie Whitelaw, Jim Prior, Francis Pym, John Peyton, Lord Hailsham and Lord Carrington.

Hailsham kept a note of the discussion, which survives in his papers. It shows that all present recognised that the 1922 was going to demand either a vote of confidence in the leader or a leadership election. Jim Prior, reflecting Ted Heath's view, wanted neither of these options. But the others thought this was an untenable position.

'Willie expressed fear lest Ducann [*sic*] cd win on (2)',[14] wrote Hailsham. His full stop after '(2)' made it clear that they were talking about du Cann winning in a second ballot. This was a forecast also being made on the backbenches.

Although du Cann was clearly coming into the frame as a strong candidate, Carrington, Hailsham and Whitelaw said they could not work with him. Carrington reported on his lunchtime conversation with Harold Macmillan.

Apparently the former Prime Minister was dismissive of du Cann, saying, 'Why not ask Tiny Rowland straight away?' This was a reference to du Cann's controversial business ties with Roland 'Tiny' Rowland. The two were respectively Chairman and Chief Executive of Lonhro, a buccaneering trading company with extensive interests in Africa.

Hailsham's note of this 12 November meeting is revealing. For a start, it makes no mention of Margaret Thatcher, who was not being even considered by this group. It shows that the key figures in the Tory hierarchy regarded du Cann as the number one threat to Heath. He was seen as both the likely winner of a leadership election and as the arbiter of whether or not there would be such an election.

As things turned out, du Cann quickly got his way on the election objective. He fought for and won a decision that there would be an early leadership contest. The date for the ballot was set for 4 February 1975, with nominations closing two weeks earlier.

But who, apart from the determinedly immovable Ted would be nominated?

Margaret Thatcher had declared her willingness to stand but was not yet certain to do so. Indeed, she was so uncertain about her prospects that in early December she offered to withdraw from the contest in order to let du Cann have a clear run. She made this offer of withdrawal to Nigel Fisher, the MP for Surbiton, and a member of the 1922 Committee. He was a mild, middle-of-the-road back-bencher who had developed a far from mild antipathy to Heath. This dated from an extraordinary display of rudeness to Fisher at a dinner party in 10 Downing Street when the Prime Minister told him he was 'plain ignorant' in front of other guests.[15] It had been Heath's stock in trade to hand out gratuitous insults to colleagues with whom he disagreed. It was hardly surprising that the insulted became the activists in the campaign to defenestrate him.

In late November Nigel Fisher began gathering signatures among his colleagues to a letter urging Edward du Cann to stand for the leadership. After two days, twenty-five MPs including Airey Neave had signed it and another thirty indicated their willingness to do so. In the middle of this exercise, Fisher saw Margaret Thatcher. It is unlikely that she had anything over fifty potential supporters at this stage, and in any case she had no campaign manager to count her numbers. When she heard Nigel Fisher's account of how well his canvassing for du Cann was going she said, 'Please give Edward my firm assurance that I will withdraw my name if he decides to stand'.[16]

Although it sounds out of character for Margaret Thatcher to back down from any sort of challenge, Edward du Cann was not surprised when Nigel Fisher brought him the news of her firm assurance. 'I think it was a pure mathematical calculation on her part', he has recalled. 'I had the votes. She did not.'[17]

Edward du Cann was a rare bird in the parliamentary aviary. But could he fly all the way to 10 Downing Street? He had some good credentials as a former Treasury minister and Party Chairman. He was a capable speaker and had formidable skills at chairing meetings. But he had enemies too, who engaged in a whispering campaign against him. They included Willie Whitelaw, who let it be known that he would never serve in a du Cann government; Peter Walker, a former business associate who murmured unhelpfully about du Cann's City of London reputation; and above all Ted Heath, who had sacked him from the Party Chairmanship and excluded him from the 1970–1974 government.

Everyone in the parliamentary party knew that Heath and du Cann were chalk and cheese. One was a rude man; the other was smooth man. Du Cann was master of the art of oleaginous compliments to colleagues. One of the many stories of a 'du Canning' was about his greeting a new member, Commander John Kerans RN,* with the words, 'I understand you served in submarines: how brave!'[18] Another, surely apocryphal, tale consisted of du Cann being asked the time, and replying, 'And what time would you like it to be?'[19]

Du Cann's over-polished courtesy was seen by his colleagues as a stylistic quirk rather than as a serious fault. He might not have been everyone's choice but his stature was thought to be higher than Margaret Thatcher's. She was the only declared candidate, but even as an undeclared candidate he was believed to have a far better chance of beating Heath. Nigel Fisher was not the only experienced colleague to take this view. Airey Neave,† the Member for Abingdon,

---

* Commander John Kerans DSO RN (1915–1985), Conservative MP for Hartlepool, 1949–1964. As Captain of HMS *Amethyst* he led a spectacular escape from Chinese Communist forces on the Yangtze River in 1949. He was immortalised in a Holywood movie based on the episode, *The Yangtze Incident*.
† Airey Neave DSO MC (1916–1979). Prisoner of war 1940–1942. First British officer to escape successfully from Colditz. Conservative MP for Abingdon 1953–1979. Leadership campaign manager for Margaret Thatcher 1975 and head of her office 1975–1979. Assassinated by Irish National Liberation Army March 1979.

had also offered his services to du Cann as his potential campaign manager. Among younger Members, Peter Tapsell was organising support for him. A key factor in this gathering momentum was that the Tory leadership was still regarded by many MPs as a male preserve. Edward du Cann seemed to be the most competent *man* available for the job, which was one reason why the odds on him were shortening.

Throughout the months of November and December, du Cann remained politely ambiguous towards all overtures. He had one good reason for his aloofness. As Chairman of the 1922 Committee he was the umpire of the leadership election. He did not wish to jeopardise this position. He feared he might be accused of having used his role improperly if he switched to becoming a challenger.

These arguments had less force after the machinery for the election on 4 February was agreed and in place. So when Nigel Fisher came down to du Cann's home in Somerset at the beginning of the year, the hesitant candidate was still open to persuasion. However, there was a new problem. It was the attitude of his wife, Sally du Cann. The couple were in the middle of marital difficulties, which later ended in divorce. The future of their country house was one of the issues in dispute. As Nigel Fisher produced his round-robin letter, signed by supporters, it became clear that the candidate's most important supporter was refusing to countenance a leadership bid. 'Sally took Nigel out for a walk and told him she was utterly opposed to the idea,' recalled Edward du Cann, 'and once she said that, I accepted it completely. My wife's objections were the chief reason why I told Nigel to drop it.'[20]

Before Nigel Fisher finally dropped it, he arranged a meeting between Margaret Thatcher and Edward du Cann. This clandestine rendezvous had the effect of extracting a new and quite different assurance – this time from him to her. She wanted to hear from his own lips that he definitely would not stand.

The meeting took place at du Cann's house in Westminster, 14 Lord North Street. Denis Thatcher accompanied his wife. As Edward du Cann recalled it:

It was of course an entirely private meeting between the three of us. I remember it as rather tense at first. Margaret and Denis sat on the edge of the sofa in my drawing room almost as if they were a housekeeper and a butler applying for a job. After I assured them that I was certainly not going to be a candidate they relaxed. It became quite clear that if my decision was final then she was going to run. No one else knew this. I took away the strong impression that Denis was her only confidant in on the secret and that the two of them were very excited.[21]

Edward du Cann's impressions were correct. Margaret Thatcher had taken quite a battering at the hands of Ted Heath's camp since she had told him of her intention to stand against him. There had been several covert attempts to undermine her. Of these, the most damaging exercise in black propaganda had been Peter Walker's use of a pre-election interview she gave to a somewhat obscure magazine, *Pre-Retirement Choice.* In this interview she had advised its readers to buy canned food, particularly tins of 'the expensive proteins: ham, tongue, salmon, mackerel, sardines', as a hedge against inflation.[22]

This dull story was spun into a scandal by well-orchestrated accusations that Margaret Thatcher was a 'food hoarder' – a term with unpleasant associations from the days of rationing in the Second World War. The claims had echoes of the 'milk snatcher' uproar with the added ingredient of snobbery. The implication was that the Grantham grocer's daughter was selfishly stocking up her own larder, 'acting against the public interest'. This accusation was solemnly made on television by the former Conservative Chief Whip, Martin Redmayne, who had become the Deputy Chairman of Harrods.[23]

In rebuttal, Margaret Thatcher no less solemnly invited a posse of Fleet Street journalists to report on the modest contents of her food cupboard at her Flood Street home. The episode says volumes about the febrile atmosphere of fear and feuding that her leadership challenge had triggered at the highest levels of the Tory Party.

After a week or two of media hysteria, the synthetic indignation evaporated. It is unlikely to have changed a single vote in the election, but it rattled Margaret Thatcher at the time. 'I was bitterly upset by it', she recalled. 'Sometimes I was near to tears. Sometimes I was shaking with anger.'[24]

The bruises from the food-hoarder affair meant that the Thatcher family had a downcast Christmas. Denis was having business worries because of boardroom troubles at Burmah Oil. But there were hopeful signs too. A small but gathering band of supporters following in Peter Morrison's footsteps came to see Mrs Thatcher to assure her of their votes. These early declarers included

Geoffrey Finsberg, Robin Cooke, Bill Shelton, John Gorst, David Crouch, Hugh Rossi and William Rees-Davies. None of them carried great weight in the party, and no one was organising or counting them. But their arrival as the outriders of a support movement was a further sign that a spontaneous Thatcher bandwagon was beginning to roll.

Although the Heath camp had shown itself capable of malevolence over the food-hoarder row, it was proving incapable of picking up fresh support. Among the new intakes of younger MPs elected in February and October 1974, dissatisfaction with the status quo was growing. Heath was looking like goods too damaged to be re-elected. Yet he held pole position partly because his potential challengers had too many weaknesses, and partly because he still controlled the levers of power within the party. This gave him the only team of colleagues who seemed capable of running an effective election campaign. This changed the moment Airey Neave became Margaret Thatcher's campaign manager. Why he got there and how he carried out the job for her is an intriguing story, which greatly enhanced his House of Commons reputation as a man of mystery.

ENTER AIREY NEAVE

Many of his fellow-Conservative MPs were baffled by Airey Neave. He was variously described as 'a sound man', 'a shadowy figure' and 'a good operator'.[25] His soundness derived from his war record, whose highlights were to have been decorated with the MC, DSO and Croix de Guerre. He was the first British officer to have escaped and made a 'home run' from Colditz.

The shadowy side of Neave came from the widespread belief that he had worked in the post-war years for MI5, and still maintained close links with the intelligence community. This may have been an impression he himself liked to cultivate. He would have fitted in well as a character from the 'Circus' in John Le Carré's novels. Even Neave's way of walking and talking had an air of invisibility. He moved along the corridors of the House of Commons like a crab scuttling towards crevices in the walls. He murmured rather than spoke in elliptical half sentences. Extracting a point of view from him was like fishing for a moonbeam.

Was he on the left or right of the party? For or against the EEC? Supporting which contender in the leadership election? The answers were in the evasive.

One fact that did become known about Airey Neave was his intense dislike of Ted Heath. This was hardly a singular distinction, but the story of their falling out (later denied by Heath) formed part of the apocrypha of leader vilification. According to the smoking-room stories (encouraged by discreet nods and winks from the injured party), Neave had suffered a heart attack in 1959 and went to explain to Chief Whip Heath that for medical reasons he could not continue to serve as a junior minister in Macmillan's government. 'You're finished then', was Heath's cold response.[26]

Whatever words were actually used on that occasion, there was a lasting resentment between the two men. A further cause of enmity was that Neave felt he had been unfairly denied a knighthood. This was a grievance shared by several other non-'Knights of the Shires'. The impression was given that Airey Neave was energised into hyperactive plotting against Heath for reasons that were more personal than political.

Willie Whitelaw, Keith Joseph and Edward du Cann were all approached by Airey Neave with the offer of his services as their campaign manager. The spectrum of views held by these potential contestants suggests that Neave's overtures to them were not motivated by ideological constraints. His primary objective was to get rid of Heath.

In this role Neave had done well, with the assistance of his friend Nigel Fisher,[*] in collecting almost seventy pledged supporters for du Cann. The scorecard was far from reliable due to the duplicity of many members of the electorate. Even so, Neave's figures were at least three times better than the much vaguer list of supporters Margaret Thatcher's fey and rather ineffective PPS, Fergus Montgomery, claimed were for her.

In mid-January 1975, the rumours, numbers, odds and runners were sharply clarified by the game-changing withdrawal of Edward du Cann. But only Margaret and Denis Thatcher and Edward du Cann knew it was coming. A few hours before the public announcement, Neave had a conversation with Bill Shelton, the MP for Streatham, who was counting the Thatcher pledges, suggesting that they should come to 'some arrangement', by which du Cann's votes could be merged with her votes. The agreement was easily reached and consisted

---

* Nigel Fisher (1913–1996), Conservative MP for Hitchin 1950–1955 and Surbiton 1955–1983. Member of the 1922 Executive 1972–1979.

of Shelton stepping down to a number two role and Neave being appointed as the number one campaign manager. All it required was the approval of the candidate herself.

Airey Neave came to see Margaret Thatcher after a late-night division at the House on 15 January. In the manner of a George Smiley, he asked who was running her campaign. Entering into the spirit of dissimulation, she replied that she did not really have a campaign. It is hard to decide whether the question or the answer was more disingenuous. What happened next, by Margaret Thatcher's account, was: 'Airey said: "I think I had better do it for you." I agreed with enthusiasm. I knew this meant he would swing as many du Cann supporters as possible behind me.'[27]

Her instant trust in Airey Neave was surprising after the way he had been hawking himself around to other candidates. But she had known and liked him ever since their first encounters at meetings of the Conservative Candidates Association in 1950–1951. They had been in the same chambers at the bar. All her life she had a romantic view of war heroes and secret-service operatives. For her, he was the right man at the right time.

With the appointment of Airey Neave to run her campaign, Margaret Thatcher's leadership prospects were transformed. She was no longer a stalking horse, but a serious runner with credible supporters, organisers and voters. No one could be sure what was going to happen in round one or round two (if it came to that) of the ballot. But the sheer unpredictability of the contest made her an exciting candidate as the end game began.

A STUNNING RESULT ON THE FIRST BALLOT

For the next three weeks, events moved at break-neck speed. Airey Neave ran by far the subtlest and smoothest campaign. Its key ingredients were discreet canvassing, accurate counting, confidential meetings with the candidate and calculated misinformation. By contrast, Heath met no undecided MPs on a one-to-one basis. He felt it demeaning to solicit votes. When he came to conduct a Christmas carol concert in Broadstairs, just before Christmas, I had a few moments alone with him and suggested he should talk to some of his new colleagues from the 1974 intakes, privately. 'No I don't think so, actually', he replied. 'They all know where I stand.'[28]

On reflection he relented, allowing his Parliamentary Private Secretary Tim Kitson to organise a series of dinners in a private room at Bucks Club throughout January. These were stilted affairs, attended by around twenty colleagues at a time, with deferential questions from the guests and wooden answers from the leader. The exercise did little or nothing to change the long-held feelings of animosity towards Heath that had been nurtured by so many for so long.

Just before nominations closed, Hugh Fraser threw his hat into the ring. For a while, this was thought to be a blow to the Thatcher camp, who feared that their candidate's votes would be siphoned off to him. But such fears were misplaced. Although he had been an effective Secretary of State in Macmillan's government, he was not a serious contender. A romantic Highlander, the younger brother of Lord Lovat, Fraser was a mixture of original ideas, quixotic ambition and a tendency to knock over the card table when he was holding the aces. Unfortunately, at this stage of his career he held no court cards, let alone aces.

Hugh Fraser was contemptuous of Heath but cautiously admiring towards Thatcher. Nevertheless, he felt Britain was not ready for a woman prime minister, particularly one who had shown so little interest in foreign affairs, a frequently heard complaint against her. But he thought Margaret Thatcher's time might yet come and that she would make a good Chancellor of the Exchequer in a future government headed by Willie Whitelaw.

That last opinion was being increasingly voiced by Tory MPs who had been listening to Margaret Thatcher's speeches on the Finance Bill. The best of these came on 22 January when she was leading the opposition's attack on the Budget proposals for a Capital Transfer Tax.

In the early part of the debate she had attacked Denis Healey with a staunch defence of the right of families to pass on inheritance from generation to generation. 'Why does the Chancellor take such objection to such efforts for one's children?' she asked. 'Some think of it as a duty and a privilege.'[29]

Responding in the wind-up of the debate the following day, Healey counter-attacked her use of the word privilege, using a colourful metaphor. Comparing Margaret Thatcher to the legendary heroine of the Spanish Civil War, he mockingly described her as 'La Pasionara of privilege', who had decided to 'see her party tagged as the party of the rich few'.[30]

In the midst of an uproar of points of order, Margaret Thatcher came back with a knockout blow. 'Some Chancellors are macroeconomic. Other Chancellors are fiscal. This one is just plain cheap.'[31]

Her back-benchers roared approval, chanting 'cheap, cheap, cheap' at the discomfited Healey, who looked as crestfallen as a school bully who had been thrown to the ground by a girl wrestler.

The Conservatives were electrified by this momentary surge in their morale. Margaret Thatcher instinctively turned up the voltage, delivering a final flurry of thunderbolts at the Capital Transfer Tax which she denounced because it would affect 'not only the one in a thousand to whom he referred but everyone, including people born like I was with no privilege at all. It will affect us as well as the Socialist millionaires.'

Her conclusion was that CTT would damage private businesses, farming, woodlands and shipping; and it would also damage

> the very nature of our society by concentrating power and property in the hands of the State . . . We believe that the future of freedom is inseparable from a wide distribution of private property among the people . . . We can say little for this tax. It should be withdrawn.[32]

The vehemence of this four-word crescendo would have delighted her old Oxford speaking tutor, Mrs Gatehouse.

Many of us listening from the backbenches to this fighting speech saw that Margaret Thatcher had seized the initiative in the leadership contest. Up to this moment the campaign had been a prosaic affair characterised by grubby attempts at character assassination, unsuccessful efforts to persuade the unwilling to stand and dubious number counting. Suddenly a passionate candidate had lifted the battle to the higher ground of beliefs and principles.

The Tory party of the mid-1970s had become mired in defeatism. Buffeted by events and outmanoeuvred by union militancy it had lost its confidence. On that day in the House of Commons Margaret Thatcher was an inspirational force. Her crushing of Healey was the talk of the tea room for the next few hours. So was her championship of inheritance, family businesses and private property as essential ingredients in what she called 'the future of freedom'.

I recall Teddy Taylor, the MP for Glasgow Cathcart, saying 'we've heard the voice of leadership today', as he declared he would probably vote for her.

This was a considerable surprise, for Teddy Taylor was thought to be a loyal admirer of Heath, even though he had resigned as a junior minister from his government on the issue of devolution. It was one of several indications that Margaret Thatcher's speech had turned votes in her favour. The press gallery caught the new mood too. *The Times* reported, 'Far fewer members . . . are speaking dismissively of a woman's candidature for the party leadership than they did a fortnight ago, when she announced her challenge'.[33]

With less than two weeks to go until the first ballot, Airey Neave and his core group of six or seven ardent Thatcherites began canvassing with skill and sophistication. It was the ideal role for an intelligence officer well versed in the tradecraft of deceiving the enemy. Neave's basic tactic was to pretend that his candidate was not gaining enough ground, and to tell all and sundry that 'Ted's bound to win'.[34] These predictions upset a good many colleagues who thought little of Margaret Thatcher, but would like to see Willie Whitelaw, Jim Prior, Francis Pym or A.N. Other take over the leadership. Norman Tebbit was one of Neave's key lieutenants in the dark art of persuading the electorate to vote for Thatcher in order to open up the contest for a second ballot. 'I talked round quite a few colleagues into voting for Margaret on these grounds', he recalled. One of these voters, according to Tebbit, was Michael Heseltine.[35]

The most Machiavellian manoeuvres were handled by Airey Neave himself. In a conversation with me, he said that Margaret was 'doing well, but not nearly well enough'. Because I was known to be a close friend of Hugh Fraser, he asked me if I could persuade Hugh 'to slip one or two of his votes to Margaret'.[36] The impression Neave was trying to disseminate was that his candidate was well short of the support needed to win.

I also witnessed a late-night conversation between Airey Neave and Sir John Rodgers. The latter, somewhat in his cups, kept repeating that he was 'loyal to Ted, but fed up with him . . . the man needs a jolt to show he can't take us for granted'.

'Then jolt him by voting for Margaret. She won't win, but she'll give him a fright', said Neave.

At the time he was saying this, he knew from his double- and treble-checked canvassing returns that his scorecard showed 120 certain votes for Thatcher, and only 80 for Heath. But Rogers fell for it, and then felt guilty; huffing and puffing for months afterwards that he had been 'tricked' into not voting for Ted.[37]

It is doubtful whether Margaret Thatcher ever knew the dark secrets of Neave's dissimulation techniques. She wisely stayed aloof from the horse-trading. She saw any colleague who asked to meet her, and gave a few press interviews. For most of the time, she concentrated on the Finance Bill and confided only in Denis.

In comparison with Airey Neave's tireless subterranean operations, the organisers of Ted Heath's campaign (his Parliamentary Private Secretaries, Tim Kitson and Kenneth Baker) were overconfident and overbearing. Like their boss, they simply did not believe that a former Prime Minister could be beaten by an inexperienced woman. They were also lulled into a false sense of security by Neave's misinformation about the strength of the support he knew was pledged to Margaret Thatcher. So, in the belief that their man was home and dry, the Heathites made little extra effort in the closing days before the ballot. Cheered up still further by some evidence that backing for the incumbent leader was firming up at the last moment, Ted Heath and his team stayed aloof, waiting in tranquillity for the result.

On the day of the first ballot, Margaret Thatcher had a lunch date at Rothschild's Bank, which had been arranged by the thirty-two-year-old Norman Lamont MP who worked for them.* 'Let's vote together and then go to your bank', she told him, giving him the impression as they went into Committee Room 14 to mark their ballot papers that she was taking a close interest in which name he put his cross against.

Their lunch was not a success. Every member of the Rothschild family, with the exception of Evelyn de Rothschild, had found an excuse to be absent. The non-Rothschild executives took it upon themselves to be 'incredibly rude' about the economic ideas their guest supported. 'Don't ever take me to that red bank again', she said to Lamont. On the way back to the House of Commons she saw an *Evening Standard* placard saying 'Constituencies rally to Heath'. 'That's Ted stirring up the press against me', she complained with a touch of nervousness in her voice.[38]

The ballot closed at 3.30 p.m. on 5 February. The result, when it came some ten minutes later, was a bombshell. Airey Neave came to the waiting Margaret

---

* Norman Lamont (1942–), Conservative MP for Kingston-upon-Thames, 1972–1997; Financial Secretary to the Treasury, 1986–1989; Chief Secretary to the Treasury, 1989–1990; Chancellor of the Exchequer, 1990–1993. Created Lord Lamont, 1998.

Thatcher and said in his soft voice: 'It's good news. You're ahead in the poll. You've got 130 votes to Ted's 119.' Hugh Fraser had 16 votes.[39]

Margaret Thatcher was stunned but exhilarated. She had never quite believed she would do it, and certainly not by such a convincing margin. Heath resigned as Leader of the Opposition immediately. Although a second ballot was required under the rules, most insiders thought Margaret Thatcher was now unstoppable, as she only had to pick up thirty-one fresh votes to achieve victory.

Whilst privately ecstatic about her success, the hot favourite for the run-off was careful to avoid any hint of presumptuous triumphalism. While being toasted by her supporters, she quietly returned to her tasks and duties. 'Here's to our future leader – where is she?' was the cry of her fan club as they raised their silver tankards of champagne to her in the smoking room.[40]

The answer, which took some time to emerge, was that she had returned to the Committee Stage of the Finance Bill. And there she stayed, speaking and voting on complex amendments until almost midnight. For her, even in the hour of near-triumph, it was business as usual – with the second ballot fixed for 11 February.

REFLECTION

'Tis not in mortals to command success;
But we'll do more, Sempronius, we'll deserve it.

(Joseph Addison, *Cato, A Tragedy*, Act I, Scene 2)

Addison's lines are the true explanation of why Margaret Thatcher was catapulted into an unassailable position in the leadership race. For some years afterwards, particularly during the troughs of her time as Leader of the Opposition, it was fashionable to say that she was just lucky. Not true. By her courage, her early declaration and her professionalism in the debates on the Finance Bill, she earned her emergence as the winner of the first ballot.

Whatever role luck played, it was a small one. Her greatest piece of good fortune was that Enoch Powell had quixotically ruled himself out of the running by giving up his Wolverhampton seat in January 1974, and advising the electorate to vote Labour. Had he still been a Conservative MP, he would have won the contest hands down. She was helped by the decisions of Whitelaw and du Cann not to enter the first round of the race. Her greatest bonus was the curmudgeonly character of Ted Heath, who accumulated such a large anti-vote. But other people's mistakes did not turn her into a champion. As the race came down to the wire, she galloped ahead because of the very qualities her earliest supporters among those toffs and Treasury specialists for Thatcher had identified in her. In spite of the prejudice against women in the Tory Party of the 1970s, she was the bravest, the brightest and the best of the candidates.

She deserved her victory.

11

Leader of the Opposition
A fragile beginning

WINNING THE FINAL ROUND

The second ballot for the leadership of the Conservative Party was almost a non-event. From the outside, the media did its best to make the contest look as though it would be a close race. Inside the House of Commons, most Tory MPs knew it was all over bar the shouting. The only betting was on the size of Margaret Thatcher's majority.

Predictably, Willie Whitelaw threw his hat into the ring as the unity candidate, but he was too late. At least half the Conservative Party was uniting behind the victor of the first ballot. The other half was splitting to candidates besides Whitelaw. This lack of solidarity behind a single 'stop Thatcher' candidate was largely due to further Machiavellian manoeuvres by Airey Neave. He despatched closet Thatcherites, notably the far from neutral Chief Whip Humphrey Atkins, to encourage other shadow cabinet ministers to stand in the second ballot. The line taken with these not-so-reluctant *débutantes* was that they should put down a marker in this election so as to be well positioned for the next leadership contest if Thatcher were to implode. This appeal to political vanity brought three more hats into the ring from Jim Prior, Geoffrey Howe and John Peyton. The anti-Margaret forces were now well and truly divided. The trio of new contenders guaranteed that Whitelaw could not muster enough votes to mount a serious challenge to the front-runner.

By contrast, Margaret Thatcher was on a roll. She was the only candidate with momentum and charisma. Once it was realised by the wider public that Britain might be about to have the first-ever woman political leader of a major Western democracy, astonishment turned to excitement.

During the week between the first and second ballots, I decided to take soundings among the executive committee of my constituency Conservative

Association. About thirty Thanet East Tory activists turned up. They had on the whole been staunch supporters of local boy Ted Heath, whom some of them had known since childhood. Now two-thirds of them were gung-ho for Margaret Thatcher, who they variously described as 'gutsy', 'rather beautiful', 'strong enough to give Wilson hell', 'an imaginative choice' and 'a winner'.[1] After this test of grass-roots opinion, I returned to Westminster and cast my vote for the lady.

Other colleagues had similar experiences. The establishment wanted decent old Whitelaw, but exciting innovative Thatcher was the people's candidate. She romped home with 146 votes to Willie Whitelaw's seventy-nine votes. Geoffrey Howe, nineteen votes, Jim Prior, nineteen votes, and John Peyton, eleven votes, trailed far behind her. Britain had a new Leader of the Opposition.

There were some interesting surprises during her first few hours in her new role. Her soft style to MPs during the campaign was replaced by a bossy manner at her first press conference. She gave brisk one-liners as replies to questions. Asked about foreign affairs, she coquettishly answered, 'I am all for them'. Her staccato responses kept the event moving too fast for most of the press corps, who she chivvied along with commands, 'Come along now, next question, next question'. She also pronounced: 'You chaps don't like short, direct answers. Men like long, rambling, waffling answers.'[2]

After the press conference she attended a celebration party at the Pimlico home of her deputy campaign manager, Bill Shelton, followed by a working dinner with Chief Whip Humphrey Atkins. Denis seemed to have been dumped in the middle of the new leader's progress. He was found wandering by himself in a House of Commons corridor by Norman Tebbit, who took him to dinner.

An unattractive surprise was the venom of some of those who had voted against her. Ian Gilmour was, and remained, vitriolic in his condemnation of the party's choice, saying that night in his cups, 'We've gone mad. She won't last . . . she can't last.'[3] There seemed to be an uncomfortable number of heads nodding in agreement at his table in the smoking room.

Labour, in general, was cock-a-hoop about the Tory choice. My election night featured a drink in the 'Kremlin' bar with my Labour pair, Alec Woodall, the Member for Hemsworth, and a group of his fellow mining MPs from Yorkshire. They repeated over and over again the line that the new Tory Leader would prove 'bloody unelectable'.[4] This was the received wisdom on the government benches for many more months.

On the night of 11 February, the House was busy voting in numerous divisions. One of them was in the Finance Bill Committee of which Margaret Thatcher was still a member. So she took part in a 10.20 p.m. vote on an amendment. After it, the Labour Chairman, Richard Crawshaw, congratulated her. She replied with a few leave-taking words that combined charm and asperity. 'I think that, due to circumstances beyond my control, I have been called to higher things and, therefore, may not be with the Committee very much longer', she began, going on to say that progress on the bill seemed to get slower when she was absent because 'women are always very economical in their speeches'.[5]

At around midnight, she came home to Flood Street and popped in to see Carol, who was in bed in a neighbour's spare room. 'I was half-asleep when she knocked on the door and I can't remember exactly what we said to each other. But I do recall that she instantly looked the part: the aura of power about her was almost like a halo.'[6]

Her daughter's beatification was premature. As the congratulations and celebrations faded away, the reality soon dawned that the victory had brought Margaret Thatcher a difficult and divided inheritance.

AN UNCERTAIN START

Margaret Thatcher got off to a shaky start as Leader of the Opposition. The parliamentary party did not unite behind her. The shadow cabinet, which she altered only slightly, simmered uneasily with divisions and discontent. She made maladroit changes at the top of Conservative Central Office. Airey Neave, who she appointed head of her private office, was conspicuously less successful in this role than he had been as her campaign manager. The greatest disappointment was that she failed to establish a leader's ascendancy in the House of Commons.

Although these weaknesses were considerable they were mitigated by other factors. Ted Heath helped her by his volcanic sulking. The emollient Willie Whitelaw, her deputy, was a paragon of public loyalty tinged with occasional private disparagements. The constituency associations were more enthusiastic about her than the parliamentarians. On the wider stage, the media were favourable to her novelty and sympathetic to her problems. Yet even taking account of these positive factors, her position remained fragile.

The morning after she was elected, Margaret Thatcher called on Ted Heath at his home in Wilton Street. It was never going to be an easy encounter. She offered him a place in her shadow cabinet, hoping he would turn it down. He did. Her second olive branch was an invitation for him to lead the Conservative campaign in the referendum on Europe. He rejected that too. Then she asked him for advice on how to handle the press. He refused to comment. The meeting was over in less than five minutes.

Heath behaved rudely as well as abruptly. Just before the appointment he was seen by his PPS, Tim Kitson, piling up books on two out of the three chairs in his study to make it impossible for his visitor to take a seat. He did not rise from behind his desk when Margaret Thatcher entered the room. She had to move the books in order to find somewhere to sit down. According to one account, he replied to both her offers in the monosyllables of a petulant child: 'Shan't' and 'Won't'. 'What can I say?' she then asked him. 'There is nothing to say', he replied.[7]

With the dialogue at an end, Margaret Thatcher left the room. She hung around downstairs talking inconsequentially to Tim Kitson for another quarter of an hour in order to diminish the risk of bad publicity from the reporters waiting outside. Her first attempt at rapprochement had failed completely, as did other peace moves towards Ted Heath in the next few months. The problem was that the deposed leader remained in such high dudgeon that he declined to speak not just to his successor, but to all his old friends who agreed to serve in her shadow cabinet. Even Willie Whitelaw, Jim Prior and Peter Carrington found that they were 'sent to Coventry' by their old boss for several months.

Margaret Thatcher did not take her chance to reshape the shadow cabinet. Caution ruled her. She neither rocked the boat nor brought fresh faces into it. This was partly because there was no pool of outstanding talent on the Tory back benches from which a new leader could easily pick replacement shadow cabinet ministers. The net result was that the reshuffle was minimal. Only Peter Walker was sacked, although two other front-benchers retired. The most interesting appointments were Reggie Maudling as Shadow Foreign Secretary, Geoffrey Howe as Shadow Chancellor, and Airey Neave as spokesman for Northern Ireland, which he combined with being head of her private office.

Airey Neave, so conspiratorially adroit at planning the election that made Margaret Thatcher leader, became conspiratorially paranoiac about plots to undermine her. His brooding mistrust created an unnecessarily tense atmosphere.

I myself ran into trouble with Neave about a month after his appointment when he called me into his office to ask why I was being 'disloyal to the boss'. As evidence for this crime he produced a copy of *Private Eye*. It reported my attendance at a dinner party in Beirut at which various Middle Easterners, while discussing the 1975 Sinai Accord between Israel and Egypt, wanted to know which sections or subsections of the draft agreement were supported by Margaret Thatcher.

At a late hour in this convivial evening I was reported, alas accurately, as saying, 'She knows so little about the Middle East, she probably thinks that Sinai is the plural of Sinus'.[8] Although I explained that this rather feeble quip was intended only as a light-hearted aside for private hearing, Neave insisted that I should formally apologise to my leader. He suggested I should do this in the Aye lobby at the 10 p.m. division, superfluously adding, 'She'll be wearing a green dress'. When I duly made my rendezvous with the lady in green and ate my humble pie, Margaret Thatcher was charmingly insouciant about the episode. 'Oh don't worry at all. Keith and I say the most frightful things about each other at dinner parties', was her response.[9]

As this story shows, Margaret Thatcher went out of her way to be agreeable to her back-benchers including those who had voted or even joked against her. Acutely aware of Heath's mistakes, she made concerted efforts to be congenial where he had seemed curmudgeonly. She worked hard at remembering the names of even her obscurest colleagues, often asking after their wives and children.

This was not natural territory to her, but her solicitousness was appreciated. Several MPs, when they were having family or health problems, were touched to be sent handwritten notes from her. I received two such letters when I was in hospital with a typhoid infection for eight weeks. These personal kindnesses helped her to keep the party steady during those early months when she was not making much headway as Leader of the Opposition across the floor of the House of Commons.

In the gladiatorial combat of Prime Minister's Questions, quick repartee, a ready wit and a feel for the mood of the House are vital skills for dominating the frequently boisterous atmosphere. Despite her earlier successes in parliamentary debates, Margaret Thatcher often lacked those skills while Leader of the Opposition. Time and again her troops left the chamber after PMQs feeling deflated. I recall one such down moment in the tea room when Cranley Onslow, later to become Chairman of the 1922 Committee, observed, 'Hasn't quite got the pitch of the wicket yet, has she?' To which Nicholas Budgen replied, 'It's the pitch of her voice that's more worrying'.[10]

Her shrill voice was a problem. She overcame it by taking lessons from a speech therapist recommended by Gordon Reece who taught her breathing techniques. These and the repeated chanting of the mysterious word 'Ingakokka' deepened her tones. Reece also tutored her for television appearances with visual recommendations such as, 'Avoid lots of jewellery near the face . . . Watch out for background colours which clash with your outfit.'[11]

But while her style in the media improved, the substance of her speeches in the House of Commons did not. Some of her earliest parliamentary performances in her new role were a near disaster.

On 22 May 1975 she moved an opposition motion condemning the government's failure to curb the accelerating rate of inflation. As this was 21.7 per cent and rising, her target should have been easy to hit. Instead, she delivered a turgid recital of statistics, which bored the House and offered no alternative policies. Harold Wilson had no trouble running rings round her. She had a bad press for the speech. The *Sunday Times* described it as 'a disappointing flop . . . it lacked fizz and originality and her voice had its usual garden-party quality'.[12]

The combination of disappointing parliamentary performances and a divided shadow cabinet meant that Margaret Thatcher's base of support in Westminster looked insecure. Willie Whitelaw loyally deflected the rumblings of criticism, but even he became affronted from time to time by her confrontational methods of man-management. One such flashpoint in the early weeks of her leadership was the sudden dismissal of the Director General of Central Office, Michael Wolff.

This row was pointless and easily avoidable. Michael Wolff was a decent and thoughtful Conservative Party administrator who had previously been a *Telegraph* leader writer and chief researcher to Randolph Churchill for the first two volumes of his mammoth filial biography of Sir Winston. The only fault in Wolff was that he had been appointed to the top job at Central Office by Ted Heath. For this reason alone Margaret Thatcher sacked him.

What she did not seem to know was that in the wiring of the Conservative establishment, Michael Wolff and his wife Rosemary belonged to a network of powerful friends. None of them would have quarrelled with the leader's right to have her own man at the head of the party's administration. But there are right and wrong ways of making such changes. Instead of easing Wolff out, or changing his responsibilities, she fired him with a summary brutality that made her look spiteful. That was the view of Jim Prior who nearly resigned over the issue.

Also protesting vigorously on Wolff's behalf were Willie Whitelaw, Peter Carrington, Ian Gilmour and Geoffrey Howe. In retrospect, the fuss looked like a storm in a tea-cup, but at the time it was a serious revolt. On the night of the firing, I recall an incandescent Jim Prior banging the wood panels on the walls of the division lobby and refusing to vote for an opposition motion on the Finance Bill as he said over and over again, 'Vindictive and nasty! Vindictive and nasty!'[13]

Perhaps *The Times* was right to describe Michael Wolff's dismissal as 'the act of a down-right fool'.[14] It was a misjudgement on Margaret Thatcher's part to have stirred up major ill feeling in her shadow cabinet over a minor personality issue. It was an early warning sign that the way she handled people could make her seem an unpleasant character.

By contrast, she was running a happy ship in her private office. She inherited one private secretary from Ted Heath, Caroline Stephens, who organised her diary and became her closest and most trusted aide for the next fifteen years. Another key figure was her constituency secretary, Alison Ward. She looked after the personal aspects of Margaret Thatcher's life, such as hair appointments, clothes and liaison with her family. From the *Daily Telegraph* came twenty-five-year-old Richard Ryder, an exceptionally talented writer and administrator.* He gradually emerged as the Leader of the Opposition's *de facto* chief of staff, his influence waxing as Airey Neave's waned. Richard Ryder and Caroline Stephens married in 1981 after an office romance that was discreetly encouraged by their boss. Margaret Thatcher in the role of Cupid sounds unlikely casting, but in this matchmaking endeavour her arrows found their mark.

---

* Richard Ryder (1949–), Political Secretary to the Leader of the Opposition, 1975–1979; Political Secretary to Prime Minister, 1979–1981; married Prime Minister's diary secretary, Caroline Stephens, 1981; Conservative MP for Mid Norfolk, 1983–1997. Created Lord Ryder of Wensum, 1997.

This inner team formed a genuine affection for the leader they served so well. They noticed one or two interesting features of her evolving character. Some of these qualities became well known in her Downing Street years, while others never quite emerged in full view yet remained a central part of Margaret Thatcher's personality.

First, she was a good listener in one-on-one meetings when she wanted to learn something, but a poor one in large groups where she wanted to get her way. The shadow cabinet was the uneasiest of these wider gatherings, partly because she talked too much herself and paid too little attention to the views of her colleagues.

Second, she could be surprisingly disorganised in her allocation of priorities and time. She was a poor delegator of tasks, and over-generous in the attention she paid to those who agreed with her. She had her early court favourites, such as Alfred Sherman from the CPS, the Soviet expert Robert Conquest and the former Labour MP turned *News of the World* columnist Woodrow Wyatt.

Third, beneath her outer carapace of simple certainties and self-belief there lay an inner level of insecurity and vulnerability. Some of her insecurities were social. On her way out to a dinner party given by Lord and Lady Carrington, she anxiously asked her secretary Caroline Stephens, 'Do you think I should wear white gloves?'[15]

She had other sartorial qualms and questions before attending events at which members of the royal family would be present. She was helped with some of these problems by advice from Lady Tilney, the wife of the Conservative MP for Liverpool Wavertree, Sir John Tilney.* However helpful that advice was, Margaret Thatcher, the Grantham dressmaker's daughter, always had a good dress sense of her own. As Guinevere Tilney told her friends, 'Margaret has an instinctive flair for colours and quality designs'.[16]

Another area of insecurity was intellectual inadequacy. Margaret Thatcher felt she had a good brain but not a great mind. This humility gave her an

---

* There was a Grantham connection in this relationship. Sir John Tilney's sister, Susan Agnes Rhodes Tilney (1897–1964) married Colonel Henry Brace DSO MC, 15th Hussars. They lived in Grantham. He was Deputy Lieutenant of Lincolnshire in 1944. Mrs Brace served on the Grantham town council with Alfred Roberts and knew Margaret Thatcher as a child. She wrote to Conservative Central Office in February 1949 recommending Margaret as the prospective Conservative candidate for Dartford.

exaggerated respect for exceptionally clever colleagues such as Keith Joseph and Ian Gilmour. Realising that she had to live off other people's ideas, she was constantly seeking reassurance from intellectuals who would provide her with the philosophical fire-power she needed to reinforce her own instincts.

As for her vulnerabilities, she rarely showed them outside her inner circle of core aides. She could be hurt by personalised criticism, by family worries, by condescension from arrogant parliamentarians and by rejection from people she wanted to be on her side of the argument but who were not. She showed her bruised feelings in a revealing interview with *Woman's World* in September 1978:

> 'There are times when I get home at night and everything has got on top of me when I shed a few tears, silently, alone.' She says she is a very emotional person. 'I have never known a person to be insensitive about things which are wounding and hurtful and I am no exception.'[17]

These weaker aspects of Margaret Thatcher's personality made her a gentler and more attractive figure to the handful of people around her who were in the know. Because her leadership of the opposition was so insecure in the early days, the chinks in her armour were visible to insiders. The impregnable, invincible Iron Lady was a character who had yet to make her appearance, not only in the pages of the *Red Star* newspaper (which invented the nickname in 1976), but also on the stage of British politics. To many waiting in the wings, she was still thought of as an interim leader who might not last the course.

Although her speeches were not going down well at Westminster, she was having more of an impact in the country. But even to the most adoring of Tory audiences she was repeating old formulas in new words. There was no ideological revolution of fresh ideas and new politics which eventually emerged as Thatcherism. She promised to fight socialist extremism, to champion thrifty self-reliance and to create wealth before it was distributed. The only novelty in such views was that they were being proclaimed by a leader who was a woman. If she had a more radical agenda in those early days, it was almost invisible.

She had one or two campaigning successes. On her first visit to Scotland she was given an enthusiastic welcome by some of the largest crowds ever seen in the centre of Edinburgh. In South London she broke the then convention that party leaders did not campaign in by-elections when she came down to support the Conservative candidate, Peter Bottomley, in West Woolwich. When he won the seat in June 1975 by overturning a Labour majority of 3,500 it was the first electoral success the party had achieved for two years. Margaret Thatcher was so excited by this first sign of progress under her leadership that she gave a vigorous 'V' for victory sign to the media. To their amusement, she put her two fingers up the wrong way round. Even after her mistake was explained to her, she had difficulty in understanding why she had made an obscene gesture.

Despite the Woolwich by-election reducing the government's overall majority from four to three, inside 10 Downing Street there was a growing confidence that the novice Leader of the Opposition was proving no match for the experienced Prime Minister. Harold Wilson's principal briefer for Prime Minister's Questions was Bernard Donoughue. He recalled:

> We couldn't believe our luck. At first Harold was quite nervous about having to face a new Tory leader. He resented Heath's departure, saying, 'I've watched that man for ten years, and I know every move he's going to make. Now I've got to learn the whole thing over again'. But after a few months of dealing with Margaret he knew she couldn't lay a glove on him. He was too wily and she was too wooden. She just kept reading out prepared questions, which weren't holding the House.[18]

Her lack of spontaneity at the despatch box was causing a slow burn of discontent on the back benches behind her. The murmurings were increasing. Questions ranging from 'Have we made a terrible mistake?' to 'How can we help her to do better?'[19] kept being asked among Tory MPs.

As one symptom of these troubled times I recall an anxious discussion at the summer meeting of the Alf Bates club. This was a dining group of Conservative colleagues who had been elected to the House in 1974. It was organised by Peter Morrison, who humorously named the club after a long-haired Labour MP whose left-wing views had particularly riled him. Besides Peter and myself, its members included Michael Spicer, Sir George Young, Alan Clark, Alastair Goodlad, Tim Renton, Leon Brittan, John Moore and several others. The question that we discussed at the end of July 1975 was, 'Will the lady last?'

On the whole, we thought she would, at least for a while. But there was no ringing endorsement of our leader except from her uber-loyalists, Morrison and Moore. All of us wanted her to succeed, yet there was hanging in the air a worried feeling that she might prove to be only a temporary occupant of her position. As we dispersed for the long summer recess of 1975, the trumpets for Margaret Thatcher were giving an uncertain sound.

PERSONAL GLIMPSES

In the summer of 1976, I began dating Carol Thatcher. Our relationship became serious, lasting for over three years. It was not greeted with unqualified enthusiasm by the Leader of the Opposition, aka 'Mum'. She advised her twenty-two-year-old daughter to be careful of an involvement with the thirty-three-year-old bachelor MP for Thanet East. This warning was given after she had seen us talking rather too intensely over a jug of Pimm's at a summer drinks party hosted by John Moore and his wife Sheila, at their home in Wimbledon.

Romancing the boss's daughter was always likely to be a risky journey, but young love is oblivious to risk. What Stendhal calls *L'égoisme à deux* takes no notice of warnings or chilly noises of parental disapproval. Carol and I pressed on regardless. After a few months there was a thaw in the temperature, and I was invited to Sunday lunch at Scotney Castle, a National Trust property in Kent where Margaret and Denis Thatcher rented a flat.

My welcome was mixed. Denis was characteristically genial, asking knowledgeable questions about 'my patch', his phrase for my constituency. Atlas sold a lot of paint in Ramsgate to customers I knew, so that was a point of conversation. By contrast, Mark was in a sulk, so made no conversation at all. Carol was cross with her brother. Ignoring these sibling tensions, Margaret wanted to talk shop. This meant a serious conversation about the Middle East, 'a subject on which I seem to remember you think I don't know very much about', she said with a glare rather than a twinkle in her eye. She had just come back from a visit there, thankfully not to Sinai but to Damascus and Cairo.

After a monologue on the politics of the region, she mentioned that after her meeting with the Syrian President, Hafez al-Assad, his Ambassador, Adnan Omran, had presented her with an elaborately jewelled insignia in Islamic calligraphy. 'There it is', she said, pointing to a golden frame hanging above the mantelpiece in the dining room. 'Is your Arabic good enough to tell me what it says?' Perhaps unfortunately, my limited linguistic skills were equal to this task. 'It says: "There is only one God and his name is Allah".'

'Oh my goodness!' said Margaret, looking flustered, evidently unaware that she had been exhibiting the first teaching of the Koran on her wall. 'Just as well we didn't ask the padre to lunch', joked Denis.

'Or the constituents from Finchley', I added in the same bantering tone. This was supposed to be a light-hearted reference to the high percentage of Jewish voters in her Finchley electorate. Margaret was not amused. Fixing me with a gimlet stare, she said in a reproving tone, 'I will invite anyone I like to lunch here'.

Despite my *faux pas*, I enjoyed this and other visits to Scotney. Denis and Carol were warm and endearing characters. Neither adjective seemed appropriate for Margaret, yet she was attractive because of her looks and her energy. She was an excellent if monomaniac hostess, insisting on doing all the wine pouring, cooking and washing up herself, interspersed with imperious commands to the onlookers such as, 'Watch out!', 'Move your elbows, dear!', 'Look sharp!', 'Out of the way!' and 'Drink up!'

Her specialities were Sunday roasts and coronation chicken. She bustled around the kitchen at high speed like a television chef on fast forward. With the same acceleration, she cooked breakfast every morning for Denis, who could get pernickety if his bacon was not grilled in a certain way.

My perception of life *chez* Thatcher was that it was never dull but never relaxed. Even when politics were not being discussed, intensity ruled. Super-woman ran her home super-efficiently. She bossed her family around a great deal, but none of them seemed particularly responsive to her commands. Denis withdrew behind the sports pages of the *Daily Telegraph*. Carol withdrew from the line of fire of too much maternal criticism. Mark wanted too much maternal attention. Dysfunctionality ruled. Everything in their lives was subordinated to the challenges of being Leader of the Opposition. Margaret was permanently as taut as a piano wire. She seemed admirable, but abnormal. I was probably at fault too, for being excessively on edge.

As an occasional insider to Thatcher family life, I sometimes saw unexpected sides to the outwardly tough matriarch. Three worth mentioning were glimpses of her frugality, vulnerability and maternal affection.

The frugality appeared on an evening when I bought four tickets for a performance at the National Theatre of Noël Coward's *Blithe Spirit*. She had somehow assumed that I had been able to get these tickets as free house seats for Denis and herself, because my sister Maria Aitken was in the cast playing the lead role of Elvira. When Carol corrected this impression during the evening, Margaret declared, 'I insist on going halves with you'. I brushed this offer aside, and despite her not-so-mild protests I refused to tell her what the cost of the tickets had been. She was not so easily thwarted. The next day, in my pigeonhole at the Members' Lobby, she sent me a blank cheque signed 'Margaret H Thatcher'. She became cross with me after discovering from her bank statement that I never filled it in or cashed it.

The vulnerability was well hidden, but it was there. One night, after an 11.30 p.m. vote in the House, I dropped Carol home at Flood Street. Margaret was on her own in the sitting room reading some papers. I put my head round the door to say goodnight, and saw that she was red-eyed, visibly upset. So I asked what was the matter. 'Nothing really', she sniffed. 'One of our colleagues was unbelievably unpleasant to me in the division lobby . . . said I was wrecking the party . . . ' This seemed such an unlikely cause of tears that I treated it rather insouciantly. 'He was probably pissed', I said. 'Don't let it get to you.' 'I hurt too, you know', she said, getting up and leaving the room. It was the first sign to me that the Iron Lady had a soft centre.

As for maternal affection, I had observed early on in my relationship with Carol that the usual outward signs of mother–daughter tenderness were rare. However, there was an inner bond of some strength as the following story of a skiing weekend illustrated.

In the winter of 1978 Carol was given a ten-day holiday in the Swiss resort of Verbier by her parents. I planned to come and join her there for a long week-end in the middle of it. Because of problems with airline seat availability at the height of the skiing season, my travel plans only worked if I flew back to London on a Monday evening flight from Geneva. Unfortunately, after the tickets had been bought, this particular Monday turned out to be a date unexpectedly chosen by the opposition for some contentious parliamentary voting. It required all Conservative MPs to be present in the House on a running three-line whip from 3.30 p.m. onwards. As I could not be on the ski slopes and in the division lobbies at the same time, and as no alternative flights were available, my week-end with Carol in Verbier had to be cancelled, to our great disappointment.

Although I accepted the disappointment, Carol in Verbier did not. Unknown to me, she telephoned her mother with a wail of protest about the unfairness of the opposition's three-line whip and its wrecking effects on our romantic weekend. Margaret's heart evidently melted. A cheerful Carol came on the line with the announcement, 'Mum says she can change the voting for Monday'. 'That's impossible', I replied. I was wrong. For at the last minute the opposition day business was switched and the three-line whip was miraculously dropped. Carol and I had a wonderful weekend together in the joys of the Alps.

The day after my return I was back in the division lobbies of the House of Commons when I saw the Leader of the Opposition a few feet away from me. I went over and started to say thank you for her amazing favour in re-arranging the parliamentary business. 'Sshh!' she said, putting a finger to her lips and giving me a theatrical wink. 'Did you two have fun?' 'Great fun', I replied. 'Come and tell me about it, then.'

Five minutes later I was sitting in an armchair drinking Scotch with Margaret Thatcher in the Leader of the Opposition's office. Kicking off her shoes, she brushed aside my thanks by saying that her Chief Whip, Humphrey Atkins, had wanted to change the opposition's voting plans anyway. Then she wanted to know everything about Verbier, asking me about snow conditions, ski runs, restaurants, the local fondue and whether Carol had any other friends or skiing companions. 'I get so worried about Carol being out there all on her own', she explained in an anxious voice. Even more poignantly, as I was leaving her office Margaret said, 'You won't tell Carol that I was worrying about her, will you? She will think I am being overbearing.'

The relationship between Mark and his mother was over-indulgent. Margaret was constantly fussing about her son's health, his failure to pass his accountancy exams and his perilous finances. She paid off his overdraft at least twice in the mid-1970s. She worried about his personal safety when driving motor-cars long before the 1982 episode of him getting temporarily lost in the Sahara on a rally. In 1979, she became tearful when late at night Mark had not returned from a day on the test-driving track of the Williams Formula One team. Margaret was beside herself, getting me to call my friend Frank Williams to make sure that Mark had not been injured.

I liked what I saw of Margaret as a mother and Denis as a father. Some of my best glimpses of them were at Scotney Castle, which had beautiful grounds. Looking out of the window one morning, I saw Margaret and Denis strolling around the garden holding hands. It struck me that this was the first time I had seen any two members of the family in warm human contact. They were not a tactile foursome. Hugs, cuddles and kisses never seemed to be on their agenda. Years later I asked Mark if my impression was correct. 'Yes,' he said, 'Mum was not in the slightest bit tactile. But she communicated her love by the way she looked at you.'[20]

For all such loving glances, good communications within the family deteriorated in quantity and quality once Margaret Thatcher became Leader of the Opposition. She was such a totally absorbed public figure that there was little or no time for private relaxation, even with her nearest and dearest. Did she have any true friend in whom she confided and trusted, apart from Denis? I suspected not. Her shadow cabinet colleagues may have been the recipients of political confidences, but there was no indication that she showed them any personal intimacy or even warmth. The same was true of her office team. With the possible exception of Cynthia Crawford ('Crawfie'), who later became something of a confidante through her feminine skills as a PA and dresser, Margaret Thatcher's inner circle of staffers were professionally but not personally close to her.

Endearingly, she had a great appreciation for the virtue of loyalty. Anyone who gave it to her received it back abundantly, particularly if they were going through a bad patch. When her former PPS, Fergus Montgomery MP, was accused of shoplifting, Margaret Thatcher sought him out on the day after he was charged and said: 'Fergus, you stay beside me all the time in the House today. I want everyone to see that I know you are innocent.'*[21]

A more colourful recipient of Margaret Thatcher's loyalty was a remarkable parliamentary character known as 'The one-armed bandit'. He was William Rees-Davies QC MP, whose constituency of Thanet West adjoined mine.

Billy was a flamboyant original. In his heyday he had been a fast bowler in county cricket, a war hero who had lost an arm on the battlefield, a big-time gambler and a controversial criminal barrister. During the late 1970s, he managed to get himself into a series of well-publicised scrapes. His troubles included a police scandal, an unpaid debts controversy, a row with his tenants

---

* On 4 April 1977, Fergus Montgomery was charged with stealing two books from the Army & Navy Stores in Victoria. He was convicted and fined £70. He appealed and in December had his conviction overturned.

over bed bugs in his house in Greece and a drink-driving charge. He was reprimanded by a judge for being at the races when he should have been in court. There were problems within his constituency association, which threatened to de-select him. Some of his local difficulties stemmed from his vociferous opposition to Ted Heath, a fellow resident of Thanet.

Perhaps because of his anti-Heath feelings, Billy Rees-Davies became one of the earliest and staunchest supporters of Margaret Thatcher. He was not exactly her cup of tea, but because of his enthusiasm for backing her as a leadership candidate, she reciprocated his loyalty. So when de-selection rumours were threatening to end his career, Billy asked for, and received, the leader's personal help.

The circumstances in which the help was given were hilarious. Billy hosted a New Year's Eve party at his country house at Monkton-in-Thanet. Apart from Margaret and Denis Thatcher and myself, the guest list consisted of the entire executive of the Thanet West Conservative Association. As the clock ticked towards midnight, the disgruntled anti-Billy faction, pacified by the presence of the party leader, began to express the view that their Member of Parliament was perhaps not such a bad chap after all. The leader strongly agreed. Champagne flowed. Good-will increased.

At about 11.45 p.m., Billy rang the ship's bell that stood in the hall of his house, and called on the Chairman of the Thanet West Conservative Association, Councillor Harry Anish, to say a few words. The Chairman expressed the opinion that in these festive circumstances, with the Leader of the Conservative Party being in attendance, it might be appropriate to let bygones be bygones, and to pass a vote of confidence in our Member, wishing him and our leader a Happy New Year. 'Yes please', said Margaret Thatcher loudly. The vote was immediately carried by acclamation. We all sang, 'For he's a jolly good fellow' and then 'For *she's* a jolly good fellow', until the clock struck twelve and it was time for 'Auld Lang Syne'.

It must have been one of the most unusual and unconstitutional constituency association meetings in the history of the Conservative Party, but it did the trick. There was no more talk of de-selection, and Billy Rees-Davies duly survived for another Parliament as the Member for Thanet West.

As Margaret Thatcher departed into the night for her drive across Kent back to Scotney, someone asked her what she thought of Thanet's two Members of Parliament. 'They are both excellent MPs – with unusual talents',[22] was her verdict. Whatever she really felt, she had shown loyalty to a friend under pressure, and been marvellously effective with the rank and file members of the Conservative Party.

REFLECTION

It was easy to underestimate Margaret Thatcher during the early stages of her leadership of the opposition.

Although she had the highest constitutional respect for Parliament, she was never really comfortable as a parliamentarian. She had no feel, let alone love, for the House of Commons. She was impatient with its atmospherics, and with many of its Honourable Members. She had her occasional one-off successes at the despatch box, but she did not instinctively go with the flow of the House or tune into its moods. This was the cause of her continuous underperforming in the gladiatorial contests of Prime Minister's Questions. She was over-prepared, and lacking in the spontaneous cut and thrust that is essential for success at PMQs. 'Too bandbox' was the view of Barbara Castle, watching Margaret Thatcher with some degree of feminist sympathy from the Labour front bench. 'When finally she . . . fires her shaft, it never completely misses, but is never (or very, very rarely) deadly.'[23]

This same weakness of not being in command of her party in Parliament applied to her lack of dominance at meetings of the shadow cabinet. 'The atmosphere was often uneasy because Margaret was too careful and not strong enough to take on the old guard', recalled John Nott, who was one of the few kindred spirits she promoted to her top team. 'Most of the Pyms, Priors, Carringtons, Gilmours and their ilk believed she would fail, and that sanity would return in the form of a consensus-minded replacement.'[24]

This feeling that Margaret Thatcher was merely an interim leader prevailed in many other metropolitan quarters. The intellectual elite in the Conservative Research Department, headed in 1975 by Chris Patten, referred to her as 'Hilda'. Snobbery about her voice and her clothes, as well as her middle name, were among the many condescensions she had to bear. Julian Critchley suggested that she should be written to as 'The Leader of the Opposition, c/o Dickins & Jones'.[25]

Yet at the same time as the old guard, the metropolitan elite and the social snobs in the Tory party were turning up their noses at Margaret Thatcher, a much larger swathe of public opinion was warming to her. Her unique status as the first woman party leader in any Western democracy gave her an aura of interest and charisma that few male politicians could match. She used it to communicate her vote-winning potential not in the usual currency of specific promises, but by proclaiming her personal values and beliefs.

There were signs from polls and by-election results that Middle England liked what it saw in this side of Margaret Thatcher. A large section of the electorate also knew in its heart of hearts that something must be done to halt the slow decline of their country, and to break the stranglehold of union power. But did the new Tory leader have the strength and the support to tackle these enormous problems?

On such crucial questions the national jury was undecided. People disliked Harold Wilson's government. But the leap from his cynicism to Margaret Thatcher's certainties was a step too far, at least in the mid-term of a Parliament that looked as though it could muddle on for most of the next five years.

There were three factors running in Margaret Thatcher's favour. The first was her novelty. The second was her ability to communicate impressively in big set speeches and on television. The third was her interest in new ideas and solutions. Even with these advantages, she continued to be thwarted by her inability to shine in Parliament. Her apparent failure in this arena worsened with the arrival of a new Labour leader, James Callaghan. He was surprisingly effective as a Prime Minister who for many months ran rings round an inexperienced Leader of the Opposition.

Despite a hairline majority and a perilous inheritance of insecurity in most of the important votes in the House of Commons, Jim Callaghan managed to keep Margaret Thatcher at bay for three frustrating years. She did not lead her party in Parliament well during this fragile period, until the 'winter of discontent' changed the atmosphere.

12

Three frustrating years

PARTY CONFERENCES AND FOREIGN VISITS

In the world beyond the House of Commons, Margaret Thatcher performed better as the new Leader of the Opposition. She was consistently effective with the faithful at constituency rallies and regional gatherings. Although this part of politics is the equivalent of preaching to the choir, she did it well. Indeed, the earliest sign that she might have star quality as a national leader came at her first party conference. In October 1975 at the Blackpool Winter Gardens, over four thousand delegates (the best crowd since 1963) came to inspect the leader they had not expected to be chosen. Even by the sceptical standards of the media commentators she was a hit.

She had vision and humour in her text. Its preparation was an agony but its reception was a triumph. The opening was endearingly humble as she recalled coming to her first conference in 1946 when Winston Churchill was leader. She moved briskly through tributes to all her predecessors including Ted Heath, 'Who successfully led the party to victory in 1970 and brilliantly led the nation into Europe in 1973'.[1] This was generous, considering Heath had refused to attend a reconciliation meeting organised by Willie Whitelaw two nights earlier in the Imperial Hotel. Her unreciprocated graciousness brought the audience to its feet, many expecting at least a handshake from the ex-leader sitting a few feet away from her on the platform. But Heath remained motionless and expressionless as a sphinx. The coldness of his snub increased the warmth for her as she developed her themes of economics and personal freedom.

> Let me give you my vision. A man's right to work as he will to spend what he earns to own property to have the State as servant and not as master these are the British

inheritance. They are the essence of a free economy. And on that freedom all our other freedoms depend.

Her knockabout moments went down well too with an amusing analogy likening the Labour Party to a pub which was running out of mild beer: 'If someone doesn't do something soon, all that's left will be bitter. And all that's bitter will be Left.'

After emphasising the importance of wealth creation in order to spend money on the sick and handicapped, and the primacy of law and order, she boldly upheld the right to be unequal in economic and personal development. Her peroration was the philosophy of her Grantham upbringing writ large:

> I have tried to tell you something of my personal vision, my belief in the standards on which this nation was greatly built, on which it greatly thrived, and from which in recent years it has greatly fallen away. We are coming, I think, to yet another turning point in our long history. We can go on as we have been going and continue down. Or we can stop – and with a decisive act of will we can say 'Enough!'[2]

In those days a Tory conference always gave a rapturous ovation to the closing speech from the leader, but this acclaim was explosive in its enthusiasm. The reason for such excitement was partly down to her ability to express her own and the party's frustrations over a failed socialist economy in which inflation had just reached the rate of 26.9 per cent. More importantly, Margaret Thatcher tapped into deep wells of instinctive Tory beliefs with her championship of self-reliance, a smaller state, and the economic right to be better rewarded for hard work and effort.

I recall the high emotions her speech produced in one of my constituency delegates from Thanet East. He was David Pettit, a greengrocer from Ramsgate. As we walked away from the Winter Gardens he hopped from one leg to the other and twisted himself around in dance-steps of delight, saying over and over again: 'She spoke for me! She spoke for the man in the street! She spoke for my customers!' Alfred Roberts would have been too restrained to do the dance, but he would surely have enthused over the speech for the same reasons as the greengrocer from Ramsgate. Middle England had found a voice. As the *Daily Mail* commented in its leader the following day: 'If this is "lurching to the Right", as her critics claim, 90 per cent of the population lurched that way long ago.'[3]

The speech had been crafted by several wordsmiths but she was the only one who counted since she completely dominated the agonising process of its creation. The most exotic recruit to her speech-writing team was the playwright Ronald Millar.* He was summoned to Blackpool at short notice by Gordon Reece with the brief to 'make the whole text flow along', as Margaret Thatcher put it.[4] This was no mean task since she herself was constantly altering its flow.

In his amusing autobiography *A View from the Wings*, Millar recaptured the scene: a combination of the neurotic, the heroic and the comic, as he and his fellow writers Chris Patten and Adam Ridley wrote and rewrote into the small hours of the morning. The leader of the party attacked and changed their draft pages, which were spread out on tables, chairs and even over the carpet across the suite. An added complication was that since Margaret Thatcher did not do humour, the jokes that Millar wrote for her had to be explained and rehearsed in laborious detail. In this speech the line about mild and bitter beer took a lot of polishing, since she had never tasted either. The exhausting process went on until ten past five when Denis came in and ordered his wife to bed. It was the first illustration of a much-repeated saying among her inner circle: 'No one ever writes a speech *for* Margaret Thatcher. They write it *with* her.'[5]

Just before the speech started a highly nervous Margaret Thatcher said to Ronnie Millar, 'I wish it was over'. He thought: 'She looked young and vulnerable and pretty and scared. I felt suddenly protective.'[6]

When it was finished she was at first uplifted by the acclamation. But two hours later she plunged herself into the depths of insecurity about whether she could repeat the performance at next year's conference. 'Brighton could be the most dreadful anti-climax', she fretted.[7]

According to Millar:

This was too much for Denis. 'My God, woman, you've just had a bloody great triumph and here you are worrying yourself sick about next year! I'll get the others, shall I? Then

---

* Ronald Millar was writing speeches for Ted Heath when he met Margaret Thatcher for the first time at the Carlton Club in 1972. She was at the centre of the 'milk snatcher' row and the miners were on strike. Dining by candlelight during a power cut, Millar recalled, 'She looked radiant and ridiculously young' (Ronald Millar, *A View from the Wings*, p. 219).

you can settle down for another all-night session. I mean, obviously, there's no time to be lost . . .' I slipped away. So long as she had this man around she was going to be all right.[8]

Further away from home, Margaret Thatcher delivered speeches of quality in New York, Washington, Zurich and Hanover. These visits broadened her experience of foreign policy as she started to meet international leaders of the day including Presidents Gerald Ford and Jimmy Carter, French Prime Minister Jacques Chirac and Helmut Kohl, future Chancellor of West Germany. All of them seemed fascinated to meet this new phenomenon among Western democracies, a potential woman prime minister, but not all were impressed.

Jimmy Carter, who normally declined to meet opposition leaders, welcomed her for a forty-five minute discourse in the Oval Office, but was surprised when she used two-thirds of it to argue what a mistake he was making with his efforts to negotiate a nuclear test ban treaty.

One early American visitor to London was won over by the Thatcher energy and vision. He was US Secretary of State Dr Henry Kissinger, who breakfasted with her at Claridge's a week after she had won the leadership election. He had been trying to meet her since 1972, on the recommendation of his wife Nancy.

Connecting for the first time on 18 February 1975, Kissinger was impressed by Margaret Thatcher's ardent support for the 'special relationship' and her staunch anti-communism. She asked him what he thought was the major problem facing the world now that the Vietnam War was over. He mentioned the Latin American debt crisis. 'Why is that a problem?' she asked. 'You borrow money. You have to pay it back.'[9] She may have seemed simplistic in some of her opinions, but Kissinger saw the point of her, ahead of any other world statesman.

He sat down to breakfast with her expecting to be underwhelmed, since the night before one or two of his Tory grandee friends had filled him up with their views on Margaret Thatcher which were 'distinctly jaundiced'.[10] But the US Secretary of State was impressed by her forthright personality. Even so he retained doubts, planted by his UK establishment friends, about her electability. Three months after the Claridge's meeting Kissinger advised President Gerald Ford, 'I don't think Margaret Thatcher will last'.[11] This view of the Leader of the Opposition's prospects evidently improved for during the years 1976–1978 Kissinger organised dinner parties in honour of Margaret Thatcher every time she came to Washington. His guests were luminaries of the foreign-policy establishment, such as Senators Sam Nunn and Richard Lugar; senior White House aides; editors from *Time, Newsweek* and the *New York Times*; Kay Graham, the owner of the *Washington Post*; and the Chief Justice of the United States Supreme Court, Warren Earl Burger.

One of the reasons why Henry and Nancy Kissinger went out of their way to be so hospitable was that they were irritated on her behalf by the lack of hospitality extended to her by the British Ambassador to Washington, Peter Jay. This criticism may have been misplaced. Jay seems to have done his best to be helpful on Margaret Thatcher's visits to Washington. But if there was a certain coolness between the Ambassador and the Leader of the Opposition, it was understandable. For Peter Jay was a political appointee with unusually close connections to the Labour government. His father-in-law, James Callaghan, was the new Prime Minister. He presented a formidable obstacle to Margaret Thatcher's progress.

OUTMANOEUVRED BY JAMES CALLAGHAN

It might have been predicted that the unexpected retirement of Harold Wilson in March 1976 would have helped Margaret Thatcher. Far from it. Her perform-ances from the despatch box became noticeably worse as she went head to head with James Callaghan.

She got off to a bad start on the day Wilson announced his departure. It was an occasion when the traditions of the House expected the Leader of the Opposition to join graciously in the tributes to the retiring Prime Minister. Instead, she completely misread the mood and slipped into partisan jibes demanding an immediate election. It was a mistake that brought frowns from her own side and protests from Labour. The word in the tea room afterwards was that she had showed no feel for Parliament.

This word increased as she lost clash after clash with Callaghan. His technique was to don the mantle of a wise elder statesman brushing aside the clamourings of an over-eager challenger. His condescension infuriated her. 'I am sure that one day the right hon. Lady will understand these things a little better', was his patronising put-down when she tried to interrogate him about government borrowing.[12]

As Callaghan's authority in the House increased, she had greater difficulty in penetrating his armour. On one occasion she attacked him for his 'avuncular flannel', but he genially brushed her aside: 'I have often thought of the right hon. Lady in many ways, but never as my niece.'[13]

Although Callaghan's flannelling was surprisingly successful, the Labour government hit a dangerous rock in March 1977. The devolution issue turned sour when it lost the support of Welsh and Scottish Nationalist MPs. This caused parliamentary chaos for a while. Margaret Thatcher tabled a motion of no confidence. But Callaghan was able to cobble up a deal with the Liberals. Some Conservative back-benchers thought their leader should have done the same. She was adamantly opposed to the thought, saying privately, 'never, but never, would I consider a coalition from which could only come irresolute and debilitating government'.[14]

Callaghan's deal, later called the Lib–Lab pact, saved his government and enabled him to defeat the opposition's motion with some ease. He was helped by Margaret Thatcher's opening speech in the debate, which by her own admission was one of the worst she ever made. It produced many negative reactions. I remember the grimaces and cringes on our back benches as she faltered through her mediocre script.

'They'll be passing a no confidence motion on *us* after this', muttered the MP for Canterbury, David Crouch, amidst the half-hearted 'hear, hears' when Mrs Thatcher resumed her seat.[15]

In the Distinguished Strangers' Gallery an eminent Washington columnist Joseph Alsop was listening to the debate. I had tea with him afterwards in the Pugin Room. 'I came because I heard she was the great white hope', drawled Alsop. 'I'm going away thinking she's not up to it.'[16]

Joe Alsop's opinion was becoming the received wisdom in sceptical Tory circles. Edward du Cann, keeping his ear to the ground among Conservative MPs, recalled 'continuous and considerable sniping against Margaret by a wide spectrum of the colleagues . . . a recurring theme among several of them was "we've made a mistake: how can we undo it?"'[17]

One way of undoing it, which received a surprising amount of support, was the notion of a government of national unity. This had been floated first by Ted Heath when he was sinking towards defeat in October 1974. In the 1976–1978 period it was revived by various eminent business leaders, by *The Times* and even by Harold Macmillan, who broke thirteen years of ex-prime ministerial silence. Margaret Thatcher went to see him a few days later 'to see what he really thought'.[18] Their meeting was not a great success. She called it 'pleasantly inconclusive'. He returned from it to Chatsworth, where his hostess the Duchess of Devonshire asked him, 'Did you talk?' 'No, she did', was Macmillan's tart response.[19]

The general populace, however, did appear ready to listen to Margaret Thatcher's message. She continued her practice of campaigning alongside the Conservative candidate in by-elections, and enjoyed a string of successes as large Labour majorities were overturned in seats as diverse as Walsall North, Workington, Stetchford and Ashfield. Her arguments for reining back public spending were gaining ground, apparently even within the Labour government. For the Chancellor, Denis Healey, under pressure from the International Monetary Fund (IMF) had to implement a stringent programme of expenditure cuts, while Jim Callaghan bravely told his party conference that governments could no longer spend their way out of a recession.

The feeling that the Conservatives were winning the debate, in the country if not in the House of Commons, was confirmed by a succession of encouraging opinion polls. The most favourable of these, which showed a leap in the Tory lead over Labour to a margin of 48–39 per cent, came after Margaret Thatcher made a calculated intervention on the taboo subject of immigration.

Ever since the furore created by Enoch Powell's 'Rivers of Blood' speech in 1968, the rising level of voter concern about immigration numbers had become the 'elephant in the room' of British politics. For nearly ten years there was an uneasy silence from the Tory front bench on race and immigration issues. The Shadow Home Secretary Willie Whitelaw spoke, if at all, on the subject in woolly bromides.

On 27 January 1978, without any consultation with her colleagues, Margaret Thatcher answered a question about immigration on *World in Action* with unusual clarity:

People are really rather afraid that this country might be rather swamped by people with a different culture . . . So, if you want good race relations, you have got to allay people's fears on numbers . . . So, we do have to hold out the prospect of an end to immigration, except of course, for compassionate cases. Therefore we have to look at the numbers who have a right to come in.[20]

Coming two days after an episode of racial violence in Wolverhampton, the emotive word 'swamped' caused excitable reaction. The Chancellor, Denis Healey, accused Margaret Thatcher of 'stirring up the muddy waters of racial prejudice'. The Home Secretary, Merlyn Rees, claimed she was 'making respectable racial hatred'. The Liberal Party leader, David Steel, said that her remarks were 'really quite wicked'.[21] Willie Whitelaw was furious and briefly considered resignation.

But whatever the political elite was saying, the public reacted favourably. The 11 per cent surge to the Tories in the opinion polls, an unexpected win for the Conservative candidate in the Ilford North by-election and other evidence from market research organisations all confirmed that Margaret Thatcher had struck a populist chord. Even though the Conservative Party's policy on immigration hardly changed, it sounded as though its leader wanted a new approach. She had followed her instincts, defied her colleagues and successfully made her point. This was to be a pattern she repeated many more times both in opposition and in government. The element of surprise in Margaret Thatcher's personality was beginning to be appreciated.

NEW POLICIES AND PHILOSOPHIES

During her four years as Leader of the Opposition there was a constant tug of war between two perceptions of Margaret Thatcher. The positive perception was that of a conviction politician who was gradually winning support from the electorate by her courageous openness to new ideas about how to tackle Britain's decline. The negative image of her, ardently promoted by her opponents, portrayed her as the stereotype of a narrow, shrill, suburban right-winger who could never win an election.

This tug of war was not resolved until the 'winter of discontent' in early 1979. In the meantime, the debate about her raged on with peaks and troughs on both sides of the argument.

One of the first peaks, which led to a short-term surge in her support, was her attack on the Soviet Union. This was delivered in two speeches on home Tory territory, to an audience of the faithful in Kensington and Chelsea. Until these broadsides, she had been noticeably cautious in foreign-policy matters. She had dutifully supported NATO and the Anglo-American alliance, while rather less dutifully campaigning for a 'Yes' vote in the 1975 referendum on Britain's membership of the EEC. But when she came out as a critic of Soviet expansion and portrayed herself as a passionate opponent of détente, she ruffled many feathers, not least in her own shadow cabinet.

Margaret Thatcher had a long history, going back to her Grantham days, of attacking communism. In her Chelsea speech, inspired by the writings of Herbert Agar, Alexander Solzhenitsyn and Robert Conquest, she championed the predicament of dissidents in the Soviet Union. She warned that on this subject the Helsinki Agreement consisted of vague words rather than clear action.

In her Kensington speech six months later, she went much further, attacking the Soviet military build-up around the world:

> She's [Russia's] ruled by a dictatorship of patient, far-sighted determined men who are rapidly making their country the foremost naval and military power in the world. They are not doing this solely for the sake of self-defence. A huge land-locked country like Russia does not need to build the most powerful navy in the world just to guard its own frontiers. No. The Russians are bent on world dominance, and they are rapidly acquiring the means to become the most powerful imperial nation the world has seen. . . . The men in the Soviet politburo don't have to worry about the ebb and flow of public opinion. They put guns before butter, while we put just about everything before guns. They know that they are a superpower in only one sense – the military sense. They are a failure in human and economic terms.[22]

The men in the Soviet politburo were not amused by this unexpected onslaught from a Western political leader. They disliked being described as 'a dictatorship' and resented the challenge to their détente and defence strategy. Affronted by Margaret Thatcher, they decided to counter-attack with ridicule. A few days after her speech, the Soviet army newspaper *Red Star* came up with the worst insult they could think of. They dubbed her the 'Iron Lady'.[23]

The epithet made headlines around the world. Margaret Thatcher revelled in it. 'They never did me a greater favour', she commented.[24] In the polls, her leadership rating climbed by seven points. She was hailed as a heroine of anti-Sovietism around the world from the dissidents of Eastern Europe to the leaders of China. But the speech played unfavourably inside her shadow cabinet.

Reggie Maudling, the Shadow Foreign Secretary, had already had one private row with her about making anti-Moscow speeches without consulting him. Now he protested even more vehemently against her 'violent and sustained attack on the Soviet Government'.[25] It is likely that several other members of the shadow cabinet agreed with him, for it was the general view of the foreign-policy establishment that détente with the Soviet Union should be supported.

Maudling was out of sympathy with his leader on incomes policy, trade-union reform and now on her policy towards the Soviet Union. To make matters worse, he made a joke – apparently at her expense – at a shadow cabinet meeting in November 1976. She reported to her colleagues that she had been unimpressed by the President-elect of the United States, Jimmy Carter, at their first meeting, 'but sometimes the job can make the man'.

'Yes,' observed Reggie Maudling, 'I remember Winston's remark – if you feed a grub on royal jelly, it will grow into a Queen Bee.'

His jibe produced an icy stare from Margaret Thatcher and suppressed mirth among several colleagues. 'I did not fancy Reggie's chances in the next reshuffle', commented Jim Prior.[26]

This prediction came true a few weeks later when Maudling was sacked from the front bench after an angry encounter in which she told him, 'You're getting in my way'.[27]

The same thought was in her mind when she moved Michael Heseltine from his portfolio at Industry where his interventionist views were at odds with hers. He reluctantly accepted a less palatable role as Shadow Environment Secretary but only after extracting a pledge that he would not be appointed to this post in government.

Two weeks later, the Shadow Scottish Secretary Alick Buchanan-Smith resigned in disagreement with Margaret Thatcher's opposition to Scottish devolution. His right-wing replacement, Teddy Taylor, was on the opposite side of the issue to Willie Whitelaw and Francis Pym who were supporters of devolution. Other discordant voices, particularly Ian Gilmour (Shadow Defence Secretary) and Jim Prior (Shadow Employment Secretary), were critical of the opposition's far from clear policies on the economy and the trade unions. One way and another the shadow cabinet was not a happy ship.

To a small group of insiders it was clear that Margaret Thatcher was passionate about reversing Britain's decline with radical new policies on the unions and the economy. But she was too cautious to allow her real thinking on these issues to surface in the shape of policy commitments.

On the unions, she encouraged two informal advisers, John Hoskyns and Norman Strauss, to produce a paper titled *Stepping Stones*, which advocated a confrontational strategy. Its main policy suggestions were legislation to outlaw the closed shop, secondary picketing and legal immunities for the trade unions. Even when presented in the mildest of forms, this agenda sharply divided the shadow cabinet. Peter Thorneycroft, Jim Prior, Ian Gilmour, Lord Carrington and Francis Pym did their best to block *Stepping Stones*, even though it had the backing of Keith Joseph, Willie Whitelaw, Geoffrey Howe and the leader herself.

John Hoskyns recalled:

> Margaret's heart was entirely in the right place in supporting our radical reforms, but she never allowed *Stepping Stones* to be published, nor did she accept its ideas publicly until the Winter of Discontent had completely changed the climate of public opinion. So until late 1978 we were just going round in impotent circles on union reform, even though she knew all too well what had to be done.[28]

This same mixture of private radicalism and public caution prevailed in Margaret Thatcher's mixed messages on the economy. Off the record, when speaking to small gatherings of colleagues, she communicated her support for free markets, free wage bargaining, lower taxes, the abolition of exchange controls, big reductions in public expenditure and tight control of the money supply. But the specifics of these virtues were not openly spelt out by her. The only policy document the Conservative Party produced while she was Leader of the Opposition was *The Right Approach* (1977). She herself called it 'a fudge – but temporarily palatable'.[29]

On the crucial question of whether a Thatcher government would adopt an incomes policy, there was a vague public impression that she would go along with it in the interests of national unity. However, in many private conversations she said exactly the opposite.

This was not a dishonest approach. It was the different expression of Margaret Thatcher's short-term political head and her long-term philosophical heart. One perceptive observer of this phenomenon was Enoch Powell, who saw the contradictions as the product of a feminine mind:

> The consonance between thoughts and words is something in which she is basically not interested. This – as well as being a woman – enables her year after year to live with

something, with a cross on a paper at the back of her mind saying, 'I don't agree with that, I don't like it . . . but I can't do anything about it at the moment.' . . . It's more the mood of a person who says, 'I don't like that. When I can settle accounts with that, I will settle account with it.'[30]

It is possible that Enoch Powell's perception of this ambivalence in Margaret Thatcher came from listening to her at private gatherings of an organisation to which they both belonged in the 1976–1979 period – the Conservative Philosophy Group (CPG). Although her attendance at its meetings was intermittent, she revealed more of herself than was on display to the general public by her interest in the philosophical ideas and values championed by the group.

Margaret Thatcher began coming to the CPG because Airey Neave suspected its meetings were being used for plotting against her. This paranoia on his part surfaced in May 1975, when he asked me to come and see him. 'Are you running some sort of subversive right-wing operation against the leader?' he asked. 'What's this I hear about you starting up a splinter group to keep on supporting Hugh Fraser?'[31]

This was one of many wires that were getting crossed in the fragile aftermath of her election as Tory leader. Hugh Fraser, the least successful of first-round contestants, had started chairing the new CPG, whose principal organisers were the philosopher Roger Scruton, the Cambridge don Dr John Casey and myself. As we had lined up speakers of the calibre of Robert Blake, Friedrich Hayek, Michael Oakeshott, Milton Friedman, Hugh Trevor-Roper, Hugh Thomas, Peregrine Worsthorne, Anthony Quinton, Richard Nixon and Paul Johnson, it was not difficult to persuade the head of the leader's office that the purpose of the CPG was to generate new ideas for the party, not to open old wounds. Margaret Thatcher was evidently so persuaded, because a few days later a slightly sheepish Airey Neave asked me, 'Do you think the leader could be invited to join your group?' The answer was of course yes, so I sent her an invitation to our next supper, which she promptly accepted.

Her participation in CPG meetings revealed some interesting angles on her then unknown personality. It became clear that she loved to argue, often with a vigour that could startle the assembled company. One evening Professor H.W.R. Wade, Master of Gonville and Caius College, Cambridge, delivered a paper favouring a British Bill of Human Rights, which he said was necessary 'to protect us from political extremes'.

'But on our side we are never extreme', objected Margaret Thatcher. Professor Wade begged to differ, and was able to cite one or two examples of actions by previous Conservative governments that he thought fell into this category. This set off a vehement clash of opinions between the two of them. Their exchanges became so heated that Professor Michael Oakeshott mischievously started a diversion. Seeing on my mantelpiece a Victorian gilded birdcage containing two miniature linnets, he wound it up. As the clockwork songbirds chirruped away, several members of the group dissolved into laughter. But Margaret Thatcher was not to be distracted by these noises off. She kept firing her salvos until Bill Wade and the linnets subsided into silence.

Another lively evening, which found the Leader of the Opposition in full voice, began with a paper from Dr Edward Norman about the relations between church and state. Somehow this worked round to an argument about whether Christians had a duty to fight for the state even if its government became communist.

Professor Hugh Trevor-Roper, an old adversary of Dr Norman, said he couldn't see what all the fuss was about. He reminded us that when the Barbarians had sacked Rome, the Christians had promptly signed on for service in the Barbarian army.

'You're being deliberately provocative,' declared Margaret Thatcher, 'but do go on. This is fun.'

Enoch Powell intervened to say that he would fight for England even if it had a communist government.

'But you would only fight to defend the right values?' said the Leader of the Opposition in a tone of command rather than inquiry. 'Values exist in a transcendental realm beyond space and time', replied Powell. 'They can neither be defended nor destroyed.'

Margaret Thatcher gazed at him as though this was the most extraordinary statement she'd ever heard. 'Construct, Enoch dear, construct – don't destruct',[32] she ordered.

More or less at this point the division bell pealed in my home at Lord North Street. We were on a two-line whip. Most of us, including the Leader of the Opposition, were paired and stayed on. But a handful of MPs, including Enoch Powell, who had become a member of the United Ulster Unionist Party, had to go and vote.

'You shouldn't have left us, Enoch dear', was Margaret Thatcher's parting shot. 'You would have had a pair this evening.'[33]

As these vignettes show, her appearances at CPG evenings had their moments of amusement. She communicated some attractive sides of her personality in this private setting. Her warmth, her willingness to debate ideas and the radical strength of her political instincts manifested themselves in a form that was a refreshing contrast to the chilly caution of her Dresden china image. Among like-minded friends she relaxed more, and also looked a more interesting future prime minister.

Margaret Thatcher's participation in the CPG was indicative of her enthusiasm for seeking out a framework of moral and intellectual values for her future policies. But it was not nearly as influential as the two think tanks that she listened to most – the Centre for Policy Studies (CPS), chaired by Keith Joseph, and the Institute for Economic Affairs (IEA), chaired by Ralph Harris. She attended seminars and speaker events organised by both institutions, occasionally asking questions and frequently taking notes.

There is little doubt that the two most important thinkers who influenced Margaret Thatcher in her quest for fresh ideas were Friedrich Hayek and Milton Friedman. Yet she was never either a fully committed Hayekian or Friedmanite. The practicalities of British politics, coupled with her own instinctive caution, ensured that she did not fully embrace anyone's academic theory or philosophy. Yet she owed much to both these gurus who were introduced or re-introduced to her in the late 1970s.

While an Oxford undergraduate, Margaret Thatcher read Hayek's *Road to Serfdom* when it was first published in 1944. However, she had ignored the book's fervent anti-socialism during her first fifteen years in Parliament, making many compromises with the leftist orthodoxy of the times when she served as Education Secretary in Ted Heath's government. But Keith Joseph and the CPS reconverted her to Hayek's political *credo*.

There is a story of Margaret Thatcher visiting the consensus-leaning Conservative Research Department, where she cut short a researcher's presentation by pulling out of her handbag a copy of Hayek's *The Constitution of Liberty*. 'This is what we believe', she declared as she slammed the book down on the table.[34]

Many of her convictions were inspired by Hayek's writings, particularly her zeal to roll back the frontiers of the socialist state in Britain. In their later exchanges of correspondence, Margaret Thatcher paid tribute to her reliance on Hayekian thought. 'We are indebted to your economic ideas and philosophy', she wrote to her intellectual hero from 10 Downing Street twelve months after becoming Prime Minister. Four years later she made him a Companion of Honour in the 1984 Birthday Honours List.

Friedrich Hayek was important as a philosopher-king to the Thatcherite movement, but he was never a monetarist. This part of the opposition's new thinking on economic policy came largely from Milton Friedman. He preached his gospel of public expenditure cuts and tight control of the money supply. Margaret Thatcher listened to him at both the CPG and the IEA in 1978. Ralph Harris has recalled from the latter occasion how 'Mrs Thatcher hung on his words like a schoolgirl, carefully writing down everything he said and asking intelligent but elementary questions, as though it was all quite new to her'.[35]

For all her keen studies of Hayek and Friedman, Margaret Thatcher did not use either of them as direct sources for policy-making. As she well realised, the specific application of their ideas would be a dangerous hostage to fortune in electoral politics. Nevertheless, their influences made themselves felt in her self presentations of the kind of national leader she would turn out to be.

The values she proclaimed were a mixture of economic freedom and social conservatism. She advocated free choice, free enterprise and a throwing off of the shackles of socialist governance. Common-sense economics and sound rule of law disciplines were the key points on her compass. But rarely did these themes translate into specific proposals. Instead, she expressed her beliefs through the image of her personality.

Her most important tool in wooing the electorate was her self-projection. Many voters did not warm to her personality, but an increasing number were won over by the strength of it. What you saw was what you got – an immensely hard-working, determined and professional political leader. Away from the bear-pit of the House of Commons, where she faltered too often, she was beginning to sound like a capable Prime Minister-in-waiting. This improving perception of her owed much to her growing trust in a trio of image-makers – Tim Bell, Gordon Reece and Ronnie Millar. The results of their labours were a long time coming, and might not have come at all had it not been for the extraordinary events that became known as the 'winter of discontent'.

That winter was some eight months away in the spring of 1978. It was a time when Margaret Thatcher did not look like a sure-fire winner for the next general election. The opinion polls were narrowing. Jim Callaghan was maintaining his ascendency in the Commons, and the economy was starting to recover. This last factor was the wild card. Two years of IMF-imposed discipline on the public finances had given Denis Healey enough leeway to make some modest tax cuts in his April Budget. All of a sudden, the sinking ship of government by Lib–Lab pact appeared more seaworthy.

Astonishingly, considering its failures of policy and governance in the previous four years, Labour began to look electable. The party even showed a small lead in the polls later in the summer, while the Prime Minister's personal approval ratings climbed ten or twelve points above those of the Leader of the Opposition.

These signs and portents unnerved many Conservatives. Instead of concentrating their fire on the most unsuccessful government in living memory, they began a renewed round of grumbling about matters such as Margaret Thatcher's hats and vocal chords. It was the summer of Tory discontent and the lowest point of her leadership.

REFLECTION

As Parliament went into recess in July 1978, the discontent over Margaret Thatcher was reaching new levels of turbulence among Conservative MPs. Three years after she had been elected Leader of the Opposition she was looking alarmingly close to being a failure at the job. Why did she do so badly, particularly in a period when the Labour government of the day was in such dire straits?

The answer to this question may have more to do with the plight of the country than the political abilities of Margaret Thatcher. The mid-1970s found Britain in a demoralised, chaotic and confused state. We were rightly called 'The sick man of Europe', but no one in the front line of politics knew how to cure the sickness. Successive Conservative and Labour governments had failed at this task. The endemic problems of soaring inflation, union militancy, low productivity and unsustainable levels of public expenditure remained in place. Worse than any of this was the shattering loss of national self-confidence.

Although as Leader of the Opposition Margaret Thatcher tried to articulate solutions to the crisis, her voice and her views were not nearly as coherent as they became once she was established as Prime Minister. She had three major difficulties. Her party was not united behind her. Her skills at presentation, particularly in the House of Commons, were often unconvincing. And, she herself had not worked out what the right policies were for halting Britain's decline.

One last obstacle to her progress towards No. 10 was the considerable figure of James Callaghan. All polling data suggested that the electorate trusted him far more than they trusted her to pull Britain back from the abyss. He was often called 'The best Conservative Prime Minister we never had'. Considering the poor cards he held in terms of a fractious party, explosive wage demands, anarchic unions and no parliamentary majority, he was astonishingly successful in playing his hand as a respected national leader. Had he called a general election in either the summer or early autumn of 1978 he would probably have won it, thereby relegating Margaret Thatcher to a footnote in political history. She always said she would only get one chance from the electorate as Leader of the Opposition. In the period May–October 1978 she looked as though she was going to blow it.

But as often happens in politics, the game was changed by unexpected developments. These were the events of the 'winter of discontent' and the wave of reaction they unleashed among the electorate. Because Margaret Thatcher kept her nerve during the troughs of opposition, she was ready to ride on the crest of this wave. Its turbulence seemed to vindicate much of what she had been saying and standing for during her most difficult years as leader of her party.

13

Last lap to the election

THE IMPORTANCE OF THE LAUGHING BOYS

Before the tide turned in Margaret Thatcher's favour during the 'winter of discontent', there were another six months of choppy political waters to be navigated. It was a time when she needed friends. She found three of her best ones in the world of advertising, PR and the theatre. They were Tim Bell, Gordon Reece and Ronnie Millar. She called the first two 'my laughing boys', a label which might just have well been extended to all three of them, since it was Millar who provided the best of the humour. As a triumvirate, they were deadly serious about delivering the missing weapon in the Leader of the Opposition's arsenal – the presentational skills which could deliver victory at the coming election.

In the summer of 1978, Margaret Thatcher was doing badly in the House of Commons. In late July she had come off noticeably worse in a joust with Jim Callaghan, which was designed to draw the battle lines for the expected autumn election. Opening the debate, Callaghan launched an attack on the Leader of the Opposition's ability to govern. He accused her of being 'All over the shop on this issue of pay', 'insulting the intelligence of the British people with her one-sentence solutions to deep-seated problems' and setting out a foreign policy based on 'prejudice and dislike'.[1] His peroration was designed to portray the Leader of the Opposition as a divisive figure who would split the country.

He concluded:

> The right hon. Lady has led the Conservative Party for three years and under her leadership people still do not know what the Conservatives stand for. They do not know because she does not know . . . The Tory Party once aspired to lead one nation and to speak for one nation. Now the Tory Party, many of its members reluctant and

sullen, has to listen to the language of division the whole time. The British people have come to know that they achieve most when they work together in unison, in social justice and in fair play.[2]

Margaret Thatcher missed her chance to make a vigorous rebuttal of the Prime Minister's attack. Instead of a debating speech from a fighter, the House was given an analysis of government statistics by a lecturer. Callaghan had instructed his back-benchers not to interrupt her. The result was that she spoke in an eerie silence that made her tone sound 'nervous and faltering'.[3] According to one discomfited member of her shadow cabinet, Norman St John-Stevas, 'The speech showed that she had no feel whatever for the mood of the House'.[4] It was a disaster.

As she ran through a tedious recital of the comparative economic figures from the Conservative record of 1961–1964 (pointedly omitting the Heath government period of 1970–1974), the restive back-benchers behind her were the visible proof of Callaghan's claim that her own party was 'reluctant and sullen'.[5]

It was an unhappy parliamentary occasion for the Tories, made unhappier by the wind-up speech for the government by the Chancellor, Denis Healey. Posing as a prophet of doom, he condemned Margaret Thatcher for her 'deep psychological obsession with conflict and confrontation', and funereally proclaimed the debate as 'a historical occasion' because it was her last speech as Leader of the Conservative Party. 'The axes and knives are already been sharpened.' She and her party were 'in the last stages of decay . . . riding to certain defeat'.[6]

Although the fever of what he evidently thought was an imminent election made Healey's forecasts look silly in hindsight, at the time both he and Callaghan touched many a Tory nerve with their attacks on the Leader of the Opposition. I well remember the negative reactions among colleagues to her speech, which even her strongest supporters were describing as 'off form' or 'dull'. Most of us thought she had confirmed her increasingly poor reputation for failing to rise to the occasion in these big set-piece debates. 'But we're stuck with her now, until she loses',[7] said Nicholas Fairbairn, the colourful Scottish Member for Kinross and Perthshire. It was exactly the sort of gloomy judgement passed on Ted Heath in early 1974.

Although this extreme pessimism was a minority view within the party, as we dispersed for the long summer recess the mood was more of foreboding than anticipation. Most Tory MPs thought an election was coming in the autumn, and many felt that the chances of winning it were at best fifty–fifty. These anxieties were heightened by opinion polls in early August showing that Labour was ahead with a four-point lead.

August is a month that is usually helpful to the government of the day. But 1978 was an exception because the 'laughing boys', led by Tim Bell, took the initiative of introducing into British politics the first example of negative campaigning. Their initial poster was so effective that it derailed Callaghan's plans for an early election.

The name the 'laughing boys' derived from a lunch party at the Thatcher's country flat in Scotney Castle in July 1978. Its main objective was for election photographs to be taken of the leader looking relaxed *en famille*. However, the image of a happy family was difficult to portray on this particular morning because all four Thatchers were in a vile temper. Denis was irate because he had been ordered to cancel his Sunday game of golf. Margaret was furious because Denis had spontaneously invited the barrister Tricia Murray, wife of the DJ Pete Murray, to stay on for lunch after doing an interview for a book she was writing on Margaret Thatcher. The presence of this unexpected guest thwarted the leader's plan to discuss election tactics with her key media advisers. As for Mark and Carol, they were having a quarrel of their own which put both of them in bolshie moods. However, their bad temper was offset by the arrival of Messrs Bell, Reece and Millar in the sunniest of moods. They had turned up early in the vicinity of Scotney, and to kill time had polished off a couple of bottles of champagne in a local pub.

While downing the champagne, Ronnie Millar regaled his friends with an anecdote from his naval days about a commander whose invariable wardroom order was 'I'll have a piece of gin, please'. On arrival in the drawing room of Scotney, when Margaret Thatcher asked Millar what he would like to drink, he again imitated the commander's punch-line. This sent Reece and Bell into paroxysms of merriment. Unaware of the champagne, and oblivious to the point of the joke, the lady was bemused but pretended to be amused. She promptly christened the jesters 'my laughing boys', and the name stuck. On the day, it relieved the tension, which was a task they all became good at during the next twelve years.

Margaret Thatcher already trusted Ronnie Millar, a playwright friend of Noël Coward, who had been sculpting the best lines in her conference speeches since 1975. She had also come to depend on Gordon Reece, a television producer who softened her image, deepened her voice, advised her on clothes and accompanied her on media interviews. She had appointed him Director of Publicity at Central Office in early 1978. For his part, Reece venerated Margaret Thatcher with devotion not far short of idolatry. This spirit of adoration soon spread to Tim Bell, who was the toughest and savviest of the 'laughing boys'. He had entered the advertising industry straight from his North London grammar school, and climbed the ladder fast by his creative originality on big campaigns. In the summer of 1978 he was Managing Director of Saatchi and Saatchi,*[8] which Reece chose to handle the Conservative Party account.

Tim Bell, who was the only Conservative voter in the hierarchy of Saatchi and Saatchi, soon hit it off with Margaret Thatcher, who found him a kindred spirit. They shared similar grammar school backgrounds, an aversion to consensus politics and a preference for blunt speaking. At their first meeting, in her room at the House of Commons, she told him: 'You will find that politicians have very large fingers and very large toes. You must be frightfully careful not to tread on them by accident.'

Bell respectfully agreed to watch his step among the political classes. Then she startled him with more personal advice: 'I, however, have no fingers and no toes, and I insist you tell me the truth at all times, however painful you think it might be for me.'

Her final warning was: 'If you paint a picture of me that isn't true, and I get elected, then I won't be able to do what I want because people will expect me to do something else.' As Bell was leaving after this unusual interview, Margaret Thatcher asked him: 'What's your favourite poem?'

' "If", by Rudyard Kipling'.

'Mine, too', she replied.

From day one, she and Bell bonded.[9]

---

* In the 1970s, Saatchi and Saatchi was a small advertising agency winning acclaim for its creativity. Founded by the eponymous brothers Charles and Maurice, it grew by acquisition and by the energy of its Managing Director, Tim Bell. When approached by Gordon Reece about handling the Conservative Party account, the brothers said privately, 'We've never voted Tory in our life. You'll have to do it, Tim'.

It was still unusual in the 1970s for political parties to rely on advertising men, although the Tories had used Colman Prentis and Varley in the 1959 election. But Margaret Thatcher took an intuitive decision to use the industry's most innovative tactics and to trust Tim Bell. He suggested a strategy that consisted of appealing to voters' instincts with emotional messages and hitting Labour hard by going on the attack. Both themes were present in the poster he unveiled to the Leader of the Opposition that Sunday afternoon at Scotney.

The poster, destined to become a political legend, showed a dole queue tailing off into the distance. The slogan above it read 'Labour isn't working'. Bell told her it was a *double entendre*. 'What's this *double entendre* that's too subtle for me to get?' she demanded. It was patiently explained to her that neither the Labour government nor the unemployed were working. Then she found a different objection. 'Surely, it's all wrong that the biggest thing on this poster is the name of the opposition? Why are we promoting them?' Tim Bell argued back: 'We're not promoting the opposition. We are demolishing Labour.'[10] Eventually she saw the point, and gave the go-ahead. Although the poster went up on only twenty sites around the country, it caused a sensation.

Small news often becomes big news in sleepy August. With election jitters in the air, Labour launched a frenzy of protests against the poster, which only served to heighten its impact. The images were reproduced so often on television and in the press that Tim Bell later boasted that the Tories received £5 million of free publicity at a cash cost of only £50,000. Even the disclosure that the poster dole queue consisted of Hendon Young Conservatives posing for Saatchi and Saatchi cameras did not dilute its message. For the campaign reminded millions that the fear of rising unemployment was an issue on which the Labour government was electorally vulnerable.

No one took this reminder more seriously than Jim Callaghan. Having raised expectations that he would call an election, even to the point of singing the old music-hall song 'There was I, waiting at the church . . .' to the TUC conference on 5 September, he changed his mind. Two days later, he announced he would address the nation on television. 'I don't imagine that he's making a ministerial broadcast to say he's *not* going to hold an election', said Margaret Thatcher, who was on a tour of marginal seats in the West Midlands.[11] Minutes later she took a call from No. 10 Downing Street giving her advance notice that this was precisely what was going to happen. The Prime Minister had blinked.

That evening he solemnly announced to the nation that there would be no autumn election.

It is one of the mysteries of twentieth-century politics why Jim Callaghan backed away from going to the country. One explanation was that the Saatchi and Saatchi poster unnerved him. A second was that he felt less sure than the pollsters and most other observers that he would win the electorate's support. A third was that he thought he could gamble on an improvement in the economy over the winter months, winning the co-operation of the unions for a policy of pay restraint. But the most private, and perhaps most telling, explanation was the one he gave to his Downing Street aide, Tom McNally. 'In the history books, having been Prime Minister for three years rather than two looks a lot better.' When this unguarded Callaghan aside was passed on to Bernard Donoughue, the head of the Prime Minister's Policy Unit at No. 10, he observed: 'That's the ring of the true Jim.' Callaghan's desire to record against his name 'Prime Minister 1976–1979' was the decisive factor in postponing the date of polling day.[12]

When she received the news of the delay, Margaret Thatcher initially felt frustrated. She rang up Tim Bell to grumble about her sense of anti-climax, but soon shifted gear to discussing how the extra time could best be used. 'We were all on the go button,' he recalled, 'but once she began saying in a matter of fact way that we would just have to start all over again, we knuckled down and began preparing a completely new set of party political broadcasts for the New Year.'[13]

PPBs, as they were known, were considered to be a major force in shifting the allegiances of voters in the 1970s. The Tories were allocated five of them, each ten minutes long, during the election campaign itself, and two more in the weeks before polling day was announced. The 'laughing boys' seized these opportunities with relish. But their first priority was to extract the best possible performances from the leader.

Tim Bell recalled:

We treated her like a film star from the word go. She could have been Sophia Loren in terms of flowers, hairdos and compliments. Mind you, she saw through it. One day we were filming a PPB that was designed to reassure people that it would be all right to have a woman's finger on the nuclear trigger. As she couldn't understand what the fuss was about, it wasn't easy to get her into the right mood for the filming. But Ronnie Millar had written a script which contained the line, 'Whether we like it or not, we are the parents and the children of the nuclear generation'. He rehearsed her over and over again to get her intonation right. Eventually she said rather crossly, 'The trouble with you lot is that you think I'm Anna Neagle'.*[14]

'You lot' delivered the goods for Margaret Thatcher and the Conservative Party because she came to trust them completely. All three of them were in love with her politically and to some extent personally. Ronnie Millar's finest hours as her in-house wordsmith, or 'Ronniefier' of her speeches, came in her early years as Prime Minister, but he was effective in opposition, too. He got upset when some of his best efforts were discarded by her saying 'It's not me, dear', but she learned to let him down gently, explaining to other members of her team, 'Ronnie's very sensitive, you know'.[15]

Gordon Reece and Tim Bell could not be categorised as sensitive plants, and her handling of them could be rougher. There was one explosive episode when both of them were fired for a serious transgression.

In the summer of 1978, Conservative Central Office received a letter from the BBC, asking if the Leader of the Opposition would participate in televised debates with the Prime Minister and the leader of the Liberal Party, during the election campaign. Reece and Bell thought this was a bad idea because their boss had most to lose in a contest with Callaghan. They also saw no merit in giving equality of airtime to the despised Liberals. So Gordon Reece wrote back to the BBC turning them down.

After receiving acceptances from Jim Callaghan and David Steel, the BBC tried again with a second letter, which puzzled Margaret Thatcher because Reece had not shown her the original correspondence. She asked him what had happened to the first letter. 'Oh well, we answered it', he said rather nervously. 'You see, in image terms Callaghan's a rather avuncular figure, and you can be a very hard fighter. So we thought it wouldn't look nice on television for him to be seen getting beaten up by this . . .'

---

* Anna Neagle (1904–1986), popular stage and screen actress renowned for playing real-life British heroines such as Edith Cavell and Queen Victoria. She was at the height of her fame and box-office success during the Second World War and post-war years.

'By this tough bitchy housewife', snapped Margaret Thatcher.

'Well, er, I wouldn't put it quite like that . . .', faltered Reece.

'Let me understand something here', said the Leader of the Opposition, with her voice rising to earthquake level eight on the Richter scale. 'You got this letter from the BBC and you answered it without asking me. Get out! Get out, and take Tim with you! Get out!'

The two delinquents beat a hasty retreat from Flood Street, escorted to the door by a somewhat worse-for-wear Denis, who whispered, 'She'll be all right tomorrow'.[16]

His assurance gave little consolation to Reece and Bell. Shaken by the lady's seismic wrath, they assumed their relationship with her had been terminated. So they spent the rest of the night drowning their sorrows.

The following morning, at seven-thirty, their respective hangovers were interrupted by calls from Caroline Stephens, who controlled the Leader of the Opposition's diary: 'Could you be at Flood Street by nine?' When they presented themselves it was business as usual. Without a word of explanation, recrimination or apology, Margaret Thatcher never mentioned the BBC debates again.

Although television had counted in previous elections, by 1979 it was expected to be the dominant force in the coming contest. Margaret Thatcher was lucky to have three such consummate media professionals guiding her through the new age of animated PPBs and rolling electronic news bulletins. She relied on her experts completely. Her head told her she had to defer to them technically; her heart said she could trust them personally.

Tim Bell said:

I think it was because we understood the loneliness of her position as leader. Almost everyone political around her wanted something from her, or even wanted her to lose. We only wanted her to win. We understood her, almost loved her, as a woman – which helped. And all three of us were absolutely sound in our agreement with her convictions. We were pretty much the original 'One of us' group.[17]

What this group could not know as they re-scripted and re-shot all five of the election campaign PPBs in the autumn of 1978 was that events on the street were about to deliver a whole lot more of 'us' into Margaret Thatcher's political corner.

THE WINTER OF DISCONTENT

The 'winter of discontent' was preceded by an autumn of division for the Tories. The Party Conference in October highlighted the split between Heathite and Thatcherite Conservatism. Predictably, the most troublesome issues were incomes policy and trade-union policy. On the first, Ted Heath spoke in support of the government's 5 per cent pay norm, while Margaret Thatcher was known to favour free collective bargaining. On the second, Jim Prior was in favour of a 'softly, softly' approach to trade-union reform, while his leader wanted to legislate for secret ballots before strike action, the withdrawal of benefits for strikers' families and the outlawing of the closed shop. It was becoming increasingly difficult to paper over these cracks with a façade of shadow cabinet unity.

A third divisive issue was the renewal of sanctions on Rhodesia, which caused a row at the conference and the rebellion of 114 Tory MPs in an autumn vote in the House of Commons. These splits took their toll. Immediately after the conference season, Labour moved ahead by five and a half points in the opinion polls.[18] On 26 October the Conservatives lost a by-election at Berwick and East Lothian that they were expected to win. In early November, Gallup reported that Margaret Thatcher's personal approval had fallen to 33 per cent. When asked whether she or Ted Heath would make the better prime minister, a sample of voters polled by MORI for the *Daily Express* preferred Heath by a margin of 22 percentage points.[19]

As 1978 drew to a close, Margaret Thatcher's tenure on the leadership of her party looked shaky. She had her loyalists, but there were nowhere near enough of them to make her secure. Several of the MPs who had voted for her in 1975 were growing uncertain in their support three and a half years later. A few had privately recanted. But Margaret Thatcher, who could at least be confident that there would be no leadership challenge to her position before the imminent election, ignored the negative atmosphere and exuded an artificial air of invincibility.

To Norman Tebbit, one member of the 'Gang of Four' who helped her prepare for Prime Minister's Questions, she breezed: 'How are you – not depressed? Good. We'll beat the bastards yet.' Even the ultra-loyal Tebbit was startled by her defiance. 'She swore so rarely that I was taken aback', he recalled. 'But there was certainly an air of defeatism at that time.'[20]

Like Queen Victoria, Margaret Thatcher was not interested in the possibilities of defeat. Even so, December weekends at Scotney must have had uneasy moments. 'We were behind in the polls and seemed all too willing to behave like a permanent Opposition', she recalled. 'We still had a long way to go.'[21]

Suddenly, there were unexpected pre- and post-Christmas developments on the industrial front that changed the outlook. The government's 5 per cent pay limit, which had been hanging together by the slenderest of gossamer threads, fell apart in December when the health-service unions and local authority workers rejected it with the announcement that they would strike in the New Year. In January the Transport and General Workers' Union called the road-haulage drivers out in pursuit of an outrageous 25 per cent pay claim. The oil-tanker drivers followed suit. NHS manual workers (including refuse collectors, porters, cleaners and mortuary assistants) made up the next wave of strikers.

By the middle of January the country was in chaos. Lack of fuel deliveries meant power cuts at a time of extreme cold. Unable to have goods delivered in or out by road transport, many businesses shut down. Schools closed. Hospitals accepted only emergency cases. Scenes of violent picketing outside factories, docks and power plants shocked the nation's television viewers. The worst symptoms of the unrest were the rotting piles of garbage on the streets and dead bodies being prevented from burial by pickets outside hospitals. The face of trade-union militancy had never looked uglier as the excesses spread towards anarchy.

On 22 January, the union leaders called out 1.5 million workers for a National Day of Action. It was the biggest stoppage since the General Strike of 1926. The government's reaction to such events was one of impotence and incompetence.

In the middle of these upheavals Jim Callaghan attended a G7 Summit in Guadeloupe. It was bad PR for the Prime Minister to be televised in shirt sleeves, relaxing alongside Valéry Giscard d'Estaing, Helmut Schmidt and Jimmy Carter in the Caribbean sunshine while Britain shivered in the turmoil back home. But Callaghan made these images infinitely worse by his complacent underplaying of the chaos when he returned. 'Crisis? What Crisis?' was the headline of the *Sun*'s report on his press conference at Heathrow Airport.[22]

Although he did not use these actual words, the journalistic licence cunningly suggested to the *Sun*'s editor, Larry Lamb, by Tim Bell was a fair portrayal of the Prime Minister's attempt to minimise the scale of the problem. Callaghan never fully recovered from this gaffe.

As the havoc surged to new heights, Margaret Thatcher's natural instinct was to go for the government's jugular. But a combination of her own caution and the restraining advice of her colleagues caused her to handle the drama more skilfully.

The great turning point in Margaret Thatcher's relationship with the British electorate came with a party political broadcast on 17 January 1979. It was not the message she had planned to deliver. The PPB that had been filmed but rejected at the last minute was confrontational. The one that she actually gave was consensual. She took a lot of persuasion to take the second option.

'You know what you're doing, don't you?' she said to her three speech-writers, Ronnie Millar, Chris Patten and Tim Bell, who came in to see her with the new text, accompanied by Peter Thorneycroft, the Party Chairman. 'You're asking me to let Callaghan off the hook.' 'No,' said Thorneycroft gently, 'we're asking you to put country before party.'[23] This patriotic argument won her round. The filmed PPB was binned. In its place she gave a completely new speech, straight to camera from her room in the House of Commons.

'Yes, technically, this is a Party Political Broadcast on behalf of the Conservative Party', she opened, as these words in the formal title faded from the nation's screens.

> But tonight I don't propose to use the time to make party political points. I do not think you would want me to do so. The crisis that our country faces is too serious for that. And it is our country, the whole nation, that faces this crisis, not just one party or even one government. This is no time to put party before country. I start from there.[24]

Having donned the mantle of a unifying national leader, Margaret Thatcher offered the opposition's support for the government if they would legislate to introduce a ban on secondary picketing, the funding of strike ballots and no-strike agreements in essential services. She had made these proposals when speaking in the Commons on the previous day. The Prime Minister, in thrall to the unions who were the backers and backbone of the Labour Party, had brushed her cross-party deal aside. But as she repeated the offer on television, she seized the moral superiority of speaking for Britain.

The case is now surely overwhelming; there will be no solution to our difficulties which does not include some restriction on the power of the unions. And if that case is overwhelming, then in the national interest surely government and opposition should make common cause on this one issue.

She concluded with the punch-line, 'We have to learn again to be one nation, or one day we shall be no nation'.[25]

It took time for Margaret Thatcher to realise what a resounding success this broadcast had been. One of the quickest and most surprisingly favourable reactions came from Jim Callaghan. The next day, as the Leader of the Opposition and the Prime Minister walked down the aisle of Westminster Abbey together after attending a memorial service, Callaghan said to her: 'That was a damned good broadcast you did last night . . . I wish I'd said it. Well done.'[26]

Margaret Thatcher gave him a cool response, thinking she was being patronised. But within a few seconds she was getting the same message again. By chance I was standing close to her near the West Door of the Abbey. 'Will you walk out with me?' she asked. So I escorted her through the throng of photographers to her car, congratulating her on the broadcast, and telling her I had watched it at a South London pub in Kennington. 'Everyone was quiet,' I said, 'and when you finished with that line about "one nation or no nation", a lot of people at the bar clapped.'

'Our people?' she asked.

'No, just ordinary working men in the pub.'

'Well . . .' she said. 'That's quite something, isn't it?'[27]

Soon she was hearing similar assessments from many sources.

The 'laughing boys' were exultant. Tim Bell came to believe 'this broadcast won the election'.[28]

It certainly swung the polls her way. Suddenly the Conservatives were nineteen points ahead of Labour, and Margaret Thatcher's personal ratings leapt by fifteen points to 48 per cent.[29] The 'winter of discontent' had transformed her from divisive voice to national leader in waiting. As the government's woes multiplied, she prepared for the final push to victory.

THE VOTE OF NO CONFIDENCE

For a Leader of the Opposition whose job it was to defeat the incumbent government, Margaret Thatcher was surprisingly hesitant about delivering the coup *de grâce.* It was caution that made her hold back. Most of her back-benchers had no such reservations. I vividly remember the mood of angry impatience that surged through the 1922 Committee meetings during the 'winter of discontent'. At one of them, Julian Amery echoed the call his father Leo Amery had made in the 1940 debate about Neville Chamberlain: 'In the name of God, go!'[30]

Amery junior was the toast of the smoking room after that filial blast on the trumpet. But the leader herself was giving an uncertain sound. Her reasoning was, 'We were extremely reluctant to put down a Motion of No Confidence until we were assured of its likely success'.[31] It was not an argument that had much appeal to her rank and file MPs. During one boisterous late-night sitting in early March a group of us broke into 'Why are we waiting?' whenever a member of the shadow cabinet came anywhere near our part of the tea room. The Conservative Parliamentary Party was beginning to resemble those scenes of order, counter-order and disorder immortalised in Macaulay's *Lays of Ancient Rome* when:

Those behind cried 'Forward!'
And those before cried 'Back!'[32]

What was holding Margaret Thatcher back was her attempt to make sense of the grubby calculations on the changing parliamentary arithmetic. After the chaos of the 'winter of discontent', Labour was dealt another lethal blow by the collapse of its devolution policy. Referenda on the issue in Wales and Scotland on 1 March produced negative results. As a consequence it looked as though MPs from the nationalist parties would no longer be willing to prop up the government. The Liberals now wanted an early election following the breakdown of the Lib–Lab pact. These underminings of the tenuous allegiances that had allowed Labour to survive for the past few months meant that the government no longer had the votes to keep on getting its business though in the House of Commons.

The absence of a majority did not, however, ensure that Labour could be dislodged. All depended on the twelve Northern Ireland MPs who were split in at least three different directions. Margaret Thatcher declared herself implacably opposed to doing deals with any of these factions that might tie her hands as Prime Minister. Nevertheless her Shadow Northern Ireland Secretary, Airey

Neave, did secretly put out feelers to the ten United Ulster Unionists. However, since this party was far from united, not unanimously unionist and not entirely drawn from Ulster (Enoch Powell having become one of its MPs), the outcome of Neave's horse trading was shrouded in swirling Irish mists.

By the third week in March, the clamour from the back benches became irresistible. Even though the arithmetic of predicted voting did not clearly add up in her methodical mind to the desired figure, and even though she feared that a failed result would prolong the life of the Labour government until the autumn, Margaret Thatcher reluctantly took the plunge and tabled the opposition motion: 'This House has no confidence in Her Majesty's Government.'[33]

The no confidence debate produced the most exciting parliamentary night in living memory. As one of the youngest MPs, I sat throughout the 1974–1979 session on the third bench below the gangway which junior Tories had to share with the United Ulster Unionists. On 28 March this gave me one of the best seats in the House for witnessing the extraordinary gyrations of the Northern Ireland MPs who eventually decided the outcome of the motion.

Margaret Thatcher opened the debate with one of the more pedestrian speeches of her career. For once it did not matter. There was so much electricity in the chamber that a low-voltage performance by the Leader of the Opposition seemed almost irrelevant. Her twenty-nine-minute analysis of why the British economy had been in decline for the past five years was heard in bored silence. Only her final lines got a cheer:

> What condemns the Prime Minister now is the justified feeling that the substance of matters before the House takes second place to the survival of the Government. That feeling is widespread, and it robs the Government and the Prime Minister of authority, credibility and dignity.[34]

Despite his tattered authority, for the sixth time in their past two years of major parliamentary clashes, the Prime Minister outshone the Leader of the Opposition. Jim Callaghan was on chipper form, teasing Margaret Thatcher for hanging back from tabling her no confidence motion until after she had discovered that the Liberals and the Scottish Nationalists would be voting for it. 'She found the courage of their convictions.'[35]

But this was a day when votes, not words, counted. On the Ulster Unionist bench there was much whispering and manoeuvring as the evening wore on.

It was clear that Enoch Powell was doing his utmost to persuade his colleagues to abstain. The Reverend Ian Paisley, my next-door neighbour on the bench, shifted his not inconsiderable bulk upwards, downwards and sideways with such animation during these *sotto voce* arguments that I was bounced around on the same strip of taut green leather bench like a tennis ball.

Much of the debate was taken up with speeches from Members representing outlying reaches of the United Kingdom with constituencies like the Western Isles, Carmarthen, Renfrewshire, Antrim South, Caernarvon and Down North. During one of these orations I muttered that the speaker was as 'wet as hell', only to be chided by the Reverend Paisley with the reproach, 'Hell is not wet!'[36]

Satanic or at least sinister rumours were circulating in the bars and corridors of the Palace of Westminster all day long. One was that Labour's terminally ill MP for Batley and Morley, Sir Alfred Broughton, had been brought down from his deathbed in Yorkshire, but had died on the journey. However, once his ambulance was sighted in Palace Yard, it was claimed his vote could still be 'nodded through' (the procedure for allowing sick members of the precincts to be counted in divisions), even if he was dead. This would have been taking to extreme the convention that no one legally dies within the precincts of Parliament.

Like several of the hysterical stories ground out by the rumour mill in the closing hours of the debate, this one was nonsense. Jim Callaghan and his Chief Whip had already decided that it would be morally wrong to subject the dying Broughton to a 400-mile round trip down the M1 and back. So neither his ambulance nor his vote existed.

Great anger was caused to Margaret Thatcher in the middle of these tensions when the opposition's Deputy Chief Whip, Bernard 'Jack' Weatherill, offered to pair with Broughton. He was attempting to honour a previous pledge that pairs would always be granted to seriously ill Members on either side. But the government's Deputy Chief Whip, Walter Harrison, refused the offer for equally honourable reasons.* So there was no change in the numbers, although there was a change for the worse in Thatcher–Weatherill relations, as later events were to show.

---

* The dramatic moves and counter-moves between Weatherill and Harrison were chronicled with considerable historical accuracy in the play *This House* by James Graham, which had a long run at the National Theatre in 2012–2013.

Even without Sir Alfred Broughton, the experts calculated that Labour would win because they could count on the support of two anti-Unionist MPs from Northern Ireland. They were Gerry Fitt, the leader of the Social Democratic Labour Party, and Frank Maguire, a Republican with no love for the Tory government that had interned him for three years under the Special Powers Act.

As MP for Fermanagh and South Tyrone, Maguire was known only for his absence and silence. In the five years since being elected, he had not made his maiden speech. However, when he arrived in the Palace of Westminster, apparently to cast his vote for the government, the Ulster Unionists on the bench beside me worked themselves into a frenzy of excitement. 'Beelzebub is here!' declared Robert Bradford, 'Labour will be home and dry now!' This became the received arithmetical wisdom in many quarters after the sighting of the maverick Mr Maguire was confirmed.

A devilish feud between Gerry Fitt and Frank Maguire was to send the arithmetic astray at the last moment. But no one understood this at the time. Instead, the rumours multiplied while both the climatic and the political temperature climbed.

The House of Commons was a hellish place on the night of 28 March. Not only was the chamber as packed and hot as Dante's *Inferno*, almost everyone was hungry. The 'winter of discontent' had spread to the catering department whose employees walked out on strike on the busiest night for years. Fearing that vital votes could get lost if MPs went in search of outside nourishment, the Conservative and Labour whips banned all their members from leaving the building. This left most of us with empty stomachs, although Margaret Thatcher dined comfortably on a food hamper sent in from Fortnum and Mason.

The wind-up of the debate was both passionate and hilarious thanks largely to Michael Foot, who teased the leaders of the Scottish Nationalist Party (Donald Stewart) and the Liberal Party (David Steel). Foot accused Margaret Thatcher of leading 'her troops into battle snugly concealed behind a Scottish Nationalist shield, with the boy David holding her hand'.[37] She was about the only MP present who did not laugh. Her po-face may have been due to her failure to understand the joke or to her expectation that the motion would be narrowly defeated.

The aye lobby for the big division was excitable to the point of near hysteria, but not in the bubble around Margaret Thatcher. Her Chief Whip Humphrey Atkins gave her bad news. Labour had polled at full strength, boosted by the votes of Frank Maguire and Gerry Fitt. A couple of Tories had broken the ban on going out to dinner and had not returned from White's Club. Labour would hang on by a two- or three-vote majority reported the deeply apologetic Atkins.

Sitting on the front bench awaiting the announcement of the voting figures, the Leader of the Opposition cut a dejected figure. Suddenly there was a whisper passed along by members of the shadow cabinet bench that made her sit up. It was a report from her PPS that the vote was tied. Seconds later there was a thumbs-up sign from Tony Berry, the Conservative whip who had been counting the Labour votes in the no lobby.

There was a moment of disbelief followed by an exultant roar from the Tory benches. Humphrey Atkins reversed his pessimism, shouting to his boss, somewhat superfluously by that stage: 'We've won!'

In the final tally, Labour had one MP too ill to vote (Broughton). The two missing Tories, one of them Winston Churchill, Sir Winston's grandson, returned from White's in the nick of time, while the two feuding Irishmen killed the Labour government they supported by actions of complete illogicality. At the last moment, Frank Maguire said he had 'come over the water to abstain in person',[38] and did just that. Gerry Fitt announced that he could not vote to keep the Labour government in office, although he would campaign vigorously to get it re-elected. As a result of these illogical declarations, the government lost two vital votes.

The result was announced in a stentorian bellow by the 6ft 7in former Guards officer turned Tory whip, Spencer Le Marchant: 'The Ayes to the right 311. The Noes to the left 310. So the Ayes have it.' Pandemonium *in excelsis*! The government had fallen.

It was the first time a vote of confidence had been lost in the House of Commons since the defeat of Ramsay MacDonald's first Labour government in 1924. We back-bench Tories celebrated well into the small hours. More circumspectly, Margaret Thatcher had a quick glass of wine in the whips' office before leaving for Flood Street under increased police protection, telling her family assembled there, 'I've got a lot of work to do now'.[39]

It was a parliamentary night to remember.

REFLECTION

The 'winter of discontent' broke the mould of British politics. Before it, Margaret Thatcher was a doubtful bet to become the next prime minister. Once it lurched out of control, she was a certainty.

Her conviction that the unions had to be defeated was never explicitly spelt out on the last lap of the election. Yet somehow she communicated to the public that she would be strong enough to rise to the challenge. The force of her personality sent out this message. The voters were far from sure that they liked her, but they sensed that they needed her. There was a growing feeling that Labour had become too tired as a government to handle the union militants. The time had come for a strict headmistress who would impose national discipline and restore order.

Margaret Thatcher grew in public stature and private confidence as her views were vindicated by events. Even so, she still had to win the battle to establish her credentials for leading a new government to the electorate. It was interesting that she chose as her right-hand men for this task a trio of anti-establishment mavericks, who were complete outsiders from the political class. 'You know why we get on so well with the old bat?' Tim Bell rhetorically asked a friend. 'None of us want to be politicians.'[40]

It was one of the paradoxes of Margaret Thatcher, herself a totally professional careerist in politics, that she had a poor opinion of most other professional politicians. They were accustomed to hedging their bets, trimming their sails and seeking the common ground of consensus. She despised all three of these practices. She wanted complete commitment and was unafraid of confrontation. So she looked around for fellow warriors, or at least fellow challengers of the accepted wisdom. She ran her party in the last months before the election rather in the way that she came to run her government. She rummaged around in the pool of talent available to her until she found abilities she admired, combined with a zeal that matched her own instincts. This was an unorthodox, almost revolutionary, form of leadership for the Tory Party, but the times were so serious that she got away with it.

After winning the vote of no confidence, she was out on a limb more than ever in terms of being ahead of her party. But as the next few weeks were to demonstrate, she was in tune with the instincts of the majority of the voters.

14

The final ascent to No. 10

WAITING BEFORE THE OFF

Immediately after the no confidence debate, the Conservative lead in the opinion polls was between 9 and 13 per cent.[1] No political party had ever entered a general election with such an advantage. Margaret Thatcher and her inner circle immediately recognised that the contest was theirs to lose. They resolved to make the campaign as low-key as possible. Dullness and safety were the order of the day. No lurches to the right. No controversial pledges. No gaffes. No rocking the boat. Such a strategy did not fit easily with Margaret Thatcher's combative personality but she played the game in order to win the match.

Before campaigning began, Airey Neave was assassinated by the Irish National Liberation Army, a breakaway faction of the IRA. On the afternoon of 30 March Margaret Thatcher was attending a routine function in her constituency when the senior Conservative Central Office Press Officer, Derek Howe, told her, 'I think you ought to know that a bomb has gone off in the precincts of the House of Commons, in the garage they think. At least one person has been very seriously injured, but we don't know who.'[2] Within an hour it was confirmed that the victim was Airey Neave. A bomb had been placed underneath his Vauxhall Cavalier with a tilt switch, which ignited the explosion as the car was climbing up the exit ramp of the car park. Neave was trapped in the shattered wreckage for half an hour before being cut free and rushed to Westminster Hospital.

Margaret Thatcher received the news at the BBC where she was preparing to record a party political broadcast. She cancelled it. Numb with shock, she returned to her office in the House of Commons where she was told that Neave had died on the operating table. 'Thank God one doesn't know when one wakes up in the morning what will happen before one goes to bed at night', she murmured to her staff.[3] Then she withdrew into her inner sanctum to compose a handwritten tribute, which went out as a press release. She described Neave as 'One of freedom's warriors. Courageous, staunch, true, he lived for his beliefs and now he has died for them. A gentle, brave and unassuming man, he was a very dear friend.'[4]

The assassination of Airey Neave came as a huge blow to Margaret Thatcher. Even though he had become less influential with her in the last year or so, he was still an important confidant as her Shadow Secretary of State for Northern Ireland. She never forgot the great debt she owed him for managing her campaign in the 1975 leadership election. He was as close a personal friend as she ever had in politics. But she kept her grieving for him in private. Outwardly, she was steady as a rock as she returned to the political and professional challenge of preparing for the election.

Polling date was set for 3 May, which made the nine-week campaigning period the longest ever seen in British politics. In line with the safety-first tactics that had been agreed, a decision was taken that the leader should not start electioneering too soon. So for the first ten days of April, Margaret Thatcher had nothing to do. This was a role to which she was utterly unaccustomed. She did it badly. Her private office team was stressed out by her fretting and fuming over irrelevant details during this phoney-war period. Eventually, one of her secretaries suggested to Ronnie Millar that perhaps he could ease the pressure by taking the boss out to dinner and the theatre.

Unaccustomed though they were to thespian evenings, Margaret and Denis Thatcher made three visits to the theatre – in one week. These outings organised by Ronnie Millar were not an unqualified success but they did manage to provide a distraction from politics. The three shows Millar selected were *The Two Ronnies* at the London Palladium, *Annie* at the Victoria Palace and *Evita* at the Prince Edward. In different ways they all gave glimpses of the human side of Margaret Thatcher on the eve of the greatest battle of her political life.

At *The Two Ronnies* Denis loved every moment of the jokes but Margaret got few of them. The humour she did understand was too blue for her taste. But she enjoyed the chorus line of Ziegfeld-style dancing girls in glittering sequined gowns and feathers, murmuring to Millar, 'I love this sort of thing . . . So pretty.'[5] It was a reminder that she always had an eye for feminine glamour.

Meeting the cast backstage went with the territory of being a Prime Minister-in-waiting. She proved good at luvvie flattery, laying it on with a trowel even when she had not been enamoured with the show. But after the musical *Annie*, she found her skills tested by the child actress in the title role who wept uncontrollably when congratulated on her performance. The leader of the Conservative Party embraced the sobbing child while her mother explained that she was upset because under the employment laws for juvenile actors she had to take a break from the part for three months.

'My dear, you mustn't take on so, you'll be back again before you can say Jack Robinson', said Margaret Thatcher. 'Time will fly, it always does. Meanwhile, you know what you must do.' The howling Annie asked through her tears what she should do.

'You must write a diary, that's what you must do', was the brisk response. According to Ronnie Millar, 'The child was so stunned by this mysterious advice she stopped crying instantly, and Margaret was hailed as a miracle worker by the entire company.'[6]

After her third night out in the West End, to see *Evita*, the life of Eva Peron, with music by Andrew Lloyd Webber and lyrics by Tim Rice, stirred by 'Don't cry for me, Argentina', the hit song of the show, Margaret Thatcher wrote a letter of thanks to her host. 'I was thinking, if a woman like that [Eva Peron] can get to the top without any morals, how high could someone get who has one or two?'[7]

Away from the bright lights of the theatre, a serious issue at this time for both the Prime Minister and the Leader of the Opposition was how to make arrangements for the handover of power – should there be one. Although the Sir Humphreys at the top of the civil service had for decades taken pride in the smoothness of earlier transitions, the last one had gone horribly wrong.

When the Conservatives lost power in 1974, the incoming aides to the new Prime Minister, Harold Wilson, exchanged angry words and, in one case, actual physical blows with the outgoing political staff of Ted Heath. Jim Callaghan, who knew about these kerfuffles, was determined that no such unseemly incidents should occur again. So he instructed his Principal Private Secretary, Kenneth Stowe, to make contact with Margaret Thatcher's office for discussions on how to ensure a smooth transition.

Kenneth Stowe had won the trust of the Leader of the Opposition some months earlier, but only after bearing the brunt of her anger. This episode says much about three weaknesses in her personality. Her tendency to fly off the handle too easily; her capacity to get the wrong end of the stick; and her reluctance to apologise.

The trouble had its origins in a disputed parliamentary vote when Harold Lever, Labour Chief Secretary to the Treasury, had allegedly broken his pair. The fall-out over the incident was so serious that all co-operation between the opposition and the government about parliamentary business was suspended on Margaret Thatcher's instructions. She was right to retaliate. But the House of Commons cannot function without some dialogue between 'the usual channels' (a circumlocution meaning the secretary of the Chief Whip negotiating matters of parliamentary business with the opposition whips' office), so sooner or later an accommodation had to be reached.

After a long and bitter delay, a meeting to settle the row was held between the Prime Minister and the Leader of the Opposition. Michael Foot, as Leader of the House, was also in attendance. Kenneth Stowe took notes. He described it as 'a painful discussion'.[8] But in the end, the protagonists found a way to move on. As a good civil servant does, Kenneth Stowe had his record of the meeting typed up and sent to the principal discussants.

When Margaret Thatcher read the notes taken by the Prime Minister's Private Secretary, she exploded. Kenneth Stowe was summoned to her office in the House of Commons. 'She was in a bit of a Paddy to put it mildly', he recalled. 'Her opening words to me were: "You didn't tell me you brought a tape recorder into my room."'

'I didn't tell you because I didn't take one', replied Stowe.

'I don't believe you', was the furious retort. 'You must have had a tape recorder to have taken down my words so exactly!'

A strenuous argument followed. 'She was seriously angry – no question,' recalled Stowe, 'but in the end I convinced her that I had noted her words accurately simply because it was part of my trade to be able to do so.'[9]

In accordance with her pattern of handling the aftermath of unpleasant rows in which she turned out to be wrong, Margaret Thatcher never apologised for her accusation. But she did manage to cast a warm mantle of compensatory gratitude over Stowe, accepting that his handwritten note was solely responsible for the impeccable accuracy of the record. 'She was eventually very grateful that I had got her actual words down correctly', he recalled. 'That was the beginning of a very trusting relationship between Margaret Thatcher and myself.'[10]

The bonds of trust that were forged in this unusual way were to prove invaluable in the preparations for the handover of power. Richard Ryder, the political head of the Leader of the Opposition's office, made several visits to No. 10 in the weeks before the election. He reported back to his boss in detail. As a result of her decisions about the allocation of offices, the layout of her own rooms and her plans for working practices, the transition from Jim Callaghan's No. 10 to Margaret Thatcher's No. 10 became the easiest and smoothest in modern times.

SOFT-CENTRE CAMPAIGNING

The Conservative election campaign was formally launched with the publication of the party's manifesto.

In contrast with all other manifestos in political memory, the one she unveiled was remarkably short on specific commitments. It had no title. It was like a user-friendly philosophy stall setting out the themes she had been emphasising in her speeches for the past four years. Lower taxes, lower public spending, less state control, and the upholding of Parliament and the rule of law were its broad principles. Denis Healey quipped that looking for policy commitments in this manifesto was 'like looking for a black cat in a coal cellar in the dark'.[11]

This was a fair comment, except in a surprising area. One result of the 'winter of discontent' was that Margaret Thatcher won her battle with Jim Prior and most of the shadow cabinet over trade-union law reform. So she did promise in the manifesto to introduce limits on secondary picketing, compensation for workers dismissed for not joining a closed shop and postal ballots for union elections. This was nowhere near as radical an agenda as the one she really wanted on union reform, but it was progress.

On incomes policy, the manifesto was as murky as Healey's dark coal cellar. That was not what the leader desired, but she had to defer to her colleagues, particularly to the Party Chairman, Peter Thorneycroft, who had moved into pole position as the preserver of quiet equilibrium in the election. This meant manoeuvring Margaret Thatcher away from controversial territory. It was no easy task.

The Thorneycroft strategy worked for a while. Due to a three-day suspension of hostilities for the Easter weekend, the Tory campaign as controlled by Central Office was made as brief (sixteen days) and as uneventful as possible. Of course the leader had to be kept busy around the country with a programme of events. But on the whole the emphasis in her schedule was on soft photo opportunities not hard politics.

She did factory tours with particular panache. At a Kleeneze brush manufacturing plant in Bristol she performed pantomime imitations of sweeping away the cobwebs and applying a new broom. In a Leicester clothing factory she surprised everyone by sitting down at a sewing machine and stitching the pockets on a blue overall with the seamstress skills she had learned from her mother. In Bourneville she wrapped Cadbury's chocolates with a deft touch. The horde of accompanying paparazzi loved these images. She looked good in them, but away from the cameras she was growing bitter at being confined to soft centres.

While posing at the Cadbury factory, she learned that Peter Thorneycroft was insisting on a major cut in the speech she was due to deliver that night in Birmingham, the second major rally of the election. The passage he wanted to censor was an indictment of union malpractices, which had been drafted for her by the historian and convert from Labour Paul Johnson. The Party Chairman thought it was 'too provocative'.[12] After a blazing row with him on the telephone, Margaret Thatcher furiously tore out the offending pages from the prepared text. It was the first of many frictions she had with the high command at Central Office.

Her worst clash with Thorneycroft came in the last weekend of the campaign. She was relaxing after a successful day in Glasgow when he sent her a message via his Deputy Chairman, Janet Young, that he wanted to invite Ted Heath to join her at her final press conference on Monday. This caused an eruption.

'Scared rabbits! They're running scared,' Margaret Thatcher exploded, 'that's what's the matter with them! The very idea! How *dare* they!'[13]

She continued in this vein not only for the rest of the evening but for most of the next twelve hours. As Denis confided to a friend the following morning: 'This business of Ted appearing on the same platform with the Boss. She hasn't slept a wink all night. I've never seen her in such a state.'[14]

The state continued until she returned to London. Peter Thorneycroft and other members of the hierarchy made one last attempt to persuade her to share a slot with Ted Heath. Her refusal was so vigorous that the plan was shelved.

The reason for the suggestion that the past and present leaders of the Conservative Party should present a united front was that the opinion polls had gone wobbly. After weeks of psephological evidence that the Tories were in a comfortable lead, Central Office received advance warning that a NOP poll to be published on 1 May would show Labour was scraping ahead by 43.1 per cent to 42.4 per cent.[15] Most members of the leader's immediate entourage went into a state of panic over these findings. Margaret Thatcher was the exception. After being told about the figures, she kept silent for about a minute, and then said quietly, 'I don't think I believe this'.[16] She was right. The NOP findings were a rogue poll. All the other polls confirmed the trend with predictions that the Tories would beat Labour by an average lead of between 4 and 7 per cent.[17]

In the final week Conservative-supporting newspapers, particularly the *Sun*, stepped up the aggression level of their attacks on Labour. But for Margaret Thatcher, soft-centre campaigning continued to be the order of the day. There was one exception, when she did her only major one-on-one television interview with Denis Tuohy of *TV Eye* on 24 April 1979. He gave her a rough ride, which she made look rougher by talking over his questions as if trying to drown him out. The clashes, both in full flow without giving way, broke all records for what is known in the jargon of broadcasters as 'simultaneous speech'. It was virtually the only time throughout the election when she gave the impression of having a combative personality.

Although Jim Callaghan did his best to portray his opponent as a dangerous right-wing ideologue, he was not cutting much ice with the floating voters. She continued with her royal progress of photo-calls. The most memorable of these was a visit to a farm in Norfolk, when she cuddled a newly born calf in her arms for thirteen minutes. She might have gone on longer posing for new camera angles, had not Denis warned that if they were not careful they could have a dead calf on their hands. 'It's not for me, it's for the photographers', she explained. 'They are the really important people in this election.'[18]

The priority given to cameramen, calves and chocolates was largely the work of her image consultant, Gordon Reece. He knew exactly what he was doing. Some years later he confided to me that he had been influenced by a minor classic of American reporting on the 1968 presidential election, *The Selling of the President* by Joe McGinnis.[19] This told how Richard Nixon had been carefully packaged to avoid sharp questioning by the liberal media.

Margaret Thatcher herself had no qualms about taking such questions, but she had been discomfited by the hostile interrogation she had received at the hands of Denis Tuohy. When it was over, she complained to Gordon Reece about one weakness that she thought was his fault. 'Gordon,' she said piercingly, as she swept past the cameras, 'I understand you were here yesterday. Why was I advised to wear beige when there is beige in the studio set?' As he began stumbling out an explanation she raised an imperious hand: 'Let's leave that for later.'[20] She was determined to be mistress in her own house, even when it came to the tricks of the image trade which Reece had taught her.

During the final days of the campaign she exuded the air of Prime Minister-in-waiting with increasing confidence. On the last Sunday before polling day, there was a rally of Conservative trade unionists at Wembley. She entered the hall to a chorus of 'Hello Dolly' – with new words by Ronnie Millar and recorded by Vince Hill. It began:

> Hello, Maggie,
> Well, hello, Maggie,
> Now you're really on the road to Number 10 . . .

Fourteen lines later it ended:

> So here's to you, Maggie,
> Give 'em the old one-two, Maggie,
> Maggie, we're right behind you all the way![21]

The penultimate line puzzled the star of the show. 'What does "give 'em the old one-two" mean? What's an old one-two?' she asked. Millar had to explain that it was a boxing term for a knockout.[22]

Margaret Thatcher liked winning arguments with knockout blows rather than on points, but that was not how she presented her case in her final party political broadcast. She decided to play it safe – literally.

Her last words to the nation on the eve of the election were not just softly, softly; they were sugary, sugary:

Let us make this a country safe to work in; let us make this a country safe to walk in; let us make it a country safe to grow up in; let us make it a country safe to grow old in . . . May this land of ours, which we love so much, find dignity and greatness and peace again.[23]

'Amen', said one of my irreverent supporters in Thanet East to a group of us gathered round a television set to watch this performance. It was a let-down. The breathy pauses reeked of ham acting stuffed with sentimentality. 'It's not quite like the Margaret Thatcher I know', I commented to my party workers.[24]

But how well did anybody know her?

ON THE EVE OF POWER

During the election I had two telephone conversations with Margaret Thatcher. They were mainly chats about what the canvass returns were showing in my constituency (a clear swing to the Conservatives of about 5 per cent) and how her speeches were playing on television. Among other topics she complained about the invisibility of her shadow cabinet, singling out the exception of Teddy Taylor, who she said was showing himself to be 'a bonny fighter' in Scotland.

These exchanges took place during the visits of Carol who was staying at my house in Thanet for much of the campaign. After the second call the thought struck me that the next time I spoke to Margaret she would be Prime Minister. She sounded totally confident of this destiny when I wished her good luck. 'Not luck. We'll win because we deserve to win', she said.[25]

Her certainty triggered a mood of uncertainty in me. Even after four years of scrutiny as Leader of the Opposition, I thought she would arrive in 10 Downing Street as the 'Unknown Prime Minister'. Neither her colleagues nor the country had really come to terms with her extraordinary personality, let alone the impact it might make on unforeseen events. I had spent more time with her at closer quarters than most back-benchers, but even so I was making the mistake of seriously underestimating her. Yet this underestimation of Margaret Thatcher was widely shared in 1979, partly through ignorance and partly because she had kept some aspects of her personality and plans carefully hidden.

I remember quite well what I thought about her on the eve of the election. It was a mixture of the intriguing, the exciting and the worrying. If my picture now seems too negative with the wisdom of hindsight, it was made up not only of my own observations but also of many parliamentary and personal views, which were insider talk at the time.

On the parliamentary front, I saw Margaret Thatcher as the least collegiate politician I had ever met. This was because she had no friends. Naturally she had legions of acquaintances with whom she was friendly, and a handful she trusted. But these were professional relationships. She could work with anyone if it served her purpose, but she relaxed with no one. She had no interests beyond politics. The concept of a disinterested personal relationship or a private hinterland was beyond her ken.

The intensity of her focus on the political tasks in hand seemed both admirable and alarming. Admirable because there was a huge job to be done in pulling Britain out of the slough of despond and disintegration into which it had descended. Alarming because government was thought to require a team effort, and she was no team player. Could she hold together her cabinet colleagues, her party supporters and ultimately the electorate while delivering the medicine that would bring the country back to recovery? Could she win over the House of Commons as Prime Minister?

Many people, including a large section of her parliamentary party, feared that she might be too confrontational a leader to achieve these goals.

Confrontation came naturally to her. 'I don't think we should bother too much with the centre ground', she said in an unguarded moment during a meeting of the CPG at my house in 1977.[26] 'I couldn't waste any time having internal arguments', she told the *Observer* a few weeks before the election in the context of needing a cabinet of like-minded colleagues.[27] This must have been the reason she so fiercely resisted Peter Thorneycroft's suggestion that she should share a platform with Ted Heath in the closing stages of the campaign.

By chance, Ted Heath came down to visit his father and stepmother in Broadstairs the weekend before election day. I took a walk with him from Will Heath's house in Dumpton Park Drive down to a pub in Viking Bay. For the previous three weeks Ted had been a highly visible figure on the nation's television screens. Late in the day he had transformed himself into an exemplary loyalist, speaking mainly on foreign affairs. There was speculation that he might be signalling a willingness to be the next Foreign Secretary. Without asking about this directly, I said that his contribution to the campaign effort had made many people hope that there could be reconciliation in the air between him and Margaret Thatcher.

'Hmm . . .', responded Ted Heath. 'Are they really saying that?' I nodded. There was a long silence. 'She'd find it difficult', he eventually said. 'She's a hater, you know. Probably hates me.' I was bold enough to say that I thought it looked the other way round. 'She can't separate the political from the personal, you see', Heath responded. 'She always takes the narrow view. Doesn't realise that you have to make compromises. She bears grudges.'[28]

Although this was rich coming from him it was probably an accurate view. In private I had heard Margaret Thatcher being scathing about MPs whose main fault seemed to be that they had stood against her in the election (Jim Prior and John Peyton), or stood up to her in arguments (Michael Heseltine). She could get surprisingly personal. 'In the shadow cabinet she had to win every single argument and ram it home,' said her admirer Norman St John-Stevas, 'and she could be quite bitter about those who she disagreed with.'[29] But in line with the conventional hypocrisy of politics she was pleasantly agreeable to these same colleagues in public.

Another exercise in her art of dissembling was that Margaret Thatcher presented herself in the election as a moderate consensualist. There were no signs that she would confront the miners, privatise huge swathes of industry, scrap incomes policy or demand rebates from the European Union. Yet she had been quite willing to talk privately about such ideas. She just kept them in the closet, along with her personal likes and dislikes. Everything was subordinated to winning the next election.

This dissonance between the public and private Margaret Thatcher extended into personal issues. I thought she was a more attractive character than the world perceived. I saw her as courageous, kind, feminine and considerate to the least important people in her orbit. Yet I knew there was also an unpleasant streak in her, which manifested itself in her bullying manner towards colleagues she thought were being slipshod in their preparations for policy discussions. At least she only punched people who boxed at her weight.

On the good side, the greatest plus was her courage. This was visible not just on the big stage, where she dared to challenge Ted Heath for the leadership and delivered brave speeches on foreign and domestic policy. She was also fearless in her approach to a host of smaller decisions. To give just one example:

In 1978 I helped to organise Richard Nixon's first visit to Europe following his resignation from the presidency after Watergate. At that time he was an international pariah. The Foreign Secretary, David Owen, tried to block his private visit. The Speaker of the House of Commons cancelled a planned reception for him. Two ex-prime ministers, Ted Heath and Harold Macmillan, refused to meet the former President.

In the middle of all these rejections from the great and the good, I asked Margaret Thatcher whether she would be willing to see Nixon. She replied unhesitatingly, 'Of course I would be delighted to meet him'. When I reported her attitude to the nervous Speaker, George Thomas, he did a *volte-face* about the cancellation of his party. 'What a woman! What courage!' he exclaimed. 'That puts a completely different complexion on matters. I think I shall give my reception after all.' At Speaker's House Margaret Thatcher struck up a good relationship with Richard Nixon, later receiving him in 10 Downing Street when she became Prime Minister.[30] It was not the first or the last time that her 'infection of a good courage'[31] changed events.

Another plus was her kindness. She had a soft touch for anyone down on their luck, ill, bereaved or suffering any kind of adversity. Once she became the Iron Lady, this image eclipsed her gentler side. But compassion was a real part of her private personality, despite all the noise in the opposite direction. I saw this myself in several small ways: concern for my dying godfather, Selwyn Lloyd; a couple of kind notes when I was in hospital; caring for Airey Neave's widow, Diana; sending flowers and letters to the families of other sick or dying colleagues; insisting the Central Office staffers took days off when they had family problems such as a sick child. Her later image as an uncaring prime minister had some political validity, but at a personal level she cared.

One other aspect of the lesser-known Margaret Thatcher was her consideration for those who worked for her. In those days, the Leader of the Opposition's office was an overworked, highly stressed crucible of controversy. I knew two of the key figures working there quite well – Richard Ryder, the *de facto* head of her private office, and Caroline Stephens, her personal assistant. Clam-like in their discretion, they were experts in managing her personality. It was a more tumultuous force than they ever let on, but equally forceful was the mutual respect. Just as no man is a hero to his valet, no political leader is without flaws to their private office, but she was something of an exception to this adage.

Margaret Thatcher was always a considerate boss. She could be short on apologies after she had gone over the top during a drama, but to her staff she was long on gentleness and kindness. Those two words are not naturally associated with the Iron Lady, but in her time as Leader of the Opposition they were true.

As for her feminine side, this was obvious in many ways starting with her good dress sense, her eye for colours and her interest in curtains, fabrics and furnishings. I remember when she came to a family lunch in my mother's home, how she spent five minutes commenting with some expertise on a hand-painted Chinese wallpaper in the dining room, running her fingers delicately over the flow of the artist's brush strokes.

As for other aspects of her femininity, it did not require much in the way of male imagination to see Margaret Thatcher as a woman of sensuality as well as strength. We were photographed walking away from Westminster Abbey after Selwyn Lloyd's memorial service. Taken shortly before the general election of 1979, her hat is tilted at a jaunty angle; her confident eyes, her wide hips, her full yet trim figure and her elegant ankles all convey the impression of a fine-looking woman.

Being a woman political leader caused huge reactions in the political and media arena, but I could see that this almost unique status was of little interest to her. She was underwhelmed by the cause of feminism. She asked for and gave no quarter in arguments with her male colleagues. This put them at a disadvantage because they did not know how to answer her vigorous point scoring, let alone her diatribes.

She was at her most obnoxious when tearing a strip off a colleague, partly because she had no idea how to do this, except by going on and on with increasing unpleasantness.

Denis, who took his fair share of tongue-lashings, once said to me, 'You just have to let her bollockings flow over you. Even the right royal ones don't last that long.'[32]

On one occasion when I received a right royal bollocking from Margaret Thatcher while she was Leader of the Opposition, it was an alarming experience. Late one evening in the House of Commons, she called me into her office and in tones of fury erupted: 'I hear you told Willie Whitelaw he was like one of Pavlov's dogs. Well, let me tell you . . .' Three minutes later, by which time the flow of molten lava had covered Willie's war record, disloyalty to colleagues, my arrogance, his hurt feelings, the importance of party unity and goodness knows what else, I finally got a word in edgeways.

I replied that I had not said what she thought I said. This seemed to infuriate her even more. Larger rockets were fired in my direction. But I stood my ground and insisted that my comment had merely been that the opposition had made 'a Pavlovian response' to a government announcement about the handling of complaints against the police. This was some way from attacking Willie Whitelaw personally.

Margaret Thatcher took no notice. She banged on as if I had compared her deputy to Adolf Hitler. 'But it's in *Hansard*', I protested. 'When you read it you'll see that its mild stuff and not offensive. I'm sorry if Willie took it the wrong way.' The realisation that my criticism of Whitelaw had not been a private *ad hominem* row but a public argument about policy on the floor of the House of Commons slowed her down – but not much. Mount Vesuvius went on rumbling but stopped erupting. The bollocking was over.

The following day the official record confirmed that my comment had indeed been a mild and impersonal one. Perhaps it was a misjudgement on my part, but nothing that remotely justified all that rage from Margaret Thatcher. Within a week she was going out of her way to be pleasant to me – which I sensed was her way of correcting her over-reaction. She hated to admit she had been in the wrong.

This minor incident was not uncharacteristic of Margaret Thatcher with her dander up. There were several colleagues who had been bruised by her voluble and personalised criticism. Ironically, one of them was Willie Whitelaw, who in 1976 moaned to friends, 'I have never been spoken to that way in my life', after she had lambasted him for not knowing his Home Office brief properly.[33]

There was a special skill in handling Margaret Thatcher which few of her political colleagues acquired in opposition, although one or two became adept at it in government. She had fewer people around her between 1975 and 1979 who knew how to cope with her volatility. They were Caroline Stephens, Richard Ryder, Ronnie Millar, Gordon Reece and Tim Bell. In their different ways they each brought out the best of her by understanding through the prism of her femininity not only her high peaks of achievement but also her low moments of vulnerability. And of course there was Denis. He put up with a lot but he was the rock of trust on which her ultimate confidences were reposed.

As polling day loomed, there was a growing sense that Britain was facing a watershed election. Whatever their political allegiances, most people knew that we could not go on with the economic and political failure that had characterised the locust years of the 1970s. One key figure who understood that the tectonic plates of political Britain were shifting was James Callaghan. In the closing phase of the campaign he made one or two comments to his staff that revealed his understanding of what was happening in the mood of the electorate. When his speech-writer served him up a draft that included a personal attack on his opponent, he rejected it, saying, 'I'm not going to go for Mrs Thatcher like that. In a week or so she may be Prime Minister of Britain.'[34]

Bernard Donoghue, the Prime Minister's closest political aide, detected a growing respect in Callaghan's mind for what Margaret Thatcher was saying in her election speeches and broadcasts. Even when the polls suggested the gap between the parties was narrowing Callaghan remained privately sceptical about his own prospects. Driving back from a Labour Party rally in the last week before polling day, Donoghue offered the view that victory could yet be theirs if the momentum continued. As the car rounded Parliament Square, the Prime Minister disagreed:

> Every thirty years or so there comes a sea change in politics . . . Then it does not matter what you say or do. There is a shift in what the public wants and what it approves. I suspect there is now such a sea change – and it is for Mrs Thatcher.[35]

That sea change was the final ingredient in Margaret Thatcher on the eve of the election. She was riding to power on the crest of a wave. The force was with her, and it was exciting to watch. She generated her own electricity which both attracted and repelled. If you were anywhere near her field you felt the current. You sensed that she was going to give the nation a shock – but would it energise the body politic or make it fall apart? She was sure of the answer, but most members of her party in Parliament, whatever they might hope or fear, were much less certain.

VICTORY

There was no lack of certainty about the result in Margaret Thatcher's mind as polling day dawned, although she professed to be nervous. After casting her vote at nine in the morning in Chelsea Town Hall for the Conservative Candidate Nicholas Scott, she tried a laboured jest: 'We never count our chickens before they are hatched, and we don't count No. 10 Downing Street before it is thatched.'[36] She wrote the line herself. Jokes were still uncertain instruments in her hands.

The polls and the papers were good. Her most ardent new supporter in the media, the *Sun*, for the first time urged its largely Labour readership, 'Vote Tory This Time – It's the Only Way to Stop the Rot'.[37] Rupert Murdoch had initially been anti-Thatcher in her early days as opposition leader, but scenting her success, he had come round. So had the swing voters. All the final opinion polls put her in the lead by margins of between 2 and 10.5 per cent. But she was careful to suppress her optimism as she spent the afternoon doing the usual tour of committee rooms in her Finchley constituency. Then she returned to Flood Street for the unusual luxury of a nap.

By the time she arrived, shortly after midnight, at Barnet Town Hall for the Finchley count, the trend of the early results was encouraging. It seemed clear that the Tories would form the next government. The predictions of the majority were rising. But Margaret Thatcher made no premature comment. She sat in a side room watching the television coverage, making notes of the returns in the briefing book Conservative Central Office had prepared for her. She could now count her chickens as they hatched, and long before her own result was announced she was certain she would be the next prime minister.

Because of a temporarily mislaid ballot box, Finchley declared late at 2.25 a.m. Margaret Thatcher more than doubled her majority, winning by 7,878 votes.[38] She said she was 'cautiously optimistic' about the national result, which she revised to 'optimistic' when she arrived to cheering crowds at Central Office just before 4.00 a.m.

Amidst the scenes of triumph, a BBC radio reporter caught her saying it was 'all very exciting . . . but somehow one is calm about it because you have to be'.[39] Calmness in the eye of the storm of rejoicing was her trademark on that blissful dawn. She made a point of formally thanking every available Central Office staffer and party volunteer. Only once did she let her emotions show. She drew Ronnie Millar aside and asked him what he had prepared as a draft statement for her to deliver on the steps of No. 10 Downing Street.

He suggested she should quote the words of a prayer attributed to St Francis of Assisi:

Where there is discord, may we bring harmony, where there is error, may we bring truth, where there is doubt, may we bring faith, and where there is despair, may we bring hope.[40]

According to Ronnie Millar, 'The lady rarely shows her deep feelings but this, on a night of high tension and the constant switchback of emotion, proved too much. Her eyes swam. She blew her nose.'[41]

As she sat down with her constituency secretary, Alison Ward, to get the lines typed, Alison began crying too. After these private tears, it was back to Flood Street for public cheers at 5 a.m. There, she snatched a couple of hours of sleep.

When the final results were analysed, the Conservatives were home and dry with a comfortable overall majority of forty-three seats. The national swing was 5.1 per cent – regionally higher in the South (7.7. per cent) than in the North (4.2. per cent).[42] The worst blow of the night was that the Shadow Secretary of State for Scotland, Teddy Taylor, lost his seat to Labour in Glasgow Cathcart. But with that exception, the electoral sea change predicted by Jim Callaghan had taken place.

At 11.30 a.m. on Friday 4 May Margaret Thatcher returned to Central Office, where Tim Bell and Gordon Reece advised her that she should not use the prayer of St Francis because it sounded 'far too pious'.[43] She consulted Ronnie Millar, who told her to ignore them, invoking the name of Winston Churchill, which seemed to persuade her.

'What shall I tell the boys?' she asked.

'Tell them it's too soon to get cold feet until you've kissed hands.'[44]

She decided to stay with the St Francis script.

On television it was reported that Jim Callaghan had gone to Buckingham Palace to surrender his seals of office. Half an hour later, the phone rang. It was Ted Heath, wanting to offer his congratulations. Margaret Thatcher decided not to take the call. 'Thank him very much', was her instruction. The phone rang again. Everyone stiffened. 'You're not going to believe this', said Caroline Stephens. 'Wrong number.'[45]

With the tension rising, Margaret Thatcher kicked off her shoes and flexed her toes. Denis asked whether she had confused Buckingham Palace with a Hindu temple. She glared at him but put her shoes back on. Just after three o'clock the call came from the Queen's Private Secretary, Sir Philip Moore.

'Right. We're off', she said as she replaced the receiver.

'Prime Minister . . .' began Mark.

'Not yet, dear', reproved his mother.

'No', chipped in Denis. 'The car might break down.'

'In that case, I shall walk', said the Prime Minister-elect, with theatrical firmness.[46]

As she was driven out of Smith Square, she had the idea of using the car telephone to reach out to the defeated Teddy Taylor. He was amazed to be told she was calling while en route for the Palace. Her words of commiseration and kindness at such a moment moved him to tears.[47]

After a forty-five minute audience with the Queen, Prime Minister Margaret Thatcher arrived at Downing Street. She paused amidst a *melée* of cameras to deliver the apocryphal prayer of St Francis. Her tone was the opposite of triumphalism. It was also the opposite of what she planned to do in government. As she must have known, 'Where there is discord, may we bring harmony' was the antithesis of her conviction politics.

Just before she crossed the threshold of No. 10, a reporter shouted, 'Have you any thoughts, Mrs Thatcher, at this moment about Mrs Pankhurst* and your own mentor in political life – your own father?'

Despite the oddity of this pairing, the last two words evidently struck a chord. Ignoring Mrs Pankhurst, the new Prime Minister seized her chance to pay tribute to Alfred Roberts. She responded:

> Well, of course, I just owe almost everything to my own father. I really do. He brought me up to believe all the things that I do believe and they're just the values on which I've fought the election. And it's passionately interesting for me that the things I learned in a small town, in a very modest home, are just the things that I believe have won the election.[48]

Invoking her humble roots was a good public relations touch. But the tasks that awaited her on the other side of No. 10's front door would soon show different dimensions of her personality than the humility and the prayer of St Francis.

---

* Emmeline Pankhurst (1858–1928) was a suffragette leader who fought for women's voting rights in the early twentieth century.

REFLECTION

Although Margaret Thatcher won the 1979 election, the main force that drove her to victory was neither her policies nor her leadership nor her image; it was the 'winter of discontent'.

The voters most affected by this national melodrama were the group known to pollsters as C2s. They were the skilled working class, fast becoming disillusioned with Labour for giving in to union militants who stopped them earning higher pay for longer hours of work. Many of these C2s were readers of the *Sun*, which was why the paper's editor, Larry Lamb, worked so closely with Tim Bell and Gordon Reece before and during the election.[49]

Lamb's view of his readers was that many of them saw in Margaret Thatcher the values that they themselves aspired to. They liked her because she was self-made, hard working, ambitious, determined, patriotic and hating Britain's slide into anarchic decline. The big hurdle these readers and voters had to overcome was that they and their families were traditionally Labour voters. The big push in Margaret Thatcher's speeches, broadcasts and newspaper coverage was persuading them 'to cross the Rubicon',[50] as she put it, and vote Conservative for the first time.

Post-election analysis of the voting figures showed that this strategy succeeded. Amongst C2 or skilled working-class voters, the Tories achieved a swing of 11 per cent. With the C3, or unskilled working class, the swing to the Conservatives was 9 per cent. This was twice as big as swing as the rest of the electorate gave Margaret Thatcher.[51]

She broke new ground by capturing votes that had never before been won from Labour by the Conservative Party. This blue-collar support stayed solidly behind her for most of the 1980s. It was the bedrock on which she built her revolution. It gave her a mandate for breaking with the middle-way consensus that had governed Britain since 1945.

No one would have guessed this if they had tuned in to the prayer of St Francis of Assisi that the new Prime Minister read out on the threshold of 10 Downing Street. It was an ill-judged lurch into uncharacteristic hypocrisy. For the saint's apocryphal words did not represent the true thoughts or the real instincts of Margaret Thatcher – as the world would soon discover.

15

First moves as Prime Minister

MAKING A START

'Well, Ken, what do I do now?' were almost the first words spoken by Margaret Thatcher after she crossed the threshold of No. 10 Downing Street.[1] They were addressed to her Principal Private Secretary, Kenneth Stowe, whom she had come to know and trust from her occasional dealings with him as Leader of the Opposition.

He was waiting for her on the other side of the famous front door, while she delivered her Francis of Assisi message to the media. Crammed into the entrance hall with him was the entire hundred-strong prime ministerial staff, from tea ladies to top civil servants. As they applauded the arrival of their new boss, Margaret Thatcher seemed touched by the warmth and size of her reception committee. After exchanging pleasantries with them, Stowe led her to the Cabinet Room where a number of briefing papers were laid out for her, starting with the procedures for nuclear weapons and urgent security issues. The Cabinet Secretary, Sir John Hunt, took her through these briefs. Her work as Prime Minister had begun.

'Well prepared, brisk, thoroughly business-like and knowing exactly what she wanted', was Kenneth Stowe's characterisation of Margaret Thatcher's first hours in No. 10. Her immediate priority was forming the government. The great offices of state went to William Whitelaw (Home Secretary), Lord Carrington (Foreign Secretary) and Sir Geoffrey Howe (Chancellor of the Exchequer). There had been speculation in the press that she might invite Ted Heath to be Foreign Secretary, but this was not a thought she entertained seriously. She did mention it to Kenneth Stowe at the outset of her cabinet making, but only in the context of how she should tell Heath that he was *not* going to be offered the Foreign Office. She sent a handwritten letter to his home by despatch rider, explaining that after thinking 'long and deeply about the post of Foreign Secretary' she had 'decided to offer it to Peter Carrington who – as I am sure you will agree – will do the job superbly'.[2] As she told her Private Secretary before writing to Heath: 'I can't have him in the cabinet because he will be patronising me all the time.'[3]

Margaret Thatcher hated to be patronised. That was why she excluded from her first cabinet one other senior figure who she thought, on past form, was likely to offend her in this way. He was John Peyton, the Shadow Leader of the House, whose pedantic style of elaborate sarcasm she disliked. She gave the Leadership of the House to the more colourful Norman St John-Stevas, whose jokes about 'The Leaderene' and 'The Blessed Margaret' were thought, at least in his own opinion, to provide him with a special niche in her affections as a licensed court jester.

The surprise of her first cabinet appointments lay in their caution. Most of the new ministers were given the posts they had been shadowing in opposition. There was no tilt to the right. Some ardent Thatcherites, such as Nicholas Ridley and Jock Bruce-Gardyne, were disappointed. They were predicting that she would pick a team containing many whole-hearted supporters of her reforming agenda.

Instead, she appointed a traditional Tory cabinet most of whom had built their careers in the Macmillan, Douglas-Home and Heath administrations. The political commentators, as always obsessively interested in the class backgrounds of ministers, gleefully pointed out that the new twenty-two-member cabinet contained twenty Oxbridge graduates; six Old Etonians; three Wykehamists; six former Guards officers; five barristers; three baronets; two hereditary peers; and seven substantial landowners. Just two ministers, aside from Margaret Thatcher, had been educated at state schools – John Biffen and Peter Walker.[4] She was the only woman. Feminism, radicalism and monetarism did not seem well represented in the Prime Minister's brave new world.

These appearances were somewhat deceptive. Superficially, she appeared to have picked a cabinet with a built-in majority of the laid back and the luke-warm in their attitudes to Thatcherism. James Prior (Employment); Francis Pym (Defence); Sir Ian Gilmour (Lord Privy Seal and Lord Carrington's deputy in the House of Commons); Mark Carlisle (Education); David Howell (Energy); Peter Walker (Agriculture); George Younger (Scotland); Lord Hailsham (Lord Chancellor); and Lord Soames (Leader of the House of Lords) were a mixture

of sceptics and consensualists of the old school. They seemed unlikely to be
ardent followers of the Prime Minister down the roads of confronting the unions
or replacing Keynesian economics with the doctrines of Milton Friedman.

There were, however, other counter-balancing factors in the early architecture of Thatcherism. She handpicked an inner group of Treasury and spending
department ministers whom she treated as her praetorian guard. They held
most of the positions on the vital E (for Economic) Committee of the Cabinet.
She had weekly breakfast meetings with them to discuss both the tactics and
the strategy of adherence to the monetarist faith. These insiders included
Sir Geoffrey Howe (Chancellor of the Exchequer); John Biffen (Chief Secretary
to the Treasury); Sir Keith Joseph (Industry); Patrick Jenkin (Health and
Social Security); and John Nott (Trade). Outside the cabinet two influential
keepers of the monetarist flame were Nigel Lawson (Financial Secretary to the
Treasury) and Ian Gow (Parliamentary Private Secretary).

By far the most important torchbearer for change in the government was
the Prime Minister herself. She was the personification of Edmund Burke's
dictum 'One man with conviction makes a majority'.[5] If there were any doubts
that the pressures of power might dilute Margaret Thatcher's zeal as a reformer,
they were dispelled by her first parliamentary appearance eleven days after
winning the election. Opening the traditional debate on the Queen's Speech,
she outlined the government's legislative programme for the year ahead with
an extraordinary display of political passion.

Listening to this firecracker of a performance from the back benches, I was
one of several MPs present on whom it dawned that Margaret Thatcher was
determined to upset the apple-cart of the old consensus politics. Watching
Tory grandees like Francis Pym and Ian Gilmour shift uneasily in their seats on
the front bench as their leader crushed interruptions and powered ahead with
her agenda of economic priorities, I wondered how well some of them supported
the tone in which she was moving 'The Gracious Speech'.

After reminding the House that she had won this 'watershed election . . . with
a difference of about 2 million votes between the two parties, which was the
largest difference since 1935', Margaret Thatcher unveiled the agenda of reform
that she had been careful not to spell out with specific details during the election.
Public expenditure would be cut. Income tax would be reduced by the Budget
in one month's time. Every council tenant would have the right to buy their

home at a substantial discount with 100 per cent mortgage. Grammar schools would be preserved. Trade-union powers would be curbed. The public sector would be reduced. The Price Commission and the Community Land Act would be abolished. State holdings in industry would be sold. The government's strategy was to restore the balance between the individual and the state.[6]

The fervour with which she delivered her speech (which she had written herself) left the House stunned – with admiration if you were on her side, or with amazement if you were not. These categories were not necessarily defined by political loyalties. I recall going to the tea room soon after the Prime Minister sat down. A Scottish Labour MP, Dr J. Dickson 'Dick' Mabon, said, 'What courage! She's exactly what the voters are crying out for.'[7]

Several Tories were more hesitant. 'She needs hosing down with the waters of reality', said William van Straubenzee, the Conservative Member for Wokingham, whose penchant for Episcopalian platitudes earned him the nick-name 'The Bishop'.[8] Tony Benn captured the mood on the Left when in his diary he described her oration as 'the most rumbustious, rampaging right-wing speech I've heard from the Government Front Bench in the whole of my life'.[9]

The Budget on 12 June was also bolder and more right wing than most observers had imagined possible. Although the economic weather was becom-ing increasingly stormy, with inflation at 10 per cent and rising, the unity of purpose between the Prime Minister and her Chancellor was steadfast. The relationship between Margaret Thatcher and Sir Geoffrey Howe was eventually to turn sour and to bring about her downfall. But in the 1979–1981 period they worked hand in glove together, even if it was her hand pushing into his glove.

Between them they constructed a budget that cut public expenditure by £3.5 billion; brought the top rate of tax down from 83 per cent to 60 per cent, and the standard rate from 33 to 30 per cent; lifted pay and dividend restraints; and abolished exchange controls.[10] This last move, which was completed in three stages by October, was a radical affirmation of faith in free markets. Lifting all restrictions on the movement of capital could have caused the collapse of sterling. In fact the international markets sent the pound rising, but the move had been a close call with Margaret Thatcher temporarily becoming more hesitant than Geoffrey Howe on the eve of the final announcement.

There were prices to be paid for these displays of boldness. In order to afford the cuts in direct taxation, VAT was massively increased as the existing rates of

8 and 12.5 per cent were unified at 15 per cent.[11] Inflation, boosted by soaring oil prices, more than doubled, from 10.3 per cent to 21.9 per cent in the first year after the Budget. Interest rates soared to 17 per cent.[12] Unemployment began climbing towards what was thought to be a frightening forecast of two million. Also starting to rise were the number of doubters in the cabinet.

HANDLING HER CABINET

Handling her cabinet was not one of Margaret Thatcher's strengths. Eventually it became one of the main causes of her downfall. But in her early weeks of power she was a good practitioner of collegiate government. The old hands compared her favourably with Ted Heath, who had been far more restrictive in suppressing wide-ranging debate on policy issues.

By contrast, the new Prime Minister enjoyed a good argument around the cabinet table. She liked to open the discussion on a particular topic herself, usually rather forcefully. She was not backward in interrupting the voices that disagreed with the line she had taken. Later in her premiership this style was regarded as somewhat intimidating by newcomers to the cabinet. But at the beginning she was surrounded by older and more experienced colleagues who could not easily be intimidated. So the shared decision-making process was rather effective, owing much to the skills of Willie Whitelaw. He was a past master at summing up cabinet deliberations in a way that kept the dissenters mollified while guiding the decision in the direction the Prime Minister wanted. When reaching this goal proved particularly tricky, Willie had a habit of tugging his eyebrow with his right hand as if to pull himself and his audience to the desired conclusion. It was an engaging quirk that seemed to achieve the right result.

It was sometimes said that Margaret Thatcher never quite understood the concept of cabinet government, and lost the art of it when Whitelaw retired, following a minor stroke, in 1988. Her weakness was spotted early by one leading political figure who had never served with her. Enoch Powell joked over dinner one evening in my home:

The problem is that cabinet government is the ultimate men's team game. All those public schoolboys were trained from childhood to play in football teams, cricket teams, regimental teams and at the top of politics in the cabinet team. But she's a woman. She thinks quite differently. Women fight for their men, their children, their homes, but they don't play in teams. So it's hardly surprising she doesn't know how to be captain of a team. She has no concept of *primus inter pares*. She's what Hollywood calls a Lone Ranger.[13]

Some members of her cabinet were unable to dodge the Lone Ranger's bullets. To a minister she felt was ineffective, she could be insufferably rude, even in the presence of his departmental officials. This was below the belt by all previous standards of prime ministerial behaviour. But Margaret Thatcher did not play by the Queensberry or any other set of rules when she was in a fighting mood.

Among the earliest targets for the rough edge of her tongue were the Department of Energy and its Secretary of State, David Howell. He was a cerebral and courteous Old Etonian, with useful ministerial experience as Willie Whitelaw's no. 2 in Northern Ireland during the Heath government. Thatcherite in his economic thinking, Howell had headed Margaret Thatcher's speech-writing team in opposition to her considerable satisfaction. Yet in government, he found he could do nothing right in the eyes of the Prime Minister. He recalled:

> She was instantly hostile to everything and everyone in my department. It was almost as if she had declared UDI* from us. She saw Energy as a gigantic temple of inefficient, high-spending nationalised industries, particularly coal, electricity and nuclear power. She thought North Sea oil was a bureaucratic mess. She disliked the Permanent Secretary and the Deputy Permanent Secretary. She was unpleasant and rude to me. It just got more and more rough.[14]

This was not just the bruised reaction of a beleaguered cabinet minister. David Howell's Parliamentary Under-Secretary was Norman Lamont. He was so upset by the Prime Minister's belligerence at her meetings with Energy ministers that he went to see Sir Keith Joseph to make a private complaint about it. 'Oh, I've felt the lash too', said Joseph with amused insouciance. 'You see, she deals in creative destruction to make her point.'[15]

---

* Unilateral Declaration of Independence – a label created by Ian Smith's regime in Rhodesia when it declared UDI from Britain on 11 November 1965.

At this early stage in the life of the government, the personality flaws of Margaret Thatcher as an occasional bully were hidden from the world, although they later became notorious because of her treatment of Sir Geoffrey Howe. But within the inner circle, her rudeness to her senior colleagues, even in cabinet, could seem shocking. 'It's not just an error,' she snapped at Lord Carrington when he apologised for some minor failing by the Foreign Office, 'it's incompetence, and it comes from the top.'[16]

'Isn't he awful? Isn't he awful!' was her heckling of the Lord Chancellor, Lord Hailsham, as he tried to explain to the cabinet why high-court judges merited their salaries and pensions. When she spotted Lord Soames glancing at his watch during a late-morning discussion of civil-service pay (for which he was responsible), the Prime Minister sniped, 'If you want to go to lunch, Christopher – you can go now'.[17] And to more than one minister who seemed to be relying too heavily on his departmental brief, her rebuke was, 'Your civil servants have got at you again. I'm not surprised.'[18]

These snipings were never recorded in the cabinet minutes. But so many of them are well remembered that there is no doubt that Margaret Thatcher could display an unpleasant edge to her style of leadership. Its saving grace was that she mostly reserved her bullying for people her own size. It was the grandees of the Tory Party rather than junior ministers and officials who bore the brunt of her rough style. But it could get nasty. After one rumpus involving next week's business in the House of Commons, a shaken Norman St John-Stevas left the cabinet room making the comment, 'No one will ever believe it is like this!'[19]

One of Margaret Thatcher's most unbelievable outbursts in cabinet during the government's early months came on Tuesday 20 November 1979. Patrick Jenkin, the Secretary of State for Health and Social Security, was due to move the second reading in the House that afternoon of a Social Security Bill that would lead to significant reductions in public expenditure. He outlined the main points of the legislation to his colleagues. 'Where are the cuts in benefits for strikers' families?' demanded the Prime Minister. Patrick Jenkin replied that the Legislation Committee of the Cabinet, chaired by Willie Whitelaw, had come to a clear decision that this issue should be dealt with in a separate Social Security Bill during the next session of Parliament.

'Why not in this one?' demanded the Prime Minister. After the same explanation, the matter might have rested on this note of disappointment, but for an intervention from the Leader of the House of Commons, Norman St John-Stevas. He commented that in fact there were powers given to the Secretary of State in the small print of the schedules of the existing bill which would allow him to cut benefits for strikers' families.

'Good. Do it at once!' said Margaret Thatcher.

'Then I shall have to tell the House in my speech this afternoon', replied Jenkin.

'No you won't. Let them find out', was the retort from the Prime Minister.

There then followed a fierce argument. Patrick Jenkin said that he could not and would not conceal from Parliament the intention to use such a politically sensitive power.

'Yes you can. Just let them find out!' Margaret Thatcher kept repeating. Patrick Jenkin stuck to his ground, despite the hard pounding. 'Well none of us are going to get to St Margaret's until we've settled this', declared the furious Prime Minister. She was referring to a memorial service at St Margaret's, Westminster, which many of the cabinet were scheduled to attend at 12 noon.

In an acrimonious discussion, Willie Whitelaw and Lord Carrington supported Jenkin, saying that no Secretary of State could possibly get away with the course of action suggested. Faced with the opposition of these two heavyweights, Margaret Thatcher gave way – but with bad grace.

'She became extremely snarly,' recalled Patrick Jenkin, 'and as she swept out of the Cabinet Room on her way to St Margaret's she practically shouted at me: "This is the worst decision we've made since we've been in government!"' [20]

Immediately after this scene, an upset Jenkin walked across to No. 11 Downing Street with his old friend the Chancellor of the Exchequer. 'Well, Patrick,' said Geoffrey Howe consolingly, 'you've seen the downside now – but the upside is well worth it.' [21]

This did not remain Howe's point of view during his later years in the cabinet. But at the time his words were a good guide for himself and for other senior ministers. They had their rough passages with Margaret Thatcher, but most of them believed in the upside of her leadership.

CHALLENGING THE CIVIL SERVICE

Yes Minister had not been invented as a television series in 1979, but the culture it caricatured was already firmly embedded in Margaret Thatcher's mind as a reality. She came to power with an instinctive distrust of the civil service, born of her unhappy experiences at the Department of Education. She never lost this attitude towards the Whitehall machine, yet more and more she came to rely on a small number of individual civil servants whom she saw as kindred spirits of talent and energy. This paradox between her suspicion of the institution and her enthusiasm for individuals within it gradually gave her government the feel of a guerrilla army headed by a rebel leader.

'You're not being seduced by your Martians, are you?'[22] This was the question she put to her Parliamentary Under Secretary of State at the Department of Employment, Peter Morrison, in the autumn of 1979. The imagery was revealing. For one part of Margaret Thatcher liked to believe that civil servants lived on another planet. She was determined to attack it, to reduce the number of aliens and to 'de-privilege' them. These star wars had mixed results, but they quickly highlighted the impact of the Prime Minister's personality on the government machine.

One immediate target for her reforming zeal was the Department of the Civil Service. She put a freeze on its recruitment; cut its jobs by 14 per cent; and created her own Efficiency Unit, under Sir Derek Rayner, the Managing Director of Marks & Spencer, whose departmental scrutinies found savings of over £200 million. These upheavals caused grief for Sir Ian Bancroft, Permanent Secretary at the Department of the Civil Service, who became the Sir Humphrey she loved to hate.

Their first conflict came in June 1979, when she was told by him that her Principal Private Secretary, Kenneth Stowe, would be moving to Belfast as Permanent Secretary of the Northern Ireland Department, at the end of the month. Margaret Thatcher resisted the departure of a first-class Private Secretary who had been with her for only three weeks. Ian Bancroft resisted back, explaining that Stowe's new post was his promotion to a higher civil-service grade. The Prime Minister retaliated with the argument that he could surely be awarded the higher grade in his existing post. Bancroft objected, which she thought was unreasonable.* The deadlock was only broken when Bancroft played what was called 'the sympathy card'. He argued that after four years at No. 10 serving three prime ministers, Stowe needed to spend more time with his young family.

---

* Margaret Thatcher eventually won this argument but in slower time. The post of Private Secretary to the Prime Minister has now been upgraded to the rank of a Permanent Secretary.

It was a little-known side of Margaret Thatcher that she was extremely considerate to the family needs of her staff. So she gave way gracefully to Kenneth
Stowe, whom she honoured with a farewell dinner, but she behaved grudgingly
to Bancroft. Her grudge against him worsened after a disastrous evening which
she later described as 'one of the most dismal occasions of my entire time in
government'.[23]

According to Lord Carrington, who was present at this memorably awful
event, the prospects for it could not have been more positive. How it all went
wrong is a revealing story about Margaret Thatcher's personality.

In early 1980, she invited all Whitehall's Permanent Secretaries and their
wives to dinner at No. 10. 'No Prime Minister had ever done such a thing before',
recalled Carrington. 'The mandarins were immensely flattered. They were eating
out of her hand. They would have done anything for her – that is until she got
up to speak.'

Margaret Thatcher's idea of an after-dinner speech to this select gathering
of Britain's top civil servants was to tell them that they were a useless and
inefficient bunch who should stop obstructing the government, and do what
they were told. The twenty-three Sir Humphreys were not the only ones to be
affronted. 'I was appalled', said Carrington. 'It was so silly for such a clever
woman to be so gratuitously rude. She could have got her point across in any
number of better ways, but instead she showed her worst side in a stream of
governessy hatred.'[24]

Inevitably, the response to this opening diatribe was a cool one. Sir Ian
Bancroft, as Head of the Civil Service, made the first speech of reply. In the view
of the Prime Minister this was 'a menu of complaints and negative attitudes',[25]
while the question and answer session went from bad to worse.

This ill-humoured soirée happened to take place the day after a terrorist
siege of the Iranian Embassy had been ended by the Special Air Service (SAS)
making a dramatic rescue of the hostages. One of the Permanent Secretaries at
the dinner, Sir Frank Cooper, from the Ministry of Defence, temporarily slipped
out of the room during the question period. As he left, Sir Lawrence Airey, the
Second Permanent Secretary of the Treasury, muttered that he hoped Frank had
gone to summon the SAS to rescue the present company of hostages. Margaret
Thatcher overheard, and did not appreciate the joke.

Sir Lawrence Airey was soon afterwards moved out of Whitehall to become
Chairman of the Board of Inland Revenue. At least he fared better than Bancroft,

who retired early after his entire department was closed down in 1981, its functions delegated to the Cabinet Office and the Treasury. But in its short-term impact and in its longer-term effects, Margaret Thatcher's dinner for Whitehall's top brass was an unmitigated disaster.

The Prime Minister's restless interventionism did not stop at clashes with Permanent Secretaries. She embarked on a tour of all the major government departments. At the lower levels of Whitehall these visitations were popular events. Margaret Thatcher had a charming, almost royal touch when it came to meeting junior members of staff, thanking them for their work and appreciating their contribution to the government. But when she moved into meetings with the higher echelons of senior officials, the visiting princess could turn into a tigress. She pounced on individuals, gnawing away at them on points of detail as if she wanted to demonstrate that she was better briefed than the departmental experts. Some of them were reduced to jelly by this experience. Others fought back.

During one of her earliest visits, to Jim Prior's Department of Employment, an outstanding Deputy Secretary responsible for policy and trade-union law, Donald Derx, became locked into an argument with her about the law on secondary picketing. Frustrated by her ignorance, he eventually silenced her with the question, 'Prime Minister, do you really want to know the facts?' Derx never climbed higher on the civil-service promotion ladder after this exchange. Jim Prior blamed his blockage on the 'black mark' Derx received that afternoon.[26]

Margaret Thatcher did want to know the facts, but how they were conveyed to her was an art form that the ablest communicators in Whitehall soon mastered. She responded best to clever energetic officials who offered her advice in the form of positive solutions rather than negative caution. She preferred feisty advisers who spoke their minds bluntly. She was impatient with polished circumlocutions of the 'with great respect, Prime Minister' variety.

The Permanent Secretary at the Foreign and Commonwealth Office, Sir Michael Palliser,* was a particular *bête noire* of hers. She disliked both his Europhile views and his fastidiously diplomatic style of presentation. She preferred to test policy by argument and engagement. Her reactions were abrasive, with a bias

---

* Sir Michael Palliser (1922–2012), Permanent Secretary FCO and Head of Diplomatic Service 1975–1982. A passionate Europhile who was Britain's first Ambassador to the EEC (1973–1975) and married to the daughter of one of the founding fathers of the EU – Paul-Henri Spaak.

against smooth men who she thought sounded condescending when they sought to reassure her that the status quo was working. Her hostility to Palliser resulted in him being denied the life peerage that FCO Permanent Secretaries were accustomed to receive on their retirement. Many people, including many top Mandarins, thought that her treatment of Palliser was 'very unfair'.[27]

First impressions counted heavily in these encounters. Cecil Parkinson, a junior trade minister in 1979, gave an amusing illustration of the Prime Minister's instant reactions to civil servants. When she made her visit to the Department of Trade, he sat next to her as she grilled each of its senior officials on the opposite side of the table about their responsibilities and objectives. He recalled:

> She had a list of the officials present, and she made a mark under their names as they spoke. Some of them were noted with a dotted line and others with a solid line. I soon realised that the dots were for the baddies as she saw them, and the line for the goodies. There were only two categories and everyone fitted into one or the other.[28]

Although her methods of shaking up Whitehall were unusual, the mandarins got the message. The new Prime Minister was determined to impose her vision and her will on the entire government machine.

REFLECTION

At the beginning of her eleven and a half year reign at No. 10 Downing Street, Margaret Thatcher's style of leadership was a perplexing mixture of intuition, caution, angry reactions and courageous initiatives.

Her personality was a work in progress that many were observing, but few understanding. She was respected for her dedication, but not yet for her judgement. She had won an election, but it was unclear how long she would last as Prime Minister. She had a strong sense of mission, but a weak grasp of how best to accomplish it.

The weakness, well perceived by her, was that she had to manage a cabinet and a civil service that were far from committed to her cause. As she grappled with the complexities of government, she recognised one simplicity: she would have to fight on many fronts to deliver the regeneration of Britain she had promised to the electorate.

Margaret Thatcher was no stranger to fighting difficult battles. Throughout her career she had struggled, often against tremendous odds, to circumvent the forces of prejudice, condescension and obstructionism that flourished against a rising woman politician within the elitist worlds of Westminster and Whitehall. Having defeated them by her rise to the top and to the unique status of becoming the first woman leader of a major Western democracy, she ought to have been able to throw off most of the insecurities and pressures for compromise that had troubled her even when Leader of the Opposition. Yet those experiences had both scarred and energised her. Now that she was Prime Minister, she continued to think of herself as an outsider who had to fight her ground every inch of the way.

The outsider did not display the smooth personality, which so often characterises successful politicians. She used harsh words, sharp elbows and rough edges to accomplish her mission. The abrasive side of her nature could hurt those who got in her way or to whom she took an immediate dislike. Her penchant for instant judgement led to many unfairnesses. 'I usually make up my mind about people within thirty seconds and 99 times out of a 100 I'm right', she told her Cabinet Secretary, Sir Robert Armstrong.[29]*

This self-caricature was absurd, yet it did surface in her early days at No. 10. There were encounters at which she made up her mind far too quickly and negatively about minister X or civil servant Y, with dire consequences for their careers. The Prime Minister's intuition tended to be final.

Her first administration was an uncomfortable coalition of true believers and disloyal unbelievers. Inexperience caused her to appoint too many ministers in the latter category. She was also weighed down by a large middle ground of cabinet colleagues and senior Whitehall officials who saw their roles as complaisant managers of Britain's decline. As she was dedicated to reversing it, there was immediate tension between her energetic radicalism and the centrist inertia of many of those around her.

The story of how she conquered this inertia is inspirational in some phases, unattractive in others. But before she could move forward on the most substantive parts of her mission, she first had to climb a steep curve of learning how to govern.

---

* Sir Robert Armstrong (1927–), Secretary of the Cabinet, 1979–1987, and Head of the Home Civil Service, 1983–1987 (Joint Head, 1981–1983); created Baron Armstrong of Ilminster, 1988.

16

The learning curve

INSIDE NO. 10

On her first evening as Prime Minister, Margaret Thatcher hosted a small supper party, which signalled the tone for her way of working at No. 10. It was both hospitable and frugal; inclusive of official and political staffers; warm yet businesslike; and it ended early because there was more work to be done long into the night.

In 1979, No. 10 was a modest centre of government in comparison to the giant octopus it extended to during the Blair premiership. With less than a hundred staff, it was minuscule in relation to the White House or the Elysée Palace. It had no computers, no mobile phones and faced no demands from a twenty-four-hour news cycle. It had the feel of a private house whose hub was the appropriately named Private Office, manned with collegiate teamwork by six of Whitehall's best and brightest high flyers. Margaret Thatcher brought only a handful of outsiders with her. One was her Political Secretary, Richard Ryder, who from his base in the Leader of the Opposition's office had been discreetly planning the transition with Ken Stowe for some weeks.

Another pivotal newcomer was Caroline Stephens, an experienced former secretary to various Conservative MPs, including Ted Heath. She was the daughter of the Clerk of the Parliaments, a background that had helped to make her a strong member of the Thatcher team in the past four years of opposition. At No. 10 her title was Diary Secretary, but her remit was more like that of senior executive assistant, confidante and conduit for private messages. Denis made sure everyone had a glass of wine, and Margaret Thatcher spooned out the shepherd's pie, which had been cooked at her Flood Street home and motored over to Downing Street.

This intimate group of guests at the first supper was supplemented during the first few weeks by additional political appointees, particularly Ian Gow, the Prime Minister's Parliamentary Private Secretary, or PPS; John Hoskyns, the Head of her Policy Unit; and David Wolfson, a personal aide whose independent wealth had helped to elevate him to the notional position of Chief of Staff at the Political Office. However, in this role his activity level became imperceptible. 'As time went on, he did less and less',[1] said Kenneth Stowe. Wolfson's habit of knocking off work at 6 p.m. in order to play bridge at the Reform Club was not in harmony with the intense work ethic of his boss.

Margaret Thatcher's understanding of the civil service had been limited to her experiences of officials at the Department of Education. They were an insular breed; incorrigibly leftist in their political attitudes, and ineffably superior in their disdain for a right-wing secretary of state. As a result of her unhappy clashes with the educational priesthood of Curzon Street, the Prime Minister entered No. 10 with the mistaken suspicion that the whole of Whitehall would be similarly adversarial. But she became so impressed by the intellectual excellence and prodigious industry of the team of private secretaries working round the clock to serve her that she began singling out other exceptional talents inside the civil-service machine. 'She was after capable managers, not just skilful policy advisers',[2] said her Cabinet Secretary, Sir Robert Armstrong. In that spirit, the Prime Minister developed an almost Leninist zeal for assembling a small band of outstanding officials who would help her drive the government towards her goal of rebuilding Britain's national purpose and pride.

The Downing Street team she inherited had been handpicked by two outgoing senior civil servants, the Principal Private Secretary and the Cabinet Secretary. Both positions changed within weeks of Margaret Thatcher's arrival, not at her request but because of the civil service's timetable of rotations and retirements. So she had to appoint successors to these two vital positions, largely on the basis of her intuition.

Having failed in her efforts to keep Kenneth Stowe, she chose as his successor Clive Whitmore, a Ministry of Defence technocrat. A high-flying former grammar-school boy from Surrey, he had impressed the Prime Minister when he gave her his department's briefing on the nuclear deterrent. For three tumultuous years, which included the Falklands War, they worked together efficiently in a professional relationship that never became personally close. It ended when she promoted Whitmore, at the unusually young age of forty-seven, to be Permanent Secretary of his old department.

Her choice for the top job in the civil service was Sir Robert Armstrong. 'I want you to succeed John Hunt as my Cabinet Secretary, and I would like you to know that I haven't thought of having anyone else', was how she opened her meeting with him on 9 July 1979. It was both flattering and surprising to Armstrong. He was far from confident of being appointed. His closeness to Ted Heath, when working as the Prime Minister's Private Secretary from 1970–1974, was expected by some to count against him.

Although Armstrong had experienced some difficult moments when handling the Heath–Thatcher relationship, she had come to like and trust him. It also helped that they went back a long time, for they had overlapped at Oxford in 1946 as fellow members of the Bach Choir, conducted by Sir Thomas Armstrong, Robert's father. The meeting at which he was appointed ended on a musical note when Robert Armstrong asked whether it would be possible to combine his duties as Cabinet Secretary with the role of Secretary to the Directors of Covent Garden. 'Of course you must continue at the Opera, but please take me some time,' replied the Prime Minister. Her first Royal Opera House evening with him was to a performance of Mozart's *Cosi Fan Tutte*, which she much enjoyed, but observed that, 'the plot is rather immoral!'[3]

The plot at No. 10 Downing Street was soon being driven by Margaret Thatcher's principles – moral, political and personal. On the personal front, she was noticeably solicitous towards her staff, both in small acts of kindness towards individuals at moments of trouble and in the motherly interest she took in them at all times. She made great efforts to know about the family lives of her team, because she wanted to create a happy atmosphere within her own circle. Beyond the walls of No. 10 and Chequers, she made little attempt to do this in her wider worlds of Westminster, Whitehall or the cabinet.

'She was vinegary with her cabinet, but honey with her staff', observed one of her private secretaries seconded from the Foreign Office, Bryan Cartledge. 'I think the reason why at that time No. 10 worked so very well as a unit was because it was small, and everyone knew everyone else.'[4]

Work had always been the driving force of Margaret Thatcher's life, and it reached its zenith during her early months of power. All prime ministers are over-burdened, but she doubled the normal workload by the intensity of her attention to detail, her critical questioning and her enthusiasm for seeking alternative sources of advice. The equivalent of the royal sceptre as her instrument of rule was the Prime Minister's box or boxes. These were the red-leather containers of paperwork which went up to her flat at night and got 'done' in the early hours of the morning. The word 'done' covered a variety of actions, such as decisions approved, appointments confirmed, minutes noted and briefing papers absorbed.

No prime minister in living memory had tackled their boxes with the voracious industry shown by Margaret Thatcher. 'She reads every paper she gets and never fails to write a comment on it', said one of her private secretaries. '"No!", "Nonsense", "Needs more briefing" or "Do this again" are what she's constantly writing.'[5] She was also frequently asking her private office to send out notes beginning, 'The Prime Minister wants to know why . . .' or 'The Prime Minister's view is . . .' The effect of such missives was electrifying. No previous head of the government had ever been so personally involved and interventionist in the workings of Whitehall departments.

Another of her innovations was a regular demand to see the authors of the papers that flowed through her red boxes. At these encounters, her style was to cross-examine the official she was meeting, often with the aggression of a barrister attacking a hostile witness. It was trial by ordeal, her way of satisfying herself that a proposal or a presentation could stand the test of adversarial argument.

One newcomer who found himself enduring this baptism of fire was thirty-six-year-old Terry Burns. The son of a Durham miner, who had become a professor at the London Business School, Burns was unexpectedly recruited into Whitehall in 1979 as Chief Economic Adviser to the Treasury. He was preparing to give the cabinet a presentation on the outlook for the economy when Margaret Thatcher summoned him to Downing Street for a one-on-one grilling. Burns recalled:

It was the most frightening experience of my life at that point. I was drained by her directness and the intensity of her questioning. There were no short answers to the points she was raising, but she didn't want long answers. And she jumped around. If I responded with details, she switched to principles. If I talked about principles, she demanded details. All the time she was prodding to discover my instincts and to test my knowledge. It was without doubt the most exhausting yet also the most exhilarating meeting I had ever had.[6]

Margaret Thatcher's early style of government consisted not only of testing her officials and ministers but also of setting an example. The certainties of her own moral compass were her driving force, not least in the important arena of reducing public expenditure.

To set an example, she made a point of switching off the lights in unoccupied rooms at No. 10. Such gestures, which included cutting the number of photocopiers in her office, were her 'ludicrous obsession that we must get the economy right by small savings of candle ends',[7] according to John Hoskyns. Whether or not she was obsessive, she sent out several early signals about the need for frugality with small items of government expenditure.

One bee in her bonnet was the necessity of cutting down the number of civil servants that prime ministers had traditionally taken abroad as their entourage on overseas trips. So when she made her first visit to France, she insisted that her party had to fit into a Hawker Siddeley HS-125 corporate jet with seating for eight passengers. When they landed at Le Bourget, the French Prime Minister and his large entourage could hardly believe their eyes when this tiny aircraft halted at the red carpet and disgorged Margaret Thatcher, Lord Carrington, her Private Secretary, her Special Branch protection officer and three Foreign Office officials.[8]

Another candle end that caught her eye was a note in one of her red boxes asking her to approve the sum of £1,836, which the Property Services Agency had spent on refurbishments to her flat above No. 10 shortly before her arrival. Although this was not a large sum for cleaning and making minor improvements to the Prime Minister's official residence, she queried it and asked for further and better particulars.

A Private Secretary sent her a minute on 25 June 1979 detailing the refurbishment costs. Alongside the charges of £209 for replacing crockery and £464 for replacing linen and pillows, he commented: 'I find these figures almost impossible to believe.'

'So do I!' scribbled Margaret Thatcher, at the foot of the page. 'I could use my own [linen] and my own crockery . . . Bearing in mind we only use one bedroom, can the rest go back into stock?' Highlighting another item costing

£19 that she thought should not be paid for by the taxpayer, she instructed, 'I will pay for the ironing board myself'.[9]

This marginalia emerging from the red boxes highlighted the Prime Minister's eye for detail and also her insistence on being her own woman at No. 10. She was determined not to become a prisoner of what was later called, 'the bubble' of official life and advice. To avoid this, she made determined efforts to break away from the grip of the machine. It was her wish to receive alternative streams of advice from outside sources, which the private secretaries called the 'voices'. She also forged a bond with one or two insiders on her team whose contact with the wider world caused her to label them 'my bridge builders'.[10]

BRIDGE BUILDERS AND VOICES

The two most important bridge builders from No. 10 to the wider world were Ian Gow and Bernard Ingham, respectively her Parliamentary Private Secretary and her Press Secretary. Both were remarkable English characters who could have stepped from the pages of Dickens or Thackeray. Their idiosyncrasies, their formidable abilities and their near-idolatry for their boss made them pivotal players in communicating the personality of the Prime Minister to parliamentarians and the media.

Ian Gow's idiosyncrasies were his engagingly eccentric camouflage for his dedicated professionalism. He pretended to be such a caricature of a period-piece politician that he looked unlikely to have much rapport with Margaret Thatcher. With his half-moon spectacles, old-fashioned waistcoats, gold watch chain, orotund manner of speaking and enthusiasm for White Ladies (the cocktail), Gow could have been amusingly portrayed in a *Spy* cartoon of the Victorian era. As he hardly knew the Prime Minister when she came to power in 1979, he was unsurprised but unhappy for the first three days after the election when his name did not appear even in the most junior lists of ministerial appointments.

But Margaret Thatcher had noticed Ian Gow's relentless harrying of the Labour government for their profligacy with public expenditure. His mordant House of Commons wit and his quaint mannerisms appealed to her. So did his background as a former officer in the 15th/19th Hussars serving in Ulster at the height of the troubles; as an old-fashioned country solicitor specialising in wills and trusts; and as a churchwarden in his local parish church. Almost as an afterthought to her administration making, she appointed Ian Gow to the unpaid post of her PPS, without at the time fully appreciating either his unusual gifts or the importance of the job he had to do.

Although Margaret Thatcher had been an MP for twenty years, she never really understood the spirit of the House, let alone the spirits of her own back-benchers. She was too intense, too short on humour, too impatient, perhaps too womanly in a man's world to fully understand the changing moods of the parliamentary village. By contrast, Ian Gow adored Westminster life. He became a master of Commons procedure and traditions. His quirky style combined with his granite integrity won him friends in many quarters. Above all, he was a man of principle, which soon endeared him to the woman of principle who had become his boss.

Gow worked longer hours than anyone other than the Prime Minister in No. 10, for he would arrive there before 7 a.m. and would often not depart until after midnight. He had three great strengths.

The first was his encyclopaedic knowledge of the Conservative Parliamentary Party, whose MPs affectionately nicknamed him 'Supergrass'. He reported their murmurings and mischiefs with a humorous fidelity that appealed to Margaret Thatcher's enjoyment of gossip, and kept her attuned to her power base with a depth of understanding that was never again achieved after Gow left her inner circle with a ministerial promotion in 1983.

Second, he achieved a personal rapport with her that was unequalled by any other political colleague. Over late-night tumblers of Famous Grouse whisky in the flat above No. 10, he reinforced her own convictions. For in every major policy area, from relations with the EEC to balancing the public finances, Gow was a hardliner with the driest of dry views, which were often more arid than her own.

Third, he was a straight arrow who won her absolute trust. He exercised immense influence over her in matters that ranged from who she should invite to dinner to who would make good ministers. The appointment of his erratic but endearing friend Alan Clark* to the government in 1983 spoke volumes for

---

* Rt Hon. Alan Clark (1928–1999), barrister, diarist and historian; Conservative MP for Plymouth Sutton, 1974–1992, and Kensington and Chelsea, 1997–1999; PUSS, Department of Employment, 1983–1986; Minister for Trade, 1986–1989; Minister of State, Ministry of Defence, 1989–1992. Debonair, dashing and forever dicing with danger in his private life, Alan was one of my closest parliamentary friends. In his diaries he describes me as 'my old standby for many a dirty trick'. Always life-enhancing but rarely reliable, Alan stood out as a colourful bird of paradise in a monochrome House of Commons.

Gow's powers of persuasion over 'The Queen's First Minister', as he pedantically insisted on calling her.

Margaret Thatcher developed an extraordinary chemistry with her closest advisers. The only ones who approached the Gow level of professional intimacy were her Private Secretary and Adviser on Foreign Affairs, Charles Powell, from 1983 onwards, and Bernard Ingham who started his eleven-year reign as Press Secretary in October 1979.

Ingham said:

> If ever there was a Prime Minister who needed a Press Secretary it was he, because it became clear at my interview for the job that she had absolutely no interest in the media except to grumble about it. She talked non-stop on this theme for twenty minutes, and her only brief to me was to say that she wanted me to get over her policies to the people who would believe in them.[11]

This was an odd instruction to a professional civil servant who had never been a Tory voter. Ingham was a blunt-speaking Yorkshireman who had served as a labour correspondent for the *Guardian* before joining the Government Information Service. However, he had been drifting away from his Labour roots because of his antipathy towards the abuses of power by militant trade unions. 'I'd had enough of us being laughed at as a country', he recalled. 'I wanted to see reform, which was what Mrs Thatcher was offering even though it was far removed from Toryism.'

The new Press Secretary was amazed by the lack of interest his boss took in newspapers. To overcome this he produced his own daily digest of press cuttings which he insisted she looked at every morning, usually sitting alongside her to make sure she did so.

The dossier was almost her only window on the media. Whereas most prime ministers tend to worry a great deal about their own press coverage, Margaret Thatcher was gloriously insouciant to it. However she did care about the impact of her policies. It was of no concern to her that they upset the liberal consensus of the commentators. 'You and I, Bernard, are not smooth people',[12] she said to him early on in their relationship. This was an essential ingredient in their bonding. 'She was straight, direct, and tactless – probably the most tactless woman I've ever met in my life', recalled Ingham. He replicated these qualities when dealing, sometimes rather brutally, with the self-perpetuating oligarchy of political correspondents known as the 'Lobby'. They had access to the daily Downing Street press briefings, which Ingham conducted unattributably in a colourful style that was strikingly personal. Becoming an advocate for the Prime Minister's convictions with the zeal of a convert, he would think nothing of rubbishing a hostile reporter's question as 'bunkum and balderdash', or of planting stories detrimental to ministers who were falling out of his boss's favour. This last practice caused much grief inside the cabinet.

At one meeting of ministers in the autumn of 1980, the Prime Minister grumbled that her government was being damaged by a spate of leaks. 'Most of them coming straight from here', muttered Lord Soames in a *voce* that was far from *sotto*. 'What did you say, Christopher?' demanded the Prime Minister. The Leader of the House of Lords was bold enough to repeat his grievance, to which she retorted: 'No. We never leak.'[13] If she believed that, she believed anything.

As the economic climate worsened in 1980–1981, the practice of leaking and counter-leaking intensified. Bernard Ingham was a tougher player of this game than anyone else. His loyalty to the Prime Minister and his disloyalty to those members of her government about whom she had expressed doubts stretched the limits of civil-service neutrality. But she always protected him, and he always championed her. It was a relationship that transcended the usual boundaries. Nevertheless, through Ingham she did indeed 'get over her policies to the people'. He was a vital and successful player in communicating what Margaret Thatcher stood for and believed in. This was largely because he came to share in the same beliefs. He thought of her as 'a liberator' who gave ordinary British people new freedoms, opportunities and prosperity.[14]

The most unorthodox source of strength in Margaret Thatcher's first years as Prime Minister were the 'voices'. This was the civil servants' term for the shadowy and changing cast of characters who somehow communicated with her out of hours in unrecorded meetings or telephone calls, and through unofficial channels. As she loved to surprise, she would often cite these voices at important decision-making meetings by saying 'I hear that . . .' or by pulling a sheet of paper out of her handbag, from which she quoted as proof that she had authoritative sources of advice from experts outside the government machine.

Some civil servants were thrown by the 'voices'. Others welcomed them as a sign that the Prime Minister was on top of a game other than their own. Her first Private Secretary, Kenneth Stowe, was delighted to discover that the Managing Director of Morgan Stanley, John Sparrow, was writing her a weekly report of the City's reaction to the government's economic policies. Various eminent industrialists like Sir Arnold Weinstock of GEC, Sir Hector Laing of United Biscuits, Sir James Hanson of Hanson PLC and Sir Marcus Seiff, Chairman of Marks & Spencer,* also had their own hot lines to her. So did Enoch Powell, who was brought in to see her by Ian Gow, via the back door of No. 10, for at least six unrecorded meetings with the Prime Minister during her first two years.[15]

At a less lofty level of political and economic advice, the cleaning lady of the flat above No. 10 was frequently mentioned as an authentic representative of *vox populi*. The most persistent telephone caller was Woodrow Wyatt, a former Labour MP, *News of the World* columnist, horse-racing expert and wide-ranging man about town. The private office dubbed him 'the Concierge' because he was always passing on so much gossip, but Wyatt was also her channel to Rupert Murdoch, and a strong reinforcer of her political convictions.

On the foreign-policy front there were many voices. The Foreign Office were disconcerted that she paid so much attention to calls from Senator Jesse Helms Jr., the right-wing chairman of the US Senate Foreign Relations Committee. She also listened to the Soviet expert Robert Conquest and the former Foreign Office minister in Harold Wilson's government, Lord Chalfont. Paul Johnson sent her historical perspectives on issues of the day. Professor Peter Bauer of the London School of Economics advised her on the need to make drastic reductions in Britain's foreign-aid budget. 'Our aid is a process by which poor people in rich countries give money to rich people in poor countries', he told her.[16†]

An important foreign-affairs interlocutor who came into his own at the time of the Falklands War was Professor Hugh Thomas, author of a seminal book on the Spanish Civil War. He was chosen by her to replace Keith Joseph as Chairman of the Centre for Policy Studies, which remained her favourite think

---

* The Prime Minister not only listened to them, but she elevated them all to the House of Lords.

† When Margaret Thatcher tried to implement Professor Bauer's recommendations for cuts in the foreign-aid budget in 1980–1981 she was thwarted by Lord Carrington who threatened to resign as Foreign Secretary over the issue. There were limits to the influence of the 'voices'.

tank. 'Your main job is to keep Alfred under control', said the Prime Minister, referring to Alfred Sherman, its research director. He was another of the private voices who bombarded her with memoranda, saying that her economic policies were not going nearly far enough.

Hugh Thomas wrote many speeches for Margaret Thatcher, a process that could be exhausting since she would argue fiercely about her ideas and the words she should use to express them late into the night. Thomas recalled:

> I remember one particularly long discussion on whether the word 'prone' or 'supine' was right for the context of a speech. I really enjoyed working with her because of her directness, her original views and her interest in the historical roots of a problem. I think she regarded the preparation for a speech as the way to test her policies by intellectual debate.[17]

Once someone in her orbit was established as a 'voice', she would call them up to seek their opinions on a wide range of subjects, sometimes those on which they had no particular expertise. At an early stage in her arguments with Lord Carrington about how to handle Rhodesia, Hugh Thomas was surprised to have his kitchen supper interrupted by the Prime Minister on the line, asking him detailed questions about Ian Smith and Bishop Muzorewa.

'Who on earth were you talking to about Rhodesia?' asked Hugh Thomas's wife, Vanessa, when the call had ended.

'Margaret Thatcher.'

'But you don't know anything about Rhodesia.'

'I don't – but she trusts my judgement.'[18]

That was the point of the 'voices'. They were people whose judgement she trusted, often much more so than the judgement of the major departments of state, like the Ministry of Defence and the Foreign Office. It was unprecedented for a prime minister to engage in so much second-guessing of her own ministers and officials.

Eventually, this brought her into serious conflicts, most notoriously at the time of the clash between her Chancellor, Nigel Lawson, and her economic adviser, Professor Alan Walters, in 1990.* But at the beginning of her premiership, her

---

* See Chapter 30.

wide-ranging contacts with the 'voices' seemed a refreshing innovation. She clearly felt that to implement the reforms that were required to change Britain, she needed additional sources of advice in order to challenge the consensualist wisdom of Whitehall. Closed government was being challenged by open argument. It was an intriguing and attractive characteristic of the new Prime Minister.

OLD STRIPEY AND STUBBORNNESS

The red boxes of official papers sent up to the Prime Minister's flat by her private office every evening included one of a noticeably different size and colour. It was known as 'Old Stripey', because it had a large blue stripe across its lid. Margaret Thatcher always opened this box first. Only she and her Principal Private Secretary had a key to it. This was because 'Old Stripey' contained daily top-secret reports from the intelligence services and other highly sensitive material deemed to be for the eyes only of the Prime Minister.

She was known by her staff to be 'utterly fascinated'[19] by the product from MI5, MI6 and GCHQ. Her fascination increased because she built a close relationship with two outstanding security chiefs of that era. One was Sir Maurice Oldfield, 'C' or head of the Secret Intelligence Service, popularly known as MI6. The other was Sir Antony Duff, Director-General of MI5, the domestic Security Service.

Also, in the age of IRA terrorism, she needed regular briefings on the threats in Northern Ireland. A description of how intensely she applied her mind to these issues came from Kenneth Stowe, who brought in the Northern Ireland Office's Director and Controller of Intelligence, David Lanthorne, to brief her on a specific problem. 'I vividly recall this meeting because it completely dispelled the legend that Margaret Thatcher was a bad listener', said Stowe. 'David Lanthorne briefed her for twenty minutes. She said not a word. Sitting on the edge of her chair, she kept her eyes on him with total concentration, absorbing everything.'[20]

Although her absorption with security issues was commendable, it also led her to some questionable judgements involving both MI5 and GCHQ. One early over-reaction by her, which shocked the security services, centred on the case of Sir Anthony Blunt.

Blunt had been recruited by Russian intelligence while at Cambridge University in the 1930s. In the 1940s, he acted as a Soviet agent at the same time as he was working for MI5. He passed many wartime secrets to Russian intelligence.

After 1945, he left MI5 to work as an art historian. Then in 1952, he was appointed Surveyor of the Queen's Pictures. In 1964, the government of the day offered Sir Anthony Blunt immunity from prosecution provided that he co-operated in the inquiries of the security authorities. Blunt accepted the offer. Buckingham Palace was also briefed on the immunity deal, which enabled Blunt to continue with his duties there for the next fifteen years.

This was the status quo that Margaret Thatcher inherited and was briefed about as an incoming prime minister. But in October 1979 the journalist Andrew Boyle outed Blunt in a book, which gave rise to a written Parliamentary Question. The public had become familiar with Third Man, Fourth Man, Fifth Man revelations from the Philby, Maclean and Burgess era of Cambridge spies in the 1950s, so no great stir was caused by Boyle's book. The written Parliamentary Question could easily have been dealt with in the time-honoured formula, which maintains that it is long-established government practice not to provide answers to questions affecting national security.

Instead of playing it safe, Margaret Thatcher overruled the Director of MI5, Sir Michael Hanley, and went public on Blunt. She confirmed in the House of Commons that he had been a Soviet agent. This caused a sensation. There was a parliamentary debate in which she spoke uneasily and unconvincingly as she set out a selective version of the Blunt story. The net effect was that a flood of further revelations on security matters followed with other MI5 operatives, most notably Peter Wright in his book *Spycatcher*, telling their stories, much to the Prime Minister's anger. None of these revelations were prevented, and no other former spy since has been offered immunity from prosecution in return for co-operation with the authorities.

This useful mechanism was made useless by Margaret Thatcher's decision to break the seal of confidentiality on the Blunt deal in the interests of openness. The irony was that she never again advocated any other form of openness or scrutiny in relation to the security services. One practitioner in this field described her handling of the Blunt affair as 'Mrs Thatcher's rush of blood to the head'.[21] Margaret Thatcher hated to admit that she ever made any errors of judgement. She became positively proprietorial towards the security services. This led her to make further mistakes in relation to GCHQ and MI5.

In 1980, she became so angry about the selective strikes and pay demands of workers at GCHQ that she refused to settle the civil-service pay dispute that had given rise to the problem. It became such a personal issue to her that she overruled the sensible settlement negotiated with the unions by Lord Soames, the minister responsible for the civil service. The Soames settlement figure of a 7.5 per cent pay deal was only 1 per cent above the Treasury guideline. Most ministers, including the Chancellor, Sir Geoffrey Howe, were minded to accept it. But at a stormy cabinet meeting, Margaret Thatcher threatened to resign if the Soames deal went through. Willie Whitelaw had to use all his skills as a trouble-shooter to calm her down. A few weeks later, he persuaded the Prime Minister to accept the original Soames figure. Her intransigence cost the government around £400 million. The strike ended, but so did the career of Lord Soames. She sacked him at the next reshuffle, apparently for the crime of being right about GCHQ and the other civil-service unions.

Prime ministerial stubbornness and the security services continued to go hand in hand. A later episode involving GCHQ in her second term arose when she became determined to ban its employees from being members of a trade union. Her view was that working for any part of the government's security services was incompatible with being a trade unionist. Even when Sir Robert Armstrong had negotiated a compromise by which GCHQ staff could retain their union membership after signing a no-strike agreement (a deal which had prevailed for many years with the police), Margaret Thatcher refused to countenance it. The affair ended messily, with high-court judgments going both ways, the sacking of some GCHQ workers and eventually a Pyrrhic victory for the government. The outcome caused considerable uneasiness, not least for Sir Geoffrey Howe, who blamed the mess on the Prime Minister's 'absolutist instinct'.

'It was probably the clearest example I had seen so far of one of Margaret's most tragic failings: an inability to appreciate, still less accommodate, someone else's patriotism', he commented. 'A citizen, she seemed to feel, could never safely be allowed to carry more than one card in his or her pocket, and at GCHQ that could only be Her Majesty's card.'[22]

One final example of the Prime Minister's 'absolutist instinct' in relation to the security services came over another side of the fall-out to the Blunt affair. Her 'rush of blood to the head' had caused a rush of articles and books about the curious goings-on at MI5 in the 1950s. Some of these publications were cleared by No. 10. although they had obviously been sourced from retired MI5 officers. One of them, Peter Wright, then decided to publish his memoirs,

Spycatcher, in Australia where he had gone to live. Margaret Thatcher rightly felt that *Spycatcher* was a serious breach of the duty of confidentiality imposed on all former employees of the security services. She wrongly decided to fight in the Australian courts to get the book publication suppressed.

Her appointed representative in this colonial-minded and therefore doomed endeavour was Sir Robert Armstrong, the Cabinet Secretary. He received something of a mauling in the witness box at the hands of a pugnacious young Sydney lawyer, Malcolm Turnbull, who later rose on the Australian political ladder to become a senior minister and Leader of the Opposition. The Prime Minister solicitously called up Robert Armstrong in Australia two or three times to encourage him as the trial progressed. It ended in ignominious defeat for the British government as the Australian courts, predictably, permitted the publication of *Spycatcher*. When the Cabinet Secretary returned home, Margaret Thatcher called him into her study and presented him with two bottles of Scotch whisky. It was her way of apologising for despatching him across the world on a mission made impossible by her own stubbornness.

As a result of such episodes, the Prime Minister's reverence for the security services became something of an in-joke among the cognoscenti of Whitehall. It was not unconnected to her avid readership of the works of John Le Carré and Frederick Forsyth. Her later Chancellor of the Exchequer, Nigel Lawson, found it positively comical to discover how besotted she was by the secret agencies, their establishments and their hardware. He saw public spending on them as 'one of the very few areas of public life virtually untouched by the rigours of the Thatcher era'.[23]

Some of this hush-hush expenditure avoided cuts by being carefully concealed, with her connivance, in the Defence, Foreign Office and Home Office budgets. Larger sums were authorised, under her chairmanship, by the so-called Secret Vote Committee. This was so secret that it never actually met! Paying generously for the products of 'Old Stripey' was an example of how she was learning to get her own way by unorthodox methods.

A FAVOUR FOR RUPERT MURDOCH

One of the most questionable episodes of Margaret Thatcher's first two years as Prime Minister was her bending of the rules on monopolies and mergers in order to allow Rupert Murdoch to purchase *The Times* and the *Sunday Times*. It illustrated both her political dependence on Murdoch's newspapers and her political ruthlessness in imposing her will on the government and its legal procedures.

The drama began, as far as Margaret Thatcher was concerned, when Rupert Murdoch came to lunch at Chequers on 4 January 1980. A detailed, if circumspect, note of record was taken by Bernard Ingham who, on the instructions of the Prime Minister, did not circulate it outside the private office of No. 10. This account of the conversation marked 'Commercial – In Confidence' makes it clear that 'the main purpose of Mr Murdoch's visit was to brief the Prime Minister on his bid for *Times* newspapers'. Using this privileged access, Murdoch described the success of the *Sunday Times* (even in the depths of a recession it was turning away advertising), but stressed the high-risk nature of his bid by explaining that he could lose £50 million of his resources because, 'turning round a £13–£17 million loss was a formidable undertaking at a time of deep industrial recession'.[24]

These observations about losses were the note of record's coded reference to the massive legal obstacle in the way of a bid by Rupert Murdoch. Because he already owned the *Sun* and the *News of the World*, his bid had to be referred to the Monopolies and Mergers Commission (MMC) in accordance with the Fair Trading Act of 1973. It would have been amazing if this problem had not been mentioned at Chequers by either the Prime Minister or Mr Murdoch. Equally amazing would have been no mention of the only route by which the Murdoch bid might be exempted from an MMC reference. This exemption could be granted if the newspaper, which was the subject of the bid, was making such large losses that it was 'not economic as a going concern'.[25]

In the course of a long conversation about the bid for *The Times* and the *Sunday Times*, the notion that two such straight talkers as Margaret Thatcher and Rupert Murdoch would not have discussed either the MMC obstacle or the possible exemption from it was fanciful. The Prime Minister had no such inhibition when she came to chair the cabinet committee on the bid for *The Times* newspapers on 26 January 1981. For in her usual forceful style, she opened the discussion by emphasising that although the bid must be referred to the MMC, 'There was an exception to this rule under S.58 (3)(a) of the Fair Trading Act, which gave the Secretary of State discretion to decide whether a reference should be made if he were satisfied that certain criteria were met'.[26]

The Secretary of State for Trade who was so pointedly reminded of his discretion in this way was John Biffen. His problem was that he could only grant his exemption if he was satisfied that neither *The Times* nor the *Sunday Times* was economic as a going concern. He told the committee that he was satisfied of this, but added 'though only in the case of *The Times* was the issue clear cut'.[27]

When he announced his decision to grant Rupert Murdoch's bid an exemption from being referred to the MMC, John Biffen faced a parliamentary storm in the shape of an Emergency Commons Debate. All speakers from the opposition parties, and several from the government's side, questioned how he could possibly have decided that the profitable *Sunday Times* was not a going concern.

As a Conservative back-bencher who spoke and voted against John Biffen's decision, I had a friendly private disagreement with him after the debate. He was charmingly embarrassed. 'Ah well, there's a political dimension to this.' He smiled, pointing with his right index finger to the ceiling.[28]

Woodrow Wyatt produced a blunter explanation for the collusion with Murdoch: 'I had bent the rules for him . . . Through Margaret I got it arranged that the deal didn't go to the Monopolies Commission, which almost certainly would have blocked it.'[29]

The episode was not one of Margaret Thatcher's finest hours, but in the dark days of 1981 she needed the support of Murdoch's newspapers. She was ready to be a ruthless player of prime ministerial hardball in order to get her way.

PERSONALITY TRAITS ON AND OFF DUTY

Margaret Thatcher became increasingly skilful at getting her way, but the methods by which she achieved this revealed a complex personality. It was a myth that she was over-confident. As a later Principal Private Secretary, Robin Butler,*

---

* Robin Butler, Baron Butler of Brockwell (1938–), Private Secretary to Edward Heath, 1972–1974; Private Secretary to Harold Wilson, 1974–1975; Principal Private Secretary to Prime Minister Margaret Thatcher, 1982–1985; Secretary of the Cabinet and Head of the Home Civil Service, 1988–1998; created Life Peer, 1998.

perceptively observed: 'The key to her style was that she did not have excessive confidence. On the contrary, she lacked self-confidence. That was why she was so assertive. She had to pump herself up with adrenalin before any big occasion.'[30]

The same applied on many small occasions too. Because she lacked confidence, she felt she needed to master a brief right down to the smallest details before she went into a meeting. This over-preparation, accomplished by the burning of much midnight oil, enabled her to browbeat her ministers. One of her techniques was to fire questions at them about some obscure fact in a footnote to the main briefing paper under discussion. If they did not know the answer, she belittled them. This was her way of dominating her colleagues by exhibiting her own expertise on the minutiae of the subject.

Domination was only one of her personality traits. She used it a great deal in public or semi-public battles. But in private she deployed subtler and more feminine wiles. They included judicious flattery, harmless flirtatiousness and even elaborately staged 'poor me' performances designed to elicit protective support at predominantly masculine meetings. She played the card of being a lone woman quite unscrupulously, often exploiting the inhibitions of some men to argue back against her. Her femininity, which she used as a technique when it suited her, was real. She liked her clothes to be admired, and was susceptible to the good looks of attractive colleagues. She enjoyed male flattery and gallantry, particularly when she could turn it to good use by winning a concession.

Although she was open to strong argument, she hardly ever conceded a point during the exchanges. However, a day or so later, she might present the same point as her own view, as if she had never argued against it.

When she flared up, she could sometimes pick on a minister or an official, and insult them quite gratuitously. 'Have you actually read this paper, Chief Secretary?' she once asked John Biffen.[31] To a senior civil servant who kept silent during an all-day discussion on public expenditure she acidly enquired, 'Do you speak, Mr Jones?' She increased the pressure at the lunch break by asking him, 'Do you eat, Mr Jones?'[32]

Her sharpness and rudeness in such rough and tumbles were often utterly unfair. She seemed to have a mental block against ever saying she was sorry. But occasionally she would at a later stage make a compensatory move, such as writing the victim a pleasant note on a different subject. Or she would invite someone who might be nursing hurt feelings up to her flat for a drink. This was the nearest she came to either apologising or relaxing.

She enjoyed an hour of Whitehall and Westminster gossip over an evening whisky, or occasionally going out to someone else's home for a meal. Her favourite excursions were to the Carringtons' country house at Bledlow, whose proximity to Chequers sometimes seemed a mixed blessing to her hosts. Or she would drop in for supper to Ian and Jane Gow's tiny Kennington *pied à terre* in South London. The only problem with their hospitality was that on summer evenings the Prime Minister enjoyed drinking *al fresco* on the Gow's patio. This alarmed her protection officers, because the patio was overlooked by council tower blocks, but it did not alarm her. 'Snipers taking pot shots at Chester Way!' (the Gow's street) she scoffed. 'I shall need a lot of convincing about that.'[33]

Other forms of R&R were never on her agenda. She had no idea how to relax. She had no hobbies, no hinterland and no close friends with 'an old shoe' quality of comfortable familiarity. Recharging her batteries was a practice she had never heard of. She kept going at full throttle on a combination of extra adrenalin and extra work. But despite her protestations that she needed neither sleep nor holidays, there were times when her closest aides inside No. 10 thought she was physically and emotionally frazzled. Even when these signs of exhaustion coincided with the doldrums of August, the problem of persuading her that she needed a break was not easily solved – as the story of her first prime ministerial holiday in Scotland demonstrated.

DOG DAYS ON ISLAY

During her first August in office, she kept the wheels of power turning, partly by inventing tasks and summoning briefing papers. But in response to some gentle prodding from Ian Gow and others, she did finally agree to take a short holiday; the question was where?

The resourceful Gow telephoned Peter Morrison and enquired whether he could possibly put up a couple of extra guests 'on that family island of yours in Scotland'.[34] Morrison immediately agreed, thinking that he was offering a bed to Mr and Mrs Gow. He was surprised when the prospective guests were revealed to be the Prime Minister and Mr Denis Thatcher.

Professing an unexpected enthusiasm for Scottish scenery ('I love the Highlands and Islands'[35]), Margaret Thatcher set out for Islay House, Islay. This was an eighteenth-century mansion on a 73,000 acre estate owned by Peter Morrison's father, Lord Margadale, looking out to sea across Loch Indaal on the most southerly tip of the Hebrides. Because the prime ministerial visit was at short notice, the twenty-four bedrooms of Islay House were already full with younger Morrisons and their friends, but the master bedroom was gladly vacated by Lord Margadale. The guest of honour enjoyed her first hours on the island with a short walk to the shores of the loch followed by a visit to a local distillery where samples of the local malt whisky were savoured by Denis.

It was the custom at Islay House for charades to be played after dinner. The Prime Minister sat uneasily through one round of these theatricals. She then retired to her bedroom, which was situated immediately above the wood-panelled ballroom where the games were taking place. The clan Morrison in full post-prandial cry were not a quiet family. With the decibels rising, they were surprised that their festivities were interrupted by some sharp knocks from the ceiling. For some reason no one associated these signals with the Prime Minister's wish to have peace and quiet in her bedroom above.

The revels continued, moving from charades to a game called 'Pull the Key'. This consisted of tying the large Victorian house key on a string, passing the string down every girl's dress and up every man's trousers as they stood in a line. Then at the *moment critique*, the key was pulled down the line accompanied by the inevitable cacophony of squeals, shouts and loud laughter.

The noise was more than Margaret Thatcher could bear. Unable to concentrate on her reading, she decided to take a nocturnal walk. So she donned her cloak and strode out into the gloaming. Thinking she had gone to bed, her Scotland Yard close protection detail had set off for a local pub. So the Prime Minister, believing she knew the geography of Islay from an earlier visit in her opposition days, strode out across the heather alone and unaccompanied.

There was, however, one police officer still on duty in the vicinity of Islay House. He was a dog handler from Strathclyde Police, tasked with keeping dangerous intruders away from the Prime Minister. This constable and his dog maintained their vigil on a hillock several hundred yards away. It was a lonely night shift until suddenly around 11.30 p.m. he spotted a hooded figure marching briskly across the moor. In the gloaming it was impossible to see anything more than the outline shape and direction of the walker, who by this time was heading back towards Islay House.

The policeman shouted a challenge to the suspected intruder. There was no response. So he let his dog off the leash. Seconds later the Alsatian pounced on the hooded figure, who was knocked backwards and pinned to the ground. As the handler arrived on the scene he was horrified to discover that the suspect captured under his dog's paws was none other than the British Prime Minister.

Alas, there is no record of the dialogue between the police officer and the Prime Minister. All that is known is that a dishevelled Margaret Thatcher, an apologetic constable and a tail-wagging Alsatian arrived back at Islay House together shortly before midnight.

Peter Morrison led the profuse apologies and tried to treat the incident with humour. But the lady was not for joking. 'Her cloak was dirty, she was shaken up and pretty fed up', he recalled later. 'She went straight to bed. But the next day, in a chilly sort of way, she was good about it. She never wanted it mentioned again. So, of course, I hushed it up.'[36]

All was forgiven and forgotten. The incident passed into legend among her inner circle, with the punch-line question: 'How on earth did the dog dare?' This was a variation on an earlier jest by Lord Carrington who interrupted a colleague talking hypothetically about 'If the Prime Minister was run over by a bus . . .' with the interjection, 'The bus would not dare'.[37]

REFLECTION

The analogy of the bus was to be tested in the coming months as various fast-moving political vehicles did their best to flatten Margaret Thatcher. Both on the economy and in foreign policy, she was about to travel through dangerous territory.

The reasons why she showed such strength in standing up to these pressures are to be found in the power of her personality. She was certain about her objectives. She had the character to stick to her guns. She surrounded herself with an inner core of staff and advisers who she felt were supporters and believers in her mission to restore Britain's pride as a nation. And she psyched herself up with adrenalin to the point where she positively relished being opposed.

There was an interesting difference between the perception of Margaret Thatcher inside the government she was leading and the wider perception of her by the country. Those who had voted for her wanted her to succeed after the chaos of the 'winter of discontent'. But for all the good-will towards her, the jury was out and the suspicion was widespread that she might not be capable of dealing with the unions and the economic problems. Inside the Tory Party, the hesitations about her were palpable. Ted Heath remained a brooding presence poised to ferment trouble. He was by no means the only brooder.

John Hoskyns, less than a month after his appointment as Head of the Prime Minister's Policy Unit, met a senior City friend at a Rifle Brigade regimental dinner, who asked him: 'Is it true you're now working for Mrs Thatcher? . . . You must be the most frightful shit.'[38] Hoskyns noted in his diary that the remark 'captured perfectly the ambivalent attitude of my friends towards the new government and its leader'.[39]

The ambivalence was however lessening at the heart of government in White-hall. For every Sir Humphrey who was being obstructive in the face of the new broom, there were several younger deputy secretaries or assistant secretaries who were being singled out by her as 'good doers'.[40]

They encountered her up close in the abrasive decision-making meetings that she used to hammer out policies. They saw, as the world came to see, that their new boss had extraordinary qualities of energy, courage and determination to change Britain. 'There's a feeling round here of "*Enfin, nous avons un maître*",'[41] said a rising young star of the Foreign Office, David Gore-Booth, echoing the words of French bureaucrats soon after the arrival of Napoleon in Paris in 1792.

However hard Margaret Thatcher was trying to become master in her own house, her climb up the learning curve of government was proving more difficult than she expected, in two areas.

One was the economy, which was responding far too slowly to the medicine she had prescribed for it. The other was foreign policy, where her inexperience brought her into much creative tension with her Foreign Secretary, Lord Carrington.

17

First steps in foreign affairs

LEARNING FROM LORD CARRINGTON

Margaret Thatcher and Lord Carrington had an occasionally stormy but generally successful relationship as Prime Minister and Foreign Secretary. Because they both had strong wills and short fuses, they had many fierce arguments. One of the most heated of their rows blew up in Washington, DC, a few minutes before the start of a summit with the recently inaugurated President Ronald Reagan in February 1981.

The Prime Minister was in a state of tense excitement about her meeting with the new leader of the free world. She had encountered Reagan twice on his visits to London, when she was in opposition and he was in the wilderness as an ex-Governor of California. She had taken a shine to his good looks, his courtly gallantry and his conservative credentials. Now he was in the White House she hoped that they might be able to energise the UK–US 'special relationship', making it far more productive than it had been in the first twenty months of her premiership, working in harness with Reagan's predecessor, President Jimmy Carter.

With these aspirations in mind, Margaret Thatcher brought a strong team to Washington on her RAF VC10. Along with her Foreign Secretary, she was accompanied by Sir Robert Armstrong (Secretary to the Cabinet), Sir Michael Palliser (Permanent Secretary at the Foreign Office) and Sir Frank Cooper (Permanent Secretary at the Ministry of Defence). All of them had submitted briefing papers, which she studied and annotated with her habitual diligence.

The Prime Minister rose early at Blair House* on the morning of Thursday 26 February to put in some extra preparation for her 10 a.m. *tête à tête* with

---

* Blair House is the US President's guest house where foreign heads of state and heads of government stay during official visits. Built in 1824, the red-brick mansion stands across Pennsylvania Avenue from the White House.

President Reagan. As it was not known which subjects he might raise in their discussion, she carefully reviewed the briefing papers prepared for her by the Foreign Office. One on the Middle East aroused her disapproval. She made a number of harsh comments about it over breakfast to Sir Michael Palliser, whose laconic replies did not calm her indignation. So she asked Carrington to join them. Before he could sit down, she said accusingly: 'Your policy on Palestine is going to lose us the next election.'

'I rather thought it was the government's policy on Palestine', answered the Foreign Secretary.

His urbanity increased her irascibility. She let fly with a string of offensive remarks about 'the moral cowardice' of the Foreign Office, and then returned to the impact of its Palestinian proposals on domestic politics.

'What's more, not only is your Palestine policy going to lose us the next election,' she hectored Carrington, 'it is going to lose me my seat in Finchley . . . I will definitely lose my seat in Finchley because of this stuff', she shouted, slamming the briefing paper down on the table.

Now it was Carrington's turn to get angry. 'If you think that British foreign policy should be based on whether you will lose your seat in Finchley, you need a new Foreign Secretary', he retorted, storming out of the room and slamming the door.[1]

After this upheaval there was, to put it mildly, a chill between the two senior members of the British delegation as they headed off to the White House for their summit with the President of the United States. It was non-speaks in the Ambassador's Rolls-Royce on the short journey across Pennsylvania Avenue. But the civilities were restored after the *tête a tête* and the welcoming ceremonies. The Prime Minister murmured to her Foreign Secretary: 'I don't think we did very well this morning, did we?' It was, by her standards, an apology.

What may have been behind the Prime Minister's aggression at Blair House was an anxiety that the strongly pro-Israeli Ronald Reagan was going to ask her awkward questions about the British proposals for progress on the Israel–Palestine issue. But the broad-brush President was not interested in getting down to such detail. He simply wanted to throw a warm mantle of welcome around his fellow-conservative head of government. So the summit, which dealt with few issues of substance, apart from the President's determination to resist the spread of communism in Latin America, passed off as a great success. Nevertheless, the early morning row had highlighted Margaret Thatcher's fear that Carrington, as she put it, 'was intent on pursuing lines which I knew would in practice be quite fruitless, given the President's unshakable commitment to a limited number of positions'.[2] In fact, Carrington had no such intention, so the eruption had been needless and pointless.

Lord Carrington was too grand and secure a figure to become unduly bothered by an up and downer with his boss. As at Blair House, he could at times be baffled by her rudeness and wrong-headedness. But he also saw her strength of will and determination. He said:

> I admired her enormously, particularly her courage and her character. I understood that in her passion to change things, she decided to ignore people, sometimes trample over people, who told her she couldn't or shouldn't take such a course. But the problem was that if you do that when you're wrong, you can get into serious trouble.[3]

There was quite a lot of trampling in the early days of the Carrington–Thatcher foreign-policy partnership. She was hostile to the Foreign Office as an institution and to some of its leading mandarins. She behaved unfairly to its Permanent Secretary, Sir Michael Palliser, mainly because his elaborately polite style jarred with her preference for a rough and tumble argument. This was all too often based, at least in her first two or three years as Prime Minister, on ill-informed prejudices. Carrington explained:

> You had to be pretty quick with her because her instincts on foreign policy were often wrong, but her brain was very good. So you had to get to her before those instincts had pre-empted the brain. If you didn't reach her early enough, it took quite a struggle before her heart would rather grudgingly yield to her highly intelligent head. By golly it was hard work sometimes![4]

One area of hard work was policy towards the Soviet Union. Margaret Thatcher felt the Foreign Office was soft towards the Kremlin. 'You don't have anyone in your department who knows anything about the Russians', she told Carrington contemptuously.

'You're absolutely wrong. I have two outstanding experts. Come and meet them', he replied. The following evening at 6 p.m. Margaret Thatcher came round

to the Foreign Office to have a drink with its top Sovietologists, Christopher
Mallaby and Rodric Braithwaite.

Carrington had warned his mandarins about her propensity to interrupt
and, sure enough, within seconds of Mallaby's opening presentation he found
himself being contradicted by the Prime Minister. He pressed on regardless
with the magisterial rebuff: 'If I may just be allowed to continue . . .' By the time
he and Braithwaite had finished, she was captivated. 'She was so impressed that
from then on she sidelined her gurus', claimed Carrington.[5] This was not entirely
correct, for she continued to listen to her private anti-Soviet voices such as
Robert Conquest. But at least she gave more weight to the departmental advice
for a while.

Two weeks after this meeting, the Prime Minister and her Foreign Secretary
made a refuelling stop in Moscow on their way to the G7 summit held in Tokyo.
To their surprise, half the Politburo of the Soviet Union, headed by Prime
Minister Alexei Kosygin, turned out to meet her. They gave an unscheduled
dinner in her honour in an aircraft hanger. After listening to a speech of
diplomatic bromides from the Soviet leader, Margaret Thatcher responded
with a sharp and detailed reply. Looking magnificent in her cobalt blue suit
and matching hat, she fired off a salvo of questions, vigorously interrupting
the answers.

One of her major concerns was the plight of the Vietnamese boat people,
which was causing problems to the British colony of Hong Kong. The Prime
Minister said that what was happening was a disgrace not only to the regime in
Vietnam, but to communism as a whole. Surely the Soviet Union could exercise
its influence to put a stop to it? Premier 'Cosy Gin', as Carrington nicknamed
Kosygin, gave a watery smile and the excuse that the boat people 'were all
drug-takers or criminals'. Margaret Thatcher interrupted him: 'What, one
million of them? Is communism so bad that a million have to take drugs to steal
to live?'[6] The subject was immediately dropped. According to Carrington, 'The
Politburo's eyes were out on stalks as she told them off on issue after issue.
They were mesmerised. They were astonished at being beaten over the head,
but they saw her strength and quality.'[7]

The Prime Minister was also awarded a star-quality rating in Tokyo, where
over a thousand journalists turned out at the airport to report on the phenomenon
of a woman leader. But she was underwhelmed by her first experience of global

summitry. Prior to departure for Tokyo, her major preoccupation had been to ensure that the British delegation was the smallest of the participating G7 countries. She made her Private Secretary for Overseas Affairs, Bryan Cartledge, count and recount the size of the other delegations in the hope that they would all be larger. 'In the end, we were only the second smallest', he recalled. 'We were beaten by the Canadians. She was very cross about that.'[8]

Her frugality about the size of her official party might have seemed an odd preoccupation had it not been for the pointlessness of the summit. Carrington said:

It was useless, a complete waste of time – nothing agreed, nothing achieved. She was bemused by the stupidity of it all. We both found it impossible to tell whether the Japanese Prime Minister chairing the conference, Masayoshi Ohira, was asleep or awake. The only point to it all was that she did meet President Carter for the first time. She was a bit bemused by him.[9]

Carrington was her tutor on her geopolitical learning curve. Sometimes he handled her as a father figure, sometimes as her leading man, sometimes as her in-house humorist. One occasion when he made her laugh came during a Downing Street meeting with Chairman Hua Guofeng, the immediate successor to Chairman Mao. The Chinese leader opened the discussion with a fifty-minute monologue, not allowing the Prime Minister to get a word in edgeways. Carrington passed her a note saying: 'You are speaking too much, as usual.' She opened this missive just as Chairman Hua was saying, 'Now I come to the tragedy of the Holocaust . . .' He must have been baffled by the Prime Minister pulling out her handkerchief to suppress a fit of giggles. Those inscrutable British![10]

Usually, however, it was Margaret Thatcher who seized the lion's share of the dialogue during such meetings. On at least a couple of occasions Carrington had to pass her a note saying, 'He's come 1,000 miles. Let him say something.' She took such teasing well; partly because, up to a point, she was amused by the irreverence of an authentic toff, and partly because she respected his foreign-policy expertise. As a former UK High Commissioner in Australia, First Lord of the Admiralty, Secretary of State for Defence, an international banker and a director of Rio Tinto Zinc, he had come to know the world and almost everyone of importance in it. To bring the new Prime Minister up to the same level of understanding was his greatest challenge. Carrington recalled:

> Frankly, there were times when I found her intensely irritating. Her prejudices were sometimes extraordinary. She seemed to believe all blacks were communists. When we were on our first trip to Africa together, she put on a pair of dark glasses just before our VC10 touched down at Lusaka. 'What on earth are those for?' I asked, since we were landing in darkness. 'I am absolutely certain that they are going to throw acid in my face', she replied. 'I told her not to be so silly, and that an African crowd would be much more likely to cheer her. That is exactly what happened.'[11]

The Thatcher–Carrington preparations for the Commonwealth Heads of Government Meeting (CHOGM) in Lusaka were particularly fraught. The most important issue on the agenda was Rhodesia. She had strong views on its future, a problem which had proved intractable to successive British governments ever since the regime of Ian Smith had made its Unilateral Declaration of Independence (UDI) on 11 November 1965. Thirteen years later Ian Smith reached a power-sharing agreement with the leaders of the two more moderate African parties. This was ratified in the April 1979 election, with Bishop Muzorewa becoming Prime Minister, but was boycotted by the two major African nationalist parties, and condemned by most international opinion. But Margaret Thatcher's personal emissary to Rhodesia, the former Colonial Secretary Viscount Boyd of Merton, reported that the elections had been fair and valid.

After reading Boyd's report, Margaret Thatcher's instincts were to recognise the Smith–Muzorewa settlement. Carrington persuaded her otherwise. It was a U-turn that required all his formidable skills of argument. He recalled:

> We had several flaming rows. In the end she listened to the evidence, which was that every single Commonwealth country as well as the United States and Europe would not wear the solution she wanted. But she still did not give way completely, until we were on the flight to Lusaka. While we were having dinner in mid-air, I said to her that I thought the best result we would get from the conference would be to pull off a damage-limitation exercise. She claimed she'd never heard of such a phrase – 'typical Foreign Office language', she called it – and then she said, 'I want to do better than that'.[12]

It was the first clear sign that the Carrington tutorials on Africa might be beginning to work.

RHODESIA

Solving the problem of Rhodesia was Margaret Thatcher's first major success as Prime Minister at home or abroad. After her initial obduracy she turned out to be a surprisingly pragmatic operator in the unfamiliar waters of African diplomacy. She showed courage, charm and considerable flexibility in achieving the desired result.

She was frightened and worried when she arrived in Lusaka. Although her fears of having acid thrown in her face proved groundless, as Carrington had assured her, it still took courage to walk into the crowds (without her dark glasses) and to have to face a hostile media conference. In the airport chaos she became separated from her staff, including her Press Secretary, Henry James. She was unwell because of a stomach bug, and nearly fainted. Yet she gave as good as she got from the hostile Zambian journalists, who treated her as a colonial cardboard cut-out, and described her as 'a racist'.[13] But the British press corps thought she showed grace and spirit under the pressure of her interrogation. John Simpson of the BBC reported that she had given 'a magnificent performance'.[14]

The atmosphere at the Commonwealth Heads of Government Meeting was more friendly. Margaret Thatcher's mistrust of Africa softened under the warmth of the welcome she received. This had a lot to do with the Queen's skill at presiding over the social side of the conference. Also, the presidents of the 'frontline' states, namely Botswana, Mozambique and Zambia, were politically more accommodating in private than they sounded in their public statements. Many of the other twenty-seven heads of government attending were also helpful in nudging the main protagonists towards an agreement.

The most positive leader was the host of the conference, President Kenneth Kaunda of Zambia. He went out of his way to cajole his fellow Africans into accepting the British proposals they did not initially like. He also charmed Margaret Thatcher (or did she charm him?) in a session of dance-floor diplomacy. The photographs of the quickstep between the Zambian President and the British Prime Minister came to symbolise their good rapport. According to Denis Thatcher, their whirl round the ballroom 'turned the trick' at the conference.[15]

In reality, the trick was turned by the surprise reversal of what was widely assumed to be Margaret Thatcher's position on Rhodesia. She accepted a bold plan, the brainchild of an imaginative FCO official, Robin Renwick, that Britain should abandon its impotent role as the colonial power and assume a powerful new role as the decolonising power. To the astonishment of the assembled heads of government, the Prime Minister announced that the Smith–Muzorewa settlement would be abandoned. Britain would take the driving seat in delivering black majority rule, not the United Nations. Rhodesia would first resort to its pre-UDI colonial status with a British governor who would supervise direct elections policed by British troops. The future constitutional arrangements would be decided by a British-chaired conference at Lancaster House in London with the key African politicians, Robert Mugabe and Joshua Nkomo at the table. It was a U-turn but it was a U-turn on her terms. Some of the Africans were unenthusiastic but once Kaunda backed the plan, declaring that 'the Iron Lady has brought a ray of hope on the dark horizon', they all fell into line.[16]

Margaret Thatcher had misgivings about the plan she endorsed. The way she read out her part of the communiqué at the end of the conference was in a head-down, high-speed monotone, far removed from her usual vocal range when handing down the commandments of conviction politics. But in the excitement of getting the deal, she finally became committed to it. Having arrived in Lusaka fearful, she left hopeful. As Carrington put it: 'She didn't really believe that we would ever agree a final settlement, but once she saw there was a real hope of getting an agreement she went for it.'[17]

When the long-running Rhodesia saga moved to London in September, the Prime Minister left the details of the Lancaster House constitutional conference to her Foreign Secretary. It took sixteen weeks of arduous negotiations between the parties. It was not her show, but she did play two key cards in it with clarity and courage.

First, she remained determinedly aloof from the negotiating process. The white Rhodesians, egged on by the Rhodesia Lobby in London, had always expected that she would act as a final court of appeal through which her 'kith and kin' might be able to extract some last-minute concessions. She would have none of it. She was firm in the commitment she had made in Lusaka to black majority rule.

Second, she took a considerable risk, when the civil war was still raging in Rhodesia, in sending Lord Soames out to Salisbury as Governor. He and the small contingent of British troops protecting him could easily have been engulfed in the violence. But the gamble was taken and it worked. Soames was able to supervise free, fair and peaceful elections in February 1980. They produced a decisive result. Robert Mugabe became Prime Minister, and power was formally transferred from Britain to an independent Zimbabwe on 17 April 1980.

Watching the independence ceremony on television with her Parliamentary Private Secretary, Ian Gow, Margaret Thatcher wept as the Union Jack was lowered. 'The poor Queen', she said. 'Do you realise the number of colonies that have been handed over from the British Empire since she came to the throne?'[18]

For the next fifteen or so years, there seemed few reasons for shedding tears over Zimbabwe. Although it quickly became a one-party state, the worst fears of the pessimists were not realised. The civil war ended, black- and white-owned farms flourished, the population was well fed, infant mortality halved, secondary school places quadrupled. Although Mugabe made many speeches about his Marxist credo, not an acre of land was confiscated and not a single business was compulsorily nationalised. As a mixed economy it was relatively successful. Only at the end of the century did Mugabe emerge as a tyrannical dictator who launched violence against white farmers, seizing their land and handing it over to his cronies. He also brutalised his people with cruel oppression and starvation.

So what looked like a diplomatic triumph in 1980 had turned to ashes by the early twenty-first century. Margaret Thatcher cannot be blamed for this tragedy, which unfolded long after she left power. In the period when Zimbabwean independence took root, she won high praise for her statescraft. In her heart of hearts, she might well have preferred to maintain British colonial rule or a power-sharing regime along Smith–Muzorewa lines. But these were not options. Given the politics of Africa at the time of the Lusaka conference in 1979, she found the best solution. Sadly, it lasted for only one generation.

EUROPE

'I came to realise that Margaret Thatcher didn't really like people whose mother tongue was not English', said Lord Carrington. 'She mistrusted Europeans, and her dealings with them were often very embarrassing because she was so rude to everyone.'[19]

Although mistrust and bad manners were often at the forefront of Margaret Thatcher's many arguments with her fellow heads of government in Europe, it should be recorded that the opening blows of rudeness were struck against her, not by her. The perpetrators were the leaders of France and Germany.

Her first foreign visitor to Downing Street in May 1979 was the German Chancellor, Helmut Schmidt. She initially found him an attractive personality, and was dismayed when he patronised her with a condescending attitude. However, in the *folie de grandeur* stakes, he was soon overtaken by President Valéry Giscard d'Estaing of France. As the host of the European Council summit in Strasbourg in June, the French President went out of his way to snub the British Prime Minister by not sitting next to her at any meal. He also insisted on being served first, as head of state, instead of yielding this courtesy to Europe's first woman leader, as most participants expected. 'Silly of him', said Carrington. 'Everyone commented unfavourably.'[20]

The Strasbourg summit was not about slights against Margaret Thatcher, but about an issue of substance that she regarded as a high priority. It later became known as 'The Bloody British Question', or BBQ, although needless to say it was not so described in the Foreign Office briefing paper prepared for the Prime Minister by Sir Michael Butler, UK Representative to the European Community in Brussels.

Margaret Thatcher was dissatisfied with Butler's paper, which she thought was too ready to make compromises on the question of Britain's contribution to the community budget. So she commissioned an alternative briefing paper from the Treasury. Its author was a young Assistant Under Secretary, Peter Middleton, whom she summoned to Chequers to be interrogated on it. This was a testing experience, but he made such a favourable impression on the Prime Minister that it led to his meteoric rise, four years later, to the top job in his department as Permanent Secretary. For Middleton was the original architect of the case Margaret Thatcher launched at Strasbourg for the return of 'our money'.

The 'our money' campaign had its roots in the complex imbalances between British import levies and Common Agricultural Policy (CAP) benefits within the EU budget. It was common ground that those structural imbalances should be redressed by a budget rebate to Britain. What was not common ground was the amount of the rebate (£1 billion a year according to Middleton's figures) and the priority that should be given to it.

Margaret Thatcher came to Strasbourg spoiling for a fight. She wanted the British budget rebate to be taken as the first item on the agenda, and to be separated from all the rest of the horse-trading on budgetary issues. This was not the Franco-German way of doing business. President Giscard d'Estaing and Chancellor Helmut Schmidt resented Margaret Thatcher's nationalistic approach. They were dismissive towards her, and only grudgingly agreed to consider the issue at their next meeting.

Lord Carrington thought that the European leaders' attitude to her was 'Pretty stupid . . . enormously short-sighted and selfish'.[21] By contrast, Margaret Thatcher was rather pleased with herself. 'I felt that I had made an impression as someone who meant business', she said.[22]

Between the Strasbourg summit in June and the next European Council at Dublin in November, the British Prime Minister sounded increasingly determined. She let it be known that she was considering withholding Britain's VAT payments to the Community – which would have been illegal. Delivering the 1979 Winston Churchill Memorial Lecture in Luxembourg on 18 October, she described the treatment of Britain over the European Community budget as 'demonstrably unjust' and 'politically indefensible'. She continued: 'I cannot play Sister Bountiful to the Community while my own electorate are being asked to forgo improvements in the fields of health, education, welfare and the rest.'[23]

At the Dublin Council meeting in November, Sister Bountiful became Sister Aggressive. She was offered a £350 million rebate, which the Europeans thought was their first move in a bargaining negotiation. She rejected it contemptuously as 'a third of a loaf'.[24] Thereafter, she spent the rest of the evening upbraiding her fellow heads of government in what Carrington described as 'a rant',[25] in a repetitious flow of rhetoric with the constant refrain, 'It's my money I want back'.[26]

Helmut Schmidt pretended to fall asleep. Giscard d'Estaing read a newspaper. According to Roy Jenkins, the President of the European Commission, 'She kept us all round the dinner table for four interminable hours . . . She spoke without pause, but not without repetition . . . It was obvious to everyone except her that she wasn't making progress and was alienating people.'[27]

The alienation was a two-way street. The friction of personalities was one problem. The lordly Giscard d'Estaing could not bear the over-loquacious lady he privately derided as 'la fille d'épicier'. Helmut Schmidt was no less contemptuous of the anti-communitarian attitudes of the grocer's daughter. He walked out of the Dublin dinner shaking with rage saying: 'I can't stand this any longer . . . I can't deal with someone like that.'[28]

But Margaret Thatcher was not flustered by either Gallic scorn or Teutonic tantrums. She was proud to be distrustful towards what she later called 'The Franco-German carve up of Europe'.[29]

Deep in her psyche she was still the patriotic Grantham girl who remembered the war all too well. If she sounded like a Little Englander it was because that was her character. She saw everything through the prism of British interests, a position she and the majority of her electorate thought was entirely right and proper for a British Prime Minister.

The morning after the disastrous dinner in Dublin, Margaret Thatcher returned to the fray with still more detailed arguments on the unfairness of Britain's treatment in the EEC budget. Five minutes before the final session of the summit broke up, she reluctantly agreed to a postponement of the issue until the next meeting in Luxembourg, which took place in April 1980. There she was offered a rebate of £750 million, which her Foreign Office advisers thought was a fair deal. To considerable astonishment, she turned it down flat on the grounds that it was only a two-year deal. This imperious 'No' to three-quarters of the loaf she had been seeking stunned her own team as much as the European leaders. Now it was Giscard's turn to walk out in a bad temper. 'I will not allow such a contemptible spectacle to occur again', was his parting shot.[30]

Margaret Thatcher seemed to be enjoying her isolation. She told BBC Radio 4 that she was pleased that the Europeans were calling her a 'she-de Gaulle'.[31] She received a good reception to her statement on the Luxembourg summit from the House of Commons. The image of British Maggie giving the bureaucrats of Brussels a good handbagging* played well across the country. It was also a welcome diversion from the economic troubles at home as well as the negotiating realities within the EEC. For domestic reasons of their own, the French and Germans were anxious to settle the budget question. For all the umbrage taken by the French and German leaders, the argument was about a comparatively

---

* The term 'handbagging', now defined in the *Oxford English Dictionary* as 'an idiom for asserting oneself and ruthlessly attacking one's opponent', first entered the lexicon of politics at the time of Margaret Thatcher's aggressive arguments about the British rebate at the EEC summit meetings.

small amount of money measured against EEC finances. So on 30 May a new round of negotiations took place at the Council of Foreign Ministers – without Margaret Thatcher.

The British negotiators, Lord Carrington and his House of Commons spokesman Ian Gilmour, did better than expected. They improved the rebate terms by £50 million, and extended them into a third year. So they returned from their all-night negotiations in Brussels with some satisfaction, only to be greeted at Chequers by an extremely dissatisfied Margaret Thatcher, who did not even offer them a cup of coffee. 'Had we been bailiffs arriving to take possession of the furniture,' recalled Ian Gilmour, 'we would probably have been more cordially received. The Prime Minister was like a firework whose fuse had already been lit; we could almost hear the sizzling.'[32]

The fireworks chastened Carrington. His Assistant Private Secretary, Stephen Wall, remembered 'his mixture of exasperation tinged with reluctant admiration, that after he and Gilmour had negotiated for days and nights, and secured a deal . . . Margaret Thatcher should treat them as if they were schoolboys who had failed to produce their homework to the standard required.'[33]

In the end, the schoolboys outwitted their schoolmistress. Gilmour ignored the Prime Minister's fulminations and briefed the press that a diplomatic triumph had been achieved. Carrington put his foot down in cabinet and insisted that the deal he had signed in Brussels must be honoured. Faced with such a rebellion, well supported by other senior figures in the government, Margaret Thatcher had to back down. It was almost the only occasion in her first year of power when the collective will of her colleagues forced her into a course of action to which she was strongly opposed.

These early experiences of EEC summitry did not teach Margaret Thatcher the lessons she might have learned from them. She should have realised that progress in European diplomacy is not always achievable by advancing like a battle-tank with all guns firing. She would not have liked the French phrase *reculer pour mieux sauter*, but she needed to know that more subtle methods of negotiating could achieve the desired results.

Subtlety did not come easily to her personality. It was one of the reasons why the politics of Europe eventually became her downfall. But whatever annoyance she caused by her trenchant style of negotiating in 1979–1980, she did deliver a budget rebate for Britain that was far larger than anyone had expected. So in the short term, her undiplomatic diplomacy paid off. It was a substantial and enduring achievement.

A SLOW START TO THE SPECIAL RELATIONSHIP

The highest priority for Margaret Thatcher in foreign policy was strengthening the Anglo-American alliance – a cause in which she had believed passionately ever since her wartime childhood in Grantham when US servicemen had been a memorable presence in the town. But by 1979 the special nature of this alliance was now fading. According to a CIA report written for President Carter in October 1979, 'The "Special Relationship" between the United States and the United Kingdom, finally, has lost much of its meaning. The United States is no longer significantly closer to Britain than to its other major allies.'[34] President Jimmy Carter annotated this observation with the comment, 'Partly accurate, partly fallacious'.[35]

The same ambivalence characterised his attitude to the new British Prime Minister. A week after her election, the US National Security Adviser, Zbigniew Brzezinski, sent the President a memorandum advising him, 'It will take patience to deal with Mrs Thatcher's hard-driving nature and her tendency to hector'.[36]

Carter seems to have found this warning accurate. 'A tough lady! Highly opinionated, strong willed, cannot admit that she doesn't know something', was his private comment after seeing her at the G7 summit in Tokyo.[37]

Their next encounter came on her visit to Washington in early December. America was in the throes of the Iranian hostage crisis created by the seizure of the US Embassy and fifty-two American diplomats in Tehran. Margaret Thatcher mistakenly took the view that this was a domestic problem for America, on which a visiting foreign leader should not publicly comment. Lord Carrington had to work hard to change her mind. But he succeeded.

At the arrival ceremonies on the White House lawn, the Prime Minister came out with a ringing statement of solidarity. 'At times like this you are entitled to look to your friends for support. We are your friends, we do support you. And we shall support you. Let there be no doubt about that.'[38]

After these words, which resonated profoundly with Washington's need for reassurance from close allies, the rest of the Prime Minister's visit was a triumphal progress. She was serenaded at a White House banquet in her honour by a choir that included Kirk Douglas and Secretary of State Cyrus Vance. She was acclaimed for her address to Congress and for her speech to the Foreign Policy Association of New York. There was a section in both audiences that virtually fell in love with Margaret Thatcher's personality. Her forthright style of answering questions and her robust views on issues ranging from free-market economics to Soviet expansionism created a fan club of American conservatives which grew for many years.

During the twenty months while they were in office together, President Jimmy Carter and Margaret Thatcher got on better than either of them expected. She admired his Christian faith, scientific knowledge and personal sincerity. But she thought he was inadequate in his understanding of economics and of the Soviet threat.

After the Soviet invasion of Afghanistan he felt she was the weaker partner, sheltering behind legalities and technicalities in order to avoid imposing the toughest possible sanctions. 'I would hope that you would not be so, excuse me using the word, adamant', he said to her during a 28 December call to Chequers when the British seemed to be having too many reservations about a US draft of a Security Council Resolution.[39] Evidently, the President had not learned in his dealings with the British Prime Minister that it was in her nature to be 'adamant' about most things.

Despite their differences of political and diplomatic outlook, the two leaders did much useful business together. Among their strategic agreements was the replacement of Britain's ageing Polaris nuclear missile system with the purchase of Trident, and a deal which allowed a large US expansion of its military facilities on the British island of Diego Garcia. But Jimmy Carter and Margaret Thatcher were never kindred spirits. That personal rapport and the revival of the 'special relationship' that went with it had to await the election of Ronald Reagan.

REFLECTION

The Carrington–Thatcher partnership was a fruitful one for British foreign policy. For all her inexperience, she did jolt him and the diplomatic establishment into more robust stances. For all his amusing cynicism, he was strong enough to stand up to her when she was being impossible. As a result, they jointly had some considerable successes on Rhodesia, on the British budgetary rebate in Europe and in strengthening the 'special relationship' with the United States. Yet sometimes their co-operation resembled that of a patrician trainer working with a headstrong racehorse. Carrington could cajole or turn her away from what he regarded as a disastrous course. But he never managed to restrain her from her rudeness, particularly to the Germans.

'My dear Peter, please explain me something about Mrs Thatcher', enquired the new German Chancellor, Helmut Kohl, after a couple of bruising European summits with her. 'Could you tell me why she treats me as though I was the most junior and least important member of her cabinet?'

'My dear Helmut,' replied Carrington, 'she treats all of us like that – and you are lucky, for she would be far worse if you really were in her cabinet.'[40]

The reasons why Margaret Thatcher never established good relations with the four Franco-German leaders she had to deal with – Giscard, Mitterrand, Schmidt and Kohl – were a combination of the visceral, the political and the personal. As a child of the Second World War, she could not forget the shadows of Nazi Germany and Vichy France. She had moved on, but not nearly as far as most British people who had been teenagers in the dark days of the 1940s when England stood alone.

What might have convinced her to change her attitudes would have been a willingness on the part of the key European leaders to engage with her in forensic arguments about issues on the agenda of the EEC. But these leaders were broad-brush declarers of intent, while she was a master of detail. This was a gulf that could not be bridged. She became as contemptuous towards them as she could be towards her own ministers when she realised they had not done their homework. There could be no dialogue and no meeting of minds between Margaret Thatcher and those who had not studied their briefs, however eminent they might be.

The only one of the big four in Europe for whom she developed a soft spot was President Mitterrand. Initially, this was a personal feeling, strengthened later by his helpfulness during the Falklands War. When he made his first visit to Chequers soon after his election in May 1981, the President and the Prime Minister struck up a warm *entente cordiale*. As Mitterrand was driving away, her Cabinet Secretary, Robert Armstrong, congratulated her on how well the discussions had gone. 'Yes', replied Margaret Thatcher, and then, after a short pause, 'He likes women, you know.'[41]

The unexpected comment reflected a strange dimension to Margaret Thatcher's foreign policy. The statesmen she could best do business with were the men she found attractive – Reagan, Gorbachev and Mitterrand. Those she found unattractive, notably the corpulent Kohl, the reptilian Giscard and the anaemic Carter, were consigned to the outer regions of her likes and dislikes. Looks counted with her. This may have had something to do with the differences between the ways she treated her Foreign Secretaries. The lugubrious Francis Pym and the podgy, discursive Geoffrey Howe were not her type. The trim, amusing Lord Carrington had much more appeal to her. Their arguments were vigorous, but they enjoyed each other's company without the slightest traces of rancour.

She liked and learned much from Carrington. Yet it is intriguing that she never invited him to rejoin her government after his later honourable resignation over the Falklands,* which was only a transient blot on his escutcheon. His restoration to her cabinet would have been easy before or after he became Secretary General of NATO. Perhaps the real problem was that she wanted to be her own Foreign Secretary. She would not have welcomed a foreign-affairs heavyweight in the senior ranks of her government, particularly one who would have managed to restrain her approach to Europe from being so confrontational. This was a pity, because Carrington was a statesman whose partnership with her contributed much to her early successes.

---

* See Chapter 19, 'The Falklands War: the prelude'.

18

Storm clouds on the economy and in the cabinet

THE GATHERING STORM

Margaret Thatcher's determination to cure Britain's deep-rooted economic sickness came to be symbolised by her words to the Conservative Conference of October 1980: 'You turn if you want to – the lady's not for turning.'[1] Although greeted with thunderous applause by the rank and file of the party, there were many in her cabinet who thought them foolhardy. For by this time unemployment was over 2 million, inflation had risen to 13 per cent and the recession was worsening. The government's main weapons in the battle to restore prudence to the nation's finances were controlling the money supply and reducing public expenditure. Neither was working.

There was a widespread expectation that the realities of the recession, especially the rise in unemployment, would force a change of strategy in the management of the economy. But the Prime Minister had staked her reputation on not initiating the kind of U-turn that had brought about the political demise of Ted Heath. Moreover, she was far more resolute than he had been in her certainty that she must stick to the course she had set. The big question, not resolved until the autumn of 1981, was: would her cabinet stick with her?

Although the cabinet was portrayed as being divided into the wets and the drys this was largely a caricature of Margaret Thatcher's own making. She enjoyed the mystique of being an embattled crusader against her adversaries. But the reality was that her praetorian guard of Treasury ministers and like-minded colleagues on the 'E' or Economic Committee of the cabinet backed her strategy. So did two other bulwarks of support in the shape of William Whitelaw and Lord Carrington. 'As every other nostrum for reversing our economic decline had failed, we thought we had better let her get on with what she wanted to do', was how Carrington described their position.[2] So, with the connivance of her Home and Foreign Secretaries, the cabinet itself rarely discussed economic policy for the first two years of the Thatcher government's existence. The Wets (Jim Prior, Francis Pym, Lord Soames, Norman St John-Stevas, Ian Gilmour, Peter Walker and later allies) huffed, puffed and leaked, but they never came close to bringing the house down. In the meantime, the Chancellor and the Prime Minister went ahead with implementing their master plan.

But what exactly was their strategy? In the beginning it was said to be all about monetarism. But measuring, let alone controlling, the money supply proved an elusive failure. The principal yardstick was called £M3, which meant all money in circulation including notes, coins and bank deposits. In 1980, £M3 soared to 18 per cent, three times the government's target of 6 per cent. Ian Gilmour had a point when he commented that monetarism was 'the uncontrollable in pursuit of the indefinable'.[3] Margaret Thatcher was stung by his criticism, tartly noting that the Wets were finding 'the wayward behaviour of £M3 a suitable subject for mockery at dinner parties'.[4] She insisted that the monetary squeeze was bringing down inflation and working more effectively than the £M3 figures suggested.

The second cornerstone of the strategy was reducing public expenditure. Sir Geoffrey Howe did make cuts of over £3 billion in his 1979 and 1980 budgets, but these were overwhelmed by overspending in Defence and Health; by the high cost of subsidising nationalised industries; and by burgeoning wage claims in the public sector, particularly those granted by the Clegg Commission,* whose awards Margaret Thatcher had promised to honour in the heat of the election campaign. The net result was that public spending kept on rising.

Some order in all this chaos looked as though it might be imposed by the Medium Term Financial Strategy (MTFS). It was the brainchild of the intellectually assertive Nigel Lawson, still only a junior minister in the Treasury. Margaret Thatcher, who was in awe of first-class minds in general and Nigel Lawson's in particular, bought the idea of MTFS. It was supposed to be a set of iron-clad rules setting fixed targets for monetary growth and public expenditure

---

* Standing Commission on Pay Comparability, 1979–1980, set up by James Callaghan to settle the 'winter of discontent' pay disputes and chaired by Hugh Clegg, Professor of Industrial Relations at Warwick University.

reductions for several years ahead, replacing the usual one-year forecast. But who would deliver performance in line with the MTFS rules? The Prime Minister took the challenge personally. 'The MTFS would only influence expectations in so far as people believed in our determination to stick to it', she declared. 'Its credibility depended . . . on the quality of my own commitment, about which I would leave no-one in doubt. I would not bow to demands to reflate.'[5]

It was the recognition of Margaret Thatcher's commitment not to make a U-turn that proved the game changer. Although she was vilified for her inflexibility, stubbornness, heartlessness and even for practising 'sado-monetarism',[6] somewhere deep down in the political subconscious of the British people there was a recognition that her determination should be given its chance.

The 'winter of discontent' remained such a bad memory that a majority of the electorate, rather like Whitelaw and Carrington, were willing to try Margaret Thatcher's prescriptions for reforming the economy. But to a sizeable minority, including many within her party, her remedies seemed divisive.

Around this time the acronym 'TINA' entered the political vocabulary. It was derived from briefings Margaret Thatcher gave to Conservative MPs and others, vehemently repeating the phrase, 'There is no alternative'. It rang true because the Wets had not come up with any coherent plan B for the economy that did not involve paying for the extra expenditure they wanted by printing more money. But TINA also became an irreverent nickname for the Prime Minister. I remember using it myself on the Terrace of the House of Commons one spring evening in 1981, only to be rebuked by Donald Thompson, the MP for Sowerby. He was a hands-on Yorkshire butcher who still chopped up carcasses and delivered cuts of meat to his customers on Saturdays. 'Aye, Jonathan, but TINA is bloody well right – isn't she?'[7]

Belatedly and perhaps too grudgingly I was beginning to agree. So were many other Tory MPs who were not paid up members of the 'one of us' Thatcherite fan club. But thanks to Ian Gow's assiduous efforts among back-benchers, the Prime Minister was much better supported by her parliamentary party than she was by her cabinet. What was starting to make an impact was the very ingredient Margaret Thatcher had mocked her critics for lacking – courage in backing the economic strategy. While the Wets fretted and fumed, often in a hand-wringing style that was unattractive, she was ploughing her own lonely furrow with such personalised determination that she warmed hearts even if she did not change minds.

There were, however, many unanswered questions about the strategy. The biggest one was: what was the government going to do to curb the excessive wage demands and the excessive powers of the trade unions?

OUTFLANKING JIM PRIOR

Jim Prior was Margaret Thatcher's most formidable opponent within her cabinet during her early years as Prime Minister. How she outflanked him, sidelined him and emasculated his influence is a story that provides revealing insights into her personality.

The unanswered political question of the 1970s was: who governs Britain? The circumstances in which the governments of both Ted Heath and James Callaghan lost power suggested that union leaders rather than elected politicians were calling the shots on economic and industrial policy. Margaret Thatcher was determined to reverse this, and believed she had a mandate to do so. But so long as Jim Prior was her Secretary of State for Employment, she was thwarted in her reforming zeal to sort out the unions. Another problem in their relationship was that he was effectively the leader of the Wets, and their only voice on the 'E' committee.

Jim Prior liked to play up to his image of a Suffolk farmer. He was authentic in this role, but he was a far cleverer operator than might be imagined from his rubicund countenance and genial manner. As a middle-way Conservative in the Harold Macmillan mould, he had an abhorrence of high unemployment. Prior was by temperament a seeker after consensualist solutions to the political problems of the day. He had invested much time and energy in building bridges with the leading trade unionists. Sincere in his determination to avoid a return to the scenarios of the three-day week or the 'winter of discontent', he thought he could gently nudge the unions towards greater moderation by personal diplomacy. So he followed a 'softly, softly' approach on the issue of trade-union law reform. As he took up this position in the cabinet with what might be called a 'stubbornly, stubbornly' attitude, this put him on a collision course with Margaret Thatcher.

Their first collision came over the Employment Bill of 1980, which did not go nearly as far as the Prime Minister wanted in curbing the excesses of trade-union power. She and most Tory back-benchers hoped to see secondary strike action outlawed, the closed shop banned and the legal immunities of trade unions from civil damages removed. Prior had a more modest agenda. His bill gave increased rights of appeal to workers against the operation of closed shops, but did not outlaw the closed shop itself. Secondary picketing was made illegal, but secondary strike action remained lawful. Trade-union immunities were untouched.

Margaret Thatcher, who had long ago accepted the case for wholesale reform of trade-union privileges, as set out in John Hoskyns' unpublished policy document *Stepping Stones*, did her utmost to persuade Prior and the cabinet to toughen the legislation. She lost the early battles, but found other routes for winning the war.

One fundamental problem was that the personalities of Margaret Thatcher and Jim Prior were chalk and cheese. When she appointed him to her cabinet they had an argument about who should become his junior ministers. 'I'm determined to have *someone* with backbone in your department',[8] she told him, insisting on the appointment of Patrick Mayhew as his Parliamentary Under-Secretary. In fact, Mayhew's backbone leant more in the direction of Prior than Thatcher, but at the time her note of menace was clear. The difficulty was that from day one the Prime Minister thought her Secretary of State for Employment was an appeaser. She described him in pejorative terms. 'Jim Prior was an example of a political type that had dominated and, in my view, damaged the post-war Tory Party. I call such figures "the false squire". They have all the outward show of a John Bull – ruddy face, white hair, bluff manner – but inwardly they are political calculators who see the task of Conservatives as one of retreating gracefully before the Left's inevitable advance.'[9]

For his part, Prior could not stand Margaret Thatcher's shrill combativeness when challenging his proposals:

> Margaret not only starts with a spirit of confrontation but continues with it right through the argument. It is not a style which endears and perhaps even less so when the challenger is a woman and the challenged is a man. I have to confess that I found it very difficult to stomach, and this form of male chauvinism was obviously one of my failings.[10]

Prior's 'confession' is almost the only recorded example of any male minister or official admitting to suppressed feelings of misogynism as a result of being told off by Margaret Thatcher. There were probably numerous examples of such emotions. The Attorney General, Peter Rawlinson, acknowledged having them late in life with the wry comment that his hostile reactions to her cost him the Lord Chancellorship.[11] Men of that generation sometimes did find it hard to accept an abrasive and upbraiding style from a woman – even a woman prime minister. The fault was theirs. At least Jim Prior had the grace to admit it.

The Prior–Thatcher quarrels may have been exacerbated by a clash of styles, but at the core of their disputes lay a clash of wills. In February 1980, when the Employment Bill was going through its committee stages, the Prime Minister put heavy pressure on Prior to introduce a new clause outlawing secondary strike action. She even, through Ian Gow, solicited votes in the lobbies for what he called 'Margaret's amendments' to the government's own bill. This subversive activity failed. But it was becoming a parliamentary 'Alice in Wonderland', where the PPS to the Prime Minister was seen to be fermenting opposition to the legislation proposed by the Secretary of State for Employment.

Meanwhile, a strike accompanied by secondary picketing at the British Steel Corporation was causing serious national difficulties. In response Margaret Thatcher tried to pre-empt the main Employment Bill with an emergency one-clause bill to ban secondary picketing immediately. Prior felt that this would be a panic response, and was prepared to resign over it. So, the day before the vital 'E' committee meeting on 13 February, he embarked on a major lobbying exercise of his colleagues, persuading Willie Whitelaw, Lord Carrington, Michael Heseltine, Peter Walker, Lord Hailsham, Ian Gilmour and Norman St John-Stevas to support it.

The result was that Prior got his way. His 'softly, softly' line held. It was one of the rare examples of a rebellion by the Wets gaining a victory. But their success was short-lived. Margaret Thatcher hated her defeat, and came up with a new initiative of her own to signal her willingness to take tougher action against the unions.

Twenty-four hours after she had lost the argument with her cabinet, she made a surprise announcement at Prime Minister's Questions that the government would soon be cutting welfare benefits for strikers. Jim Prior was 'amazed' by this announcement, but grudgingly admired the cunning of her pre-emptive move. 'She was determined to get it on the record in case, when it came to the crunch, the wets prevailed', he commented. 'And that was quite often her way of doing things. Very effective.'[12]

The label the Wets originated from Prior–Thatcher tensions. She got into the habit of scrawling the adjective 'wet' in the margins of memoranda and letters from him when she was Leader of the Opposition. Prior saw the accusation of wetness as a badge of honour. He boasted of it to journalists. As a result, the word came to be a generic term for those who harboured serious doubts about the economic policies of Margaret Thatcher in her first three years as Prime Minister.

Jim Prior's doubts went far further than employment legislation issues. On that front, he suffered more defeats. He thought his 1980 Employment Bill was to be the government's last word on law reforms affecting the trade unions. Margaret Thatcher decreed it was to be the first step. Before the bill was on the statute book, the government published a green paper indicating that further curbs on the closed shop and other measures were in the pipeline. But as Prior was still refusing to end the legal immunities of trade unions, a priority reform for her, it became clear that he was a cabinet minister who would have to be reshuffled to some other job as soon as practicable.

Prior's lame-duck status was none too subtly announced to the world by a process that could well have been called 'death by a thousand leaks'. It was a form of slow torture applied to several other ministers over the next few years, but the Secretary of State for Employment was the prototype victim. What happened was that a trickle and then a steady flow of press stories started to appear, reporting in various formats that Prior was not up to the job, losing the confidence of the Prime Minister, failing to reform the unions and likely to be banished to Northern Ireland. There was an element of tit for tat in this war of attrition, since Prior himself was a fountain of indiscretion when it came to letting journalists know about his misgivings over the government's economic strategy.

However, he was not the only such fountain. Others spouted higher and more artistically. One of the most voluble wets, Norman St John-Stevas, was sacked from the cabinet in January 1981 for being leaker-in-chief, although the charge was later somewhat unconvincingly withdrawn by the Prime Minister.

The Downing Street official often blamed for black propaganda activities against ministers was her new Press Secretary, Bernard Ingham. He was far too professional a civil servant to do any negative briefing without higher authority. Most of the leaking was done by other hands and voices with access to Margaret Thatcher's frequent fulminations against her colleagues.

The firing of Norman St John-Stevas, like the eighteenth-century execution of Admiral Byng, was widely seen as a move by the Prime Minister '*pour encourager les autres*'.[13] Soon after it, Jim Prior had a meeting with her that he regarded as his effort to get back into a reasonable working relationship with his boss. He decided to tackle the problem of leaks and counter-leaks.

'I know you think I leak things to the press, and yes, I sometimes do, deliberately at times and by mistake on others', he began. 'But, of course, so do you.'

'Oh no, Jim, I never leak', she replied.

'Well, if you tell me that I must accept it, but in that case your officials and press people certainly leak for you.'

'Oh, that is quite wrong: they never know anything, so how could they leak?'[14]

The straight-faced effrontery of this answer amazed Prior. He eventually came round to the view that the Prime Minister was in denial, because she simply never thought that any disclosure by herself could be a leak. 'If she said it,' he concluded, 'how could there be any question of a leak?'[15] This view might explain her handling of the Westland crisis and other unsavoury leak episodes at later stages of her time at No. 10.

With leaks, as with so many manoeuvres of power, the cards were always stacked in favour of the Prime Minister. She ran rings around Jim Prior, calling his bluff when he rumbled about resigning over economic policy, and when he made initial noises about refusing to serve as Secretary of State for Northern Ireland. She sent Whitelaw to rebuke him for disloyalty and for 'holding a pistol to the PM's head'.[16] This caused Prior to back down and left him looking foolish.

In general, Jim Prior was always more of a bluffer than a plotter. He saw life differently from Margaret Thatcher. He thought her leadership had created 'the most divided Conservative cabinet ever'.[17] But, apart from doing a great deal of private grumbling, he kept his head down in his department and did not foment these divisions, except when she attacked him for being too soft or too wet with the unions. For her part, she saw him as a lightweight figure. This was unfair in most people's eyes, but not in hers. She liked to remind her inner circle that he had only received nineteen votes in the 1975 Tory leadership election. She never believed he had the fire-power to cause the slightest threat to her position. So in slow time she undermined him, marginalised him and moved him to a peripheral role in the cabinet. His last attempt to cause serious trouble was over the 1981 Budget.

THE COURAGE OF THE 1981 BUDGET

The 1981 Budget was a major turning point in the reputation of the government and of Margaret Thatcher. It did not look that way at the time, for it received one of the worst receptions of any Budget in modern times. Yet, seen with the wisdom of hindsight, this was the political event that confirmed beyond doubt that 'The lady's not for turning' on economic strategy. It crushed the wets in the cabinet, and marked the end of Britain's long and dismal record of economic decline since the early 1960s. Also it demonstrated that the Prime Minister and her Chancellor of the Exchequer deserved recognition for political courage. For it was a time when they stood alone against the prevailing opinion of the pundits, the political elite and the general populace, but they were proved right.

Just before the Christmas parliamentary recess in December 1980, Ian Gow organised a small private dinner in the House of Commons for the Prime Minister to get to know more of her new MPs. One of them asked her about the atmosphere at cabinet meetings. 'Well, really it's very lonely', she replied. 'It's really Geoffrey and me against the rest of them.'[18]

This feeling of isolation grew worse. In the same pre-Christmas period she asked Brian Griffiths,* Professor of Banking at City University, to come to see her. He was one of her academic 'voices' on economic policy, but was unprepared for the depths of her worries. 'Twice she came close to tears', he recalled. 'She felt that Geoffrey was getting it wrong, always trying to find a middle way under the influence of Treasury Keynesians like Sir Douglas Watt. She was in a despondent mood.'[19]

Loss of confidence in her Chancellor was increased by the gloomy news he kept reporting to her at their weekly bilaterals. In the early weeks of the New Year it emerged that all the national economic indicators were far worse than

---

* Brian Griffiths (1941–), Professor of Banking and International Finance, City University, 1977; Head of Prime Minister's Policy Unit, 1985–1990; created Lord Griffiths of Fforest-fach, 1991.

anyone had expected. The main problem was public borrowing. The high costs of subsidising the nationalised industries and of rising unemployment benefit meant that the Public Sector Borrowing Requirement (PSBR) was forecast to reach £11.5 billion. By March this forecast had increased to £14.5 billion. Margaret Thatcher had frequently proclaimed the need to cut the PSBR, but now it was soaring out of control. Would she grasp the nettle of bringing it down by higher taxation?

A new recruit to her team of advisers in January 1981 was a little-known economist, Professor Alan Walters. On his first morning at No. 10 he was given a clear signal by the Prime Minister that she thought her Chancellor's backbone needed stiffening. 'What should she do about Geoffrey?' Walters recorded in his diary. 'Who could she promote. No one. Said come and see me whenever you like.'[20]

Professor Walters' proximity to the seat of power initially troubled the Chancellor, or at least his wife. 'Elspeth clearly peeved at me being in No. 10',[21] he wrote, after a tense encounter with Lady Howe. He was an unsettling Cassandra, making good use of his access to argue that to restore prudence to the national finances, a PSBR of £10 billion was imperative, which he thought required new taxes of £4 billion. When he pressed for this at a meeting between the Chancellor and the Prime Minister on 13 February, Margaret Thatcher reacted angrily, exclaiming that she had not been elected to put up taxes. 'Nor had I',[22] responded Sir Geoffrey Howe, but he went on in his dogged way to agree with Walters and to outline the options for raising the necessary extra taxation.

Gradually, the Prime Minister came round to the Howe–Walters view. On this occasion the Professor and the Chancellor were singing from the same hymn sheet. Another key voice was that of John Hoskyns, the head of the Prime Minister's Policy Unit, who favoured a draconian Budget. So did the inner Treasury team of officials. But none of these advisers were elected politicians. As Margaret Thatcher tartly told Hoskyns at one point in the heated discussions: 'It's all very well for you. You don't have to stand up and sell this in the House.'[23]

Her caution was understandable. The strategy she was about to endorse was likely to be rejected by the majority of her cabinet and by most Members of Parliament. It flew in the face of Keynesian economics and the received wisdom of pundits and commentators. Their prevailing view was that at a time of rising unemployment and deepening recession it would be politically impossible to apply the thumbscrews of higher taxation and deflation to an already depressed economy.

Margaret Thatcher saw the risks. But she continued to be swayed by Alan Walters, who convinced her that to get the economy moving out of recession the highest priority was lower interest rates, which would be impossible without lower borrowing, which could only be achieved by higher taxation. In the end this argument, backed to the hilt by Hoskyns, Howe and the Treasury, won her support. 'Its consequences for my administration were unpredictable', she recalled. 'Yet I knew in my heart of hearts that there was only one right decision, and that it now had to be made.'[24]

Once the strategy was agreed, Geoffrey Howe implemented it with skill and courage. Instead of raising the standard rate of income tax, as the Prime Minister had accepted might be necessary, he decided to freeze all personal allowances and tax thresholds. She described this as 'an extraordinarily bold move when inflation remained at 13 per cent'.[25] Other painful measure included double-indexing the tax rates on alcohol, tobacco, cars and vehicle excise duties. Extra taxes on banks and North Sea oil companies completed a tough package, which reduced the PSBR forecast by £4 billion from £14.5 billion (6 per cent of GDP) to £10.5 billion (4.5 per cent of GDP). As a plan it was admirable for its prudence, but no one knew how it would be received politically. Shortly before the 1981 Budget was unveiled to the world, the Prime Minister confided to Alan Walters: 'You know, Alan, they may get rid of me for this.' But, she added, it would be a worthwhile cause. 'At least I shall have gone knowing I did the right thing.'[26]

The first test of whether these apocalyptic misgivings might prove justified came on the morning of the Budget, when its details were revealed to the full cabinet. It is one of the traditions of British politics that the First and Second Lords of the Treasury (the Prime Minister and the Chancellor) keep their ministerial colleagues completely in the dark about the Budget until some three hours before it is presented to the House of Commons and the world. This secrecy is said to be essential to prevent profiteering by speculators. In 1981, secrecy was imperative to avoid a rebellion by cabinet ministers.

The chief potential rebel, although he turned out to be ineffective in this role, was Jim Prior. As a courtesy to his position, Geoffrey Howe decided to brief him on the eve of Budget day. The Secretary of State for Employment was appalled. 'I told him [Howe] that I thought it was awful and absolutely misjudged', recalled Prior. 'It was far too restrictive, the PSBR was being cut by far too much, and it would add to unemployment. I couldn't say anything bad enough about it.'[27]

The following morning, Prior shared his negative views with two other leading wets in the Cabinet – Ian Gilmour and Peter Walker. They talked about resigning over the Budget, but it was just talk. This was the nearest they came to a rebellion. At the cabinet meeting Prior was 'interestingly incoherent', according to Howe.[28] But as the three musketeers neither fired a shot nor produced a strategic alternative, their revolt fizzled out with barely a whimper. Led by the loyal Whitelaw, all other Ministers closed ranks behind the Chancellor and the Prime Minister. Gilmour and Prior said afterwards that they regretted not having handed in their resignations, but these were afterthoughts. At the time it was game, set and match to the Budget makers, although Alan Walters presciently noted in his diary that evening: 'All hell breaks loose. The Wets are up in arms. We'll have a hot summer.'[29]

The views of the commenting classes on the Budget were indeed hot and hostile. Geoffrey Howe was given a rough ride by Tory back-benchers at the meeting of the Finance Committee immediately after his speech. One of them, Peter Tapsell, demanded his resignation, calling the Budget 'economically illiterate'.[30]

The press, from the *Financial Times* to the *Sun*, were almost as negative. The unkindest cut of all came in a letter to *The Times,* signed by no less than 364 economists. They forecast that the government's policies would 'deepen the depression, erode the industrial base of our economy and threaten its social and political stability'.[31]

Margaret Thatcher took not the slightest notice of these prophets of doom. She slammed the 364 economists:

Their confidence in the accuracy of their own predictions leaves me breathless. But having myself been brought up over the shop, I sometimes wonder whether they back their forecasts with their money. For I can't help noticing that those who have to do just that – the investing institutions which have to show performance from their judgement – are giving us a very different message.[32]

It was a dubious argument to contrast academic economists with professional investors, but the Prime Minister, buoyed up by a rise in the stock market, and scornful toward her academic attackers, was in a mood for taking no prisoners. Mocking her critics, she trumpeted her convictions as if she was Joan of Arc issuing a call to the faithful: 'I do not greatly care what people say about me . . . This is the road I am resolved to follow. This is the path I must go. I ask all who have the spirit – the bold, the steadfast, and the young in heart – to stand and join with me as we go forward.'[33]

This speech to the Conservative Central Council in Bournemouth three weeks after the Budget made a great impact. John Hoskyns, who sat up with her, helping her write it long into the early hours of the Saturday morning when she delivered it, believed that she was turning the Budget into a statement of her personal will power. 'She was getting across the message that she was far tougher and stronger than anyone had thought.'[34]

This power of her personality changed the game. The wets were routed. The stock market was rallying. The opposition was in disarray after the formation of a new Social Democratic Party (SDP) discordantly headed by four ex-Labour cabinet ministers; Roy Jenkins, David Owen, Shirley Williams and Bill Rodgers. The only political leader who seemed to be certain where the country should be going was Margaret Thatcher. But as events were to show, she was still a vulnerable Prime Minister.

THE VULNERABLE PRIME MINISTER

Although Margaret Thatcher's ringing enthusiasm for the 1981 Budget strategy produced some good results, such as growing City confidence, better press coverage and some early signs of increasing industrial output, negative forces were at work too. The government had to cave in to a potential miners' strike over pit closures* because coal stocks were so low. Industrial action by the Civil Servants Union was ended only by an expensive pay settlement. Unemployment continued to rise towards three million.

The most troublesome problem was an outbreak of rioting, first in Brixton, South London, then in Moss Side, Manchester, and most seriously of all in

---

* See Chapter 26, 'Unions and miners'.

Toxteth, Liverpool. The opposition and the government's internal critics within the Conservative Party seized on the argument that the Thatcher–Howe economic policy was causing these social disturbances. The Prime Minister was having none of it. She identified with the victims. 'Oh, those poor shopkeepers!' was her immediate reaction on seeing the television coverage of the looting in Toxteth.[35]

She regarded the unrest as a police matter, and was adamant in asserting that the paramount imperatives were to stop the violence, uphold the law and punish the lawbreakers. This was right, but initially she seemed unable to express any concern for the need to look more deeply into the background to the disturbances. She delivered a disastrous party political broadcast on 8 July, in which she came across as nervous, insensitive and irrelevant. As The Times said in its leader on 10 July, 'Not for the first time she was unable to strike the right note when a broad sense of understanding was required'.[36]

Michael Heseltine, hastily appointed Minister for Merseyside, wanted to reduce unemployment in the riot-torn areas with a wide-scale policy of industrial interventionism. The Prime Minister gave him a chilly reception, privately telling Alan Walters that Heseltine was 'a very vain man – sees Toxteth as a basis for projecting himself'.[37] At a meeting of the 'E' Committee on 15 July, Jim Prior made an impassioned plea for an extra £1 billion of public expenditure to fight unemployment.

In the middle of these tensions, the full cabinet met on 23 July to discuss the outlook for the autumn spending round. The battle lines were drawn in advance. Spending ministers had submitted bids for extra expenditure of over £6.5 billion. The Treasury put in a paper demanding further extra cuts of £5 billion in 1982–1983, over and above the already reduced totals published in a white paper at the time of the Budget. Against the background of the riots and the unemployment figures it looked as though the meeting was going to be the political equivalent of the shoot-out at the OK Corral. Margaret Thatcher knew how high the stakes were. Just before she went down from her flat to chair the cabinet, she told Denis that she would not remain as Prime Minister unless her colleagues saw the strategy through.[38]

Her fears of an explosive meeting were justified. After Geoffrey Howe had summarised his proposal for a programme of £5 billion of further cuts, Michael Heseltine, the Environment Secretary, led the charge against the Chancellor.

Speaking after a night of fresh rioting in Toxteth, Heseltine said that Howe's proposals would cause despair in the inner cities and bring electoral disaster for the government. He advocated a pay freeze. This would have been an astonishing U-turn. Nevertheless this heresy, striking at the root of everything that Margaret Thatcher stood for, was also supported by Peter Walker and Lord Soames. Worse was to come from the Lord Chancellor, Lord Hailsham, who spoke in doom-laden language about how in the 1930s unemployment had given birth to Herbert Hoover's Great Depression in the United States and Hitler's Nazi Party in Germany. Without making the same comparison, Jim Prior, Francis Pym and Ian Gilmour were almost as pessimistic about the government's strategy.

With the temperature rising, Margaret Thatcher became 'extremely angry', particularly as some of her most trusted allies defected to the wets. She was astonished when John Biffen switched sides for the first time, saying that public spending should be allowed to rise. An even worse betrayal in her eyes came from John Nott, who launched a withering attack on the Treasury's figures. 'All at once,' Margaret Thatcher recalled, 'the whole strategy was at issue. It was as if tempers suddenly broke.'[39]

These bitter divisions brought the government to the brink of a disastrous split. Feuds with the wets had been a festering sore for over two years, but suddenly they were winning by a clear and outspoken majority. Willie Whitelaw did his best to paper over the cracks with a loyal summing up. Yet even he, after rejecting the pay freeze, gave a warning against breaking the tolerance of society.[40]

Margaret Thatcher had to face the reality that only she and three of her twenty-three cabinet ministers, Geoffrey Howe, Keith Joseph and Leon Brittan, the new Chief Secretary to the Treasury, fully supported her economic strategy. She closed the cabinet on a subdued note, instructing the Chancellor to produce a new paper setting out both sides of the argument. She made a fervent plea for secrecy, particularly about a pay freeze being discussed. She retired from the fray as a wounded Prime Minister. Her wounds hurt. The late summer of 1981 was the lowest point of her time in 10 Downing Street, apart from the dark days when she was ousted from power some nine years later.

Throughout August she had forebodings of a serious threat to her position, discussing it melodramatically with trusted members of her inner circle. 'The men in grey suits have been to see me', she told Tim Bell, describing how a deputation of party elders led by Lord Thorneycroft had come to give her a warning that support for her policies was collapsing. 'They want me out.'[41]

In similar vein, she gave a gloomy vision of her future employment prospects to her Economic Affairs Private Secretary, Michael Scholar: 'I can always get a job', she told him. 'I can always scrub floors. And I will if they kick me out.'[42]

This wild talk worried her staff. Her closest personal aide, Caroline Stephens, asked Ronnie Millar to come in and talk about the Prime Minister's 'physical and mental exhaustion, harsh public image and alienation from her friends'.[43] Millar was usually a soothing presence. But he evidently felt so upset about his heroine's prospects that he co-authored with John Hoskyns and David Wolfson a blistering private submission to her, entitled 'Your Political Survival'. This passed into folklore as 'The blockbuster memorandum'.[44] It had a profound effect on Margaret Thatcher.

BLOCKBUSTERED INTO RESHUFFLING THE CABINET

The blockbuster memorandum offended Margaret Thatcher. This was understandable, since it was probably the most brutal internal communication ever sent to any Prime Minister from members of the No. 10 Downing Street staff. Yet, although many of its words were personally offensive, their message was politically effective. It made disagreeable reading, but it resulted in Margaret Thatcher taking decisive steps to achieve the objective of its title, 'Your Political Survival'.

The headlines on the various sections of the memo must have come as a shock to her. They included these statements:

'You lack management competence'
'Your own leadership style is wrong'
'The result is an unhappy ship'
'You have an absolute duty to change the way you operate.'

The specifics were worse than the rebukes. In the paragraph about leadership style, the authors pulled no punches:

You break every rule of good man-management. You bully your weaker colleagues. You criticise colleagues in front of each other and in front of their officials. They can't answer back without appearing disrespectful, in front of others, to a woman and to a Prime Minister. You abuse that situation.[45]

The blockbuster was right on these counts, but Margaret Thatcher did not immediately see it that way. 'I got your letter. No one has ever written a letter like that to a Prime Minister before', she hissed to Hoskyns in a moment of fury, believing him to be its principal author. In fact, it had been a genuine collaborative effort by the 'Westwell Three', as Margaret Thatcher crossly called the signatories. Her label derived from David Wolfson's country house in Westwell, Oxfordshire, where the triumvirate had composed their memorandum.

Their message was most effective in its political recommendations. While praising her for launching 'a near-revolution in the private sector', it warned that an internal revolt 'threatens your own position'. It also urged her to make a radical reconstruction of her cabinet, and to sack Peter Thorneycroft as Party Chairman. 'You need a new Chairman, a younger man who is totally loyal to you, and you need him fast.' The most devastating part of the blockbuster was its conclusion, which baldly stated that unless she accepted the authors' advice she would soon be ousted, going into the history books only with the prize for being the 'Best Loser'.[46]

Once her temper had cooled, Margaret Thatcher saw John Hoskyns and David Wolfson to discuss their criticisms of her. Although not himself present at this meeting, Alan Walters' diary entry for Wednesday 26 August reported the essential outcome of it: 'JH & DW saw PM until 11.30. She was very shaken – realises she has to change – V. tired and needed holiday. MUST (2) [make] bold and decisive move to fire Thorneycroft . . . Reshuffle being discussed.'[47]

Although she resented being hauled over the coals so brutally by insiders she considered as loyalists, Margaret Thatcher took their political advice seriously, for she followed their main recommendations on reshuffling the cabinet and changing the party chairmanship. As for their more personal suggestions, she was too angered by them to change her style of man-management. It remained her long-term Achilles heel. But in the short term, the men she needed to manage most carefully were away for the next few weeks. Their absences from the policy-making battlefield demonstrated the truth of an old parliamentary saying, 'Nothing succeeds like recess'.

The summer recess of 1981 was a hot and happy one. The nation was entranced by the wedding of the Prince of Wales and Lady Diana Spencer at St Paul's Cathedral on 29 July. The inner-city riots evaporated as mysteriously as they had started. The grandest and most troublesome Tory ministers dispersed to their country houses, grouse moors or villas in Tuscany. Politics and economics seemed to fall off the agenda. Even the holiday-averse Prime Minister eventually shut up shop to spend a few days in the cool of the Swiss Alps. She was biding her time and planning her revenge against her foes.

The cabinet that had so bad-temperedly split over public spending in July never met again with the same membership. The blockbuster memorandum persuaded Margaret Thatcher that she must reassert her authority by wielding her axe. So, on 14 September 1981, while Parliament was still in recess, she sacked three prominent figures from the cabinet, moved seven others and changed the party chairmanship. The net effect was to shift the balance of power in the government towards a more loyal group of ministers who supported her policies and philosophy.

The three dismissals – Mark Carlisle, Ian Gilmour and Lord Soames – she regarded as wets. Two of them did not go quietly. Immediately after his sacking, Gilmour strode out of No. 10 to tell the awaiting journalists that 'It does no harm to throw the occasional man overboard, but it does not do much good if you are steering full speed ahead for the rocks.'[48]

Lord Soames, the hero of the Rhodesia crisis, Winston Churchill's son-in-law, and a Tory grandee to the triggers of his Purdeys, let the Prime Minister have it with both barrels. In what must have been one of the angriest cabinet dismissal interviews of all time, Soames sent her private secretary out of the room and then opened fire. For twenty minutes he gave her a hard pounding for her mishandling of the civil-service strike and her rudeness to colleagues. Both charges were true. But she was impervious because she had come to dislike Soames with a personalised intensity. She retaliated in her memoirs by writing: 'I got the distinct impression that he felt the natural order of things were being violated and that he was, in effect, being dismissed by his housemaid.'[49]

Another cabinet heavyweight was almost as upset as Soames – but for being moved to a less influential post. This was Jim Prior, the Employment Secretary. He wanted to stay at the centre of economic decision-making. She wanted to shift the arch wet away from it. So she offered Prior the job of Secretary of State for Northern Ireland. As he had been leaking to the press for weeks that he would never accept such a move, this folly caused him no little difficulty. After a couple of hours of hesitation, he realised that his bluff had been called. He knew he would look cowardly if he refused the place of honour and danger. But he did negotiate the retention of his seat on the 'E' committee – where he was to be consistently outmanoeuvred and outvoted. From that time on, Prior's influence as a leading wet went into continuous decline.

The new arrivals in the cabinet were kindred political spirits who shared the Prime Minister's convictions. Nigel Lawson, who had been hugely influential in the junior post of Financial Secretary to the Treasury, was given his own portfolio as Secretary of State for Energy. Norman Tebbit, razor sharp in tongue and mind, replaced Prior. The most surprising promotion was that of Cecil Parkinson. Although almost invisible to the watchers of political form because he travelled so much as a junior trade minister, he had caught Margaret Thatcher's eye by his charm, competence and good looks. He replaced Peter Thorneycroft as Chairman of the Party and was given the right to attend the cabinet as Paymaster General.

Other ministers who were moved included Patrick Jenkin to Industry, Norman Fowler to the Department of Health and Social Security, and David Howell – a demotion – to Transport. Baroness Young replaced Soames as Leader of the House of Lords. She was the only woman ever appointed to the cabinet by Margaret Thatcher, but she lasted a mere twenty months. Promoting women ministers never came high on the Prime Minister's agenda.

This reshuffle reduced Margaret Thatcher's vulnerability to rebellion from her own senior colleagues. She still did not have a majority of 'true believers' in her own cabinet. But she had said in the past, 'Give me six strong men and true, and I will get through'.[50] Now at last she had them.

Even though she had buttressed her position against internal revolts like the one that temporarily destabilised her grip on 23 July, external pressures were continuing to take their toll. By the turn of the year, interest rates surged back to 16 per cent and unemployment climbed above three million. On 26 January 1982, the day when this symbolically dreadful figure was announced, Margaret Thatcher had to face Prime Minister's Questions in a House of Commons she knew would erupt with hostility towards her.

She made her final preparations for the ordeal with her Economic Affairs Private Secretary, Michael Scholar. He was no Thatcherite politically, but on this occasion his civil servant's neutrality soared to the highest realms of admiration. He recalled:

> As we sat there in her room at the House with the clock ticking towards 3.15, I could feel the heat coming from her body. I saw that she was perspiring. And I thought: 'By God, this woman is brave. How I admire her courage to go out and face what will be a howling mob.' I knew the worry she felt about the continuous rise, rise, rise in the unemployment figures. But she held her nerve.[51]

Strong nerves were required in the country as well as in the Commons when the opinion polls declared Margaret Thatcher to be the most unpopular Prime Minister in living memory, with a rating of 25 per cent. Appalling by-election results were also deepening the Tory gloom. The Liberals won North West Croydon with a swing of 24 per cent. Shirley Williams overturned a Conservative majority of 18,000 to capture the blue-chip seat of Crosby in Lancashire for the SDP. The sudden emergence of third-party politics was complicating the mid-term picture. The prospects of the government holding on to power at the next election with an overall majority looked bleak. The received wisdom in Westminster, Whitehall and Fleet Street was that Margaret Thatcher would be a one-term prime minister.

REFLECTION

The year of 1981 was Margaret Thatcher's darkest hour. Her economic strategy appeared to be failing. Her authority over her cabinet was crumbling. Her man-management of her colleagues was as dreadful as the blockbuster memorandum had portrayed it. The words 'An unhappy ship' were inadequate to describe the plummeting morale within the government.

Although she was shaken by the storm clouds that surrounded her, the Prime Minister did not lose her self-belief or her capacity for decisive action. The cabinet reshuffle of September 1981 was a major turning point in her leadership. It had two dimensions: sending out signals that she was sticking to a revolution in economics and starting a revolution of political attitudes.

The economic revolution was already starting to work by the spring of 1982, as the fruits of the 1981 Budget began to appear. The figures for GDP growth, productivity and lower inflation began to move in the right direction. Although unemployment remained stubbornly high, it was in fact peaking. Moreover, the country seemed more resilient than the cabinet in its attitudes towards the deep-seated problems that Margaret Thatcher was determined to solve.

These changing attitudes were reflected in the September 1981 reshuffle. Grandees, wets, and the 'softly, softly' approach to the unions were purged. Self-made men, hard-liners and tougher approaches were in the ascendant. It became clear that the Prime Minister had gained control of her cabinet. By her own certainty and by the lack of a coherent plan B, she managed to win a grudging national acceptance that there really was no alternative. TINA was alive and flourishing, even if far from secure in electoral expectations. That security was to come via the totally unexpected route of the South Atlantic.

19

The Falklands War I
The prelude

SABOTAGING THE LEASEBACK OPTION

Three weeks after becoming Prime Minister, Margaret Thatcher invited her two most senior cabinet colleagues and their wives to Sunday lunch at Chequers. This was intended to be a celebratory occasion in the afterglow of election victory. It began in that spirit, for it would be difficult not to enjoy the company of four such agreeable guests as Willie and Celia Whitelaw, and Peter and Iona Carrington, with Denis mixing the pre-lunch gin and tonics.

Despite the good intentions of those present, the occasion passed into legend as the 'thermonuclear lunch'.[1] The trigger for the explosion was the subject of the Falkland Islands as raised by the Foreign Secretary.

While eating the first course, Lord Carrington, in his languid style of conversation, observed that one of the problems sitting on his desk was what to do about the Falklands. 'I think we will soon be in trouble if we go on having meetings about them with the Argentines without saying anything at all', he said. 'One of the options which seems to me worth exploring is a leaseback arrangement similar to what we have in Hong Kong.'[2]

The Prime Minister was not merely opposed to such a suggestion. She was appalled by it. She erupted in anger, and spent the next ten minutes denouncing the very idea of exploring a Hong Kong solution for the Falklands. 'I remember her shouting, "That's the trouble with your Foreign Office. Everyone in it is so bloody wet!"' Carrington recalled. 'And it got worse. She banged on the table, and went on and on and how typical it was of me and the F.O. "to want to give away Britain's possessions".'

With the eyes of Lady Carrington and Mrs Whitelaw rolling in astonishment at this performance, it was Denis who cooled the temperature by saying to his wife: 'I think you're being a little extravagant, my dear.'[3]

Despite this 'thermonuclear' attack at Chequers, Carrington persisted in his efforts to find a way round the Prime Minister's objections. He wrote to her formally on 20 September 1979 saying that a form of leaseback was the best solution to the Falklands. She scribbled on the top of his letter, 'I cannot possibly agree to the line the Foreign Secretary is proposing'.[4]

Undeflected by this further rebuff, Carrington returned to the leaseback option at two later meetings of the Overseas and Defence committee of the cabinet in October 1979 and March 1980. Margaret Thatcher eventually gave some ground to the extent of allowing the Foreign Office to begin exploratory discussions with Argentina. Carrington allocated responsibility for this initiative to his Minister of State, Nicholas Ridley, who was believed to be a kindred spirit of the Prime Minister's. She had spoken of him as 'one of us' in her opposition days after finding herself in agreement with the free-market views he expressed at meetings of the Economic Dining Club.

Having established this good rapport with his leader, Nicholas Ridley was disappointed not to have been made a Treasury minister. But Margaret Thatcher sugared the pill by telling him that she needed 'one sound man' in a department she regarded as notoriously weak.[5] She also told him that she mistrusted Carrington's economic views and needed an ally 'to keep him on the straight and narrow'. This amused the Foreign Secretary:

> She had no idea what my views were on economics. They were practically non-existent! Also, she didn't realise that in those days the F.O. hardly ever discussed economics. So, poor old Nick had nothing much to do until I asked him to take charge of the Falklands.[6]

For Ridley, this was a poisoned chalice. Notoriously tactless in domestic politics, he showed similar lack of finesse on his first foray into international diplomacy. He was too blunt with the Falkland Islanders telling them with a hint of menace that they must 'take the consequences' of being unwilling to make a deal on sovereignty.[7] He was prematurely accommodating to the Argentines, provisionally agreeing a ninety-nine-year leaseback agreement with their Deputy Foreign Minister, Commodore Carlos Cavandoli, at secret talks with him in New York and Geneva.

When he reported this deal back to the OD committee, the Prime Minister was suspicious and nervous. She was recorded by the Cabinet Secretary as saying, 'My fear is an awful row from our backbenches'.[8] Regrettably she helped to turn her fear into a reality. For when Nicholas Ridley declared his negotiating hand in a statement to the House of Commons on 2 December 1980, he could never have guessed that the fierce opposition to his proposals had been orchestrated not only by the Falkland Islanders but also by the Prime Minister's Parliamentary Private Secretary.

Ian Gow mounted a discreet operation. 'Are you sound on the Falklands, Jonathan?' he asked me the day before Ridley's statement. Like most back-benchers, I did not realise there was an issue on this obscure colony to be sound or unsound about. 'Then I suggest you have a word with Amery', said Ian with a knowing twinkle. 'He knows the score.'[9]

Julian Amery, a former Foreign Office minister and son of Winston Churchill's Colonial Secretary, Leo Amery, was one of the last bastions of the imperial mindset surviving in the House of Commons of the 1980s. His inside information about the Falklands was interesting, as he was well briefed on the recent deliberations of the OD Committee of the cabinet. According to Amery's account, Nicholas Ridley had presented his Falklands leaseback proposal to OD and had narrowly got it through, thanks to support from Lord Carrington and the Defence Secretary, Francis Pym. However, the Prime Minister had strong reservations. Although expressing them forcefully, she had only managed to insist that any final decision must be subject to the consent of the Islanders, whose wishes must be 'paramount'.[10] This was a blocking card equivalent to the ace of trumps. Even so, she remained anxious. So she asked her Parliamentary Private Secretary to approach Julian Amery and other like-minded colleagues to make sure that the Islanders' views were well represented when Nicholas Ridley made his statement to the House.

Ian Gow did his job well. Fortified by this nudging from No. 10, Julian Amery organised one faction of the parliamentary revolt against Ridley's plan. Other factions were put on full alert by the Falkland Islands' lobbying office in London, which had supporters in all parties at Westminster. The result was that when Nicholas Ridley made his statement he was savaged by an ambush led by angry Tories such as Julian Amery, Sir Bernard Braine, Peter Tapsell and Viscount Cranborne. They were backed by senior opposition Privy Councillors Douglas Jay and Peter Shore (Labour), Russell Johnston (Liberal) and Donald

Stewart, the leader of the Scottish Nationalist Party. All of them vigorously opposed the government's policy.

Sitting in the House that afternoon, I had never before seen such a mauling of a minister. The noise levels of hostile barracking were at full volume. Nicholas Ridley did not help his case by using a sarcastic tone when soft answers might have turned away wrath. But his pitch had been queered. Not a single government back-bencher had been encouraged by the whips to support him, and several had been briefed to attack him. At the end of thirty minutes worth of virulent questioning of his statement amidst repeated appeals for 'Order!' from the Speaker, leaseback was well and truly sunk.

'I think the PM will be well pleased',[11] boomed a cheerful Julian Amery, as we walked out of the chamber together. She probably was. Amery talked openly about the guidance he had been given by Ian Gow. It was not the first or the last example of how Margaret Thatcher sometimes undermined her ministers by surreptitiously getting her aides to brief against them.

The collapse of the leaseback deal sent its own message to the military junta in Buenos Aires. In an erratic way they were already flexing their muscles over *Las Malvinas*, as they called the Falklands. Now they deduced that Britain lacked the will and the means to defend the Islands by military force. Failure to disabuse the Argentines of this impression was a mistake for which Margaret Thatcher was partly responsible. She had insisted on substantial defence cuts in 1981, appointing a new Defence Secretary, John Nott, to implement the reductions in the defence budget that his predecessor Francis Pym had avoided by threatening resignation.

She did not take enough interest in the strategic implications of Nott's cost-cutting plans. He decided that his axe would fall on the surface fleet. The expensive aircraft carriers *Hermes* and *Invincible* were to go. A more political decision was the scrapping of the Royal Navy's ice patrol ship in the South Atlantic, HMS *Endurance*. Its decommissioning saved only £3 million but the symbolism of this cut was diplomatically disastrous. As Carrington warned in three separate minutes to Nott, the withdrawal of *Endurance*'s minor military capabilities (two helicopters, twenty Royal Marines and four Ack-Ack guns) might be interpreted as a strategic weakening of Britain's commitment to the Islanders.[12]

Margaret Thatcher did not intervene in these Ministry of Defence versus Foreign Office exchanges about HMS *Endurance*. She was dismissive of the ship's military capabilities, saying that it could only go 'pop, pop, pop'[13] to Ridley's successor, Richard Luce. On 9 February 1982 she endorsed the withdrawal of *Endurance* when answering a Parliamentary Question from her predecessor, Jim Callaghan. He had handled a previous episode of sabre-rattling by the Argentines in 1977 by sending a submarine to the Falklands. Eventually, Margaret Thatcher followed his example on 28 March 1982, with a similar order to the Navy, but by then it was a case of too little, too late.

Earlier in the year a confusing series of events had been unfolding in the South Atlantic. They included more threatening noises from the junta; an unauthorised landing by Argentine scrap-metal dealers on the island of South Georgia on 20 December 1981; a suspiciously anodyne session of Anglo-Argentine talks at the UN in January 1982; and some aggressive editorials in the Buenos Aires newspapers demanding the return of *Las Malvinas*.

These signs of trouble were complacently misinterpreted by the Foreign Office. The Prime Minister did not have her eye on the ball either. But on 3 March she did annotate one telegram from the British Embassy in Buenos Aires, reporting on Argentine press speculation with the words, 'We must make contingency plans'.[14] Yet neither she nor anyone else in her government did anything to follow this up for the next three weeks. This was an omission which seemed of low significance in Whitehall but it had high consequences in Argentina. For the month of March was the last window of opportunity in which any moves or messages of deterrence could have been sent to the military junta. Alas nothing was done.

PARLIAMENT'S WAR

Margaret Thatcher was caught off guard by the junta's preparations to invade the Islands. In the last days of March she began to focus on the signs of impending hostilities. On Sunday 29 March, she sent two nuclear-powered submarines and two frigates to reinforce HMS *Endurance*, which was on one of her last patrols before decommissioning. But the submarines would take two weeks to reach the South Atlantic. The Prime Minister was worried, but she still did not believe an invasion was imminent.

Her false optimism was shattered when, on the evening of Wednesday 31 March, she received a call in her office at the House of Commons saying that the Defence Secretary wanted an immediate meeting to discuss the Falklands. The news brought by John Nott was shattering. He reported that the Argentine Fleet had put to sea and was likely to invade the Islands by Friday 2 April. 'If they are invaded, we have got to get them back', declared the Prime Minister, only to be told that in the view of the Ministry of Defence the Falklands could not be retaken once they had been seized. For her, this was a shameful prospect.[15]

The gloom of the meeting deepened, partly because most of those attending it were indecisive junior ministers. Lord Carrington was away in Israel so the Foreign Office was represented by Humphrey Atkins and Richard Luce, both briefed to propose well-meaning but ineffective diplomatic moves. The Chief of Defence Staff, Admiral of the Fleet Sir Terence Lewin, was visiting New Zealand so military advice was transmitted through two pessimistic civilians – John Nott and the MoD's Permanent Under-Secretary, Sir Frank Cooper. They advised that the Islands, once seized by the Argentines, could not be recaptured. Margaret Thatcher expressed her feelings of outrage, but they were feelings made more painful by her growing realisation of impotence.

Then, like a dramatic moment in a play, a surprise intruder took centre stage and changed the plot. He was Admiral Sir Henry Leach, the First Sea Lord and Chief of the Naval Staff. For reasons of MoD protocol, he had not been asked to attend the meeting. But once he heard it was taking place he decided he was coming anyway, so he turned up at the House of Commons, arrayed in the splendour of the First Sea Lord's full dress uniform,* which he was wearing for a ceremonial dinner later that evening.

A hiatus occurred at the St Stephens entrance to the House of Commons when the Admiral's medals, out of sight beneath his overcoat, set off the metal detector alarms. An inflexible police constable insisted on detaining the First Sea Lord for twenty minutes in a side room. Rescued by Ian Gow, he eventually reached the Prime Minister's office in a foul temper. 'He erupted into the room', was how Sir Antony Acland, Deputy Under-Secretary of State at the Foreign and Commonwealth Office, described the Admiral's entry.[16]

---

* There is a conflict of evidence on the attire worn by Sir Henry Leach. Most accounts, including the one given to me by Ian Gow, say he was in full dress uniform. Margaret Thatcher describes him in her memoirs as wearing 'civilian dress'. Her official biographer, Charles Moore, says he was in 'his admiral's day uniform'.

After the Prime Minister had summarised the discussion so far she asked Sir Henry Leach what the Royal Navy could do. 'I can put together a Task Force of destroyers, frigates, landing craft and support vessels. It will be led by the aircraft carriers HMS *Hermes* and HMS *Invincible*. It can be ready to leave in forty-eight hours', replied the Admiral, assuring her that such a force could retake the Islands.[17] 'Not only can we do it, we will be the laughing stock of the world if we don't do it', declared Sir Henry. His certainty contradicted the pessimism of the military options the Prime Minister had been given a few minutes earlier by the Defence Secretary. She seized on the optimistic scenario because the First Sea Lord's strategy was just what she wanted to hear. It transformed the dynamics of her meeting.

Two factors emerged that evening which were to govern the decision-making process in the early stages of the Falklands War. The first was the readiness of the Royal Navy. The second was the resolution of the Prime Minister.

The Royal Navy was expecting the unexpected ahead of any other part of the government. Admiral Leach and the Commander in Chief of the Fleet, Admiral Sir John Fieldhouse, had been taking a prescient view of the developing situation on the Falklands for over a week, ever since it had first been mooted in Whitehall that submarines might have to be despatched to the South Atlantic as a precautionary measure. The Admirals and their staffs had used the week to work up much larger contingency plans, a move which was made easier by the participation of many British warships in a large NATO exercise already taking place off Gibraltar. So Sir Henry Leach's remarkable confidence in the Royal Navy's preparedness to despatch a task force was well founded. It was based on some clever forward thinking and planning for a fleet that was already at sea on the NATO exercise.[18]

Fortified by the report given to her by the First Sea Lord, Margaret Thatcher was decisive and resolute. She immediately authorised the Navy to prepare the task force to sail, subject to the approval of the cabinet the following morning. But for all her ringing endorsement of the Leach plan, when the meeting ended and she was left alone in the room with John Nott, the Prime Minister asked: 'Can we really do this, John?'

The Defence Secretary was far from certain, given the general doubts that were being expressed in his department by everyone other than the First Sea Lord.

'I just don't know yet, Prime Minister', replied Nott. 'I've had no formal advice. But these Islands are 8,000 miles away, and we can't be sure that we can handle the logistics.'

'John, we must!'[19] was the response.

Her firmness set the tone during the hectic meetings and preparations of the next forty-eight hours. Events were moving so fast that big decisions were taken on the hoof by military chiefs reporting directly to the Prime Minister. The civil service, apart from the No. 10 private secretaries, were largely out of the loop. Margaret Thatcher had an instinctive trust in the professionalism of the armed forces, and she urged them on with a resolution that they found inspirational.

For all her decisiveness, the Prime Minister's confidence was far from impregnable in those early days as the risks were pointed out to her. On Friday 2 April, the landing of the Argentine invasion force on the Falklands was confirmed. Outwardly the business of peace-time government was continuing as usual at No. 10. According to her diary, Margaret Thatcher was scheduled to host a lunch for university vice-chancellors. The Minister of State for Higher Education who had arranged it, William Waldegrave, assumed that the event would be cancelled. Not so. Over lunch in the small dining room, Margaret Thatcher explained to the great men of academia how they should run their universities, all the time reading urgent notes on the Falklands brought in by private secretaries. The vice-chancellors departed, looking somewhat shell shocked. Alone in the room with Waldegrave, the Prime Minister gripped his arm and confided, 'William, the problem is we shall have no proper air cover'.[20]

The political situation at home initially looked almost as fragile as the military prospects on the islands. The House of Commons was recalled for an emergency debate on the morning of Saturday 3 April. Before the sitting began, Conservative back-benchers met in a crowded upstairs committee room. The mood was indignant. As one of the sixty or so MPs present, I well recall the number of times phrases like 'national humiliation', 'day of shame', 'catalogue of missed warnings', 'guilty men' and 'hour of infamy' rang through the air. Several older colleagues spoke of the dangers of 'another Suez'. One lone voice said it had been a black day 'but one which could yet end in glory'.[21] But the overall tone was almost entirely negative and critical. The Chief Whip, Michael Jopling, who took notes throughout, left the room looking shaken. The same was true of the Prime Minister, whose car was booed as it passed through the gates of the Palace of Westminster.[22]

Margaret Thatcher had recovered her composure by the time she rose to speak in the debate. She knew from an overnight opinion poll that 60 per cent of the public were blaming her for allowing the debacle to take place. She was aware that some of her back-benchers were now calling for ministerial blood. Even some senior figures in the government were ridiculing the idea of recapturing the Islands. The Chancellor, Sir Geoffrey Howe, joked on the day after the invasion that Britain was at war but that it would 'probably be over by tea time'.[23]

Another cabinet minister harbouring doubts was John Biffen. As he was a good friend I chatted to him shortly before the debate began and asked him what he thought. 'This will be our poor man's Vietnam', was his sardonic reply.[24] It was, to put it mildly, a disconcerting response. It later emerged that on the previous day the Prime Minister had gone round the cabinet table asking every one of her colleagues if they supported sending the task force. All said yes apart from Biffen. Although he was the sole dissenter there were several others who supressed their misgivings. Margaret Thatcher enjoyed saying in later life that the cabinet were 'rock solid – afterwards'.[25]

The Prime Minister struck the right notes of gravity and decisive action when she opened the debate. It seemed a somewhat low-key speech, perhaps because she was tired and also because hers was almost the most moderate voice on that morning of high emotion. Just how high those emotions were running became apparent from the roar of approval that went up from all parts of the House when she condemned 'this unprovoked aggression by the Government of Argentina against British territory. It has not a shred of justification and not a scrap of legality.'[26] Another thunder of 'hear, hear' greeted her crucial announcement: 'A large Task Force will sail as soon as all preparations are complete. HMS *Invincible* will be in the lead and will leave port on Monday.'[27]

With the possibility of war now looming, Parliament went into patriotic overdrive. The Leader of the Opposition, Michael Foot, soared to heights of impassioned eloquence as he proclaimed it was Britain's 'moral duty, political duty and every other kind of duty'[28] to repel the Argentine invaders. From his bellicose speech, and from almost every other contribution to the debate, the overriding impression was that the House of Commons had become united in its determination to reverse the Argentine seizure of the Islands by British military force.

The fall-back position that the despatch of the fleet was a diplomatic bargaining chip rather than an instrument of retaliation evaporated during the debate. The one or two voices that entered caveats about the difficulties of waging a war across 8,000 miles of ocean were given a rough ride. 'Let us hear no more about logistics – how difficult it is to travel long distances', declared Sir Edward du Cann, Chairman of the 1922 Committee. 'I do not remember the Duke of Wellington whining about Torres Vedras. We have nothing to lose now except our honour. I am clear that that is safe in the hands of my right hon. Friend.'[29]

Margaret Thatcher was seen to be nodding at this implication that the war and the nation's honour had been personally entrusted to her. In the next speech, Enoch Powell made the same point in memorably chilling language.

> The Prime Minister, shortly after she came into office, received a soubriquet as the 'Iron Lady'. It arose in the context of remarks which she made about defence against the Soviet Union and its allies; but there was no reason to suppose that the right hon. Lady did not welcome and, indeed, take pride in that description. In the next week or two this House, the nation, and the right hon. Lady herself will learn of what metal she is made.[30]

Margaret Thatcher's body language as she heard Enoch Powell's challenge was a combination of nodding and squirming. Watching her, I sensed at the time that his thrust had gone deep. If she ever had any doubts about crossing the Rubicon to war, they were removed by the House of Commons on that Saturday morning. Some commentators subsequently described the parliamentary mood as 'jingoistic', 'gung-ho for war' and completely 'over the top'. But as one who was present in the chamber throughout the debate, I had no doubt that MPs from every corner of the political spectrum were reflecting the feelings they had already heard voiced in their constituencies. The country would not settle for anything less than the eviction of the Argentine invaders from the Falklands. As a result there was remarkably little difference in the tone of the speeches, whether they came from the unilateralist left (Michael Foot) or the imperialist right (Julian Amery). It was a genuinely British response to an outrage against British people by a foreign dictatorship in violation of international law. Margaret Thatcher had reflected those attitudes and her instincts were confirmed by a united Parliament. She had swung all parties behind her decision to send a task force. But as Enoch Powell had hinted, any weakening in this resolve would put her own political future in peril.

In the hours immediately following the debate, the patriotic unity of the public speeches in the chamber was diluted by many expressions of private cynicism in the corridors and committee rooms of the Palace of Westminster. 'She'll be out if she don't deliver what she promised, and she'll be in for a long time if she do',[31] was the opinion of Alec Woodall, the Labour MP for Hemsworth. He was an ex-miner, a staunch old Labour patriot and a personal friend as my House of Commons pair.

Another interesting opinion that afternoon came from Nicholas Ridley. I found him sitting morosely in the smoking room nursing an outsize brandy.

'I blame the Tory Right', he grumbled. 'But for them we could have avoided this bloody mess.'

'Do you include Margaret in "them"?' I asked.

'Yes she was part of it. But now we've got to back her to the hilt.'[32]

In some Tory circles there was less straightforwardness, and more vindictiveness. The disaster of the debate had been the winding-up speech of John Nott, who seemed to lose his nerve and the high ground of the argument. He made the great mistake of attacking the previous Labour government for alleged inconsistencies in their earlier handling of the Falklands. After many interruptions, which he did not handle well, he sat down amidst raucous calls of 'Resign!' – some from his own back benches. This was rough stuff for a government on the brink of committing the nation's armed forces to a war, but worse was to come.

Immediately after the debate ended, Margaret Thatcher convened a meeting of senior ministerial colleagues in her House of Commons office behind the Speaker's chair. Although John Nott was shaken by the mauling his speech had received a few minutes earlier, he was calm in comparison to some others present, notably Willie Whitelaw, described as being 'in a frightful flap', and the Chief Whip, Michael Jopling, who excitably reported that the party was 'in a state of chaos',[33] with rebellions and resignations of the whip imminent. Margaret Thatcher agreed with her Chief Whip's suggestion that the best way to steady her parliamentary troops would be to call an immediate party meeting in Committee Room 10, to be addressed by both the Defence and Foreign Secretaries.

This was a misjudgement. The meeting, which along with over a hundred Tory back-benchers I attended, began in the atmosphere of a lynch mob, as unprecedented boos and catcalls greeted the entry of the two cabinet ministers. Even when the hysteria subsided, the tone of the questioning was subversive. Alan Clark caught the atmosphere in his diary when he wrote contemptuously about 'the predictable front men making their coded statements whose real purpose was to prepare the way for a coup if events should lead to humiliation or disaster'.[34]

I drew different conclusions from this tense gathering. The 'predictable front men' identified by Alan Clark were vocal, but their circumlocutions made them sound weak and unreliable. Moreover, by that mysterious process of character analysis, which the House of Commons performs on its members, some of the most hostile speakers had long been identified as third raters. By contrast, there were well-respected colleagues speaking up quietly and sensibly for the task-force strategy. But they were in a numerical minority.

Carrington answered questions capably at this meeting, but misread the signals from it. As a peer, he had the disadvantage of not being able to know the characters and reputations of his Commons questioners. Schooled only in the genteel politeness of the Upper House, he was unnerved by the rough and tumble of the elected representatives' rudeness. He was being attacked by men of straw but was unable to differentiate them from the colleagues who carried weight. So instead of shrugging off the often silly criticisms of his department, he became despondent.[35]

Over the weekend, Carrington consulted his friends on whether he should resign. The Prime Minister wanted him to stay, and said so in her usual forthright manner. Over lunch at Dorneywood on Sunday 4 April, the Home Secretary offered the same advice, but less forthrightly. 'Oh, you know Willie. He tried to dissuade me – but not too hard', recalled Carrington.[36]

Another elder statesman who advised him to remain in his post was former Prime Minister and Foreign Secretary Lord Home. But his support was unwittingly undermined by his wife. Just after he thought he had persuaded Carrington to stay, he left the room to go to the lavatory. Elizabeth Home entered. Carrington asked what she thought he should do. 'Oh well, Alec has told me that if he was in your position he wouldn't have the faintest hesitation but to resign', blurted out Lady Home.[37]

If there were any doubts after that they were dispelled by a third member of the family, Charles Douglas-Home. As editor of *The Times*, he wrote a hostile leader attacking the Foreign Secretary, which was published on Monday 5 April. For Carrington, it was the final straw. A few hours later he insisted on tendering his resignation. 'I think I was doing the Prime Minister a favour', he said. 'Someone had to carry the can, and I thought it was right that it should be me.'*[38]

Margaret Thatcher was aghast at his decision. To this day opinions are divided on whether he was right or wrong to go. Carrington was not to blame for the Argentine invasion. He had done his best to pursue the leaseback option within weeks of taking office. He had minuted three warnings about the dangers in withdrawing HMS *Endurance* from the South Atlantic. He would have played a much firmer hand in the diplomatic manoeuvres that preceded the war than his successor Francis Pym. If there had to be ministerial bloodletting, John Nott was the obvious candidate, particularly after his catastrophic speech in the 3 April Commons debate. He too offered his resignation, but the Prime Minister could not afford the departure of two such senior colleagues. So Carrington, out of *noblesse oblige*, went; Nott, out of political necessity, stayed.

After Carrington had fallen on his sword, Margaret Thatcher had to choose a new foreign secretary. She had a brief flirtation with the idea of appointing Julian Amery, whose right-wing views were in tune with her own, and whose robust speech in the emergency debate had struck a chord in all parts of the House. But more cautious counsels from Willie Whitelaw prevailed. Although she had little regard for the judgement or the steel of Francis Pym, who had disappointed her as a wet and as an unimpressive Defence Secretary, she gave the job to him. As she later observed, she discovered she 'had exchanged an amusing Whig for a gloomy one'.[39] Worse than his gloom was his temperament.

---

* Carrington had tried to 'carry the can' at an earlier stage of his career. In 1954 he offered his resignation as a junior minister over the Crichel Down affair. His boss, the Agriculture Minister Sir Thomas Dugdale, resigned for this episode which is often cited as the classic case of ministerial responsibility being honourably accepted. Carrington's friends, notably Selwyn Lloyd and Alec Douglas-Home, said to me in later years that they thought he always had pangs of guilt for not having resigned with Dugdale. Perhaps the memory of Crichel influenced his Falklands resignation.

He had suffered one nervous breakdown during his parliamentary career and was notorious for his mood swings.

Unlike Carrington, Pym had no rapport with the Prime Minister. While admiring his good war record honoured by his Military Cross, she disliked him for the condescendingly snobbish attitudes she felt he had shown towards her in the past. Their awkward relationship was further soured by the undercurrents of press and parliamentary opinions that Pym would be her likely successor at No. 10 if the Falklands mission ended in failure. For all these reasons the new Foreign Secretary was in the uneasiest of partnerships with the Prime Minister as they contemplated the prospects for the war to which Parliament had committed them.

SEEING OFF HAIG

One of the most vivid images at the start of the Falklands War was the sailing of the task force on Monday 5 April. As the grey hulls of the aircraft carriers HMS *Invincible* and HMS *Hermes* and their accompanying escort of destroyers and frigates slipped their moorings and headed out to sea from Portsmouth harbour, it was clear to many that if these warships returned without achieving the retaking of the Falkland Islands it would mean the end of Margaret Thatcher as Prime Minister.

She recognised this reality. There is no evidence that she gave any particular concern to her personal position. It was restoring Britain's honour that motivated her actions. She was old enough to remember the fiasco of Suez in 1956, when a military force to recover the canal had been despatched and humiliatingly withdrawn without its objectives being achieved. The retired Prime Minister Winston Churchill delivered his memorable epitaph on the Suez failure: 'I am not sure I would have dared to start, but I am sure I should not have dared to stop.'[40]

These Churchillian words were quoted several times by Margaret Thatcher to Ian Gow in the week she ordered the despatch of the task force. From the day she received full parliamentary backing for her bold move, nothing less than the return of the Falklands to British administration and sovereignty would do. She never faltered in this purpose. Moreover, from the beginning she saw clearly that diplomatic compromise was likely to be impossible for either side.

If General Galtieri and his junta backed down without securing Argentine sovereignty over *Las Malvinas* they would fall. If the task force returned without restoring British rule to the Falklands, she would fall. Understanding these high stakes, she did not weaken in her conviction that there was no credible alternative to war, even though she had to pay lip service to the quest for a negotiated settlement.

The Prime Minister had to work hard to keep political, domestic and international public opinion on her side. Inside her own party at Westminster the number of dissenting voices started to increase after the task force sailed.

Some ten days after the 2 April Parliamentary debate, Chief Whip Michael Jopling sent a note to the Foreign Secretary reporting that he had sounded out twenty-eight MPs on their reactions to events in the Falklands. Twenty-one of them were out of tune with the Prime Minister's instincts. They ranged from Robert Rhodes James ('Is hopelessly defeatist, depressed and disloyal') to Ken Clarke ('Hopes nobody thinks we are to fight the Argentinians') to Marcus Kimball ('Let the Argentinians have the Falklands with as little fuss as possible') and Ian Gilmour ('We are making a big mistake. It will make Suez look like common sense').[41]

Such wobbles in her own ranks coupled with considerable scepticism in Washington and other allied capitals meant that despite her view that war was inevitable, Margaret Thatcher had to maintain an elaborate façade of pretence that she was keeping the diplomatic options open.

This was made easier by an unexpected triumph for Britain at the United Nations. One day after the invasion, the UK Permanent Representative to the United Nations, Sir Anthony Parsons, succeeded in obtaining the necessary two-thirds majority in favour of UN Security Council Resolution 502, which condemned the Argentine invasion and called for the withdrawal of the occupying troops pending a diplomatic solution. The final vote, from Jordan, that ensured the passing of UN Security Council Resolution 502 was secured by Margaret Thatcher's personal appeal in a last-minute telephone call to King Hussein.[42]

The Security Council Resolution strengthened Britain's moral position. The parliamentary indignation in London had initially been compared by a US State Department official to a Gilbert and Sullivan operetta.[43] Now it was ratified as an internationally important stand of high principle against aggression.

Margaret Thatcher was no great admirer of the UN, but now she was grateful for the legitimacy it had conferred on her decision to send the task force. 'All the Argentines have to do', she repeated many times, 'is honour UN Security Council Resolution 502.'[44] It was an irony that the Foreign Office professionals of whom she was so often suspicious dealt her a winning hand in the battle to persuade the world of the rightness of her cause.

Despite having scored such a quick victory at the United Nations in New York, Margaret Thatcher had greater difficulty in winning hearts and minds in Washington. Ambivalence and confusion were reigning within the Reagan administration over the Falklands. The State Department saw Argentina as a key ally in its strategy to roll back communism and socialism in Latin America. Influenced by the pro-Argentine US Permanent Representative to the United Nations, Ambassador Jeane Kirkpatrick, there had been considerable sympathy for the junta's demand for sovereignty over the islands. On the night of the invasion, Kirkpatrick had dined as guest of honour at the Argentine embassy, an engagement which infuriated the Prime Minister when she heard about it.[45] But whatever some voices in the State Department were saying, Margaret Thatcher believed that President Reagan himself would be unequivocal in his support for Britain. He was not. Although he had tried to be helpful a few hours before the invasion by making what turned out to be an ineffective telephone plea to General Galtieri, Reagan seemed reluctant to tilt US policy one way or the other in this quarrel between two allies.

As he headed off for an Easter vacation in Barbados at the home of his old Hollywood friend Claudette Colbert, the President remained non-committal about the Falklands crisis. At a meeting of the National Security Planning Group on 7 April, Reagan talked the problem over with most of his top foreign-policy team including Secretary of State Alexander Haig, Defense Secretary Caspar Weinberger, UN Ambassador Jeane Kirkpatrick and National Security Advisor Judge William Clark. According to one of those present, NSC staffer Jim Rentschler, the President said, 'It seems to me we have an opportunity to do some good here. The main thing we have to do is to get these two brawlers out of the bar.'[46] However later in the meeting, under pressure from Jeane Kirkpatrick not to favour the British, Reagan responded, 'Look, I would love to stay friends with Argentina but I think our first loyalty, our first order of business if worst comes to worst, is to side with the Brits'.[47]

With the meeting ending hurriedly because the President, casually dressed in a blazer and sports shirt, was visibly anxious to get away to Barbados, the decision was taken that the Secretary of State should set off on a peace mission. In a move designed to imitate Henry Kissinger's famous shuttle diplomacy between the Arabs and Israelis in the mid-1970s, Haig proposed that he should visit London and Buenos Aires in order to negotiate a settlement between the two capitals.

Displeased by this indication that the United States was appearing to take a neutral stance towards the conflict, the Prime Minister nevertheless agreed to welcome Haig as a friend and ally, but not as any kind of mediator. However, within hours of his arrival in London the Secretary of State made it clear to the Prime Minister that he had indeed come to mediate. She was having none of it.

Over dinner at No. 10 on the evening of 8 April, Haig unveiled his settlement plan. As he chain-smoked underneath two paintings of Nelson and Wellington that had been displayed especially for this occasion on the Prime Minister's instructions, the US Secretary of State attempted to persuade her to accept some form of what he called neutral 'interim administration of the Islands'. This vague proposition involved establishing a Canadian or American presence if the Argentines withdrew their troops, while negotiations about sovereignty continued. According to the diary of Jim Rentschler who accompanied Haig to the No. 10 dinner, Margaret Thatcher listened to these proposals and then exploded.

'Wooliness', she spat contemptuously, her voice rising with indignation and high colour flushing in her cheeks.

> I did not dispatch a fleet to install some nebulous arrangement which would have no authority . . . Interim authority! – to do *what*? I beg you, I beg you to remember that in 1938 Neville Chamberlain sat at this same table discussing an arrangement which sounds very like the one you are asking me to accept: and were I to do so, I would be censured in the House of Commons – and properly so! Britain simply will not reward aggression – that is the lesson we have learned from 1938.[48]

The lessons of appeasement were always at the forefront of Margaret Thatcher's mind in her continuing dealings with Alexander Haig. If he faced an uphill task with her, he soon found he had a higher mountain to climb with the Argentines.

From London he flew to Buenos Aires, where he thought he had agreed some concessions with one part of the junta, only to have them publicly sabotaged by another. But Haig persisted in a new demand, when he returned to Downing Street on 12 April, for Britain to accept a revised idea of an interim joint admin-istration and to halt the task force while the details were worked out.

'Unthinkable', retorted the Prime Minister. 'One simply doesn't trust burglars who have tried once to steal property. No, Al, no, absolutely not, the fleet must steam on!'[49]

On 13 April, Haig left London with his mission in ruins. 'He was obviously very depressed', commented Margaret Thatcher, not entirely sympathetically.[50] But the Secretary of State had identified from his talks in London the one British cabinet minister who might have some sympathy for the American peace plan. This was the Foreign Secretary, Francis Pym, who Haig invited to Washington on 23 April. Tremendous pressure was applied to get Pym to accept yet another variation of the proposals for halting the task force, an Argentine withdrawal from the Islands and the setting out of an interim authority, which would now include representatives from the Argentine government.

To Margaret Thatcher's horror, Francis Pym was persuaded to recommend that this package should be accepted. She regarded it as 'conditional surrender', above all because it did not restore either British rule or sovereignty. But Pym insisted that his recommendation should be discussed by the war cabinet, which had been set up three weeks earlier. Before this meeting took place at 6 p.m. on the evening of 24 April Margaret Thatcher met alone with her deputy, Willie Whitelaw, and told him that if the Foreign Secretary's proposals were accepted, she would resign.[51]

Although Whitelaw backed his Prime Minister, the war cabinet was fraught and tense. Francis Pym, supported by a Foreign Office team, advocated the new proposals. He made a strong case for their acceptance, arguing that they could be presented as the American plan to avert war.

Margaret Thatcher realised the magnitude of the problem with which Pym's recommendation confronted her. She was in serious danger of being isolated and defeated. To avoid this, she made an intensive study of the document known as 'Haig Two', which had reached her five hours earlier. She went through the text clause by clause as if she was a prosecuting counsel cross-examining each line of a dossier in meticulous forensic detail. Among the fiercest points of her interrogation she asked: Why had we not insisted on a minimum of self-determination for the Islanders? Why had we accepted almost unlimited Argentine immigration and acquisition of property on an equal basis with the existing Falklanders? How come we had accepted various terms, which had previously been rejected out of hand? Her mastery of detail was impressive, but Pym held his ground. Although the members of the war cabinet stayed on her side, it was clear that a menacing disagreement had built up between the Prime Minister and the Foreign Secretary.[52]

The stalemate was broken by the Defence Secretary, John Nott. He made the suggestion that the British government should not respond to 'Haig Two'. Instead, it should request that the draft be put to the Argentines first. If the junta accepted it, which Margaret Thatcher did not believe they would, then the 'Haig Two' document could be put before Parliament on that basis. Sir Nicholas Henderson, the British Ambassador to Washington, thought that Nott's suggestion was a masterstroke, calling it 'a finesse of which Talleyrand would have been proud'.[53] The Prime Minister was not in the least proud of it but she temporarily and unhappily bowed to Pym's pressure, allowing the diplomatic ball to fall into Argentina's court.

The junta in Buenos Aires did not disappoint Margaret Thatcher. On 29 April they rejected 'Haig Two' out of hand. The Secretary of State's 32,000-mile peace shuttle had ended in failure. Despite further fruitless overtures to the Argentine Foreign Minister, Nicanor Costa Mendez, the die was now cast for war.[54]

One other development contributed to the inevitability of a fight for the Falklands. While Haig had been pursuing his frustrating negotiations, American public opinion had been shifting towards Britain. On Capitol Hill and on the television talk shows, the UK's two ambassadors, Anthony Parsons at the United Nations and Nicholas Henderson in Washington, had been highly effective in converting influential voices to Margaret Thatcher's cause. On 29 April the US Senate by seventy-nine to one votes passed a resolution stating that the US 'cannot stand neutral' and must help Britain achieve 'full withdrawal' of Argentine forces.[55] The US Defense Secretary, Caspar W. Weinberger, on his own initiative ordered that maximum military assistance should be given to the British. His help included full access to US intelligence; the code-breaking of Argentine military signals; unlimited use of fuel and spares from the US base on Ascension Island; and accelerated purchase of American Sidewinder missiles which were to prove one of the most effective weapons in the conflict.[56] The Anglophile Secretary of the US Navy, John Lehman, was also extremely helpful to Britain's Royal Navy at a working level of co-operation.

Finally President Reagan came off the fence. Although privately he never quite lost his air of bemused detachment about what he called 'that little ice-cold bunch of land down there',[57] he did change his position. After a private discussion with Caspar Weinberger, Reagan told him, 'Give Maggie everything she needs to get on with it'.[58]

After chairing a meeting of his National Security Council on 29 April, when it was formally decided to take 'an explicit pro-UK tilt', the President wrote to the Prime Minister to inform her of this new policy direction. He agreed not to publish the full text of 'Haig Two', 'because of the difficulty that might cause you', and ended his message with these helpful words: 'We will leave no doubt that Her Majesty's Government worked with us in good faith, and was left with no choice but to proceed with military action based on the right of self defence.'[59] As he wrote in his private diary, 'I don't think Margaret Thatcher should be asked to concede any more.'[60]

Making concessions to Argentina had never been on the Prime Minister's agenda since that rumbustious morning in the House of Commons, when Parliament had given its full backing to the sending of the task force. She had always been certain that the Argentines would refuse to compromise over their illegal occupation of the Islands. She was no less uncompromising herself in her determination to remove them by military force. But she had to avoid sounding obdurate. As she later recalled, 'We . . . had to stand firm against the pressure to make unacceptable compromises, while avoiding the appearance of intransigence.'[61]

This posture of outwardly pretending to be flexible while inwardly remaining resolute was Margaret Thatcher's hardest challenge of the diplomatic phase of the conflict. If any other British politician of the twentieth century, with the exception of Churchill, had been Prime Minister when the doves of Washington were putting on the pressure for concessions, it is likely that they would have given ground. Margaret Thatcher gave none. 'That's one hell of a tough lady', said Haig as he returned to his hotel after his first meeting with her on the Falklands crisis.[62] She would need to get tougher still, but she had won the first round. The task force sailed on.

REFLECTION

Margaret Thatcher's personality was the driving force throughout all her preliminary moves and responses to the Falklands crisis.

Once the Islands had been invaded the instinctive reactions of her leadership were courageous. The strengths of her character and her determination were an inspiration to the military preparations for war and to the avoidance of an unprincipled diplomatic settlement.

Yet the uncomfortable truth has to be faced that the stubbornness of Margaret Thatcher's earlier attitude and her inexperience in foreign affairs killed off all the opportunities between May 1979 and March 1982 for the conflict to be avoided.

During this phase of the drama Lord Carrington was in the right and the Prime Minister was in the wrong. The leaseback solution was a workable and sensible option. If she had backed it at an early stage, she could have achieved an honourable settlement of the dispute. This would have meant encouraging Lord Carrington and Nicholas Ridley in their negotiations; persuading the majority of her back-benchers to accept them; and selling the deal to the Falkland Islanders. Only the last hurdle would have presented a serious difficulty. But most Falklanders would surely have seen the merit of a ninety-nine-year or even a 999-year lease (both were discussed in Ridley's talks) granting full British administration to the Islands while ceding British sovereignty. What had worked well in over-populated Hong Kong could have worked even better in Britain's under-populated South Atlantic dependencies.

The might have beens of history are eternally debatable. But this one is easier than most on which to reach a judgement. Margaret Thatcher deserves the highest praise for winning the Falklands War. She has been fortunate to escape censure for bungling her opportunity to make an earlier peace.

Throughout 1979–1980 she either thwarted or undermined every effort to reach a Hong Kong-type settlement with the elected government of Argentina.

The 'thermonuclear lunch' at Chequers in May 1979 was worse than Denis Thatcher's phrase 'a little extravagant' in its incandescent rejection of the leaseback option. Hanging Nicholas Ridley out to dry, let alone undermining him in December 1980 with the help of her Parliamentary Private Secretary Ian Gow, were extraordinary acts of prime ministerial sabotage.

She also invented the doctrine that the views of the 1,800 Falkland Islanders should be 'paramount' in exercising a veto over leaseback. In fact the residents of the colony were never fully or formally asked to consider a Hong Kong option. She also failed to understand the political symbolism of HMS *Endurance*.

The debate over Margaret Thatcher's initial handling of the Falklands problem will continue for centuries to come. My judgement is that she got the pre-invasion stage of the story badly wrong, and then got the post-invasion chapter gloriously right. Both sides of the coin are explicable by the vehemence of her personality.

In between part one and part two there were grey areas of intelligence failures and Whitehall inertia during the first three months of 1982. If there were mistakes in this period they were not made by the Prime Minister. The Franks Committee of Inquiry into the war concluded in the final sentence of its report, 'we would not be justified in attaching any criticism or blame to the present Government for the Argentine Junta's decision to commit its act of unprovoked aggression in the invasion of the Falkland Islands on 2 April 1982'.[63]

This may have been a generous exoneration of some of the intelligence failings in the weeks leading up to the invasion, but as the Prime Minister was never alerted by the Joint Intelligence Committee to the dangerous situation evolving inside the junta, she cannot be faulted for not responding to it.

The strangest omission by the British government in the days leading up to the invasion was its failure to send an ultimatum to the junta in Buenos Aires. In their book *The Falklands War*, Max Hastings and Simon Jenkins highlight this error describing it as 'one of the mysteries of the pre-invasion week . . . known still to exercise a number of those present at Thatcher's various crisis meetings'.[64] The authors ascribe it and other weaknesses to the Prime Minister's inexperience in defence and foreign affairs. This is fair comment.

Having from the outset rejected the only workable proposal for the Falklands – leaseback – Margaret Thatcher had no policy for dealing with either the run-up to the invasion or the invasion itself. She only stumbled upon a policy after Admiral Sir Henry Leach had made his dramatic entry into her meeting in the House of Commons on 28 March, and told her that Britain could and should despatch a task force. Once the sending of the task force became a reality, Margaret Thatcher's resolution and tenacity were the strengths that delivered clarity in diplomacy and victory in war.

On the diplomatic front, she was right to deal brutally with the mish-mash of muddled proposals for a negotiated settlement that were initially served up to her by the US Secretary of State, Alexander Haig. His task was made infinitely harder by the confused and contradictory responses made to him by the junta.

One of Margaret Thatcher's assets throughout the crisis was that she read the minds of her enemies in Buenos Aires with remarkable accuracy. She grasped, apparently by intuition, that General Galtieri and his military colleagues could never accept any sort of diplomatic compromise that involved Argentine troops withdrawing from the Islands they had invaded. So, whatever she said during the various moves and counter-moves by Alexander Haig and other international intermediaries, Britain's Prime Minister was filled with an inner certainty that the Islands would have to be recaptured by Britain's armed forces. She somehow communicated this certainty down the chain of command to the officers and men of the task force. Even when the risks they faced looked daunting, they knew they could rely on clear and committed leadership from No. 10 Downing Street. As the task force sailed on, Margaret Thatcher's courage was to prove a major factor in its ultimate success.

20

The Falklands War II
Into the fighting

MILITARY AND POLITICAL PREPARATIONS

'How do you actually run a war?' Margaret Thatcher asked Sir Frank Cooper, the Permanent Secretary of the Ministry of Defence, over a gin and tonic in the flat above 10 Downing Street just twenty-four hours after the parliamentary debate, which had backed her decision to send the task force.[1] She put a similar question to Harold Macmillan when he came to offer his ex-Prime Minister's support and counsel, two days later. The result of their advice was that she set up the smallest possible war cabinet – so small that it excluded the Chancellor of the Exchequer, Geoffrey Howe. His feelings were hurt by his omission. It was partly due to Macmillan's argument that there was no role for the Treasury in a cause where national honour transcended all financial concerns. A second reason was that the Prime Minister's antennae had deduced that Howe might be more eager to find a compromise than to support her war aims.

Four out of the five ministerial members of the war cabinet picked themselves. They were the Prime Minister; her de facto deputy, Willie Whitelaw; the Defence Secretary, John Nott; the new Foreign Secretary, Francis Pym; and Cecil Parkinson. The last name caused some surprise. Parkinson had been an effective junior minister for Trade, but he was a new arrival at the top table of politics, having just joined the cabinet as Chairman of the Conservative Party and Paymaster General. In the previous few months he had become something of a Thatcher court favourite. Westminster gossip said he owed his promotion to his maintee idol good looks. A more substantive reason was that he had made an impressive contribution as a member of the top-secret cabinet sub-committee, which took the decision to acquire the Trident nuclear missile system. Also, John Nott strongly recommended Parkinson for membership of the war cabinet.

Margaret Thatcher agreed, later saying that she had picked him because he was 'brilliantly effective in dealing with pubic relations'.[2]

The war cabinet, known to Whitehall by the initials ODSA,* met every week-day at 9.30 in the morning, and at weekends at Chequers. It was observed by insiders that ODSA was notable for being the one and only important Whitehall committee throughout her premiership where Margaret Thatcher listened much more than she talked. This was because she grasped that her role as a war leader was to give political direction to the overall strategy of the campaign, and then to let the military get on with it. She was guided on all the naval and military aspects of the campaign by the representative of the Armed Services in the war cabinet, Admiral Sir Terence Lewin. With his quiet charm and authoritative expertise he built a close rapport with the Prime Minister. Lewin and all the service chiefs were pleasantly surprised by her committed backing for their tactics. She in turn developed an almost emotional reverence for their pro-fessional judgement. It was political and military teamwork at its best. Lloyd George in the First World War and Churchill in the Second World War did not have anything like as harmonious a relationship with the top brass as Margaret Thatcher enjoyed with Admiral Lewin and his senior colleagues.

The excellence of the Prime Minister's rapport with her naval and military commanders was not matched by her confidence in the two most important political colleagues in the war cabinet.

After John Nott's disastrous speech in the Falklands debate, she was edgy about him for the first weeks of the campaign. He was a mercurial politician at the best of times, sometimes capable of surprising mood swings. She thought of him as 'a mixture of gold, dross and mercury',[3] which was not the ideal metallurgical alloy for the war test envisaged by Enoch Powell. Yet the accord between the Prime Minister and her Defence Secretary improved as the Falklands campaign progressed. Despite one or two disagreements, John Nott became a strong member of her team. He was a far steadier and more supportive colleague, in her eyes, than the Foreign Secretary.

Perhaps because he had seen the horrors of battle at first hand in the Second World War, Francis Pym was zealous, even over-zealous, to find a diplomatic

---

* The Overseas and Defence Committee of the Cabinet created a South Atlantic Sub-Committee, hence ODSA.

solution to the Falklands problem. He thought he was doing his duty in going the extra mile for peace. She thought he was willing to sell out for peace at any price. These tensions simmered unhappily between them for the duration of the crisis.

There were, however, both visible and invisible bulwarks of support for the Prime Minister on the verge of war. Denis was a rock whose military experience combined with a husband's love provided unseen dimensions of strength in the lonely hours of night in the flat. Many of those hours were spent glued to the BBC World Service news bulletins, adding prime ministerial sleeplessness to restlessness.

Another rock was Ian Gow, who recognised from the outset 'the loneliness of your task', as he described it in a hand-written note to his boss on 8 April. He told her that he was one of many 'who, whatever the future holds in store, will be forever thankful for having had the privilege of trying to help the finest chief, the most resolute and far-sighted leader, and the kindest friend that any man could hope to serve'.[4]

The tenor of suppressed emotion in this and many other communications to and about Margaret Thatcher at this time reflected the rising tension of a nation going to war. One concern, often expressed but never directly to her face, was the question: how would she cope with the experience of taking responsibility for heavy casualties?

SOUTH GEORGIA, THE *BELGRANO* AND THE *SHEFFIELD*

In the month of April, most of the war cabinet's time had to be devoted to diplomacy, while the military tackled the huge logistical challenges of preparing to fight a war 8,000 miles from home. Against the advice of the Royal Navy, the politicians at the war cabinet wanted to start the campaign with what looked like an easy victory. As the first strike in the conflict, they decided to recapture South Georgia before moving on to the Falklands, because this would please domestic public opinion and send a signal of resolve to the Argentines. In spite of strong reservations expressed by Admiral Sir John Fieldhouse, the Commander in Chief of the Fleet, Margaret Thatcher authorised what had been seen as a low-risk operation to evict the occupying Argentines on South Georgia. She was horrified to be given a situation report that suggested that the plan had gone wrong.

On the afternoon of 22 April, John Nott and Admiral Lewin told the Prime Minister that the British SAS and SBS units who had landed on the island were in serious difficulty. In appalling weather, two of their helicopters had crashed, leaving some of the toughest men in Britain's Special Forces stranded in an Antarctic blizzard, too weak to continue. On being told that there was a possibility that seventeen lives might be lost, the Prime Minister wept. She then had to go out to speak at a dinner given by the Lord Mayor of London at the Mansion House. As she was leaving Downing Street in a miserable mood, her private secretary rushed out with the good news that a third helicopter had managed to land in the treacherous conditions, and had rescued the SAS and SBS units without loss. 'As I carried on out of No 10 and left for the dinner I walked on air', she recalled.[5]

The Prime Minister's first brush with the risks of war in a hostile climate moved from near-disaster to total triumph. In the next few hours, fresh contingents of Special Forces and Royal Marines landed on South Georgia. After heavy exchanges of fire, they disabled an Argentine submarine, accepted the surrender of the garrison and hauled up the Union Jack. The war cabinet's first military move had been a high-risk gamble, but it paid off. John Nott announced the news late at night on 25 April outside No. 10.

After he had read the MoD communiqué, journalists began questioning him for further details. Margaret Thatcher interrupted her Defence Secretary to give the media a piece of her mind. 'Rejoice! Just rejoice!' she declared in a tone that might have been sounding the Reveille, as she rolled the Rs of the imperative verbs. 'Just rejoice at the news, and congratulate our forces and the marines . . . Rejoice!'[6]

In the context this was a rebuke to the reporters rather than an exultation of war. Margaret Thatcher, who well knew that the recapture of South Georgia had been a perilously close drama, was more relieved than triumphant.

Four days later, the war cabinet took what turned out to be the most controversial decision of the entire conflict. Britain had declared a Maritime Exclusion Zone (MEZ) of 200 nautical miles around the Falklands, warning that any Argentine warship inside it was liable to be sunk. This MEZ had been superseded by a further British warning that any ship operating in the area of the task force would be attacked. This created the Total Exclusion Zone (TEZ), which came into force on 30 April 1982.

On 2 May, the British naval commander in the South Atlantic, Admiral 'Sandy' Woodward, reported that the Argentine cruiser *General Belgrano* with two destroyer escorts was operating on the edge of the TEZ, engaged in 'a classic pincer movement' against the task force.[7] He requested permission to order a nearby British submarine, HMS *Conqueror*, to attack the *General Belgrano*. The request, brought to a meeting at Chequers of the war cabinet by Admiral Lewin, was one of the quickest decisions of the conflict.

Standing in the Great Hall of the house before lunch, Margaret Thatcher listened to Lewin's endorsement of the proposed attack and then asked all those present whether they thought the *General Belgrano* should be sunk. Willie Whitelaw, Cecil Parkinson, John Nott, Michael Havers, the Attorney General and Sir Antony Acland, the new Permanent Under-Secretary of State at the Foreign Office, substituting for Francis Pym, who was in New York, were unanimous that permission should be granted.

The discussion took no more than fifteen minutes. 'I had no hesitations at all', recalled Acland. 'The direction in which it was going was irrelevant, it could perfectly well turn round, it had two escort vessels with Exocet missiles, and they were very nearly in range of the Task Force which was coming south-west down the Atlantic towards the Falklands.'[8]

With its orders authorised by the war cabinet, HMS *Conqueror* torpedoed the *General Belgrano*, which sank with the loss of 321 of its crew. The Argentine destroyer escorts, apparently fearing that they might be the next targets, headed immediately back to port instead of rescuing survivors. As a result the scale of the losses was greater than anticipated; a tragedy that had repercussions at home and abroad.

At home, Margaret Thatcher was accused of acting illegally or even of committing a war crime, because the *General Belgrano* was sunk just outside the TEZ at a moment when it was steering away from the task force. Another charge was that the sinking had been ordered in order to sabotage a peace plan that was being organised by the Peruvian government. Both accusations were without substance. The war cabinet had not even heard of the Peruvian peace initiative, which was almost identical to the Haig proposals that had already been rejected. As for the *General Belgrano*'s zig-zag course and position, these were irrelevant, given the warnings that had been issued to the Argentines. Margaret Thatcher and her colleagues simply accepted the military advice they were given by Admirals Woodward and Lewin. This advice turned out to be correct. For, after the sinking of the *General Belgrano*, all the ships of the Argentine Navy, including its aircraft carrier the *Veinte Cinco de Mayo*, returned to port and made no further attempt to threaten the task force. So, by its future protection of British ships and men, the decision to attack the *General Belgrano* proved to be one of the most important military actions of the war. Margaret Thatcher deserves credit not criticism for taking the right decision.

Internationally, the perception was different. The heavy loss of life among the *General Belgrano*'s sailors caused a loss of sympathy for Britain at the United Nations. The Irish, Italian and West German governments all wavered in their backing. The Irish Defence Minister described Britain as 'the aggressor'.[9] However, these stirrings of anti-British sentiment diminished after the news of Argentine retaliation, which resulted in the sinking of HMS *Sheffield* two days later.

I well remember the sombre hush that fell over the House of Commons at 10.56 p.m. on the night of 4 May when John Nott made an emergency statement on the loss. With Margaret Thatcher sitting alongside him on the front bench looking stunned and sorrowful with her head bowed, Nott reported how HMS *Sheffield*, a Type 42 destroyer, had been hit by a single Exocet missile launched from an Argentine aircraft. The fire had spread out of control and the order had to be given to abandon ship. The statement estimated that twelve of the crew were missing.[10]

As MPs heard this grim news in silence, it was clear that on both sides of the conflict the war had entered a new phase of hostilities.

Immediately after the statement Margaret Thatcher had a private meeting with Enoch Powell in her room at the Commons. 'It is a relief to be able to talk to you. There is nobody else I can talk to like this', she said. It was an encounter at which she spoke emotionally, not only about the human losses on HMS *Sheffield* but also about the political pressures within her cabinet, which she feared would now be pushing her towards an unacceptable settlement. Powell urged her to stand firm, and assured her that in accordance with his Privy Councillor's oath he would keep their conversation secret. 'Enoch, I would trust you with the life of my child', was the Prime Minister's response.[11]

The over-wrought language was perhaps an indication of the degree of Margaret Thatcher's distress. She had been warned that casualties would be inevitable in the war, but this was her first major experience of them. She had told her staff that the blow she most dreaded was the loss of a ship. Now she was bearing the burden of knowing that the *Sheffield* was the first British warship to be sunk by enemy action since the Second World War. Up until this moment, her experience of war had been confined to images. Suddenly she was confronted with its reality.

Retiring to the privacy of her flat under the eaves of Downing Street, Margaret Thatcher broke down in floods of tears. She was overwhelmed by what were perhaps maternal emotions over the loss of young lives. As she said through her sobs, the sailors drowned in the South Atlantic were about the same age as her twenty-two-year old son Mark, who was now with her in the sitting room. He and Denis did their best to comfort her. But after a while Denis grew tetchy in response to his wife's overwrought reactions. 'What are you making all this fuss for?' he asked. 'When there's a war on you've got to expect things not to go right all the time.'[12]

Mark had gentler and more sensitive reactions. He was staying at No. 10, so he sat up late with his mother, and rose with her too, awakened by the ringing of her bedside telephone at 5 a.m. The call from the duty clerk reported that the death toll from the *Sheffield* had risen to twenty. Seeing the impact on his mother, Mark brought her a cup of tea and sat in the bedroom with her in a time of silent emotion. 'I could see that she was suffering', he recalled. 'I think it helped her to have a member of the family beside her sharing in her feelings. It wasn't necessary to say anything.'[13]

MORE DIPLOMATIC WOBBLES

A few hours later, the Prime Minister called her full cabinet into emergency session on the morning of 5 May. Her ministers were also shaken by the sinking of the *Sheffield*. They had awkward military questions for Admiral Lewin, such as: Why were our ships so vulnerable to Argentine missiles? Was the task force too close to the mainland? Could a landing really be made on the Islands?

Most of the cabinet were reassured by the answers they received on these questions, although one minister, Patrick Jenkin, voiced the minority view that the sinking of the *Sheffield* meant that Britain should offer a cease-fire.

The loss of life over the *Belgrano* had increased the diplomatic pressure for a settlement, which was now coming from three combined sources – a peace plan from Peru; its acceptance by Francis Pym; and its advocacy by the US State Department and the White House.

Margaret Thatcher reported to the cabinet that she had just received a message from President Reagan, which asked her to accept the Peruvian peace proposals. It had arrived at a bad moment, soon after she had been told that the *Sheffield* was on fire. She did not tell her ministers how angry she had been with the President of the United States for piling on what she later called 'this constant pressure to weaken our stance'.[14]

Affronted by Reagan's demands to find a compromise, she sat down and composed a blistering reply that pulled no punches about her disappointment with him. This furious missive was never sent.

The draft in her own handwriting has survived in her private papers. It is revealing about the true anger of the Prime Minister's mood during her most vulnerable period in early May. The main issue on which she parted company from the President and his Secretary of State was the Islanders' right to self-determination. Margaret Thatcher wrote:

> You say that your suggestions are faithful to the basic principles we most protect. I wish they were but alas they are not. The present proposals do not provide a right to self-determination, although it is fundamental to democracy and was enjoyed by the Islanders up to the moment of invasion. We asked that it should be included. The reply contained in Mr Haig's letter to Francis Pym was that it could not because the Argentines would not accept it. So our principles are no longer what we believe, nor those we were elected to serve, but what the dictator will accept.[15]

These words were cut out of the final version of the reply she sent to President Reagan because she was persuaded by cooler heads that it 'revealed perhaps too much of my frustration'.[16] But even in its watered down form her response was a rebuke.

She complained about the US efforts to bulldoze Britain into compromise, making a personal appeal to Reagan as 'the only person who will understand the significance of what I am trying to say'. Her message was the familiar theme that at stake were great issues of legal and moral principle. There could be no solution to the Falklands crisis that did not 'provide unambiguously for a right to self-determination'.[17] She was not going to desert the Islands without establishing this right.

Although the Prime Minister was resolute in her refusal to consider diplomatic compromises that eroded British sovereignty or the Islanders' right to determine their own future, she gave more credence to the Peruvian peace plan than she admitted at the time. This was partly because of the American pressure, and partly because she had been listening to a Peruvian back channel operated by her friend and speech writer Professor Hugh Thomas.

Hugh Thomas was an expert on Latin America and an acclaimed author of books on Cuba, Mexico and the Spanish Civil War. He had extensive contacts across the South American continent, and enjoyed a close relationship with the Prime Minister of Peru, Manuel Ulloa Elías. Throughout April and most of May, Thomas and Ulloa telephoned each other every day. The important messages from these conversations were reported directly to Margaret Thatcher by Hugh Thomas, who in turn relayed her thoughts to his high Peruvian source.

This back channel stayed secret, but it became known to Washington. The US State Department was so concerned by this that they despatched the Minister at the US Embassy in London, Ed Streator, to talk to Hugh Thomas. As the two men knew each other socially, Thomas was unsurprised by the contact, but became startled when Streator began asking him about his regular communications with Manuel Ulloa. 'How do you know about them?' asked Thomas. 'We are a global power', was Streator's reply. When this was passed on to Margaret Thatcher, she told Hugh Thomas, 'Ring me at Chequers. They listen in less, there.'[18]

If the Americans had been listening to the dialogue between the British and Peruvian prime ministers, as conducted through Hugh Thomas, they would have receive only limited encouragement. But Margaret Thatcher took the Peruvian proposals more seriously than she acknowledged in her memoirs. Intriguingly, she showed some willingness to agree to the idea of what was called an 'Argentine Resident' in the Falklands. This would have been the equivalent of the British Resident in the Gulf, a former diplomatic posting to the Trucial Oman States. Because it had no legal impact on sovereignty, the idea had little appeal in Buenos Aires. But it did show that the Prime Minister was willing to give some ground. She was getting a better understanding of the Argentine junta's mindset from the Peruvian Prime Minister's nocturnal phone conversations with Hugh Thomas ('sometimes with the unmistakable sound of castanets in the background')[19] than she was from her own Foreign Office. On one occasion she asked Thomas why Manuel Ulloa was so well informed and insightful about the inner workings of the junta. 'Prime Minister, you have to realise that like every successful Peruvian, he has an Argentine second wife', was the reply.

One of the more dramatic products of the Peruvian back channel came on the night of 2 May, when Manuel Ulloa telephoned Hugh Thomas to report that the *General Belgrano* had been sunk. Thomas immediately called Margaret Thatcher (who was out at a dinner), and passed on this news to her Principal Private Secretary. 'Are you sure he said it had been *sunk*?' asked Clive Whitmore. Apparently, No. 10 knew that the *General Belgrano* had been hit by the torpedo attack from HMS *Conqueror*. But the first confirmation of the cruiser's sinking came from the co-operative Peruvian Prime Minister. Back channels have their uses.

Through more conventional diplomatic channels, the Peruvian peace plan began giving Margaret Thatcher a serious problem. Not only was she being pressurised by President Reagan to accept it. Her Foreign Secretary, Francis Pym, returned from New York on 4 May with a renewed determination to secure a cessation of hostilities. The basis on which Pym advocated a peace deal was effectively a revised version of the 'Haig Two' proposals, which had already been rejected by the Prime Minister and the war cabinet.

The revisions were slight, but this time they had the imprimatur of President Fernando Belaúnde of Peru, who was Argentina's closest ally in Latin America.

At a meeting of the full cabinet on 5 May, Pym received a more positive response than he had been given when the war cabinet turned down almost the same package on 23 April. Margaret Thatcher herself remained 'deeply unhappy about the US–Peruvian proposals'.[20] But her cabinet, by a counted majority of twenty to two, wanted the talking to continue. So, biting her lip she had to tell the House of Commons the following day that the government was making 'a very constructive response' to the Peruvian initiative.[21] Her words on the printed page of the official report are deceptive for her tone could hardly have been less constructive. She was also visibly dismayed by the cheers of left-wing Labour MPs at this apparent reversal of her uncompromising stance. For the next few hours the Prime Minister's strategy on the Falklands was on a knife edge.

The collapse of her strategy was averted by the machismo of the junta in Buenos Aires. Had they accepted the Peruvian plan, Margaret Thatcher would have been on the ropes, for she would have been pushed into a messy compromise which failed to secure her key objectives of restoring British sovereignty and administration to the Islands. But fortunately for her, the junta had become emboldened by the sinking of the *Sheffield* and upped the ante. Instead of doing a deal with President Belaúnde, the Argentine Foreign Minister Nicanor Costa Méndez criticised the details of the Peruvian plan and wanted further negotiations in New York.

During a stormy debate in the House of Commons, a disappointed Francis Pym said that but for the junta's intransigence there could have been 'an immediate cease-fire'. He was given a rough ride by his back-benchers for going on to say, 'If one phase of diplomatic effort has been brought to an end . . . another phase is already under way in New York'.[22]

Margaret Thatcher well understood that she had been passing through a forty-eight-hour period of political peril for her own survival. She was furious with Francis Pym for bouncing her into a semi-endorsement of the US–Peruvian proposal. It would have meant the end of British sovereignty over the Falklands, some form of UN trusteeship administering the Islands and a climb down from her high principles for the long-term governance of the colony would have to be shared with Argentina. She had come perilously close to being forced to sign up to this.

One trusted aide in whom she confided her fears and her fury was her PPS, Ian Gow. He in turn passed them on to a number of trusted back-bench friends, who included Tony Buck, Alan Clark, Jim Spicer and myself. That was one of the reasons why Francis Pym was greeted with groans and cries of 'No' when he said that another phase of diplomacy would continue in New York. But even allowing for Ian Gow's orchestration of it, there was always a strong body of parliamentary opinion which felt that a settlement anywhere near the Peruvian or indeed the American terms would be a defeat for Britain and its prime minister.

The Americans however had not given up. On 13 May, Ronald Reagan telephoned Margaret Thatcher in what must have been one of the most acrimonious conversations ever to take place between a US president and a British prime minster. The call began agreeably, with Reagan saying that he understood that the negotiating positions between the two sides were now quite close.

Thatcher firmly told him that this was not the case and gave him a detailed explanation of the British position. Detail was never Reagan's strong point. He moved on to say he was worried about rumours that British forces were planning an attack on the Argentine mainland. Not true, he was told. Then he asked Margaret Thatcher to hold off on further military action to give more time for the UN to devolve the negotiations. This was too much for her. 'Argentina attacked our ships only yesterday', she retorted. 'We cannot delay military options simply because of negotiations.'

Reagan's next ploy was to comment that international opinion might see the conflict as a David versus Goliath struggle with Britain in the role of Goliath. 'This could hardly be true at a distance of 8,000 miles', was her riposte. Then she lambasted the President, asking if he would like Americans to live under a brutal dictatorship like the junta; pointing out the length of time that many of the Islanders had lived on the Falklands; and lecturing him on the strategic importance of the Islands if the Panama Canal was enclosed.

Margaret Thatcher called these exchanges 'a difficult conversation'.[23]

President Reagan wrote more emolliently in his diary, 'Talked to Margaret but don't think I persuaded her against further action'.[24]

The British Ambassador to Washington, Sir Nicholas Henderson, commented, 'I can't see Reagan getting on to her on the phone again in a hurry'.[25]

Although there was clarity from Margaret Thatcher, the Argentines were making their responses to the various settlement proposals as clear as mud. The junta consisted of fifty-four people divided into groups and sub-groups which frequently contradicted each other. The number of their interlocutors was multiplying too. To Haig's considerable annoyance, the Secretary General of the United Nations, Javier Perez de Cuellar, launched his own variation of the American and Peruvian proposals, while the US Ambassador to the United Nations, Jeane Kirkpatrick, had a private dialogue with Argentine diplomats about possible peace terms. This mixture of overtures gave the junta the opportunity to play one negotiation off against another, and also to play for time.

Margaret Thatcher knew that time was running out. She was acutely conscious of the limited window of opportunity afforded by the South Atlantic weather patterns. With her war cabinet she had given approval on 8 May to the military's plan for an amphibious landing at San Carlos Bay in the Falklands. The remaining units of the task force were given orders to sail south from Ascension Island.

On 12 May the requisitioned liner *Queen Elizabeth II* left Portsmouth carrying 3,000 men of the Welsh and Scots Guards to reinforce the Marines and Paratroopers who would launch the first wave of the assault and establish the beach-head.

With these military moves so far advanced, and the landing on the Falklands planned for 21 May (almost the last possible date for weather reasons), the Prime Minister grew increasingly irritated with those who kept urging her to make further diplomatic concessions. President Reagan was not the only one to catch the rough edge of her tongue on this issue. At a meeting of the war cabinet at Chequers on 17 May, she was bitterly sharp with Francis Pym and his team of senior Foreign Office diplomats who were drafting a final ultimatum to Argentina.

The unpleasant wrangling at this meeting showed Margaret Thatcher at her most aggressive. At various moments she accused the five Foreign Office representatives, Sir Anthony Parsons, Sir Nicholas Henderson, Sir Michael Palliser, Sir Antony Acland and Francis Pym of 'being wet, ready to sell out, unsupportive of British interests' and lacking resolution. At one point she asked, 'Did the Foreign Office have no principles?' For good measure, she added the insult that while the Foreign Office 'were content to be dishonest and consult with dishonest people, she was honest'.[26]

At this moment, John Nott attacked her for being unfair. She counter-attacked, shouting him down for being rude! These rough tactics described by various participants as: 'A totally horrendous bull session', or more loftily as 'Mrs Thatcher's High Noon with the FO',[27] caused its most senior official to offer his resignation. 'At one moment when I thought she was being unnecessarily critical', recalled Antony Acland, 'I said, "If you want to get another Permanent Under-Secretary, for heavens sake do".' After a long pause, the Prime Minister backed down. 'All right, no more Foreign Office bashing', she replied in a grudging tone.

It was on the tip of Acland's tongue to say, 'I don't know how long that will last, Prime Minister', but he restrained himself to, 'Thank you very much'.[28] The incident was symptomatic of her belligerent style towards the diplomatic service even though the record suggests that it served her well throughout the crisis.

The picture conveyed by the various accounts of this day at Chequers suggests a warmongering Prime Minister beating off an appeasement-minded Foreign

Office. It was not that simple. No one at this Chequers gathering had any real expectations that the junta would yield to the British ultimatum. But the Foreign Office team wanted to draft a document demonstrating 'beyond peradventure', as one of them kept saying, that the UK had gone to the furthest possible limits in offering every reasonable option to avoid war.[29] Margaret Thatcher regarded this exercise as a waste of time, with the added danger that it might trigger a new round of arguments to delay the landing of task-force troops on the Falkland Islands. A few days earlier she had sat on the front bench during a House of Commons debate on 13 May visibly seething as Francis Pym, followed by Ted Heath, had made out the case for further negotiations.

There was, however, one moment in this debate when the Prime Minister perked up. Her body language and her nodding signified complete agreement with what was the second major contribution by Enoch Powell to Parliament's consideration of the Falklands crisis. During the initial debate on 3 April he had sent shivers down many a spine when he had asserted in his compelling counter-tenor that the next few weeks would find out what metal the Iron Lady was made of. Now, in this 13 May debate, he rounded on Francis Pym, issuing a veiled demand for his resignation on the grounds that the Foreign Secretary had made concessions radically different from the basis on which the task force had been despatched. 'If people doubt that . . .', continued Powell in tones ringing with menace, 'let them visualise the task force sailing back up the Atlantic and into Portsmouth harbour. Would those who sent them, would those who comprise that force, say "We achieved the purposes for which we set sail"? Of course not.'[30]

Although some dissented from Enoch Powell's argument, Margaret Thatcher wholeheartedly agreed with it. In case there was any doubt about it, her energetic PPS, Ian Gow, bustled around the committee-room corridor just before the 1922 Committee of Conservative back-benchers held its weekly meeting. He was handing out the Hansard transcripts of this second warning from Enoch the Oracle, telling all and sundry that 'The Lady has taken it to heart'.[31] Once again the Foreign Secretary was clearly in the Prime Minister's bad books. Not surprisingly Pym had a bruising reception at the 1922, which he left to shouts of 'No surrender!' and 'No appeasement', after his poorly received remarks. I was one of the louder shouters. A couple of days later, Ian Gow sidled up to me and murmured in his quaint style: 'The Queen's First Minister has asked me to thank the Honourable Member for Thanet South for his most welcome support at the 1922 Committee.'[32]

Because of the tension between the Prime Minister and her Foreign Secretary, there was considerable ambiguity in the British government's position during the week before the task force landed its men on the Falklands. However, there was no such ambivalence in the mind of Margaret Thatcher. Two days before she went head to head with her senior diplomats in that highly charged session at Chequers, she addressed a conference of Scottish Conservatives at Perth. She told them 'I should not be doing my duty if I did not warn you in the simplest and clearest terms . . . a negotiated settlement may prove to be unsustainable'.[33]

She was right in her warning for, as expected, the Argentine junta rejected Britain's final ultimatum on 19 May. The search for a peaceful settlement was over. The Prime Minister announced this to the House of Commons, and simultaneously published a white paper setting out the history of the failed peace process. She also withdrew any concessions that had been offered during the abortive negotiations. The decks were now cleared for war.[34]

REFLECTION

The unity in Parliament that greeted the publication of the white paper was a vindication of Margaret Thatcher's strategy. From the outset she had consistently believed that diplomatic negotiations would never end the Argentine occupation of the Falklands. She faced massive pressure from the Americans, the UN and her own Foreign Secretary to back down from this stance but, apart from one brief wobble caused by the cabinet vote on 5 May, she refused to do so. As a result of her steadfast determination she kept faith with both the Falkland Islanders and with the will of Parliament.

It is hard to believe that any other politician would have remained so straightforward in purpose and so single minded in commitment. It was the force of her personality and the strength of her certainty that enabled her to stand firm. The people who appreciated this most were the men who were about to do the fighting.

21

The Falklands War III
Victory

THE BATTLE FOR THE FALKLANDS

Margaret Thatcher had an exceptionally good relationship with the military. Somehow it filtered down from senior commanders to junior officers and through the ranks that this Prime Minister was hewn from a block of granite quite different from other politicians. In the context of fighting a war, her moral certainty, determination and absolute support for 'our boys', as she often called them, was a boost to their morale. She also strengthened the senior commanders by not second guessing their plans.

On 18 May, the Prime Minister and the war cabinet gathered in the Ministry of Defence to receive a final briefing from the Chiefs of Staff on the prospects for landing Royal Marines and Paratroopers of the task force at the chosen location of San Carlos Bay. It was made clear, for the first time to the politicians, how enormous the risks were, given the threat posed by the Argentine Air Force. If the Prime Minister was shaken, she did not show it. She asked many questions to increase her understanding of the situation, but not in any way to challenge the tactics that she strongly supported. 'Her biggest concern in her questioning was to make sure the number of casualties would be minimised', recalled the Cabinet Secretary, Sir Robert Armstrong.[1]

Once the political decision to approve the sending in of the task force had been taken by the war cabinet and endorsed by the full cabinet, the die was cast. The date of the landing, 21 May, was a closely guarded secret. On that day, as the counter-invasion got under way, Margaret Thatcher, as MP for Finchley, was scheduled to be carrying out constituency engagements. She had to open a warehouse, accept a bouquet of roses, meet a delegation of local residents concerned about a planning problem and give a speech at the retirement party of her agent. The next day, Carol asked her how on earth she could carry out her constituency programme looking so calm and unruffled in the press photographs. 'Of course, all my thoughts were in the South Atlantic. I was desperately worried . . . it was just so important that the landing went right', her mother replied. 'But if I hadn't gone to the function people would have thought something was wrong – I had to carry on as normal.'[2]

Margaret Thatcher kept up a brave front of looking normal. But on her way to Finchley she was thrown by one early piece of bad news from the landing ground: two Gazelle helicopters had been shot down with three fatalities. She went ahead with the warehouse opening at which a Royal Marines band was playing. Their martial music was too much for her at the moment when she knew the Marines were approaching the beaches in their landing craft. By the time she left she was fighting back tears of anxiety. But during a later constituency engagement, a retirement party for her agent, there came better news. The beach-head had been established at San Carlos Bay. 'That's it. That's what I've been waiting for all day. Let's go!' declared Margaret Thatcher in uplifted spirits.[3] As she walked back into Downing Street she paused to tell the expectant crowd: 'These are nervous days, but we have marvellous fighting forces; everyone is behind them. We are fighting a just cause, and we wish them Godspeed.'[4]

On the beaches of San Carlos the landings went better than expected, with 4,000 Marines and Paras coming safely ashore. But in San Carlos Bay the ships of the task force were coming under sustained and sometimes devastating attack. The British commanders had underestimated the courage and effectiveness of the Argentine pilots, while overestimating the fire-power and reliability of the task force's air defences.

In the first hours of daylight the frigate HMS *Ardent* was sunk, another frigate HMS *Argonaut* was badly damaged, and so was the destroyer HMS *Brilliant*. In the middle of the fiercest fighting the Royal Navy had seen since the Second World War, Margaret Thatcher visited the Fleet Headquarters at Northwood. She understood at first hand from briefings in the Operations Room the savagery of the attacks by the Argentine's Mirage, Skyhawk, Pucara and Aermacchi aircraft flying across San Carlos water at suicidally low heights to direct their bombs and missiles at the British ships.

'I did my best to seem confident', she later recalled. But her inner feelings were different. She could hardly believe that the *Canberra*, requisitioned as a troop ship for 3,000 men, could survive the constant bombardment aimed at her. She well understood that this phase of the battle was finely balanced. As she left Northwood to return to Chequers, the Prime Minister drew aside the task-force commander, Admiral Sir John Fieldhouse. When they were out of earshot she asked him, 'How long can we go on taking this kind of punishment?'[5] His verbatim reply was not recorded, but seems to have been a mixture of continuing anxiety combined with the reassurance that the Argentine Air Force were taking heavy losses from the British Harriers and their US-supplied Sidewinder missiles.

Although Margaret Thatcher's weekend at Chequers and the week ahead of her were fraught with worry, she stuck to her self-imposed rule of not telephoning task-force headquarters at Northwood to ask for news. This restraint was admirable but it created its own tensions. Late at night in the flat above No. 10, surrounded only by her family, Carol asked her mother a question about the day's progress and was given the anguished reply: 'I wish I knew, I wish I knew.' To which Denis calmly responded, 'That is how it is in a war'.[6]

The early reports the Prime Minister did receive in the first few days after the landing at San Carlos Bay often contained bad news. On Tuesday 25 May she was working late in her room in the House of Commons when John Nott came in to tell her that the destroyer HMS *Coventry* had been bombed by Argentine aircraft and was sinking. Nineteen of the crew were lost.

Later that night the duty clerk at No. 10 told her that the 18,000-ton roll-on-roll-off container ship the *Atlantic Conveyor* had been hit by two Exocet missiles and was sinking. Margaret Thatcher knew that this ship contained some of the most vital re-supplies of the war including nineteen Harrier aircraft, four Chinook and seven Wessex helicopters, essential to the movement of troops.

The loss of the *Atlantic Conveyor* caused her a sleepless night of worry, inflamed by an Argentine radio report that one of Britain's two aircraft carriers, HMS *Illustrious*, had been attacked and damaged. In the midst of these traumas, Denis woke up to find his wife sitting on the end of the bed in floods of tears. 'Oh no, oh no! Another ship! All my young men!' she sobbed. He sat down beside her and said, 'That's what war's like, love. I've been in one. I know.'[7]

Her son as well as her husband helped to calm her down. Mark pinned a *billet doux* to her pillow with the words, 'Mum, I'm so sorry. Love M', followed by some lines by Kipling she had taught him to recite as a child:

Dear-bought and clear, a thousand year,
Our fathers' title runs.
Make we likewise their sacrifice,
Defrauding not our sons.[8]

When morning came, the sacrifices were not quite as bad as the Prime
Minister had feared. The radio report of an attack on *Illustrious* turned out to
be a false alarm. Although the *Atlantic Conveyor* had been sunk, her cargo of
Harriers had been flown to safety two days earlier. But the six Wessex and
three Chinook helicopters, winter tents for 4,500 men, runway and fuelling
equipment were at the bottom of the South Atlantic along with the ship, the
ship's captain and eleven members of the crew. These losses were a severe blow
to the logistics of moving Marines and Paras across East Falkland towards the
capital of Port Stanley.

On the ground at San Carlos, the bridgehead was well established but the
land campaign was taking time to get under way. The delays led to acute frustrations at 10 Downing Street. For the first and only time in the war there were
tensions between the Prime Minister and her Chiefs of Staff. Some members
of the war cabinet fretted openly that the land forces were being too cautious
and that their commander, delayed on board the liner *Queen Elizabeth II*,
requisitioned as a troop ship, was taking too long to arrive. 'It might have been
quicker by gondola', was Margaret Thatcher's tart comment.[9]

The Prime Minister's impatience boiled over into making one bad judgement.
Shortly before the major landings began, Admiral Lewin reported that there
was an opportunity to sink the enemy aircraft carrier *Veinticinco de Mayo*.
It posed a potential threat to the ships of the task force, and was a legitimate
target. But the carrier was within Argentine territorial waters. Margaret Thatcher
was in favour of attacking her. John Nott took the opposite view. He recalled:

We had an enormous argument. I said that we were going to recapture the Islands
within a month anyway. If we sank the *Veinticinco de Mayo* in its own territorial waters,
it would cause international uproar and turn the whole of South America against us.
In the end, I carried my case with the war cabinet. It was our only major disagreement.[10]

While this naval argument was taking place in London, the military took a
bold initiative in the land war by sending the 2nd battalion of the Parachute

Regiment out of the bridgehead with orders to capture Darwin and Goose Green. Margaret Thatcher was incandescent with the BBC when news of the imminent movement towards Goose Green was broadcast on the World Service before 2nd Para had launched their attack. Possibly as a result of these leaks, British casualties were heavier than expected. They included the battalion commander Colonel 'H' Jones, who was awarded a posthumous Victoria Cross after the recapture of Goose Green. Margaret Thatcher was said to be more troubled by his death than by any other loss of the war, with the exception of the sinking of HMS *Sheffield*.[11]

On 31 May, Admiral John Pointdexter, the Deputy National Security Advisor at the White House, telephoned Robert Armstrong to set up a call on the hot-line between the President and the Prime Minister. As it was hastily arranged, neither the Cabinet Secretary nor the Prime Minister were fully briefed about what would be on the agenda, although Margaret Thatcher may have had some indications from the British Embassy in Washington that Reagan was likely to suggest a cease-fire.

The call began affably enough, with the President congratulating the Prime Minister on demonstrating to the world that unprovoked aggression did not pay, and asking, 'How's it going down there?'

He received a ten-minute monologue in reply. When Margaret Thatcher paused for breath, Reagan broke his silence to ask a further question about the military situation. He was answered with a second lengthy monologue. During this part of the conversation, Reagan held up the receiver to his staff in the Oval Office, with his hand over the mouthpiece, and said with a grin, 'Isn't she marvellous?'[12]

Eventually, the President was able to intervene for long enough to indicate the purpose of his call. He said he wanted to share 'some of our ideas on how we might capitalise on the success you've had with a diplomatic initiative'. He seemed to be suggesting that a contact group could be used as intermediaries between the combatants. 'I think an effort to show what we're all still willing to seek a settlement . . . would undercut the effort of . . . the leftists in South America who are actively seeking to exploit this crisis. Now, I'm thinking about this plan . . .'

The Prime Minister reacted badly. She was not going to consider further diplomacy. She interrupted the President before he had begun to explain what his plan might be. 'This is democracy and our island', she declared, 'and the very worst thing for democracy would be if we failed now.'

'Yes . . .' began Reagan, only to be interrupted again before he had opened the sentence.

'Ron, I'm not handing over', blazed Margaret Thatcher. 'I'm not handing over the island now. I can't lose the lives and blood of our soldiers to hand the islands over to a contact [group]. It's not possible.'

'Margaret, but I thought that part of this proposal . . .'

'You are surely not asking me, Ron, after we've lost some of our finest young men, you are surely not saying, that after the Argentine withdrawal, that our forces, and our administration, become immediately idle? I had to go to immense distances and mobilise half my country. I just had to go.'

'Margaret, I . . .'

'I wonder if anyone over there realises, I'd like to ask them. Just supposing Alaska was invaded? Now you've put all your people up there to retake it and someone suggested that a contact could come in . . . you wouldn't do it!'

'No, no, although, Margaret, I have to say I don't quite think Alaska is a similar situation.'

'More or less so', she snapped back.

'Yes, well . . . Well, Margaret, I know that I've intruded and I know how . . .'[13]

As the call ended it was clear that the President of the United States had been driven into stumbling silence by the irresistible force of Margaret Thatcher. 'He came off sounding even more of a wimp than Jimmy Carter',[14] was the comment of NSC aide, Jim Rentschler, who had been listening to the call. Reagan's presentation had been so inadequate that it was far from clear to the listeners on the hot-line in No. 10 what the American proposal had actually been. When the Cabinet Secretary, Robert Armstrong, later sought clarification from Admiral Pointdexter, the Deputy National Security adviser said, chuckling: 'Well, we won't try that again! You see, we had a disagreeable message to convey to you Brits and, because it was disagreeable, we thought it had better be delivered by the President to the Prime Minister personally. Unfortunately, the President wasn't able to get a word in edgeways!'[15]

In the immediate aftermath of the hot-line call, Margaret Thatcher was in a furious temper. She called the British Ambassador in Washington, Sir Nicholas Henderson, to berate him for not giving her proper warning about what Reagan

The Roberts family on the day Margaret's father became Mayor of Grantham, November 1945. From left to right: Muriel, Alfred, Beatrice and Margaret.

All smiles at a Kent
Conservative dance
from three candidates
in the 1950 election:
Margaret Roberts (*left*)
Ted Heath (*centre*) and
Pat Hornsby-Smith (*right*),
1950.

Margaret Roberts, Conservative
Candidate for Dartford canvasses
a voter during the 1951 General
Election in Attlee Drive.

On their Wedding Day, 13 December 1951, Margaret and Denis Thatcher emerge from Wesley's Chapel, Mile End Road, London.

9 November 1959, Margaret Thatcher watches her children Carol and Mark playing together in unusual harmony.

The new Member of Parliament for Finchley (elected 1959) becomes the first of her intake to be appointed a junior minister in 1961. She is Parliamentary Secretary at the Ministry of Pensions and National Insurance.

Margaret Thatcher flutters her fingers to the press after defeating Ted Heath on the first ballot of the Tory leadership election, February 1975.

Leading the Conservative campaign for a Yes Vote in the 1975 Referendum vote on Britain's EEC membership in uneasy alliance with Ted Heath.

4 May 1979, the morning of victory. Prime Minister-elect Margaret Thatcher waves to the crowd outside her home in Flood Street.

Her first diplomatic success was solving the crisis over Rhodesia, 1979–80. It began by winning over Zambia's President Kenneth Kaunda at the Commonwealth Heads of Government conference in Lusaka. Denis said that this dance 'took the trick.'

Political campaigning in 1980 with Ian Gow MP. He was her first Parliamentary Private Secretary (1979–83), and her wisest, wittiest and warmest supporter until his assassination by the IRA in 1990.

Margaret Thatcher and her most influential Foreign Secretary Lord Carrington leaving Heathrow for yet another contentious European Summit meeting, June 1980. Immediately behind them is the Cabinet Secretary Sir Robert Armstrong.

Engaging with King Fahd of Saudi Arabia, April 1981. Her secret communications with him won Britain the multi-billion Al Yamamah defence exports contract, which secured over 50,000 jobs in the UK.

'He likes women, you know' was Margaret Thatcher's comment to her Cabinet Secretary Sir Robert Armstrong after her first meeting with President François Mitterrand of France. Charles Powell, her closest and longest serving Private Secretary, 1983–1990, is on the right behind Mitterrand.

Visiting 'Our Boys' at Port Stanley in January 1983, seven months after the liberation of the Falkland Islands.

Welcoming Mikhail Gorbachev to Chequers, December 1984. Sparks flew during their five-hour lunch, but they built a relationship, which helped bring about the ending of the Cold War.

The Iron Lady test-drives Britain's new Challenger tank, September 1986. As usual she had a photogenic eye for striking attire and a patriotic setting.

Taking Russia by storm and charm. Margaret Thatcher's visit to Moscow (seen here with monks from the Trinity Sergius Monastery at Zagorsk) established her as an icon of Western freedom to the people of the Soviet Union, March 1987.

Facing questions from the media in 1986 alongside her formidable Press Secretary Bernard Ingham. 'You and I, Bernard, are not smooth people,' she told him.

The President and the Prime Minister enjoying each other's company on the patio of the White House, July 1987. Together they strengthened the Special Relationship to a level unequalled since the days of Roosevelt and Churchill.

Deceptively warm smiles from her Cabinet in July 1989. But away from the camera the personality clashes were becoming explosive. They resulted in the resignation of her Foreign Secretary Sir Geoffrey Howe and her Chancellor Nigel Lawson.

Dear Margaret - As you can see, I agree with every word you are saying. I always do. Warmest Friendship.
Sincerely Ron

(*Top*) Speaking at her No. 10 Downing Street dinner in honour of President Reagan with Secretary of State George Shultz on her left, July 1988. (*Bottom*) Leaving Downing Street for the last time as Prime Minister, 28 November 1990.

The Queen arrives at Claridge's to attend Margaret Thatcher's 70th Birthday party on 16 October 1995.

With all good wishes
1996.
Margaret T.

Windswept on Rannoch Moor.
Margaret Thatcher on 'The Craiggie',
the highest peak on the Scottish
estate of Lord Pearson of Rannoch.
The expression on her face may
reflect the pain and poignancy
of her enforced retirement years.

'I just want to show him we won',
said Margaret Thatcher as she
posed for this photograph in front
of a statue of Lenin in the woods
of Sir James Goldsmith's estate at
Montjeu in France, in 1997. *Left
to right*: Denis Thatcher, Biddy
Cash, Margaret Thatcher and
Sir James Goldsmith. Amateur
picture taken by Bill Cash MP.

Arriving early for the opening of Parliament, the recently widowed Baroness Thatcher of Kesteven looks a lonely figure in the House of Lords, 26 November 2003.

Surrounded by Chelsea Pensioners in February 2008 at the Royal Hospital, which became her second home in old age and the last resting place for her ashes.

was going to say. She was indignant about the President. She kept repeating that she was 'dismayed by his attitude' and 'most upset'.

'We have lost a lot of blood and it's the best blood', Margaret Thatcher expostulated. 'Do they not realise that it is an issue of principle? We cannot surrender principles for expediency.' She ended by denouncing the President's call as, 'pure Haigism'.[16]

In fact, this was a time when US policy towards the UK over the Falklands was neither pure nor clear. It was more like 'duck soup', a phrase from a Marx Brothers movie that Alexander Haig had applied to the confused military situation on the Islands. It might just as well have been used to describe the confused state of play in Washington.

The Pentagon, under the Anglophile Caspar Weinberger, was being extra-ordinarily helpful to Britain's armed forces. So was the CIA in providing invaluable signals intelligence (SIGINT) from Argentina. However, in the State Department's offices at Foggy Bottom there was just fog, thickened by feuding and miscommunication of the key foreign-policy players of the administration, Alexander Haig, Jeane Kirkpatrick and the President's National Security Adviser, Judge William P. Clark. Their difficulties were set to get worse. Thatcher and Reagan were scheduled to meet again after their non-dialogue on the hot-line, at the G7 summit at Versailles. The Prime Minister, preparing for the encounter, told Sir Nicholas Henderson that she would be very reasonable in her con-versation with the President, 'provided I get my way'.[17] She did.

Before she met the President of the United States, Margaret Thatcher made a final effort to communicate with the President of Argentina. On 2 June, the day on which she flew to Paris to attend the G7 meeting, she drafted a telegram to General Galtieri:

> I am sending you this personal message because I want to be sure that you fully under-stand the situation and the choice which now faces your country, your government and yourself.
>
> The decisive battle in the Falkland Islands (Malvinas) is about to begin. With your military experience you must be in no doubt as to the outcome. In a few days, the British flag will once again be flying over Port Stanley. In a few days also, your eyes and mine will be reading the casualty lists. On my side, grief will be tempered by the knowledge that these men died for freedom, justice, and the rule of law. And on your side? Only you can answer that.[18]

This eloquent draft message, for some unknown reason, was never sent. If it had been delivered, the moral clarity of the Prime Minister would have been unlikely to elicit a comparable reply from the confused and chaotic leadership in Buenos Aires. Nor was it yet clear whether the leadership of the United States had seen the issues of the Falklands in the same stark right versus wrong terms that were being so bluntly stated to Galtieri.

There were no note-takers or officials present at the one-on-one meeting that took place between Margaret Thatcher and Ronald Reagan in the US Ambassador's residence on the rue du Faubourg St Honoré on Thursday 3 June. But the important result was that Reagan came to recognise that there would be no movement from Britain about a cease-fire, let alone a settlement, on the Falklands until after the recapture of Port Stanley. So the President reaffirmed his support for the Prime Minister, thus causing intense irritation to Alexander Haig who reportedly flew into a rage, threatening to resign.

It was not the only problem the US Secretary of State was having in Paris. At the United Nations, a resolution had been tabled in early June by Panama and Spain calling for an immediate cease-fire in the Falklands. It came to the vote on Friday 4 June. Britain vetoed it. So did the United States. But seconds after the vote, US Ambassador Jeane Kirkpatrick announced she had voted the wrong way. In Paris, Alexander Haig had changed his mind and decided to abstain on the resolution. But this instruction reached Mrs Kirkpatrick too late, as she explained to incredulous reporters at the UN. 'You don't understand it? I don't understand it either', she declared on the record.[19]

This American ineptitude looked even worse when members of the press asked President Reagan about the *volte-face* at the UN, just as he was sitting down to lunch, next to Margaret Thatcher, at the Palace of Versailles. As he had not been briefed on the flip-flop of Jeane Kirkpatrick in New York, the President offered the lame response, 'You've caught me a long way from there'. Margaret Thatcher, astonished by the President's ignorance, was more skilful at not explaining the inexplicable as the reporters tried to question her. 'I do not give interviews over lunch', she grandly retorted, making it sound like she was upholding the rules of social etiquette.[20]

In any case she had more pressing military issues on her mind. Having seen off the American, G7 and UN pressures for a cease-fire with considerable determination she was now awaiting the final push of British forces towards the recapture of Port Stanley and the Falkland Islands.

VICTORY

It took some fierce fighting on the Islands before the mission could be accomplished. During the last week of the conflict, Margaret Thatcher had to rely mainly on the radio for news as she continued her resolve not to telephone the HQ at Northwood while the battle was under way.

Some of the news was tragic. The landing ship *Sir Galahad*, carrying troops and munitions, was attacked by Argentine Skyhawks killing fifty-one servicemen (mostly from the Welsh Guards) and injuring forty-six others, many with terrible burns. The Prime Minister heard about the *Sir Galahad* disaster as she was welcoming President Reagan to Britain. His visit, which included a horse ride with the Queen at Windsor and an address to both Houses of Parliament, passed off smoothly and ceremoniously. But the differences over Falklands diplomacy had left rifts in the 'special relationship', which took later efforts by both the President and Prime Minister to heal.*

After Reagan's departure, Margaret Thatcher presided over the last meeting of the war cabinet before the final push on Port Stanley began on Friday 11 June. The military decisions about the assault's timing and method were left entirely to the land forces commander, Major-General Jeremy Moore. The next day the Prime Minister, dressed in black, watched a rain-soaked Trooping of the Colour on Horse Guards' Parade. 'There was so much to mourn', was how she put it as the latest casualties were weighing heavily on her mind.[21]

After the Trooping, she gave a lunch party for some thirty children of her personal 10 Downing Street staff. Apart from their parents, only a handful of adults were present, including John Nott and Rex Hunt, the deposed Governor of the Falklands. Nott asked his hostess who had prepared the lunch. 'Oh, I did', replied the Prime Minister. 'I stayed up late last night to put a meal together.'[22] Even in the middle of a war, Margaret Thatcher found the energy to be kind and hospitable to the families of her inner circle of staffers.

---

* See Chapter 25.

Later that afternoon, she drove to Northwood to be briefed on the early stages of the battles around Port Stanley. She learned that after meeting some fierce resistance, British forces were achieving all their military objectives. By the following morning, the Argentine conscripts were retreating in large numbers. When the war cabinet met on Monday 14 June, ministers were startled by the speed of the enemy's collapse. Their defeat was now a certainty. Margaret Thatcher's preoccupation for the next few hours was when and how to announce it.

Since the Falklands War had effectively begun in the House of Commons, and since many of its most dramatic moments had unfolded there, she took the decision to declare victory in the same arena. In order to make this declaration a total surprise, she instructed that throughout the day all military information from the Islands was to be kept under a strict embargo of secrecy.

Even though the final surrender terms had not been signed in Port Stanley, the Prime Minister arrived at Westminster around 9.30 p.m. on the night of 14 June to prepare to deliver her unscheduled announcement to the House. So unexpected was her arrival that she found her room locked. She had to hang around in the corridors for several farcical minutes until the Chief Whip's assistant, Murdo Maclean, could find a spare key.

Once admitted to her office, she wrote out her own speaking note which had to begin with the words, 'On a point of order, Mr Speaker'. Under an archaic rule, this was the only way she could intervene in the proceedings of the House at that hour. No one was expecting a dramatic prime ministerial intervention after a routine 10 p.m. division. Many MPs were heading for their cars and their beds, until the whips passed the word round that there was going to be a statement on the Falklands after the vote. 'What is it about?' was a frequent question in the lobbies. Although it was known that the military operations were going well, the general expectation among MPs was that there would be several more days of fighting before the Islands were recaptured.

At 10.12 p.m., Margaret Thatcher rose from her place on the front bench and said:

On a point of order, Mr Speaker. May I give the House the latest information about the battle of the Falklands? After successful attacks last night, General Moore decided to press forward. The Argentines retreated. Our forces reached the outskirts of Port

Stanley. Large numbers of Argentine soldiers threw down their weapons. They are reported to be flying white flags over Port Stanley. Our troops have been ordered not to fire except in self-defence. Talks are now in progress between General Menendez and our Deputy Commander, Brigadier Waters, about the surrender of the Argentine forces on East and West Falkland. I shall report further to the House tomorrow.[23]

Immediately, there were gasps of astonishment, followed by a roar of cheering, stamping and waving of order papers. At first, the enthusiasm seemed to be coming mainly from the Tory benches. But Michael Foot, as Leader of the Opposition, quickly made the celebrations universal, with a generous tribute to the British forces, 'and, if I may say so, to the right Hon. Lady'.[24]

A mere seventy-two days after the tempestuous debate at the nadir of Britain's Falklands shame, the House of Commons was united in celebrating our Falklands victory. It was a momentous parliamentary occasion. The cheers rolled on and on, fuelled by a combination of surprise, relief and heartfelt rejoicing.

A few moments later, we all tumbled joyfully out of the chamber. I bumped into Alan Clark and slapped him on the back, congratulating him on his many robust speeches and broadcasts throughout the crisis. 'Don't suck up to me', he said. 'Come on, let's see if we can blow a kiss to the Lady.' With that, we both legged it through the aye lobby corridor to the back of the Speaker's chair, where Margaret Thatcher was just emerging surrounded by a crush of ministerial acolytes. 'Hear, hear, hear!' I boomed in her direction from three yards away. Her face lit up with a golden smile.

Alan Clark got even closer. He was far bolder and almost passionate in his compliments. 'Prime Minister only you could have done this', he began. 'Your place in history is assured.' He tilted his upper body and knees forward in a cross between a bow and a genuflection.

'If you'd been wearing a cloak you'd have thrown it on the ground in front of her', I teased him afterwards.[25] Clark was right to seize his moment for praising her. He reflected the mood of the House and of the country.

The festive mood continued in the Prime Minister's room in the Commons. The key politicians in the war cabinet, along with Robert Armstrong, Antony Acland and Admiral Lewin, assembled there. Denis Thatcher poured out generous libations of champagne. Willie Whitelaw proposed a toast. 'I don't want to make a speech, but I do want to congratulate you, Margaret', he began. 'I don't think any other politician in the country would have done what you decided to do, to embark on this enterprise and to bring it to a successful conclusion.'[26] The Prime Minister was too overcome to reply. Her tears may have been tears of joy, but they were surely mingled with tears of relief. The Falklands War had been won but, as the Duke of Wellington said of Waterloo, 'It was a damned close run thing'.[27]

REFLECTION

The Falklands War will go down in history as Margaret Thatcher's finest hour. She well deserved the acclaim she received for her constitutional propriety, her commitment to redeeming Britain's national honour and her personal courage.

The constitutional arrangements were impeccable. Later in her time as Prime Minister, she was sometimes accused of riding roughshod over her cabinet, failing to respect Parliament and even of running an 'elective dictatorship'.* None of these criticisms could be applied to her conduct of the conflict. She set up the right form of governance. The small war cabinet sought authority on all major decisions from the full cabinet. The civil and military sides of the administration worked in harmony. The advice of the Chiefs of Staff was always followed. The reporting to Parliament was punctilious.

Margaret Thatcher's constitutional propriety in leading the Falklands War contrasts sharply with Tony Blair's much-criticised 'sofa government' – his alleged manipulation of small groups of ministers during the Iraq War, twenty-one years later.

From the beginning the Falklands conflict was fought with a remarkable degree of parliamentary and public approval. Margaret Thatcher tapped into those feelings with an instinctive sense that national honour was the real prize at stake. Once the task force had sailed she realised, almost alone among the country's senior politicians, that there could be no going back without the recapturing of the Islands by military force. She read the minds of the junta in

---

* The phrase was originally coined by Lord Hailsham in an earlier context to describe the power of a government with a large majority. It was often applied to the Thatcher style of leadership in her second and third terms.

Buenos Aires far more clearly than various American, UN and British diplomats. They earnestly hoped that reasonableness and willingness to compromise would prevail. She understood that these hopes had no chance of being fulfilled.

Even with that understanding, it took immense courage on the part of the British Prime Minister to keep saying 'No' forcefully to the well-meaning if muddled peace seekers; particularly Haig, Pym and assorted intermediaries.

If her diplomatic steadfastness was remarkable, it was matched by her unflinching willingness to accept the military risks. If a British aircraft carrier had been lost, the whole operation might have been regarded as a failure, and her resolution would have been condemned as recklessness.

Did her determination show a courage that could only have been displayed by a woman? Her Defence Secretary, John Nott, thinks so.

> This was undoubtedly a woman's war. Margaret Thatcher did not have any traces of men's hesitancy. She had made up her mind to get the Falkland Islands back, to avenge our national dishonour. I cannot think of any recent male Prime Minister – Macmillan, Heath, Callaghan – who would not have sought a settlement. Margaret only pretended to do this. She went along with the diplomatic games played by Haig and company because to win she had to be seen to be trying diplomacy. But once faced with the crisis, she shut her mind to the risks of conducting such an operation 8,000 miles away. Her refusal to compromise was instinctive and un-masculine.[28]

The instincts of the Prime Minister were not without a maternal dimension. During the battle she revealed a tearful softness over casualties. Before the hostilities began, she 'was hugely concerned over the individual deaths of servicemen, that she knew would happen', recalled Cecil Parkinson. 'Her abiding preoccupation was that losses must be kept to the minimum.'[29] But once that preoccupation had been made clear to the military, she never wavered.

In the end, it was her courage that counted. It is academic whether it was the heart of a lion or a lioness that produced it. As Willie Whitelaw said on the night of victory, only she could have done it. By succeeding, she changed the mood of the country, the landscape of politics and her legacy to history.

The Falklands War was the turning point in Margaret Thatcher's story.

22

After the Falklands

THE CHANGING OF THE POLITICAL LANDSCAPE

The political rewards for Margaret Thatcher from the Falklands were enormous, but she was too cautious to exploit them quickly. With two years to go before the 1979 Parliament ran its full term, she dismissed the speculation that she might make an early dash to the polls in a 'khaki election'.[1] Instead, she engaged in a more subtle form of political opportunism. She exploited to the full the growing perception of her strong personality.

The Iron Lady and the Lady Not for Turning had been two uncertain stereotypes when they first made their appearances. After the Falklands they were not only accepted; they merged into two sides of the same re-valued coin.

Enoch Powell was the first to articulate this. Using the metaphor of metallurgy he had deployed in the epic parliamentary debate at the start of the war, he rose at Prime Minister's Questions on 17 June to remind the House how he had predicted that the Falklands crisis should determine what metal the Iron Lady was made of. With theatrical solemnity Professor Powell announced the results of his experiment: 'It shows that the substance under test consists of ferrous metal of the highest quality, that it is of exceptional tensile strength, is highly resistant to wear and tear and to stress, and may be used with advantage for all national purposes.'* Margaret Thatcher glowed at Powell's tribute. 'I am very grateful indeed to the right hon. Gentleman. I agree with every word he said', she replied.[2]

---

* Ian Gow framed the two Enoch Powell quotations about the metal of the Prime Minister during the Falklands crisis. She was so delighted that she hung them on the walls of her study at No. 10.

It took her no time to develop a link between the resolution she had demon-strated in the South Atlantic and the resolution that would be required to solve the most pressing economic, industrial and political issues at home.

The summer of 1982 was a festival of Falklands jubilation. One by one, the big ships of the task force came home – HMS *Illustrious, Hermes, Fearless, Intrepid* and the *Canberra* – amid scenes of high emotion at Portsmouth and Plymouth. One image that I vividly recall from the television news was that of a burly Marine coming ashore from HMS *Fearless* to embrace his wife with tears streaming down his face as he repeated 'Best bloody country in the world, this!'[3]

Margaret Thatcher tapped into these manifestations of national pride. In one of her first speeches after the war, at Cheltenham Racecourse, she alluded to the connection between conflicts to come at home and the war that had just been fought:

> We have ceased to be a nation in retreat. We have instead a newfound confidence – born in the economic battles at home and tested and found true 8,000 miles away . . . We rejoice that Britain has rekindled that spirit which has fired her for generations past and which today has begun to burn as brightly as before.[4]

Outwardly she seemed hyped up during the weeks of post-Falklands euphoria. Inwardly she was tired, perhaps suffering from a temporary burn-out after some seventy-two days of intense pressure and sleepless nights. She admitted as much to friends and family.

She became tetchy about post-Falklands pinpricks. She was incandescent with the BBC for its 'unpatriotic' (they said 'even-handed') reporting; insulted by the suggestions from Tam Dalyell MP that she had ordered the sinking of the *General Belgrano* to thwart the Peruvian peace initiative; and irritated with the Archbishop of Canterbury, Dr Robert Runcie, for including prayers for the Argentine dead in the Falklands Memorial Service at St Paul's Cathedral.

She was also dismayed at having to allow the setting up of a committee of senior Privy Councillors under the Chairmanship of Lord Franks, inquiring into the way the government handled the crisis in the period leading up to the conflict. Six months later, Franks came to the conclusion that the invasion could not have been anticipated or prevented by Britain since the Argentines themselves only decided to seize the Islands at a very late date. This exoneration was diplomatically generous but politically wise, even if a few critics called it a whitewash. For the Franks Committee deliberated against a background of national gratitude for a job well done. Although there clearly had been errors of judgement in political and intelligence areas before the war, none of the blame for them was apportioned to the Prime Minister. Margaret Thatcher's Falklands' luck held.

Her popularity was at its zenith when Parliament went into recess at the end of July. But she needed a rest so unusually for her she took a proper holiday, staying for ten days at a chateau in the Swiss Alps owned by Lady Glover.* On return, the Prime Minister was admitted to the Fitzroy Nuffield Hospital in Bryanston Square for surgery on her varicose veins. She discharged herself the same day as the operation, wearing trousers for the only time in her years at No. 10. Her general practitioner, Dr John Henderson, told reporters that he was 'completely overwhelmed . . . by the way Mrs Thatcher has recovered. She is really behaving as if nothing had happened . . . she simply won't allow herself to be ill'.[5]

What she was allowing herself to do was to rise above the political fray. For the next few months she soared to an extraordinary status somewhere between 'she who must be obeyed' and 'she who should not be criticised'. This was not achieved by wrapping herself in the Union Jack. She was circumspect about her triumph as a war leader, confining the Falklands to no more than a few sentences at the end of her speech to the Conservative Party Conference in October. Instead she entered the artificial world of soft imaging.

This was a strategic move suggested by Tim Bell to counter-balance her reputation as a Warrior Queen. Suddenly the women's magazines and the women's pages of the tabloids were full of prime ministerial interviews accentuating her feminine side – her hair, her favourite recipes, her clothes, her feelings as a mother, her taste in novels and her enjoyment of TV serials. The readers of *Vogue*, *Woman*, *Woman's Own*, the *Sun*, the *Sunday People* and the *News of the World* may have lapped this up. Those who knew the real

---

* Margaret Eleanor Glover, heiress wife of Sir Douglas Glover (1908–1982), former Conservative MP for Ormskirk, 1953–1970. 'The Widow Glover', as she was known in the No. 10 private office, had inherited from her first husband the 2,000-acre Schloss Freudenberg estate in Switzerland. It became Margaret Thatcher's favourite holiday retreat.

Margaret Thatcher had a double take or two when she professed to watch television drama series, read many novels, and to like nothing more than to just potter in the kitchen or the garden.

This charm offensive extended to the broadcast media. She appeared on both ITV and BBC children's programmes, achieving one of the highest-ever viewing audiences for her starring role on *Jim'll Fix It* with Jimmy Savile. Her memories of the Falklands campaign often featured in these broadcasts, particularly on the Remembrance Sunday edition of *Songs of Praise*, when she talked about the lives lost at Goose Green, and chose as her favourite memorial hymn:

O valiant hearts who to your glory came
Through dust of conflict and through battle flame[6]

She also relived the Falklands War in front of the television cameras when she made her first visit to the Islands in January 1983. It was an emotional tour of battlefields and war graves combined with meeting servicemen and enjoying parties hosted by grateful Falklanders. There were touches of comedy too, such as her insistence at rising at 5 a.m. on the morning of her departure with the demand, 'I haven't seen a penguin. I must see a penguin before I leave.'[7] Her energy levels exhausted everyone, not least Denis, who at one point had to restrain her from inspecting some discarded boxes of ammunition. 'For God's sake, woman, don't get out and count them.'[8]

If her non-political image needed any further polishing, it got it from a BBC documentary, *The Woman at No. 10*, shown in March 1983. This was soft journalism extended to soft furnishings. It drew comparisons with Jackie Kennedy's televised presentation of the White House a generation earlier. The complaisant interviewer on this prime ministerial guided tour of No. 10 was one of her favourite spiritual gurus, the anthropologist Sir Laurens van der Post, who had been a Chelsea neighbour in her Flood Street days. He gave her *carte blanche* to talk about her favourite paintings, porcelain and predecessors.

She seized her opportunities. 'I thought of Wellington very much because I was very upset at the people who lost their lives in the Falklands', she said, pointing to one portrait of the victor of Waterloo. 'The great Lord Salisbury was Prime Minister for thirteen years', was her comment on another picture on the walls of No. 10. Sitting in a chair in the Cabinet Room, she gestured towards a painting of Sir Robert Walpole: 'It is a great comfort to many of us that he stayed here for twenty-one years.'[9]

The not so subliminal message was that Margaret Thatcher had woven herself into the tapestry of Britain's military and political history. Like Walpole, Wellington, Salisbury and Churchill, she would be around for a long time.

The electorate had already taken this message on board. Before the Falklands she was rated as the country's most unpopular prime minister since polling was invented. With both Labour and the SDP well ahead of her, winning by-elections in Tory strongholds up to March 1982, her chances of remaining at No. 10 looked slender. One year later she bestrode the political landscape like a colossus. The polls proclaimed it and the public knew it. This success was not all down to the Falklands factor. She appeared to be winning on two other battlefields that the voters cared about – the economy and the trade unions.

THE ECONOMY AND THE UNIONS

The economy was on the move before the Falklands War started. Sir Geoffrey Howe's bold budget of 1981 had begun to produce its medicinal results. The most worrying symptom of the British disease, rising inflation, was being cured. By the end of 1982, the headline rate of inflation had fallen to below 5 per cent. After the price rise panics of the 1970s, when the Retail Price Index had fluctuated between 8 and 24 per cent, this stability was reassuring. With interest rates also coming down and living standards on the rise for those in work, Margaret Thatcher's economic policy was beginning to be credited with delivering at least some of what she had promised.

What was not being delivered was a reduction in unemployment. In August 1982 it soared to 3.3 million. Such a figure would have previously been a harbinger of electoral disaster for any government. Old hands still worried on this score. In the middle of the post-Falklands festivities, when the earliest voices began predicting a second term for Margaret Thatcher, her loyal deputy Willie Whitelaw was heard to warn: 'Nobody has ever won an election before with three million on the dole.'[10] But Norman Tebbit, who had joined the cabinet as Employment Secretary in September 1981, took a more sanguine view, persuading the Prime Minister that the jobless figure had reached a plateau, and that in any case the public were coming round to a different view of the causes of unemployment. Tebbit was right on both counts.

The sea change in the public's perception of unemployment was one of the most remarkable consequences of Margaret Thatcher's style of leadership. In the politics of the 1950s, 1960s and 1970s, governments had always been blamed for putting people out of work. In her didactic way of telling home truths, the Prime Minister had been sending out the message that jobs were lost by lack of international competitiveness, by over-manning, by the follies of mis-management and, above all, by trade-union militancy. Gradually it became clear that the public was starting to believe her. From their own experiences of daily life, the majority of the electorate grudgingly accepted that she was correct. Unemployment became the dog that did not bark in the night.

The domestic arena where Margaret Thatcher scored her most convincing victories was in confronting the power of the unions. The unions helped her by inflicting some of the worse damage on themselves. She accelerated the twilight of their authority by changing the law.

In January 1982, Norman Tebbit produced the government's second instalment of trade-union reform. He only just managed to have his Employ-ment Bill accepted by the cabinet after Margaret Thatcher had crushed the doubting voices by summing up vigorously in support of her abrasive new Employment Secretary. In fact the 'Chingford skin-head', as his detractors called him, produced a more subtle package than the Tory right were hoping for. The bill removed the immunity of trade-union funds from actions for damages resulting from secondary or sympathetic strike actions. It also tightened the restrictions on closed shops and made it easier for employers to dismiss per-sistent trouble-makers. Norman Tebbit wanted to make union ballots compulsory before strike action could be called. But Margaret Thatcher's political caution caused her to take a gradualist approach. She postponed such radical changes until 1984. Her moderation ensured a comparatively easy passage for the bill through Parliament.

Her first test of strength with the unions came over the 1980 steel strike. The British Steel Corporation (BSC) was faced with a demand for a 20 per cent wage increase, which could not possibly be paid on any economic basis. The steel unions, who called a strike in support of their pay claim, came to No. 10 to ask the government to help BSC settle the dispute with 'new money'.[11] Margaret Thatcher firmly pointed out that there was no such thing.

In the first three months of the strike, steel stocks diminished and officials at the Department of Industry pressed their Secretary of State, Sir Keith Joseph, to settle the dispute by finding extra pockets of pubic money. For all his strict monetarist principles, Sir Keith was inclined to see all sides of the question too easily, so he returned at least three times to No. 10 to try and get the Prime Minister's agreement to a strike settling formula. She would have none of it. 'Don't wobble, Keith',[12] she instructed. Her determination won the day.

In the thirteenth week of the strike, steel stocks mysteriously began to rise because private companies discovered how to import steel in containers using non-union ports. By April the unions settled their pay claim for a disappointing increase – 3 per cent below the rate of inflation. The strike was broken – the first time this had happened to a major union for over twenty years. It was a seminal moment in the power struggle between Margaret Thatcher and the unions, reinforced soon after the Falklands victory when in 1982 she saw off the strikers in two other fiefdoms – the railways and the National Health Service.

In spite of such successes, Margaret Thatcher did not have everything her own way. She continued to look for deeper cuts in public spending. In the summer of 1982, her Downing Street think tank, the Central Policy Review Staff (CPRS), produced a paper packed with radical ideas. It called for funding the NHS with a new system of private health insurance; charging for visits to the doctor; ending state funding for all institutions of higher education, and slashing the social security budget by stopping all welfare benefits from rising with inflation. When this wish list was circulated around Whitehall, according to Nigel Lawson, 'it caused the nearest thing to a cabinet riot in the history of the Thatcher administration'.[13] The wets and the traditionalists were united in denouncing the CPRS proposals, which were largely backed by an accompanying paper from the Treasury.

Ministers attacked these ideas from all points on the political compass. The usually supportive Lord Hailsham called them 'the worst mistake the Government has made since it came to power'.[14] The resident contrarian, Peter Walker, went ballistic in his criticisms and organised the cabinet opposition. He leaked the CPRS paper and the details of the ministerial rebellion against it to The Economist,[15] whose story caused an explosion.

Margaret Thatcher's handling of this foreseeable furore revealed aspects of her personality which were unedifying. They included poor judgement and deceit. Not only should it have been obvious to her that the CPRS agenda could not possibly have been acceptable politically, but she was warned of this by the most neutral and favourable source of advice, her own private office at No. 10.

The Treasury civil servant who had been appointed as her Private Secretary for Economic Affairs was Michael Scholar. He immediately saw the dangers of the paper, and tried to persuade the head of the CPRS, John Sparrow, to tone down the right-wing radicalism. But the Prime Minister had the bit between her teeth, and rejected all recommendations to dilute the proposals or to restrict their dissemination. 'Does anyone imagine she would have dared to circulate the paper if it hadn't been for Falklands euphoria?'[16] Jim Prior privately asked his colleagues. This correctly identified hubris was followed by the inevitable nemesis. The cabinet was never going to agree to the onslaught on educational, welfare and NHS spending that the Prime Minister was implicitly advocating. She had to retreat under heavy fire. Some of it became personal. 'Why on earth did you allow this paper to be circulated?' she was asked, towards the end of the angry cabinet meeting of 9 September. 'I didn't', she replied defensively, pointing her finger at her Private Secretary, who was sitting at the end of the room. 'Michael circulated it.'[17]

This was untrue. Michael Scholar had done his best to persuade the Prime Minister to avoid the confrontation that was now taking place. He kept silent, and bore the opprobrium as all eyes turned reproachfully towards him. Although he was far too good a Private Secretary to deny his Prime Minister, he privately felt that Margaret Thatcher had let herself down.

In the face of the near riot by most of her cabinet ministers, the Prime Minister had to give up. She yielded with another display of bad grace, saying in a petulant tone, 'All right then, shelve it'.[18]

It was not quite her last attempt to investigate ways of radically reforming the NHS. Soon after this reversal in cabinet, she returned to the subject at a time when the Health Secretary, Norman Fowler, was out of the country studying the worldwide AIDS crisis. In his absence, the Prime Minister reached out to the Permanent Secretary at the Department of Health and Social Security, Sir Kenneth Stowe, commissioning him to produce a brief on the question of whether there were more sustainable ways of running Britain's health-care system with the users of the service contributing more towards its cost.

Norman Fowler, on return from his travels, was not best pleased to discover that his department was preparing a memorandum for the Prime Minister on how the whole basis of the NHS might be changed. He need not have worried. Ken Stowe, well trusted by Margaret Thatcher since his time as her first Private Secretary at No. 10, produced a magisterially thorough report. The inescapable conclusion to be drawn from it was that the upheavals involved in root and branch reforms of the NHS would be so dramatic that they would make the reforms themselves virtually unworkable.

After Ken Stowe had presented his report and discussed it with the Prime Minister, she eventually gave a deep sigh and said, 'Ken, the problem is there's no constituency for change'.[19]

Her caution seemed admirably pragmatic to the Permanent Secretary. 'In terms of her personality', recalled Sir Kenneth Stowe, 'this was a good illustration of how this hard-driving, indefatigable, unstoppable Prime Minister could suddenly see that there were buffers in the way of what she wanted to do and that there was no point in hitting them.'[20]

A few weeks later she finally killed off the speculation that she had plans to overhaul the health-care system by making a pledge in her party-conference speech that 'the National Health Service is safe with us'.[21]

This episode showed that within Margaret Thatcher the radical reformer and the cautious realist could co-exist as two sides of her personality. But the earlier story of the cabinet row over the CPRS proposals also showed that she could behave badly when she did not get her way.

THE BEGINNINGS OF PRIVATISATION

The cautious and the radical sides of Margaret Thatcher's personality were evenly balanced when it came to launching what has been called 'the jewel in the crown'[22] of her domestic policy. This was privatisation, a policy that was popular at home and copied extensively around the world. Yet the Prime Minister needed a lot of convincing before she took her first tentative steps towards putting the idea into practice. During her first three years in power, she not only hesitated, she disliked the word privatisation so much that she refused to use it, sticking rigidly to the more negative and politically divisive term 'denationalisation'. Yet as success bred success, she came to see that privatisation was one of her most important innovations, and also one of her most enduring legacies.

Although privatisation had been talked about while she was Leader of the Opposition, nothing much came of those discussions. However, she did set up a cabinet sub-committee in 1979 labelled 'E (DL)', whose initials stood for economic disposals. It made an unimpressive start, disposing of a mixed bag of assets such as the British Freight Corporation, various motorway service stations and buildings owned by the water authorities.

There were many ministers who made a contribution to the success of privatisation, but the cabinet colleague who persuaded Margaret Thatcher to implement the policy on the boldest scale was Patrick Jenkin, the Secretary of State for Industry. He was responsible for six nationalised industries. The largest of them, British Telecom, wanted to raise £28 billion to invest in new digital technology. 'There's no way you'll ever get that from the Treasury,' Jenkin told the BT chairman, Sir George Jefferson, 'but this bird might fly if we could sell shares in it on the stock market.'[23]

Once a privatisation plan had been devised, Patrick Jenkin presented it to the Prime Minister, who was sceptical. 'Why do we have to do it in one go?' she objected. 'Why not do it separately in each of BT's fifty-one areas? That would allow competition.'[24]

After two meetings Patrick Jenkin persuaded her that the fifty-one areas she kept talking about were irrelevant lines on the map. So she gave her blessing to the whole-scale privatisation of BT. Because of the huge sums of new capital required (selling the first 50.2 per cent of the company's shares eventually raised £3.9 billion), this sale was delayed until November 1984.

In the months after the Falklands, Margaret Thatcher not only approved what she still called the 'denationalisation' of BT, she also gave the green light for the much quicker, if smaller, public offerings of shares in British Aerospace, Cable and Wireless, Amersham International, Britoil and Associated British Ports.

Apart from the enormous breakthrough of the BT share flotation decision, the biggest privatisation in the first term of Margaret Thatcher's government was the British National Oil Corporation (BNOC). At first she was surprisingly reluctant to allow this to take place, rejecting it twice in cabinet committees, apparently on the instinctive but incredible grounds 'that Britain would some-how lose control of part of her oil'.[25] However, the new Energy Secretary, Nigel Lawson, eventually won her round and 51 per cent of BNOC was privatised as Britoil in November 1982, with the share placing proceeds of £549 million going to the Treasury.

From then on, Margaret Thatcher's confidence in the policy grew. She had seen the future for privatisation, and became totally committed to it once she knew it worked. 'Already we have done more to roll back the frontiers of socialism than any previous Conservative Government', she told the 1982 Tory conference, 'and in the next Parliament we intend to do a lot more.'[26] She did.

Another part of the revolution where Margaret Thatcher believed she was energetically rolling back socialism concerned the sale of council houses. Her 1980 Housing Act had established the 'Right to Buy'. As a result, over 370,000 families living in council houses had bought their own homes at a substantial discount by the autumn of 1982. '. . . this is the largest transfer of assets from the State to the family in British history', she proclaimed. 'And this really will be an irreversible shift of power to the people.'[27]

The sale of council houses was such a popular policy that it was visibly shifting political support from traditional Labour voters to Thatcher's Tories. In my own Kent constituency, over two hundred 'right to buy' applications a month were flowing in from the poorest housing estates in Ramsgate by the turn of the year. The Labour Party, both locally and nationally, were vociferous in their opposition to these sales. Margaret Thatcher hit back equally vociferously, declaring that her opponents would never dare to reverse the policy 'because they know we are right, because they know it is what people want'.[28]

On the doorsteps of council homes this controversy attracted far more interest than any other political topic. As the MP for a deprived district of South East England with one of the highest concentrations of council housing in the region, I soon recognised that Margaret Thatcher had struck vote-winning gold. My agent and chairman calculated that in the South Thanet constituency approximately 3,000 traditionally Labour-supporting households, grateful for or eagerly waiting for their right to buy, had shifted their allegiance to the Conservatives by the summer of 1983. The only dedicated opponents of the policy seemed to be the Kent Miners and the Socialist Workers Party. Margaret Thatcher was firmly on the side of the council tenants.

THE SUICIDE OF THE OPPOSITION

The Labour Party were not only digging their own political graves over council-house sales, they seemed to have a death wish in several other policy areas. Their leader, Michael Foot, had in his heyday been a left-wing firebrand and a coruscating parliamentary debater. Charming, courageous and brilliant as a former newspaper editor and book reviewer, he was utterly unconvincing in the role of an alternative prime minister.

As his fighting speech in the historic debate at the start of the Falklands conflict demonstrated, Michael Foot was no pacifist. But he was a longstanding and passionate supporter of unilateral nuclear disarmament. His enthusiasm for this cause could not have been a greater contrast to Margaret Thatcher's championship of a strong defence policy, whose centrepiece was Britain's independent nuclear deterrent.

In the middle of her first term as Prime Minister, she chaired a subcommittee of the cabinet, which took the decision to replace Britain's Polaris nuclear weaponry with the American Trident (C4) missile system. But before it could be installed in British submarines, President Reagan started a programme of modernising the United States strategic nuclear arsenal. As a result, America planned to use a more sophisticated Trident II (D5) missile system. Did Britain wish to buy this upgraded but more expensive version?

Some senior members of the cabinet expressed doubts about Trident II, notably the Defence Secretary John Nott and the Foreign Secretary Francis Pym. Margaret Thatcher called their arguments 'feeble and unrealistic'.[29] But she had a fight on her hands, which she won by calling a meeting of the full cabinet where the doubters were outnumbered. She also launched a pre-emptive strike of her own ahead of the meeting, by declaring her personal support for the value for money of Trident II to a startled House of Commons.[30] To no one's surprise she got her way a few days later in cabinet. Her commitment to this form of nuclear weaponry was driven by national pride, always a key ingredient in her personality and her decision-making.

As part of her commitment to nuclear peace-keeping in Europe at a time when Soviet SS20 warheads were being targeted on the West, Margaret Thatcher agreed to allow the stationing of 144 US cruise missiles at Greenham Common in Berkshire and at RAF Molesworth in Cambridgeshire. Predictably, their deployment in 1983 became the focus for anti-nuclear protests. The dormant CND movement, supported for the first time by the Leader of the Opposition, became resurgent with numbers reminiscent of its Aldermaston marches in the 1960s. With relish, the Prime Minister picked up the gauntlet thrown down by demonstrators, such as the Greenham Common Women for Peace who encamped on the perimeter of the cruise-missile base.

'We really are a true peace movement ourselves', she riposted at a London press conference with Chancellor Helmut Kohl of Germany, in February 1983. 'We are the true disarmers, in that we stand for all-sided disarmament, but on a basis of balance.'[31] Her annexation of her opponents' labels showed that she had learned a trick from an earlier Tory leader, Benjamin Disraeli, when he famously taunted: 'We have caught the Whigs bathing and run away with their clothes.'[32]

The nakedness of the opposition was painfully exposed on defence. Margaret Thatcher exploited it by promoting Michael Heseltine to Defence Secretary in January 1983. She was mistrustful of him, but she recognised his talent for public relations. He used it ruthlessly in caricaturing both the well-meaning leftism of the peace campaigners and the muddled unilateralism of official opposition. By the time the coming election began to loom in the national consciousness, the gulf between Labour and Conservative policy on national security had never looked wider. Overshadowing the day-to-day argument on defence, Margaret Thatcher held the trump card of her military resolution in the Falklands. She barely needed to play it.

For different reasons, the Alliance of the Liberal and Social Democratic Parties were faring little better than Labour against Margaret Thatcher in the popularity stakes. The SDP leader, Roy Jenkins, was well past his prime when he was returned to Parliament in a by-election. His interventions in the House of Commons seemed as dated as his plummy voice and pompous mannerisms. David Owen was a more incisive, but also a more divisive, figure within the Alliance. Margaret Thatcher respected him, and had been grateful for his support in debates during Falklands War. But his internal squabbles with the Liberal leader, David Steel, soon gave the Alliance the appearance of a marriage of inconvenience. It looked too fractious to be relevant to the long-term governance of Britain.

By the spring of 1983 Margaret Thatcher should have known that she could win a general election whenever she decided to call one. Yet she was curiously hesitant to make this move. Conservative Central Office, under the chairmanship of Cecil Parkinson, was gung-ho for an early poll as soon as possible after the 1983 electoral register came into force in February that year. The party's experts believed that the new constituency boundaries were worth thirty extra seats to the Tories. Even more important, the polls showed the government to be some fourteen and twenty points, respectively, ahead of Labour and the Alliance, with the gap growing.

Tempted by these portents, the Prime Minister flirted with the idea of a late spring election. At the annual dinner of the Confederation of British Industry, she fanned the flames of poll fever by emulating Jim Callaghan's incursion into music-hall lyrics. In October 1978 he had inflicted upon the TUC conference his rendition of an old ditty about the expectant bridegroom: 'There was I, a-waiting at the Church.' In April 1983 Margaret Thatcher quoted another music-hall song of the same vintage. 'Some say Maggie may ... others say Maggie may not.'[33] No one had told her that the heroine of these verses was a Liverpool prostitute.

While her party managers kept up the pressure for June, she baulked at it. 'I must not be boxed in', she told Cecil Parkinson at the end of a Chequers meeting about the manifesto and other election details in early April.[34]

One month later, again at Chequers, the party high command gathered to try and persuade her to give the green light. Willie Whitelaw, Geoffrey Howe, Norman Tebbit, Cecil Parkinson and Chief Whip Michael Jopling were there from the cabinet. Parliamentary and personal advisers included Ian Gow, Michael Spicer, Tim Bell, Gordon Reece, David Wolfson and Ferdinand Mount. All of them wanted her to go to the country. In addition to the prevailing good news from the polls, the Conservatives had won 128 seats in the local government elections on 4 May. Yet at this Chequers election summit on Sunday 8 May, Margaret Thatcher was in a most uncharacteristic mood of dither.

Her nervousness was highlighted by the silliness of her doubts. Would she be accused of cutting and running if she said yes, or of clinging to power if she said no?

How could she possibly break her promise to President Reagan that she would attend the G7 summit in Williamsburg, Virginia at the end of May? Or, if she did attend it, would she look out of place as a transitional leader lacking in authority? Political arguments highlighting the electoral advantages of attending a summit of world leaders, and historical references to the precedent set by Clement Attlee attending the Potsdam Conference during the 1945 general election campaign gradually calmed her fears.

Then she started a hare running about the negative public relations fall out from Royal Ascot, which was taking place in mid-June. Wouldn't it look terrible if the media was full of Tory ladies in huge hats and Tory toffs in tailcoats while she was on the stump fighting for re-election? Incredibly, it was her paranoia about the imaginary Ascot factor that finally made her plump for 9 June.

Just when she seemed to have chosen the date, the Prime Minister's indecision became final. She thought of a new excuse for procrastination. 'Even if I wanted to call an election', she objected, 'The Queen could hardly be available at such short notice.' Ian Gow slipped out of the room, called the Palace, and returned to report that Her Majesty would be graciously pleased to see the Prime Minister at noon the following day. As Cecil Parkinson recalled her body language, 'I am still not sure that the look she shot him was one of gratitude'.[35]

So the die was reluctantly cast. The ministerial and other guests departed. But even after most of them had left, Margaret Thatcher was seen by Ferdinand Mount sitting disconsolately by the embers of the fire in the great Tudor Hall at Chequers muttering, 'I'm not sure it's the right thing to do at all. I shall sleep on it. It's always best to sleep on these things.' To which Denis retorted, 'You can't do that, Margaret. They've all gone back to town saying it's going to be the 9th. You can't go back on that now. The horses have bolted, my dear.'[36]

Denis was right. The next day, the Prime Minister went to the Palace, the Queen agreed to the dissolution of Parliament and the election was announced for 9 June.

A LANDSLIDE VICTORY

Although the 1983 general election was effectively over before it began, Margaret Thatcher's nervous wariness about the result continued. She spent several hours at the start of the campaign clearing out boxes of clothes and clutter from No. 10 in case she was not coming back. This was a reaction guided by superstition rather than psephology for the polls continued to show that the Conservatives were in an unassailable lead of between 15 and 20 per cent.

She dominated the campaign which, in contrast to 1979, was well organised by Conservative Central Office. Almost every day began with a press conference, which she ruled with a rod of iron. In the early stages she corrected Francis Pym for suggesting that the sovereignty of the Falklands might one day be negotiable. Later, she slapped him down brutally for ruminating that landslides on the whole do not produce successful governments. Most cabinet ministers were allowed only walk-on parts at these morning conferences, since Margaret Thatcher answered nearly all the questions herself.

The rest of her electioneering day tended to be arranged for the benefit of the cameras. Photo-opportunities of the Prime Minister serving fish and chips in Yorkshire; trying out one of the earliest mobile phones (which weighed 2.2 lb, or 1 kg!) in Reading; or wading through horse manure in Cornwall. All made good footage on the evening news.

Her most awkward television moment came on BBC *Nationwide*, when a tenacious teacher, Diana Gould, repeatedly questioned her about inconsistencies in her answers as to whether the *General Belgrano* was steering towards or away from the task force when she ordered it to be torpedoed. Visibly infuriated by this unexpectedly knowledgeable interrogation from a member of the public, Margaret Thatcher came off the air firing verbal torpedoes at the programme makers. 'Only the BBC could ask a British Prime Minister why she took action to protect *our* ships against an enemy ship that was a danger to *our* boys', she expostulated.[37]

The viewers were on her side. They reacted negatively against Denis Healey talking about Margaret Thatcher having 'rejoiced in slaughter'.[38] Neil Kinnock dealt with a heckler shouting that at least Mrs Thatcher had 'showed guts' with the retort, 'It's a pity others had to leave theirs on the ground at Goose Green to prove it'.[39]

Both Labour spokesmen had to back down – Healey by apologising with the explanation that he had meant to say 'glorifying in conflict',[40] while Kinnock felt obliged to write to the Welsh Guards, the 2nd Battalion of the Parachute Regiment and to the relatives of the servicemen killed or injured at Goose Green.[41]

The battle of the manifestos was a one-sided contest. 'Somehow not an exciting document', was Margaret Thatcher's characterisation of the Conservative blueprint for the next five years.[42] It promised little apart from further privatisation and local government reform in London. 'More of the same' could well have been its title, although the Prime Minister said she preferred Tim Bell's label, 'Keep on with the change'.[43]

By contrast, the Labour manifesto lived up to its cruel caricature as 'the longest suicide note in history'. Margaret Thatcher found it an easy target for negative campaigning. She called it 'the most chilling and alien Manifesto ever put before the British people by a major political party',[44] adding for good measure, 'It would be a suicide note for Britain too'.[45] She costed Labour's public expenditure programme over the next Parliament at a price tag of between £36 and £43 billion – a figure almost equal to the total revenue from income tax. She mocked the plans for extending the nationalisation of key industries including banks, with the punch-line, 'Put your savings in your socks and they'd nationalise socks'.[46]

These attacks were so devastating that Labour candidates all over the country began losing heart. In my constituency I saw my unilateralist opponent booed off a council estate to shouts of 'Commie!' from people who were usually Labour supporters. There was no need to intervene in this private grief.

Towards the end of the campaign, even Margaret Thatcher began to pull her punches. Four days before the poll, she cancelled some of the Conservative Party's planned Sunday-newspaper advertising on grounds of thrift. Earlier, on grounds of bad taste, she had vetoed a Saatchi and Saatchi poster depicting Michael Foot as a geriatric pensioner. But she laughed at the even worse taste of the comedian Kenny Everett, who joked at a final Tory election rally in Wembley Stadium: 'Let's bomb Russia, and let's kick Michael Foot's stick away.'[47]

The final result of the 1983 general election was a landslide victory for Margaret Thatcher. In the new House of Commons she had a stunning majority of 144 over all other parties. But on closer analysis it became clear that the result was more of a disaster for Labour than a decisive vote of confidence in Thatcherism. For the Conservatives' share of the national vote was lower than it had been in 1979 – down from 43.9 per cent to 42.4 per cent. This less than stellar numerical result nevertheless converted into a torrent of Tory gains in individual constituencies, because the Alliance did so much damage to Labour. Although it won woefully few seats itself – only twenty-three – the Alliance cut Labour's vote so severely that many socialist strongholds toppled into the Conservative camp.

On election night, no one was much concerned about these psephological calculations. Under Westminster's first past the post system, winner takes all and unquestionably the big winner was Margaret Thatcher.

She was greeted at Conservative Central Office by cheering crowds and the Party Chairman, Cecil Parkinson. Then it was back to 10 Downing Street at 4.30 a.m. where the house manager greeted her with the words, 'Welcome home'. Her second term as Prime Minister had begun.

REFLECTION

It took a while for the political world to recognise that the Falklands War had transformed both the personal image and the political prospects of Margaret Thatcher.

The period May 1982 to May 1983 was an *annus mirabilis* for her, not because she was loved but because she was needed. On defence, foreign-policy and security issues, which occupied much of her time, she was thought to be taking the right decisions in the national interest, while her unilateralist opponents were seen as disastrously wrong. On economics, she was given the benefit of the doubt with the huge bonus that she was now believed to be tough enough to stand up to the union militants. That was a future confrontation everyone was expecting. It was now thought that there was a prime minister strong enough to win it.

It was clever of her image-makers to accentuate the softer side of Margaret Thatcher's character in the months running up to the election. This exercise may have convinced the many. The few knew perfectly well that the Prime Minister showed remarkably little interest or sympathy for the deprived, the marginalised and the down-on-their-luck at the lower end of society. She had other priorities. She was much more interested in delivering the rising tide that lifts all boats than finding welfare mechanisms to help those that were sinking.

One aspect of her positioning and presentational efforts in 1982–1983 was that she talked a great deal about values. The arguments about defence gave her the platform to champion the values of a free society versus Soviet society. She had no interest in co-existing with values of communism. Her line, well ahead of its time, was that 'the demise of the communist creed is inevitable because it is not a creed for human beings with spirit who wish to lead their own lives under the rule of law'.[48]

Such forthright declarations projected the Prime Minister's personality. By the time of the 1983 election the voters, if they bothered to read the remarkably content-free Tory manifesto, would only have had the vaguest idea of what a Conservative government might do. Nevertheless, they had a very clear perception of who the Conservative leader was, and what she stood for. Her values combined with her victory in the Falklands gave her a decisive majority and a second term in office. The 1983 election was the hinge of history opening the door to seven more years of Margaret Thatcher's pre-eminence on the international and domestic stages of politics.

23

Stumbling into the second term

CECIL PARKINSON AND THE SPEAKER

Margaret Thatcher's second term should have begun with huge confidence from her election victory and high competence after four years' experience at the helm of government. Instead, she was plagued by a series of difficulties with appointments, misjudgements and avoidable errors. It took her some while to steady the ship.

Her first major difficulty was caused by Cecil Parkinson. He had performed well as Party Chairman during the election, and earlier as a member of the Falklands war cabinet. He was skilful in handling her, particularly at moments of stress when her temperament became difficult. She admired his presentational skills, his good looks and his political judgement. She had complete confidence in him. So it was a pleasant but not a great surprise when on the Wednesday before polling day she said to him: 'Come and have tea tomorrow, and tell me what you would like to do in government.'[1]

She opened the conversation by saying that she intended to make him Foreign Secretary. 'Before you go any further', said Cecil Parkinson, 'I have to tell you that there is a problem.' He began to explain that he had been having an affair with his secretary, Sara Keays.

'What's the problem?' interrupted Margaret Thatcher. 'They tell me Anthony Eden jumped into bed with every good-looking woman he ever met.'[2]

Astonished by this lack of censoriousness from the Prime Minister, whom he had always thought of as 'a rather strait-laced lady from Grantham'.[3] Parkinson explained that his problem was more complicated. Sara Keays was pregnant with his child.*

---

* In her memoirs Margaret Thatcher suggested that she received this information in a letter from Colonel Keays on election day. In fact, she heard it first from Cecil Parkinson.

Although Margaret Thatcher paused on receiving this news, she did not immediately see it as an insuperable obstacle to appointing Parkinson as Foreign Secretary.[4] He demurred, and asked her to leave him out of the cabinet so that he would have some privacy in which to sort out his problems.

'But you won't have any privacy', retorted the Prime Minister. 'Every newspaper will be wanting to know why you are not in the cabinet. It will be the only story.'[5]

Cecil Parkinson reluctantly accepted her point. But he insisted that he needed privacy in order to conduct delicate negotiations about his child with Sara Keays and her family. 'It would be very difficult to do this surrounded by twenty-four-hour a day bodyguards', he said.[6]

Margaret Thatcher was so keen to keep him that she offered him the lower (and unguarded) post of Secretary of State for Trade and Industry. She also emphasised the importance of him staying married to his wife, Ann. Cecil Parkinson agreed to both points. So, having settled these matters, the Prime Minister and her still-favourite secretary of state moved on to settling the membership of the entire cabinet.

Forty-eight hours later, with the election result declared, Willie Whitelaw and the Chief Whip, Michael Jopling, came round to No. 10 to give their advice on the choosing of the new cabinet. Cecil Parkinson was already with her. Margaret Thatcher made a show of pretending that she had not already selected her cabinet the previous day. In the middle of her charade for the benefit of Whitelaw and Jopling, a call came in from the White House. The President of the United States wanted to congratulate the Prime Minister on her re-election.

As they retreated into the Downing Street garden while this transatlantic conversation took place on the hot-line, Willie Whitelaw sought to convince Cecil Parkinson that he deserved a higher place in the government.

'Look, Cecil, you absolutely must get one of the top three jobs', said Whitelaw. 'I shall tell her so myself. You must either be Chancellor, Foreign Secretary or Home Secretary. You have earned it.' With some difficulty Parkinson persuaded his benefactor to back off. 'Look, Willie, for reasons I am not free to explain, on this occasion I can't consider it',[7] he said. The Deputy Prime Minister was left puzzled.

This was not the only complicated puzzle that arose as Margaret Thatcher tried to decide who was coming or going in her new administration. She made a grave misjudgement involving the Speakership of the House of Commons.

In a foolish display of arrogance, she thought she could deliver this job to her own nominee.

As the incumbent Speaker, George Thomas, was retiring, she decided to give the post to Francis Pym, who she was intending to sack as Foreign Secretary. He was not interested. So the Prime Minister then offered it to Humphrey Atkins, who was close to her both personally and politically. He had been Chief Whip, and her clandestine supporter, during the leadership election of 1975. Smooth, handsome and ambitiously charming, Atkins was her court favourite before the rise of Cecil Parkinson. Unfortunately, he enjoyed far lower esteem among his parliamentary colleagues. He had not been a popular Chief Whip, and had resigned from the cabinet when he was No. 2 at the Foreign Office under Lord Carrington at the start of the Falklands crisis. But Margaret Thatcher retained a soft spot for Atkins, and assured him that the Speakership would be his. Accordingly, she put the word out through the whips to Conservative MPs that they should vote her choice into the chair.

This was a serious mistake. The election of a Speaker, which takes place before a new Parliament can formally open, is strictly a House of Commons matter. MPs who knew the constitutional conventions were outraged that the Prime Minister should be encroaching on their territory by trying to impose her own candidate. I well remember the furious resistance expressed in all parties to 'Maggie's poodle', as Humphrey Atkins was being called. Once the interventions of No. 10 were spotted, a bandwagon began rolling for Bernard 'Jack' Weatherill, the likeable Deputy Speaker, who looked the strongest alternative to the Prime Minister's candidate.

When she heard of the growing opposition to Humphrey Atkins, Margaret Thatcher played it rough. First she briefed against Weatherill, telling a number of colleagues that she thought he was not up to the job. This was so palpably unfair that it increased the groundswell of support for him. Then she tried to twist the arm of Robin Maxwell Hyslop, the Member for Tiverton, who had let it be known that he intended to move the motion to elect Weatherill as the new Speaker. 'Jack and I were subjected to intense and repeated pressure from the Conservative whips and No. 10 to give way to the "official candidate",' recalled Maxwell Hyslop, 'but we stood firm.'[8]

In the face of this firmness, Margaret Thatcher tried a knock-out blow. She summoned Jack Weatherill to No. 10.

'I hear you're trying to thwart me', was her opening line to him.

'I'm not thwarting anyone, Prime Minister', replied Weatherill. 'I'm simply allowing my name to go forward in the election for the new Speaker.'

'Then I will make you the senior Minister of State at the Foreign Office. How about that?'

'That would be quite wrong for me, and for you', was Weatherill's answer, arguing that it was without precedent for a sitting Deputy Speaker to leave the neutrality of the chair and re-enter party politics as a minister.

Angered by his steely integrity, Margaret Thatcher lost her temper and shouted, 'You're just being obstructive to me!'[9] The interview ended as unpleasantly as it began.

Three days later, Bernard Weatherill was elected as the new Speaker of the House of Commons with an overwhelming majority of support from all parties. 'Jack's great strength was that everybody knew that Margaret Thatcher didn't want him',[10] observed Cecil Parkinson. To have shown her hand so counter-productively was a blunder. In an attempt to cover it up, she concocted a face-saving device that allowed her aborted candidate, Humphrey Atkins, to move the motion in favour of Jack Weatherill's appointment.

This fooled no one. For days after the election, the talk of the tea room was fiercely critical of Margaret Thatcher for trying to use her muscle to control what was regarded as a purely House of Commons decision. Had she simply failed to understand that prime ministers have no right to influence the election of the Speaker? Or had her triumph at the polls blinded her to the limits of her power? Either way, she allowed herself to be seen in a bad light. Even more foolishly, she went on to show herself to be a bad loser.

Margaret Thatcher had an unattractive side to her personality – a tendency to bear grudges. Because Jack Weatherill had 'thwarted' her, she made a later attempt to undermine him, using much the same negative briefing techniques as she deployed against some of her ministers who had fallen out of favour. This was a dangerous tactic for a Prime Minister to use against a Speaker. Jack Weatherill soon rumbled what was happening, calling her efforts to discredit him by anonymous leaks a 'Black Glove' operation. As he later explained:

Black Glove is a political phrase not known to too many people . . . rather nasty things are said and written about you, and the great art is finding whose fingers are in it. Well,

I did discover this. Margaret Thatcher had her spin doctors too, notably in the person of Bernard Ingham, and some pretty unflattering articles appeared . . .[11]

When the Black Glove operation was at its dirtiest, with the *Sunday Telegraph* openly reporting that a campaign to bring about the Speaker's resignation was being orchestrated by elements in the government itself,[12] Jack Weatherill's friends started to rally round. I was one of them. As he told the story:

> One day Jonathan Aitken came to me and said, 'You realise, Mr Speaker, this is a put-up job, and they're trying to make you resign . . . You've got to go and see the editors.' I said I don't know any editors. And he said, 'Well, we do!' And the result of that was that I began seeing the editors in the evening time. They used to come and talk to me, and leading articles began to appear in the newspapers, particularly the heavy newspapers, saying how important it was to have a Speaker who would stand up to a powerful Prime Minister.

With the help of Matthew Parris, the presenter of *Weekend World* in 1988, the Speaker took the unprecedented step of appearing live on the programme to put across his message that he was 'not going to be put off in any way from doing what I believe to be my undoubted duty'.[13] What he meant by this was that he would continue to be more helpful to back-benchers on matters like granting more Private Notice Questions than Margaret Thatcher wanted. Because this made him popular with the House of Commons, she eventually saw that her war against the Speaker was rebounding on her. So she sent her PPS, Michael Alison, on a late-night mission to Weatherill, saying to him: 'Mr Speaker, the Prime Minister asks if we may have a truce.'[14]

The truce held, somewhat uneasily, for the next two and a half years. Jack Weatherill ceased to be a beleaguered Speaker once No. 10 became silent. But he remained hurt by Margaret Thatcher's treatment of him.

There is an intriguing postscript to these battles between the Prime Minister and the Speaker. It is little known that Jack Weatherill came to play an almost invisible yet pivotal part in her downfall.

On 13 November 1990, when Margaret Thatcher was highly vulnerable, Sir Geoffrey Howe made his dramatic resignation statement* to a packed and

---

* This is described in Chapter 35.

silent House of Commons, immediately after Prime Minister's Questions. He was only able to deliver it at this time and in this way because of a most helpful ruling from the Speaker.

Sir Geoffrey was planning to explain the reasons for his resignation in the course of the Queen's Speech debate, exactly as Nigel Lawson had done a year earlier. If that and similar precedents had been followed, the ex-Deputy Prime Minister would have been called at about 5.30 p.m., when the House would not have been full. His speech would have been susceptible to questions and interruptions. Given the likely reaction to his planned remarks from Thatcher loyalists, they might well have diminished if not undermined the impact of his speech.

But to his great surprise, Howe was telephoned by the Speaker's office at noon on the day of the debate. He was told that the Speaker would prefer him not to address the House in the Queen's Speech debate, but instead to explain his resignation in what was deemed to be 'a personal statement', at the start of business after questions. As the Speaker reminded the House, by tradition, personal statements may not be interrupted. So, Sir Geoffrey rose to his feet in prime time and was heard to maximum effect in pin-drop silence. The rest is history.

Was the unsolicited ruling by the Speaker just another example of his practice of being helpful to back-benchers? Or could it have been Jack Weatherill's secret revenge for those earlier threats and Black Glove operations against him by the Prime Minister?

I have often wondered.

OTHER EARLY GLITCHES

The row over the Speakership had its origins in the Prime Minister's post-election reshuffle. She wanted to give the post as a consolation prize to sweeten the pill of dismissal for Francis Pym. She had made up her mind to sack him after their conflicts of opinion during the Falklands. They were politically and temperamentally poles apart.

'Francis never understood that he needed to engage with her and argue back to her', said Lord Carrington. 'They just didn't get on.'[15]

Their lack of rapport deepened when Pym made some cack-handed remarks during the election campaign to the effect that a landslide Conservative victory might not result in a successful government. Margaret Thatcher disagreed with Pym as strongly over landslides as she had over the Falklands. She also suspected that he had been positioning himself as her successor if the war had gone wrong. To be identified as a future claimant for her throne was a guarantee of bad relations with the Prime Minister, as Michael Heseltine and Norman Tebbit were later to discover. So she fired Pym, wishing to replace him with a more compliant Foreign Secretary.

The government reshuffle after the election was limited in scope. Apart from the exit of Francis Pym, the only departures from the senior ranks of the government had been David Howell and Janet Young.

The most remarkable promotion was Leon Brittan, who rocketed upwards from Chief Secretary to the Treasury to Home Secretary, replacing Willie Whitelaw. Having been a supremely loyal deputy to Margaret Thatcher, Whitelaw was hurt to lose his important job in the cabinet and to be booted upstairs to the more marginal post of Leader of the House of Lords. He went because the Prime Minister wanted a tougher Home Secretary, in tune with her own right-wing instincts on law and order.

Unfortunately, Leon Brittan never looked convincing in the role for which she had cast him. This became apparent a month after his appointment when the government allowed an early debate in the House on the re-introduction of capital punishment. Margaret Thatcher hoped that the large intake of new Tory MPs who favoured hanging would vote with her to restore it, at least for terrorist murderers and the killing of police officers. But Leon Brittan, who had changed his previous opposition to the death penalty, made an unimpressive speech as Home Secretary in favour of bringing back the noose. In a free vote, capital punishment was rejected by an unexpectedly large all-party majority of 145.[16]

Margaret Thatcher hated to be on the losing side. According to Jim Prior (an anti-hanger), she let her feelings show in the hurly burly immediately after the result was declared:

> Her populist politics got the better of her. She shouted at Gerald Kaufman, Roy Hattersley and Peter Shore across the dispatch box that they didn't know what the people wanted, and that on the council housing estates the Labour leadership would get stick for turning down hanging.[17]

It was an odd issue for a prime minister to become so passionate about, given the practical difficulties any government would face if executions had been restored.

Another parliamentary glitch when Margaret Thatcher's wishes were not respected by the House of Commons despite her large majority concerned MPs' pay. The Review Body on Top Salaries published its recommendation that gave Members an increase of 31 per cent. Margaret Thatcher rejected this and offered a rise of 4 per cent. She lost her battle to impose this figure.

The most serious ructions came from her back-benchers. After a row with Edward du Cann who, as chairman of the 1922 Committee, was acting as the Tory MPs' shop steward, she gave way with bad grace, agreeing to a 22 per cent increase spread over the next four years. Thereafter, MPs' pay would be linked to an identified pay grade level in the civil service. But on 20 July 1983, seventy Tories rebelled and by an eight-vote majority linked their pay to a higher grade.[18]

The Prime Minister was furious. The row grew bitter, with some MPs pointing out that Margaret Thatcher could afford to be austere about her own pay (she voluntarily did not take some £10,000 of the salary to which she was entitled) because she had a rich husband. The issue was badly handled, and opened the back door to the 'padding' of MPs' allowances that eventually led to the MPs expenses scandal a generation later. At the time, it caused an avoidable rift between the Prime Minister and her parliamentary party.

More serious than any of these teething troubles was the discontent on the back benches about the government's legislative programme. The Queen's Speech had been a damp squib. The anodyne election manifesto had resulted in an unimpressive list of bills for the new Parliament to put on the statute book. The only fresh legislation of substance concerned the setting up of a Crown Prosecution Service and giving the go-ahead for cable television. This was hardly the radical fuel for the Thatcherite revolution that had been expected.

When those criticisms were voiced by six or seven back-benchers at a dinner organised just before the summer recess by the Prime Minister's new Parliamentary Private Secretary, Michael Alison (Ian Gow had been made a Housing Minister), Margaret Thatcher gave an unexpected response. 'You are right – the government is not doing enough',[19] she declared. It was an early example of her growing tendency to make a distinction between herself and the ministers she had appointed. Those of us sitting around the table in the House of Commons dining room on this particular evening just before the summer recess were amused. We came away thinking that our leader wanted the government to develop a momentum for radical change, yet claimed she was being prevented from doing so against her will by the forces of inertia around her.

She was outspoken about the failings of some of her colleagues, notably her second choice (after Parkinson) for Foreign Secretary, Sir Geoffrey Howe. She said he had 'already caught F.O.-itis'.[20]

After more in this vein, the Prime Minister left the dinner table with a memorable exit line: 'We still need a revolution, but we have too few revolutionaries. Come on!'[21]

We back-benchers rose from our seats at this exhortation, but out of politeness rather than with passion to follow Boadicea to the barricades. This was a problem for her, to which she did not pay enough attention in the months and years ahead. Prime ministers who do not take their parliamentary supporters along with them on their crusades become more at risk than they realise.

DIFFICULT PROBLEMS

Margaret Thatcher was always several steps ahead of her party when it came to implementing an agenda of radical change. She was often obstructed by a combination of intractable problems and irresolute people. Another factor was that in domestic politics she was a cautious politician as often as she was a conviction politician. She kept her powder dry for the biggest issues.

Unemployment remained the toughest nut to crack. Early in her second term it peaked at 3.3 million. Neither the Prime Minister nor her Employment Secretary, Norman Tebbit, showed much sympathy for the plight of those on the dole. In a memorable party conference speech in 1981, with Margaret Thatcher applauding alongside him, Norman Tebbit told a tale of how his father had coped with unemployment in the 1930s. 'He didn't riot. He got on his bike, and looked for work.'[22] This was the *Zeitgeist* of second-term Thatcherism.

After Norman Tebbit was promoted from Employment to the Department of Trade and Industry in October 1983, the Prime Minister became impatient with her new Employment Minister, Tom King. 'There is a limit to how much tea and sympathy can be offered to the unemployed',[23] she said.

She turned to David Young, a successful businessman who, after two and a half years advising Keith Joseph, became Chairman of the Manpower Services Commission (MSC). In this role, Young began seeing a great deal of Margaret Thatcher. 'David brings me solutions,' she said, 'others bring me problems.'[24]

The admiration was mutual. 'I had a meeting with Margaret for half an hour at the beginning of every week', Young recalled. 'Without doubt, it was the most stimulating thirty minutes of my entire schedule. I would come away from my time with her walking on air. She was so resolute, so clear sighted in what she wanted to get done.'[25]

While David Young was Chairman of the MSC, he began to make the first big dent in the unemployment figures by introducing a wide range of work schemes and training projects, notably the Youth Training Scheme (YTS). When the general economy began picking up under Lawson's 'Budget for Jobs' in 1985, the dole queues started to shrink, and the YTS eased the labour bottlenecks by providing a skilled workforce. Young was given a peerage, made Minister without Portfolio in the cabinet, and in 1985 promoted to Secretary of State for Employment. His rapid rise from outside the political system caused some jealousies among his fellow ministers.

Despite these mutterings, Margaret Thatcher liked promoting fellow revolutionaries from obscurity to stardom within her government. In addition to his initiatives for reducing unemployment, Lord Young was a major force in getting the privatisation of British Telecom accomplished. He also persuaded Margaret Thatcher and a majority of the cabinet to support the building of the Channel Tunnel. No wonder she liked him for bringing her solutions.

The most difficult problem on the Prime Minister's desk was the reform of local government and of local government finance. She could never forget that in October 1974 she had promised, as Shadow Environment Secretary, to abolish the rates. Her determination to deliver this pledge became obstructed by a succession of ministers who either could not or would not find the means to the end the Prime Minister wanted.

After two major reviews by successive Secretaries of State for the Environment, Michael Heseltine and Tom King, all that had been produced was what Margaret Thatcher called, 'the most modest of mice'.[26]

In her frustration with high-spending Labour-controlled local authorities, she took the radical step of abolishing the Greater London Council (GLC) and six other Labour-controlled big city councils. This move had been announced in the 1983 Conservative election manifesto, and seemed to be accepted by the voters. However, the detailed legislation needed to accomplish abolition was a controversial mess. The impression of political vindictiveness and administrative incompetence was hyped up in a skilful campaign of propaganda led by Labour's GLC leader, Ken Livingstone.

As the abolition legislation took a long time to pass, during which the profligate spending councils became even more profligate, the government had to introduce complex financial controls known as 'rate capping'. The issues on the government's side of the case were poorly presented, and Margaret Thatcher became frustrated that she was losing the argument on this part of her reform agenda. She sacked her Environment Secretary, Patrick Jenkin, replacing him with the more media-savvy Kenneth Baker, who had been no. 2 in the department as Local Government Minister.

Kenneth Baker and his junior minister, William Waldegrave, with extra help from Lord Rothschild, who had headed the Central Policy Review staff in the Heath government, were the original begetters of the Community Charge, later and better known as the 'poll tax'. They unveiled their idea at a Chequers seminar in March 1985. The essence of the proposal was that domestic rates should be abolished and replaced with a new tax levied at a flat rate on all resident adults. Rebates would be available to those on low incomes, although even the poorest would have to pay something in order to maintain the principle of accountability.

At this Chequers seminar Margaret Thatcher gave the go-ahead to the Community Charge. She made this endorsement too quickly, and with uncharacteristic lack of attention to detail. She was so keen to get rid of the rates, to which she had a deep-seated aversion, that she abandoned her usual practice of testing a new policy idea by hammering out all its pros and cons in vigorous argument. Nevertheless, because she had given the Community Charge her early approval, she stuck to it with a fierce tenacity that ultimately proved to be her undoing.

One early sign that she might have made a mistake came from the Chancellor of the Exchequer, Nigel Lawson. He had not been present at the Chequers seminar. But he submitted a dissenting memorandum which presciently suggested that the new tax would simply be used by many Labour-controlled local councils as a device for increasing spending and then blaming central government for the increased costs.

It was a great pity that the Prime Minister did not pay more heed to her Chancellor's objections. For his star was rising, and he had become, after her, the most important figure in the government.

HER BLUE-EYED CHANCELLOR

Margaret Thatcher made a bold move at the beginning of her second term when she appointed Nigel Lawson to be Chancellor of the Exchequer. He was an unexpected choice, having been in the cabinet only twenty-one months, with a relatively low profile outside Whitehall. She admired him for his creative work as Financial Secretary to the Treasury, when he had pioneered both the lifting of exchange controls and the invention of the Medium Term Financial Strategy. She also noticed with approval his administrative skills as Energy Secretary, when he quietly succeeded in moving massive quantities of coal from the pits to the power stations – an achievement which facilitated the defeat of the miners' strike in 1984. Above all, she thought Lawson's combination of innovative ideas and right-wing radicalism was just what the management of the economy needed.

However, her admiration did not extend to matters of personal presentation. After appointing him Chancellor, her first advice to him in the same conversation was that he should get his hair cut. He obeyed, but was not always to prove so compliant with her commands.

Margaret Thatcher's relationship with Nigel Lawson was quite different to her handling of her first Chancellor, Geoffrey Howe, who she had shifted sideways to the post of Foreign Secretary. She saw Howe as a cautious, plodding decision-maker whose understanding of economics was inferior to her own. By contrast, she thought Lawson was an intellectually brilliant economist who understood the Treasury inside out.

'I had by now come to share Nigel's high opinion of himself',[27] was her barbed explanation for promoting him over the heads of other contenders. As the comment indicates, she sensed that Lawson was unlikely to be unduly subservient towards the First Lord of the Treasury, a stance which was acceptable to her during their honeymoon period after his appointment, but which eventually led to friction and conflict.

Besides admiring Nigel Lawson's talent, Margaret Thatcher liked his bucca-neering approach to problem solving and the speed of his decision taking. She had an early taste of this three weeks after he started at the Treasury and dis-covered that public borrowing was overshooting by £3 billion a year. Courageously, Lawson proposed an immediate package of asset sales and expenditure cuts which he and the Prime Minister steered through a hesitant cabinet on 7 July. His axe fell most sharply on the Defence budget and the NHS budget, which between them yielded up £500 million.

The health cuts caused a storm, coming so soon after an election in which Margaret Thatcher had promised that the NHS would be safe in her hands. But she rode it out by arguing that prudent housekeeping to keep the NHS within its original budget was no more than 'very, very good government'.[28] The description was broadly justified because Lawson's medicine worked, and confidence grew.

By the end of the year, the economy was picking up steam. Britain was showing the fastest rate of growth in Europe, according to a December 1983 Organisation for Economic Co-operation and Development (OECD) report. Public borrowing had come under control. Margaret Thatcher claimed to be creating 'a picture of rising demand and activity levels spreading more widely through the economy, and rising investment'.[29]

This spirit of optimism was consolidated by the 1984 Budget. Business was delighted by the Chancellor's cut in corporation tax from 52 to 35 per cent over three years. Savers liked his abolition of the 15 per cent surcharge on investment income. 850,000 low-paid workers were taken out of income tax altogether by raising personal thresholds. The National Insurance surcharge, often described as a tax on jobs, was abolished.

This first Lawson Budget received an almost rapturous reception from the Prime Minister, from the press and from Parliament. Although it was very much the Chancellor's own work and cleverness, Margaret Thatcher had made three important contributions to its success. First, she had been involved in the strategic planning over suppers at No. 11 from the beginning of the budgetary process. Second, she had earlier swung a divided cabinet behind the big curbs on public expenditure and borrowing in July 1983, which made the tax reduc-tions possible. Third, she had given some last-minute presentational advice, without which the Budget would almost certainly have received much adverse press coverage.

In his efforts to broaden the base of VAT, Lawson was secretly planning a surprise move to extend the tax to newspapers and magazines. He told the Prime Minister that he was going to do this, during their final pre-Budget discussion. She saw, as he did not, the negative impact on Fleet Street that the ending of the VAT exemption for newspapers would have. 'Look, Nigel,' she said, 'this is a wonderful Budget and you should get a wonderful reception. You don't want to spoil that by putting VAT on newspapers.'[30]

It was a good example of how Margaret Thatcher's cautious political antennae were often superior to those of her senior colleagues. On this occasion, Nigel Lawson heeded her advice, dropped the proposal and, as a result, received bouquets from the press instead of the brickbats that would have been thrown at him by an industry unexpectedly required to pay £200 million a year in VAT.

The 1984 Budget was a mood changer for the government. The gloom over its early glitches lifted. Although unemployment remained stubbornly high, confidence soared in many sectors of the economy, particularly in the City of London. There was a banking bonanza from the flow of massive privatisation issues, which in the second term saw British Telecom, British Gas, Enterprise Oil, Jaguar, Rolls-Royce and British Airways return to the private sector.

The big one that got away was the Royal Mail, because Margaret Thatcher stamped her foot and ruled to Patrick Jenkin, 'You can't touch that – it's Royal'. It was an irrational attitude, which Jenkin thought 'Absolutely absurd', but he and his successors toed the line.[31]

Margaret Thatcher's personality played its part in both the strengths and the weaknesses of privatisation. Strength came from her instinctive understanding that the programme was not just a series of commercial transactions; it was an important plank in her personal philosophy that the frontiers of state socialism should be rolled back. 'Privatisation is at the centre of any programme of reclaiming territory for freedom', she asserted.[32] By 1989 she was able to claim, 'Privatisation: five industries that together were losing over £2 million a week in the public sector, now making profits of over £100 million a week in the private sector.'[33]

Yet she did not do as much as she might have done to promote freedom of competition within the architecture of privatisation. The Electricity industry simply became a series of regional monopolies, with their ownership ending up in the hands of foreigners.

As Chancellor, Nigel Lawson was a major driving force in the privatisation strategy. His battles with Sir Denis Rooke, Chairman of British Gas, who tried to obstruct the policy at every turn, became legendary. Other senior ministers such as Norman Tebbit, Patrick Jenkin and John Moore were key players too. But historically, the glory for this revolutionary, widely imitated and highly successful privatisation initiative went to Margaret Thatcher. It is seen to this day as one of the most important parts of her legacy.

Privatisation brought unexpected receipts to the Treasury of £13.5 billion during the second term. It was accompanied by cultural changes in the British economy, largely inspired by the tax cuts, incentives, deregulation and market liberalisation which the government's economic strategy encouraged.

One of the most important manifestations of these changes was the 'Big Bang' in the City of London, which introduced new technology, new foreign investment and a wave of mergers into the traditional financial sector practices of jobbing, broking and old-boy networking. The transformation created many fortunes and opportunities in the City, while in other sectors of the economy there was a similar surge in technology-led entrepreneurship.

All this activity became know as the 'Lawson boom'. Initially it was seen as a huge success, not least by Margaret Thatcher, who regarded her Chancellor as the brilliant brain masterminding what she called the 'enterprise culture'. Her views of the culture, the boom and the Chancellor were later to turn sour. But for most of her second term, Nigel Lawson was her blue-eyed boy.

REFLECTION

It was strange that so determined a prime minister should have made so accident-prone a beginning to her second term. The explanations for this faltering start were to be found in her lack of preparation, and a series of misjudgements fuelled by hubris.

Margaret Thatcher prepared assiduously for almost every action and decision she took in government. One notable exception was her failure to pay attention to the Conservative Party's 1983 election manifesto. It was a policy-lite document. Because the Tories were so far ahead in the polls, the electorate took little interest in the lack of substantive pledges for the next five years. Margaret Thatcher herself brushed aside all criticisms on this score during the campaign.

She then became highly critical of those she felt had left her with an empty cupboard of legislative proposals for the new Parliament. In fact, she herself was responsible for this vacuum.

There was a vacuum of ministers as well as measures, thanks to the troubles of Cecil Parkinson. He was a good choice for the post of Foreign Secretary, and his inability to take the job weakened the entire government. Margaret Thatcher handled his problems broadmindedly but badly. Her insistence that he should take the lower profile post of Secretary of State for Trade and Industry was a mistake. Why she believed that he would be any safer from exposure in that department than at the Foreign Office is a mystery.

The Prime Minister's intervention saved the Parkinson marriage, but only managed to preserve the Parkinson job for four more months. In October, in the middle of the Conservative Party Conference, the suppressed scandal hit the headlines with a vengeance. This was the appropriate word, since Sara Keays made disclosures in the press and in her book, *A Question of Judgement*, which reminded many of the old adage: 'Hell hath no fury like a woman scorned.'[34] In the heat of the fury, Cecil Parkinson had to resign. It would have been better for everyone if he had been allowed to do so after the election.

The Parkinson problem, like the Speakership problem, was caused by the Prime Minister's hubris. In her first term she was often insecure. In her third term she was overbearing. During the second term her personality was moving into territory somewhere between the two, with growing signs of unreasonable arrogance.

Her attitude to the Foreign Office was a constant source of friction. A few months after the Falklands she decided she should have her own foreign-policy adviser installed in No. 10. This alarmed the civil service establishment. Her new Principal Private Secretary, Robin Butler, was bold enough to have 'an enormous row'[35] with her on the issue. He lost the argument, although perhaps not as badly as he had thought, for the first No. 10 adviser on foreign affairs was Sir Anthony Parsons. He was an original and iconoclastic Foreign Office diplomat, but with sufficiently deep roots in his institution to keep the tensions between Downing Street and King Charles Street simmering gently rather than boiling over. Sir Geoffrey Howe had no such success, as will emerge in later chapters.

At one moment when working with Parsons, Margaret Thatcher made an unexpected observation. 'You know, Tony, I'm very proud that I don't belong to your class.'

'What class do you think I belong to?' asked the surprised former Ambassador to Iran and the United Nations.

'I am talking about upper middle class intellectuals who see everybody else's point of view and have none of their own' replied the Prime Minister.[36]

In that response lay both the strengths and weaknesses of Margaret Thatcher's personality. Leaving aside her distaste for intellectuals she had a real problem in seeing, let alone accommodating, a point of view other than her own. This made her seem, on a bad day, unreasonable, narrow minded or even bigoted in her apparently uncaring attitudes. Nuances and consensus had no appeal to her. She had no empathy for those adversely affected by her policies.

Yet it was rarely that simple. She liked argument. She changed her mind more often than she admitted, and listened more than most people realised. 'She could even manage to listen when she was talking',[37] claimed Robin Butler, recognising a talent in her that escaped others.

The same forces that could seem stubborn and overpowering were also the wellsprings of her courage. This was the quality that had been recognised by the country during the Falklands crisis. It would be recognised again as she grappled with her two greatest dramas on the domestic front – the fight against terrorism and the miners' strike.

24

Terrorism, Ireland and Hong Kong

FACING DOWN TERRORISM

Terrorism posed a continuous threat to Margaret Thatcher. She faced it with courage and determination. There was no finer example of her unflinching stead-fastness under attack than her reaction to the bombing of the Grand Hotel in Brighton where she was staying for the party conference in October 1984. But long before that outrage, she had to deal with other episodes of terrorist violence. The way she handled them revealed much about her character and personality.

A few weeks before she became Prime Minister, one of her closest colleagues, Airey Neave, was assassinated by a bomb, which detonated as he was driving out of the House of Commons car park. The device had been planted by the Irish National Liberation Army, a breakaway faction of the IRA. Although Margaret Thatcher's public reactions to the killing were fierce in their con-demnation of the 'common criminals'[1] who had committed the murder, her private sorrow was agonising. The tragedy was an early warning of the high risks that she and many other prominent figures were facing from Irish terrorism.

Four months after the 1979 election, the IRA terrorists struck two blows in a single day on 27 August. Earl Mountbatten, the Queen's second cousin, two members of his family and a local boy were murdered when their boat was blown up in County Sligo. At Warrenpoint, near Neary, close to the border between Northern Ireland and the Republic, two booby-trap bombs killed eighteen British soldiers from the Parachute Regiment.[2]

After writing letters to the bereaved families, Margaret Thatcher decided to visit the British troops and officers of the Royal Ulster Constabulary who were in the front-line of the fight against terrorism. Two days after the tragedy she flew to Belfast, went on a walk-about in the city centre, and visited injured soldiers in hospital. Then she took a helicopter to the heart of what was called 'bandit country' in South Armagh, where she visited army and RUC bases at Crossmaglen and Gough. Wearing, against advice, a Greenfinches camouflage jacket and beret borrowed from a female soldier of the Ulster Defence Regiment, she had to run to and from her helicopter to minimise the possibility of a sniper attack.[3] The courage and symbolism of her visit made a great impact on the people of Northern Ireland. 'From that time on, Ulster knew that we had a British Prime Minister with plenty of guts who would give no quarter to the IRA', said the Unionist politician Harry West.[4]

Another episode which enhanced Margaret Thatcher's decisiveness when dealing with terrorist issues was shown by her handling of the Iranian Embassy siege. On 30 April 1980, a group of six Iraq-trained Arab Iranian gunmen seized the embassy and captured twenty-six hostages, including a police constable who had been on duty outside and two BBC journalists who had been applying for visas. Six days later, after the gunmen had killed one hostage, throwing his body out of the embassy, the Prime Minister authorised the SAS to go in. Their operation, covered live on television, was a military success. The twenty-five surviving hostages were safely rescued; five of the gunmen were shot dead and one was captured.[5]

Mission accomplished, Margaret Thatcher went to congratulate the SAS men in their London barracks in Regent's Park. She arrived unannounced at 9.58 p.m. in evening dress, accompanied by the Director of the SAS Brigadier Peter de la Billière, Cabinet Office official Richard Hastie-Smith and Denis. The forty soldiers of the Pagoda Unit, who had carried out the raid, were stripping off their black denims and passing round cans of Tennent's lager. Suddenly they heard the startled voice of their commander, Major Jeremy Phipps, saying, 'Good evening, Prime Minister'. It was almost the only greeting she received, because a few seconds later the chimes of Big Ben started booming out from a large television set at the end of the gym, heralding the start of *News at Ten*. With typical Hereford indifference towards the visiting VIPs, the SAS men rushed over to the screen amidst cries of 'Siddown' – a command which Margaret Thatcher herself obeyed. She sat on the floor at the front of the semi-circle of soldiers, steadying herself with one hand on the shoulder of a burly trooper. Once or twice she interjected 'Isn't this exciting . . . how exciting!' as the day's dramatic events were replayed on the news. When it ended, the Prime Minister thanked the men for doing their job 'so well and so courageously',[6] staying long enough to shake hands with them, while Denis enjoyed a can of Tennent's. One of the officers thought he saw the beginnings of a love affair that evening between the Prime Minister and the SAS regiment, which at that time was little known to the general public. 'We never thought you'd let us do it', said one trooper.[7] 'I took the right decision. Terrorists must never prevail', 'she responded.'[8] The military were getting the message that the new Prime Minister would not falter in her determination to defeat terrorism.

Margaret Thatcher displayed the same determination in her confrontation with the IRA hunger strikers. As part of a series of protests against IRA terrorists not being recognised as 'political prisoners', a number of them, headed by the convicted murderer Bobby Sands, announced they would 'fast until death' in the Maze prison. The propaganda battle waged by the IRA on behalf of the hunger strikers produced an unyielding response from the Prime Minister. She rejected their claim that convicted terrorists should be granted 'political' status. Answering a question on the subject at the EEC Dublin summit in December 1980, she said bluntly: 'Murder is a crime. Carrying explosives is a crime. Maiming is a crime . . . Murder is murder is murder. It is not, and never can be, a political crime. So there is no question of political status.'[9]

Amidst rising violence in Northern Ireland, Bobby Sands and three other hunger strikers died in May 1981. Later that month, Margaret Thatcher visited the province where she was asked by a television reporter if she was prepared to see 'an endless stream of hunger strikers die'. She replied:

> That is a matter for those who go on hunger strike, and those who are encouraging them to do so. I am not urging them to go on hunger strike. I am urging them not to die . . . it is they who are sentencing their own people, to death, not me.[10]

Eventually the IRA got the message that the Lady was not for turning on terrorism. They blinked. Under pressure from the Church and from the families of fasting prisoners, the hunger strike was called off in October 1981.

During the seven months while the Sands protest lasted, the IRA killed thirteen policemen, eight British soldiers, five members of the Ulster Defence Regiment and five civilians. This was one of the bloodiest periods of the Troubles with a total of 61 people killed, 34 of them civilians.[11]

Meanwhile, the IRA was extending its terrorism to bombings in London and other mainland cities. The worst of these atrocities came in a double attack on 20 July. One bomb killed two soldiers of the Household Cavalry, injuring twenty-three others. Two hours later, a second device placed beneath the bandstand in Regent's Park killed six soldiers of the Royal Green Jackets and injured a further twenty-four people attending a lunchtime concert. The final toll was eleven dead, fifty injured and seven cavalry horses killed.[12]

On Saturday 17 December 1983, two police officers and three passers-by, including an American, were killed in a bomb attack outside Harrods. A further seventy-five were injured and a third police officer died of his injuries on Christmas Eve. Margaret Thatcher was on the scene less than an hour after the explosion. She was sickened by the sight of a teenage girl's charred body that was impacted against the window of the store. Encouraged by his wife, Denis Thatcher went Christmas shopping in Harrods forty-eight hours after the bombing.[13]

The most politically targeted of the IRA attacks was on the Grand Hotel in Brighton during the Conservative Party Conference in October 1984. Margaret Thatcher was lucky to survive it, for the bomb was planted to kill her. It destroyed the central section of the hotel, and wrecked many other rooms, including her bathroom. If she had been using it at the time, she would have been seriously injured or killed. But, night owl that she was, the early hours of the morning of Friday 12 October found her still working on the conference speech that was to be delivered a few hours later.

She said good night to her speech-writers, gave the draft a last tweak or two, and was about to turn in when her Principal Private Secretary, Robin Butler, put one last official document in front of her, saying, 'Can I give you this to look at overnight, and you can tell me by breakfast what you want done.'[14]

It was 2.50 a.m. Her quick glance at the document – about funding for the Liverpool Garden Festival – delayed her for a crucial moment or two from what might have been a fatal journey to the bathroom. For she was still in the sitting room of her suite alone with Robin Butler when at 2.54 a.m. a loud thud shook the hotel, followed by the sound of cracking masonry. Plaster fell from the ceiling. A slab of glass from a shattered window crashed onto the carpet. Margaret Thatcher immediately knew that a bomb had exploded, but did not realise the blast had been above her in the hotel. She thought a car bomb might have detonated on the sea-front, so went to look out of the window.

'Come away from the window', said Robin Butler. Before he had time to give her any further advice, she darted 'like a rabbit shooting into its burrow'[15] towards the bedroom, saying, 'I must see if Denis is all right'. Her instinctive reaction was a dangerous one, for it was immediately followed by the noise of falling masonry – fortunately not from the bedroom but from the adjacent bathroom. To the huge relief of her Private Secretary, the Prime Minister reappeared a few moments later accompanied by Denis. He was pulling on his clothes over his pyjamas. 'I've never seen so much glass in my life', said Denis, referring to the damage in the bathroom.[16]

The next few minutes seemed deceptively normal. Surprisingly, the lights were still working. Denis went back into the bedroom to get fully dressed. Robin Butler tidied up government papers. The Prime Minister went across the corridor to see if the secretaries on duty were all right. Their main concern was that they had not finished typing up the speech. Margaret Thatcher sat down in one of their chairs, murmuring to no one in particular, 'I think that was an assassination attempt, don't you?'[17]

Gradually, other figures from the hierarchy who had been sleeping in the same part of the hotel started to arrive in the secretaries' room. They included Geoffrey and Elspeth Howe, Party Chairman John Gummer and his wife Penny who was still in her nightdress, Keith Joseph in silk pyjamas and dressing gown, David Wolfson and Ronnie Millar.

Michael Alison, the Prime Minister's Parliamentary Private Secretary, and a man of strong faith, said to her quietly, 'Thank God you are all right, Margare . . .'

'I do. I do thank him', she replied.[18]

Alison recalled the scene as

Very British. Everyone kept a stiff upper lip. There were quite long silences. One or two people wondered whether a second bomb might have been primed to go off. Margaret was very steady. She asked me if the Conference Hall had been damaged. I said I didn't think it would have been as it was a quarter of a mile away. With great firmness, she said, 'Then it's important that we begin on time at 9.30'.[19]

Robin Butler, who had not heard the conversation with Michael Alison, suggested that the Prime Minister should return to London, an hour's drive away. 'I'm not leaving the area', she replied firmly.[20]

The decision on what to do next was taken out of her hands by the arrival of a fireman at 3.10 a.m., followed by Special Branch protection officers. The fireman cautiously led the Prime Minister and her party downwards out of the Grand Hotel. It was not a quick exit. One of the first routes they tried was impassable, so she had to wait in an office. After a while, it was deemed safe to descend by the main staircase. Around it, the air was swirling with cement dust, which made her cough. It covered the blue ball gown she had worn for her appearance at the Conservative Party agents' dance some six hours earlier. As the white dust settled on the dress, it gave her the appearance of a ghostly apparition as she clambered over chunks of masonry and broken furniture. Arriving in the foyer, she insisted on checking that all the reception staff on duty had been accounted for. Only after hearing that they were all safe did she agree to leave the hotel by a back exit, under heavy police protection.[21]

In the chaos outside the hotel, rumours had begun spreading that Margaret Thatcher had been killed. The sea-front was crowded with conference delegates tumbling out of nearby hotels. I was one of them, and remember staring with amazement at the gaping hole in the front of the Grand, wondering who had or had not survived. But then the word was shouted round that the Prime Minister had been seen coming down the main staircase. The cry went up, 'Maggie's safe!' Such was the relief that strangers shook hands, and clasped each other's shoulders – but in silence.

On leaving the hotel, the Prime Minister was driven to Brighton police station where she was joined by various cabinet ministers including Willie Whitelaw, Keith Joseph, Geoffrey Howe and his wife Elspeth, with Budget, their dog, John Gummer and Leon Brittan. Her security advisers tried to persuade her to return to No. 10. She would have none of it.

Margaret Thatcher changed out of her evening dress into a navy-blue suit, which her personal aide, Cynthia Crawford ('Crawfie'), had salvaged from the hotel bedroom. Then she was driven to Lewes Police College. It was so heavily surrounded by armed men with machine guns that it resembled a military bunker. Once inside, she was allocated a twin-bedded room, which she shared with Crawfie. Denis found other accommodation further down the corridor where he dossed down with Special Branch protection officers.

Before she snatched a couple of hours of sleep, Margaret Thatcher could only think of one thing to do. 'Crawfie and I knelt by the side of our beds and prayed for some time in silence.'[22]

While the Prime Minister took her brief rest, Robin Butler manned the telephone, and pieced together the news coming in from the police and party officials at the scene of the bombing. When she emerged from her room, he briefed her: 'Prime Minister, I'm afraid it's far worse than we supposed. Bodies have been taken from the wreckage. They are digging the injured Norman Tebbit out now.'[23]

From watching breakfast television news, Margaret Thatcher learned more about the night's casualties. Anthony Berry MP was dead and so was Roberta Wakeham, the wife of the Chief Whip. John Wakeham was still trapped with his legs crushed under debris. Norman Tebbit was being hauled out of the rubble in excruciating pain, along with his wife, Margaret. News of three other fatalities and many more injuries were being continuously reported. Turning away from this harrowing television coverage, Margaret Thatcher said to Robin Butler: 'Well, it's eight o'clock. The conference must begin on time at 9.30, and I must be there.'

He could not believe what he was hearing. 'Prime Minister, you can't be serious. People have been killed. You can't just go on with the conference as if nothing has happened.'

Without hesitation Margaret Thatcher answered, 'This is our opportunity to show that terrorism can always be beaten by democracy.'[24] The strength of her instincts overruled all other considerations.

On the dot of 9.30, the Prime Minister made her entrance into the Conference Centre and was greeted with an outpouring of emotional applause by the delegates, roaring their relief that she was still alive. Once the tears and cheers had receded, the emphasis from the platform was business as usual. Appropriately, but coincidentally, the first scheduled debate of the morning was about Northern Ireland. It was followed later by the leader's speech, which had to be massively rewritten by Ronnie Millar and the team of writers. Out went the traditional knockabout of jokes and jibes against the opposition. In came solemnity, a denunciation of terrorism and an appeal for national unity. She struck all the right notes:

> The bomb attack . . . was an attempt not only to disrupt and terminate our conference. It was an attempt to cripple Her Majesty's democratically elected government. That is the scale of the outrage in which we have all shared. And the fact that we are gathered here now, shocked but composed and determined, is a sign not only that this attack has failed, but that all attempts to destroy democracy by terrorism will fail.[25]

This Churchillian defiance captured the mood of the nation as well as the conference. Margaret Thatcher's coolness under fire won universal acclaim. She reflected what Britain wanted its Prime Minister to be at a time of such crisis – a beacon of courage and a symbolic assurance that the IRA would not be allowed to triumph.

For all her visible resolution in the hours after the attack, Margaret Thatcher was invisibly affected by the Brighton bombing. In the short term, she suffered the predictable reactions of shock and emotion that she had not allowed herself to display in her superbly professional television interviews and in her conference speech.

When she returned to Chequers, after visiting the injured in the Royal Sussex County Hospital, her feelings started to show. In the Intensive Care Unit, the sight of Norman and Margaret Tebbit shook her. She could only just recognise her Secretary of State for Trade and Industry as he croaked a few words through his swollen lips and face. His wife managed to communicate that she had no feeling below the neck, which they both knew meant permanent paralysis. Over dinner that evening, Margaret Thatcher told Denis that she feared she would always be haunted by the thought that Margaret Tebbit's fate might have been her fate.[26]

This mood of shock at the narrowness of her survival lasted for some time. On Sunday morning the Prime Minister went to church and was seen wiping away her tears during prayers.[27] By the time she returned to Chequers, Carol had flown in from Australia. She found her mother sitting on the terrace 'calm but seemed still shaken'. After describing the events at Brighton she said, 'This is the day I was not meant to see.'[28]

Denis appeared equally subdued. He rarely let his spiritual or emotional feelings show, but after this experience he wrote several letters to well-wishers with a line about the near miss: 'I like to think God had a hand in it.'[29] A few days afterwards he bought his wife a watch and gave it to her with a note: 'Every minute is precious.'[30]

The closeness of the brush with death left no lasting mark on Margaret Thatcher. Some observers felt that the episode decreased her self-confidence and increased her remoteness, but the evidence for this is slender. A better view is that her spirits were shaken – but not for long. She was on the road to recovery as early as ten days after the attack telling her Finchley constituents, on the twenty-fifth anniversary of her election as their MP, 'We picked ourselves up and sorted ourselves out as all good British people do.'[31]

THE ANGLO-IRISH AGREEMENT

One matter related to terrorism which needed a lot of sorting out in the aftermath of Brighton was a top-secret diplomatic initiative which she had authorised the Cabinet Secretary, Sir Robert Armstrong, to explore with his opposite number in Dublin, Dermot Nally. Their talks led to the Anglo-Irish Agreement of 1985, which laid the foundations for later historic developments.

How this began and brought about the first major breakthrough in Anglo-Irish relations for half a century is a fascinating story that says much about the quieter subtleties of Thatcherite statecraft.

A year after winning the 1979 election, Margaret Thatcher became the first British Prime Minister ever to welcome an Irish Taoiseach (Prime Minister) at No. 10 Downing Street. She was wary of her guest, Charles Haughey, the leader of the Fianna Fail governing party. He was known to have held sympathies for Republicanism in the North, which had led to him being tried and acquitted of importing arms for the IRA in the early 1970s.

Despite this inauspicious background, the Prime Minister and the Taoiseach struck up a good rapport. Blarney was a trademark of Charlie Haughey, and he excelled himself in the art of it when handing his hostess a farewell gift. For he presented her with a tea set complete with a silver spoon, inscribed with the words, 'Where there is discord may we bring harmony'. This was the opening line of the prayer attributed to St Francis of Assisi, which Margaret Thatcher had declaimed from the doorstep on No. 10 on the day she became Prime Minister.

Although her political sympathies about bringing harmony to Northern Ireland lay instinctively with the Ulster Unionists, Margaret Thatcher had also experienced good reasons for being disenchanted with them. She knew she should not keep all her eggs in the Belfast basket. So the teaspoon of charm from the Taoiseach, plus some nudging from the Foreign Office, took her to a bilateral summit in Dublin – another first for a British Prime Minister – in December 1980.

The Haughey charm continued to cast its spell over Margaret Thatcher. The summit was high powered, attended on the British side by the Foreign Secretary (Lord Carrington), the Chancellor of the Exchequer (Sir Geoffrey Howe) and the Northern Ireland Secretary (Humphrey Atkins). More surprisingly, the communiqué issued at the end of these deliberations broke new ground in diplomatic effusiveness. It made a British commitment to give 'special consideration to the totality of relationships between these islands'.[32]

Margaret Thatcher was subsequently embarrassed by these words. 'You have destroyed my credibility with the Unionists',[33] she complained to the Permanent Under-Secretary of the Northern Ireland Office, Sir Kenneth Stowe, who had drafted them. When she returned to London she engaged in some damage limitation with the Orangemen, writing an appeasing letter to Ian Paisley, and telling the pro-Unionist Ian Gow that she had been 'tripped up by the Foreign Office'.[34]

But, for all such fence mending, the Dublin summit was a turning point for Margaret Thatcher. Kenneth Stowe, in whom she had special trust because he had been her first Private Secretary at No. 10 before moving to the Northern Ireland Office, took this view of her reaction to it:

> This summit was the start of the peace process. For the first time, the Prime Minister saw that the relationship between London and Dublin was more important than the relationship between London and Belfast. This was a hard lesson for her to learn, but she got it. She realised that the troubles in Northern Ireland were not a problem that could be solved by Belfast and the British Army. She understood, even though she grumbled about it, that the words in the communiqué about 'the totality of relationships' were the beginning of wisdom.[35]

The wisdom took a while to take root, not least because Margaret Thatcher became contemptuous of Charlie Haughey and his government for their anti-British statements during the Falklands War. But the election of a new Irish government and Taoiseach, Garret FitzGerald, improved the climate. Taking the view that secret diplomacy might achieve progress, the Prime Minister authorised her Cabinet Secretary, Sir Robert Armstrong, to float a proposal to the Irish Cabinet Secretary, Dermot Nally. It was helpful that the two mandarins were already friends.

The first proposal filtered through this back channel was that the border between Ulster and the Republic of Ireland should be changed from a line to a band, five miles wide on both sides, on which police and security forces could operate when in hot pursuit of terrorist or criminal suspects. Although the Irish government rejected the idea, the fact that such a serious proposal had been put forward by the British made the Irish use the Armstrong–Nally talks as a vehicle for negotiations on other substantive issues. In no time, the two principals and their aides were meeting every two weeks.

The early cloak and dagger conditions included promises that there would be no records of the oral discussions. There would also be hush-hush arrangements for travel on false passports, and James Bond-like assignations. Nally's instructions to the Deputy Cabinet Secretary, Robert Wade-Gery, were:

> When you get to Dublin airport, take a taxi to your hotel, and at a quarter to nine the next morning, you walk along a particular street in Dublin, which is past the wall of the Taoiseach's garden, and, if it's exactly quarter to nine, the door will open as you walk past it, you step in, it'll close behind you, and we can negotiate all day.[36]

The Prime Minister, despite what Wade-Gery described as her 'intense suspicion'[37] of these negotiations between officials, allowed them to continue. She imposed two conditions. First, they were only to be conducted at their initial stages at the Cabinet Office, with no involvement by the Foreign Office or the Northern Ireland Office. Second, there were to be no suggestions of shared or diluted British sovereignty. 'Her rock was sovereignty', Robert Armstrong recalled. 'Nothing was permissible which would weaken or impair Britain's sovereignty over Northern Ireland.'[38]

The Brighton terrorist attack caused a nervous hiatus in the rounds of secret diplomacy. Margaret Thatcher hated to give any possible impression that she was being 'bombed to the negotiating table'.[39] Nevertheless, she did agree to go ahead with an Anglo-Irish summit at Chequers on 7 November 1984. She was developing a growing respect for the new Taoiseach, Dr Garret FitzGerald. Even so, their summitry came close to being a disaster because of her aggressive statements at the final press conference, on a tangential matter.

The matter arose because shortly before the summit a private Dublin think tank, the New Ireland Forum, published a report. Although it had no imprimatur from the Irish government and no direct connection with the Chequers agenda, its proposals were considered newsworthy. This report, a document of considerable earnestness and complexity, had suggested various forms of new constitutional architecture that might eventually end the troubles. Its ideas were liked more in Dublin than in London, but given its opaque language and its distant timescale, the report's contribution to the discussion could easily have been kicked into the long grass. Margaret Thatcher, however, preferred to give it another kind of kicking.

When asked about the findings of the New Ireland Forum at a post-summit press conference, she oversimplified them down to three solutions: unification, confederation or administrating the province by joint authority. In a disparaging tone of voice accompanied by an even more dismissive flicking of her wrist, she rubbished all three. 'That is out . . . That is out . . . That is out!'[40]

The Irish media immediately denounced her. Dr Garret FitzGerald described the British Prime Minister's language as 'gratuitously offensive'.[41] She pretended not to understand what the fuss was about. Anglo-Irish relations fell to a new low. The British Ambassador in Dublin was even warned that tolerance for the IRA would grow in Ireland and that the fight against terrorism had been weakened. But these appearances were deceptive.

It was Margaret Thatcher's practice, when she knew she had over-reacted, to make a conciliatory move rather than to offer an apology. So she extended an olive branch to Dr FitzGerald and re-engaged in further talks with him. She was never an enthusiast for a formal Anglo-Irish Agreement. All she really wanted from Dublin was better co-operation on security. But after pressure from leading members of the US Congress and President Reagan, she reluctantly agreed to allow the government of the Irish Republic not just the right to be consulted on Northern Ireland governance, but a new right to have a permanent role in it. The machinery for this would be a commission jointly chaired by Irish and British ministers with a presence and secretariat in Belfast. This was the centrepiece of the Anglo-Irish Agreement, which the Prime Minister and Taoiseach signed on 15 November 1985 at Hillsborough Castle in Northern Ireland.[42]

The circumstances of the signing were unsettling. 'Margaret was caught very much on the hop by the hostility of the reactions to it', recalled Tom King, who she had appointed as her new Secretary of State for Northern Ireland some six weeks earlier. 'The essence of the deal was that it had been negotiated in deepest secrecy, largely through the Armstrong–Nally* channel, and it was

---

* Sir Robert Armstrong and Dermot Nally had become so close that they designed a tie emblazoned with their initials – AN. It was presented to the Irish and British group of secret negotiators.

presented in Northern Ireland as a complete *fait accompli*. Of course, the Unionists and their supporter were bound to be furious, but she was surprised by the extent of the fury.'[43]

One unwelcome dimension to her surprise was the resignation from the government of Ian Gow, her former PPS, now a Minister of State at the Treasury. When the Prime Minister arrived at Hillsborough Castle, the first thing she did was to go to an upstairs bedroom and telephone Ian Gow. Her efforts to persuade this staunch advocate of the Unionist cause not to leave his post were unsuccessful. Part of her admired his principled stance, but it upset her on the day.

At the signing ceremony, Garret FitzGerald caused his own surprise by speaking in Gaelic. 'Margaret kept wondering what on earth he might be saying', recalled Tom King. 'I murmured to her "Could it be 'We've won?'" '

Meanwhile there was no doubt what the Unionists were saying. 'All hell was breaking loose outside the gates of Hillsborough', said King. 'The Unionists were creating a tremendous noise of hammering and shouting. This protest made it difficult to hear what was being said inside.'[44]

The protests went on and on. The Unionist parties had never expected that she would go behind their backs and strike a bargain with Dublin. Their sense of betrayal was personal. 'British we are, and British we shall remain', bellowed the Reverend Ian Paisley at a mass demonstration against the Anglo-Irish Agreement in Belfast on 24 November. 'Now Mrs Thatcher says that the Republic must have a say in our province, we say "never, never, never, never".'[45]

Paisley's Deputy, Peter Robinson, called the Agreement 'this act of political prostitution'.[46] Using the rapier rather than the bludgeon, Enoch Powell chillingly asked her in the House of Commons if she realised that 'the penalty for treachery is to fall into public contempt?' She retorted that she found his remarks 'deeply offensive'.[47]

The unkindest cut of all remained Ian Gow's resignation, which also turned out to be his death warrant. His stand against the Hillsborough agreement made him a marked man. The IRA eventually murdered him in 1990 by a bomb placed under his car in the garage of his constituency home in Eastbourne. It was the most personal loss in a long chain of bombings and other tragic events. Margaret Thatcher had increasing doubts as to whether she had been right to sign the Anglo-Irish Agreement.

By chance, I had a conversation with the Prime Minister at a family reception immediately after Ian Gow's funeral in August 1990, near his home in Sussex. She was as upset as I had ever seen her. Our talk was mainly about Ian's extraordinary personal qualities, which she was kind enough to say I had captured well in the obituary I had written in the *Guardian* a week earlier. But in an indirect reference to the Anglo-Irish Agreement, she remarked: 'We're just not getting the security and intelligence cooperation we should be getting from Dublin on the IRA.'[48]

This negative view of the way the Agreement was working came to prey on Margaret Thatcher's mind. By the time she published her memoirs in 1993, she had convinced herself that it had been a mistake. She described the results as '. . . disappointing. Our concessions alienated the Unionists without gaining the level of security cooperation we had a right to expect.'[49]

This was a premature judgement. She built better foundations for peace than she saw at the time.

ACCEPTING REALITY IN HONG KONG

The deal with the Irish government at Hillsborough in 1985 was not the only international agreement Margaret Thatcher signed against her instincts. Another 'problem left over from history', as the Chinese called it,[50] was the future of Hong Kong. The way the Prime Minister approached the issue, argued over it, mishandled it, eventually settled it and then privately condemned her own decisions revealed much about her personality.

The first meeting at which Margaret Thatcher applied her mind to Hong Kong was held at No. 10 on 28 July 1982; two days after the Falklands Thanksgiving Service at St Paul's Cathedral. As Sir Geoffrey Howe put it: 'No one had been relishing the idea of telling the Prime Minister, who had just triumphantly re-asserted sovereignty over the Falklands, that she must now consider relinquishing it over Hong Kong.'[51]

The Foreign Secretary and his team of officials who were experts on the colony had considerable difficulty in persuading the Prime Minister to enter a mind-set in which British sovereignty would have to be surrendered. But as 92 per cent of Hong Kong's territory was British by virtue of a lease from China, due to expire in 1997, it was completely unrealistic to argue that the remaining

8 per cent, Hong Kong Island and Kowloon, could survive as a colonial outpost on their own.

Despite the unreality of such arguments, Margaret Thatcher embarked on them 'in a combative and uncooperative spirit',[52] according to the wisest old China hand in Whitehall, Sir Percy Cradock. She eventually became so impressed by Cradock that she installed him in No. 10 as her personal adviser on foreign affairs. But at the start of her investigations into the problem of Hong Kong, she rubbished the recommendations given by him and the rest of the Foreign Office.

Instead of working out a negotiating position from which to start discussions with the People's Republic of China (PRC), the Prime Minister suggested that Hong Kong Island and the tip of the Kowloon Peninsula might be retained in perpetuity. She said, apparently seriously, that she did not see why it could not be defended by the British Army. She also insisted that Britain's legal rights to the tiny 'freehold' remnant of Hong Kong were unassailable. The Chinese took the opposite view of the treaties granting these rights, which had been signed between the government of Queen Victoria and the Qing dynasty in the 1840s. In any case, Beijing held all the de facto cards once the lease expired in 1997.

In addition to her remarkable assertions that Britain was in a position of military and legal strength over Hong Kong, Margaret Thatcher floated several other original ideas for the future of the colony, such as UN trusteeship, and joint rule with China. She pretended that any concessions of sovereignty to the PRC were out of the question. To maintain this impossible position she embarked on a series of discussions with her advisers, which were described as 'unstructured and abrasive'.

According to Cradock, 'The Prime Minister conducted a species of guerrilla warfare; appearing suddenly behind the lines, or firing from unconventional angles. She also often operated behind a smokescreen of her own making.'[53]

Behind the smokescreen lay a pressing engagement with reality. A summit meeting with China's leader, Deng Xiaoping, was scheduled for 24 September in Beijing. It was not a happy or successful visit for Margaret Thatcher. She was suffering from a bad cold. On the first morning of the talks she had a nasty fall on the steps of the Great Hall of the People, which was seen by many superstitious Chinese as a bad omen for the British.

Their superstitions were not all that wide of the mark. Deng reacted negatively to the arguments put forward by the Prime Minister. He was immovable on the issue of Hong Kong returning to Chinese sovereignty. He became angry when she suggested she could only consider this when the two governments had agreed arrangements that would be acceptable to Hong Kong and to the British Parliament. Rejecting this with some forcefulness, Deng said he was prepared to wait one or two years for consultations to take place, but after that China would announce its own decisions. Deng's toughness and his personal habits – chain smoking and frequent expectorations of phlegm into a spittoon – repelled Margaret Thatcher, who thought him 'cruel'.[54]

The impasse was unblocked after several months by 'the first finesse'.[55] This was the Foreign Office's description of a revised wording for the Prime Minister's views on the sovereignty question. At the Beijing summit in September 1982, Margaret Thatcher had spoken of being ready in certain circumstances to 'consider' making recommendations to Parliament on sovereignty. By March 1983, she shifted her position to say that she 'would be prepared to recommend to Parliament'. This minor change caused her much heart searching and the revisiting of absurd alternatives, such as the military defence of Hong Kong Island and holding a UN-supervised referendum as a prelude for independence. But in the end, she reluctantly agreed to the first finesse, declaring it to be 'her last word'. It was conveyed in a letter to the Chinese Prime Minister, Zhao Ziyang, who evidently appreciated such delicate nuances. The talks restarted.

For the next twelve months, a complex diplomatic minuet was played out mainly between officials in London, Beijing and Hong Kong. Sir Geoffrey Howe, who could be as inscrutable as any Chinese mandarin, used his skills to particularly good effect in the negotiations. They progressed not because of Margaret Thatcher's continuing interest, but in spite of it. She had at least one more lurch towards the politically insane option of granting independence to the freehold parts of Hong Kong. But the saner possibilities had an influential voice in her closest counsels when in January 1984 Sir Percy Cradock moved into No. 10 as Foreign Affairs Adviser to the Prime Minister.

It says a great deal about her criteria for selecting important members of her staff that Margaret Thatcher chose Cradock for this key role. He was an archetypal Foreign Office diplomat, a member of the Labour Party and he held opposite views to hers on many foreign-policy subjects, not least on Hong Kong.

'It was because of her sheer respect for his formidable intellect',[56] said David Wilson, later appointed as Governor of Hong Kong. He was a member of the negotiating team that, under Cradock's leadership, wrestled with the Chinese and English texts of the proposed agreement known as the Joint Declaration.

Although there were many difficult issues to be resolved, in the end the Prime Minister accepted the advice of Sir Percy Cradock and the Foreign Office.

'It was the real mark of quality in Margaret Thatcher that even when all her emotions were against it, and she had tried every possible form of questioning and saying "couldn't we do it some other way", she was steady when it was time to take a decision that really mattered', recalled David Wilson. 'It was then that the self-flagellation ended and she came to the right conclusions.'[57]

The final round of negotiations went right to the wire. The Foreign Secretary performed brilliant acts of brinkmanship in Beijing on the eve of his meeting with Deng Xiaoping on 31 July 1984, while the Prime Minister kept asking for more in telegrams from London. She hated the process of making concessions on points such as the remit and location of the Joint Liaison Group tasked with preparing for the handover in 1997. But the mission was accomplished more successfully than she realised at the time. The deal, encapsulated in Deng's phrase 'one country, two systems', provided Hong Kong with a stability, prosperity and continuity that served it well in its final years as a British colony, and as an autonomous region of China ever since.

'It was an *excellent* result – progress beyond all expectations' was Margaret Thatcher's verdict on the finalisation of the negotiations. Her last act was to sign the historic agreement in Beijing on 19 December 1984. On the flight from London she recited, in concert with Sir Percy Cradock and Robin Butler, the concluding lines from Tennyson's *Ulysses*, which all three of them knew by heart:

Though much is taken, much abides; and though
We are not now that strength which in old days
Moved earth and heaven; that which we are, we are;
One equal temper of heroic hearts,
Made weak by time and fate, but strong in will
To strive, to seek, to find, and not to yield.

The Tennysonian spirit seemed, at the time, a fair verdict on Britain's negotiation of the Hong Kong agreement. But it was not Margaret Thatcher's final opinion. She became retrospectively angry for having signed it.

In January 1987 she gave an astonishing ventilation of her regrets at a No. 10 meeting with Sir David Wilson. He had just been appointed to be the penultimate Governor of Hong Kong. Wilson recalled:

> There was no question of her giving me any guidance or instructions on how I should do my job as Governor. All she wanted to do was to rail on and on about the Hong Kong Agreement. She kept saying what a mistake it had been, and how terrible it was. Percy Cradock was there, and he interrupted her every so often to say, 'But Prime Minister, you agreed to this, and you were quite right.' She took no notice of him, pouring out her emotional feelings against the Chinese. I think she just wanted to get off her chest how much she had hated giving Hong Kong away and signing the agreement.

The emotional Margaret Thatcher and the realistic Prime Minister were two sides of her personality. With Hong Kong it was both inevitable and right that realism won in the end.

REFLECTION

Ireland and Hong Kong were not seen by Margaret Thatcher as foreign-policy successes. 'Like Calais for Mary Tudor, they were written on her heart',[58] said Charles Powell, who listened to more than his fair share of prime ministerial rants on these subjects.

It was a strange failing in Margaret Thatcher to underestimate two such important parts of her legacy.

With Hong Kong she held virtually no cards, yet by blustering and bluffing she secured better arrangements for the handover of the colony than any of her advisers initially expected. Her appointment of Sir Percy Cradock was a vivid illustration of her willingness to give priority to excellence, even if it was contrarian excellence in relation to her own instincts.

Credit should also go to Sir Geoffrey Howe for his ability, in this rare instance of their harmonious teamwork, to keep the Prime Minister on side. On the day he came back from his final round of successful negotiations with Deng

Xiaoping, Margaret Thatcher sang the praises of her Foreign Secretary. 'I congratulated Geoffrey in Cabinet on his return, and I meant every word.'[59]

In Ireland, Margaret Thatcher showed prescience, particularly in a period scarred by terrorist outrages, in allowing the secret Armstrong–Nally channel to lay the foundations for an agreement. Reducing her dependency on the Orange card, yet without yielding an inch of British sovereignty over Northern Ireland, was an achievement of considerable statesmanship. She was reluctant to move in this direction, resented the American pressure for it and appeared to be disavowing the whole endeavour in her retirement. But the undeniable result of the Anglo-Irish Agreement is that it gradually transformed the relationship between Dublin and London.

It took arduous work by two more prime ministers, John Major and Tony Blair, before peace came dropping slow. On her watch of the long war against IRA terrorism, Margaret Thatcher held the line courageously and opened the negotiating door constructively. She deserves credit for this twin-track approach.

Seen with the hindsight of history, it is now clear that the Anglo-Irish Agreement of 1985 paved the way for the Northern Ireland peace process initiated by John Major in 1994, followed by the Good Friday Agreement signed by Tony Blair in 1998, which culminated in the historic state visit of Queen Elizabeth II to Ireland in May 2011.

These were milestones of reconciliation made possible by the earlier acts of resolution and responsible diplomacy in the early 1980s. Margaret Thatcher is not always applauded as a peace-maker in Northern Ireland, but without her contribution the Troubles might still be with us.

Important though Hong Kong and Ireland were, they remained sideshows in comparison with her primary mission – to rebuild Britain's economic and political confidence.

25

Batting for Britain in Saudi Arabia

THE DEAL OF THE CENTURY

Towards the end of a long dinner in Riyadh on the night of 16 April 1985 King Fahd bin Abdulaziz of Saudi Arabia turned towards Margaret Thatcher, sitting on his right, and said quietly but with the unquestioned authority of an absolute monarch: 'Prime Minister, the deal is yours.'[1]

The deal, announced six months later on 26 September 26, was the largest export contract in the history of Britain. It was worth £5.2 billion at the time of signature, growing in value to over £90 billion during the next two decades. It ensured the survival of British Aerospace and many other companies in the sector, creating vital cash-flow and at least 50,000 new jobs. It inflicted a painful defeat on the French, compared by some to the commercial equivalent of a twentieth-century Waterloo, because before Margaret Thatcher's intervention Dassault had received a letter of intent to award them the same contract. It was a game changer in terms of increasing Britain's political influence and export performance across the Middle East.

The name of the deal was *Al Yamamah*. It would never have been struck without Margaret Thatcher. She achieved this triumph almost single-handedly as she deployed some of the most original, unorthodox and secretive aspects of her personality, particularly when co-operating closely with Prince Bandar bin Sultan of Saudi Arabia.

The secrecy was vital because the eventual contract touched some highly sensitive areas within the Saudi royal family, her own family, the RAF's nuclear capabilities and Britain's aerospace industry. To this day the detailed account of how the deal was won is almost unknown except to a handful of insiders. Intriguingly Margaret Thatcher did not mention the project in her memoirs, which is mysterious since it was one of her greatest achievements. But her veil of secrecy can safely now be lifted, not least because the story is entirely to the Prime Minister's credit.

FIGHTING THE FRENCH

A good starting point for the story is to be found in the tensions between the two most powerful men in Saudi Arabia – Defence Minister Prince Sultan and his elder brother King Fahd. Throughout the 1970s Prince Sultan was the sole decision-maker on all defence issues within the Kingdom. Although he respected British defence equipment suppliers, particularly British Aerospace who had since the 1950s supplied the Royal Saudi Air Force (RSAF) with Lightnings, Strikemasters and training for their pilots, Prince Sultan had become strongly pro-French. He was planning a massive re-equipment programme for the RSAF to give it both an offensive and defensive capability. This meant placing an export order for over a hundred new military aircraft. To insiders who knew about Prince Sultan's Francophilia, Mirages made by Dassault were the favourites to win it.

The British, however, remained confident of securing at least a part of the potential order. Margaret Thatcher raised this export prospect when she made her first visit to Saudi Arabia in 1981. Subsequent reports by the defence sales department of the Ministry of Defence increased her expectations that an order for Hawk trainers would be given to British Aerospace. Michael Heseltine as Defence Secretary made a visit to Riyadh and came back full of optimism. By chance he reflected this in a conversation he had in my house in 1983 with a well-connected Saudi businessman, Wafic Saïd. Both of them were my guests at a dinner I gave in honour of former President Nixon. On discovering that Wafic Saïd had Saudi Arabian interests, Heseltine talked about his recent meeting with Prince Sultan and his confidence that a big Hawk order would be coming Britain's way. 'Nothing has been agreed' said Wafic Saïd. 'I wouldn't count on anything yet.' 'Who are you?' asked Heseltine sharply. 'What do you know about it?'[2]

Some weeks later Wafic Saïd was approached by James Blyth, the head of defence sales at MoD. Saïd had no business connection with British Aerospace and was not an arms dealer. But he was known to be a close confidant of and business adviser to Prince Sultan and his family. For that reason James Blyth asked Saïd if he could find out what was happening to the Saudi aircraft order. Wafic Saïd, who was married to an English wife and was staunchly pro-British, immediately agreed to help. He raised the subject in Washington a few days later with his close friend Prince Bandar bin Sultan, the Saudi Ambassador to the United States.

After checking back with his father, Prince Bandar passed on bad news to Wafic Saïd, 'I am afraid our British friends have lost the contract', he reported. 'My father has signed a letter of intent with the French.'[3]

When James Blyth was given this information he was astounded, but his checks proved it to be correct. Dassault had indeed received from Prince Sultan a letter appointing them the suppliers of Mirage aircraft to the RSAF.

The news shook both British Aerospace and the British government at the highest levels. Margaret Thatcher wanted to know why the MoD's optimism had been so misplaced and what, if anything, could be done to win the contract back. She was advised that the only source of inside information available to the British government that had proved to be reliable was Wafic Saïd. So she asked to see him.

Wafic Saïd met the Prime Minister at No. 10 and was deeply impressed. He recalled:

'She was extremely well briefed and absolutely furious. She ran through the history of how Britain alone had been willing to provide the RSAF with Lightnings back in 1959. She said 'We trained their pilots. We taught them English. We built a close relationship with them. I will not accept that we should be kicked out by the French! This contract is vital to our aerospace industry! We must fight back.'[4]

The only advice Wafic Saïd felt able to offer was that she should have a face-to-face meeting with Prince Bandar as soon as possible. Margaret Thatcher immediately agreed to this.

Wafic Saïd gave her this good advice not just because Prince Bandar was the defence minister's son, but because he too was staunchly pro-British in his personal and aviation loyalties. He had trained as a pilot at Cranwell, retaining close friendships from his days as a Flight Lieutenant in an RAF Lightning squadron. Despite having been given the politically incorrect nickname of

'Woggie' by his fellow pilots, Bandar enjoyed their camaraderie, their humour and their English way of life. He was knowledgeable about British politics and had become a great admirer of Margaret Thatcher in the aftermath of her Falklands victory.

It took no time for this admiration to become mutual. At their first meeting Prince Bandar was immediately recognised as 'one of us'. Handsome in his looks, military in his bearing, expert in his briefing and talented in his geo-political flair for deal making, he became an immediate and enthusiastic collaborator with the Prime Minister in her drive to win back the huge aircraft order for the RSAF from the French. To an outsider this looked like mission impossible as Dassault already had Prince Sultan's letter of intent in their pocket. But Bandar was one of the few insiders who understood the tension that was growing between the King and his younger brother on defence issues. So Bandar advised Margaret Thatcher that with the right strategy she had a chance of persuading the King to reverse Saudi Arabia's plan to purchase Dassault's Mirage aircraft for the RSAF.

King Fahd was unhappy at the way his predecessor King Khaled had delegated all defence decision-making to Prince Sultan. Not only did the new king wish to reassert his monarchical authority, he also had doubts about the reliability of France as an ally.

At the prompting of Prince Bandar, Margaret Thatcher converted King Fahd to the idea that she would be rock solid as a loyal ally to Saudi Arabia. Throughout 1984 and early 1985 she sent the king a series of personal hand-written letters and secret messages. Some of them were on intelligence matters such as reports about the trouble-making intentions of the Shia leaders of Iran. Others were notes about her talks with President Reagan, Deng Xiaoping and other world leaders. King Fahd was flattered. He passed several oral messages to and from the Prime Minister using Prince Bandar as an inter-mediary. 'It is better for these communications to go outside the system', Bandar told Margaret Thatcher.[5]

THE DENIS BACK CHANNEL

In the age of recorded telephone calls and civil service procedures there is no normal method for Britain's head of government to communicate privately with a foreign head of state outside the system. But Margaret Thatcher liked listening to unofficial voices reaching out to her in unorthodox ways. She understood the Saudi royal family's love of conspiratorial secrecy. So she created a uniquely secure back channel designed to beat the system. It was called Denis.

The battle to win the *Al Yamamah* deal was nurtured, facilitated and watered by the invisible hand of Denis Thatcher. He became a pivotal player for four reasons. His wife wanted him to do it. His business acumen enabled him to understand the magnitude of the opportunity and its complexities. His patriotism caused him to love the idea of beating the French or, as he called it, 'stuffing the Frogs'.[6] He built a crucial rapport with the key executive at British Aerospace, Dick Evans, a rugby-playing kindred spirit who acted as the link man to Bandar.

Dick Evans recalled:

I had completely open access to No. 10 through Denis who was bloody marvellous. I would ring him up, usually to say that I had a message from Bandar and could I come round? In those days there was a back entrance and I'd meet Denis there. He'd take me up the staff stairs to his flat, usually about six in the evening, and I'd wait having a drink with him until the Prime Minister came up from her study. Then I'd give her Bandar's message and often take one back.[7]

These messages were partly about the positioning of the British bid for what became the *Al Yamamah* contract, but more about what King Fahd was thinking and how the Prime Minister might consider replying to him in her back-channel communications. There were also at least six unrecorded private meetings between Prince Bandar and the Prime Minister in the crucial 1984–1985 period. One of them was in Saltzburg in August 1985 when she broke her holiday in Switzerland to meet him.

Margaret Thatcher, well guided by Bandar, played the king brilliantly. She recognised that the battle for *Al Yamamah* was not really about aircraft capabilities or prices. It was a much more personal and strategic fight to convince the Saudi monarch that Prime Minister Margaret Thatcher of Britain would be a more reliable long-term ally than President François Mitterand of France.

At the time when these deliberations were taking place, Prince Bandar was becoming closer to his uncle, King Fahd, than he was to his father, Prince Sultan.

No Western observer can ever comprehend such shifts within the House of Saud which are emotional as well as political. But on the political front, Prince Bandar as the Saudi Ambassador to Washington was also handling another dimension of the Kingdom's aircraft buying strategy.

The Saudis' highest priority was to equip the RSAF with American F15E fighter jets. Ambassador Bandar not only reported that Congress would never allow the sale of F15E because of pressure from the Israeli lobby; he also orally conveyed a personal message to the king from President Reagan which in effect said, 'Sorry about the Congress: if I were you I would buy the British Tornados.'[8]

Although the deal was now moving Britain's way, inside the rival camps of companies, agents, promoters, fixers and commission takers in Saudi Arabia there was a fierce dogfight about the merits of Tornados versus Mirages. With more than a little help from the Bandar–Evans–Denis back channel the British Prime Minister gave the strongest of assurances about the continuity of Tornado spares, ammunition supplies and pilot training.

King Fahd was almost convinced to buy British but at a key moment in the debate he asked his now favourite nephew, Bandar, for his expert assessment of the two aircraft from the point of view of a former pilot. 'Each aircraft has its pros and cons,' said Prince Bandar, 'but this is a strategic issue. The key question is: in times of difficulty who will stand behind Saudi Arabia, Thatcher or Mitterand?'[9]

At the moment when King Fahd was squaring up to this decision he was told that the following day Margaret Thatcher's aircraft would be refuelling in Bahrain on its way back from a visit to Malaysia and India. The king suggested that the British Prime Minister should make her stopover in Riyadh, telling Bandar that he might be willing to agree the aircraft deal with her. Seizing the moment Bandar called Dick Evans who in turn called Michael Heseltine, Denis Thatcher and anyone else he could reach to achieve the miraculous feat of changing the flight plan for the Prime Minister's homeward journey from India. The miracle was accomplished.

Margaret Thatcher, still riding high internationally on the crest of the wave created by her Falklands victory, won King Fahd's political heart over dinner in Riyadh by the forthrightness and power of her personality. He was impressed by her mastery of the regional issues of Iran and Iraq. It also helped that he thought her a beautiful and charming woman. Around midnight the king quietly said the momentous words, 'Prime Minister the deal is yours'.[10]

DIFFICULT HURDLES TO OVERCOME

In Saudi Arabia a deal with the Government is not done until it is formally and publicly announced. So for the next six months there were intense negotiations to solve four major problems. They were: how to deliver what the Saudis wanted on an impossibly tight schedule; how the contract should be paid for; how to solve what was known as the Tornado nuclear issue; and how to handle Mark Thatcher.

It was the last problem which worried Denis and motivated his continuing involvement as an invaluable channel of communication on the project. As a father he knew better than anyone else that 'the boy Mark' as he called his son was a loose cannon.

Self promoting his skills as a wheeler-dealer of influence in the Arab world, Mark had caused earlier embarrassment to his mother by inserting himself as a consultant in a construction contract in Oman won by the British company Cementation Ltd. Critical newspaper coverage resulted making unfounded suggestions of impropriety. The reporting may have been unfair but the last thing the *Al Yamamah* deal needed was similar bad headlines. Yet there was a real danger of this because Mark Thatcher the entrepreneur, having got wind of the magnitude of the contract under negotiation, was offering his services to some of the key players. What could he provide? Access and influence in theory, but in practice this was unnecessary as the Prime Minister was already totally committed to *Al Yamamah* for national interest reasons. For the same reasons Denis was already providing ample access for Dick Evans of British Aerospace and facilitating Prince Bandar's backchannel messages. As Dick Evans put it, 'Mark was a complete distraction. He brought nothing that could be helpful or useful. He simply wasn't needed. But his efforts to be involved really worried Denis who was fiercely protective of Margaret.'[11]

Denis needed an ally in his strategy to keep Mark away from making commission deals with British companies in *Al Yamamah*. Dick Evans became that ally.

It was hard work. Denis was exceedingly bloody angry that Mark was trying to become involved. He kept asking me to keep him out. I said at one stage, 'If you his father and the Prime Minister his mother can't contain him what can I do?' But between us we did. I remember one moment of madness in the flat at No. 10. I was there with Denis when Mark rang me up and said he was in a hotel in Europe standing on the balcony and that he would jump off it if he wasn't allowed in the deal. Denis just said, 'Tell him to jump!' It was the idiot son at his worst.[12]

Suicide jumps aside, such episodes of Thatcher family dysfunctionality had long been a problem. Denis solved it this time around by making sure his own son was not engaged by British Aerospace and its subcontractors. If there were any issues the Prime Minister needed to know about, fast-track access to No. 10 was provided not by her commercially ambitious and highly visible son but by her invisible and loyal husband. This protective mechanism succeeded. Contrary to some press rumours, Mark Thatcher never came close to compromising his mother's integrity. British Aerospace and is subcontractors did not make any commission or fee paying deals with him.

Away from the distractions of Mark, there were important strategic issues which needed the hands-on attention of the Prime Minister during the *Al Yamamah* negotiations. After the Saudi Defence Minister swung behind the king on the decision to buy British, the size of the deal increased dramatically. Prince Sultan now wanted to order seventy-two Tornado aircraft and thirty Hawks, insisting that half of them should be in service with the RSAF within a year. This could only be achieved by taking a number of Tornados out of the line of operational service with the RAF. The Chief of the Air Staff was summoned to No. 10 to be given this order. After he had reluctantly agreed, Air Chief Marshal Sir Keith Williamson complacently observed to the Prime Minister that the Tornado was 'such a good aircraft that it sells itself'. She was having none of it. 'I can tell you from experience, Air Chief Marshal, that nothing ever sells itself – do you hear me?'[13]

The Tornados that were taken out of the RAF's line could have presented a major obstacle to the deal. For these Interdiction Strike (IDS) version of the aircraft were designated to be the bombers that would be used to drop Britain's nuclear deterrent on Moscow in the event of all-out war with the Soviet Union. In preparation for this Armageddon scenario, eighteen of the RAF's Tornados had already been 'nuclear wired' meaning that they were installed with a top-secret integrated computer system for the carriage and release of nuclear bombs. It was these same Tornados which, on the orders of the Prime Minister, were about to be temporarily transferred from the RAF for purchase by Saudi Arabia.

If the Israelis or indeed the British Foreign Office had ever discovered that the UK government was selling nuclear-capable aircraft to an Arab air force in the Middle East, all diplomatic hell would have broken loose. But Margaret Thatcher was playing her *Al Yamamah* cards extremely close to her 10 Downing Street chest. She showed none of them to her Foreign Secretary. Instead she used the ubiquitous Prince Bandar to explain the problem to King Fahd. He gave a categorical assurance that the nuclear-wired Tornados bought by Saudi Arabia would never be used to carry nuclear bombs. This was an entirely credible promise since Saudi Arabia had no nuclear bombs. But only a trustworthy king could have given the required assurance, only a trusting Prime Minister could have accepted it and only the two of them could have kept it secret.

Once the nuclear issue had been taken care of, the most pressing issue was working out how the *Al Yamamah* deal could be paid for. This was another huge problem. Although Saudi Arabia was an oil-rich country, its civil infrastructure modernisation programme had resulted in a substantial budget deficit. So the bills for *Al Yamamah* had to be met out of a separate off-budget account financed by a unique oil for aircraft agreement. This needed the approval of the king and prime minister.

The agreement details were fiendishly complicated since Britain could not be at risk from exchange-rate or oil-rich fluctuations. Yet all the difficulties were overcome. Margaret Thatcher had to cajole a consortium of oil majors – Shell, BP and Texaco – to accept liftings from the Aramco terminals in Saudi Arabia's Eastern Province of between 200,000 and 600,000 barrels of oil per day. She also had to bang heads together at the Bank of England, the Treasury and the Ministry of Defence to set up the government to government account arrangements. It was difficult but with the Prime Minister in charge it got done.

The prices of the aircraft sold in the first tranche of *Al Yamamah* have never previously been published. They were £25.2 million for each of the seventy-two Tornados, £5.3 million for each of the thirty Hawks and £2.8 million for 30 PC9 Trainers which were added to the deal the night before the announcement. In addition to these hardware costs of just over £2 billion there were £3.2 billion worth of spares, training facilities and construction costs for new air bases.[14] Nothing like it in the history of British export deals had ever been seen before.

Astonishingly, this was only just the beginning. The Saudis made maximum use of their new off-budget finance arrangements using oil liftings. So *Al Yamamah* was renewed again and again and again. It became much more broadly based than an aircraft contract extending to naval ships and anti-terrorist facilities. Even so, only about 20 per cent of *Al Yamamah* covered military hardware. The other 80 per cent of the approximately £90 billion spent on the programme to date has gone on the construction of roads, schools, training institutes, housing, general services and infrastructure.

THE MOTIVATION OF THE PRIME MINISTER

Even Margaret Thatcher can never have foreseen, when she was politically wooing and winning King Fahd, the magnitude of what she was going to accomplish for Britain's balance of payments and exports. But in her usual clear-headed way she saw the priorities for a prime minister. They were helping British companies to win business in new overseas markets, boosting Britain's fragile aerospace industry and creating jobs in the manufacturing sector. There was also the vital interest of increasing British influence in the Middle East. She talked frankly to Dick Evans about these objectives during the saga of the *Al Yamamah* negotiations, adding one unexpected political priority – the winning of marginal seats in general elections.

In her interrogations of Evans about the industrial impact of the deal, the Prime Minister extracted from him the information that one new manufacturing job created by *Al Yamamah* at his company's factories in places like Wharton, Brough, Salmesbury and Kingston created another twenty new jobs in the aerospace supply chain. These jobs were secured for subcontractors, principally in Lancashire and the wider North West of England, also stretching down into the West Midlands.

'Do you realise how powerful your company is, Dick?' Margaret Thatcher asked him. 'No British political party can be elected to power unless they win the key marginals. You represent to me the largest number of critical seats in the key areas of the North West and the West Midlands.' Ticking off a number of named constituencies on her fingers she asserted, 'Jobs in towns and cities like these are absolutely vital to national prosperity and to our government's electoral prospects'.[15]

The concept of *Al Yamamah* as an engine for winning domestic elections may not have occurred to anyone else but Margaret Thatcher the perceptive and sometimes parochial politician. But she also kept her side of her strategic bargain with King Fahd as Margaret Thatcher the international statesman.

For when Saudi Arabia tottered and swayed at the prospect of being the next target for Saddam Hussein in the days after his 1990 invasion of Kuwait, Margaret Thatcher was the Kingdom's earliest and most robust defender. She despatched some of the first British forces and aircraft to the Gulf – many of them landing at the new bases built under the *Al Yamamah* contract. She also most effectively exhorted the first Bush administration to put its military might behind Saudi Arabia, delivering the memorable line to the President, 'George, this is no time to go wobbly'.* As always, she was a loyal and far-sighted international ally.

Margaret Thatcher pulled off large export deals for many British companies in many countries. She saw this as a vital part of her role as Prime Minister, often describing it as 'Batting for Britain'. In Saudi Arabia she played her finest captain's innings.

REFLECTION

Al Yamamah was a triumph for Margaret Thatcher but it was not without subsequent controversy. Because of the jobs created there was always bi-partisan support for the contract in Parliament. But some MPs and journalists took a hostile stance, attacking the project on the political grounds that it was an unsavoury arms deal with a reactionary monarchy. There were also allegations of corruption linked to the deal, including unsubstantiated insinuations that Mark Thatcher had benefited from it.

Most of these claims, although published by some British newspapers, originally surfaced in underground Arab magazines such as *Sourakia*. The informants for these stories often had axes to grind that were linked to some score settling between factions within the Kingdom. So assessing the reliability of such reports was difficult.

---

* See Chapter 35.

Inevitably it was true that some individual Saudis and Saudi companies made fortunes from *Al Yamamah*. Commissions, consultancies and success fees are the way of life in the Middle East, par for the course on business deals great and small. Did Mark Thatcher benefit in this way? The allegation has always been denied and not an iota of proof has ever been produced to underline these denials. I believe them, first because it is so difficult to see what value he could possibly have added to any part of the project, and second because Denis worked so hard to keep his son out of the deal.

In 1992 I was appointed Minister of State for Defence by Prime Minister John Major and given responsibility for *Al Yamamah* which by then was in its seventh year of operation. I had long talks and negotiations with King Fahd and Prince Sultan which resulted in *Al Yamamah Two*, the first of several massive extensions of the contract which continues to this day. In that job* I learned many *Al Yamamah* secrets, none of which yielded anything but credit to Margaret Thatcher. During my meetings in Riyadh I sometimes had the impression that King Fahd would much rather be negotiating with her than with me, so often did he refer to her personality and even her beauty in the warmest of terms!

The Public Accounts Committee (PAC) in the House of Commons, under the chairmanship of the former Labour Treasury minister Robert Sheldon, conducted its own report on *Al Yamamah* in 1992. It gave the financial aspects of the project handled by the British government a clean bill of health. But the PAC report was never published, not because of any financial irregularities but because the nuclear wiring of the Tornados sold to Saudi Arabia was then deemed to be far too sensitive a secret to be revealed.

Some of the key figures in the deal stayed close to Margaret Thatcher. King Fahd invited her to Riyadh soon after she ceased to be Prime Minister. He paid her the unprecedented compliment of meeting her at the front steps of her arriving aircraft accompanied by his entire cabinet.

Prince Bandar was a regular visitor to her in retirement. Wafic Saïd became a lifelong friend, often having her to stay at Tusmore, his Oxfordshire estate.

---

* Like many other people linked to *Al Yamamah* I was subjected to vague press insinuations that I was corruptly involved in the deal. This was completely untrue. The only allegations to this effect were withdrawn in the High Court in June 1997.

During her last years Margaret Thatcher enjoyed long breaks in the Clock House of Tusmore, accompanied by her carers.

Sir Richard Evans, as he became, remained a confidant of Denis Thatcher, often dining with him or *à trois* with Bill Deedes in the East India Club. 'Denis was one of the heroes of *Al Yamamah*', said Evans. 'His only motives for being so incredibly helpful was that he loved his wife and he loved his country. He was the best British patriot I ever saw.'

Patriotism explains much about Margaret as well as Denis Thatcher over their roles in the *Al Yamamah* story. She took patriotic risks in her dealings with the Saudis but they paid off handsomely in terms of jobs, exports and a revived, indeed a saved, aerospace industry for Britain. Why did she omit any mention of this success story from her memoirs? Perhaps she felt vulnerable about Mark's rumoured involvement. She need not have done. As usual she was in the dark about her son's business activities. Had she been in the know, she would have been grateful that Denis protected her from filial embarrassment while playing his usual quiet but pivotal role as her loyal consort. In this instance both Thatchers deserve praise for steering the largest export contract of the twentieth century from France to Britain.

26

Unions and miners

STEPPING STONES TOWARDS SOLVING THE PROBLEM

The most important achievement of Margaret Thatcher's second term as Prime Minister was the defeat of the National Union of Mineworkers' strike in 1984–1985. It exorcised the demon of militant trade unionism, which had done such damage to the economy throughout the 1970s, and driven two prime ministers – Ted Heath and James Callaghan – from office.

Yet, although the economic and constitutional benefits to the nation from victory in the miners' strike were enormous, there were two surprises about Margaret Thatcher's handling of the union militancy problem. The first was how cautiously and falteringly she initially faced up to it. The second was how little credit she and her government were given for solving it. These paradoxes deserve explanation.

From the time when she replaced Ted Heath as Tory leader, Margaret Thatcher realised that she would one day have to confront the union extremists. Unfortunately, she had no coherent idea how or when to do this. The clarity of decision-making that was usually the hallmark of her personality was noticeably absent from her early attitude towards trade-union issues. Her main difficulty was that she was boxed in by a combination of political history, parliamentary fears and cabinet caution.

In the light of 1970s political experience, the conventional wisdom of the Tory Party was that picking a fight with the unions was the kiss of political death. At one of Margaret Thatcher's early shadow cabinet meetings, Lord Carrington quoted Harold Macmillan's dictum: 'No Government should ever take on the Brigade of Guards, the Vatican or the National Union of Mineworkers.'[1]

As Ted Heath had just lost the February 1974 election because of his unsuccessful battle with the miners, the axiom seemed to have been proved. So if there was any strategy at all within the Conservative Party towards the unions in the mid-1970s it was the 'softly, softly' approach personified by Jim Prior. Margaret Thatcher instinctively believed it was inadequate, but for a long while did nothing to change it.

The first stirrings of change came at the end of 1977 when she read a confidential briefing paper titled *Stepping Stones*. Its authors, who had been introduced to her by Keith Joseph, were two independent-minded businessmen, John Hoskyns and Norman Strauss.

Their central message was that a future Conservative government would have no chance of halting Britain's economic decline unless it was prepared to implement a determined strategy in facing down the excesses of union power. Hoskyns described it as

> a shit or bust strategy . . . we set out to convince Margaret that it was no use trying to be a Heath Mark II, even if she kept her nerve a bit longer than he did. We were offering something completely different, saying that the unions had to be confronted and that the union militants would have to be destroyed. Without the resolve to do this her efforts to revive the economy would be a case of 'steady as she sinks!'[2]

Margaret Thatcher liked blunt-speaking men of action who offered her solutions along the lines of her own instincts. So when *Stepping Stones* was presented to her by Hoskyns and Strauss, over a four-hour meeting in her office in the House of Commons on 24 November 1977, she was enthusiastic. 'It's the best thing we've had for many years',[3] she told Willie Whitelaw. But the paper was a long way from being accepted as Tory policy.

Although a *Stepping Stones* steering group was set up, its main achievement was to steer the radical ideas of Hoskyns and Strauss into a brick wall. This impasse came because of skilful opposition from Jim Prior, Peter Thorneycroft, Chris Patten, Ian Gilmour and other doves. The paper would probably have sunk without trace but for the 'winter of discontent'. That gave Margaret Thatcher the opportunity to resurrect the *Stepping Stones* strategy and to seize on one of its principal recommendations, which Hoskyns, a former army officer, called, 'The charge of the Light Brigade approach'.[4] This was the tactic of presenting the Callaghan government's appeasement of the unions as the major reason why the Labour Party should not be re-elected. Instead of being on the defensive about the Conservatives' inability to govern because of fear of union conflict, Margaret Thatcher went on the attack with her willingness to fight the dragon of union power. It was a bold move. Its timing was in tune with the mood of the electorate, even if her message made her senior colleagues uneasy.

This adoption of the *Stepping Stones* agenda brought John Hoskyns and his confrontational ideas back into fashion. After the general election of 1979 he was appointed Head of the Prime Minister's Policy Unit at Number 10. His arrival in what should have been a position of great influence meant that a beach-head for the strategy of challenging the unions had been established at the heart of the government's policy-making.

The strategy remained marooned on the beach for many months. This was largely due to Jim Prior whose even gentler approach in government as Employment Secretary meant that little was done to tackle the abuses of union power. As a result the Thatcher government's first Employment Act of 1980 was modest in its scope. It restricted the closed shop, but did not ban it. It outlawed secondary picketing, but not secondary strike action. It encouraged secret ballots, but did not make them compulsory. Although the Prime Minister publicly defended the legislation as 'modest and sensible'[5] and 'a very good start'[6] her real views were quite different. She became fed up with Prior, who she felt was thwarting the *Stepping Stones* agenda at every turn. So she moved her Employment Secretary to Northern Ireland, replacing him with Norman Tebbit, whose Employment Act of 1982 widened the scope of reform by making unions liable for damages.

During her first term, Margaret Thatcher had some successes in her dealings with the unions and one major failure. Pay demands became more realistic. Fear of unemployment after the 1981 Budget created a more moderate wage-bargaining climate. Some strikes, notably by train drivers and by health-service workers, ended in stalemate or even humiliation for their organisers. But the atmospherics of industrial relations remained tense. This was because of one elephant, which was not only in the room – it trumpeted its early defeat on the government. The elephant was the National Union of Mineworkers (NUM).

The NUM was Britain's most powerful and most militant union. In the first eighteen months of the Conservative government it won pay rises for its members of 30 per cent. In 1981 it threatened to strike over a proposal by the National Coal Board to close twenty-three uneconomic pits. The Prime Minister wanted to back the National Coal Board. But she had to make a swift U-turn. She discovered that coal stocks at power stations were much lower than expected.

In various cabinet committees Margaret Thatcher fulminated against Sir Derek Ezra, the National Coal Board Chairman, for failing to move sufficient quantities of coal from the pitheads to the electricity generating stations. She was almost as critical of her first Energy Secretary, David Howell. It was hardly the Prime Minister's fault that the coal was in the wrong place, but she took it personally. Yet in her despair she was decisive. When she learned that the country would only have thirteen weeks of electricity supplies before coal stocks ran out and the nation would be facing power cuts, she knew she was beaten. To her chagrin, she had to retreat before the battle started. 'Bring it to an end, David, make the necessary concessions', she instructed Howell.[7] They were expensive. The government had to find £300 million in extra subsidies to keep the twenty-three loss-making pits open. It was a major reversal for the Prime Minister's strategy to reform the financing of the nationalised industries. She had been defeated by the NUM.

The miners exulted in their easy victory. Amidst their crowing they elected, as their new NUM President, Arthur Scargill. In contrast to his moderate predecessor Joe Gormley, Scargill was a Marxist militant whose skill as a rabble-rousing orator was equalled by his determination to overthrow the elected government. He declared this openly. 'A fight-back against this Government's policies will inevitably take place outside rather than inside Parliament', Scargill told the annual conference of the National Union of Mineworkers in Perth. 'Extra-parliamentary action will be the only course open to the working class and the Labour movement.'[8]

Alerted to Arthur Scargill's intentions, Margaret Thatcher was certain that she would have to face a miners' strike. Even though John Hoskyns left her team at No. 10 in disillusionment in early 1981, she revived his *Stepping Stones* credo that confrontation was inevitable. So she prepared for it with great care, starting with an instruction to her new Energy Secretary, Nigel Lawson, to increase the movement of coal from the pitheads to the power stations. This was a wise move, because the miners' strike of 1984 was destined to become the turning point in the unresolved struggle between union power and government authority.

ARTHUR SCARGILL'S CHALLENGE

Margaret Thatcher not only saw the miners' strike coming, she regarded it as an unavoidable clash between hard-left militancy and common-sense economics. She was right. Arthur Scargill was an ideological extremist who wanted the strike for political reasons, leading it with contempt for the democratic rules of his own union and disregard for the interests of his members. Short of bringing General Galtieri over from Argentina to lead the NUM, there could not have been a more obtuse and stubborn opponent for Margaret Thatcher in her battle against the abuses of union power. But even if the fight was essential, it was a sad one with melancholy consequences and many lasting scars.

Having lost her opening battle with the NUM, the Prime Minister was determined to win the longer-term war. Her first dispositions involved making three strategic appointments that showed her prescience about the power struggle that was bound to come.

The day after the 1983 general election, she chose Peter Walker to be her Secretary of State for Energy. He was not her cup of tea politically. As a leading wet, he had opposed most of her economic policy and was a notorious leaker against her, principally to his friend Mark Schreiber of *The Economist*. But Walker had skills the Prime Minister needed – bustling energy, administrative drive and a capacity for ruthless media management. She told him on the day of his appointment that a Scargill-led strike was to be expected, and that his talent as 'a skilled communicator' would be useful in retaining public support for the government's case when the NUM militants went on the attack.[9]

The government's economic case was overwhelming. The coal industry was losing over £200 million a year in 1984. Three-quarters of its pits were uneconomic, and many of them would have to be closed.

To keep herself fully briefed on what was happening in and around the country's coalmines, Margaret Thatcher reached out to sources wider than the management of the National Coal Board. In January 1984, she asked to see two MPs who were the only Conservatives in the House of Commons whose constituencies covered an entire coalfield. They were Peter Rees (Dover and Deal), and myself (Thanet South). Between us, we represented the 3,000 strong workforce of the small but ultra-militant Kent pits.

The Prime Minister was surprised to learn that the Kent miners were such aggressive supporters of Arthur Scargill that there was no hope of persuading them to act or vote moderately. She wanted answers to detailed questions about where and how the coal they produced was being delivered. When I said that most of it seemed to be piling up at the pithead, which was unnecessary because Richborough Power Station – only six miles away – had plenty of spare storage capacity, Margaret Thatcher's eyes gleamed. 'We will make sure that Walter Marshall gets that information,' she said to her Private Secretary, 'won't we?'[10]

This was an interesting intervention by the Prime Minister. Sir Walter Marshall was the new Chairman of the Central Electricity Generating Board (CEGB). He had become No. 10's favourite nationalised industry leader after a successful stint as head of the UK Energy Authority. Margaret Thatcher liked his 'get up and go' spirit, so she promoted him to the Chairmanship of the CEGB. She gave him instructions to keep the power stations fully stocked with coal, diesel fuels and industry chemicals in case a strike was called by the NUM.

Marshall rose to the challenge and performed his task with vigour. He was an inspired choice by the Prime Minister, and a key player in the eventual defeat of the strike. It is interesting that she was in touch with him about as detailed a matter as coal deliveries to Richborough Power Station three months before the strike was called.

When Peter Rees and I were fielding a barrage of questions from Margaret Thatcher about the Kent miners, I told her that the Betteshanger pit near Dover was producing the most expensive coal in Britain, since its losses were more than £400 per ton.

She sounded shocked. 'That can't go on', she said. 'You should go and see Ian MacGregor and make sure he is aware of it. And you should invite him to speak to that Conservative Philosophy Group of yours as soon as possible.'[11]

Perhaps that response indicated that Margaret Thatcher had early doubts about the communication skills of her third key appointee for the battle with Scargill – the new Chairman of the National Coal Board. Sir Ian MacGregor was a seventy-year-old Scottish-born American industrialist with a reputation for toughness.* During his career in the United States his track record included

---

* Sir Ian MacGregor (1912–1998), Director British Leyland, 1977; Chairman British Steel, 1980; Chairman National Coal Board, 1983–1985. Arthur Scargill branded him 'the American butcher of British industry'. McGregor replied that he was 'a plastic surgeon' whose job was to 'try to rebuild damaged features' (*New York Times*, 15 April 1998).

breaking a two-year strike by the United Mineworkers. In the UK, he had served for two years as Chairman of British Steel, where he had converted huge losses into profit, but at a cost of making half the workforce redundant. This earned him the soubriquet 'Mac the Knife'.[12]

When Ian MacGregor addressed the Conservative Philosophy Group it was soon apparent that he had little talent for speaking or answering questions. His dour appearance and his corporate American jargon – 'I don't give a diddly-squat for the press' – put him on a different planet from the world of politics. He seemed insensitive to any wider issues relating to the mining industry other than the figures 'at the all-important bottom line' of the NCB's annual accounts. He told us 'kow-towing to the unions pervades our entire management, our board, and stops only at my feet'.[13] His image as a hard man evidently appealed to the confrontational instincts of Arthur Scargill, who greeted MacGregor's arrival at the NCB as that of 'A Yankee steel butcher waiting in the wings, waiting to chop us to pieces'.[14]

This was not a cry of fear. It was a trumpet call to battle. Scargill was a revolutionary who longed to repeat a triumph he had enjoyed as a local union leader at Saltley Coke Works in 1972, when the mass picketing he had organised caused the Heath government to cave in to the miners. This time the humiliation of the Thatcher government was Scargill's target. He relished the prospect of an all-out coal strike. His problem was that he could not persuade his fellow miners to vote for one.

In his first two years as NUM President, Scargill called his members to ballot for a national strike on three occasions. Each time, he had failed to get the 55 per cent majority required by the union's constitution. In March 1984, when the NCB announced its plan for closing another twenty uneconomic pits, Scargill managed to orchestrate a national strike without a national ballot. His method was to get the most militant coalfields – Yorkshire, Scotland and Kent – to walk out and then to send mass pickets to other regions to coerce them into joining the chain of strike action.

There was a turning point at the beginning of these walkout and picketing activities, when Margaret Thatcher rumbled Scargill's strategy and responded instinctively to his challenge. The moment came when Ian MacGregor arrived for a meeting at No. 10 that had nothing to do with the coal industry. Wearing his hat as Chairman of British Steel, he had come to lobby the government about a proposal to build a privately financed Channel-crossing road bridge. But before opening his presentation, MacGregor told the Prime Minister that the NUM had just launched strike action at several coalfields. He said that the position was particularly worrying in the East Midlands, because many miners there did not want to join the strike but had been prevented from going to their jobs at the pitheads by aggressive picketing from NUM militants.

Margaret Thatcher was appalled. 'Get me the Home Secretary!' she told the Downing Street switchboard operator. When Leon Brittan came on the line, he was asked whether he knew what was happening. 'You must speak to the Chief Constable of Nottingham immediately', instructed the Prime Minister, 'and tell him that the government expects him to uphold the lawful right of working men to go to work.'[15]

Present in the room when she gave this order was her Private Secretary, Andrew Turnbull. He was in no doubt that this was a turning point. He said:

> Had she not given that signal, history would have been completely different. She realised at once that the battle she had been expecting had begun. Up to then, the police were being cautious. But when they were told their duty, they did it. And from then on at No. 10 we were on a war footing.[16]

The war footing was largely invisible. Externally, the government wanted to preserve the fiction that this was an industrial dispute between the NCB and the NUM. Internally, Margaret Thatcher knew that her credibility, and Britain's, depended on not being defeated by Arthur Scargill. So, behind the scenes she exercised an extraordinary degree of hands-on control over the response to the miners' strike, sometimes using men and methods that were highly unorthodox.

The Prime Minister's problem was that she never had complete confidence in either of the two figures who were fronting the strike on behalf of the NCB and the Department of Energy. Ian MacGregor was so inept at the skills of politics and public relations that for all his determination to improve the industry's bottom line, he looked like an accident waiting to happen. Peter Walker had plenty of PR and political experience, but he was a notoriously semi-detached wet from the Jim Prior School of softly, softly conciliation. Margaret Thatcher feared that either or both of these front men might sell the pass at any moment.

To prevent this happening, she put in place her own political, administrative and clandestine machinery to ensure victory.

The political will to defeat Scargill was led by the Prime Minister, although her most influential supporter was Nicholas Ridley, then only a Minister of State at the Department of Industry. He was the hard-line strategist in whom she placed her greatest trust. But the impetus for implementing the strategy came straight from the top. 'For the best part of a year, at least half of the Prime Minister's working day was devoted to the miners' strike', recalled Andrew Turnbull. 'She kept the pressure up at a level of intensity comparable to the Falklands, with a constant flow of ministerial meetings, ad hoc meetings, and meetings of MISC 101, the key cabinet committee.'[17]

MISC 101, administratively headed by a capable Cabinet Office Deputy-Secretary, Peter Gregson, was the clearing-house and co-ordinating committee that delivered the goods. It ensured that coal stocks at the power stations stayed at an all-time high; that the CEGB generators kept running at full steam; and that police forces were well co-ordinated and well equipped in their operations to contain the violence of the flying pickets.

One vital factor in winning the battle on the many fronts where it was being joined was to make sure the NUM was kept isolated. If the strike had been supported for reasons of solidarity by other unions, Margaret Thatcher's government might well have been as badly humiliated as Ted Heath's was ten years earlier. The Prime Minister herself was sometimes dangerously combative in wishing to make premature legal challenges using the government's new powers. This might have triggered support for Scargill from other unions, but wiser counsels prevailed at MISC 101 and elsewhere. In any case, she was a model of restraint compared with Arthur Scargill, who had few friends in the union movement. He managed to lose them, and to alienate many rank and file members in his own NUM, by a series of bad mistakes and bombastic claims.

Scargill's first mistake was to call the strike in the spring, when coal stocks were plentiful and demand for electricity waning. If he had launched his offensive in the autumn, the supplies to the power stations might have run worryingly low before the end of the winter.

The second and greater mistake was Scargill's refusal to hold a national ballot of NUM members. This split the moderate Nottinghamshire miners from the rest of the union. It also ensured that other potentially sympathetic unions, such as the power and transport workers, refused to back the strike.

The third negative perception of Scargill's leadership was his encouragement of the escalating violence on the picket lines. The worst example of this occurred on 29 May 1984, outside the Orgreave Coke Works in South Yorkshire, when Scargill organised mass picketing to prevent coke convoys reaching Scunthorpe steelworks. For several hours over 6,000 pickets and 1,700 riot police fought pitched battles of a size and ferocity not seen since the English Civil War. Although the police remained in control, at least seventy people were seriously injured in the clashes.[18] The television coverage of these scenes appalled Margaret Thatcher, who denounced the violence in a speech the following day during a visit to Banbury Cattle Market. She called it 'an attempt to substitute the rule of the mob for the rule of law, and it must not succeed'.[19]

Throughout the year-long strike, Margaret Thatcher continued to worry that Ian MacGregor was inadequate at putting across the NCB's economic argument for pit closures. This should have been an easy task considering that Scargill's position was that no pit should ever be closed no matter how much money it was losing. Yet MacGregor was constantly out-manoeuvred by the NUM in the propaganda battle. His worse moment of media ineptitude was to be photographed covering his head with a newspaper in an effort to avoid reporters' questions.

After many such gaffes, the Prime Minister could bear it no longer. Using as an intermediary David Young – her newly appointed Minister without Portfolio – she sent her favourite public relations guru, Tim Bell, to act as a mentor to Ian MacGregor. More riskily, she brought in a most unorthodox adviser, David Hart, to perform dark arts in the heat of the miners' strike, which made a considerable contribution to her eventual victory over Arthur Scargill.

DAVID HART: HER SECRET BLUE PIMPERNEL

David Hart was the most exotic figure ever to penetrate the inner circle of advisers to Margaret Thatcher. He had initially attracted her interest in the mid-1970s by making generous donations to her favourite think tank, the Centre for Policy Studies. Later, with some encouragement from Ian Gow, he sent her briefing notes on topical issues.

The opinions in these briefs were alleged 'to come straight from the lips of those parts of the general populace which your officials cannot reach'. For David Hart claimed to run an unofficial intelligence service, whose agents ranged from working miners in Nottinghamshire to roller-blading West Indians in Brixton. Both sources reported to HQ Hart at Claridge's Hotel in Mayfair, and their views were conveyed to the Prime Minister as 'the word on the street'.[20] This 'word' was suspiciously supportive of the most robust opinions of Margaret Thatcher. She could sometimes be a sucker for the notion that she had a hot-line to the man in the street, the cleaner of her flat at No. 10 being her primary fountain of such wisdom. So she was delighted to have her prejudices confirmed by Hart's proletarian voices, telling him in one early morning phone call, 'Gosh, you do cheer one up'.[21]

By cheering up the Prime Minister with his well-crafted blend of street-wise reporting and worldly-wise flattery, Hart's bulletins gained increasing credibility with her, much to the dismay of her private office. 'She pays far too much attention to him', her new Political Secretary, Stephen Sherbourne, was told. 'He's a spiv. Give him a wide berth.'[22]

Son of the successful Ansbacher merchant banker 'Boy' Hart, David Hart had in his first thirty-eight years been an anarchic Eton schoolboy, an avant-garde film-maker, a poet, a playwright, a financier and a bankrupt. After settling with his creditors, he had re-emerged as a property developer with a personal helicopter, a suite at Claridge's and a country estate in Suffolk. I had known him well since we had been in the same house at school. Nothing usually surprised me about his maverick waywardness. But in 1984 I grew astonished at his increasingly influential role in helping the Prime Minister to win the miners' strike.

Eccentric in behaviour, unconventional in dress and contrarian in his thinking, David Hart was passionate in his right-wing politics. Like Margaret Thatcher, he saw the Scargill strike as a make or break crisis for Britain. Unlike her, he had a high opinion of Ian MacGregor, whom he befriended at a time when Peter Walker was refusing to speak to the NCB Chairman.

Taking MacGregor's side in this quarrel, Hart managed to plant in the Prime Minister's mind the notion that the Energy Secretary was planning to betray her by making an early settlement of the dispute with the NUM. This was considered such a subversive theory that the normally mild-mannered Andrew Turnbull had a stand-up row with Hart about it. Along with other members of the private office, Turnbull tried to block him from meeting the Prime Minister. But Hart overcame the obstacles placed in his way by officialdom. With the help of Ronnie Millar, he managed to gain access to Margaret Thatcher to discuss his take on the miners' strike, usually late at night in her flat at No. 10.

At the first of these encounters, Margaret Thatcher was surprised by the oddity of her visitor's appearance. Sporting a Mafioso moustache, a scruffy pair of sneakers, a Savile Row pinstripe suit and puffing on a Monte Cristo cigar, Hart lived up to Ronnie Millar's description of him as 'a kind of Blue Pimpernel'.[23] But enjoying, as she often did, receiving undercover despatches from unorthodox sources, the Prime Minister soon became intrigued by what Hart had to tell her from his missions behind the front-lines of the Nottinghamshire miners.

Initially disguising himself as a miner in T-shirt, tattered blue jeans and the same scruffy sneakers he was wearing at No. 10, Hart established his presence in one or two Nottinghamshire pubs, where an increasing band of anti-Scargill rebels congregated after working their shifts in the East Midlands pits. Hart's technique was to play dominoes with them, to lose, to pay for his losses in pints of beer and, above all, to take snuff with them. This was his trump card. Many miners, because of the rules against smoking down the pit, were heavy snuff users. So was Hart, who had formed this rarefied habit in his schooldays to circumnavigate the rules against smoking at Eton.

Men who take snuff together bond together, or so Margaret Thatcher was persuaded. She was shaken by Hart's stories of the brutal intimidation the Nottingham miners were suffering. She was impressed that he had used his own money to found and grow the National Working Miners' Committee, which she later described as 'an important development in the history of the working miners' movement'.[24]

Both the Prime Minister and her improbable undercover agent to the working miners understood the strategic importance of keeping the coal moving from the Nottinghamshire pits to the power stations. If this supply line could be increased, Scargill would be defeated; if it was broken, coal stocks would run out.

Because the stakes were so high, Margaret Thatcher gave David Hart her personal encouragement for his clandestine activities. He used more of his own money to expand the National Working Miners' Committee. He provided protection by ex-SAS men for the families of working miners in Nottinghamshire.

His most important coup was financing two Yorkshire miners to bring a successful legal action against the NUM, which resulted in a High Court ruling that the strike in Yorkshire could not be described as official. When the NUM ignored this ruling, Hart's lawyers obtained a writ for contempt of court against them. He flew to Blackpool in his helicopter and arranged for it to be served on a startled Arthur Scargill live on television, in the middle of a debate on the floor of the Labour Party Conference.[25] This was not only a sensational public relations coup; it resulted in the High Court fining Scargill £1,000 and the NUM £200,000. Scargill's fine was paid anonymously, but to avoid its assets being sequestered, the union sent a representative to ask for funds from Colonel Gaddafi of Libya.[26]

The NUM also received a sizeable donation from a committee of Soviet miners. With the help of the Secret Intelligence Service, whose co-operation could only have been authorised at the highest levels of government, David Hart obtained the documentary evidence of a letter signed by a senior member of the Politburo authorising the transfer of these funds to the NUM. He later framed the letter, hanging it as an historical exhibit in the cloakroom of his Suffolk home. During the strike he used his evidence of the Politburo funds to start a whispering campaign in the Nottinghamshire coalfield. The allegation that Scargill was in the pay of Moscow* spread like wildfire. It disgusted many Notts miners, alienating more of them from the NUM and causing an increasing number to return to work.

Throughout this period, Hart continued to make secret visits to Margaret Thatcher's flat above No. 10, and to brief her by telephone on a secure line from Ronnie Millar's home. He also had regular 'John Le Carré'-style walks[27] around St James's Park with her Political Secretary, Stephen Sherbourne, passing on nuggets of information from his growing network of working miners. According to the head of the Prime Minister's Policy Unit, Ferdinand Mount, Margaret Thatcher enjoyed her contact at late hours with the raffish Hart. 'Like all Prime Ministers, she often felt isolated and longed to see a fresh face who would tell her something different, though David's face and general demeanour towards the end of the day could scarcely be described as fresh.'[28]

---

* For new revelations on Moscow's side of this story see the author's interview with Mikhail Gorbachev, Chapter 28.

On one of these nocturnal visits a refreshed Hart attempted to make a pass at the Prime Minister, telling her that he thought she was 'incredibly beautiful and sexy'. She fended him off with the rebuke, 'Don't be such a silly boy'.[29] But she could not have been entirely displeased by his compliment, for she continued to use him both as an intelligence gatherer and as her link man to the anti-Scargill miners of Nottingham, whose coal production was steadily increasing.

After the strike, Hart was invited to join her speech-writing team for a while. Eventually, she was persuaded that he was too much of an unguided missile, and refused him further access after he was reported as having presented himself as her personal representative to a US defence corporation. But in her memoirs she complimented him as 'a friend who was making a great effort to help the working miners', from whom she learned 'a good deal informally about what was happening on the ground'.[30]

Margaret Thatcher's subterranean encouragement of David Hart's activities highlighted her own nervousness about the outcome of the miners' strike for most of 1984. She was troubled by what she called the 'laid-back optimism' of Peter Walker.[31] However, the sanguine views of her Secretary of State for Energy were confirmed when she held a secret meeting on the subject of power-station endurance with the CEGB chairman, Sir Walter Marshall. He gave her the good news that the power stations could be kept running until at least June 1985, and probably until November or even later. The Prime Minister was delighted, although she took on board the all-important rider that Marshall's forecasts depended on the continuing supply of coal from the Nottinghamshire pits. No wonder she concentrated on encouraging the working miners in both her public speeches and in her private initiatives through David Hart. As Margaret Thatcher's 'Blue Pimpernel', he had his niche in an important chapter of her history.

THE NACODS CRISIS AND THE COLLAPSE OF THE STRIKE

The Nottinghamshire and Derbyshire miners were just starting to trickle back to work in significant numbers when Margaret Thatcher's expectation of victory was threatened by the possibility of a strike by National Association of Colliery Overmen, Deputies and Shotfirers (NACODS). This was the obscure and small union of safety overseers whose supervision was required by law before coal could be mined from any pit. The membership of NACODS suddenly voted for strike action by an 82 per cent majority because a tactical error had been made by the NCB management.

For the first six months of the dispute, NACODS' maintenance and safety workers kept the pits open. Those who decided not to cross the NUM picket lines continued to be paid in the interests of expediency. Suddenly, the NCB announced that it would stop paying the comparatively few supervisors who refused to defy NUM pickets. This brought NACODS, until now keeping its distance from the NUM, to the brink of a strike in solidarity with Scargill. This would have been a disaster for the government's strategy because without the NACODS men carrying out their safety checks, the working miners could not go down the pits.

Margaret Thatcher was horrified by this development. Ian MacGregor's lack of political nous was responsible for it. He said he couldn't care less whether NACODS walked out. In his view Scargill was going to be beaten anyway.

By contrast, the Prime Minister felt it was vital to keep the moderate Nottinghamshire miners bringing up the coal. She was furious with the NCB chairman for his obstinacy. 'We were in danger of losing everything because of a silly mistake', was how she put it.[32]

Correcting the mistake was not easy. Margaret Thatcher was anxious to preserve the fiction that the government was keeping above the fray of the strike, which was still being presented as just an industrial dispute between the NCB and the NUM. She pretended not to be exerting any kind of interventionist influence on the NCB management. But the NACODS crisis was so serious she had to do just that.

By chance, the crisis came to a head in the middle of the Conservative Party Conference. There was a meeting on NACODS in the Prime Minister's suite in the Grand Hotel, Brighton, on the very evening when some four hours later the IRA bomb exploded. The conclusion of the meeting was that NACODS must be bought off with whatever was needed to keep the mines working. Norman Tebbit, the Secretary of State for Trade and Industry, was deputed to telephone Ian MacGregor to persuade him to make a better offer to NACODS. MacGregor did not agree. The conversation became acrimonious, with Tebbit saying: 'You've got to give in. You've got to give NACODS what they want.'

'Is that an instruction, Secretary of State?' replied MacGregor, repeating his question with a touch of menace in his voice.

Pushed to this brink, Tebbit backed off, at least to the extent of passing the receiver to Tim Bell, saying, 'Go on, you tell him'. By this time Tim Bell had developed a close relationship with Ian MacGregor, so was able to say to him, after some cajoling, 'C'mon, Mac. At the end of the day we're all working for these people. Let's do what they ask.' 'OK, then', grumped MacGregor. 'I'll hold my nose and do it.'[33]

What was then done by the NCB was to make greater concessions to NACODS than had been offered to the NUM, including an independent review of pit closures. If Scargill had been cleverer he would have accepted the NACODS terms for the NUM and declared that he had won the strike. But he had his own political agenda, which went far beyond improving the conditions for NUM members. So he bombastically rejected any settlement that did not result in the unconditional withdrawal of all pit closures. The result was to hand unconditional victory to Margaret Thatcher.

Once the NACODS crisis was over, the government only had to wait for the strike to crumble. Disillusionment with Scargill was growing in many mining communities. His antics with Libyan and Soviet paymasters contributed to his unpopularity. A greater cause of discontent was that after seven months of strike action with no discernible progress, many miners were fed up and hard up. As the economic pressures on their families mounted, they faced a bleak Christmas. They were becoming incredulous about Scargill's forecasts that coal stocks at the power stations were running out and that the government would soon crumble. Margaret Thatcher's resolution sounded far more real.

By November 1984 there was little doubt as to who was winning the battle. The NCB, again guided by the not-so-invisible hand of the Prime Minister, operating via David Young and Tim Bell, offered a handsome bonus to those miners who returned to work by 19 November. Over 11,000 of them did so. By the end of the year, 70,000 out of 180,000 miners were working, and the coal they produced was getting to the power stations.

Nevertheless, the violence and the intimidation continued, with one death and many injuries. An angry Margaret Thatcher became overtly interventionist in response to initiatives to settle the strike. She upped the ante of the NCB's negotiating position by insisting that it must receive a written guarantee from the NUM saying that management alone would be the decision-makers on pit closures. 'Let us get it written down', she said in a January television interview. 'I want it dead straight, honest and no fudging.'[34]

She was attacked by Neil Kinnock for being 'a stubborn Salome who wants the miners' heads on a plate'.[35] This was not a million miles from the truth – even if Arthur Scargill was improbably cast as John the Baptist.

By mid-January 110,000 out of 180,000 miners were back at work. Scargill, however, was in total denial about his inevitable defeat. His NUM bully boys continued to victimise 'scabs', often in brutal ways that ranged from sticking screwdrivers into their testicles to fire-bombing their homes. Appalled by such violence, Margaret Thatcher became preoccupied with the plight of the working miners, and discussed plans to welcome their representatives to No. 10. Reluctantly, she accepted Peter Walker's advice that it would be unwise to do this while there was still fighting on the picket lines. But she made her sympathies clear in a letter of 4 February 1985 to the wife of a working miner, promising her that there would be 'no betrayal of the working miners to whom we owe so much'.[36]

The strike finally collapsed almost a year after it had begun. Bowing to reality on 3 March 1985, an NUM delegate conference voted, against Arthur Scargill's advice, for the return to work that had already happened. Amidst emotional scenes of brass bands playing and banners held aloft, virtually all the miners still on strike marched back to the pitheads the next day. The exceptions were the Kent miners who stayed out for another six weeks.

One evening in the House of Commons in early April, Margaret Thatcher asked me why my NUM constituents were being so stubborn. 'Because they think Arthur Scargill is a wet for giving way', I replied. She did not find this amusing. 'But he did not give way! He was crushed', she retorted with eyes blazing.[37]

LOSERS BUT NO VICTORS

The crushing of Arthur Scargill was essential, because he had led the miners over a precipice for reasons of political extremism, which had little to do with their economic interests. Outside his own introverted circle of NUM militants, few people agreed with his views or his tactics. So his defeat by Margaret Thatcher might have been expected to be seen as another popular victory for her. This was not the way it turned out.

Economically, the NCB's and the government's side of the case was overwhelming. Only Scargill could have argued with a straight face that no pit could ever be closed for financial reasons. Margaret Thatcher was right to claim that the miners' strike was political in the sense, as she put it, that 'Marxists wanted to defy the law of the land in order to defy the laws of economics'.[38]

Legally, the new trade-union legislation introduced by Norman Tebbit and vigorously backed by the Prime Minister was crucially important in defeating the strike. The total immunity at law conferred on trade unions in 1906 had been changed by the 1982 Employment Act which required a strike ballot to be held before immunity could be claimed. As a result of this reform, the NUM was vulnerable for having claimed their strike was official without the required ballot. The sequestration of NUM assets that was ordered for contempt of court because of this breach of the law was one of the turning points in the dispute. It could not have happened without Margaret Thatcher's earlier support, against the wishes of most of her cabinet in 1981, for 'Tebbit's Law' as it was called.

Symbolically, the Prime Minister's victory over the NUM was much more than the breaking of a strike: it was the breaking of a spell. Ever since the demise of the Heath government at the hands of the miners in 1974, it had become part of the mythology of British politics that a democratically elected government could not defeat an industrial challenge from the NUM. Margaret Thatcher exploded that myth. She had decisively answered, as Heath had failed to do, the neuralgic question: 'Who governs Britain?'

Politically, at least in the House of Commons, the exchanges on the miners' strike highlighted the government's dominance over the Labour opposition. This was not just a matter of numbers in the division lobbies. Nor was it because Margaret Thatcher seemed particularly effective at the despatch box. Her ascendancy was established because Neil Kinnock, the newly elected Leader of the Opposition, looked so weak.

From the start of the dispute, Kinnock found himself in an invidious position after Scargill had avoided the constitutionally required national ballot. As a new Labour leader, dependent on NUM votes, and as the MP for a mining constituency, Kinnock could not bring himself to condemn the strike. So for a year's worth of parliamentary duelling in debates and at Prime Minister's

Questions, the Leader of the Opposition had to evade, equivocate, bluster and fudge.

Margaret Thatcher made mincemeat of him. In one of her more memorable assaults towards the end of the strike, she taunted Kinnock:

> Throughout the strike, the right hon. Gentleman has had the choice between standing up to the NUM leadership and keeping silent. He has kept silent. When the leadership of the NUM called a strike without a ballot, in defiance of union rules, the right honourable Gentleman stayed silent. When pickets tried by violence to close down the pits in Nottinghamshire and elsewhere, against the democratically expressed wishes of the local miners, the right hon. Gentleman stayed silent. When the NUM tried to impose mob rule at Orgreave, the right hon. Gentleman stayed silent . . .[39]

Kinnock might have done better if he had stayed as silent as a Trappist monk. Instead, he played his hand with a windy verbosity that exposed not only the weakness of his position, but also the inadequacy of his abilities. Long before the strike ended, there were several MPs on the Labour benches saying that he was a loser who would never make a prime minister. Kinnock never recovered from his bellicose ambivalence in facing both ways on Scargill's militants.

After trouncing all her adversaries during the miners' strike, Margaret Thatcher must have been expecting to collect a dividend of electoral popularity. Yet, although the polls showed the public to be strongly anti-Scargill, the ratings for the Prime Minister recorded no gains. To some, this was mystifying. The government's authority had increased, the sovereignty of Parliament had been restored, the defeat of union power met with widespread approval and the economy could look forward to an unprecedented era of industrial peace. So why was Margaret Thatcher not basking in the same sort of acclaim she enjoyed after the Falklands?

The answer was that she overplayed her hand. She was right to be vitriolic about Scargill, but wrong to sound so totally unsympathetic to the NUM rank and file who supported him. This was a distinction that could have been subtly exploited, but when her dander was up, Margaret Thatcher did not do subtlety. Indeed, through the red mist of her anger she came perilously close to blurring the lines between her battle against Argentine military invaders and her battle against British miners.

Addressing the 1922 Committee of Conservative back-benchers in July 1984, she became so carried away on the tide of her anti-Scargill rhetoric that she drew a parallel between the Falklands War and the miners' strike, saying that, 'At the time of the conflict they had to fight the enemy without; but the enemy within, much more difficult to fight, was just as dangerous to liberty'.[40]

The thought may have been right, but the words on the lips of a Prime Minister were wrong. Sitting in a packed Committee Room 14 of the House of Commons when she delivered this onslaught, I saw several winces across the faces of her colleagues. The tribal banging on desks by her enthusiasts easily drowned out the sharp intakes of breath among her doubters. But the doubters were right in at least one important cultural respect.

When the miners' strike was finally over, with even the militants in Kent and other enclaves returning to work, the end result had the air of a melancholy wake, not a glorious victory.

For the mining communities suffered greatly as a consequence of Scargill's folly. Pit closures multiplied, bitter enmities festered, jobs vanished in the tens of thousands, suicide rates tragically soared and a whole way of life ground to a sad halt in many parts of Britain.

Margaret Thatcher had little or no sympathy for such feelings. But a clear majority of the British public did. Their sympathy showed in opinion polls, donations to miners' families' charities, and in the success of plays and movies such as *Billy Elliott* and *Brassed Off*. There was even a joint demonisation of Margaret Thatcher and Arthur Scargill, who were voted respectively Man and Woman of the Year by listeners of the *Today* programme and lampooned as a composite hate figure, 'Martha Scarthatch'. None of this worried the Prime Minister, who often saw being hated as a badge of honour. But it changed her domestic image by permanently adding the dimension of harshness to toughness in many people's political judgement of her. It was a great pity that she never followed Winston Churchill's famous advice, 'In victory; magnanimity'.

REFLECTION

In the judgement of history the outcome of the miners' strike was of fundamental importance. The power struggle against union militancy had to be fought and had to be won. The British had instinctively known this ever since the three-day week, the 'winter of discontent' and many disastrous episodes of industrial chaos in between. So when the chips were down and the consequences of Scargill winning his miners' strike challenge were faced by the public, most voters, whatever their political loyalties, wanted him to be defeated.

It was therefore a strange paradox that Margaret Thatcher gained no victor's laurels. She may have been cheered by the few, but the many reacted with sullen ingratitude. The Conservative government fell to third place in the opinion polls – well behind Labour and the Alliance. By the same yardstick of political measurement, Margaret Thatcher herself fell rather than rose in public esteem, particularly in the North. Nevertheless, she had done what was right, indeed essential, for the future health of parliamentary government and economic well-being in Britain. However melancholy the human side-effects in mining communities, defeating the Scargill strike was the most important and enduring achievement of the Prime Minister's second term.

27

Strengthening the Special Relationship with Ronald Reagan

THE GOLD SEAM AND THE FAULT-LINE

In her second term there were important new challenges on the international stage for Margaret Thatcher. She tackled them from a position of greater prestige than any British prime minister since Winston Churchill. For her triumph in the Falklands had given her the status of a superstar in the foreign-policy and geopolitical power elites of the world. She understood how to parley this stardom into global influence.

There was a gold seam and a fault-line in Margaret Thatcher's conduct of foreign policy. Both owed a great deal to her Grantham upbringing at the height of the Second World War. The gold seam was her instinctive respect for the United States combined with a genuine if occasionally exasperated friendship with its fortieth president, Ronald Reagan. Together they created the strongest chapter of the US–UK 'special relationship' since the days of Winston Churchill and Franklin Delano Roosevelt.

The fault-line was her instinctive dislike and distrust of the Germans. Her views about them were formulated in the Grantham of the 1940s. She was at her most impressionable age. Britain was at war as a great nation-state. Churchill's broadcasts thrilled her patriotic pride. She could see how strongly the English-speaking peoples were united in their determination to overcome the tyranny of Nazi Germany. By day, air-crews from Canada, Australia, New Zealand, South Africa and above all America came and went through Grantham on leave or on duty. By night, the roar of their Lancaster or Troop Carrier aircraft were heard overhead the town as they flew in and out of the forty-nine RAF and USAF bases in Lincolnshire. Sometimes the roar of the Luftwaffe aircraft came the other way, inflicting 386 raids on Grantham with eighty-nine killed as well as 191 injured.

Crouching under the kitchen table that doubled up as an air-raid shelter in the Roberts family home at North Parade, this was the world in which Margaret grew up. By the time she was prime minister, four decades later, most of that world had moved on. But some parts of her personality remained unmoved. Her romantic patriotism, her pro-American idealism, her veneration for military courage and her longings for Churchillian big picture policy-making surfaced regularly in her life at No. 10. These traits were most discernible in her attitudes and approach to foreign policy.

Lord Carrington recalled:

> I honestly came to think that she was only able to relate to people whose mother tongue was the English language. Americans first, Old Commonwealth second including up to a point the South Africans. But after that, with one or two exceptions like the Israelis, she could not enter the foreign mind-set. She was impatient with their whole attitude and approach. She would give them her view – pretty vigorously. It was rare for her to accept their view. Language was at the heart of this problem, particularly her inability to respond to the nuances of what Europeans were saying.[1]

For all her nationalism, it would be wrong to portray Margaret Thatcher as a stubborn Little Englander with a closed mind. She was usually but not invariably open to argument – which she enjoyed as an essential part of her decision-making process. Hammered out on the anvil of realpolitik, her prejudices could soften or sharpen, depending on who was hammering with or against her. 'And provided they got to her early enough', said Carrington.[2]

This was a curious way of making foreign policy, but on the gold seam of the UK's relations with the US it worked well because the Prime Minister's instincts, interests and intellect were usually in alignment.

Even so, there were bumps in the road. During the eight years of the Reagan Presidency that began in 1981, there were some serious disagreements between London and Washington. Yet the way they were handled showed the strength of the 'special relationship', and the warmth of the rapport between the occupants of the White House and No. 10 Downing Street. By contrast, Margaret Thatcher's fault-lines with Germany and the EEC turned increasingly cold and sour.

The explanation for these differences lay largely in the personality of Margaret Thatcher. Her formative experiences in Grantham were one part of it, but two other ingredients counted more. The first was her idealistic view of the United States as the economic and political superpower that could be relied upon to uphold the values of freedom and the rule of law. The second was that she saw Ronald Reagan as the politically and personally attractive champion of those values. She was as patient with his simplicities as she was impatient with the EEC's complexities. To understand why US–UK co-operation climbed to its highest post-war peak during the 1980s, it is important to understand the chemistry between the President and the Prime Minister. That was the X-factor that breathed new life into the relationship, making it so productive and so special.

THE PERSONAL CHEMISTRY

The 'special relationship', now approaching its seventy-fifth birthday, has a long history of charming irrelevancies about how warm the personal relations were between US President X and British Prime Minister Y. Much of it is collaborative fiction organised between aides and journalists who love to embellish the legend of how well the two leaders bonded during various leisurely pursuits; from walks in the Camp David woods to watching basketball in Ohio. But the Thatcher–Reagan rapport really was different. The most interesting difference was not the obvious one: that he was a man's man while she was a feminine woman. The profound and enduring difference was that they could have formidable and forthrightly expressed disagreements, yet build the UK–US relationship into greater strengths of co-operation than at any time since she first saw it from the impressionable vantage of a Grantham schoolgirl.

To the superficial eye, Ronald Reagan and Margaret Thatcher were an odd couple. It is difficult to imagine two more different characters. He was the blue-sky Californian who felt safest when sticking to broad principles and cue-carded stories. He could be a great communicator, but was limited in his intellectual reach. Full of folksy charm, he disliked detail, argument and confrontation.

She was the polar opposite. Chillingly analytical in her absorption of briefing material, she relished confrontational debate on points of detail. One of her personal mottos was 'I argue therefore I am'.[3] On her home turf she was scathing about politicians who had not mastered their briefs, or who tried to soft soap her with touches of humour that she could rarely see the point of. She had to discipline herself into a personality makeover to get along with Reagan, but she managed it.

The odd couple first met in on 9 April 1975, when Reagan was passing through London as part of his preparations to run for the 1976 Republican presidential nomination. He made a number of calls on Westminster politicians, including the newly elected Leader of the Opposition.

Their meeting in her room at the House of Commons was scheduled to take forty-five minutes, but lasted for an hour and a half. The reason why they got on so well originated in a glowing recommendation of Reagan from Denis, who had heard him talking at an Institute of Directors conference some years earlier.

The handsome Governor of California soon won the admiration of Margaret Thatcher with his good looks, good humour and good conservative views. 'It was evident from our first words that we were soul mates when it came to reducing government and expanding freedom',[4] was Reagan's take on the potential future prime minister of Britain. He described her in his next weekly radio broadcast, *Viewpoint*, as 'a woman of charm and poise and also strength. The British like their politicians to stand for something and she does'.[5]

Margaret Thatcher was equally complimentary. 'I was immediately won over by his charm, directness and sense of humour', she wrote afterwards.[6]

The good impressions continued at a distance, but were put to their first real test when Margaret Thatcher flew to Washington on 25 February 1981 for three days of talks and ceremonial meetings with the newly inaugurated President Reagan. For all the media briefings about their 'personal friendship', the two leaders did not know each other well, and used the formal terms 'Mr President' and ' Madam Prime Minister' throughout their conversations during this visit.

In her preparations before coming to Washington, Margaret Thatcher held Chequers seminars and immersed herself in foreign-policy briefing papers to bring herself up to speed with the new president's agenda. She was, according to one member of her team, 'on a complete high' and 'tremendously worked up about seeing Reagan alone'.[7] She had demanded information about his reading habits, his priorities and his intellectual interests. The answers to these inquiries yielded a thin harvest. Margaret Thatcher was gently warned that the President liked to see himself as a chairman of a board of governors and not as a hands-on manager of the government like a prime minister. This was good advice because at the first Reagan–Thatcher summit there were no debates about policy issues and no strategic *tour d'horizon* of the international scene. The Prime Minister was amazed at the President's broad-brush approach, but she played her game according to his rules.

Since the game turned out to be one of mood music, both leaders performed good tunes. At a black-tie dinner at the British Embassy on the night of 27 February, the Prime Minister quoted Charles Dickens's description of Americans as 'By nature frank, brave, cordial, hospitable and affectionate'. Turning to Reagan with an expansive flourish, she continued, 'That seems to me, Mr President, to be a prefect description of the man who has been my host for the last 48 hours.' Abandoning her prepared text, she spoke emotionally about 'two o'clock in the morning courage', when the toughest and loneliest decisions have to be taken by a president. She assured him, 'When those moments come, we here in this room, on both sides of the Atlantic, have in you total faith that you will make the decision which is right for protecting the liberty of common humanity in the future'.[8]

Reagan was visibly moved by this tribute, particularly the passage about two o'clock in the morning courage. So his off-the-cuff opening began, 'Prime Minister, Bob Hope [who was sitting at a table a few feet away] will know what I mean when I speak in the language of my previous occupation and say, you're a hard act to follow'. The laughter and applause that followed this thespian compliment was genuine. So was Reagan's entry in his private diary that night. 'Dinner at British Embassy. Truly a warm & beautiful occasion.'[9]

Margaret Thatcher reciprocated these warm feelings. In an emphatic handwritten thank you letter to the British Ambassador, Sir Nicholas Henderson, she wrote: 'There will never be a happier party than the one you gave at the Embassy – all due to you both . . . I have great confidence in the President. I believe he will do the things he wants to do – and he won't give up.'[10]

The following day, after the Thatchers and the Reagans met alone for morning coffee in the family quarters of the White House, the President again recorded sentimental thoughts: 'I believe a real friendship exists between the P.M., her family & us – certainly we feel that way, & I'm sure they do.'[11]

It was not quite love at first sight despite the best efforts of the spin doctors to make it sound that way. Margaret Thatcher was underwhelmed by the Reagan mind. Later in their relationship she sometimes became upset by some of Reagan's policies – on the Falklands, on economic sanctions against the Soviet Union and on Grenada. But the two leaders saw eye to eye on virtually everything else. And when they differed, after the temperature had cooled, they could agree to disagree with complete lack of rancour. As Reagan disarmingly put it, 'I don't think any of the disagreements have survived as disagreements once we could talk to each other. Some of them might have been the result of distance and not having heard the entire story, and when it is told, then everything is just fine.'[12]

Living happily ever after is more of a Reagan legend than a Thatcher one, for she could sometimes be contemptuous towards those who took policy positions when they had not briefed themselves fully. But she was careful not to give way to such upbraidings in her dealings with the President of the United States. As a result, the 'special relationship' became fruitful and powerful in the years 1981 to 1989, reaching decisions that galvanised the Western Alliance and brought benefits to both Ronald Reagan's America and Margaret Thatcher's Britain.

ISLANDS AND TENSIONS

In spite of the growing bonds of personal chemistry between Margaret Thatcher and Ronald Reagan, there were three international episodes that temporarily threatened to dent if not damage the US–UK 'special relationship'. They were: the Falklands crisis, the invasion of Grenada and the bombing of Libya. All presented serious problems, in which the personality of Margaret Thatcher was pivotal. Yet all were solved more swiftly and subtly than might have been expected.

As recorded in earlier chapters, President Reagan had to suppress splits within his administration, and misgivings of his own in order to give Margaret Thatcher the support she needed in the Falklands War. But despite the early Washington wobbles, Britain in the end received the American weaponry and intelligence it needed to re-take the Islands.

Later developments in the Falklands produced fresh UK–US tensions. Once a new democratically elected government had been installed in Buenos Aires, the US wanted to support it by voting for a UN resolution calling for renewed negotiations on the future of the Islands. Margaret Thatcher tried to persuade the US to oppose the UN plan. Ronald Reagan ignored her plea. 'He was getting a little bit fed up with her imperious attitude in the matter', commented George Shultz.[13]

A subsequent problem was the question of easing the US embargo on arms sales to Argentina. Margaret Thatcher was against it, and was tactically clever in her blocking manoeuvre. Four years after the conflict, the Pentagon and State Departments had prepared a relaxation of the embargo. It awaited only the President's approval. Just when this looked a mere formality, the British Prime Minister came to Camp David on 15 November 1986 to discuss nuclear arms issues arising from the Reagan–Gorbachev summit in Reykjavik. At the end of a long agenda, Margaret Thatcher casually slipped into the conversation a last-minute item about the South Atlantic. According to Geoffrey Smith, writing for *The Times*: 'Oh, arms to Argentina', she said, for all the world like a housewife checking that she had not forgotten some last minute piece of shopping. 'You won't, will you?' To the horror of his officials, Reagan fell for it. 'No', he replied. 'We won't.' So, in one short sentence he killed months of careful preparation within his administration.[14]

Another island that caused a second flashpoint in US–UK relations was Grenada. In this tiny Caribbean country, an independent nation within the Commonwealth whose Head of State was Queen Elizabeth II, a Marxist elected government was overthrown in a coup by other Marxists. When this happened, the Reagan administration decided to invade Grenada to restore order. The pretext used was a combination of alleged fears for the safety of American students on the island, and the alleged need to respond to a request for military intervention from the Organisation of Eastern Caribbean States (OECS), a group of neighbouring islands. The US President notified the British Prime Minister that he was considering the OECS request. He asked her for her thoughts and advice.

Margaret Thatcher received this presidential communication as she was on her way out to a dinner on Monday 24 October 1983. It was a farewell event in honour of the retiring US Ambassador to the Court of St James, John J. Louis Jr. The American Ambassador was just as much in the dark as the British Prime Minister about developments in Grenada. By the time she was back from toasting the departing envoy, a second message arrived from the President. It said that the US invasion of Grenada was about to begin.

Margaret Thatcher went ballistic. After a short midnight meeting with her Foreign Secretary, Geoffrey Howe, and her Defence Secretary, Michael Heseltine (both dumbfounded by the US action), she telephoned President Reagan on the hot-line. He had to withdraw from a meeting of Congressional leaders to go into a side room to take the Prime Minister's call. His side of it was all too audible.

'I could hear him plain as day', recalled Senator Howard Baker. He said, 'Margaret . . .' Long pause. 'But Margaret . . .', and he came back sort of sheepish and said, 'Mrs Thatcher has strong reservations about this'.[15]

They may have been strong, but they were too late. As Reagan wrote in his diary that night, 'Margaret Thatcher called. She's upset & doesn't think we should do it. I couldn't tell her that it had started.'[16]

The episode caused the British government no little embarrassment. 'Humiliation in Grenada' is the title of the relevant chapter in Geoffrey Howe's memoirs. The Prime Minister shared his frustrations. 'I felt dismayed and let down by what had happened', she recalled. 'At best, the British Government had been made to look impotent: at worst, we looked deceitful.'[17]

At Westminster, Labour's Shadow Foreign Secretary, Denis Healey, exploited this discomfort to the full. 'The British people will not relish the spectacle of their Prime Minister allowing President Reagan to walk all over her', he said, successfully applying for an emergency debate on Grenada.[18]

In the middle of this parliamentary storm, Margaret Thatcher was called from her seat on the front bench to take a call from the White House. 'I was not in the sunniest of moods', she remembered.[19] Sensing the frozen atmosphere from her opening; 'Hello, Margaret Thatcher here', Reagan did his best to spread a little sunshine with a folksy quip from his Western movies days.

'If I were there, Margaret,' he began, 'I'd throw my hat in the door before I came in.'

'There's no need to do that', she replied, failing to understand the allusion until it was explained to her afterwards.[20]

The chilliness of her response appeared to unnerve the President. He was used to being cajoled, charmed or vigorously interrupted by Margaret Thatcher. 'The cold shoulder treatment was something new . . . momentarily he seemed to panic', was how the American historian Richard Aldous portrayed the moment.[21]

For the next three minutes Reagan delivered a stumbling monologue explaining why the invasion of Grenada needed to be planned with great speed and secrecy to avoid leaks. 'But I want you to know it was no feeling on our part of lack of confidence at your end', he assured the Prime Minister. 'It's at our end.'[22]

At the Westminster end of the line, the President's words were falling on unforgiving ears. He tried again and again to elicit sympathy and understanding from his 'special relationship' partner, but on this occasion she remained the Iceberg Lady. Finally Reagan offered one last apology: 'I'm sorry for any embarrassment that we caused you, but please understand that it was just our fear of our own weakness over here with regard to secrecy.'

Margaret Thatcher kept her distance. 'It was very kind of you to have rung, Ron', she replied, noticeably not accepting his apology. 'I must return to the debate in the House. It is a bit tricky.'

Realising this was his cue to ride off into the sunset, Reagan delivered his last line: 'All right! Go get 'em. Eat 'em alive', he exhorted the Prime Minister.

'Goodbye', she replied, as the curtain fell on the unhappy Grenada episode of their relationship.[23]

It was a misunderstanding on both sides. The White House never grasped the British sensitivities about the Commonwealth, the role of the Queen (who was said to be much offended) or the importance of not misleading Parliament, as Sir Geoffrey Howe had inadvertently done. Margaret Thatcher was excessively hurt about not being let into the secret by Reagan.

'That man! After all I've done for him, he didn't even consult me', she grumbled to one of her Downing Street voices on security issues, Brian Crozier.[24]

She also exaggerated the illegal bellicosity of the invasion, telling the Irish Taioseach, Garret FitzGerald, that Grenada was as bad as the Soviet take-overs of Hungary and Czechoslovakia. 'The Americans are worse than the Soviets', she claimed.[25]

In reality, the return to stability of Grenada was a limited and brief operation of US military power. After her ruffled feathers had been given time to settle, Margaret Thatcher came to realise this herself. But she also realised that she had to put in some extra spadework to get the 'special relationship' back on track.

1984 began badly for Anglo-American relations. There was a tiff about retaliatory action by US forces in Lebanon, punishing the Syrians for their role in terrorist attacks on a US Marine barracks in Beirut. Margaret Thatcher unsuccessfully urged caution and was criticised inside the White House for not standing firm with the US.

A few weeks later a visit to Washington by President Mitterrand was presented as though France was America's new best friend in the Western alliance. Influential commentators were tipped the wink by the White House that the Reagan–Thatcher honeymoon was fading. *The Economist* published a two-part report on the dire straits of their relations under the headline 'Say Something, If Only Goodbye'.[26] An unnamed White House source was quoted as saying in the context of Grenada, 'As usual, our boys lost their lives saving the world from communism, and all we get from London is prissy criticism'.[27]

Although no great admirer of the magazine, the Prime Minister read these articles and did not enjoy being castigated for her 'prissy criticism'. She began looking for an opportunity to mend her fences with the President, and took it with skill when he came to London for the G7 Economic Summit in June.

Ronald Reagan was effectively running for re-election in the summer of 1984, and the London summit provided him with a boost to his prospects. However, this was not a certain outcome because several of the G7 leaders wished to use the event as an opportunity to attack US economic policy for its high interest rates and soaring budget deficit. The Canadian Prime Minister Pierre Trudeau and French President François Mitterrand led the charge against the US President, who was not at his best in explaining America's role in the world economy.

There was a real danger that the G7 communiqué would criticise the US economic strategy, but from the chair Margaret Thatcher blocked this by acting as the President's shield, defender and restored best friend. 'Margaret handled the meetings brilliantly', wrote Reagan in his diary. 'More protests by Pierre and François. There was blood on the floor, but not ours.'[28]

Some of the protests at the summit were wounding to the Prime Minister, who came in for scathing criticism from Pierre Trudeau for her 'heavy-handed and undemocratic'[29] conduct of the meeting in the chair. Reagan thought the Canadian Premier was out of line and expressed his sympathy to Margaret Thatcher as they left the room. 'Oh, women know when men are being childish', she riposted.[30]

Further indications of restored harmony between the British and American leaders came at the fortieth anniversary celebrations of the D-Day landings, where the President's speech at Pointe du Hoc on 6 June brought tears to Margaret Thatcher's eyes. Tears of laughter followed three nights later when Reagan the actor memorably recited 'The Shooting of Dan McGrew' to Queen

Elizabeth The Queen Mother at a Buckingham Palace dinner party, after discovering that she knew and loved the poems of Robert W. Service.

Over the next few months, personal messages, handwritten notes and phone calls flowed both ways between No. 10 and the Oval Office. They covered such topics as his support during the miners' strike, his sympathy after the Brighton bombing and her best wishes for his re-election. 'I've got my fingers crossed, my toes crossed, my everything crossed', Thatcher told Sandra Day O'Connor,* giving a pantomime performance to America's first woman Supreme Court Justice from Britain's first woman Prime Minister[31] a few days before the 1984 presidential election. Reagan won it by a landslide.

There were, however, at least two more episodes in which the wires of the 'special relationship' nearly got crossed. They were the bombing of Libya and the offer of a nuclear-free world to Mikhail Gorbachev.[†]

THE BOMBING OF LIBYA

Of all the tests of commitment to the Anglo-American alliance that Margaret Thatcher had to face, the bombing of Libya was the one she passed with the boldest resolve. The decisions she had to take were not easy. But they brought her the greenest of garlands in Washington.

In April 1986, President Reagan decided to order an air strike against Colonel Gaddafi in Tripoli in retaliation for various acts of state-sponsored Libyan terrorism in Europe. The final provocation was a bomb attack on a West Berlin nightclub on 5 April. The La Belle discotheque was frequented by US servicemen and was packed with nearly 500 people. Two Americans and a Turkish civilian died. Over 230 people were injured, including fifty off-duty US soldiers. The Americans requested permission for their bases in Britain to be used by the F1-11 aircraft leading the retaliatory raid.

Margaret Thatcher was in a weakened position on the UK domestic scene because of the Westland affair and other troubles.[‡] She also had initial reservations

---

* Sandra Day O'Connor (1930–), United States Supreme Court justice, 1981–2006. Prior to her appointment by President Ronald Reagan in 1981, she was a judge in Arizona.
† See Chapter 28.
‡ See Chapter 29.

about the legality of the American raid, which was difficult to justify as an act of self-defence within the terms of the UN Charter. When she started to take soundings among her cabinet, she found that some of her staunchest allies could not be depended on to support the proposed US action. The Foreign Office was strongly against it, believing that British embassies across the Middle East would be burned and that British interests in the region would be ruined.

In the middle of these secret internal arguments that were raging in Whitehall on Monday 14 April, the Prime Minister called me into her room at the House of Commons to ask what I thought would be the effect of the use of Britain's USAF bases on the decision-makers in Saudi Arabia – particularly on King Fahd, whom I knew well.

'The Saudis will criticise Britain publicly, but that will be all', I replied. 'King Fahd loathes Gaddafi and will privately be far from sorry. There will be no repercussions commercially or diplomatically.'[32] Margaret Thatcher asked me one or two supplementary questions but reacted non-committally. In fact, she had already made up her mind to authorise the use of Britain's bases after talks at the weekend with General Vernon Walters, United States Ambassador to the United Nations, who had been sent to London as a special presidential envoy.

According to her Foreign Affairs Private Secretary, Charles Powell, Margaret Thatcher had slept on the problem overnight. 'She came down to the office early next morning and announced that we simply must accede to the American request: "That's what Allies are for." '[33]

All the other American allies in Europe had a different opinion. Only Britain granted the United States F1-11 aircraft overflying rights or related facilities. This isolation from France, Germany, Spain and Italy fortified rather than diminished Margaret Thatcher's resolve. Yet she knew she would be facing a lot of trouble from public media and parliamentary opinion for her solidarity with President Reagan. When the bombers were on their way from RAF Lakenheath in Suffolk to Tripoli, she seemed uncharacteristically nervous. As she attended a book launch at the offices of *The Economist* to celebrate the publication of Walter Bagehot's works edited by Norman St John-Stevas, the magazine's editor, Andrew Knight, expressed his concern about how pale she looked. 'Since my complexion is never ruddy, I must have appeared like Banquo's ghost', she later recalled.[34]

Despite her wan appearance and Libyan worries, Margaret Thatcher put on a sparkling performance at the book launch with elegant praise for both Bagehot and Norman St John-Stevas. It was the last friendly reception she received for some time.

Although the American airstrike was successful, the inevitable civilian casualties resulted in a dreadful public relations backlash. Even the Prime Minister's most loyal ministers showed signs of rebellion. Complaints about the US action and about not being consulted as a cabinet came from Norman Tebbit, Nigel Lawson, Douglas Hurd, John Biffen and Kenneth Baker. But the Prime Minister stood firm, telling her colleagues: 'This is the right decision in the long-term interests of Britain. The US keeps hundreds of thousands of troops in Europe to defend Europe. She is entitled to ask to use our bases.'[35]

If her reception in the cabinet was difficult, it was far rougher in the House of Commons on the afternoon following the raid. She was almost universally condemned with the tone set by the Liberal Party Leader, David Steel, who told the Prime Minister that she had turned 'the British bulldog into a Reagan poodle'.[36]

As it happened, the only supportive voice on either side of the House was my own. I thanked her during Prime Minister's Questions for 'the difficult but wholly correct decision'.[37] The rest was mostly hostility. After the exchanges, Ted Heath chided me far from pleasantly in the Members' Lobby: 'Sucking up to the headmistress, I suppose.'[38]

In fact, the 'headmistress' turned out to be vindicated by subsequent events. The outrage of Colonel Gaddafi's rhetoric after the raid was followed by a noticeable decline in Libyan terrorism for several years. The indignation in Britain turned out to be ephemeral, whereas the gratitude from Washington was euphoric. President Reagan, whose poll approval ratings in the US soared to 77 per cent for his decision to authorise the air strike, was loud in his praise for his favourite ally. 'PM Thatcher as always was right solidly behind us', he said.[39] The *New York Times* reflected the national mood with a front-page story headlined 'Anglophilia Rules'.[40]

On Capitol Hill there was an unexpected bonus for British interests, when the Senate passed a revised US–British extradition treaty that removed the immunity for terrorists who claimed that their crimes had been politic-ally motivated. This revision had been stuck in the Senate Foreign Relations

Committee since July 1985, thanks to Irish lobby support for IRA suspects seeking protection from extradition.

After Libya, that support crumbled and Reagan himself spelt out the message in a Radio Address to the Nation on Terrorism: 'Rejection of this treaty would be an affront to British Prime Minister Margaret Thatcher, one European leader who at great political risk stood shoulder to shoulder with us during our operations against Gadhafi's terrorism.'[41]

In that atmosphere the Senate ratified the UK–US Supplementary Extradition Treaty by eighty-seven votes to ten. President Reagan called Margaret Thatcher at a dinner party in London to give her the good news. He recorded in his diary, 'She's delighted'.[42]

REFLECTION

The Libyan episode need not have become the bellwether test of the 'special relationship', but it did. The United States could have inflicted just as much damage on Libyan compounds and installations from carrier-based aircraft, or from F-111s using longer in-flight refuelling arrangements. But there was something about Margaret Thatcher's lonely courage in the face of public hostility towards their cause that won the hearts of the American people. She was already a standard bearer to political conservatives for her free-market economic policies.

Libya made her a popular heroine on a far wider front. Her instinctive belief, 'that's what Allies are for', was a personal credo not a political calculation. It was the rock on which the equally instinctive Ronald Reagan built his trust in her.

Although there were to be other squalls and stormy moments in their partnership – not least over how to handle disarmament proposals to the Soviet Union – the foundations of that rock always stayed firm. Because of it, Margaret Thatcher has a special place in the history of the 'special relationship'.

28

Starting to win the Cold War

WHY THE IRON LADY WAS FOR TURNING

A surprising visitor to No. 10 Downing Street in the summer of 1982 was the former US President Richard Nixon.* He was still regarded as 'disgraced' in his own country as the scars from his resignation over Watergate were far from healed. But Margaret Thatcher held Nixon's foreign-policy expertise in high esteem. So in their hour-long one-on-one talk she picked his brain on a subject he was well qualified to discuss – how to engage with the Soviet Union at a time when its Cold War rhetoric seemed more hostile to the West than ever before. Nixon advised her:

> The Soviets will listen to you before they listen to us. They see you as strong, they see you as a tough right winger, which they always respect. They know you've got a lot of clout with our, frankly, inexperienced White House. With your credentials, you can bring a new realism into East–West relations which are right now stuck in a ruck.[1]

Nixon was skilful at flattering the British Prime Minister. He also had a perceptive feel for the statecraft of dealing with the Soviet Union. So Margaret Thatcher listened carefully to his advice, which included pithy one-liners such as: 'Get to know your enemy'; 'Find the young comers in the Kremlin'; 'Unsettle the satellites'; 'Contain, confront, and then be ready to make deals for hard headed détente'.[2]

---

* As the former president's biographer, I arranged this appointment; not through the usual channels, but via private communications with Margaret Thatcher's diary secretary, Caroline Stephens. This was known as the 'handbag route'. It worked, although the Foreign Office advised the Prime Minister not to see Mr Nixon. She took no notice of their advice.

The Nixon recommendations seem to have been heeded by Margaret Thatcher. They were a reminder that in this area of foreign policy the Iron Lady was a listening Lady. She may have been overly dismissive towards the predictable advice she received from the Foreign Office, but she did pay a lot of attention to her voices who spoke or wrote to her about the Soviet Union. Besides Nixon, they included Brian Crozier, Robert Conquest, Hugh Thomas, Robert Moss and the Chief Rabbi Immanuel Jakobovits. They were pushing at an unexpectedly open door to the Prime Minister's mind. For, well ahead of most of her contemporaries, Margaret Thatcher instinctively felt that change was coming to the Soviet Union. She was searching for an agent of such change long before she met Mikhail Gorbachev.

The first tangible evidence of her search came when she organised a Chequers seminar on the Soviet Union in September 1983. Her reaction to the suggested list of invitees was contemptuous, as she minuted:

This is NOT the way I want it. I am not interested in gathering in every junior minister, nor everyone who has ever dealt with the subject at the FO. The FO must do their preparation before. I want also some people who have really studied Russia – the Russian mind – and who have some experience of living there. More than half the people on the list know less than I do.[3]

Accelerated by this prime ministerial prodding, the Chequers seminar assembled some outstanding people and papers. However, only one of them, Canon Michael Bourdeaux,* dared to predict that, 'We may one day see the collapse of the Soviet system from within'.[4] The general summary, whose key sentence was underlined by Margaret Thatcher, concluded that although the Soviet leadership faced many problems, these were not 'on such a scale as to compel them to change course drastically, still less change the system'.[5]

Despite this pessimism within the foreign-policy establishment, Margaret Thatcher reiterated her belief that somewhere within the monolithic and apparently immobile Soviet system there were individuals of spirit who wanted to bring about change. She mentioned in this context writers and dissidents.

---

* The Revd Canon Dr Michael Bourdeaux was the founder of Keston College, an institute for the study of religion in communist countries.

But were there any kindred reformers within the government? Professor Archie Brown,* one of the external Soviet experts invited to Chequers, reported that the newest and youngest member of the Politburo was 'The most hopeful choice from the point of view of both Soviet citizens and the outside world'. His name was Mikhail Gorbachev.

Identifying him at this early stage meant 'our September seminar at Chequers was, therefore, more important than we knew', according to the Foreign Secretary Sir Geoffrey Howe, who came to see Margaret Thatcher's subsequent relations with Gorbachev as 'her greatest achievement in Foreign Affairs'.[6]

At the time, however, the identification of Gorbachev was no more than a vaguely hopeful sighting on the long-distance radar screen of Margaret Thatcher's foreign policy. This was becoming more and more personalised. She kept her diplomatic cards increasingly tightly held within No. 10. In late 1983 she appointed a new private secretary, Charles Powell, who was to become her closest aide and confidant for the last seven years of her premiership.

Charles Powell had the appearance of a quintessentially Foreign Office man, but he appealed to Margaret Thatcher because of his steeliness of character and originality of mind. Moreover, his personal views were in harmony with her political purposes.

They first struck up a rapport in Bonn in 1975. She was making her first visit to Germany as Leader of the Opposition. It fell to Powell as First Secretary at the British Embassy to arrange her schedule. It culminated in them both sitting up late into the night to hear the result of the Woolwich West by-election – a surprise gain for the Conservatives which raised the leader's spirits. Most of the talking that evening was done by the vivacious Mrs Carla Powell for whom Margaret Thatcher developed a life-long affection. She also took a favourable view of the thirty-three-year old Charles Powell, whose good looks, Oxford first and unorthodox opinions on the primacy of British national interests all impressed her.

The admiration was mutual. 'From that visit I formed the view that Margaret Thatcher was a good thing', he recalled. 'I never shared the prevailing Foreign

---

* Professor Archie Brown (1938–), Oxford University Professor of Politics, Director of St Antony's College Russian and Eastern European Centre. At the time of the Chequers seminar, he was the Oxford University lecturer on Soviet institutions.

Office wisdom that she was a ghastly, narrow middle-class housewife. I thought Britain needed her no-nonsense, reforming approach.'

During his next career stints as a Special Counsellor on the Rhodesia negotiations, and in Brussels as a Counsellor in the Office of the UK Representative to the European Community, Powell continued to catch the Prime Minister's eye. In the latter job he managed to communicate his well-informed Euroscepticism to her. This might have impeded his progress on the career ladder of the Diplomatic Service. It did him a power of good when he was interviewed for the post of Foreign Affairs Private Secretary at No. 10.

She thought he 'talked far too much',[7] but did not see any other candidate. Once appointed, Powell went from strength to strength. His rapport with his boss grew into an almost mystical bond based initially on shared political instincts and on the shared laughter and *joie de vivre* provided by Carla. The Prime Minister used to introduce her to guests at No. 10 receptions with the qualification, 'She's Italian, you know'.[8] The vital ingredient in the bonding was Charles Powell's talent for reading Margaret Thatcher's mind. He then communicated it across Whitehall and the world in minutes, which conveyed her will-power in his linguistic power. This process became so perfected that in the words of one senior China expert at the FCO, Sir Percy Cradock, 'It was sometimes equally difficult to establish where Mrs Thatcher ended and where Charles Powell began'.[9]

Less than a year after Powell joined the elite team of No. 10 private secretaries, Margaret Thatcher was flexing her wings with increasing vigour as a Prime Minister who was her own Foreign Secretary. She was taking more and more of her own foreign-policy initiatives, not least in the neglected field of East–West relations.

In February 1984, Margaret Thatcher made her first visit as Prime Minister behind the Iron Curtain. If her journey to Hungary was intended to be a move towards unsettling the satellites, it proved successful, and was followed by several later forays into the capital cities of Soviet-controlled Eastern Europe. In Budapest she was given what she called 'A warm, even passionate, welcome' from the shoppers in the central covered market.[10] The experience, and some of her conversations with individual Hungarians, reaffirmed her belief that the thawing of the Cold War would come from establishing a warmer understanding of the societies in the pivotal countries behind the Iron Curtain.

Another influence on Margaret Thatcher's willingness to engage with the Soviet Union at this time came through top-secret intelligence based on disclosures from Oleg Gordievsky. He was a senior KGB official who had become a double agent working for Britain's Secret Intelligence Service – MI6. Gordievsky reported only a few weeks earlier, in November 1983, that Soviet aircraft had moved to combat-readiness for a nuclear strike against the West. These astonishing preparations arose from a mistaken over-reaction to a routine NATO annual exercise code named 'Able Archer 83'. The Soviet high command had wrongly concluded that the NATO war games were the prelude to a real war. Margaret Thatcher's reaction to these top-secret reports was to conclude that the West needed far more effective channels of communication with Moscow.[11]

Ten days after her visit to Hungary, Margaret Thatcher travelled to Moscow to attend the funeral of the Soviet leader, Yuri Andropov, on 14 February 1984. On the flight, she immersed herself in the Foreign Office briefing papers, at one point making the comment: 'Are there no young Russian leaders? They don't seem to come out of the kindergarten until they're 65.'[12]

At the long and cold obsequies for Andropov, Margaret Thatcher had a fortuitous encounter with the young Soviet leader who was to change the destiny of his country and the world. This was Mikhail Gorbachev, who paid her a small gesture of respect not because she was the British Prime Minister but because he noticed her courtesy at the funeral.

Under the Kremlin's arrangements, visiting Western dignitaries were not allocated seats. They had to stand in a VIP enclosure in Red Square for over an hour as the funeral cortège and its military escort passed by. Most of the foreign leaders kept warm by stamping their feet and talking amongst themselves. Margaret Thatcher was freezing, too. But sensibly shod in fur-lined boots, she kept her distance from the other VIPs,* standing alone in exemplary stillness and silence. Her respectful demeanour and her bows to the coffin were appreciated by Gorbachev.

A protégé of the deceased General Secretary, he was a rising figure in the Politburo, but virtually unknown in the West. At the end of the ceremonies, he approached the Prime Minister and gallantly escorted her to a warm room.

---

* An additional reason why she kept her distance was that she was trying to avoid the Palestinian leader, Yasser Arafat, whom she regarded as a terrorist.

'I remember how you took care of me. It was frosty and I was wearing thin stockings and a light suit',[13] she recalled on the next occasion they met.

Some hours after this encounter, Margaret Thatcher realised that her escort had been the man identified at her seminar as a potential future leader of the Soviet Union. So she intensified her efforts to invite him to visit Britain. For reasons of diplomatic protocol, this could only be done through the auspices of a somewhat obscure body, the Anglo-Soviet Parliamentary group chaired by the backbench Tory MP Sir Anthony Kershaw. 'Who the hell is Mr Gorbachev?'[14] demanded Sir Anthony, when asked to issue the invitation. It was accepted with alacrity by the recipient, despite some obstruction from Andrei Gromyko, the Soviet Foreign Minister. 'I had an unpleasant conversation with Gromyko', Gorbachev recalled. 'He would not delegate anybody to help prepare the visit, and would not send anyone on the trip with me. He thought the Ministry of Foreign Affairs does not need that.'[15]

Back in Britain, Margaret Thatcher surprised her Foreign Office advisers by raising the status of Gorbachev's mission. Instead of the customary short call at No. 10 that was granted to foreign political figures below the rank of head of government, she invited the intriguing Soviet visitor to Chequers for what turned into a five-hour lunch, attended by a galaxy of senior cabinet ministers, officials and Russian experts.

'I knew exactly what she was doing', recalled Gorbachev. 'Our intelligence was very active in Britain. We knew that the government was trying to discern what would happen in the Soviet Union after General Secretary Chernenko,* who was not expected to live for long by Margaret Thatcher. She had brought a doctor with her to Andropov's funeral, and he had diagnosed Chernenko's shortness of breath as chronic emphysema. This doctor gave her a prognosis on Chernenko's life expectation which turned out to be remarkably accurate.'[16]

Although Gorbachev gives the credit for the arranging of his visit to British intelligence, it was just as much due to Margaret Thatcher's political and personal intuition. She had sensed that her benefactor at Andropov's funeral might turn

---

* Konstantin Ustinovich Chernenko (1911–1985) had been a full member of the Soviet Politburo since 1978. He succeeded Yuri Andropov as General Secretary of the Communist Party Central Committee and Head of State of the USSR in February 1984. He died of emphysema thirteen months later.

out to be a new kind of Soviet leader, with fresh ideas and a radical outlook. This was the reason she invited him to Britain and to Chequers. He so much exceeded her expectations that the Gorbachev visit became the opening move in a relationship that helped to change the world.

THE CHEQUERS OVERTURE TO MIKHAIL GORBACHEV

At 12.30 p.m. on 16 December 1984, Mikhail and Raisa Gorbachev arrived at Chequers for Sunday lunch with Margaret Thatcher. Charles Powell recalled:

> It was an extraordinary moment. Nobody had much clue what to expect. Gorbachev came to us as a new member of the Politburo. He'd only been to the West before on a visit to Canada. Very intelligently, Mrs Thatcher invited him with his wife – it was a new departure for a Soviet leader to be travelling with his wife – and within seconds of him arriving in the Great Hall of Chequers you knew that this was an entirely different kind of Russian leader. Here was a man bursting with energy, beaming, bouncing on the balls of his feet, obviously proud of his smartly dressed wife, and ready to engage in argument. Everyone present just simply had to change gear.[17]

The Prime Minister moved into a gear so high that it became frankness bordering on rudeness. After introducing him to her other British guests, who included six cabinet ministers, she decided to set what she thought would be the right tone for the occasion.

'Mr Gorbachev, I want our relationship to get off to a good start', declared Margaret Thatcher only moments after offering her guest a pre-lunch drink.

> I want there to be no misunderstanding between us. So I must tell you that I hate Communism. I hate it because it brings neither freedom, nor justice, nor prosperity to the people. But if you Russians must have it, then you are entitled to it – secure within your own borders.[18]

Bernard Ingham, the No. 10 Press Secretary who was no slouch at blunt speaking himself, witnessed these words and their effect on the Soviet visitor. 'I saw that Mr Gorbachev was absolutely astounded,' he recalled, 'first by Mrs Thatcher's directness and secondly by her saying that Russians could have Communism behind their own borders.'[19]

The frankness did startle Mikhail Gorbachev. He also had few clues of what to expect from this encounter. He had been denied a briefing from the Soviet Foreign Ministry because of jealousy about his trip on the part of the veteran Foreign Minister, Andrei Gromyko. So he had made his preparations alone with his wife, Raisa Maksimovna,* at their seaside home in Pitsunda.

Mrs Gorbacheva looked horrified as she listened to the translation of the Prime Minister's opening salvo, and her feelings became more hostile after the party had sat down to lunch, with Margaret Thatcher continuing her no-holds-barred style of aggressive interrogation. As Mikhail Gorbachev described the growing tension: 'We sat down to lunch in the not particularly spacious dining room of Chequers. Margaret and I were on one side of the table, Denis and Raisa on the other. Very quickly the argument between me and Margaret became very heated.'[20]

The argument, described by the Prime Minister as 'a vigorous two-way debate',[21] seemed rather stronger than that to the Gorbachevs. The heat was initially generated by points and counterpoints in a discussion about the merits of the centralised Soviet economic system versus the advantages of the decentralised Western models of free enterprise. From this, the questioning by Margaret Thatcher focused on the high percentage of Soviet government expenditure on military equipment, and became sharper. 'She was accusing the Soviet Union of all sorts of unfair things', recalled Gorbachev. 'I did not accuse Britain of anything. But she became so heated that at one moment she turned away from me. So I turned away from her, too. We were almost back to back.'[22]

Reliving the moment in his Moscow office thirty years after the event, in his interview for this biography Mikhail Gorbachev acted out the scene of two offended protagonists turning their backs on each other in high dudgeon.

He continued:

Then I caught Raisa's eye across the table, and her lips moved to say 'It's over!', and for a moment I wondered if we should leave. But then I thought to myself, 'We are guests

---

* Raisa Maximovna Gorbacheva (1932–1999), graduate of the Moscow State Pedagogical Insitute with an advanced degree in Philosphy. Raisa's sense of style and dynamic personality caught the attention of the Prime Minister, who was not always interested in the wives of her visitors or her cabinet ministers.

here, the conversation must continue'. I said quite firmly to the Prime Minister: 'Mrs Thatcher, I know you are a person with an acute mind and high personal principles. Please bear in mind that I am the same kind of person.' She reacted with just a nod, so then I said, 'Let me assure you that I have not come here with instructions from the Politburo to persuade you to become a member of the Communist Party'.

Reliving the moment as Mikhail Gorbachev the amateur impressionist, he imitated the sound of Margaret Thatcher bursting into laughter: '"Whoarrhaha!" she cried, and then others laughed too. So the tension was broken, and the discussion continued, although it soon hotted up again but in better ways.'

A second altercation arose after Gorbachev claimed that under the communist system, citizens of the Soviet Union lived 'joyfully'. Margaret Thatcher swooped on that assertion by asking, in that case, 'Why did the Soviet authorities not allow its people to leave the country as easily as they could leave Britain?'[23]

This started a lively debate on the prohibitions imposed on Soviet Jews who wanted to emigrate to Israel. Well briefed on this topic by her friend the Chief Rabbi, Margaret Thatcher gave her guest the 'hair dryer treatment', with blast after blast of facts and statistics about Moscow's treatment of the *refuseniks*. Gorbachev, although unprepared for the vigour of the exchange, came back confidently with the claim that '89 per cent' of those who applied to emigrate from the Soviet Union were allowed to do so. This was not a true statistic. But with a diplomatic *politesse* that she did not always exhibit, Margaret Thatcher let it pass, not least because Gorbachev added, 'and we are thinking about that',[24] which she interpreted as a sign that there might be further relaxations in Jewish emigration.

After lunch the Prime Minister accompanied only by her Foreign Secretary, Geoffrey Howe, her Private Secretary, Charles Powell, and her interpreter took Mikhail Gorbachev and three of his party to a sitting room for coffee. This private session was scheduled for thirty minutes, but lasted for over two and a half hours. It began with the two principals settling into large armchairs by the fireplace. Margaret Thatcher took off her patent leather shoes, tucked her feet under the chair cushion and pulled some papers out of her handbag. Gorbachev reached for a folder and took out a memorandum headed, 'On Conversation with Thatcher'. But then he suddenly had second thoughts and asked, 'Could we do without these papers?'

'Gladly', replied the Prime Minister, returning her briefing notes to her handbag.[25]

The two leaders set off on an unstructured agenda. The first highlight was a passionate plea from Gorbachev for disarmament and an ending of the Cold War. Unaccustomed as she was to not being able to get a word in edgeways, Margaret Thatcher eventually managed to raise one topical symptom of Cold War trouble-making, which was the Soviet funding of the miners' strike led by Arthur Scargill, then in its tenth month.

'Your trade unions are helping our coal miners with money', she said. 'The strike continues. It is doing great damage to the economy of England. For the time being, I take that quite calmly. But I request that your trade unions should cease the financial support, otherwise we will resort to sanctions.'[26]

According to his aide, Leonid Zamyatin,* Gorbachev was visibly taken aback, and said that he had 'nothing to do with the trade unions'.[27]

At this point, 'Margaret got pretty rowdy',[28] according to Gorbachev, as she claimed that the money going from Moscow's trade unions to Scargill's National Union of Mineworkers must have had the blessing of the Politburo. 'No, this is an internal matter', replied her Soviet visitor. 'You may be able to direct your trade unions, but we can't.' Sparks flew from all directions in the Chequers drawing room on this subject. 'I think, looking back on it, that both of us were being disingenuous', was Mikhail Gorbachev's retrospective opinion. 'This matter was not a Politburo decision, but the Politburo were aware of it.'[29]

The most important area of engagement at this first meeting between the two leaders was arms control. Gorbachev threw himself into this subject, offering his views on disarmament with a passion that sounded both new and sincere. This part of the discussion also became heated and personal. 'Mrs Thatcher, you are a modern and forward-looking woman leader. Don't you feel uncomfortable sitting on top of such a huge Western arsenal of nuclear weapons?' asked Gorbachev, having produced from his pocket a diagram with his own markings in green ink, which illustrated all the millions who would be killed if these weapons were fired.

---

* Leonid Mitrofanovich Zamyatin (1922–), Soviet diplomat since 1946. Head of the International Information Department of the Central Committee, 1978–1986; Ambassador of the USSR to Britain, 1986–1991.

The Prime Minister was not going to let her guest get away with such a rhetorical debater's question. 'She immediate counter-attacked me. She wouldn't give an inch. Neither of us allowed the other to get the edge', was Gorbachev's version of their argument. 'But in the end I think we both greatly valued these exchanges.'[30]

Margaret Thatcher must have been interested in her guest's surprisingly sweeping ideas for mutual disarmament, but she did not respond as positively to them as he had hoped. She was aware that the Soviet Union's leaders were greatly worried by President Reagan's plans for a Strategic Defence Initiative (SDI). This worry was discernible in the mood music of the conversations at Chequers. Gorbachev knew that the British Prime Minister had concerns of her own about SDI, on which she differed from Reagan because she did not see this so-called 'Star Wars' technology as a means of eliminating all nuclear weapons. Nevertheless, she was determined not to let her Soviet visitor get the faintest impression that there were disagreements on this issue between Washington and London.

'Do not waste my time', she warned Gorbachev, 'on trying to persuade me to say to Ron Reagan: "Do not go ahead with SDI. That will get nowhere."'[31]

In fact, nobody's time was wasted at Chequers on Sunday 16 December. It had been a major breakthrough of diplomatic communication and personal chemistry.

Charles Powell, the highly overworked note-taker throughout the five hours worth of talks, recalled:

> Gorbachev made an extraordinary impression. He was such a contrast to the succession of Kremlin geriatrics like Brezhnev, Andropov and Chernenko. He talked and argued like a top Western politician. He didn't need briefs or notes or advisers. He just sat there and slugged it out with her. I think he was using the meeting as an anvil on which he could hammer out his new ideas until they were 'Thatcher tested', conscious that she would be a channel to President Reagan.[32]

Such a channel was sorely needed, since the Americans and the Soviets were not speaking to each other at the highest levels. Their communications had broken down since President Reagan had given great offence to the Kremlin's leaders by describing their country as an 'Evil Empire . . . the focus of evil in the modern world'.[33]

As he left the Prime Minister's country house at the unexpectedly late time of 5.50 p.m., Gorbachev quoted an old Russian proverb: 'Mountain folk cannot live without guests any more than they can live without air. But if the guests stay longer than necessary, they choke.'[34]

Far from choking, Margaret Thatcher was immensely cheered by the rapport that she had been able to establish with the rising Politburo member she expected to emerge as the next Soviet leader. As his car was heading down the Chequers drive, she gave an ecstatic debriefing on the private talks to her senior aides.

'He sounds like a man you can do business with', observed Bernard Ingham.

'Yes, he certainly is', replied the Prime Minister.

'Can I say that to the press?' Bernard Ingham asked.[35]

That was how the phrase went round the world, with Margaret Thatcher using it herself the following day in a BBC interview: 'I like Mr Gorbachev. We can do business together.'[36]

When these words were translated to the object of them, he was pleased. Mikhail Gorbachev recalled:

I had no complaint! In fact, I used the same language when I reported to the Politburo very positively on my British visit. There was a lot of discussion and debate around the table, which I summed up by telling my colleagues, 'We should continue to do business with Margaret Thatcher. And we did!'[37]

BRIDGE BUILDING BETWEEN MOSCOW AND WASHINGTON

The first business, after the success of her dialogue at Chequers with Mikhail Gorbachev, was for Margaret Thatcher to make the most of her opportunities as a bridge builder between Moscow and Washington. To take the initiative in this role, she had to fulfil a schedule of intercontinental travelling that was heroic even by the standards of prime ministerial aviation.

In the space of six days she held talks with Russian, Chinese and American leaders on three continents. Her fifty-five hours of flying time included sectors from London to Beijing to sign the Hong Kong agreement; from Beijing to Hong Kong to reassure its people that they had not been sold out; from Hong Kong to Hawaii, where she insisted on a nocturnal visit to Pearl Harbor; from Hawaii to Washington; and finally a helicopter flight from Washington to Camp David.[38] President Reagan was waiting at the aircraft steps to greet her with a kiss on the cheek and a lift in his golf cart. 'I sometimes thought I was directing *Gone with the Wind*', commented Bernard Ingham.[39]

The Camp David discussions were difficult but ended in a considerable diplomatic success for Margaret Thatcher. After she had briefed the President on her positive view of Gorbachev, SDI dominated the agenda. 'This was the first occasion on which I had heard President Reagan speaking about SDI', she recalled. 'He did so with passion. He was at his most idealistic.'[40]

This was a polite way of saying she thought he was wrong. Reagan had developed an optimistic view of SDI, believing it could eliminate all nuclear weapons and end the Cold War. As a scientist, Margaret Thatcher felt this was nonsense. She was in favour of further SDI research, but she feared that reliance on deployed SDI technology would undermine all other forms of nuclear deterrence, including Britain's Trident. She argued long and hard to change the President's mind, but with no success.

Charles Powell captured the tiring atmospherics: 'I saw the President's eyes stray towards the clock calculating how many more minutes to a Martini and lunch as she rampaged on about the finer details of the Anti-Ballistic Missile Treaty.'[41] The official White House minutes suggest that the Martinis, even when they came, afforded no respite: 'During the cocktail session before lunch, the President, Mrs Thatcher and Ambassador Price continued discussions at some length.'[42]

In the end, the length and perseverance of the Prime Minister's arguments resulted in a breakthrough. Towards the end of the afternoon, she and Powell concocted a draft statement that she read out to the President. It consisted of four points:

1   The US and Western aim is to maintain balance: i.e. not achieve superiority, while taking account of Soviet developments.
2   SDI-related deployment, in view of treaty obligations, would be a matter for negotiations.
3   The overall aim is to enhance not undercut deterrence.
4   East–West negotiations should aim to achieve security with reduced levels of offensive systems on both sides.

Reagan accepted these points with almost casual nonchalance, saying he hoped 'they would quell reports of disagreements between us'.[43]

The formula worked. The President noted in his diary he hoped, on 'Star Wars', that he 'had eased some concerns she had'.[44]

The Prime Minister evidently felt she had secured a much bigger deal. She announced publicly that she had received assurances that the United States would not deploy SDI unilaterally and would not abandon deterrence. In the community of diplomats and nuclear weapons experts in NATO capitals there was considerable relief at Margaret Thatcher's achievement over SDI. And probably in Moscow as well.

Three months later, the Prime Minister was back in Moscow for another funeral for another General Secretary – Konstantin Chernenko. He was succeeded after only thirteen months in the top job at the Kremlin by Mikhail Gorbachev. Margaret Thatcher had an hour with the new Soviet leader after the ceremony, which was twice as long a session as the appointment time given to any other VIP attending the funeral. At this second Gorbachev–Thatcher meeting, they did not do any substantial business together but their rapport continued to build, and she again relayed her favourable impressions of Gorbachev to the White House.

According to the US Secretary of State, James Baker, her assessment that the Soviet Union now had a completely new kind of leader had 'a profound influence' on the US plans for its strategy and summitry.[45]

Prompted by these positive reports on Mikhail Gorbachev, the United States began feeling its way to a better relationship with the Soviet Union. For all his public rhetoric about the 'Evil Empire', Reagan had been trying since the start of his Presidency to engage in private handwritten correspondence with Brezhnev, Andropov and Chernenko. He was disappointed when these personal letters received only the most stilted of replies. 'The trouble is, they keep dying on me', he lamented in his 'aw-shucks' style to White House Deputy Chief of Staff Mike Deaver.[46]

Once Gorbachev was firmly installed in the Kremlin, Reagan reached out to him and arranged a US–Soviet summit in Geneva. There is no doubt that Margaret Thatcher's positive views on Gorbachev helped to encourage the setting up of this meeting. President Reagan acknowledged this at the time and in his memoirs.

Immediately after his return from the Geneva summit, the President convened a meeting of the National Security Council. His opening words to the NSC were: 'Maggie was right. We can do business with this man.'[47]

On the Gorbachev side of the summit, Margaret Thatcher had been a helpful interlocutor with her insistence to him that President Reagan was absolutely sincere in his idealistic quest for peaceful nuclear disarmament.

To both leaders her preliminary diplomacy was a positive influence in getting the Geneva summit off to a good start. Once Reagan and Gorbachev began meeting directly, the role played by the British Prime Minister inevitably diminished. Yet, throughout an important period of pre-summit diplomacy, Margaret Thatcher had seized her moment and her seat at the top table with the superpowers.

Between the Chequers lunch with Gorbachev in December 1984 and the Geneva summit of November 1985, she had been one of the most important players on the world stage. She was not the creator of the new chapter of US–Soviet relations, but she was an important catalyst in helping to bring it about so swiftly. There was still much more for her to do in both Washington and Moscow.

DIFFERENCES WITH REAGAN
OVER SDI AND REYKJAVIK

Margaret Thatcher was at cross-purposes with Ronald Reagan over SDI for most of the 1980s. Their differences were a source of considerable mutual irritation. Nevertheless, they preserved a façade of agreement through some testing episodes. But by the time she came to write her memoirs, Margaret Thatcher made a major historical U-turn on this issue. She asserted in 1993 that, 'Ronald Reagan's original decision on SDI was the single most important of his presidency . . . [it] was to prove central to the West's victory in the Cold War.'[48] She did not take this attitude while she was in power. The gap between her revisionism in hindsight and her view of SDI at the time needs an explanation.

Margaret Thatcher supported SDI so long as it was only confined to the testing laboratory. As a scientist she had little faith in SDI 'Star Wars' technology. As a strategist, she feared its deployment would wreck all other forms of deterrence, including Britain's Trident, and leave Western Europe dangerously exposed to Soviet military expansionism. When she first tried to explain her anxieties to President Reagan, he was unsympathetic. Nevertheless, he quietened her down by agreeing to the reassuring statement issued from Camp David in December 1984. This bought time but not Margaret Thatcher's silence. Knowing that the President was a true and total believer in the power of SDI to end the nuclear arms race, she returned to an attack on the roots of his 'Star Wars' faith. Having failed to move him in private, she embarked on the risky course of undermining his strategy in public.

An invitation to address a joint session of the US Congress on 20 February 1985 provided the opportunity for her manoeuvre. It took the form not of a full-frontal assault on SDI, but of a passionate defence of the existing arrangements for nuclear deterrence, which had kept the peace in Europe for the past forty years. The text for her speech was not drafted by the Foreign Office. It owed much to the contribution of the Prime Minister's hawkish Downing Street voices, including Lord Chalfont, George Urban and Hugh Thomas. One telling passage ran:

> Our task is not only to prevent nuclear war, but to prevent conventional war as well [applause]. No-one understood the importance of deterrence more clearly than Winston Churchill, when in his last speech to you he said: 'Be careful above all things not to let go of the atomic weapon until you are sure and more than sure that other means of preserving peace are in your hands!'[49]

Most of the Senators and Congressmen present gave this cheer-leading for nuclear deterrence a standing ovation. But the White House was annoyed by it, and by her more specific criticisms of SDI at a meeting with the President the following day.

'You know, she's really missing the point', Reagan said to his National Security Adviser, Robert 'Bud' McFarlane, after the discussion. 'And she's doing us a lot of damage with all this sniping about it.'[50]

Another burst of British sniper fire against SDI came from the Foreign Secretary, Geoffrey Howe, who made a speech in London warning of the dangers 'in creating a new Maginot line of the 21st century in space'. The analogy, and the detailed critique of the 'Star Wars' technology that accompanied it, caused, in Howe's words, 'a transatlantic explosion'.[51]

The domestic part of the explosion erupted in No. 10 Downing Street where the Prime Minister was so furious with her Foreign Secretary that she telephoned President Reagan to apologise on his behalf. She was almost as furious with Charles Powell, who had fallen asleep while beginning to look through the draft of Howe's speech on the plane coming back from Chernenko's funeral. As a result, the speech was 'cleared' by No. 10 without ever having been read by the Prime Minister or her Private Secretary. Margaret Thatcher's wrath at these sins of omission and commission was volcanic, but no one's career was destroyed by the eruption.

Whatever the rights and wrongs of this incident, the Prime Minister did not cease her barrage of veiled and not so veiled criticism of SDI. Speaking at an arms control seminar in Washington in July 1985, she delivered another stern warning that SDI would undermine the justification for nuclear defence in Europe. She repeated this argument at such length that even the President's good-natured patience was sorely tried. 'Boy, she's a great talker, not a great listener', he commented in an aside to the Director of the US Arms Control Agency, Kenneth Adelman.[52]

Over lunch after the seminar, Margaret Thatcher went so far in her expressions of concern about SDI that she received an unusual rebuff from President Reagan. She was once again repeating her anxieties that his dream of using the new technology to eliminate nuclear weapons would cause a new arms race in conventional weapons. 'If you follow that logic to its implied conclusion', she told him, 'you expose a dramatic conventional imbalance, do you not? And would we not have to restore that balance at considerable expense?' Reagan stared straight back into her eyes and replied, 'Yes, that's exactly what I imagined'.[53]

It was clear to those present that a magisterial rebuke had been delivered to the British Prime Minister by the American President. As 'Bud' McFarlane recounted: 'It was rather an awkward silence there while both sides absorbed the weight of what had just been exchanged. I think the staffs of both sides agreed that this had better never get out.'[54]

The tension created by this exchange between the two leaders took some efforts to dispel. A few hours after the rebuff from Reagan, McFarlane called on Margaret Thatcher in the British Embassy. No record of their conversation is available, but the surrounding correspondence with its cryptic reference to secrecy ('I shall of course treat what you said with the greatest possible discretion', wrote the Prime Minister) suggested that a high-level deal was struck.

According to historian Richard Aldous, 'McFarlane had bought Thatcher's silence'.[55] He persuaded her to keep her doubts about SDI to herself in the run-up to the Geneva summit. This would also keep Reagan's conservative critics quiescent in Washington and preserve the unity of the Western alliance in the eyes of the Soviets.

As a reward, McFarlane suggested that British companies might be able to win $300 million a year's worth of SDI research contracts. 'You know, there may be something in this after all', was Margaret Thatcher's response to this enticing prospect.[56] However, the end result was that UK firms won a disappointingly smaller slice of the SDI research budget, worth around $40 million in total.

There was one further and far greater disappointment for Britain's Prime Minister related to SDI, although paradoxically it paved the way to the Cold War breakthrough, which she had been hoping for. The moment of maximum distress came when Margaret Thatcher was briefed on the progress of the second Reagan–Gorbachev summit while it was being held at Reykjavik on the weekend of 11–12 October 1986.

'My own reaction when I heard how far the Americans had been prepared to go was as if there had been an earthquake beneath my feet', was how she described her response to the news from the summit.[57] Her Chief Whip, Michael Jopling, who was with her in the room when she received the briefing, 'never saw her more incandescent'.[58]

The cause of this near-panic was Margaret Thatcher's discovery that Ronald Reagan had offered over a ten-year period to eliminate all nuclear weapons from the US arsenal. He was willing to dispense with America's nuclear bombs, cruise missiles, intermediate missiles and submarine-launched missiles – which would inevitably have included Britain's US-built Trident system. Mikhail Gorbachev had provisionally agreed to carry out the same elimination process from the Soviet nuclear forces. But just when this momentous disarmament deal was about to be struck, Gorbachev inserted a new requirement. He insisted that SDI should be confined to laboratory testing, and must never be deployed. Reagan refused to drop his pet project. As both leaders dug in their heels, the Reykjavik summit ended in an impasse with no agreement.

As she absorbed the news of the concessions the Americans had been prepared to make, Margaret Thatcher's views on what had so nearly happened at Reykjavik became apocalyptic. 'The whole thing was shaking', she recalled. 'We hadn't a defence anymore. I thought, "My goodness me, I must get over".'[59] Two weeks later she was back again with President Reagan in Camp David seeking his reassurance.

At the time of this meeting, Reagan was at the lowest point of his Presidency, due to the Iran–Contra scandal that threatened to become another Watergate. Margaret Thatcher proved to be the staunchest of the President's defenders. 'I believe implicitly in the President's total integrity on that subject',[60] she told a Washington press conference at a time when no one else was willing to give such an endorsement. Reagan was delighted by the Prime Minister's support, which made it even easier for him to give her what she wanted.

Margaret Thatcher had come to Camp David in order to ensure that Britain's Trident programme would go ahead, and that the United States would continue to back NATO's policy of nuclear deterrence. She was successful in both objectives, although at a lower level of commitment than she wanted. In the short term, the White House agreed the joint statement she had sought. It gave her the ideal headline in the following day's *Sunday Times*: 'Thatcher Wins Reagan Pledge to Sell Trident.'[61]

But she admitted to 'a gnawing anxiety'[62] that sooner or later US policy might revert to the kind of Reykjavik horse-trading that could leave Britain stranded outside America's nuclear umbrella of protection.

Within the priesthood of nuclear warfare specialists, Margaret Thatcher's obsession with maintaining a high level of nuclear deterrence looked exaggerated. For, in reality, the concept had never been seriously threatened. To those who understood its technical complexities, SDI was never likely to be deployed, and unlikely to bring about the abolition of all other nuclear weapons. 'Star Wars' technology was for starry-eyed believers in a futuristic world, which existed only in a few people's imaginations in 1986. Yet the most devoted of these imaginative visionaries was the President of the United States. His simple faith led him to call Gorbachev's bluff with absolute conviction at Reykjavik. And the bluff worked magnificently.

SDI had only ever been a cosmic gambling chip. But because Reagan played it so convincingly, the Soviet Union realised they had lost the game disastrously.

After Reykjavik, Gorbachev knew his country could not afford to join an arms race in space. His dialogue with Margaret Thatcher had been instrumental in persuading the Soviet leader that Reagan meant business both in his toughness over SDI and in his sincere desire for meaningful disarmament. Partly by chance, and partly by the force of her personality, Margaret Thatcher had been the most effective intermediary between East and West at a pivotal moment in history.

If there was a moment when the Cold War ended, it can be dated at the turn of the year 1986–1987. Out-bluffed at Reykjavik, Gorbachev accepted that the Soviet Union could no longer pay the bills with money it did not have, for increasingly expensive and sophisticated nuclear armaments. Instead, he knew he had to embark on a plan B consisting of a new reform programme domestically and a new foreign policy internationally. It was no coincidence that he wanted to discuss and do this business with Margaret Thatcher.

STAR PERFORMANCE IN MOSCOW

Margaret Thatcher's four-day visit to Moscow, which began on Saturday 28 March 1987, was the stuff of which diplomatic legends are made. Its iconic television imagery struck a mysterious chord with the peoples of the Soviet Union, and may have made a deeper contribution to the coming collapse of communism than anyone realised at the time.

More concretely, her thirteen hours of talks and meetings with Mikhail Gorbachev forged an extraordinary bond between the two leaders. Their impassioned arguments flowed like molten lava, and the political landscape of East–West understanding began to shift. Whether measured by its short-term impact or by its long-term implications, this was the most important Anglo-Soviet summit in twentieth-century history.

Because of the dialogue that had been progressing since the Chequers Sunday lunch of December 1984, Margaret Thatcher was granted unusual latitude in the arrangements for her visit. 'She was my guest. I told her she could go anywhere she wanted, and see anyone she chose to see', recalled Mikhail Gorbachev. 'In the spirit of *glasnost* [openness] there were no restrictions on her.'[63]

No such freedom had been granted to any Western visitor since the creation of the Soviet Union. Determined to make the most of it, Margaret Thatcher's opening request was to be allowed to inspect the headquarters of the country's Anti-Ballistic Missile system in Krasnogorsk. The Russian Defence Ministry said 'yes', but the schedulers at 10 Downing Street had to drop the plan because the travelling time would have taken the Prime Minister out of Moscow for too long. But even without a tour of the top-secret ABM bases, her visit was packed with symbolic, visual and political breakthroughs, most of them live on world television.

Much thought went into Margaret Thatcher's wardrobe for Russia. She had three key helpers on this sartorial side – Carla Powell, Cynthia Crawford and Margaret King, Fashion Director of Aquascutum. Of these, the most daring and amusing was Mrs Powell. 'You have big boobs like mine', she told the Prime Minister, 'so you need a new look with high padded shoulders to set them off.' In search of this new image, Carla scoured boutiques and brought to No. 10 the designer Victor Edelstein. He created the first prototypes, at cost price, of the colourful dresses, coats and jackets with regally high padding around the neck and shoulders, which became part of the Thatcher legend. Mrs Powell introduced her compatriot Vanda Ferragamo, who designed special shoes for the Prime Minister's very narrow feet. Another Italian friend, Olga Polizzi, daughter of Lord Forte, offered advice. Carol Price, the wife of the American Ambassador, contributed some transatlantic chic for the Prime Minister's new look. The result was a wardrobe that helped Margaret Thatcher to project herself as a superstar on the world stage.

From the moment she arrived at Moscow Airport in a black fox fur hat and tailored black coat she radiated the aura of a Hollywood Czarina. The vast bouquet of red roses presented to her as she stepped onto the tarmac added the final touch of colour and so accentuated the elegance of her look. Well over a hundred million Soviet viewers watched her arrival on state television. Some of them talk about it to this day, explaining how the presence of a strong woman Prime Minister on Russian soil evoked ancestral memories of Catherine the Great.

The first full day of Margaret Thatcher's visit was Sunday 29 March. She began it by driving fifty miles north of Moscow to the Russian Orthodox Monastery of Zagorsk. The melodious richness of the monks' chants, the gold and purple vestments of the priests, the veneration of icons, the lighting of candles and the swinging censers pouring forth clouds of incense were, as she put it, 'A far cry from the Sunday service at Finkin Street Methodist Church in Grantham'.[64] But she took part in the spiritual fervour of the liturgy, at least to the extent of lighting a candle before the shrine of St Anthony and kneeling to say prayers at the high altar. All this was filmed live on television; a diplomatic first for a communist system which was still suppressing or at least restricting the Christian religion. 'You would think the Russians would not have been delighted by [this],' said the British Ambassador, Sir Bryan Cartledge, 'but they took it on the chin.'[65]

After the monastery, it was off to a Moscow housing estate where she was cheered by thousands as she came out of a 'typical' family home. Next stop was a supermarket whose largely empty shelves presented her with a buying problem. She solved it by purchasing a tin of pilchards – ironically a dish for which she had developed an aversion from the days of her Oxford landlady's unappetising fish breakfasts. In the evening she attended the Bolshoi Ballet's performance of *Swan Lake*, followed by a small private dinner with Mikhail and Raisa Gorbachev. The atmosphere was relaxed, with the Soviet leader in a joke-cracking mood. 'Why didn't you bring your son Mark?' he asked his guest. 'There are plenty of deserts here for him to get lost in.'[66]

The formal seven hours of Thatcher–Gorbachev talks covered a wide range of subjects including the Soviet occupation of Afghanistan, arms control, economic reforms and the emigration of Soviet Jews to Israel. But the substance of the agenda was transcended by the style in which it was discussed. Bryan Cartledge observed:

> She and Gorbachev charmed each other. He found her very charming and she found him very charming, and they got on like a house on fire. To an extent which gave rise to some pretty risqué Russian jokes at the time . . . There can never have been a case where two heads of government so radiated a kind of chemistry between them. You could see sparks flying off. They both liked talking. They both liked the sound of their own voices. They were both very difficult to interrupt. But they both managed to interrupt each other, and they had met their match.[67]

With two such political pugilists going hammer and tongs at each other, the match was spectacular even if it had no clear winner. But away from the formal talks, Margaret Thatcher scored victory after victory in the eyes of the Soviet public. From giving a lunch party for anti-government dissidents to drawing huge crowds, she was a magnet for attention and often adulation. Her greatest triumph was her television appearance.

To universal surprise, Gorbachev agreed that the Prime Minister could give a broadcast live on television that would be free from censorship. 'Yes, I took a risk, but it was my deliberate choice because I wanted her and everyone else to see that my policy of *Glasnost* was not a trick,' recalled Gorbachev, 'and by participating in the programme she was actually helping me to prove that our openness was working.'[68]

The programme was a huge surprise to both the Soviet government and the Soviet viewing public. The broadcasting authorities had expected her to deliver a monologue to camera, like one of their own leaders. But Margaret Thatcher enjoyed the cut and thrust of lively argument. So she insisted on her chosen format, which was to be questioned as if she was on a Western political talk show, by three Moscow journalists, two of whom were former army generals.

These interviewers were ponderous and long-winded in their party-line questions. They were not expecting a spontaneous debate in which the British Prime Minister would challenge them, contradict them and barely let them finish a sentence without forceful interruption. In a section of the programme devoted to nuclear weapons, one of the generals tried to raise the issue of an accidental outbreak of nuclear hostilities, asking to know who would be in charge of the West's Pershing missiles.

Margaret Thatcher replied:

> *One moment!* There are more nuclear weapons in the Soviet Union than any other country in the world. You have more intercontinental ballistic missiles and warheads than the West. You started intermediate weapons; we did not have any. You have more short-range ones than we have. You have more than anyone else and *you* say there is a risk of nuclear accident? *One moment!*

The three stooges could not cope with this kind of combative debating on live television. After a while, they subsided into softer territory, asking personal questions about her diet, her work habits and how she coped with so little sleep. Even on these anodyne subjects her frankness seemed remarkably refreshing to Soviet viewers, not least to Mikhail Gorbachev who was watching the live broadcast in the Kremlin. He recalled:

I had to give full credit to Margaret. My reaction to the programme was that our three journalists lost out – totally. She won almost every point that was raised. Some of the people around me thought we had given her too much freedom but 'no', I said – 'that's *Glasnost* in action'.[69]

The wider pubic applauded the freedom of this memorable broadcast. As the British Ambassador reported:

The Russians were absolutely captivated by this. For weeks afterwards people would come up to me and say 'Your Prime Minister is so wonderful. We'll never forget that debate on television. She told us things we didn't know, and she showed us how it should be done'.[70]

Margaret Thatcher emerged from her Moscow visit with the stature of an icon. The effects of her symbolism blazed a trail for some of the key freedoms that were becoming crucially important in the populist struggles that were taking place inside the Soviet Union. In her ground-breaking television interview she had personified the values of free and open debate, even in the sensitive area of nuclear security. She had given encouragement to freedom of religion, and hope to freedom of emigration. On these and other areas of policy she was able to change the Soviet mindset, as Gorbachev has obliquely acknowledged:

Mrs Thatcher was not an easy partner for us, and her fierce anti-communism would often hinder her from taking a more realistic view on various issues. Still, one must admit that in a number of cases she was able to substantiate her charges with facts, which eventually led us to review and criticise some of our own approaches.[71]

REFLECTION

Margaret Thatcher's political intimacy with Gorbachev came from an early recognition that, for all their ideological differences, they were kindred spirits. They were both outsiders, loners, buccaneers and fighters against the system they had inherited in their respective countries. Strong in their beliefs, they each had gifts of engagement that involved passionate argument without personal quarrelling.

At another level there was, in the view of some observers, a frisson of flirtatious sexuality in their relationship. For there were moments during their meetings and joint appearances when Margaret Thatcher could turn on an electrifying femininity, manifested in slightly coquettish forms of speech, moves and gestures. This was noticed by aides close to Gorbachev, such as Ambassador Leonid Zamyatin who observed how the Prime Minister showed off her legs to good advantage: 'Mrs Thatcher had a definite womanish feeling towards Gorbachev.'[72]

It was amplified with jokes that were more ribald than diplomatic by thousands of ordinary Russians on the street. Gorbachev–Thatcher 'chemistry' was a topic of humour and gossip for years after the Moscow visit.

In the field of substantive achievement, Margaret Thatcher believed she was playing a pivotal role in world history by her efforts to build bridges of understanding between Reagan and Gorbachev. No other American President and no other Soviet Chairman ever had the benefit of such an effective intermediary as Margaret Thatcher. She enlarged the area of confidence between the superpowers by the energy of her efforts to explain their leaders one to the other.

Always she was first and last America's ally, yet she combined this with being Gorbachev's only Western confidante. The value of the contribution showed up in many phases during the thawing of the Cold War: before and after Geneva, before and after Reykjavik, and in the immediate run-up to the Intermediate-Range Nuclear Forces (INF) Treaty of December 1987.

On 7 December, when Gorbachev was on his way to Washington to sign this treaty, he stopped off for a two-hour lunch with Margaret Thatcher at RAF Brize Norton. It was a valuable preliminary canter over the jumps he would have to take at his summit with Reagan. The Prime Minister gave the Soviet leader a difficult time over Afghanistan, human rights and what would happen after the INF Treaty. She did not appear to make much progress, but when she telephoned her report on the conversation to the Oval Office, President Reagan expressed satisfaction that the Prime Minister had 'clearly softened him up'.[73]

If there was such a softening process, it had good results. The signing of the INF treaty was the first time the superpowers had reduced their nuclear forces, abolishing an entire class of weapons such as the Pershing and SS-20 missiles. Important new rules for verification were agreed. Perhaps the most surprising indirect achievement was that two months later Gorbachev announced the withdrawal of Soviet forces from Afghanistan. Suddenly the world was beginning to feel a much safer place.

Margaret Thatcher had made a real contribution to that process. In terms of the Western alliance she was always a junior partner rather than a principal, an interlocutor not an initiator. But even so, she was a peacemaker who played a key part in bringing the Cold War to an end. It was one of her finest foreign-policy achievements.

29

Rumblings of discontent

TENSIONS WITH MINISTERS

Margaret Thatcher's international successes in Moscow and Washington created favourable television coverage around the world. But they were mismatched by a lack of support at home for her government's achievements. Most of her second term was marred by poor ratings in the opinion polls, infighting within Whitehall and uneasy bickering inside the Conservative Parliamentary Party. In retrospect, these difficulties look minor in importance, particularly as they melted away in the run-up to the 1987 general election, which resulted in her third sweeping victory. Yet a divisive cloud of unpopularity hung over Margaret Thatcher's leadership in the country and in the House of Commons for a large part of her second term, much of it due to the polarising impact of her personality.

Three power centres of British government never warmed to Margaret Thatcher, even though she was respected in them. These were the cabinet, the civil service and Parliament. In all cases the feelings of disdain were mutual, even though they were mitigated by many individual exceptions.

The cabinet she created at the beginning of her second term started out with instinctive loyalty to the Prime Minister. How she eroded that bedrock of support is an indictment of her skills, or lack of them, as a manager of colleagues. Her failure did not happen because her senior ministers were inclined to challenge her. Nor were they starry-eyed believers in the constitutional doctrine that the head of the government is merely first among equals. This had been an academic myth for most of the twentieth century. Yet, although among practical politicians the paramountcy of the Prime Minister was well established, the marginalisation of the cabinet was not.

In her first term, Margaret Thatcher had shown respect for collective cabinet discussions. Throughout the Falklands conflict, she chaired the war cabinet and the full cabinet with impeccable constitutional propriety. But the combination of victory over the Argentines and winning a big majority at the 1983 general election brought hubris to her style of leadership.

It became the Prime Minister's practice to grill her ministers on the work of their department with an intensity that too easily lurched into aggression. 'I think sometimes a Prime Minister should be intimidating', she observed in a television interview. 'There's not much point in being a weak floppy thing in the chair, is there?'[1]

Accusations of weakness, wetness, feebleness and lack of guts were the sort of shooting from the hip charges she often made with great vehemence in tirades against her senior colleagues. A strong character could argue back at her, or occasionally silence her completely. Carrington walked out of the room at least three times in the middle of what he called 'her dreadful rows'.[2] There were many of these angry altercations, but surprisingly few fight backs by those she was attacking.

One of the more spectacular eruptions followed by a counter-eruption came during the 1985 arguments over the privatisation of British Leyland. Norman Tebbit, still at the helm of the Department of Trade and Industry although convalescing from his Brighton bomb injuries, was against selling off Land Rover as a separate company. The Prime Minister took the opposite view. At one heated moment, she overruled her Secretary of State. Norman Tebbit was furious. 'If you think you can do my job better than I can, then do it!' he shouted, throwing his papers on the floor and making for the door. 'Margaret was completely shaken', said Norman Lamont, Tebbit's junior minister at the DTI and the only other person present in the Prime Minister's study. 'She was obviously alarmed that she had managed to upset him so badly, and at a time when he was not in the best of health. She climbed down immediately.' As a result, Land Rover was not sold off separately from the rest of the British Leyland group.[3]

Another minister who stood up to Margaret Thatcher robustly was Nigel Lawson. At one memorable moment in full cabinet, he told her to 'Shut up and listen – for once'.[4] On these occasions she was chastened – at least for a while. But they were the rare exceptions. Most cabinet ministers were either too respectful or too fearful to clash swords with a woman prime minister. They shut up in silence rather than put up with resistance, often with a growing sense of resentment.

One way or another, the cabinet was not a happy ship. Some of its unhappiness came from the growing and often unpleasantly handled dominance Margaret Thatcher exerted over her colleagues. It was lampooned in the satirical television programme *Spitting Image*, which portrayed the Prime Minister as a bullying dominatrix in a gangster's pin-striped suit continuously berating her cringing ministers into submission.

One memorable sketch on the show involved the Prime Minister dining with her puppet cabinet in a restaurant as the waitress took the order, addressing the Prime Minister as 'Sir'. 'I will have the steak', said Thatcher. 'And what about the vegetables?' 'Oh, they'll have the same as me', answered Thatcher.[5]

This caricature was uncomfortably close to the truth. For the reality was that Margaret Thatcher did despise a great many of her colleagues. She showed this by being gratuitously rude to them in front of their own officials; never apologising for her tirades; rarely praising them when they had done something well; and often undermining them through anonymous briefings to journalists.

A classic example of this was the denigration of John Biffen when Leader of the House as 'a semi-detached member of the Government'.[6] This phrase, which emerged from a Bernard Ingham lobby briefing, appeared all over the newspapers in May 1986. To no one's surprise Biffen was completely detached and sacked from the cabinet in the next reshuffle. Perhaps he deserved this fate, since in some of his own comments to the press he had been imprudently critical of his boss. But there were many loyal and supportive members of the cabinet whose dismissals were leaked well in advance of their execution dates. It was a cruel and capricious way of running a government.

To give a rounded picture of Margaret Thatcher's man-management techniques it should be said that there were some key figures she never undermined, even when they were under-performing. Sir Keith Joseph was one of them, largely because of her political and personal affection for him, which dated back to the 1960s. She also had great admiration for his intellect, if not for his political skills. Willie Whitelaw was a protected species too, deservedly so, since he was such a bulwark of support for her leadership. As for her changing cast of court favourites, like Cecil Parkinson, John Moore, Norman Tebbit and Lord Young, they had their difficult moments with their boss. All of them, even Joseph, Whitelaw and Carrington, felt the rough edge of the Prime Minister's tongue when she disagreed with them, or thought they had not done their homework over some point on which she had been better briefed. There was always a lurking anger in Margaret Thatcher making her liable to pounce unexpectedly at ministerial meetings. 'It was rather like going into a cage with a leopard', said her Principal Private Secretary, Robin Butler. 'You believed that the leopard was friendly and house-trained and that you would come to no harm. But you would always be worried that things might take a turn for the worse and that you could get your arm bitten off.'[7]

Fear of the Prime Minister's bite was not conducive to good collegiate relationships in the cabinet. Junior ministers also found her rather terrifying if they attended an *ad hoc* meeting and dared to disagree with her views. But if they were well briefed and good at presenting their case they could survive and prosper, for she was keen to identify talent and to promote it. She could be admirably protective of a young minister who she thought was coming under fire unfairly.

An entertaining example of this came when William Waldegrave, then a junior Parliamentary Under-Secretary at the Department of the Environment, was hauled in front of her at No. 10 at the instigation of Norman Tebbit for a dressing down – or worse. Waldegrave's crime had been to negotiate an agreement in Brussels which reduced the number of parts per million of exhaust gases permitted for British Leyland cars. In the middle of this nocturnal negotiation, Norman Tebbit, who as Secretary of State for Trade was in charge of the car industry, telephoned Waldegrave with an instruction to change his negotiating brief, and to agree to a deal which would have been further in favour of British Leyland's out-of-date technology. Waldegrave refused and settled within his brief.

For this heinous offence, the Parliamentary Under-Secretary of State for the Environment was summoned to see the Prime Minister, flanked by Norman Tebbit, Nicholas Ridley (Secretary of State for Transport), Patrick Jenkin (Secretary of State for the Environment) and various officials. There was a courtroom flavour to the occasion, with Norman Tebbit taking the role of counsel for the prosecution. Tebbit's opening attack on William Waldegrave was so vitriolic that Nicholas Ridley intervened to say that no colleague should refer to another colleague in such terms. The atmosphere became electric.

Margaret Thatcher, who had done her homework, seemed to be relishing it. She began to purr – dangerously. She said:

> Now, Norman, I am a chemist and will explain it to you. You see, here it is: they refer to CO and NOx. Those are gases, Norman. And here it says some numbers with 'ppm' after them – that's parts per million, Norman. And here is what William settled at, and you see it is between the numbers we allowed him. Oh, and here is your name, Norman. You were at the committee and agreed the numbers!

The prosecution collapsed without the defendant having said a word. As the attendees left the Cabinet Room, the Prime Minister gripped William Waldegrave by the elbow and whispered into his ear, 'I always look after my young people, William'.[8]

Such support for a junior minister in trouble was an endearing feature of Margaret Thatcher's style of governance, but it was counter-balanced by less attractive dimensions of her personality. She liked to divide and rule. She wanted to hog the limelight and take the credit for herself. Thanks to the dedication of her two key Downing Street aides, Bernard Ingham and Charles Powell, she was able to achieve these goals quite easily, sidelining even her most important ministers in the process.

Geoffrey Howe, who was downgraded in the Prime Minister's esteem from the bold Chancellor of 1979–1983 to the bullied Foreign Secretary of 1983–1989 caught the essence of her dominance with a clever analogy. According to Howe, the cabinet could be compared to the solar system. The Prime Minister was the sun. Ministers revolved around her, but in their own orbits. They were not allowed to shine in their own right or to constellate together as a planetary team.[9]

In such a system a large number of ministerial stars burned out, fell out or were kicked out by the Sun Queen. The turnover of the cabinet was numerically astonishing. No less than thirty-six senior ministers left the government between 1979 and 1990. When Margaret Thatcher finally resigned after eleven years as Prime Minister, she was the only survivor of the original cabinet she had formed in May 1979. The attrition rate was not a creditable feature of her leadership.

Some of the ministerial departures were right for a variety of reasons. Others were wrong, and would have not happened under a different kind of prime minister. But the most exotic and egocentric exit from Margaret Thatcher's government was that of Michael Heseltine.

CLASHING WITH HESELTINE

Michael Heseltine and Margaret Thatcher were chalk and cheese. She mistrusted his character, questioned his motives, deplored his showmanship, disliked his interventionist policies and saw his vaulting ambition as a constant threat. He was initially more covert in his antipathy towards her, deep seated though it was. As time went on his alienation soured into antagonism. Long before Westland was on the agenda of British politics, Hezza versus Maggie was a train crash of personalities waiting to happen.

If there was an early event that set Margaret Thatcher's suspicions of Heseltine in stone, it was the mace incident of 27 May 1976. This consisted of him losing his temper late at night in the House of Commons, seizing the ceremonial mace and brandishing it menacingly at the Labour government on the benches opposite. She was sitting alongside Heseltine on the front bench as Leader of the Opposition when he exploded at the announcement of a one-vote majority for the government on its bill to nationalise the aircraft and shipbuilding industries. As the Conservative Party's industry spokesman, he had expected to win the division because of Labour defections. He believed he had been cheated out of his victory by chicanery on the part of the Labour whips over the counting of sick and unpaired votes. Whatever the rights and wrongs of this controversy, Heseltine made himself look like a fanatic from *The Planet of the Apes* by grabbing the ceremonial mace and shaking it in the manner of an aggressive gorilla towards the government Chief Whip. The parliamentary sketch writers mocked Heseltine with the nickname 'Tarzan' – which stuck. Among MPs there were more frowns than laughs. To the constitutionally minded, Tarzan's excesses seemed a contempt of the House, because the mace is the symbol of the Crown in Parliament.

Heseltine was lucky that television cameras were not permitted at Westminster in the 1970s, or his moment of madness would have been preserved for posterity. As it was, the episode was fairly soon forgotten – but not by Margaret

Thatcher. She was affronted by her Industry spokesman's mace-waving idiocy and wanted to sack him from her shadow cabinet. She was persuaded not to do this by Jim Prior and William Whitelaw.

There was some friction in their relationship between 1979 and 1983, particularly when Heseltine expanded one part of his duties as Environment Secretary into the aggrandised role (as she saw it) of Minister for Merseyside. Even though she ignored most of his interventionist recommendations for reviving Liverpool, his public relations skills won her reluctant respect. In 1983 she moved him to Defence where he was good at winning the presentational battles against CND protestors over the stationing of cruise missiles on UK soil. However, she also became resentful of his energetic self-promotion, and jealous of his oratorical talent for rousing the faithful at Conservative Party conferences.

This resentment became a two-way street. Margaret Thatcher excluded her Defence Secretary from most of the Anglo-American discussions on the Strategic Defence Initiative (SDI), which caused great pique on his part. Heseltine, responding to questions in Parliament from the Labour benches, launched an internal Ministry of Defence inquiry into the sinking of the *General Belgrano*, to assure himself that there was 'not a Watergate in this somewhere'.[10] The comparison was ludicrous, as the later inquiry showed. Margaret Thatcher was right to be offended by it.

She was also angry at Heseltine's use of the Defence budget for social engineering purposes. They had a row over whether to build two new frigates at the Tyneside shipyard of Swan Hunter (the best value for money option), or whether to split the order with Cammell Laird in order to create jobs on Merseyside, although at a higher cost for the taxpayer. Heseltine got his way but only by threatening to resign. This disagreement became so personal that the Defence Secretary and the Prime Minister were barely on speaking terms. As Nigel Lawson put it, 'From then on, she was as determined to do him down as he was to run his Department in his own way'.[11]

These tensions became so visible that in October 1985 the *Sunday Times* reported that Heseltine 'could even be brewing up towards a spectacular resignation'.[12] This was a prescient forecast. The reasons for these advance warnings were rooted in the festering personality clash between two hostile egos. The eventual cause of the explosion that blew them apart – technical arguments about the future of a helicopter company – had barely begun to surface.

Westland was Britain's sole helicopter manufacturing company. It had a turnover of £300 million a year, small by the standards of defence industries, but important in terms of West Country jobs. It was making losses and faced a perilous future. The Secretary of State for Trade and Industry Leon Brittan reported to the Prime Minister that Westland would go into receivership unless a new shareholder came in to inject fresh capital into the company. The Westland board, unable to find any such British investors, were inclined to accept an offer from Sikorsky Aircraft Corporation, a subsidiary of the American United Technologies Corporation and Fiat, the Italian conglomerate, who were willing to invest in the company in exchange for a 29.9 per cent shareholding.[13]

Michael Heseltine, a passionate Europhile, believed that Westland should join up with a potential consortium of European defence companies. His arguments sounded worth further consideration to a cabinet committee whose ministers, ranging from Geoffrey Howe to Norman Tebbit, gave the Defence Secretary more time to explore his European option. But Heseltine embarked on a much more dramatic course than mere exploration. He did his utmost to sabotage the deal with Sikorsky. To achieve this, on 29 November, he called a meeting of the National Armament Directors (NADS) of France, Italy, Germany and Britain, persuading them to sign a document declaring that in future they would only buy European-made helicopters. With the flames being fanned by many Heseltine leaks and press briefings, the issue flared up into a test of strength between a European versus an American solution for Westland, and a Heseltine versus Thatcher power struggle. This was how a minor issue became a major crisis. The government itself took the perfectly sensible line that the Westland board should make the final decision. This in practice meant backing the American option and overruling Michael Heseltine's manoeuvres to obtain a recommendation from the pro-European NADs.

The government decided to support the Westland board and approve the Sikorsky shareholding – which had by December 1985 become formally known as the United Technologies–Fiat shareholding – with each of these partners planning to hold 14.5 per cent of the company. This decision to approve it was taken by the cabinet's Economic Sub-Committee on 9 December by a clear majority vote. Heseltine, however, did not accept the decision and wanted the issue debated at full cabinet. Margaret Thatcher initially refused this. She cut short his attempt to raise Westland at a cabinet meeting on 12 December, on the grounds that no papers had been circulated on the issue. Heseltine was incensed and launched what she called 'a short ill tempered discussion'.[14] He may have been silenced in the cabinet room, but he continued both the argument and the ill temper at full volume.

For the next three weeks Michael Heseltine was in overdrive, leaking his version of the controversy to newspapers, bankers, industrialists, lobbyists or anyone else whom he hoped to convince that the proposed UT–Fiat investment in Westland was wrong because it was not his preferred European option. This behaviour was a flagrant violation of the rules of collective cabinet responsibility. Margaret Thatcher was furious with Heseltine, but she uncharacteristically shied away from having a meeting with him and telling him to toe the line.

At one No. 10 discussion during this period, Leon Brittan, baffled by the Prime Minister's unwillingness to see the Defence Secretary face to face, said to her, 'You've just got to lay down the law to him'. Bernard Ingham then interjected, 'You don't want to have him resigning, do you?'[15] Dread of a personality clash with Heseltine was a curious chink in the Prime Minister's armour. It had first appeared right at the start of her premiership on Saturday 5 May 1979, when he declined the cabinet post she offered him. She had decided to appoint him Secretary of State for Energy. He refused, arguing that he should stay with the Environment portfolio he had been shadowing in Opposition. Margaret Thatcher caved in immediately. Just after suffering this blow to her authority, she said to the Private Secretary who had been present at the meeting, 'I don't like one-to-one confrontations with Michael'.[16]

Heseltine had no such inhibitions. He was reckless in the determination of his desire to oppose the Prime Minister. Going out of the Cabinet Room on the 12 December row over Westland, the angry Defence Secretary encountered Charles Powell in the corridor. 'She's not going to win on this one', stormed Heseltine. 'I'm going to defeat her.' 'Oh come on', said Powell.[17]

By the turn of the year, the Prime Minister's reluctance to confront her rebellious colleague led to a stand-off. Heseltine was aggressively promoting his own European solution for Westland. It was the opposite of the government's policy, but the Defence Secretary's justification for his disobedience was that Westland had never been properly discussed by the full cabinet. Margaret Thatcher thought this was a bogus excuse for his misconduct, but was unwilling to tell him so directly. Instead, she fought Heseltine by proxy, encouraging her Secretary of State for Trade to counter-attack her Defence Secretary.

'I think this episode showed her at her worst', recalled Leon Brittan. 'She egged me on with fierce support, but she refused to argue directly with him. Far from being the Iron Lady, she proved curiously weak and indecisive.'[18]

The Prime Minister's indecision almost proved fatal. As the next moves in the saga were to show, she turned a problem into a crisis. She was willing to wound her adversary, but afraid to stop him in his tracks with a direct order. Her hesitation set the stage for a far more personal and damaging battle. Within a month, the explosion into open warfare caused two cabinet resignations, and came perilously close to forcing Margaret Thatcher out of Downing Street. After more than five years as a successful Prime Minister, the Westland crisis needlessly developed into a personal failure that took her to the brink of resignation.

THE WESTLAND CRISIS EXPLODES

On 3 January 1986, Michael Heseltine's continuing efforts to sabotage the UTC–Fiat investment in Westland took a new twist when he leaked to *The Times* his carefully orchestrated exchange of letters with Lloyds Merchant Bank, the advisers to the European consortium. In this correspondence he warned that Westland risked losing future European orders if it accepted an American partner.[19] This was a deliberate contradiction of the assurances Margaret Thatcher had given in writing to Sir John Cuckney, Westland's chairman, in a letter of 1 January 1986.[20]

Instead of confronting her Defence Secretary directly, Margaret Thatcher found a more complicated method of crushing his rebellion using leaks and legalities. Her first move was to arrange for the Solicitor General, Sir Patrick Mayhew, to write to Heseltine with an opinion querying the factual basis for his letter to the merchant bank. Mayhew's letter contained a complaint of a 'material inaccuracy' in Heseltine's correspondence.[21]

These two words, wrenched out of context, were used to damage the Defence Secretary when the Solicitor General's letter was leaked to the press. 'You LIAR' was the screaming headline in the *Sun*.[22] 'Heseltine told by Law Chief: Stick to the Facts' was the more sober version of the story in *The Times*.[23] Yet the broadsides against Heseltine misfired. For, in an extraordinary turn of events, the issue became not who lied, but who leaked.

Leaking is one of the most frequently practised arts in politics. Both Michael Heseltine and Margaret Thatcher were ruthless exponents of it. But as all players of the game should know, some kinds of leak are off limits. Perhaps the most arcane area of forbidden leaking is a Law Officer's opinion. These are supposed to be protected by the highest walls of confidentiality. Quite why this should be so is baffling to ordinary mortals. To the lawyer politicians who serve in the posts of Attorney General or Solicitor General, it is part of the mystique of their ancient offices that their legal opinions must always be cloaked in secrecy. Precious little reverence for this mystique affected the next move in the Westland saga, although precisely whodunnit, who leaked it or who should be blamed for it became an incredible fudge.

The initiative to make public the Solicitor General's view that Michael Heseltine's letter contained a 'material inaccuracy' came from the Prime Minister. She later admitted this to Parliament. 'It was vital to have accurate information in the public domain . . . It was to get that accurate information to the public domain that I gave my consent.'[24] But what exactly she gave her consent to remains murky to this day.

The way the Prime Minister's consent worked in practice was that two officials at No. 10 – Bernard Ingham and Charles Powell – were in contact with Leon Brittan's Private Secretary and his head of Information at the Department of Trade and Industry. Brittan was out of the office at a lunch when Colette Bowe, his press secretary, reached him to ask whether the Solicitor General's criticism of a 'material inaccuracy' in the Heseltine letter should be made public. Leon Brittan said that he would prefer that any such disclosure should be made by No. 10, but failing this he authorised his press office to make it public 'subject to the agreement of No. 10'.[25] He returned from lunch unaware that he had made a momentous decision. He had expressed no view about the timing or method of the disclosure. He thought he had passed the responsibility for it back to the Prime Minister who had wanted to get the 'material inaccuracy' into the public domain in the first place. 'I had no doubt whatsoever that these were her instructions', recalled Leon Brittan, 'because my officials had been told by No. 10 that she wanted the information made public.'[26]

For a layman unversed in the sacred mysteries surrounding advice from Law Officers, it is difficult to see any wrongdoing in the sequence of events outlined above. The Prime Minister wanted the Solicitor General's criticisms of Michael Heseltine's inaccurate letter to be released into the public domain. As head of the government she was entitled to authorise this release. If she had taken up this position in justification of the instructions she gave, why should there have been a fuss about it?

Unfortunately for both Margaret Thatcher and Leon Brittan, the leaking of the Solicitor General's letter produced a fuss of titanic proportions created by the Attorney General. His outrage derived from the questionable proposition that the advice of the government's Law Officers automatically assumes a unique degree of confidentiality, which can never under any circumstances be breached. On these grounds Sir Michael Havers, the Attorney General, became so indignant that he threatened to send the police into No. 10 with orders to conduct an investigation into the leak of the Solicitor General's letter, under the Official Secrets Act. Margaret Thatcher headed this off at the gates of Downing Street by setting up an internal inquiry conducted by the Cabinet Secretary, Sir Robert Armstrong. The Defence Select Committee of the House of Commons then launched its own inquiry into the imbroglio. It eventually reported that, 'the method of disclosure that was adopted, the unattributable communication of tendentious extracts from the letter, was disreputable'.[27]

Michael Heseltine may well have thought it disreputable too, but unaccustomed as he was to be more leaked against than leaking, he kept his powder dry for two more days. On Thursday 9 January he took his case on Westland to full cabinet. He did not present it well. Even his friend and ally, Geoffrey Howe, felt that the Defence Secretary on this occasion seemed unconvincing, unimpressive and so obsessive that he seemed 'faintly reminiscent of Tony Benn'.*[28]

Yet even if Heseltine failed to win support for his argument against the UTC–Fiat rescue plan for Westland, he struck deeper chords with his grievances against the Prime Minister's management of cabinet discussions. For instead of giving

---

* The former Labour cabinet minister Tony Benn had by the mid-1980s become a caricature, at least in Tory eyes, of an obsessive conspiracy theorist. Twenty years later, as a diarist and one-man show performer, he came to be regarded as a national treasure.

a clear lead, her unstructured, combative style of government had encouraged chaos to reign in the argument between two of her senior ministers. A squall about helicopters had been allowed to blow up into a tempest that was now rocking the government to its foundation.

Determined to restore her authority over the chaos for which she was at least partly responsible, Margaret Thatcher called a meeting of the cabinet on 9 January. She summed up the cabinet discussion on Westland with a firmness that had been lacking in her handling of the problem so far. The government would support the decision of the Westland board to accept the UTC–Fiat shareholding. The squabbling between ministers must stop. All government statements on Westland, past as well as future ones, must be cleared by the Cabinet Secretary. She ended by declaring, 'this matter has now been decided'.[29]

This was too much for Heseltine. 'If this is the way Government is going to be conducted, I no longer wish to be part of it', he said as he gathered up his papers and left the room.[30] Opinions of his colleagues were divided as to whether this was a sudden impulsive reaction or a carefully choreographed exit whose next moves had been well prepared.

Inside the Cabinet Room there was a stoically British display of carrying on as if nothing unusual had happened. The Prime Minister, scarcely missing a beat, led her colleagues through routine items on European Community affairs, Nigeria and Northern Ireland. Only then did she call for an unscheduled coffee break.

While some colleagues wondered whether Heseltine had come to the meeting with an open mind about remaining in the government, Margaret Thatcher had no doubt that his departure was premeditated. She may even have intended to provoke his resignation. She was certainly ready for it. Within a quarter of an hour she appointed a new Defence Secretary, George Younger. She made Malcolm Rifkind his successor as the Secretary of State for Scotland. The cabinet meeting resumed with a sensible discussion about the options for reforming the rates.

Heseltine went back to the Ministry of Defence, where he delivered a twenty-five minute statement attacking the Prime Minister for allowing 'the complete breakdown of Cabinet government'.[31] It made an exciting item on the television news bulletins for a few hours. But because the British public were not worked up about a row over the details of which international company was going to be allowed to invest in Westland, it seemed unlikely that Heseltine's resignation would significantly rock the boat. However, this was only the calm before a much more serious storm.

As Parliament reassembled on Monday 13 January 1986 after the Christmas recess, the drama of the Westland crisis shifted away from helicopters and Heseltine. It now focused on the leak of the Solicitor General's letter and who should carry the can for it. It was the received wisdom that the leak amounted to a most heinous offence. But who had committed it?

Between 13 January and 27 January Margaret Thatcher and Leon Brittan made statements, speeches and answered questions in the House of Commons about this aspect of the Westland affair. A summary of their performances might be that the Secretary of State for Trade had more right on his side but performed unconvincingly. By contrast, the Prime Minister appeared to be in worse trouble but bluffed her way back from the precipice with greater luck, but also with more uncomfortable economy of the truth.

Margaret Thatcher's first attempt at explaining her role in the Westland drama was rightly described by her biographer Hugo Young as 'probably the most unconvincing statement she ever made to the House of Commons'.[32]

Some of her back-benchers made harsher comments. Before she gave her account to Parliament on 23 January, nervous government whips circled round Westminster's bars and dining rooms drumming up support among Conservative colleagues. One of them was Alan Clark, who described in his diary the approach made to him by the Chief Whip, John Wakeham.

> Then, unexpectedly, the Chief Whip came up and sat with us. He showed me a copy of the statement. I read a few paragraphs, started a *faux-rire*. I couldn't help it. 'I'm sorry, John. I simply can't keep a straight face.' The paper passed from hand to hand. Others agreed, but were too polite to say so. How *can* she say these things without faltering? But she did.[33]

The Prime Minister may not have faltered but many of her listeners were unimpressed. She high-speed read her way through a whitewash job, claiming that all concerned at the Department of Trade and Industry and at No. 10 had 'acted in good faith'. Few believed her. One ex-minister, Alex Fletcher, asked her if she was 'satisfied that the statement she has made this afternoon has enhanced the integrity of her Government?'

'Good question!' a voice called out from the depths of the sceptical Tory back-benchers. Margaret Thatcher replied like Jim Hacker in *Yes Minister* that she had set up the Cabinet Secretary's inquiry in order to give the House 'as full an account as I possibly can because the House deserves to have it'.[34] It was bluff and nonsense.

The statement ended among many rumblings and grumblings from Conservative MPs. 'This won't do. It simply will not do', Sir Bernard Braine protested,[35] over and over again, as we trickled out of the chamber. This was the spirit of frustration in which Leon Brittan became the target of the parliamentary party's anger.

Leon Brittan had shown himself to be a cabinet minister of considerable intellect and talent. But by January 1986 he was visibly unhappy in his own skin. His confidence had been shaken some months earlier by the Prime Minister's demotion of him from Home Secretary to Trade and Industry Secretary because, as she put it, he was 'not getting the message across on television'.[36] Now his Westland duel with Michael Heseltine had left him bleeding, although not yet mortally wounded. What brought Brittan down later in the afternoon of 23 January was that his back-bench colleagues would not close ranks and support him. If there had to be a fall guy for the leak of the Solicitor General's letter, it would have to be him. The alternative sacrifice was the Prime Minister.

Unfortunately for Margaret Thatcher, the facts pointed all too inexorably towards her being the prime mover in the leak. She had initiated the Solicitor General's letter. She had wanted it to be made public. Her two key aides, Bernard Ingham and Charles Powell, had been involved in the discussions with DTI officials, which led to the now-infamous release to the Press Association.

Leon Brittan had insisted that before any disclosure was made that it should be 'subject to the agreement of No. 10'. It was so agreed. Surely Margaret Thatcher's right-hand men would not have given this agreement without the blessing of their Prime Minister? But the absence of her specific authority, however improbable, was the only explanation that might enable her to escape from censure or even resignation. Even so, her personal integrity was on the line.

Leon Brittan's career was also on the line. Soon after a poisonous meeting of Tory back-benchers at the 1922 Committee he fell on his sword. It was a combination of a witch-hunt and the search for a scapegoat – tainted by an undercurrent of anti-Semitism. Personally, I felt disgusted by the attacks of several of my colleagues. I spoke up for Leon Brittan, but was the only voice of support for him in the committee that evening. I believed what should have been obvious to anyone else, that he was being used as a lightning conductor to deflect the fire that the Prime Minister had started and inflamed.

The fire was not immediately quenched by Leon Brittan's resignation on 24 January. The opposition was able to call an emergency debate for Monday 27 January. Over the weekend Margaret Thatcher's preparations for her speech were frenetic and at times paranoid. She had to agree a form of words with Leon Brittan, who had it in his power to destroy her if her narrative shifted the blame on to him. She also had to explain away the exculpatory but still critical findings of the Cabinet Secretary's leak inquiry. She needed to protect her closest aides. Above all, she had to protect herself against what could easily have been lethal questions from the leaders of either Her Majesty's Opposition or the Heseltine opposition. The latter group was fast becoming a sizeable faction on the Conservative back benches.

The debate was due to begin at 3.30 p.m. on 27 January. At 2.30 p.m. the Prime Minister's speech was still being redrafted in the small private secretary's room at No. 10, where the throng of script-writers included Willie Whitelaw, Geoffrey Howe, John Wakeham, Nigel Wicks, the Principal Private Secretary, Ronnie Millar, Charles Powell and Bernard Ingham. 'We all needed, like so many printer's devils, to be near to the stone where the final text was being cast', recalled Howe as the final preparations became more and more intense.

Margaret Thatcher kept popping in and out of the crowded room. In a distracted moment she remarked to no one in particular, 'I may not be Prime Minister by six o'clock tonight'.[37]

Although there were immediate murmurs of dissent, the possibility was real. Even the phlegmatic Geoffrey Howe realised that the forecast could turn out to be right. 'My own heart missed a beat', he recalled as he contemplated 'the frightening thought that I might suddenly find myself taking Margaret's place.'[38]

This extraordinary outcome of the crisis continued to prey on the Prime Minister's mind. For when travelling to the House of Commons in her car she again said, this time to her Cabinet Secretary, Sir Robert Armstrong, 'You do realise, don't you Robert, that by six o'clock I may no longer be Prime Minister'.[39]

The Westland debate, which could indeed have ended Margaret Thatcher's days in No 10, turned out to be an anti-climax. She was on trial, and although she did not win an acquittal, she did achieve an escape. There were two factors that turned her into a political Houdini. The first was the unexpected failure of Neil Kinnock. The second was a late developing fervour of loyalty on her backbenches.

As Leader of the Opposition, Kinnock opened the debate in front of an open goal. All he had to do was to ask the questions whose answers would have established the Prime Minister's complicity in the leak of the Solicitor General's letter. But instead of the cold forensic interrogation that the moment required, he performed like a hot air balloon, failing to get off the ground whilst blasting his Bunsen burners at full throttle in the wrong direction. As he roared and blustered his way though a flurry of vague insults, Kinnock changed the mood of the divided Tory backbenchers from suspicion of the Prime Minister to support for her. His ranting about her 'dishonesty, duplicity, conniving and manoeuvring' not only brought the Speaker to his feet demanding the withdrawal of the unparliamentary term 'dishonesty'.[40] They also produced a surge of Conservative unity that had been noticeably absent throughout the Westland crisis.

Amidst the partisan histrionics that the Leader of the Opposition created, it was much easier for Margaret Thatcher to beat a retreat. She showed just enough candour and contrition to wriggle out of the danger zone. She told some of the truth rather than the whole truth and nothing but the truth, but she was in a parliamentary bear-pit not a court of law. Although the SDP leader, David Owen, later asked the forensic questions that should have been put to her at the start of the debate, his speech was made to a half-empty House. Margaret Thatcher was confident enough to ignore him. By then she knew the tide had turned in her favour.

Even Michael Heseltine was forced to acknowledge this. Recognising that the adversary he had been so bitterly challenging for the past few weeks had got away with it, the ex-Defence Secretary put his tongue in his cheek, professed his loyalty for the Prime Minister and declared he would be voting with the government in the ten o'clock division. The Westland crisis was over.

THAT BLOODY WOMAN

The Westland crisis did, however, leave a bad taste in many mouths. Although the general public soon forgot about the involutions and convolutions of the saga, within Whitehall and Westminster it was seen as a symptom of a more disturbing disease. A common diagnosis was that the Prime Minister's relationship with her cabinet had become too dysfunctional, while the No. 10 triumvirate who really seemed to be running the country – Margaret Thatcher, Bernard Ingham and Charles Powell – had become too powerful.

This situation was not the fault of the Prime Minister's two closest civil servants. They kept the Downing Street machine humming like a Rolls-Royce, but they were only its mechanics. It was the driver who seemed to worry less and less about which corners she cut, or which other motorists and pedestrians had to jump out of her way.

One sign of this emerging streak of recklessness in her leadership skills was her aggressive discourtesy towards parliamentary colleagues. During her first term she was respectful towards the Executive of the 1922 Committee. By the end of her second term, she could be gratuitously offensive towards members of this group when they made their annual visit to report on the mood of the party. Ironically, Ted Heath had made the same mistake in the second half of his premiership.

'No backbone! No stomach for a fight!' was how she addressed the Vice-Chairman of the 1922 Committee, Winston Churchill, after he had told her that her plans for rating reform, first announced in 1986, were unpopular with his fellow-Tory colleagues in Manchester. 'And they said my grandfather was a bully! At least he listened as much as he bullied', complained Churchill soon after his handbagging.[41]

One of Margaret Thatcher's problems in dealing with her parliamentary party was that she missed the bridge-building efforts of her most gifted Parliamentary Private Secretary, Ian Gow. He had been a tower of strength to her and to her back-benchers in her first term. His successors lacked his wit, his subtlety and his ability for establishing a politically close relationship with the Lady.

After Gow, she imposed unusual criteria on her selection of Parliamentary Private Secretaries. They must be Members of Parliament with a private income. She thought it unfair to ask for long hours of House of Commons service from someone who received no salary. Hence her subsequent choices of Michael Alison, Archie Hamilton, Mark Lennox-Boyd and Peter Morrison. This quartet of comfortably-off Old Etonians were too polite in offering reassurance to the Prime Minister at times when she needed to be confronted by back-bench criticism. Not that she listened much when it was delivered.

In early 1987, I was wheeled in to see her because I had sponsored a well-supported motion calling for parliamentary oversight of the security services. She opened the conversation, 'How can you believe this nonsense?'[42]

I ran through a list of recent failings and fiascos at MI5, and suggested that a Westminster version of the U.S. Senate Select Committee on Intelligence might have helped to prevent some of them. 'What rot!' she retorted. 'That would mean people like you poking their noses into security matters they know nothing about.'[43]

I said that she could select the parliamentary overseers, but without them there would be no external oversight. 'Absolutely wrong. There is perfectly good oversight now. I do it', she asserted with ringing certainty.[44]

On that basis there was no point in having a prolonged argument. I was more amused than affronted by this *l'état c'est moi* approach to the issue. At her behest the oversight motion was duly voted down, despite some appropriately clandestine murmurs of support for it within the security services themselves.*

Dealing with the secret world produced astonishingly proprietorial instincts in Margaret Thatcher. 'Backbenchers should have nothing to do with national security matters', she told Richard Shepherd MP when he tried to win her support for his Private Member's Bill to reform the Official Secrets Act 1911. She was wrong to take such a high-handed attitude, as later reforms bringing in new oversight procedures and a new Official Secrets Act were to prove.

High handedness was an increasingly visible feature of Margaret Thatcher's leadership but it was not accompanied by an increase in her electoral popularity. As she approached the seventh anniversary of her entry into No. 10 Downing Street, her poll ratings fell to their lowest point – 28 per cent – since the dark days of inner-city riots and Geoffrey Howe's expenditure cuts budget in 1981.

---

* Parliamentary oversight of the security services became an established feature of the UK's intelligence arrangements soon after Margaret Thatcher ceased to be Prime Minister. Since 1994, oversight has been quietly and effectively carried out by the Security and Intelligence Committee. The current Chairman is the former Foreign Secretary, The Rt Hon. Sir Malcolm Rifkind QC MP.

A succession of by-election losses was unnerving both Conservative Central Office and the Tory back benches. From Ryedale in North Yorkshire to Fulham in Central London, safe seats were falling to the Liberals and to Labour. The government was coming a poor third in the national polls. This seemed strange, for many of its policies – council-house sales, diminishing the power of the unions and the general management of the economy – were being well received. The paradox was explained by what was called 'The TBW factor'.[45] Canvassers at by-elections and local elections kept on reporting a line they heard time and again on the doorsteps. 'I would vote for you if it wasn't for that bloody woman.'

David Frost was the first to tell Margaret Thatcher, live on Sunday morning television, about the TBW factor. It was one of the rare occasions when she looked as though she had been knocked off balance in a media appearance. When she received the same message from her Party Chairman, Norman Tebbit, TBW became 'That Angry Woman'.

She found it hard to accept that her personality and her stubbornness were grating on large sections of the electorate. Still less did she like to hear from her PPS, Michael Alison, that many Tory back-benchers were openly talking about a succession race, with Michael Heseltine said to be moving up fast on the rails. Not in the least a dark horse, he travelled all over the country to speak at Conservative Association fêtes, dinners and annual general meetings in response to the cry of alarmed colleagues, 'Save Our Seats'.

His blatant ambition infuriated the Prime Minister, but it also worried her. So did the polls. As she read the runes of the political scene at the end of the summer of 1986, she knew she was in trouble. She began to plan a fight-back with a new electoral strategy.

REFLECTION

For all the rumblings of discontent chronicled in this chapter, they were mainly about issues that troubled the Westminster village, not the wider electorate. Snakes and ladders in the cabinet interested only the players at or hoping to be at the cabinet table.

Westland was more serious, but it was too complicated a squabble to interest the man on the Clapham omnibus. The controversy was eventually buried by the emollient skills of Sir Humphrey, aka Sir Robert Armstrong. He produced a report that smoothed out all the uncomfortable problems exposed by the leak of the Solicitor General's letter. His conclusions bore more that a passing comparison to Voltaire's satire *Candide*: 'All is for the best, in the best of all possible worlds.'[46]

When summoned to explain his sanguine findings by the Defence Select Committee, the Cabinet Secretary gave such a masterly performance that the *Daily Mail* reported the event with the headline, 'Mandarin 3, Parliament 0'.[47] The only difficult moment for him came when he was asked to explain the Prime Minister's admission that she had authorised the leak with her words in a parliamentary answer: 'It was to get that accurate information to the public domain that I gave my consent.'[48] Sir Robert loftily brushed this smoking gun aside with the observation that it must have been 'a slip of the tongue'.[49] The MPs on the Select Committee were so tongue-tied that they never pursued the point.

Although the Westland storm passed with no lasting damage, there was a clear perception that the loss of two senior cabinet ministers was somehow Margaret Thatcher's fault for being too autocratic and for not listening. She worried about these charges.

Although the word 're-launch' never entered her political vocabulary, she began to work hard on improving the presentation of substantive policies. The effort would deliver her a third term.

30

Into the third term

APPROACHING THE 1987 ELECTION

The developing perception of Margaret Thatcher after seven years in power was that she had become a one-woman band who did not listen to or care about anyone else's opinions. Even if this view of her was exaggerated, she herself admitted that it 'contained a grain of truth'.[1] So for a while she made an effort to re-invent herself as a prime minister with a caring and listening personality. Neither metamorphosis was entirely successful. But in the short term the make-over worked. Its key ingredients were her attempts to be a more collegiate leader; her handling of a successful party conference; and the emergence of defence and foreign-policy issues as vote winners.

In June 1986, at the urging of Willie Whitelaw and John Wakeham, Margaret Thatcher set up a strategy group of senior ministers to make plans for the next election. Headlined by the tabloids as the 'A-Team' after a topical television series, this political inner cabinet included Geoffrey Howe, Nigel Lawson and Douglas Hurd as the holders of the three great offices of state; Norman Tebbit as Party Chairman supported by his ebulliently unorthodox deputy Jeffrey Archer. The last two A-Team members were the originators of the idea, Willie Whitelaw and John Wakeham. The group's much publicised existence created an impression of united teamwork.

In fact this was something of an illusion for a rift was growing between Margaret Thatcher and Norman Tebbit. Like several other cabinet ministers, the Party Chairman was becoming vexed by the flow of hostile press stories about himself that were being planted without attribution with journalists. Following a show-down with the Prime Minister they stopped. The 'A-Team', which met every Monday morning, gradually injected some unifying co-operation into the highest ranks of government. Its finest hour was co-ordinating the Conservative Party Conference in October 1986.

Under the slogan 'The Next Moves Forward', the Bournemouth conference featured minister after minister coming to the rostrum to unveil policy proposals likely to attract voter support. Nigel Lawson stole the show with the vision of income tax reduced to twenty-five pence. He was buttressed by Douglas Hurd promising longer sentences for criminals; Norman Fowler offering big increases in hospital building; and Lord Young revealing plans to reduce youth unemployment. 'More than ever before there has been the impression of a ministerial team', reported *The Times*, adding the view that this was important because the Prime Minister's personal electoral appeal was fading.[2]

Fading is the last adjective that could be used to describe Margaret Thatcher's closing speech to the conference. She came out of her corner swinging her handbag. Attack was her method of defence. In response to the familiar allegation that the Conservatives were not a caring party, she slammed Labour for supporting strikes by NHS workers and miners who had tried to 'deprive industry, homes and pensioners of power, heat and light'. She roused the delegates with her crescendo: 'Mr President, we're not going to take any lessons in caring from people with that sort of record.'[3]

Her second wave of attack was directed at the Liberals, who had passed a motion in favour of unilateral nuclear disarmament at their party conference three weeks earlier. But her prime target was Neil Kinnock's Labour Party, which had nailed its colours to the mast of a non-nuclear defence policy and the closing of American bases in Britain.

'Let there be no doubt about the gravity of that decision', she thundered.

> You cannot be a loyal member of NATO while disavowing its fundamental strategy. A Labour Britain would be a neutralist Britain. It would be the greatest gain for the Soviet Union in forty years. And they would have got it without firing a shot.'[4]

Within days of this conference speech there was a surge of support for the government in the opinion polls. The Conservatives moved ahead of Labour by nine percentage points, and ahead of the Alliance by nineteen points. At the turn of the year there was widespread speculation that there would be a general election in 1987. Poll fever was fanned by Nigel Lawson's March budget, which cut the standard rate of income tax by 2p while boosting expenditure on the NHS. Hard on the heels of this economic good news came Margaret Thatcher's telegenic visit to Moscow. The coverage on the BBC and ITV news bulletins made a major impact on the electorate.

A few weeks afterwards, Charles Powell wrote a most un-civil servant like letter to his Foreign Office colleague Sir Bryan Cartledge, Britain's Ambassador to the Soviet Union, jokingly expressing gratitude to the Moscow Embassy for helping the Prime Minister to win a third term.[5] Behind the humour lay the truth that 1987 was one of those rare general elections whose result turned on defence and foreign policy.

After her return from Moscow, the momentum for a summer election became almost unstoppable. In late March, a formal meeting of the cabinet was followed by a political cabinet, without civil servants present, at which the options for an election date were discussed at length. Margaret Thatcher was uncharacter-istically ambivalent. At various stages of the debate she intervened in favour of both a June and a September poll. What made up her mind were the results of the local elections on 7 May. Expecting losses in many areas, the Conservatives were pleasantly surprised to make modest but nationwide gains.

After a meeting of the 'A-Team' at Chequers, the Prime Minister announced the following day that the general election would be held on 11 June. With the Tories running at just over 40 per cent in the polls and the anti-government vote helpfully divided between Labour and the Alliance at 30 and 28 per cent respectively, Margaret Thatcher looked an odds on certainty to be re-elected to power.

WINNING FOR THE THIRD TIME

Although the opinion polls suggested it would be almost impossible for the Prime Minister to lose the election, her campaign got off to a slow and shaky start. It was her idea to begin gradually. But when she realised that the opposi-tion were setting a fast pace in the vacuum left by the torpor of the Conservatives' opening week, Margaret Thatcher became tetchy. 'A slow start, however, is one thing', she grumbled. 'No start at all is quite another.'[6]

What rattled her was the professionalism of Labour's early media campaign. It was a slick operation masterminded by Peter Mandelson.* The highlight was Labour's opening party political broadcast, starring its first couple, the youthful Neil and Glenys Kinnock. As they walked hand in hand along a scenic coastal path with waves pounding below and seagulls soaring above, the freshness of the imagery seemed optimistic and futuristic. It evidently struck a chord with younger voters, because the Leader of the Opposition's poll ratings shot up by sixteen points overnight.[7]

By contrast, the rival Conservative broadcast was a tired old rehash of yesterday's Britain. It featured Winston Churchill voice-overs, newsreel clips from the Battle of Britain and Margaret Thatcher's favourite hymn, 'I Vow to Thee My Country'. The nostalgia was interspersed with excerpts from speeches by Arthur Scargill and Ken Livingstone, both sounding more like prehistoric dinosaurs than contemporary demons.

Although these television overtures from both sides were focused more on style than substance, they managed to send Margaret Thatcher's morale plummeting. 'Kinnock had a marvellous programme – it's hardly worth bothering. Let's give up, it's the end', she declared after a dishearteningly rainy day on the campaign trail in North London.

She made this melodramatic announcement to a small group of friends and family members in the flat above No. 10 at the conclusion of the first week. Carol Thatcher thought that on this particular evening her mother 'was looking more upset than I could remember for a long time'.[8] But the mood changed after a whisky or two and some upbeat contributions from Tim Bell, Lord Young and Denis. These three wise men managed to convince her that the campaign could soon be revived by a combination of banging the drum on the government's record and battering the opposition for their unilateralist defence policies.

This strategy was somewhat out of kilter with the plans prepared by Conservative Central Office. Margaret Thatcher's relationship with the Party Chairman, Norman Tebbit, had become strained. This was partly because he

---

* Peter Mandelson in 1987 was the Labour Party's Director of Communications, with responsibility for overseeing the general election campaign that year. He later became an MP and cabinet minister and European Commissioner.

was a strong enough character to stand up to her, but more because she suspected him of harbouring an ambition to be her successor. 'It was the kiss of death if she ever suspected anyone of being a potential leadership contender',[9] observed Lord Young, her Secretary of State for Employment since 1986 and her latest court favourite.

The problem did not really exist. Conservative Central Office was doing a good job. However, Margaret Thatcher's confidence was at a low ebb so she sent Lord Young as her personal ferret down every campaign rabbit hole where she suspected failings. One of the first casualties of her bark combined with Young's bite was John Wakeham. He was helping Tebbit with the organisation of ministerial media interviews in the campaign. Unfortunately, one of the first ones, his appearance on BBC Radio 4's *Election Call*, was a disaster. This at least was the opinion of the Prime Minister, who listened to it and exploded to Lord Young: 'John doesn't understand the first thing about the media. You must stop him and take charge of it yourself.'[10] This was the first of many counter-orders by Margaret Thatcher, who caused disorder by issuing them to Young without telling the recipients.

A particular area of discord was the schedule for the Prime Minister's daily tours that, according to Norman Tebbit, 'became a near disaster that threatened the campaign'.[11] Some of the troubles were caused by Margaret Thatcher's wilful refusal to stick to, or even mention, the themes of the day, which had been carefully planned, complete with press briefings, by Central Office.

Worse difficulties were encountered because of clashes between Lord Young, who acted as the Prime Minister's travelling companion, confidant and right-hand man throughout the campaign, versus Norman Tebbit, who was theoretically in charge of the overall strategy as Party Chairman. The root cause of these conflicts was that Margaret Thatcher came to believe that the election was being mismanaged and would end in her defeat. Norman Tebbit, who had the advantage of monitoring reports from constituencies around the country, was always confident of winning victory by a large majority.

The strained relations between the two camps blew up into angry hostilities on Thursday 4 June – a date that became known as 'Wobbly Thursday'. With just seven days to go before the nation voted, the *Daily Telegraph* published the latest Gallup poll, which suggested that Labour were gaining ground. The gap had allegedly narrowed to only 4 per cent, with the Conservatives slipping to 40.5 per cent, Labour rising to 36.5 per cent and the Alliance static at 21 per cent. Margaret Thatcher, whose political anxieties were exacerbated by a raw tooth nerve inflamed by an abscess, went ballistic at her regular early morning meeting in Central Office. Waving around a copy of the *Daily Telegraph*, she exploded at Norman Tebbit and his Deputy Chairman, Michael Dobbs. 'Her demeanour at that meeting was unreasoning and unreasonable and close to hysteria', recalled Dobbs. 'It was impossible to put a point or even to be listened to. It was quite clear that there was no point in saying anything . . .'[12]

Although Norman Tebbit bore the brunt of this fury, he was not alone in being on the receiving end of rough treatment that morning. The subject for the daily Central Office briefing was pensions and social security. The DHSS Minister, Norman Fowler, was upbraided for his draft press release, until David Wolfson bravely intervened to tell the Prime Minister, 'Shut up, and read it through first'.[13] If she did so, it was not apparent at the subsequent press conference which, in Margaret Thatcher's own words, 'was widely considered to be a disaster for us and I was held to blame'.[14]

The problem was not what she said but how she said it. A journalist asked her to justify her use of private health insurance to pay for having her own minor operations carried out speedily in non-NHS hospitals. This was an easy question to handle, not least because many trade unionists and Labour politicians also took out insurance for private health-care. Unfortunately, Margaret Thatcher was at her most aggressive in response. She lectured the questioner that her health-care insurance was there 'to enable me to go into hospital on the day I want, at the time I want and with the doctor I want'.[15]

Her justification was fair, but her tone with its three repetitions of the words 'I want' sounded unattractive. Many in the audience were shocked. Even Willie Whitelaw became critical of her belligerence. 'That is a woman who will never fight another election', he remarked to Michael Dobbs with prescient foresight, as they walked out of Central Office.[16]

So dark was the mood on 'Wobbly Thursday' that some of the closest members of Margaret Thatcher's entourage were on the verge of predicting that she might lose the election. 'It really did appear that we were on the run',[17] recalled Lord Young. Having never fought an election himself, Young was a novice in both campaigning and in the analysis of likely voting patterns. In the judgement of experienced professionals, these matters were going remarkably well. But Young, under pressure from an increasingly anxious Prime Minister, took a more pessimistic view. Her negativity was fuelled by Tim Bell who had been excluded from the inner team at Central Office by Norman Tebbit. In retaliation for being exiled, Bell managed to persuade Margaret Thatcher that the final advertising campaign, prepared by Saatchi and Saatchi, was not good enough and should be replaced by a new series of advertisements created by his own rival agency, Lowe Howard-Spink & Bell.

When this demand for a change of advertising strategy was passed on by Lord Young to Norman Tebbit, the Party Chairman was visibly irritated. 'Who did this?' he asked, as he was shown the new ads. 'Tell me who did it.'

'Tim Bell', answered Lord Young.

Norman Tebbit became even more irascible, not least because Bell's covert involvement as an alternative adviser on advertising to the Prime Minister had been concealed from him.

Lord Young lost his temper over the Party Chairman's attitude to Bell's work. He seized Norman Tebbit by the shoulders and started yelling at him:

> Norman, listen to me. We're about to lose this fucking election. You're going to go; I'm going to go; the whole thing is going to go. The entire election depends upon her doing fine performances for the next few days – she has to be happy.[18]

In compliance with the imperative of keeping the Prime Minster happy, Saatchi and Saatchi ads were jettisoned and Tim Bell's ideas were preferred. Much heat and hurt feelings ensued in the process.

But did the upheavals make any difference to the progress or the outcome of the election? The answer to this question is a resounding 'No!' All these dramas were the product of Margaret Thatcher's reactions to wrong or wrongly anti-cipated opinion polls.

In the middle of the 'Wobbly Thursday' hysteria, I came into Conservative Central Office to pick up some extra posters for my own campaign in Thanet. After three weeks of hard canvassing, I was certain that my result would be much the same as in 1983, possibly better. So it was amazing to hear that the Prime Minister was downcast, Lord Young was panicking and that an opinion poll to be published in the next twenty-four hours by Marplan would show that the Tory lead had been cut to 1 per cent.

When I said that this sounded complete nonsense to anyone who had been on the doorsteps talking to voters, journalistic friends treated me as if I was a foolish country bumpkin. 'The only person who agrees with you that it's all going well for the Tories is Norman Tebbit', said a sceptical Bob Carvel of the *Evening Standard*.[19]

The following day, it seemed that Aitken and Tebbit were right after all. The pundits reversed their prophesies of doom after a new poll. Marplan announced that the Conservatives had shot into a 10 per cent lead.[20] With the wisdom of hindsight, Gallup's figures of 4 June were seen to be a rogue poll. 'Wobbly Thursday' turned out to be 'Wrong Forecast Thursday'. Norman Tebbit had been right all along in his assessment that Margaret Thatcher was on course for another landslide. What guaranteed the victory was a combination of the Chancellor of the Exchequer's reassuring promises on the economy and of the Prime Minister's attacks on the incredible defence policies of the opposition.

The trickiest questions in the last days of the campaign were about how long she intended to continue as Prime Minister. Her responses oscillated between the hubristic and the humble. In the first category were her hints that she might seek a fourth term, or even still be in No. 10 at the age of seventy-five. More modestly, she told an interviewer from the *Daily Telegraph*: 'It's not for me to say I would go on and on. I have to submit myself to the judgment of the people at elections and the judgment of my party every year.'[21]

At such times it seemed there were two Margaret Thatchers addressing the voters. One side of her personality was cautious and circumspect. The other was aggressive and triumphalist. The electorate split down the middle too on lines that were geographical as well as political. For as the results were to show, South East England supported her with enthusiasm, while Scotland and northern England recorded a significant swing to Labour.

By the time she reached polling day, Margaret Thatcher had recovered her confidence and her ascendancy. She won the battle of the posters against Central Office. As a result, the nation was plastered with a slogan from Tim Bell: 'Britain's Great Again: Don't Let Labour Wreck It.' It was something of a throw-back to the 'You've never had it so good', sentiments of Harold Macmillan, but it struck a right if complacent note. So did Margaret Thatcher's eve of poll broadcast, which took fourteen hours to film, climaxing in four minutes straight-to-camera from the Prime Minister on peace and prosperity.

Although these final messages to the electorate seemed to go well, few would have dared to predict the size of the Tory landslide that was delivered on polling day. At the final count the Conservatives had an overall majority in Parliament of 102 seats. Although it was a reduction from the 144-seat victory avalanche of 1983, nevertheless a majority of over one hundred for a third term under the same leader was a magnificent result.

Terrific though the hat-trick was, among even the friendliest of insiders there were concerns that the conjurer might be unable to keep on producing the rabbits out of her Prime Ministerial hat. For Margaret Thatcher had been in an unhappy and politically negative mood for much of the campaign, despite its glorious conclusion. In the euphoria of victory all doubts were brushed aside, yet the anxieties that had arisen during the past year had not gone away.

Was her style of leadership getting too aggressive and high handed? Was there too much friction with some of her senior colleagues? Was she aware of the storm clouds that might be looming in Europe or the economy? Did she really have a vision for the next five years in government? And could she keep and build the right team to fulfil it? These questions were being only quietly asked in the joyful post-election days of summer 1987, but the anxieties that lay behind them were scented in the political ether by the discerning.

'All I can say is that it will be a jolly sight harder slog for the government than it looks right now – a jolly sight harder', Willie Whitelaw told me and his other lunch guests at Bucks Club in mid-June.[22]

'In a year she'll be so unpopular you won't believe it', Denis Thatcher told his daughter Carol, as they looked down from the flat above No. 10 on the Prime Minister acknowledging the cheers of well wishers on the Downing Street pavement.[23] These early forebodings were to prove all too accurate.

A BOLD BUT FLAWED BEGINNING

Margaret Thatcher harboured no doubts about the long-term prospects for her premiership. She enjoyed comparing herself with Lord Liverpool, the only other Prime Minister to win three consecutive elections. He held power for fifteen years in the 1820s. She implied in various sound-bites that she hoped to do even better. Moreover, she intended to make her reforming zeal more radical and more permanent. 'What's to stop us?' she crowed in her speech to the Conservative Party Conference.[24]

Her rhetorical question drew comparisons with the 'We are the masters now' boast of Sir Hartley Shawcross, a Labour minister, after his party's victory in the 1945 general election.[25]

Some of Margaret Thatcher's triumphalism was justified, for she looked an impregnable Prime Minister in the early months after her 1987 victory. Her first moves were to reshuffle her cabinet and to launch the government's legislative programme for the coming year in Parliament.

The reshuffle, although not seen in this light at the time, created a dysfunctional cabinet who became so disenchanted with their leader that they were to rebel against her some three years later.

Geoffrey Howe and Nigel Lawson stayed in place as Foreign Secretary and Chancellor. Both were suppressing deeper discontents about her leadership than she realised. The middle ranks contained a group of centrist ministers who had no ideological commitment to the Thatcherite credo. They included John Wakeham, John MacGregor, Kenneth Clarke, Malcolm Rifkind, Kenneth Baker and John Major, who joined the cabinet as Chief Secretary to the Treasury. Among the departures was the Chancellor Lord Hailsham, in honourable retirement from the Woolsack at the age of eighty.

The most surprising leaver was Norman Tebbit. He withdrew in order to provide care and financial support for his wife, Margaret, who had been paralysed in the Brighton bombing. An unspoken reason was that he too had become disenchanted with the Prime Minister's style of leadership. The frictions with Lord Young, and the jealousy of Margaret Thatcher aroused by her fear that Tebbit was nurturing secret leadership ambitions, lost the cabinet one of its most capable communicators. His departure was a more grievous blow to the stability of the government than the Prime Minister realised.

The Thatcherite wing of the government was reinforced by the return of Cecil Parkinson as Transport Minister, and the arrival of John Moore, as a telegenic young Secretary of State for Health and Social Security. Yet, if the political leanings of the cabinet were carefully analysed, there were more independent-minded pragmatists around the table than at any time since 1979. In the aura of permanence that glowed around Margaret Thatcher at the beginning of her third term, she showed no signs of understanding that there might be hazards ahead within her team.

When the new Parliament assembled on 25 June, the Prime Minister was on positively messianic form when opening the Queen's Speech debate. She declared the legislative programme to be 'one of the most substantial and radical in recent years'; attacked Neil Kinnock for clinging to 'the shibboleths of the 1930s', which had no appeal to a Britain that was 'becoming home-owning, share-owning and savings-owning'; and announced sweeping reforms in education, housing, health and local government finance.

But there were two bumpy moments in her speech. The first came when she confidently proclaimed, 'We shall abolish the domestic rates – a grossly unfair tax – and replace them with a community charge'. The benches behind her managed only a half-hearted chorus of hear, hear at this reiteration of a policy which had been dividing the Conservative party for several months in its preparatory stages. The lukewarm reception her announcement received might have registered as an amber light to a more sensitive prime minister. But later at the 1922 Committee, she laid down the law by insisting that rumblings of dissent about the 'poll tax', as many Tory MPs were already calling it, must cease because it was her flagship policy. It was an authoritarian approach, which would come to haunt her and ultimately destroy her.

The second glitch in Margaret Thatcher's performance in the Queen's Speech debate came when she was talking about her fundamental reforms of education. Referring to the legislation that would enable certain schools to opt out from local authority control, she continued: 'Those schools will be on the same financial basis as local authority schools. Their fees – I mean their finances . . .'[26]

This slip of the tongue produced uproar on the Labour benches. 'Fees! Fees! Fees!' was the sustained chant. Eventually the Speaker restored order and the Prime Minister made it clear that there would be no fees payable for these opting-out schools. What was odd about her error was that she had made the same gaffe at the start of the election campaign. Then, she had to be embarrassingly contradicted by Kenneth Baker at her first press conference in Central Office for wrongly announcing that the new schools would charge fees.

A few days later, in a conversation over a drink with Alan Clark, the two of us speculated in the context of the second rumpus about these fees whether the Prime Minister could be having health or memory problems. 'No one can stand this pace', Clark's diary records me as saying.[27] The worry was premature but not misplaced. The pressures of eight years as Prime Minister were beginning to take their toll, but only a handful of insiders noticed it.

In the early months of her third term she demanded a fast pace from her ministers. The Great Education Reform Bill, known to Tory MPs as 'Gerbil', was a Leviathan of legislation. It covered the introduction of the National Curriculum, opt-outs for schools, the introduction of City Technology Colleges and the abolition of the Inner London Education Authority. As Kenneth Baker steered it through a record-breaking 370 hours of Parliamentary debate, he was subjected to a great deal of pressure from his boss. He recalled:

> Her interest in the bill was enormous. She chaired the cabinet committee and we had very feisty rows all the time. Once I had to walk out of the room because things got so heated! But being Margaret, she didn't mind if you argued back provided you were well briefed. Our fiercest disagreements came over what should be taught in schools, for example over the Maths element in the National Curriculum, where she was a traditionalist on matters such as learning the multiplication tables.[28]

The greatest dispute concerned the Prime Minister's wish to keep the National Curriculum down to three core subjects, taking up 70 per cent of the school year. Schools would be free to choose the subjects in the remainder of the time. This was duly recorded as the decision of the Education sub-committee of the cabinet.

Baker, however, challenged these minutes on the grounds that they reflected Margaret Thatcher's personal views and not the views of the meeting. His challenge took the form of an almost unprecedented personal minute to the Prime Minister, seeking to set aside the cabinet committee's findings. A major row followed, at which Kenneth Baker had to threaten resignation before his original plan for a ten-subject National Curriculum was grudgingly allowed to stay in the bill. It was a significant climb-down by Margaret Thatcher, the first of several signs that she would find it harder to get her own way in her third-term government.

LIFE WITHOUT WHITELAW

The colleague who had done most to help her get her own way was Willie Whitelaw. But six months after the election he left the cabinet for health reasons. Attending a carol concert in Westminster Abbey just before Christmas, he collapsed with a mild stroke, which put an end to his political career. He formally resigned in January 1988. His loss was enormous to the Prime Minister and to the running of the government.

For the last twelve years of Margaret Thatcher's life, four of them as Leader of the Opposition, Whitelaw had been her shrewdest adviser. He had decided, after the 1975 leadership election, that it was his duty to give her impeccable loyalty as her deputy. In government he was extraordinarily effective in helping her to deliver her agenda and to steer through dangerous moments of decision and division.

A wealthy landowner who lived the high Tory lifestyle of shooting weekends and clubbable dinners, Whitelaw combined the mind of a clever Wykehamist with the geniality of a jovial squire. Everyone liked him, trusted him and respected his judgement. He anticipated the political moods of Westminster as instinctively as a pointer stiffening at the scent of a grouse. One of his greatest assets was his ability to sum up a discordant cabinet discussion in a unifying manner that gave the Prime Minister the decision she wanted.

Other fine qualities were his openness of character, his self-deprecating humour, his warmth and his skill in persuading Margaret Thatcher in one-on-one conversations to come round to his way of handling a problem or a personality.

A few weeks before his stroke, she coined the memorable tribute to Whitelaw: 'Every Prime Minister should have a Willie.' When she realised her *double entendre*, made unconsciously in front of her speech-writing team, she tried to swear all present to secrecy.[29] The story was too good to be kept quiet, not just because it was funny but also because it contained a great truth. For without Willie Whitelaw, Margaret Thatcher and her team of ministers would have fallen out, perhaps fallen apart, much sooner than they eventually did.

Her abrasive style of leadership was only workable because her number two was so likeable. Whitelaw was at his best as a confidant to bruised colleagues. He acted as a shoulder to cry on, as a friend at court and as a mender of fences – all done for the purpose of supporting the Prime Minister.

This support came at a price. Willie Whitelaw was a more sensitive soul than his bluff exterior suggested. During the Falklands crisis, officials from the U.S. State Department noticed his neurotic nail biting at meetings. When tensions mounted in cabinet, he was often observed to be tugging at his eyebrows 'as if he was encouraging the grey cells into action'.[30]

After particularly difficult meetings at No. 10, he would sometimes come into the Principal Private Secretary's room, collapse into a chair and bury his head in his hands, saying over and over again, 'Oh dear, oh dear, oh dear, oh DEAR!'[31]

At times of conflict with colleagues he could explode into outbursts of anger, although he was careful not to lose his temper with Margaret Thatcher. But when he let off steam in this way, his bark, although loud, had no bite. For his wrath would return to good humour as quickly as a passing summer thunderstorm.

Occasionally he could be really stubborn. 'It's absolutely not on', he would tell the Prime Minister, or 'The party just won't wear it'.[32] Then they would argue, but on these rare altercations, as often as not she would be the one to yield, because she knew that his loyalty to her was absolute, and that his judgement was excellent.

Although he liked to say 'I am a bear of small brain',[33] this was all part of his self-effacing style. He was never much of a figures man, but he had the gift of political intelligence in abundance. Margaret Thatcher respected Willie Whitelaw but she probably never fully understood how much she owed him. His premature departure was one of the reasons for her own premature departure three years later.

Surprisingly, the Prime Minister never consulted her former deputy on any subject after he left the government. He was hurt by his exclusion from her counsels. This was a mistake as well as a snub. For a little of the Whitelaw wisdom applied to the cabinet's personnel problems in the 1998–1990 period could well have avoided the blow-ups that occurred, if he had occasionally been asked to help.

Outwardly, Margaret Thatcher seemed to manage quite satisfactorily without Whitelaw as she pressed ahead with her reforming agenda. In addition to education reform, she attempted to reshape housing policy, social security and the NHS. The results were mixed.

In her first two terms her attempts to introduce policy changes into this large swathe of state activity had been minimal. Norman Fowler had altered the eligibility rules for Housing Benefit, Income Support and some other benefits so that 'deserving' groups – the elderly, the disabled and families with young children – were helped at the expense of the 'undeserving' – the young unemployed. But it brought about no slowing down in the £40 million a year cost of social security, which had soared by 40 per cent since 1979.

To reduce this, the Prime Minister brought into her 1987 cabinet John Moore. He was handsome, athletic, good on television and influenced by the ideas of American neo-conservatism. These qualities made him, for a short while, another of the Prime Minister's court favourites. She even talked of him as a potential successor. But the DHSS was to prove his political graveyard.

A month after his appointment, Margaret Thatcher had a lengthy conversation with John Moore about fundamental reforms of his department. His background in US banking and his familiarity with the writings of Milton Friedman gave him an enthusiasm for overhauling the universal benefits in Britain's welfare state such as Child Benefit. But nothing ever came of this reformist zeal, largely because the Prime Minister was too cautious to support it.

She thought once more about reforming the NHS, but was again constrained by her overriding caution that it must remain free and open to all. Although she flirted with the idea of challenging this post-war consensus, she soon backed away from it and concentrated on improving the management and delivery of health services. To this end, she set up an internal policy review that she chaired. The ministers who made up the review group were John Moore and Tony Newton from the DHSS, and Nigel Lawson and John Major from the Treasury. Their deliberations were full of contradictory views. Margaret Thatcher wanted to enlarge private medical care by giving tax relief on private health insurance. She was also willing to allow the NHS to charge for some services. In the end, these plans were watered down to allow small charges for eye tests and dental check ups. They scraped through the House of Commons by tiny majorities after Tory defections. As for tax incentives for private health insurance, they too were diluted down to a small concession for the over 65s.

One part of the problem was that on NHS reform, the Prime Minister bore more than a passing resemblance to Dr Doolittle's animal, the Pushmipullyu. At one stage, she would push for radical changes, then she pulled back with conservative caution. John Moore proved ineffective in handling her uncharacteristic ambivalence, not least because of a persistent chest infection that weakened his energy and his speaking voice. The Prime Minister's new Parliamentary Private Secretary, Archie Hamilton MP, saw these contradictions in their relationship and the policy muddles that emerged from it. 'She kept changing her mind. One minute she wanted to go further, the next she got an attack of the doubts, wanted to trim back a bit. Each time, the unfortunate John agreed, made the adjustments, came back for approval. The result was a total hotchpotch and she ended up thinking he was a wanker, and got rid of him.'[34]

In July 1988, the Prime Minister made her own adjustments. She moved John Moore away from decisions on health by splitting the huge DHSS into separate Health and Social Security departments, leaving him in charge of the latter. She appointed Kenneth Clarke to be the new Health Secretary. He was positively anti-Thatcherite in his political philosophy. Nevertheless, he proved to be an effective minister in establishing an 'internal market' within the NHS, which separated the commissioning and providing roles between District Health Authorities, NHS Trust Hospitals and GP fundholders. It cost more money, which was not what the Prime Minister wanted, but it treated more patients. As this result was not apparent during her time at No. 10, she continued to be accused of attempting to privatise the NHS. In fact her reforms, most of them Kenneth Clarke reforms, did improve the management of the NHS without changing its ethos.

During the first two years of Margaret Thatcher's third term, her government managed to maintain some momentum. But her radical zeal was flagging because she was no longer bothering to take her colleagues with her. Partly because of the loss of Willie Whitelaw, rifts were developing over the economy; over the flagship policy of replacing the rates with the Community Charge; and, above all, over Europe. At the heart of all these disagreements was the most dangerous of fault-lines within any British government – a growing alienation between the Prime Minister and the Chancellor of the Exchequer.

REFLECTION

The beginning of the third term marked a change for the worse in Margaret Thatcher's personality. She was becoming more volatile, more hubristic, more autocratic and far less willing to listen to anyone else's point of view.

These weaknesses did not prevent her, for most of the time, from being an effective national leader. If she had been US president, constitutionally set apart from the legislative branch of government, she would have had few problems. But a British prime minister has to work with the grain of the cabinet and parliamentary systems. Margaret Thatcher was increasingly ignoring these two pillars of her power. As a result, discontent was growing, but she herself remained largely oblivious to it.

The rows inside the high command of the Tory Party's election campaign were largely of Margaret Thatcher's making. She played a double game, setting Tim Bell against Norman Tebbit; Lord Young against Norman Tebbit; and Bell's company, Lowe Howard-Spink and Bell, against Saatchi and Saatchi, the appointed advertising agency of the Conservative Party.

The ructions that emerged from these clashes about 1980s ad men were far more colourful than anything that could ever have been dreamed up by the twenty-first-century creators of the iconic TV series *Mad Men*. The huge surprise in the real life 1987 feuds was the discovery that the Prime Minister had been encouraging and stirring them. Her motives for doing this seem to have been a mixture of insecurity and volatility. At various times, she worked herself up into a frenzy of passion about losing the election, a deep mistrust of Norman Tebbit and an exaggerated belief in Tim Bell. The upheavals her interventions produced were as pointless as they were unpleasant. Her over-reactions caused many insiders to ask the question: What happened to the Margaret Thatcher who was so calm, so resolute and so supportive of her team in the 1979 and 1983 general elections?

Winning a third term with a 102 parliamentary majority was such a stunning result that it quelled all unhappy memories of the campaign. Yet, right from the start of the new session, there was more than a whiff of 'trouble at t'mill' among Conservative MPs.

The trouble was over the Community Charge. The policy direction had been set by Margaret Thatcher some two years earlier, but most colleagues assumed there would be plenty of give and take in the legislation in order to eradicate the manifest unfairnesses and anomalies of a flat-rate tax. It came as a blow when at the first meeting of the 1922 Committee in the new Parliament, the Prime Minister was at her most inflexible when demanding obedient support for what she called her 'flagship policy'.

As the parliamentary party trickled out of Committee Room 14 after this address, Nicholas Budgen kept saying, 'She ain't listening. She ain't listening.'[35] It could have been the refrain of a continuous lament throughout the last three years of Thatcherism.

The other place where the key figures felt they were not being listened to was the cabinet. This was the growing problem that came to dominate the third term. It all centred on the visibly changing personality of Margaret Thatcher.

31

Trouble with Nigel Lawson

FLASHPOINTS OF PERSONALITY

Margaret Thatcher had always been a leader with a combative and argument-ative personality. Her style of doing business was abrasive but effective. Once her colleagues understood how much she relished the cut and thrust of a good row, they usually accepted her flashes of anger, even when they were unfair or unjustified, as part of her character. This acceptance was made easier because for most of her first eight years in power she conducted her disputes with vigour but without rancour.

In her third term this changed. Not only did she become sharper and ruder; against her two most senior ministers, she developed a personal animus. This soured her working relationship with them and sowed seeds of such unpleasant-ness that it damaged and eventually destroyed her premiership.

To this day, it is difficult to decide whether Margaret Thatcher's time as Prime Minister came to an end because of personality clashes or policy disagree-ments. The conventional wisdom is that she was forced out because of splits over Europe and the poll tax. Yet this is by no means the full story.

All politicians like to maintain the lofty pretence that when they fight among themselves, the battle lines are drawn over great issues of principle unrelated to individual animosities. Unfortunately, in Margaret Thatcher's third term the two became inextricably linked. Her downfall occurred because personal bitterness merged with policy disagreements. So it is important to examine both areas of trouble in explaining the real reasons why her relationships with her Chancellor and her Foreign Secretary began to unravel and eventually to explode.

Margaret Thatcher had an up-and-down relationship with Nigel Lawson. In his early period as her Chancellor they worked together in harmony as a golden partnership. Then there were bumps in the road. For a while, his popularity within the government and the Conservative Parliamentary Party was greater than hers. In the final phase, with flaws appearing on both sides, they became bitter adversaries. Yet one aspect of their collaboration never changed. She was always in awe of his brainpower.

Her admiration for his intellect was not, however, immediately equalled by her enthusiasm for his personality. This was apparent during her first term when he was still a junior minister. As Financial Secretary to the Treasury, he was the architect of the Medium Term Financial Strategy (MTFS), which was pivotal to Geoffrey Howe's Chancellorship. Yet, in 1981, she promoted Leon Brittan into the cabinet to become Howe's no. 2 as Chief Secretary to the Treasury.

As the obvious front-runner for the job, Lawson was greatly upset at being overlooked, so much so that he did not turn up at his ministerial office for several days. His absence was interpreted as sulking by some colleagues, but not by the Prime Minister who invited her devastated Financial Secretary to lunch at Chequers a week after her failure to promote him.

In a frank one-on-one conversation she listened sympathetically to his grievance and promised that she would put him in the cabinet in her next reshuffle. Lawson learned that he had been blocked by Willie Whitelaw telling the Prime Minister that he was 'too clever by half' and 'not a safe pair of hands'.[1] These fences took time to mend, but after a while both Willie Whitelaw and Margaret Thatcher were completely won round. Nigel Lawson joined the cabinet as Energy Secretary nine months later. His impressive performance in that job, which contributed much to the later victory in the miners' strike, led to his surprise appointment to the Chancellorship of the Exchequer immediately after the 1983 election.

Margaret Thatcher took a big gamble in giving the second most important post in her government to such a relatively new and controversial choice. But her bet paid off – at least for most of the second term.

The Chancellor and Prime Minister began by working well together. Lawson's strategy, evolved over four Budgets, laid the foundation for sustained growth and successful election winning. But not everything was sweetness and light between them. He was obsessively secretive, especially in his dealings with her. He wanted to be master in his own house, running the economy in a non-collegiate and idiosyncratic style of last-minute decision-making.

This was the source of the most fundamental disagreements between them. He believed that there could 'only be one Chancellor'[2] exercising suzerainty over Treasury affairs. He even asserted that the Prime Minister's historic role and title of First Lord of the Treasury was 'a myth'.[3] At the beginning of his tenure of No. 11 Downing Street Lawson kept this view to himself. But as his Chancellorship moved into its fourth, fifth and sixth years he became increasingly hostile to the notion that he was the Second Lord of the Treasury who had to obey Margaret Thatcher as his boss. This was a war of will-powers waiting to happen.

FIRST CLASH OVER THE ERM

In 1985, the Prime Minister and Chancellor had their first serious policy disagreement when he began favouring the idea that Britain should join the Exchange Rate Mechanism (ERM) of the European Monetary System (EMS). In an attempt to block the advance of what she called 'a fashionable consensus',[4] the Prime Minister convened an *ad hoc* ministerial meeting of carefully chosen colleagues who she thought would support her side of the argument.

But to her dismay, at this meeting on 13 November 1985, Nigel Lawson persuaded not just the predictably pro-EMS Geoffrey Howe (Foreign Secretary) but also Norman Tebbit (Party Chairman), John Wakeham (Chief Whip), Leon Brittan (Secretary of State for Trade and Industry) and even the ultra-loyal Willie Whitelaw (Deputy Prime Minister) to speak in favour of joining the ERM/EMS arrangement.

The arguments they expressed in favour of it were entirely economic and highly technical, focused on what was right for the exchange rate, interest rates and the control of inflation. Margaret Thatcher alone seems to have recognised the constitutional implication that the EMS/ERM might bind Britain into a structure that could lead towards a single European currency and an irreversible loss of sovereignty.

Yet she did not articulate her fears in a constitutional or indeed any sort of non-economic argument. Instead, when faced with the unexpected degree of unity of her colleagues behind a policy to which she was opposed, the Prime Minister played the theatrical card of a dramatic exit. 'I disagree. If you join the EMS, you will have to do so without me', she declared as she gathered up her papers and swept out of the room.[5]

A shaken Nigel Lawson then made his exit to No. 11, accompanied by Geoffrey Howe, Norman Tebbit and Willie Whitelaw. Describing himself as 'extremely depressed',[6] the Chancellor told his colleagues that he saw little point in carrying on and felt that he ought to resign. They urged the Chancellor to banish the thought. Whitelaw in particular assured him that by persuasion and persistence he would bring the Prime Minister round to his point of view. But this did not happen.

Margaret Thatcher's determination to resist the almost unanimous recommendation of her Chancellor and her senior colleagues in favour of joining the ERM seems to have been more visceral than logical. She received support for her stance from her new Head of Policy at No. 10, Brian Griffiths; from the Leader of the House, John Biffen, who was a long-standing supporter of floating exchange rates; and from her former adviser, Alan Walters, who had written to her suggesting that an expected fall in oil prices would mean that Britain could enter the EMS at a lower parity in six months time. But their arguments were technical, too. By contrast, Margaret Thatcher's hostility to the ERM was fundamental, fuelled by deep instincts from the well-springs of her belief in Britain's freedom to make its own national decisions. Another intuitive source of her opposition may have been her dislike of Germany's dominant vote in the ERM.

Terry Burns, who was present at the meeting on 13 November as Chief Economic Adviser to the Treasury, sensed that the real reason for the Prime Minister's apparent intransigence was that 'she just couldn't bear to be beholden to other people to determine the destiny of Britain's interest rates. She did not mind rules, but she always wanted the wriggle room that the ERM would not allow'.[7]

On his side of the argument, Nigel Lawson was down but by no means out. He regarded his defeat at the 13 November meeting as 'the saddest event of my time as Chancellor'.[8] Lawson overcame his sadness by considerable clandestine activity in preparation for joining the ERM.

This began less than a month after Margaret Thatcher had vetoed the move when on 7 December 1985 the Chancellor authorised a secret mission of senior Treasury officials to the Deutsche Bundesbank in Bonn to discuss contingency planning for Britain's membership of the ERM. Despite this and other such provisional manoeuvres, the issue of joining the ERM was kept on the shelf for nearly two years. But Nigel Lawson was biding his time. When he felt strong enough to do so he effectively joined the ERM, to use Nicholas Ridley's words, 'unilaterally and unofficially',[9] in March 1987. But to do this, he had to act by stealth without declaring his hand to the Prime Minister, using a new policy known as 'shadowing the Deutschmark'.

SHADOWING THE DEUTSCHMARK

From 1987 onwards, Nigel Lawson was in a position of great strength. Never a modest Chancellor, he believed his policies had delivered a stunning victory for the Tories and an expanding economy for the nation. He was right about the first claim. On the second he did not see that his expansion was turning into overheating. But an even greater worry was that he had become so confident of his own judgement that he launched a major change in exchange-rate policy without the agreement of the Prime Minister or the consent of the cabinet.

From March 1987, in covert furtherance of his long-held view that sterling should join the ERM, Nigel Lawson began using interest rates and interventions in the currency markets to set the pound's value at DM3. This shadowing of the Deutschmark was his way of operating sterling as if Britain had joined the ERM, even though no decision to join it had been taken by the government.

At face value, this was an act of insubordination by the Chancellor, who appeared to be deliberately deceiving the Prime Minister with this secretive course of action. Nigel Lawson claimed that he did not see it in this light. Conveniently ignoring the fact that Margaret Thatcher was First Lord of the Treasury, he insisted that he was in charge of Britain's economic policy and was fully entitled to order the Treasury and the Bank of England the carry out his instructions.

His justification was that the official policy of the government, unchanged since the days when Ted Heath was Prime Minister, was that Britain would join the ERM when the time was right. Therefore, he was entitled to prepare the ground for entry by aligning sterling with the Deutschmark immediately, keeping the pound down by instructing the Bank of England to buy other currencies.

The problem with this explanation was that Lawson well knew that Margaret Thatcher's opposition to joining the ERM was hardening. In her view, the time to sign up was certainly not in the 1980s, and might never be right. In his view, the time was so right that he was already implementing the policy. This disagreement put the Chancellor and the Prime Minister on an inevitable collision course.

Margaret Thatcher claimed to be unaware of this. In her memoirs she asserted that she only discovered her Chancellor was shadowing the Deutschmark at DM3 to the pound on Friday 20 November 1987 when journalists from the *Financial Times* provided her with chapter and verse.

'The implications of this were, of course, very serious,' she wrote. 'Nigel had pursued a personal economic policy without reference to the rest of the Government. How could I possibly trust him again?'[10]

By contrast, Nigel Lawson has strenuously denied that the Prime Minister was blindsided by his Deutschmark shadowing policy. He wrote in his memoirs, 'It was always an implausible insult to her formidable intelligence to suggest that she could possibly have been unaware of it, even if I had wished to keep her in the dark, which, of course, I did not . . . She was simply not that kind of Prime Minister.'[11]

Trying to extract the truth from these conflicting accounts is difficult. But Nigel Lawson has now admitted, in an interview for this book, that he never directly told the Prime Minister that he was shadowing the Deutschmark, until after she had been alerted to it by the *Financial Times*. His case is that she must have known about his policy since she was daily sent the Treasury's market report recording the figures of intervention by the Bank of England in the foreign-exchange markets required to support sterling.

The argument is special pleading after the event. It is correct to say that if a foreign-exchange expert had studied the confidential figures sent every evening from the Treasury to No. 10 which detail the costs of UK intervention in the currency markets, then it would have been possible to detect that the Deutschmark was being shadowed as a matter of undisclosed policy. But the Prime Minister did not know this. Her two most relevant officials at No. 10, Robin Butler, her Principal Private Secretary, and Brian Griffiths, her Head of Policy concerned with Treasury and Bank of England affairs, also did not know it.[12] It is hard to escape the conclusion that concealment took place.

So why was the Chancellor not transparent with No. 10? Why in nine months of bi-laterals did he hold back from telling the Prime Minister that he had instructed the Bank to shadow the Deutschmark? Nigel Lawson explained:

I am not a gushing person. She has half a point when she says she was not told. But I never withheld the information from her. It was all there in her red boxes with the figures sent by my Private Secretary to her Private Secretary every night.[13]

The first occasion when the Deutschmark-shadowing policy was discussed face to face by the two principals came on 8 December 1987, eighteen days after Margaret Thatcher had been given the evidence by the *Financial Times*. The meeting was a stormy one. The Chancellor found the Prime Minister in 'an extremely agitated and aggressive mood'.[14] Her angry claim that trust had broken down between them was not the only problem. She was also concerned by the £27 billion cost of the intervention since the beginning of the financial year to hold the pound below the DM3 level. She was particularly worried by the inflationary consequences of this action.

Nigel Lawson reassured her that there were no inflationary consequences because it had been his practice to fund the intervention costs not by increasing liquidity but by selling gilt-edged securities – a device known as sterilisation. This explanation had the effect of keeping Margaret Thatcher's doubts at bay for a few weeks. The episode also highlighted that she remained in awe of his technical mastery of his brief. Because of this, he was usually her superior when it came to a detailed argument about policy.

By March 1988, relations between the occupants of No. 10 and No. 11 Downing Street had deteriorated further. So had the policy of exchange-rate interventions. On Wednesday 2 March and Thursday 3 March, some $1.8bn of intervention funding was required to hold the pound to the DM3 ceiling.[15]

The following day, the Prime Minister summoned her Chancellor and read him the riot act. Once again, she repeated her worries that the scale of the intervention was too high, and that it would add to the inflationary pressures in the economy. He again insisted that because of his sterilisation activities of gilt edged sales there was no question of the intervention becoming inflationary. This time she did not accept his explanation. Nigel Lawson was effectively given a Prime Ministerial order to uncap the pound. With bad grace he obeyed, although he warned her that further intervention might be necessary if the pound rose too sharply. This caveat infuriated her.

After more strong words had been exchanged, she grudgingly backed away from her view that sterling should be allowed to float to its market level. But she insisted that any further intervention should be small, and that the Chancellor's private office should have to report on the situation to her own private office at half-hourly intervals. These commands were interspersed with personalised criticisms of deceit against Nigel Lawson, which he vigorously denied. 'It was an unpleasant meeting, and I particularly resented her manner',[16] he coldly recalled.

So bad was the blood between the two leading figures in the government at this time that the Prime Minister seriously considered sacking her Chancellor. How close she came to this dramatic execution is vividly illustrated by a story of Denis quarrelling with her in front of a friend.

In late February 1988 Denis took Dick Evans, the Managing Director of British Aerospace, to the East India Club in St James's Square. A convivial lunch was preceded by several 'snifters' at the bar before and after lunch. 'Denis had a lot to drink and I felt I should see him home,' recalled Evans, 'so we went into No. 10 by the back entrance that existed in those days via Horseguards Parade. We got there about 5.30 p.m. and went up to the private flat.'

Denis poured himself a large whisky. A few minutes later Margaret came in. The Prime Minister found her husband in an unusually aggressive mood.

'Have you done it?' he demanded. There was no clear reply, so the question was repeated at louder volume.

'What are you talking about, dear?' asked Margaret Thatcher.

Denis grew angry at her dissimilation. 'You know perfectly well what I'm talking about', he shouted. 'Have – you – done – it?' Each word was accompanied by a bang of his fist on the table. Dick Evans made his excuses and tried to leave. Both Thatchers told him to stay.

'I know what he's getting at', admitted the Prime Minister.

'Well, have you done it?' came the question for the fourth time of asking.

'No I haven't.'

'I knew you weren't going to do it. When you agreed to do it at breakfast this morning, I just knew you wouldn't. So why the hell didn't you?'

'Denis, there is a limit to the number of enemies we can afford to make.'

Dick Evans made his second attempt to depart, but the Prime Minister felt that an explanation was needed. Amidst further noises of protest from her spouse she told Evans what 'it' was.

'At breakfast this morning he persuaded me to fire Nigel Lawson', she explained, 'and I haven't done it.'[17]

The story says as much about Margaret Thatcher's caution as it does about the breakfast decision she dropped. She had good grounds of being furious with her Chancellor. But she knew he had many supporters in the parliamentary party. Another key factor was the 1988 Budget was due to be presented in eleven days' time.

Those days were difficult for the two protagonists. Press reports of their split made damaging reading. Sterling rose as high as DM3.18, and would have gone higher but for a half-point reduction of interest rates to 7.5 per cent. Margaret Thatcher believed that this cut was unwise, but accepted it as 'the price of tolerable relations with my Chancellor'.[18]

Nigel Lawson did not share the view that their relationship was becoming more tolerable. He resented the unhelpfully candid comments made by the Prime Minister to Parliament about exchange-rate policy, such as 'there is no way in which one can buck the market'.[19] He also resisted but eventually accepted a redraft originating from No. 10 of crucial paragraphs in his Budget speech on exchange-rate policy. These humiliations, as he saw them, left scars on the proud Lawson. He was seething.

When he went to Buckingham Palace for the Chancellor's traditional eve of Budget audience with the Queen, he told the Monarch that he thought it would be his last such speech, 'because the Prime Minister was making the conduct of policy impossible'.[20]

THE BOOM OR BUST BUDGET

'A provocative Budget'[21] was how Nigel Lawson himself described the radical proposals he announced to Parliament on 15 March 1988. It certainly provoked his political opponents. His Budget speech caused chaos in the House of Commons, with the sitting having to be suspended twice. The Labour Party were fierce in their denunciation of the Lawson strategy, which they said would hurt the poor and help the rich.

By contrast the Conservative Party greeted the Budget with near rapture. It reduced the basic rate of income tax to 25 per cent, and brought down the higher rate from 60 per cent to 40 per cent. All intermediate tax rates were abolished. The Chancellor sat down at the end of his speech to wave upon wave of Tory cheers after he announced in his peroration that he had delivered a balanced Budget and intended to bring income tax down to 20 per cent.

Margaret Thatcher was publicly effusive but privately doubtful about her Chancellor's strategy. Before the Budget, she warned him against announcing the future goal of a 20 per cent tax rate. She would have been content to leave the top rate at 50 per cent. Her biggest worry was the overall looseness of the financial situation and monetary policy, which she feared might lead to inflation. But she kept these doubts under wraps and joined in the chorus of praise for the Budget, which she described as 'a Humdinger . . . the obituary for the doctrine of high taxation . . . the epitaph for Socialism'.[22]

Despite these laudatory words, it soon became apparent that something was rotten in the state of the relationship between Prime Minister and Chancellor. Iron had entered Nigel Lawson's soul as a result of their quarrels over the ERM. Even when she flattered him in public or sent him handwritten notes of congratulations in private, he spurned her olive branches. 'It was never praise that I sought from her: just trust, honesty and the loyalty she expected of others' was his dismissive comment on her attempts at rapprochement.[23]

Lawson was right to complain of the Prime Minister's disloyalty, which became embarrassingly transparent during parliamentary exchanges in mid-May. This was a period when the pound was again rising against the Deutschemark despite cuts in interest rates to 8 per cent.

At Prime Minister's Questions on 12 May, she was wounded by Neil Kinnock attacking her evasiveness on exchange-rate policy. After a fusillade of blows, he cornered her with the simple question: 'Can the right hon. Lady give us a straight answer? Does the Prime Minister agree with her Chancellor of the Exchequer?'[24]

Instead of replying in the affirmative, Margaret Thatcher conspicuously avoided the question in a cloud of waffle about high living standards, growth and social services. It was a deeply damaging performance, which unsettled the markets, the financial commentators and her back-benchers.

With weekend press speculation at fever pitch about the possibility of Lawson being moved to the Foreign Office, remedial action became imperative. So Chancellor and Prime Minister met to agree a damage-limitation exercise. It consisted of cutting interest rates again to 7.5 per cent, and working out a form of words that would put sticking plaster on the perceived split that had so unnecessarily been exposed by her last answers in Parliament.

Neil Kinnock found it easy to continue his winning streak at Prime Minister's Questions. 'May I warmly welcome today's cut in interest rates and the Chancellor's victory over the Prime Minister?' was his opening line. Of course, Margaret Thatcher did not admit that she had been defeated. But her one word assent, 'Yes', to a later question about whether there was 'complete and utter unanimity' between herself and the Chancellor told its own story.[25] It was more of a self-inflicted wound for her than a victory for Lawson, but she had been badly wrong-footed.

Within a matter of weeks it was the Chancellor who was stumbling. His Budget unravelled as his tax-cutting judgement turned out to have been based on inaccurate forecasts. Unexpectedly bad export figures made the trade deficit balloon to £2.2 billion in July. Inflation doubled to 6.6 per cent and kept rising. Interest rates had to be raised by a succession of upward moves from 7.5 per cent on 17 May to 11 per cent on 8 August, and to 12 per cent on 25 August.[26] It soon became clear that Britain had moved into a nightmare scenario of overheating domestic demand, rising inflation, runs on the pound and crushingly high interest rates.

Nigel Lawson had wanted to leave the government in the warm glow of success that the first reactions to his Budget had produced. He talked to friends about his plan to retire in the expected autumn reshuffle. But the sudden crisis in the economy hit his reputation so hard that he felt he must stay at the helm.

The voices that had praised the Lawson boom in the spring were sharply criticising the Lawson bust by the autumn. Among the sharpest critics, struggling somewhat unsuccessfully to keep her comments private, was the Prime Minister.

Margaret Thatcher had been instinctively opposed to some of her Chancellor's strategic moves since the beginning of her third term. She thought he was loose on monetary policy, wrong about the ERM and incompetent in failing to keep inflation down. These opinions found their way into the press in the latter months of 1988, a development for which Lawson blamed Bernard Ingham.

Just as worrying as the policy disagreements was the increasingly personalised animosity between Chancellor and Prime Minister. She took to referring to him among members of her inner circle as 'a riverboat gambler' to which she added, 'and I won't let him gamble with the British economy'.[27] Her line was that he had gone off to the ERM casino, placed the wrong bet on inflation and lost her hard-won reputation for good economic management.

'Nigel has cost us two years', she told David Hart.[28] These and other pejorative comments were made in anger, not humour. Nigel Lawson was hurt by them: 'She was in a permanent state of resentment with me for having – as she saw it – allowed inflation to rise', he recalled, 'and she was determined to rub my nose in it.'[29]

One part of that determination involved a controversial new appointment to the staff at No. 10. The appointee was Alan Walters, whom Margaret Thatcher chose to be her personal economic adviser in July 1988. He had been in this position before, from 1981 to 1983. At that time he had quietly given her discreet advice from his low-profile post. Five years on, quietness and discretion were no longer part of the Walters style, for he had become something of a celebrity in the world of academic commentators. Some of his fame derived from his outspoken public criticism of Nigel Lawson's policies.

Margaret Thatcher brought Alan Walters back into her team as a deliberate counter-weight to the Chancellor. He took up his post in May 1989 on a two-year contract. She never seems to have understood what an insult to Nigel Lawson this appointment would be, and how likely it was to blow up into big trouble. What it meant was that the Prime Minister would have two sources of advice on the management of the economy, which on past form would often be in conflict. The potential for discord was enormous.

Realising the dangers posed by Alan Walters' appointment, the Chancellor argued strenuously against it. Margaret Thatcher, displaying a side of her personality that enjoyed dividing and ruling, refused to listen to his objections. She had lost confidence in Nigel Lawson, and was determined to have an alternative source of advice within her inner circle.

In the short term, the Alan Walters' appointment won considerable sympathy and support for Nigel Lawson. Among Tory MPs, sentiments of outrage were expressed against it.

I recall attending a stormy meeting of the back-bench finance committee at which it was said that the Prime Minister 'had gone off her rocker', and that Walters was 'a Trojan horse', 'far too big for his boots' and even 'a fifth columnist'. This last description was amusingly qualified by the Member who made it, Nicholas Budgen. 'I call him that because he seems to write five columns a week, most of them critical of the Chancellor.'[30]

What MPs could see, even if the Prime Minister could not, was that the conflict between her unelected economic adviser and her Chancellor would certainly be divisive and might be explosive.

HOWE STIRS THE ERM DISPUTE

It is unlikely that Margaret Thatcher's troubles with her Chancellor would ever have escalated to the point of threatening her tenure as Prime Minister had they not become inextricably linked to her difficulties with the Foreign Secretary.

Sir Geoffrey Howe had been simmering resentfully in his post for many months. His personal relations with Margaret Thatcher were deteriorating. There were also policy differences between them in several areas. By far the most important of these was the growing divergence in their attitudes towards Europe. In simplified terms, she was an Atlanticist, while he was a Europhile. She was increasingly sceptical about the direction in which the European Community seemed to be heading. He took the opposite view, supportively accepting much of the federalist agenda in Brussels, which was being spearheaded by the energetic new President of the European Commission, Jacques Delors.*

Against the background of these tensions, Sir Geoffrey took the far from benign decision to involve himself publicly in the row with Lawson over the European ERM. Howe had long been a strong but quiet supporter of Britain's entry into the ERM. Unfortunately, he chose to declare his hand at the most awkward of moments from the Prime Minister's point of view, right in the middle of her split with the Chancellor, which had been exposed by Neil Kinnock's questions in Parliament on 12 May 1988.

The following day, 13 May, Geoffrey Howe was speaking at the Scottish Conservative Party Conference in Perth when he departed from his prepared text. Having mentioned the time-honoured formula about joining the ERM 'when the time is right', he ad-libbed his opinion that 'We cannot forever go on adding

---

* Jacques Delors (1925–), French economist and politician, eighth President of the European Commission, and first person to serve three terms in office, 1985–1995.

that qualification to the underlying commitment'.[31] Inevitably the press made hay and many negative headlines over this evidence of a further split within the cabinet.

This was a red rag to Margaret Thatcher. She was furious with Howe for 'making mischief' on the ERM at such a sensitive time.[32] He claimed that he had no such intention, and had merely been innocently replying to points raised in a European debate by Scottish Tories. This seemed a disingenuous explanation to the Prime Minister, who thought her Foreign Secretary had been stirring up trouble and the consequent media coverage quite deliberately.

The day after his speech in Scotland, with the newspaper headlines trumpeting about the disastrous cabinet divisions over the ERM, Geoffrey Howe telephoned Margaret Thatcher at Chequers to suggest they should meet together with Nigel Lawson to 'settle the semi-public dispute'.[33] He claimed that he made the call 'in all innocence'.[34]

She thought his motives were less pure. She gave him the full blast of her fury in the belief that his purpose in asking for the meeting was so that he and the Chancellor could steamroller her into agreement with their views on the ERM. 'No, I shall certainly not see the two of you together about this', she shouted.

Howe was 'astonished by the ferocity of her reaction'.[35] He was left in no doubt about her hostility to his proposal since she repeated her refusal to meet three times. She also told him that the best thing he could now do was to keep quiet, adding for good measure, 'We were not going into the ERM at present, and that is that'.[36]

This row had far-reaching consequences a year later when Howe reopened the arguments about the ERM to mount what was later called the 'Madrid Ambush'. It consisted of a joint effort by the Foreign Secretary and the Chancellor to persuade the Prime Minister to change her mind about the ERM on the eve of a European Council Summit Meeting in Madrid.

The ambush failed, but it had severe repercussions for all parties. As the Madrid European Council Meeting itself was only tangentially concerned with the ERM, this episode is dealt with in a later chapter,* which focuses on Margaret Thatcher's growing alienation from the centralising policies of the European Community. But the issue of the ERM could not be separated from

---

* See Chapter 33.

the issues of running the British economy. From mid-1988 onwards Margaret Thatcher had put herself in the dangerous position of fighting against two of her most senior ministers on two different fronts.

This was a situation that could only end in tears. So it proved. But it took another thirty months before this passion play, born in the complexities of a technical dispute about exchange rates, ended with not one but three political crucifixions.

REFLECTION

The ERM dispute between Margaret Thatcher and her senior colleagues in the 1980s is an arcane relic of twentieth-century economic history, which has about as much relevance to contemporary politics as the Schleswig–Holstein question. This was the nineteenth-century diplomatic dispute about Danish and German principalities now remembered solely for Lord Palmerston's joke: 'Only three people have ever really understood the Schleswig–Holstein business – the Prince Consort, who is dead – a German professor, who has gone mad – and I, who have forgotten all about it.'[37]

In the same way, it now seems extraordinary that Nigel Lawson, Geoffrey Howe and Margaret Thatcher could ever have become so obsessed with the intricacies of the ERM that they fought about it as if it was the Holy Grail of the British economy. It was nothing like that important. The ERM was a technical tool for stabilising international exchange rates and keeping down inflation. What made it different was first, that it required co-operation with European central banks and, second, that most of the grey eminences of Britain's economic establishment were in favour of this move throughout the 1980s.

At the ministerial meeting on 13 November 1985, Willie Whitelaw summed up the situation by saying, 'If the Chancellor, the Governor and the Foreign Secretary are all agreed that we should join the EMS then that should be decisive. It has certainly decided me.'[38] Consensus man had spoken.

Margaret Thatcher's rejection of this unanimity and her walk-out from the meeting was as dramatic as it was unexpected. For there did not seem to be any great issue of principle on the table with which she could quarrel so vehemently. Seven years earlier she had chided Jim Callaghan for not signing up to the ERM.

Four years later she was finally persuaded by John Major and Douglas Hurd to allow her government to join it. The pros and cons of Britain's membership were always argued in technical terms such as timing, currency stability, exchange-rate fluctuations and the effect on inflation.

Sir Geoffrey Howe may well have had the cause of greater British participation in the European Community's future grand designs for European Monetary Union (EMU) on his mind, but this was not the case he stated. Equally, Margaret Thatcher never at the time took her stand against the ERM because she thought it would be a Trojan horse leading to a single currency. She may have had some silent fears in this direction, but she never expressed them. It was more likely, as Terry Burns saw at the time, that her opposition was rooted in anxieties about the loss of control, the loss of British self-government, that joining the EMS involved.

Whatever her reasons, the Prime Minister's instinctive veto on ERM membership was to prove the killer on the policy for the next five years. The harder she maintained those killer instincts, the harder Geoffrey Howe and Nigel Lawson attacked her. Their challenges opened up a dark side in Margaret Thatcher, revealing a character willing to engage in bitter personality clashes against old friends who had turned into her new foes. She preferred not to seek a collegiate solution with them, but to fight against them at every turn. The ERM dispute thus became personal, eventually with dire consequences for all three combatants in the power struggle.

But who was right on the substantive issue? History vindicates the judgement of Margaret Thatcher. For after she reluctantly agreed to allow Britain to join the ERM during the last six months of her premiership in June 1990, it soon became apparent that the policy would lead not to economic stability but to a roller-coaster ride of exchange-rate fluctuations, interest-rate surges, expensive interventions, huge losses of foreign-exchange reserves and chaos in the markets.

Eventually, Britain's membership proved so catastrophic that the then Chancellor, Norman Lamont, had to make an ignominious exit from the ERM on 'Black Wednesday', 16 September 1992. It was seen as a disaster at the time although once Britain regained control of its own economic destiny, a recovery soon followed.

One Treasury official who had a ringside seat throughout the seven-year ERM drama – first as Chief Economic Adviser to the Treasury and later as its Permanent

Secretary – was Sir Terence Burns. What was his verdict on Margaret Thatcher's opposition to joining the ERM during the Lawson–Howe era?

'Seen with the full flow of history, I believe Margaret Thatcher was right', said Terry Burns, when interviewed for this biography. 'She recognised ahead of others that the UK just could not live with the European level of interest rates.'[39]

It was one of the paradoxes of Margaret Thatcher's personality that she often reached the right judgements but enforced them in the wrong way. Some of her ministers could take this. In the third term, Nigel Lawson and Geoffrey Howe could not.

The ERM dispute was a sideshow which they promoted into a Punch and Judy show with the stage management of their Madrid ambush. In the same histrionic spirit, the Prime Minister acted out the part of the policeman wielding a truncheon. She hit them too hard with it. There were better ways of handling the problem.

Margaret Thatcher's aggressive man-management methods were an obstacle to reconciling the policy differences at the top of her government. The virtues of her arguments became clouded by the flaws in her personality. She was setting herself up for much worse trouble with her most senior colleagues.

32

Swinging towards Euroscepticism

ALWAYS A DOUBTER

Margaret Thatcher made a long crossing of the desert between her 'Yes' campaigning in the 1975 referendum on Britain's membership of the European Economic Community (EEC) and her resounding 'No! No. No!'[1] denunciations of moves towards closer European integration in 1990. During the intervening fifteen years, Europe changed far more than she did. Through her roots and her instincts she was consistently inclined towards Euroscepticism. Although the term was not invented until late in her political lifetime, there are clues running through her career, which suggest that she was never a believer in the creed which proclaimed an ever-closer British relationship with Europe.

Those clues include the nationalistic patriotism of her Grantham upbringing; her wartime enmity towards the Germans; the pro-Commonwealth zeal of her constituency speeches in Dartford and Finchley; and her lifelong commitment to the primacy of the Anglo-American alliance. Her ardour for these causes far exceeded her lukewarm endorsement of the EEC. Although, as the newly elected Leader of the Opposition she campaigned for a 'Yes' vote in the referendum of 1975, her support was punctilious rather than passionate. Her most memorable contribution was to be photographed wearing a jersey patterned with the flags of the EEC states. Yet this sartorial gesture was not matched by more substantive activities. She left the lion's share of the speech-making and campaign leadership to Ted Heath, from whom she was keeping a careful political distance in the aftermath of their leadership battle.

Some observers did notice that she stayed aloof from the enthusiasts of the 'Yes' campaign. Although present at its launch, she made no major speeches in the run-up to the referendum vote. Harold Wilson dubbed her 'The reluctant debutante'. The *Sun* drew attention to her absence with a story headlined: 'Missing: one Tory leader. Answers to the name of Margaret Thatcher. Mysteriously disappeared from the Market Referendum campaign eleven days ago.'[2]

In private there were other clues to the mystery. Her political secretary, Richard Ryder, recalled her comment 'Gosh, that was good' after watching the 'No' campaign's national broadcast. He also remembered her saying that she wished she didn't have to vote at all.[3]

Despite such occasional signs of hesitancy about Tory policy towards Europe, Margaret Thatcher did not show her true colours as a Eurosceptic until she had been Prime Minister for nine years and a Member of Parliament for nearly thirty years. Why did it take her so long?

The answer lies in the culture and climate of the Conservative Party. For most of the 1960s, 1970s and 1980s, it was essential to be pro-Europe if you were an ambitious Tory MP eager to move up the ladder of promotion. Throughout the Macmillan–Heath era, the leadership's prevailing view and slogan was 'We are the party of Europe'. There were some notable dissenters from this official line headed by Enoch Powell, Neil Marten, Robin Turton, Derek Walker-Smith and Hugh Fraser, all of whom opposed the 1972 European Communities Act. But they were a minority faction. Perhaps, as Geoffrey Howe later observed, Margaret Thatcher should have been part of this group, since he came to see her as 'a natural member' of it.[4] But she was as cautious as she was ambitious when climbing towards the top of the greasy pole. So she went along with the prevailing Europeanism to get ahead within the party.

Challenging the orthodox acceptance of British membership of the European Community was a step too far in her early years as Prime Minister. Her initial rebellion against Brussels, the 'I want my money back' battle of the budget rebate from June 1979 to May 1980, was a single-issue stand of defiance rather than a sustained challenge to the establishment consensus. But although her abrasive advocacy for a rebate may have seemed to her a simple question of budgetary fairness, she gave deeper offence to her Community partners over what they regarded as an issue of principle. They believed she was attacking the Europhile article of faith which maintained that the EEC had its 'own resources', which could not be earmarked for, let alone rebated to, individual member states.

Quite rightly, Margaret Thatcher was dismissive towards this theological concept of 'own resources'. So, by persistent in fighting she won her rebate for

Britain. This was a great achievement. Yet it left behind an atmosphere of British negativity towards Europe. This was only dispelled when the Prime Minister was persuaded to sign up for the Single European Act (SEA) of 1985. It was the one and only time when she was positively engaged in the future direction of the European Community.

DIDDLED BY THE SINGLE EUROPEAN ACT (SEA)

The SEA was a major turning point for European integration. Margaret Thatcher saw its positive benefits, the creation of a single market, but failed to realise that the small print of the legislation could be used to pave the way for European Monetary Union (EMU).

The Prime Minister was not alone in this error of judgement. It was surprising how few Eurosceptics, let alone ordinary rank and file Conservatives, saw any pitfalls ahead as the legislation went through its stages in Parliament. I was one of nine Tory MPs to vote against the second reading of the bill.* Another was my fellow Eurosceptic Teddy Taylor. By chance, he and I encountered Margaret Thatcher just after we came out of the 'No' lobby on the night of that vote. 'Why on earth are you two voting against us?' she demanded. 'Because this will be the Trojan horse for Economic and Monetary Union', replied Teddy.

'Nonsense! It is no such thing', replied the Prime Minister, who went on to give us a sharp tutorial on the trade benefits of a single European market.[5]

Within three years of this conversation, Margaret Thatcher was beginning to make a U-turn on her view of the SEA. There were two reasons for this. The first was her growing unease over the flood of European Directives and Orders, which had to be passed by the House of Commons in order to make British law conform to Brussels law. The second was Jacques Delors, the formidable new President of the European Commission, who was determined to use the SEA as the vehicle to bring about EMU.

The SEA was intended to be the driving force for an expansion of trade within the single market. Unfortunately, it was also a harmonisation force, which

---

* The nine good men and true were Jonathan Aitken, Nicholas Budgen, Edward du Cann, Roger Moate, Tony Marlow, Richard Shepherd, Teddy Taylor and Bill Walker (*Guardian*, 27 June 1986).

dragged huge areas of British commercial life, quite unnecessarily, under the burdensome umbrella of EC regulation. An almost comic example of this, which considerably upset Margaret Thatcher once she understood it, was the European directive to harmonise lawnmower noise.

The notion that Parliament had to pass new legislation to make the sound of British lawnmowers harmonise with Continental lawnmowers sounds farcical. Nevertheless, some 120 pages of densely detailed legal regulations dedicated to this purpose were solemnly presented to the House of Commons for ratification. Because this latest example of 'Brussels interference' was as understandable as it was ludicrous, we Eurosceptic MPs were able to have a field day with it.

The pressure group of backbench Tory dissidents known as the Conservative European Reform Group (Chairman J. Aitken, Secretary T. Taylor), who regularly opposed such measures, suddenly expanded well beyond the usual twenty or thirty suspects. As a turbulent House neared its 1.30 a.m. vote on the Lawnmowers (Harmonisation of Lawnmower Noise Order) Regulation 1986, it looked as though as many as seventy-five rebels might be joining us in the 'No' lobby. The possibility of a government defeat was looming – panic at the whips' office. The payroll* vote was mustered to the full, so much so that even the Prime Minister had to be dragged back from No. 10 to vote in support of the Order.

When the Prime Minister arrived at Westminster, she wanted to know, 'What is all the fuss about?' Unfortunately, she asked a group of colleagues standing around in the corridor behind the Speaker's chair, who happened to be Conservative European Reform Group supporters. She got an earful. One of the measure's most vocal critics was the Birmingham MP Anthony Beaumont-Dark, who told her in no uncertain manner that this 'idiocy' would close factories all over the West Midlands. Another excited Brummie, David Bevan MP, helpfully imitated the sound of lawnmower engines at full throttle.

Margaret Thatcher was not amused. But she got the point. 'I shall look into this immediately', she said before moving on. A few minutes later, her PPS, Michael Alison, came to tell us that the Prime Minister shared the concerns

---

* Term used to cover all ministers on the government payroll and the unpaid Parliamentary Secretaries.

of our group and would be asking the Secretary of State for Trade what could be done. The answer was nothing. Lawnmower noise was duly harmonised by a smaller-than-usual majority. But the incident did demonstrate that the Prime Minister and an increasing number of her troops were becoming anxious about the encroaching effects of the SEA.

Far more serious a threat to Margaret Thatcher's favourable view of SEA was her realisation that Jacques Delors, the new President of the European Commission (EC), was using Article 20 of the Act to promote both EMU and a single currency. In her battles against him, Margaret Thatcher had to resort to semantic arguments about what she called 'the studied ambiguity' of Article 20.[6] Her case was that it only referred to the progressive realisation of economic and monetary union, which was quite different to EMU itself. But this notional difference was not understood, let alone agreed, by any other European leader. Instead, as Delors frequently reiterated, the SEA was seen as the accepted gateway to EMU and the single currency.

Jacques Delors soon became Margaret Thatcher's *bête noire*. She knew little about him at the time of his proposed appointment, and received no guidance from the Foreign Office suggesting that this former French Finance Minister might prove to be a hostile force against the British government's interests in Europe. However, she was sufficiently wary of the suggested appointee to seek advice from a British banker who had direct experience of working with Delors on a Brussels committee. This banker was Sir Ronald Grierson. He came to breakfast with the Prime Minister on 15 October 1984, the Monday after the IRA bombing in Brighton. Having fully expected his meeting to be cancelled, Grierson found himself being intensively questioned about the potential next President of the European Commission.

'I told Margaret Thatcher that Delors would be socialist, *dirigiste*, and extremely energetic in working for closer European integration', recalled Grierson. 'This was not what she wanted to hear.'[7]

The Prime Minister ignored Sir Ronald's warnings, agreed to the Delors appointment and accepted the blandishments of the other European leaders who assured her that the SEA would be a trade measure creating the single market. Margaret Thatcher in later years claimed that she had been deceived. 'I trusted them. I believed in them. I believed this was good faith between nations co-operating together. So we got our fingers burned.'[8]

Her Foreign Affairs Private Secretary at No. 10, Charles Powell, was even blunter. He recalled:

> Frankly, we were diddled. At the time we were concentrating on the advantages of the single market. The small print of the words in the Act did not seem to be a big deal, particularly after Chancellor Kohl had assured the Prime Minister that EMU was not going to happen. We underestimated, with the wisdom of hindsight, the steady accretions and pressures that followed.[9]

This explanation that the Prime Minister and her wider entourage of expert advisers were all 'diddled' about the far-reaching constitutional implications of the SEA is difficult to accept. The fact of the matter was that the British negotiating team, led by Margaret Thatcher, agreed to an Act that gave away more British sovereignty than Ted Heath had ceded in 1973. What she may have underestimated was that Jacques Delors would so forcefully use the SEA not just to develop the single market, but also to advance the powers of the Commission, by expanding majority voting and pressing forward towards EMU.

The moment when the scales fell from Margaret Thatcher's eyes about the magnitude of Jacques Delors' grand design for an integrated government of Europe came on 6 July 1988. That was the day when Delors gave a speech to the European Parliament predicting that over the next six or seven years 'an embryo European government' would be established, and that within ten years '80 per cent of the laws affecting the economy and social policy would be passed at a European and not at a national level'.[10]

Margaret Thatcher was furious. Interviewed a few days later on the *Jimmy Young Programme*, she rubbished this scenario as 'extreme' and 'over the top'. She added that Delors was a fantasist, whose prediction of monetary union was 'some airy-fairy concept which in my view will never come in my lifetime and I hope never at all!'[11]

Infuriated by what she saw as the President of the Commission playing the role of a politician, not least in a decidedly socialist speech to the TUC Conference, Margaret Thatcher decided to launch a counter-attack. She was scheduled to deliver an address to the College of Europe in Bruges on 20 September. Sir Geoffrey Howe had suggested that she might use this occasion to deliver a 'positive' view of the EEC. But the Prime Minister and the Foreign Secretary were growing further and further apart in their attitudes towards Europe.

DISILLUSIONMENT WITH GEOFFREY HOWE

Margaret Thatcher's conversion to Euroscepticism was personal as well as political. The personal dimension came from her growing disillusionment with her Foreign Secretary. This feeling was mutual, but far rougher and nastier on her side. Her antagonistic bullying of Geoffrey Howe revealed the worst aspects of her personality.

At the beginning of their eleven-year relationship in government, the accord between Chancellor and Prime Minister was a good one, despite some moments of turbulence. In the battle to turn the British economy around they were a harmonious team, united in their strategic purpose and courageous in their political resilience. Throughout her first term, she was humbler in her certainties and more amenable to listening to the views of her senior colleague. At least twice a month Howe would go through from No. 11 on a Sunday evening for a drink with his boss alone in her flat above No. 10. These private conversations strengthened their public policy-making, which resulted in falling inflation, lower public expenditure and higher growth.

After Sir Geoffrey became Foreign Secretary his problems with Margaret Thatcher grew more difficult. They had weekly bilaterals, which demonstrated as never before that their personal styles were chalk and cheese. She was brisk and business-like, displaying an impatience to take and implement decisions. He was rambling and discursive, preferring to talk round a subject obliquely, without an outcome. Even when they did agree a course of action, he would sum it up in slow motion, often adding some qualifying phrase that nettled her. Two such phrases, used by him *ad nauseam* in her view, were 'with all due deliberate speed' and 'subject to contract and survey'.[12] Howe never recognised, let alone understood, why these clichés excited the ire of his boss.

The only third party who attended these mutually unendurable bilaterals was the Prime Minister's Foreign Affairs Private Secretary, Charles Powell. He became so concerned by the stylistic gulf between the two principals that on one occasion he took it upon himself to suggest to Sir Geoffrey that he should come to the meetings with a set agenda and a prepared speaking note. The advice went unheeded. The Foreign Secretary continued to meander indecisively, and the Prime Minister reacted with increasing aggression.

Margaret Thatcher developed the view that the change of job had changed Sir Geoffrey's personality. She felt that her once resolute Chancellor had transmogrified into a vacillating Foreign Secretary. 'His insatiable appetite for compromise led me to lash out at him in front of others', was her description of their deteriorating relationship.[13] These tongue-lashings could be vicious.

'I know what you are going to say, Geoffrey, and the answer is no',[14] is how she began one meeting. 'Your paper is twaddle, complete and utter twaddle. I don't know how you have the nerve to submit it',[15] was her opening salvo at another. 'If you know so much about industry, why don't you go and work there', was her insult to him during a presentation he made about European economic models. All these rude remarks were made in the presence of embarrassed officials.[16]

She could behave even worse in front of fellow politicians. At the time when her doubts over the SEA were growing, she called in Bill Cash, the Eurosceptic Member for Stafford. 'There were just the three of us in the room', recalled Cash. 'She didn't just give Geoffrey a handbagging. He got a massive sandbagging. She was just utterly and impossibly rude to him.'[17]

Sir Geoffrey Howe's response to these torments was usually to suffer in silence. When her rants were in full flow, he would sometimes open his red box, take out a pile of letters and sign them in front of her. Occasionally, he would gradually return to the point she had been denouncing, 'rather like a submarine coming up for air after a torpedo attack, with its conning tower wrecked and its hull badly damaged', said one observer of this warfare. 'Then it would be "bombs away" from her, all over again.'[18]

She may have intuitively understood that her Foreign Secretary was smouldering with ill-will towards her. Because neither of them ever attempted to clear the air, their mutual resentment grew worse. It was not their policy disagreements over issues such as South Africa, 'Star Wars' and above all Europe that caused their split, however much they contributed to it. What drove Margaret Thatcher up the wall with her Foreign Secretary were intangible and irrational irritations. They were perhaps best encapsulated in the French phrase 'une question de peau'. It was as though proximity to his presence had the effect of sprinkling itching powder on her skin.

Four personal aspects of Geoffrey Howe's life particularly irritated the Prime Minister's skin: his ambition, his wife, his houses and his plotting. As grievances they did not add up to serious charges on objective examination. But Margaret Thatcher became incapable of objectivity towards her most senior colleague.

After the departure from the cabinet of Willie Whitelaw, and perhaps for some while before that, Geoffrey Howe was the odds on favourite to become the next prime minister if a vacancy unexpectedly occurred at No. 10. Margaret Thatcher woke up to this reality at the time of Westland when she herself briefly thought that she might have to resign. She believed that Howe secretly harboured the ambition to succeed her, and suspiciously magnified the possibility in her mind.

She spoke of it at least once to Ian Gow in the autumn of 1988. Being a friend and fan of the Foreign Secretary, he did not demur from the idea of a Prime Minister Howe, but pointed out that it was unlikely to happen because 'Geoffrey is always so loyal'. 'Not in private he isn't,' retorted Margaret Thatcher, 'and anyway, it's out of the question that he should be my successor. He's quite past it. He will never, never, never succeed me!'[19]

The eruption of her anger so distressed Ian Gow that he quickly left the flat at No. 10 and repaired to the smoking room of the House of Commons, where he poured out his heart and the story to one or two friends, including me.[20] Our nocturnal consensus was that Thatcher–Howe relations was becoming much worse than the Macmillan–Butler antipathy of the 1950s. This eventually killed off Rab Butler's expected inheritance of the Tory crown in 1963.

One person who took the possibility of a Geoffrey Howe succession with the utmost seriousness was his wife, Elspeth. She was the personification of a familiar adage in the Westminster village: 'Margaret is bad with wives.' This was true. From her yanking handshake which pulled women she did not want to converse with past her at high speed in a reception line, to forgetting their names or talking past them with bored dismissiveness, the Prime Minister generally gave the impression in her encounters with cabinet wives that none of her colleagues had such a thing as a 'better half'.

She was more respectful towards the spouses of grandees like Celia Whitelaw or Iona Carrington. But if there was one wife who irritated her more than any other, it was Elspeth Howe.

The explanation for this tension was that Lady Howe was a formidable character in her own right. Forthright in her opinions, feminist in her sympathies, sharp-tongued in her humour and fiercely supportive of her husband in his battles, she had an inner strength that grated against Margaret Thatcher's 'Iron Lady' persona. There were no overt clashes between the two of them, although many sensed their antagonism. John Biffen memorably compared the Elspeth–Margaret relationship to that of 'two wasps in a jam jar'.[21]

Elspeth Howe kept her opinion to herself. Margaret Thatcher was less successful in this, scornfully deprecating the 'feminist views', 'the progressive attitude' and the 'equal opportunities* mindset' of the Foreign Secretary's wife. There was not much substance in these grumblings, but they did illustrate that both personally and politically Margaret Thatcher and Elspeth Howe were poles apart.[22]

A third area of bitchiness – no other word for it will do – that began to trouble Howe–Thatcher relations concerned the Foreign Secretary's official residences: No. 1 Carlton Gardens and Chevening in Kent. Because the Howes were good home-makers and hosts, they made the most of these two 'tied cottages', particularly Chevening, which is one of England's most beautiful country houses. They loved its parkland walks, its trees, its splendid eighteenth-century library, and its relaxing atmosphere of elegance and grace.

Political guests who were lucky enough to be invited to both Chequers and Chevening often said they preferred the atmosphere of Chevening. There is no suggestion that Margaret Thatcher ever had such feelings for she enjoyed Chequers to the full.

She mysteriously developed the view that the Howes were using Chevening to build up a base of support for a future leadership bid. She complained that they were using the house 'to hold court' – a phrase she used unkindly on more than one occasion.[23]

If there was a rational explanation for the Prime Ministerial jealousy that seeped out over Chevening, it may have started because several MPs returned from lunches, dinners or overnight stays with the Howes saying how much they had enjoyed themselves. Geoffrey Howe on duty could seem a rather stodgy figure. Off duty at Chevening, he relaxed into being a genial host, an amusing raconteur and a whizz at the billiards table.

If there was a serious issue that could ever make a section of the Conservative Party contemplate replacing Margaret Thatcher with Geoffrey Howe, it was

---

* Lady Howe was Deputy Chairman of the Equal Opportunities Commission 1975–1979, a Labour-created quango which elicited much scorn from Margaret Thatcher. She liked to say that her own career was a good example of how women did not need a government commission to help them achieve equal opportunity.

Europe. However improbable this imaginary threat seemed to the world, the fear of it lurked in the back of her mind. This was why her feud with the Foreign Secretary grew to be personal as well as political. So when she began working on her Bruges speech, in the summer recess of 1988, she had not one but two objectives. She wanted to check the Jacques Delors vision of a federal Europe and she wanted to checkmate the ambitions of Geoffrey Howe.

THE BRUGES SPEECH

Margaret Thatcher's speech in Bruges was a carefully crafted and powerfully phrased oration. Read in its totality, it can be seen as a balanced mixture of strong support and sharp criticism for the European Community. But, as she must have known, it was the negative parts of the speech that made the biggest headlines.

She began with a barbed jest about how her invitation to speak about Britain in Europe could be compared to 'inviting Genghis Khan to speak on the virtues of peaceful coexistence!' In the next paragraph she sounded uncomfortably like an alien invader determined to overthrow the status quo of the Community as she declared: 'Europe is not the creation of the Treaty of Rome. Nor is the European idea the property of any group or institution.'

She rowed back from that early hint of confrontation by emphasising that 'Britain does not dream of some cosy, isolated existence on the fringes of the European Community. Our destiny is in Europe, as part of the Community.'

She also highlighted the idea that east of the Iron Curtain there were nations that belonged to Europe just as much as the twelve member states in the Community. This was a visionary outlook expressed long before the communist bloc began to crumble.

The most important part of her speech was her head-on challenge to what Jacques Delors had been saying about a future government of Europe. She insisted that the way to build a successful community was by 'willing and active cooperation between independent sovereign states' and not by closer integration. She warned of the follies of trying to fit strong nation-states into 'some sort of identikit European personality', in which the Community became 'an institutional device constantly modified according to the dictates of some abstract intellectual concept . . . ossified by endless regulation'.

With her tone and language growing increasingly acerbic, she delivered two explosive sentences, which sent shock waves through many Europhile institutions and individuals:

> Working more closely together does not require power to be centralised in Brussels or decisions to be taken by an appointed bureaucracy . . . We have not successfully rolled back the frontiers of the State in Britain, only to see them re-imposed at a European level with a European super-state exercising a new dominance from Brussels.

After some sideswipes against a European Central Bank and in favour of the maintenance of frontiers to control illegal immigrants, she ended with a clarion call for 'relishing our national identity no less than our common European endeavour', and preserving 'that Atlantic community – that Europe on both sides of the Atlantic – which is our noblest inheritance and our greatest strength'.[24]

Although polite applause greeted her at the College of Europe in Bruges, as she sat down after the speech its ripple effect produced sharp polarisation. Ardent Eurosceptics wanted to throw their hats into the air. Dedicated Europhiles wanted to throw up. Margaret Thatcher had cast down a gauntlet to the governing classes of Europe, particularly to the Brussels bureaucracy of the Commission and its President, Jacques Delors. She had not named him in the speech, but she might as well have declared war on him, for she was clearly targeting him as an enemy, not far behind Arthur Scargill or General Galtieri in her demonology.

Inevitably, the Bruges speech brought adverse reactions in high European places. On the evening it was delivered Margaret Thatcher dined with the Prime Minister of Belgium, who criticised her argument with considerable force. Similar reactions came from the pro-European professionals from Britain. Sir Michael Butler, Britain's Ambassador and Permanent UK Representative to the EEC, described the Prime Minister's portrayal of a European conglomerate state dominated by Brussels bureaucrats as 'very dangerous stuff indeed'.[25] Her Foreign Secretary, Sir Geoffrey Howe, professed himself 'deeply dismayed' by the speech. He compared his own position to 'being married to a clergyman who had suddenly proclaimed his disbelief in God'.[26]

It could be argued that both the jeers and the cheers for the speech were overdone. Margaret Thatcher had made a number of justified criticisms of the

Commission's way of doing business, but she had also included a number of strikingly pro-European passages. However, two further factors caused the speech to be seen as an indictment of the Community. The first was the spin of Bernard Ingham's press briefings, which accentuated the negative hostility of her Bruges message. The second factor was that the Prime Minister herself amplified it. Excited by the effect of her critical words, she returned to them with more partisan and more chauvinistic embellishments when she addressed the Tory Party Conference three weeks later in Brighton on 14 October 1989. She began with a rather boastful description of the impact her speech had made.

> It caused a bit of a stir. [Laughter.] Indeed, from some of the reactions, you would have thought I had re-opened the Hundred Years War. [Laughter.] And from the avalanche of support, you'd have thought I'd won it single-handed. [Cheers, laughter and stamping applause from the delegates.]

Then she launched into an even sharper attack on the excesses of the Commission, firing a none-too-veiled broadside at Jacques Delors, who must have been precisely whom she had in mind when she attacked 'those who see European unity as a vehicle for spreading Socialism'.

She reworked the line that had brought her the biggest headline at Bruges, but now with extra touches of political spice. 'We haven't worked all these years to free Britain from the paralysis of Socialism only to see it creep in through the back door of central control and bureaucracy from Brussels.'

She concluded by telling the Conference, 'Ours is the true European ideal.'[27]

From the seventeen-minute standing ovation given to her speech, you might have thought that the entire Conservative Party was fired up with enthusiasm for Margaret Thatcher's new vision for Europe as defined at Bruges. In fact, she had exposed the fault-line on the issue, magnifying the tensions between Europhiles and Eurosceptics into a full-blown split.

The trouble was that the party in Parliament took a different view from the party activists at the conference. Although some fifty Eurosceptic MPs who made up the Conservative European Reform Group sent the Prime Minister a fulsome letter of congratulations on her new approach, we were in a minority. For a larger number expressed their concerns to their whips that 'Margaret had gone too far' or 'gone over the top'.[28]

A handful of Heseltine supporters claimed to be outraged by the anti-European nature of the crucial paragraphs in the speech, although perhaps they were secretly pleased that they had a new reason for championing their master's cause. For this was a time when Michael Heseltine was behaving more and more like an alternative king over the water, with his courtiers quietly counting heads while the pretender himself remained indefatigable in his speech-making, particularly in the constituencies of disaffected colleagues.

Bruges therefore turned up the heat on the simmering discontent within the party at Westminster. Europe was not the only cause of the unease. There were plenty of other reasons for restlessness about her leadership. They included the poll tax legislation, the sore feelings amongst overlooked or ignored colleagues on the backbenches and the feuds within the cabinet. These became sharper and more bitter in the aftermath of Bruges.

REFLECTION

Her swing towards Euroscepticism was accompanied by a swing towards hubris. As she approached her tenth anniversary of becoming Prime Minister, she was increasingly intolerant of dissent, especially from her most senior colleagues. But these disagreements had not yet become particularly troublesome.

If she had retired, as Denis wanted her to do, after ten years as Prime Minister, she would have departed to a level of public acclaim unequalled by any other previous occupant of No. 10. But the last thought in her head was giving up the job she loved. Having no interests outside politics, she was determined to remain at the helm. In taking such a position, she was worrying a growing number of her cabinet and parliamentary colleagues, many of whom wanted to soften her stance on both Europe and the poll tax. The most worried of all was Geoffrey Howe, who felt thwarted in his European sympathies, and frustrated in his personal ambition to succeed her. So, while she stayed on and on with rising unpleasantness towards him, he began scheming against her with increasingly clandestine cunning.

33

Boiling over on Europe

THE FALL-OUT FROM BRUGES

The Bruges speech and its aftermath revealed a three-way split at the top of the cabinet. Sir Geoffrey Howe was not merely 'dismayed'.[1] In his quiet but feline way, he was extremely angry with the Prime Minister. He found it impossible to understand how she could reconcile her trumpet blasts of Euroscepticism at Bruges and Brighton with Britain's continuing membership of the European Community.

In Howe's view, Margaret Thatcher's support for the SEA should have logically led to her support for EMU, and eventually to a single European currency. The precursor to this was entering the ERM, to ensure a reasonable degree of currency stability among member states. On a wider front, the Foreign Secretary thought that his Prime Minister's call for the European Community to be run through 'willing and active cooperation between independent sovereign states'[2] was an unrealistic misrepresentation of the status quo, which already existed, thanks to texts and treaties that Britain had signed.

If Geoffrey Howe was smouldering with what he later called his 'conflict of loyalty', Nigel Lawson was in a similar state of mind, although for different reasons. He had long been an opponent of EMU. Indeed, in November 1985 he had strongly advised the Prime Minister not to agree to any words in the SEA, which referred to it, since this would be the slippery slope towards a common currency and a common Central Bank. Margaret Thatcher ignored his advice on EMU because she thought she had reached a pragmatic understanding with Chancellor Helmut Kohl that the references to it were harmless and meaningless. This proved to be one of her greatest mistakes.

Another damaging concession, in Lawson's view, was her agreement at Hanover in June 1988 to the setting up of a committee to report on the next steps on EMU under the chairmanship of Jacques Delors. Margaret Thatcher only went along with this committee of 'wise men' because she thought it would be a good way of kicking the issue into the long grass. Unfortunately, the wise man she appointed to the committee, the Governor of the Bank of England, Robin Leigh-Pemberton, went native in her eyes and supported the Delors line. This was a Thatcher own-goal.

A more effective strategy for heading off the growing momentum towards EMU, according to Nigel Lawson, would be to reach an agreement between sovereign states to accept but then go no further with the limited stage one of the Delors plan. This involved the completion of the single market, closer monetary co-ordination with Europe and membership of the ERM for all member states. It was this last condition that brought the Chancellor, a long-standing advocate of Britain joining the ERM, back into head-on collision with the Prime Minister.

The collision was strange, because Margaret Thatcher and Nigel Lawson were united in their opposition to EMU and the single currency. That unity, by all the forces of political logic, should have led them to be equally opposed to ERM. For Jacques Delors, and the leaders of every other member state in the EC, saw ERM not just as a tool for economic management but also as the first political step towards EMU. Lawson, however, remained in denial about this political objective of ERM. He insisted that it was purely an economic mechanism, which would work by co-operation between member states. This was a massive error of judgement by the Chancellor. He should have foreseen, as Margaret Thatcher foresaw, that ERM was an instrument to subordinate the sovereignty of member states, not to encourage co-operation between them. As later events were to prove, Britain could never work with such economic subordination, hence the disastrous but inevitable exit from the ERM that the successors of the Thatcher government were forced to make in 1992.

In 1989, however, the three-way split on these issues between the Prime Minister, the Chancellor and the Foreign Secretary were creating unbearable tensions. The first two opposed the single currency and EMU. The last two supported ERM. Geoffrey Howe alone wanted EMU. Margaret Thatcher alone opposed ERM. This was a recipe for chaos. Something had to give.

In an effort to resolve this impasse, on 3 May 1989, Margaret Thatcher met Nigel Lawson for their weekly bilateral without officials present. It was a disaster. They began with a discussion about the Delors Report on EMU, which they both agreed proved a grave danger to Britain. But after that their views polarised. She was implacably opposed to his idea of setting a deadline for UK membership of the ERM, which she thought to be 'particularly damaging'.[3] It would not strengthen her chances of resisting EMU. Nor would it help her to achieve her overriding aim of reducing inflation, which she believed had been increased by the Chancellor's policy of shadowing the Deutschmark.

She continued to see the argument in highly personal terms. Joining the ERM would be perceived as a defeat for herself and a victory for her Chancellor. 'I do not want you to raise the subject ever again', she insisted with her voice rising to a crescendo. 'I must prevail.'[4]

Nigel Lawson left the room after this outburst, saying that he would end the ERM discussion then and there, but would reserve his right to return to the subject. It was a bad end to a bad meeting, with the Prime Minister's last three words, 'I must prevail', hanging like a sword of Damocles over the future of their relationship. Margaret Thatcher did prevail for the next big event in the calendar of British politics. This was the European election campaign of June 1989. It was to prove her least successful encounter with the electorate since becoming leader of the party in 1975.

The Conservative Manifesto – described by the Prime Minister as 'an un-exciting document' – was prepared by Geoffrey Howe and Chris Patten.[5] It kept to the middle ground of the increasingly uneasy Tory consensus on Europe, with carefully compromised wording about the difficult areas such as the ERM.

Margaret Thatcher never liked to fudge. So she fought the election in her own words, which often bore little relationship to the words of the manifesto. On the ERM, she told the opening press conference that she would not be joining it until inflation was back under control, to which she added 'and maybe not even then'.[6] Her departure from the carefully agreed script was interpreted as another gratuitous sideswipe at Nigel Lawson. As a result, the campaign began with a flurry of headlines about further Tory splits.

The splitter-in-chief was Ted Heath, who travelled around the country ridiculing the Bruges speech. Margaret Thatcher, by contrast, concentrated her fire on the Delors Report and returned time and again to her mantra, 'We haven't rolled back the frontiers of socialism in this country to see them re-imposed from Brussels'.[7]

Some Tory MEPs seeking re-election contradicted their leader. But she was undeterred, apparently drawing strength from the populist response to her anti-European rhetoric, which included sharp criticism of 'the utterly feeble' European Parliament itself. The campaign culminated in a Central Office poster campaign proclaiming the slogan, 'Stay at home on June 15 and you'll live on a diet of Brussels'.[8] As a message it was confusing, but the general impression was that the Tories were running against the European Community under its present management.

The voters were more concerned with the management of the British government. It was unpopular for reasons quite unconnected with Brussels. The poll tax, the return of inflation, rising interest rates and a feeling that Margaret Thatcher, after ten years as Prime Minister, might be approaching her sell-by date were the key factors in the poor results on election day, 15 June 1989. The outcome was that Labour topped the poll with 40 per cent of the vote, while the Conservative Party held on to only 34 per cent – its lowest share in any national election since the beginning of universal suffrage.

Thirteen Tory seats out of forty-five were lost, and Labour won a majority of British MEPs in the European Parliament.[9] For the first time since 1979, Conservative MPs at Westminster began to wonder out loud whether Margaret Thatcher might herself be turning into an electoral liability.

The troubles caused by the bad results in the European elections spilled over into worsening relations between the Prime Minister and her senior cabinet colleagues. The Foreign Secretary and the Chancellor had been upset by her tactics and her tone on the hustings. They wanted to rein her in from the galloping Euroscepticism that now seemed to be the course on which she was set.

Geoffrey Howe decided to take the initiative of embarking on some Machiavellian moves designed to rein in the Prime Minister. By doing so, he believed he could constrain her and change her policy towards Europe. Despite his low voltage style, he showed passion and cunning when trying to get his way.

By contrast, Margaret Thatcher showed equal if not greater passion and cunning in sticking to her new-found Eurosceptic principles. Moreover, she believed, perhaps paranoiacally, that the machinations of her Foreign Secretary were aimed at fulfilling his long-held ambition to take over her job.

The combination of passion, principles and paranoia set the scene for an episode of high drama with explosive consequences. It took place in and around Madrid.

HIGH NOON IN MADRID

'On Wednesday 14 June 1989, just twelve days before the European Council in Madrid, Geoffrey Howe and Nigel Lawson mounted an ambush.'[10] This was Margaret Thatcher's reaction to receiving a joint minute from her two most senior cabinet ministers requesting a meeting to discuss Britain's tactics at Madrid.

The two authors of the minute demanded that the Prime Minister should strike an acceptable compromise on the Delors EMU proposals by agreeing only to stage one, and thwarting progress to further stages by announcing that sterling would join the ERM by 1992.

Fuming about this 'ambush', the Prime Minister first held a meeting of her No. 10 advisers, including Sir Alan Walters and Brian Griffiths. They fortified her resolve to see off her two most senior cabinet colleagues. Then she met Howe and Lawson on 20 June, where she rejected their advice but formally agreed to 'reflect further'.[11]

The next day she sent them a paper, largely written by Alan Walters, setting out her detailed view of the conditions, which would need to be met before joining the ERM. Howe and Lawson regarded these new conditions as an obstructive delaying mechanism. They insisted on a further discussion, which took place at 8.15 on the morning of Sunday 25 June – a few hours before the Madrid summit was due to open. At this 'nasty little meeting', as Margaret Thatcher called it, passions ran high.[12]

Geoffrey Howe began by restating his demand for an announcement that Britain would enter the ERM on a fixed date. He was again rebuffed by the Prime Minister, in angry language. Then he said that if she had no time for his advice he would have no alternative but to resign. At this point Nigel Lawson chipped in to say, 'You should know, Prime Minister, that if Geoffrey goes, I must go too'.[13]

Although incandescent with internal rage at what she regarded as a well-rehearsed conspiracy to destroy her authority, Margaret Thatcher counter-bluffed with surprising coolness. In the icy silence that followed the joint resignation threats, three thoughts went through her head: 'First, I was not prepared to be blackmailed into a policy which I felt was wrong. Second, I must keep them on board if I could, at least for the moment. Third, I would never, never allow this to happen again.'[14]

Concentrating on the second of these thoughts, the Prime Minister declined to set a date for ERM entry on the grounds that to do so would give a field day to currency speculators. She then fell back on the formula she had used before, promising to 'reflect further' on what she should say at Madrid. The meeting then ended abruptly with no further discussion or agreement. The shoot-out at the Downing Street Corral was over with no dead bodies or resignations. According to Margaret Thatcher, 'They left; Geoffrey looking insufferably smug'.[15] If that was a correct description of the Foreign Secretary's demeanour, he evidently had not considered that the Prime Minister might prefer to take her revenge as a dish best served cold.

Deep-frozen would have been a better description of Howe–Thatcher relations as they travelled on the same RAF VC-10 aircraft to Madrid. They did not speak in the VIP departure lounge. On the flight they were isolated from each other in two separate compartments. Whenever the buff curtain, which divided the two entourages, slid open due to the movement of the plane, a No. 10 staffer would get up and ostentatiously close it.

On arrival at Madrid, the impression that the Prime Minister and her Foreign Secretary were at daggers drawn intensified. Their non-speaking deteriorated into political apartheid. 'Charles and Bernard, come with me',[16] was Margaret Thatcher's command to her senior aides in the airport lounge.

As the trio swept off to their hotel, their unexpected departure greatly disconcerted the British Ambassador to Spain, Lord Nicholas Gordon Lennox, who had organised an open-air supper for his eminent visitors. He was dismayed to discover that the Prime Minister did not even wish to be in the same garden as Sir Geoffrey.

She absented herself from the Embassy's party, and remained closeted in her hotel suite with Bernard Ingham and Charles Powell as they worked on the draft of her speech. 'Don't show it to anyone',[17] she instructed.

The result of this edict was that when the Prime Minister rose to deliver her opening remarks at the Madrid summit, her Foreign Secretary did not have the slightest idea what she was going to say.[18]

To the surprise of Geoffrey Howe and to most participants at Madrid, Margaret Thatcher's speech was conciliatory in tone. Privately she remained 'opposed root and branch to the whole approach of the Jacques Delors Report' on EMU.[19] Publicly, this was not apparent. For she made disarming genuflections in his direction, praising the report for its staged approach towards EMU, and announcing that Britain was ready to make an early start on stage one.

On the ERM, she spelt out Britain's conditions for joining when the time was right. Although she gave no date and said it depended on success in the fight against inflation and progress towards implementing the single market, she gave a clear although disingenuous impression of her commitment by her words, 'I can reaffirm today the United Kingdom's intention to join the ERM'.[20]

This statement went down well at the summit, although in the absence of a date for joining it was nothing new as a statement of future British policy. Nevertheless, her fellow heads of government felt they could detect a more positive approach by Margaret Thatcher. This was largely based on mood music, for she seemed unusually calm and non-confrontational in the way she contributed to the discussions. Yet whatever the change of style, there was no movement of substance. She was buying time in order to fight another day both on the European stage and within her own cabinet.

Her speech may have lulled the participants at the summit into a false complacency that the British Prime Minister had been won over to a positive view of the ERM. But she did not fool all of the people all of the time. Listening to her final press conference at Madrid was a perceptive reporter from the *Daily Telegraph*, twenty-five-year-old Boris Johnson. He recalled:

> As she bustled her way through the door, she gave a loud grunt of contemptuous exasperation. She kept her head uncharacteristically down as she read out a prepared statement at high speed. I remember that she looked distinctly sexy, with a flush about her cheeks as though she was up to something rather naughty. I thought she didn't believe a word of what she was saying. My piece reflected this, saying that she had successfully fought a rearguard action against the ever-tightening ratchet of European federation.[21]

It had indeed been a rearguard action, camouflaged in enough dissimulation to outflank her rebellious Foreign Secretary and Chancellor. She met none of their demands in Madrid. They were fooled by her deceptively mild tone.

Having roared like lions as they threatened their joint resignations on the brink of the summit, they retreated like lambs immediately after it.

Nigel Lawson even had the effrontery to observe two days later in the margins of a cabinet meeting that 'Madrid had gone rather well'. Her amused private reaction was, 'He certainly had a nerve'.[22]

The Prime Minister was much more bitter about Geoffrey Howe's imitation of sweetness and light, but she kept her own counsel. At Madrid, he had enjoyed receiving the plaudits of European leaders for transforming Margaret Thatcher's attitude.

'Congratulations, Geoffrey,' said a delighted Jacques Delors 'on having won the intellectual argument within the British Government.'[23]

This Gallic bouquet was wide of the mark. The Foreign Secretary had not won his argument with the Prime Minister. Nor did he have the slightest inkling that she might be planning to remove him from the job he loved.

THE DISMISSAL OF GEOFFREY HOWE

Hell hath no fury like a Prime Minister who feels she has been blackmailed. This was the explanation for the cabinet reshuffle that Margaret Thatcher executed a month after the Madrid summit. It was a badly botched affair, strangely reminiscent of Harold Macmillan's 'Night of the Long Knives' in July 1962. Both episodes precipitated the departure of the Prime Minister within eighteen months of their attempts to reconstruct their respective administrations.

Margaret Thatcher's July 1989 reshuffle was an emotionally charged whirligig of exits, entrances and job changes. Although numerous and extensive, the thirteen place movements around the cabinet table were of secondary importance. The primary upheaval, round which everything else revolved, was the dismissal of Geoffrey Howe from the Foreign Office.

The Foreign Secretary saw the Prime Minister alone at No. 10 on the morning of Monday 24 July. To his astonishment, he was told that he was being moved. He could either be Leader of the House of Commons, or Home Secretary. Geoffrey Howe countered by saying that he would prefer to stay at the Foreign Office. 'That option is not open', was her reply.[24] He was shattered. 'The word "shock" cannot do justice to my feelings at the way in which this was sprung on me', was how he described his reaction.[25]

Howe's outrage was understandable, but his surprise seems synthetic. There had been press rumours about his demotion, which the Prime Minister had conspicuously failed to quash. He knew that he was at loggerheads with her over European policy. He was also aware that their personal relationship had deteriorated to the point of mutual animosity. The tipping point towards his dismissal had been her anger over his manipulation of Nigel Lawson into their pre-Madrid ambush on the ERM. She saw Howe as the prime mover in this plot to blackmail her. Now she was taking her revenge.

Although he knew the Prime Minister was furious with him for his attempt to pressurise her into setting a date for joining the ERM, Howe calculated that the storm had blown over and that he was secure in his job. This self-delusion was largely due to Margaret Thatcher's ability to play to the gallery at the Madrid summit. Despite her outward emollience, she was inwardly seething. She had made up her mind to get rid of her Foreign Secretary on the day they travelled to Spain together in such frigid separation. But for tactical reasons, she had stayed her hand for a month. Now she wrapped up his dismissal in a broader reshuffle, in order to make it look as though his move was part of a strategic plan to rejuvenate the entire cabinet.

The strategy failed because media and parliamentary attention focused almost entirely on the Howe drama. His first reply was to say that he could not give the Prime Minister an answer to either of her proposals until he had talked them over with his wife Elspeth. As Lady Howe had come to loathe the Prime Minister even more than her husband did, this was hardly a positive response. It also had the effect of delaying the progress of the reshuffle, a hiatus that gave rise to increasingly feverish media speculation.

Sir Geoffrey's initial decision, backed by his wife, was to turn down both the jobs he had been offered. He drafted a pained letter of resignation, which he showed to the Chief Whip, David Waddington, who was alarmed at the prospect of such a major loss to the cabinet.

In the next few hours Waddington brokered an arrangement that would make Howe Deputy Prime Minister as well as Leader of the House. But this all depended on how well the new Deputy could work with his old boss. The two of them had a far from encouraging meeting, at which Howe said that his confidence in their future relationship had been 'greatly damaged by today's events'.[26] Margaret Thatcher replied that 'The problem was mutual'. It was hardly a reassuring start. But since Sir Geoffrey could not bear, when push came to shove, to leave the government, he accepted the best of a bad deal.

If the Prime Minister's purpose in keeping him in her cabinet was to rock the boat as little as possible, she failed. This was because the Downing Street press machine set out to disparage the new Deputy Prime Minister. In briefings by Bernard Ingham, his post was called 'a courtesy title with no constitutional status'.[27] In retaliation, Howe leaked that he had been offered and rejected Douglas Hurd's job as Home Secretary.

The media had a field day of mockery at this reshuffle chaos, which had many dimensions of further unpleasantness. Under one tabloid headline, 'Howesey Housey',[28] it was reported that the Foreign Secretary had engaged in an unedifying bargaining session with the Prime Minister about which government residence he would be allowed to live in – Chevening or Dorney-wood. In fact, there was no bargaining. Geoffrey and Elspeth Howe were understandably upset at having to move from the first house to the second for reasons that were inexplicable except as a further act of personal humiliation.

The final picture that emerged was that of an unnecessarily brutal execution of a loyal colleague, who for over ten years had occupied two great offices of state with distinction. Many recognised, although she evidently did not, that the success of Thatcherite leadership owed a great deal to Howe's dogged attention to detail. Because of this perception, he swiftly became the beneficiary of a groundswell of sympathy in the House of Commons and in the country.

I well remember Sir Geoffrey's first appearance at the despatch box as Leader of the House on 27 July 1989. He rose to make a routine announcement about the next week's parliamentary business. Before he could open his mouth, a deep-throated rumble, burgeoning into a roar, of 'hear, hear' filled the chamber. On and on it rolled from all sides of the House, lasting for well over a minute. It was a patently sincere outpouring of goodwill coming from not only Howe's well-wishers but also from his critics, who ranged from Tory Eurosceptics to Labour left-wingers. It was a spontaneous display of affection, and the high point of the ex-Foreign Secretary's parliamentary popularity.

With the Prime Minister fidgeting awkwardly alongside him on the front bench, Geoffrey Howe was overcome with emotion. He had lost his old place at the pinnacle of the government, but his rough treatment won him a niche in the sentimental feelings of Westminster, which he had never occupied before.

Margaret Thatcher would have been wise to take note of this unexpected side effect of her reshuffle. Amidst the waves of warmth for him there was also a strong undertow of hostility towards her. But by this time she had lost her political antennae when it came to the subject of Sir Geoffrey. She continued with her attitude of unpleasantness and underestimation for her new Deputy Prime Minister. The consequences of this hostility were to prove fatal.

REFLECTION

The sacking of Sir Geoffrey Howe increased the flow of poison in the relationship between him and Margaret Thatcher. She could easily have applied balm to his injured feelings. The 'Howesey Housey' row was entirely avoidable. Chevening was just as appropriate an official residence for a Deputy Prime Minister as it was for a Foreign Secretary. As these arrangements were in the gift of Margaret Thatcher, she could perfectly well have allowed the Howes to remain living close to their constituency in the country house they had come to love. But for reasons of pure spite, she was determined to displace them. Was it her intense dislike of Elspeth Howe, or paranoia about 'holding court', or imagined 'leadership plotting' that motivated the Prime Minister to behave so unpleasantly? These pinpricks against Sir Geoffrey revealed a mean streak in Margaret Thatcher's personality that had not surfaced before.

Other slights were reported that confirmed the bitter atmospherics of the reshuffle. There was an unedifying squabble as to whether or not the new Deputy Prime Minister should sit at cabinet meetings on Margaret Thatcher's left as Willie Whitelaw had done. She gave way on this with bad grace. It was clear that her main reaction to having Howe as her Deputy was to downgrade his appointment as much as possible.

These petty manoeuvres against Geoffrey Howe rebounded against Margaret Thatcher. The rest of the reshuffle was largely ignored by the media. They were so busy chronicling the stories about the Deputy Prime Minister's houses, titles and status that they underplayed the new appointments except to keep pointing out the youth and inexperience of her surprising choice to be the new Foreign Secretary – John Major.

Although the dust settled on the reshuffle during the summer parliamentary recess, it left behind a feeling that the Prime Minister had treated Sir Geoffrey

Howe unfairly. It was widely believed that her personal dislike of him had been a more important factor in her motivation than their disagreements over Europe.

Because even well-informed members of Parliament were slow to grasp the constitutional importance of the movement towards a federal Europe that Jacques Delors was proposing and Geoffrey Howe was supporting, it was easy to downgrade the reasons for Margaret Thatcher's rejection of her Foreign Secretary to matters of personality. Those frictions were real, and at times rather nasty. Yet the fundamental explanation for the great Howe–Thatcher divide was that it was all to do with past history and future vision.

Margaret Thatcher had a profound sense of Britain's legal and constitutional history as a sovereign nation-state. She woke up rather slowly to an understanding that the foundations on which the rule of law and the parliamentary system she cherished were going to be irreversibly changed by the Delors vision for European economic, monetary and, ultimately, political union. She had an utterly different vision based on her patriotic nationalism. She was mortified that she was not supported by her Foreign Secretary.

If she turned against Howe too venomously, it was because she found herself unable to separate her personal and political feelings about the greatest issue Britain had faced since the Second World War. She was way out in front of public and parliamentary opinion on the European crisis that was looming. Both would catch up with her during the next two decades, but at the time she was unappreciated for being right. The prevailing view in the late summer of 1989 was that the Prime Minister had been getting her jaundiced view of both Howe and Europe out of proportion.

A few days after the House of Commons went into recess, a surprising number of Tory MPs descended on Canterbury cricket ground to watch Kent play the Australians. This quintessentially English event was the centrepiece of the annual festival known as Canterbury Week. In August 1989, the new cricket-loving Foreign Secretary, John Major, was a noted spectator, as were a less knowledgeable gathering of parliamentarians who came to drink the Pimm's as much as to watch the play.

As an East Kent MP, I moved around the hospitality tents, and recall being amazed by how many doubts, criticisms and questions were expressed by my off-duty colleagues about the Prime Minister. Many of them were clearly getting fed up with her; not just because she had bungled the Geoffrey Howe dismissal, but for deeper reasons, such as the growing unpopularity of the poll tax, the debacle of the European elections and, above all, the feeling that she would no longer listen to her supporters. 'Is she losing her grip?' asked one MP. 'Is she becoming a liability?' inquired another. Perhaps the most prophetic comment was: 'And if she were to lose her Chancellor after another bloody Cabinet row – we're sunk!'[29]

34

Exit the Chancellor, enter the stalking horse

TRYING TO STABILISE THE GOVERNMENT

Although she pretended to put on a confident face after her ill-received Howe reshuffle, Margaret Thatcher was shaken by the public and parliamentary reaction to it. One sign that she understood the need to stabilise her government came at the first meeting of the new cabinet on 27 July. She surprised her colleagues by announcing that she now had in place the ministerial team with which she would fight the next election. She emphasised that there would be no further cabinet changes for the remainder of the parliamentary term.

It was unprecedented for any Prime Minister to tie their hands in this way, almost three years before an election was due. Margaret Thatcher had never before shared her thinking on reshuffles, or lack of them, with her colleagues. The likely explanation was that she wanted to repair the damage to her negative image as a divisive leader by appearing to work for the long haul with a united team.

There were some signs that the Prime Minister was beginning to think about bringing on a potential successor during 1989, even though she believed she would have another four or five years in power. She was far from ready to make any such choice. But at least she had decided who would *not* succeed her. At the top of her 'He will never be Prime Minister' list were her two *bêtes noires*, Michael Heseltine and Geoffrey Howe. She also ruled out those who were the same political generation as herself, saying, 'I saw no reason to hand over to anyone of roughly my age while I was fit and active'.[1] This meant that she did not envisage the leadership going to Norman Tebbit or Nigel Lawson.

A further constraint on her selection process was that she did not like the idea of passing the torch to someone who in her early days at No. 10 would have been called a 'wet' and was later characterised as 'not one of us'. This made it hard for her to favour the chances of Kenneth Clarke, Chris Patten or Kenneth Baker. As she surveyed this field of runners, most of whom had been heavily handicapped under her own rules, a dark horse started to move up on the rails. He was John Major, whose competence as a whip and as a junior Social Security minister had caught her attention. So she promoted him into the cabinet with the low-profile but testing job of Chief Secretary to the Treasury, where he proved himself to be a capable guardian of public expenditure. Also, in his unassuming way he was attractive to women and skilful in the art of feminine flattery. These qualities did him no harm on his rise in the Prime Minister's estimation.

Her assessment of her new protégé was flawed in one important respect, because somehow she managed to convince herself that John Major was a staunch Eurosceptic and a right of centre Thatcherite in his economic outlook. In fact he was neither. But because he seemed to carry no baggage his ascent was unimpeded by her usual ideological questions.[2]

One of the reasons the Prime Minister assumed he was 'one of us' was that she liked the story of his background. He was far removed from the world of Tory privilege, since he had left school at fifteen, endured youthful poverty in Brixton, and come up the hard way. So he fitted her presentational bill when it came to grooming a candidate for stardom, even though she misunderstood where his political orientation lay. This was how John Major came to make the great leap forward from Chief Secretary to the Treasury to Foreign Secretary in the July 1989 reshuffle. His elevation astonished everyone, including himself, but it immediately established his credentials as a potential successor. Inevitably, one or two senior colleagues' noses were put out of joint, particularly those of Geoffrey Howe and Nigel Lawson, over such a dramatic promotion for the most junior member of the cabinet.

John Major's tenure at the Foreign Office was a brief and uncertain one. He tried to decline the job when it was first offered to him. He felt uneasy with the culture of the FCO, which had become a demoralised department thanks to the Prime Minister's style of running foreign policy from No. 10. But whatever *angst* the new Foreign Secretary felt over his appointment, it was short lived. For in another part of the government a storm was blowing up which would sweep John Major to a higher destiny more quickly that he could have possibly imagined.

The economy was at the centre of the storm. Nigel Lawson, lauded to the skies as a great Chancellor just eighteen months earlier, was now in the depths of unpopularity as he took the blame for the grim conditions he had helped to create. Britain had the worst balance of payments deficit in its history. Inflation was the highest of any industrial country at 7.6 per cent and rising. Interest rates were 14 per cent. The protests from mortgage holders and the business world were fierce. 'This Bankrupt Chancellor' was the headline on the front page of the *Daily Mail* on 10 October 1989, five days after he put interest rates up by a full point to 15 per cent.

Some newspaper commentators speculated that in the face of such bombardment, Nigel Lawson might be looking for an escape route. But although he was under pressure, he was too proud a politician to jump ship because the sea was rough. In fact, he managed to strengthen his position in mid-October with two good speeches. The first was a barnstorming romp to the Conservative Party conference, which brought him a standing ovation. The second was an acclaimed address to the Lord Mayor's annual banquet at the Mansion House. On both occasions he sounded like a Chancellor who knew how to weather the storm.

Yet, for all the outward confidence that Nigel Lawson managed to project to the world, inwardly he was seething over a long-nurtured grievance that was troubling him both emotionally and practically. This grievance was about Margaret Thatcher's special relationship with Alan Walters.

THE PROBLEM OF ALAN WALTERS

Although she was making more effort to get along with her Chancellor, Margaret Thatcher was not in harmony with him. 'Nigel and I no longer had that broad identity of views or mutual trust which a Chancellor and Prime Minister should' was how she put it.[3] She continued to blame him for stoking the rate of inflation. They were in profound disagreement over the ERM. These divisions were frustrating Lawson more than they apparently troubled his boss. She suspected him of looking for an excuse to leave the government. To her chagrin, he found one in a convenient but artificial row about Alan Walters.

Ever since Margaret Thatcher had insisted on bringing Alan Walters back into No. 10 as her part-time economic adviser, Nigel Lawson had been spoiling for a fight on this issue. Although the Prime Minister as First Lord of the

Treasury was more than entitled to take advice from any expert she wanted on the economy, Nigel Lawson was a proprietorial Chancellor and hated to have his stewardship of the economy second-guessed by prime ministerial advisers. This resentment went wider than Alan Walters. Lawson also look a hostile stance towards Brian Griffiths, the head of the No. 10 Policy Unit, whenever he passed comments about Treasury issues.

The Chancellor's hyper-sensitive skin received a new pinprick on 18 October when the *Financial Times* reported on an article by Alan Walters which disagreed with the view that Britain should join the ERM. However, on closer investigation it became clear that the offending article had never seen the light of day until the *FT*'s story. It had been written but not published by an obscure academic journal a year before Walters was appointed as the Prime Minister's economic adviser. Far from being an attack on Lawson's current policies, the article referred to a historical controversy about the ERM eight years earlier. It should have been treated as a small storm in an old tea-cup.

Nevertheless, Nigel Lawson took umbrage as the *Financial Times* contrived to report the retrospective dispute as if it were a newsworthy and current topic. The Chancellor became hot under the collar and wanted to have an immediate confrontation over the article.

Unable to see Margaret Thatcher because she was away in Malaysia at the Commonwealth Heads of Government Conference, Nigel Lawson summoned the Prime Minister's PPS, Mark Lennox-Boyd, to No. 11 and asked him to pass an urgent message to his boss, to the effect that Alan Walters' activities were becoming so damaging to the government that they could no longer be tolerated. Lennox-Boyd thought that Nigel Lawson was merely putting down a marker for the record. A copy of the offending Alan Walters article was faxed to Kuala Lumpur, where Margaret Thatcher took a nonchalant view of it on the grounds that it had been written some months before its author formally joined her staff. 'As the article was written well before Madrid,' she minuted, 'I don't see the difficulty. Moreover, advisers ADVISE, Ministers decide policy.'[4]

Smarting from this rebuff from the Prime Minister, Nigel Lawson had to endure another torment – mockery in the House of Commons. On 24 October, Labour's Shadow Chancellor, John Smith, made one of the wittiest attacking speeches ever heard in an economic debate. He had some easy Aunt Sallies for his knockabout. The dire economic statistics. Two Chancellors, one unelected, speaking for economic policy. The saga of the official residences, in which Lawson had been the loser. According to John Smith's burlesque version of events, Margaret Thatcher had taught her ministers this lesson by her reshuffle:

> If you lose your job you get another house, but if you keep your job, you lose your house. [Laughter.] If you are not careful, you might lose both. Whatever happens, Mr Bernard Ingham – that other unaccountable source of power in Britain – will be waiting to give a friendly benediction as one moves on.[5]

This ridicule was uncomfortably near the knuckle. Watching Nigel Lawson squirm on the front bench as the whole House rocked with laughter at these jibes, it became apparent that he was quite likely to heed John Smith's parting words of advice; that the time had come for him to tell the Prime Minister 'Either back me or sack me'.[6]

LAWSON SNAPS

Within forty-eight hours of being ridiculed in Parliament, Nigel Lawson decided he could stand it no longer. He followed John Smith's advice and issued his own ultimatum to the Prime Minister. It was, in effect, 'Sack Alan Walters or I resign'.[7]

Because of her absence from London at the Commonwealth Conference, Margaret Thatcher was not confronted with the Lawson problem in its full magnitude until the morning of 26 October. At 9.00 a.m. she met him to hear his ultimatum. She pretended that she could not take his threat to resign seriously, and believed she had persuaded him to think again.

In the overcrowded day that followed, she had to fit three further meetings with him around Prime Minister's Questions and a statement on the Commonwealth Heads of Government Meeting to Parliament. But in the end, faced with having to choose between her personal economic adviser and her Chancellor of the Exchequer, Margaret Thatcher made the extraordinary decision that the Chancellor would have to be the one to depart. As she put it to Nigel Lawson, 'If Alan were to go, that would destroy *my* authority'.[8] It was a ludicrous observation, because her authority as Prime Minister had little or nothing to do with Alan Walters.

To make the situation even more ludicrous, a few hours later Alan Walters concluded that his position also had become untenable. He also resigned. It was a disastrous débâcle.

The next day's newspaper headlines were the worst of her ten years as Prime Minister: 'Thatcher Day of Disaster' (*Daily Mail*); 'Thatcher in Crisis: Government Totters' (*Daily Mirror*); 'Government in Turmoil' (*Independent*); 'Crisis for Thatcher' (*Daily Telegraph*).

Inside Parliament there was incredulous bafflement at her man-management. One old hand who put his finger on the problem was Willie Whitelaw, who wrote in a private letter to Nigel Lawson: 'She could so easily have got rid of Walters, but increasingly I fear that she simply cannot bring herself to be on the losing side of any argument. That failing may ditch us all.'[9]

The Lawson resignation did great harm to Margaret Thatcher. Her stock plummeted further as a result of a television interview she gave to the usually friendly Brian Walden on Sunday 29 October. She began by taking the unconvincing line that she had fully 'backed and supported' the Chancellor whose position, she kept insisting, was 'unassailable'; a word she repeated seven times with theatrical emphasis. Even more unconvincingly, she claimed that she could not understand why Nigel Lawson was so concerned about Alan Walters, saying, 'It is just not possible that this small particular thing could result in this particular resignation'.[10]

But when Walden finally cornered her in his relentless cross-examination style, her bravado collapsed into ignominious mumblings and non-sequiturs. It was probably the worst interview she ever gave, as the transcript shows:

BW: Do you deny that Nigel would have stayed if you had sacked Professor Alan Walters?

PM: I don't know, I don't know.

BW: You never even thought to ask him that?

PM: I . . . that is not . . . I don't know. Nigel had determined that he was going to put in his resignation, I did everything possible to stop him.

BW: But . . .

PM: I was not successful. No, you are going on asking the same question.

BW: Of course, but that's a terrible admission, Prime Minister.

PM: I have nothing further . . . I don't know . . . of course I don't know . . . I am not going on with this.

BW: I suppose I must ask you once more, just once more, did . . . you say you don't know whether you could have kept him if Walters had gone . . . did he ask you to sack Walters?

PM: I'm not going to disclose the conversations which the two of us had together . . .[11]

These floundering exchanges left a bad impression. The general public, most of whom knew nothing about Professor Walters and his views, were mystified by what seemed to be a spat about personalities. In fact, the row was rooted in far deeper issues, such as the disagreement about the ERM and who had the ultimate authority for conducting Britain's economic policy. But neither the press nor most politicians understood this. As a result, Margaret Thatcher was pilloried for her capricious handling of personnel problems with her Chancellor.

One ominous sign of the damage done by the Lawson resignation was the warning given to the Prime Minister by the Chairman of the 1922 Committee, Cranley Onslow. She met him and other members of the executive just before the prorogation of Parliament at the beginning of November. They were underwhelmed by her explanation that her Chancellor had wanted to quit anyway and was just using Walters as a pretext. Instead, one member of the committee bluntly told her that more and more colleagues were getting fed up with what he called 'the revolving door of the Carry On Downing Street Show'. He added the rider, 'and if you don't get your act together they won't let you carry on much longer'.[12] Margaret Thatcher frowned but failed to acknowledge the warning. She was probably unfamiliar with 'Carry On' humour and made no response.

There were some signs that the 1922's danger signals were heeded. The Prime Minister made a flurry of appearances in the tea room, reassuring her back-benchers that the new trio at the top were working in step with each other and with her. This was true. John Major as Chancellor, Douglas Hurd as Foreign Secretary and David Waddington as the new Home Secretary were a far more cohesive team in the great offices of state than when the strong-willed Lawson and the resentful Howe had been at the top of the government. Their quarrels had left Margaret Thatcher a wounded Prime Minister. How wounded? It was a question about to be probed by the arrival of a stalking horse.

THE STALKING HORSE

The mood among Tory MPs was irritable rather than irascible as the new session of Parliament opened in November 1989. Many colleagues were critical of the Prime Minister, but few wanted to see her ousted from No. 10. In any case, there was not the faintest consensus about a candidate suitable to succeed her. The only conceivable but still covert contender was Michael Heseltine. Yet for all his assiduous courting in the *salon des refusés* he had too few disciples and too many detractors. Trapped in his own twilight zone of being unwilling to put up, yet unable to shut up, he continued to prowl around the camps of the discontented stirring up ill-will but declining to make his own challenge. He realised that the time was not ripe for him to wield the dagger. As his closest lieutenant, Keith Hampson MP, put it, 'Michael knew perfectly well that Margaret was falling apart and that all he had to do was to wait for his moment'.[13]

A challenger of the moment that November did however emerge in the quixotic form of Sir Anthony Meyer. He was a parliamentary oddball. From a background of inherited wealth, an Oppidan scholarship at Eton and a Baronetcy, he championed extreme liberalism by Tory Party standards. An early diplomatic career with long stints in Paris and in the European Department of the Foreign Office had made him the most ardently Europhile MP on either side of the House of Commons. Besides promoting a federal union with Europe, his other lost cause was to be the only Conservative Member to oppose the recapture of the Falklands.

Outwardly fey, shy and gentle, he had an inner core of steel. This mixture of qualities, plus some heavy prompting from Ian Gilmour and other friends of Heseltine, led Meyer to put his hat into the ring as a stalking-horse candidate for the leadership election that could be called at the start of any new session of Parliament.

Margaret Thatcher had no time for Sir Anthony Meyer. When Ian Gilmour, at an early stage of the contest, coined the phrase 'the Meyerites', the Prime Minister's private reaction was: 'Meyerites! They're just Adullamites!' Baffled by this label, Ian Gow sought further and better particulars, only to be told by her, 'Cave dwellers with nowhere else to go – look it up in the Old Testament'. Biblical research produced the verse, 'All those who were distressed or discontented gathered in the cave of Adullam'. The preacher's daughter had not forgotten her scripture.[14]

Although Meyer was an absurd leadership candidate, quickly dubbed 'the stalking donkey' by many of his colleagues, his campaign was nevertheless met with serious tactics by Margaret Thatcher. She put in place an election team, which ironically was far more energetic and better organised than the team with which she defended herself against Michael Heseltine's much more serious challenge a year later. Her core supporters included George Younger as campaign manager, Kenneth Baker as cheer-leader in chief, Ian Gow, Tristan Garel Jones, Richard Ryder, Bill Shelton – her initial campaign chief in 1975 – and Mark Lennox-Boyd, her PPS.

Perhaps the most formidable operator in this team was Tristan Garel-Jones, the Deputy Chief Whip. He took leave of absence from this official post in the government in order to devote his full time to securing the re-election of the Prime Minister by her own party. The task proved more difficult than expected. 'We really had to work hard to get a good result for her', said Garel-Jones. 'It wasn't easy. At the end of the day, I was left with deep feelings of disquiet.'[15]

These anxious feelings were barely discernible to the public. On the face of it, the result looked good for Margaret Thatcher. A vote of 314 to thirty-three was by normal standards a convincing victory. But a closer examination of the figures showed that in addition to the thirty-three votes cast for Sir Anthony Meyer, another twenty-four Tory MPs had spoiled their ballot papers and three more had abstained. This meant that sixty members of her party were now opposed to the Prime Minister.

It also emerged from the sophisticated canvassing operations masterminded by Tristan Garel-Jones that a further forty-two MPs were so critical of Margaret Thatcher that they had to be 'worked on' by her campaign team before they reluctantly agreed to cast their votes in her favour. Some of these dissidents allowed themselves to be arm-twisted into the Prime Minister's camp only after making it clear that they would not support her in a subsequent election unless she changed her ways or her policies.

The most insistent demand from these invisible but audible opponents of Margaret Thatcher's leadership was that the poll tax should be scrapped. Others wanted her to soft-pedal her hostility to the European Community. Among lesser complaints, the most frequent was that she had become too aloof and had stopped listening to her own MPs.

These grievances had such a bitter edge to them that Tristan Garel-Jones decided he should pass them right to the top. With the help of Bernard Ingham, he saw the Prime Minister alone on a Sunday evening some two weeks after her apparently decisive defeat of Meyer.

'I know I'm only the Deputy Chief Whip', began Garel-Jones, 'but I've got to warn you that there are 102 of our colleagues lurking in the bushes and they're going to kill you.'[16]

After such a dramatic opening, one might have thought that the Prime Minister would wish to listen carefully. But when Garel-Jones explained the high level of discontent over the poll tax, Margaret Thatcher responded with a lecture demonstrating that she had the right policy and would not change it. Ditto on Europe. 'But all you've got to do is to pretend you like one or two people in the EEC', protested Garel-Jones. 'Can't you just dissemble a little?'

'Certainly not!' retorted the Prime Minister, who embarked on a lengthy diatribe against Delors, Kohl, Mitterrand and other European leaders. It was too much for the Spanish-born Garel-Jones. Realising he was wasting his time in a dialogue of the deaf, he made his excuses and cut short the meeting. But as he departed, he paused to repeat his warning with a theatricality worthy of Sir Laurence Olivier. 'Don't forget that a year from now, those 100 and many more assassins will rise up from the bushes', declared Tristan the prophet. To emphasise his point, he acted out the gesture of a killer flourishing his dagger and plunging it into a dying corpse. 'And they will murder you, even while you are still serving as Prime Minister.'[17]

After such a histrionic exit, Margaret Thatcher could hardly complain that she had not been warned. But, like Caesar on the Ides of March, she took no heed of the soothsayer. She felt she should devote her attention to more important matters.

GREATER EVENTS

While plotters squabbled at Westminster, great events were taking place on the world stage. In November 1989, the Berlin Wall came down, swiftly followed by the collapse of communism in Eastern Europe. These developments were both a vindication and a challenge for Margaret Thatcher.

Alone among European leaders, she had held the view since 1982 that the Iron Curtain might be cracking and that freedom for the oppressed peoples of the Warsaw Pact countries could be just around the corner of twentieth-century history. She had sensed this from her dialogues with Mikhail Gorbachev, from her visits to Hungary and Poland, and from her many private briefings from dissidents, intelligence experts and academics. In her Bruges speech she had spoken of her hope that Warsaw, Prague and Budapest would return to their roots as great European cities. Although this vision was coming to pass, it was not immediately happening in the form that Margaret Thatcher had hoped for, namely the enlargement of the European Community by the looser and wider participation of more independent nation-states.

Instead, the short-term effects of the fall of communism and the reunification of Germany brought about demands for the European Community to bind itself together in both monetary and political union. This surge in the momentum for a full-blown federalist Europe was anathema to the British Prime Minister.

She said as much at the Dublin summit in April 1990, as she highlighted the consequences of political union to the national parliaments, monarchies, heads of state and electoral systems of the member states. This ten-minute *tour d'horizon* of the problems which she described as 'a tongue in cheek' speech had the effect of sowing seeds of confusion, since it immediately became clear that there was little or no agreement at the summit about what exactly was meant by 'political union'.[18]

Margaret Thatcher also made an ill-judged attempt to block German reunification. Her obstructionism was a hopelessly lost cause. The Berlin Wall had come down amidst scenes of exultant rejoicing in the East. Chancellor Helmut Kohl's drive for reunification was enthusiastically supported by Washington and not objected to by Moscow. Margaret Thatcher's only hope of stopping Kohl was to win President Mitterand over to her corner. She lobbied the French President at a meeting in Strasbourg in December 1989, pulling maps of Germany's pre- and post-war borders out of her handbag. Pointing to Silesia, East Prussia and Pomerania, she told Mitterand: 'They'll take all of that and Czechoslovakia too!'[19]

However much he may privately have shared such fears, Mitterand was not about to break the Franco-German axis within the EU by opposing reunification. So Margaret Thatcher was left out on her own anti-German limb. She remained there in impotent isolation, often expressing her views in a style and language that gave the impression that she had become an anachronistic bigot.

In the months after the destruction of the Berlin Wall, Margaret Thatcher became obsessed with a fear of Germany, which shocked some of those who heard her express it. She was careful to let out her feelings only in private settings and conversations. But there were so many of them that the news travelled quickly. One early indication of her anti-German views came at a private lunch at the Centre for Policy Studies in December 1989. She shocked several of those present, particularly one of her informal foreign-policy advisers on Eastern Europe, George Urban, when she said to him.

> You know, George, there are things that your generation and mine ought never to forget. We've been through the war and we know perfectly well what the Germans are like, and what dictators can do, and how national character doesn't basically change.[20]

In the same vein, she clashed with the Centre for Policy Studies' Director Hugh Thomas, rebuking him for saying that German reunification marked the defeat of communism. 'Don't you realise what's happening? I've read my history, but you don't seem to understand.'[21]

Even within her own cabinet, the Prime Minister was isolated. She held a seminar at Chequers in March 1990 at which she sought to persuade the assembled company of ministers, foreign-policy specialists and academics that German reunification presented a danger to British interests and to long-term stability in Europe. Virtually everyone disagreed with her. 'Very well, very well, I am outnumbered round this table', she eventually conceded. 'I promise you that I will be sweet to the Germans, sweet to Helmut when he comes next week, but I shall not be defeated. I shall be sweet to him, but I will uphold my principles.'[22]

> It seemed as though Margaret Thatcher's principles were locked in the time warp of the Second World War. In a note of the Chequers seminar, Charles Powell solemnly recorded, surely echoing his mistress's voice: 'Some even less flattering attributes were also mentioned as an abiding part of the German character: in alphabetical order, angst,

aggressiveness, assertiveness, bullying, egotism, inferiority complex, sentimentality.' When this memorandum was embarrassingly released, *Private Eye* parodied it with its own memo along the lines of 'Germans: wear moustaches, eat sausages, drink beer in cellars, etc. etc.'[23]

The Prime Minister's prejudices were not all that far removed from the parody. She gave no credence to the view that the new generation of post-war Germany might be different from their forebears. Her line was that the national character of Germany had not changed, and that sooner or later the re-united country would exert its power, although by economic means not territorial aggression. 'Germany is thus by its very nature a destabilising rather than a stabilising force in Europe' was her judgement.[24]

The only senior colleague who shared her attitudes was her Secretary of State for Trade and Industry, Nicholas Ridley. He gave a recklessly anti-German interview to the editor of *The Spectator*, Dominic Lawson, in July 1990. In its sensational article, Ridley was recorded as saying that European Monetary Union was, 'a German racket to take over the whole of Europe . . . I'm not against giving up sovereignty in principle, but not to this lot. You might just as well give it to Adolf Hitler, frankly.'

To stir up even more mischief, the magazine's front cover portrayed Nicholas Ridley drawing a Hitler moustache on a likeness of Chancellor Helmut Kohl. In his article, Dominic Lawson opined that, 'Mr Ridley's confidence in expressing his views . . . must owe a little something to the knowledge that they are not significantly different from those of the Prime Minister'.[25] It was a fair comment. As I knew from having lunched with Nicholas Ridley a week before *The Spectator* article, he was to a large extent repeating the anti-German vitriol which he had privately heard straight from His Mistress's Voice.

Margaret Thatcher tried hard to save Nicholas's Ridley's skin as the storm raged over his interview. Her initial view was that his gaffe was not a resigning issue. 'It was an excess of honesty that ultimately brought him down', she said.[26]

The reason why he had to go was that the Chairman and Executive Committee of the 1922 Committee insisted on it. Ridley had been the high priest of political incorrectness for many an entertaining year, but the PC vultures got him in the end. He was the last keeper of the Thatcherite flame left in the cabinet, so his departure left her even more exposed.

A sadder loss came on 30 July, when Ian Gow was assassinated by an IRA bomb placed under his car in the garage of his Eastbourne home. Margaret Thatcher immediately drove down from No. 10. She spent several hours comforting Ian's widow, Jane, attending an evening mass at the family church – St Luke's, Stone Cross. Of all the terrorist killings during her years as Prime Minister, the death of Ian Gow was probably the bereavement that touched her most deeply. She had built an enduring friendship with him in the tough and early years when he was her first PPS.

He survived many difficult shared experiences, including his principled resignation over the Anglo-Irish agreement. The key to their political intimacy lay in the chemistry between their two personalities.

There has never been, and perhaps never will be, such a successful Prime Minister–PPS relationship as the one that flourished between Ian Gow and Margaret Thatcher in her first term. It was founded on two pillars: his absolute loyalty to her, and her willingness to respond to his faithful reporting on the moods and murmurings of the Conservative Party in Parliament. Only when she had moved him higher to temporary ministerial office did she realise how much she missed him. Yet he remained her confidant. Although he failed to build bridges between her and his other great friend, Geoffrey Howe, Ian Gow always stayed unsycophantically yet reverentially close to 'The Lady', as he called her. His last great service was to minimise the effect of the 1989 stalking-horse challenge. If murder had not prevented him from repeating his pivotal role a year later, it is unlikely that the Prime Minister would have narrowly lost the first round of the 1990 contest.

'Such a stalwart . . . so steadfast in his faith . . . so courageous in his convictions' were three of the phrases Margaret Thatcher used when talking to me about Ian Gow after his funeral in Eastbourne on 8 August.[27] Ian would have reciprocated the compliments. He would also have seen, more clearly than she could see, that the months ahead were going to be hard pounding for a Prime Minister who, for one reason or another, had lost virtually all her truest bondsmen.

REFLECTION

'To lose one parent, Mr Worthing, may be regarded as misfortune; to lose both looks like carelessness.' Lady Bracknell's words in Oscar Wilde's *The Importance of Being Ernest* can be adjusted to apply, all too appropriately, to Margaret Thatcher's losses of her senior cabinet colleagues in the 1989–1990 period. It may even be argued that the Prime Minister herself bore a passing resemblance to Lady Bracknell because of her domineering wilfulness, her refusal to listen and the symbolic wielding of her handbag to silence dissent.

Seen purely in terms of man-management, there is little doubt that the departures from their posts of the Foreign Secretary and the Chancellor of the Exchequer were blows to the government that could easily have been avoided. Less gratuitous rudeness; more collegiate teamwork; an observance of convention that the views of the holders of the great offices of state have primacy over the opinions of Downing Street advisers – such changes in Margaret Thatcher's style of governance could have avoided the debacle at the top of her cabinet.

But it was not that simple for two important reasons. First, the faults of personality were far from one-sided among the dysfunctional trio who headed the British government in this period. Second, the splits between them were not just about man-management. They were also about important issues of foreign and economic policy where divisions between the principal office holders ran deep. With the wisdom of hindsight and history, it is now possible to offer an answer to the question: Who was right?

What Shakespeare called 'the insolence of office'[28] grows with the years spent in occupancy of great positions. At the height of the personality clashes described in the last three chapters, Margaret Thatcher had been Prime Minister for a full decade. Nigel Lawson was the second longest serving Chancellor of the twentieth century. His six years and four months in the job were exceeded only by the seven years and one month of David Lloyd George. Geoffrey Howe had been Foreign Secretary for six years, preceded by four years as Chancellor. All three had grown not only in experience, but also in over-confident certainty that their views were right.

Geoffrey Howe and Nigel Lawson were both resentful of the Prime Minister's challenges to the received wisdom of their departments. They both thought that they were in charge of foreign and economic policy. They could be secretive, sneaky and devious in their public and private efforts to outmanoeuvre the Prime Minister in order to get their own way. Un-collegiate behaviour was by no means a one-way street among the top three figures.

Geoffrey Howe's enthusiasm for closer monetary and political union with Europe was the fault-line in his relationship with Margaret Thatcher. But it has since emerged that she was on the right side of that line, and that he was spectacularly wrong. Who today would defend Howe's championship of EMU during the 1980s, now we can so clearly see the disaster of the Eurozone and the single currency of the present day?

Similarly with Nigel Lawson, most economists would now say that his enthusiasm for Britain joining the ERM was a strategic mistake. So were his policies of shadowing the Deutschmark, and of sowing the seeds of a recklessly inflationary boom in his 1988 Budget. Again, as we look back with the perspective of history, it appears that it was the Prime Minister, not the Chancellor, who made the better judgements.

Margaret Thatcher was not always right She could be petty (as she was over the official residences); vindictive (in authorising Bernard Ingham to brief against the authority of the Deputy Prime Minister); and foolishly stubborn (in fighting to keep Alan Walters). Yet these were unhappy sideshows. On the important policy questions that separated the Prime Minister from her Foreign Secretary and her Chancellor, Margaret Thatcher has largely been vindicated by subsequent events. Whatever the errors of her tactics, and the excesses of her zeal and her language, Margaret Thatcher was right on the great issue of Britain's involvement in European Monetary and Political Union. It is the paradox of history that because she was right, she fell.

35

Countdown to the coup

THE INVASION OF KUWAIT

Margaret Thatcher's last months as Prime Minister were dominated by the two issues that brought her down: the poll tax and Europe. They were compounded by her inability to hold on to her support base within the Conservative parliamentary party. Yet, although she handled her domestic problems with a singular lack of skill and subtlety, she remained an influential figure on the world stage, particularly when shaping the West's response to the invasion of Kuwait.

On 2 August 1990, the day when Saddam Hussein invaded Kuwait and declared it to be Iraqi territory, Margaret Thatcher was at the Aspen Institute in Colorado, preparing to address its fortieth anniversary conference, which was to be opened by President George H.W. Bush. The coincidence of the two leaders being together had the effect of strengthening the Western response. The President's first reaction to the crisis was that Arab diplomacy should be given a chance to bring about the withdrawal of Iraqi forces and the restoration of the lawful government of Kuwait.

The Prime Minister was underwhelmed by this approach. During the next few weeks of the crisis she was the voice of the hawkish tendency within the Western alliance. Her most famous advice to the US President, 'Well, all right, George, but this is no time to go wobbly',[1] was given in the context of an Anglo-American disagreement about whether or not to go after two Iraqi tankers which were violating the rules of the immediate Western blockade of the Gulf. On that occasion George H.W. Bush's instinct to prefer diplomacy to naval intervention was the course of action that prevailed. But the President took the Prime Minister's phrase to heart, repeating it like a mantra almost daily to his staff, as if to prove that he would be resolute in leading the US response to the invasion. In this way the spirit of the Iron Lady hovered over the White House like a guardian angel warning against wobbliness in the build-up to the war.

Five days after the opening of the Aspen conference, Margaret Thatcher cut short a planned family holiday in Colorado in order to go to Washington for further talks on the Iraq crisis at the White House. It had been widely speculated that her influence with the new administration was waning because she did not see eye to eye with President Bush on German reunification. Although this disagreement was real, it did not prevent Margaret Thatcher from moving into her familiar role of presidential confidante on planning the international response to the invasion of Kuwait during her visit to Washington on 6 August. As she recalled: 'For all the friendship and co-operation I had had from President Reagan, I was never taken into the Americans' confidence more than I was during the two hours or so I spent that afternoon at the White House.'[2]

The Oval Office meeting began a highly restricted session attended by the President, the Prime Minister and their key aides, Brent Scowcroft, US National Security Adviser, and Charles Powell. Margaret Thatcher's main concern was how to protect Saudi Arabia. With Iraqi tanks moving up to the Saudi border, she thought the main danger was that the oil-rich kingdom would be invaded before its rulers formally asked the West for help. Fortunately, King Fahd did make the request quickly and within twenty-four hours the 82nd Airborne Division and forty-eight USAF F-15 fighters had arrived in the Eastern Province of Saudi Arabia.

Margaret Thatcher was the first to see that limited deterrence might not be enough. She was as clear in her assessment of Saddam Hussein as she had been in her view of General Galtieri. She believed that Iraqi troops would never leave Kuwait until they were thrown out and she thought the West must remain in a state of maximum preparedness to prevent Saddam from extending his invasion into Saudi Arabia. As she put it in a minute to her Defence Secretary, Tom King, on 12 April: 'We thought that Iraq would not move into Kuwait, although their forces were massing on the border. Let us not make the same mistake again. They may move into Saudi Arabia. We must be ready.'[3]

She was as good as her written word. During August, Britain dispatched one squadron of Tornado and one squadron of Jaguar combat aircraft to the region, supported by AWACs and tanker planes. The Prime Minister also authorised the despatch of the 7th Armoured Brigade, a self-supporting force of 7,500 men, including 120 tanks, a regiment of Field Artillery, a battalion of armoured infantry and anti-tank helicopters. 'My heavens, a marvellous commitment, this is really something',[4] said President Bush when she told him of Britain's decision, which was supported by a Commons vote of 437 to thirty-five.[5]

Although most of her moves were made within the secret confines of diplomatic contacts and military preparations, Margaret Thatcher's early contributions to the first Gulf War against Saddam Hussein were of pivotal importance. Fortified by her experiences during the Falklands conflict, she was at the top of her game in terms of thinking several moves ahead. Three of her initiatives deserve particular mention.

First, she insisted on the appointment of General Sir Peter de la Billière to be the commander of UK forces in the Gulf. She had known him since they struck up a good rapport in the aftermath of the siege of the Iranian Embassy in 1980, when he had been in command of the SAS. She admired both his leadership and his linguistic skills in Arabic. He was not the choice of the Ministry of Defence to be commander in the Gulf, partly because he was regarded as something of a maverick, and partly because he was one week away from retirement. But Margaret Thatcher beat off these objections, saying that she needed 'a fighting General', and that if Sir Peter was not appointed, she would make him her personal adviser on military affairs at No. 10. This threat caused the Ministry of Defence to beat a retreat. General Peter de la Billière was quickly appointed Commander of UK forces in the Gulf.[6]

Second, the Prime Minister conducted a vigorous diplomatic battle to achieve unity among Arab governments and rulers, many of whom she had come to know well. King Hussein of Jordan, who surprised everyone by supporting the Iraqi invasion, was given a right royal handbagging when he came to lunch with the Prime Minister on 31 August. It appeared to weaken his already faltering backing for Saddam Hussein.[7]

Across the Middle East, Margaret Thatcher was credited for the speed and strength of the West's response to the invasion of Kuwait. Her Defence Secretary, Tom King, made an early visit to the region as the military build up got under way. 'The Gulf rulers were all certain that it was because she persuaded President

Bush at Aspen to move immediately that Saddam did not move on into Saudi Arabia',[8] he recalled.

The same view was held by the Saudi monarch, King Fahd, who was frequently telephoned by Margaret Thatcher with advice and promises of support. A year after the conflict, I had an audience with the king in Riyadh, who said, 'Your Prime Minister was terrific – she strengthened me, she strengthened President Bush and she helped to unite the whole coalition against Saddam'.[9]

In the early stages of these preparatory moves I had a conversation about the Kuwait crisis with Margaret Thatcher after Ian Gow's funeral on 8 August. I found her resolve and commitment to the inevitable war with Saddam to be positively Churchillian. At a time when her Foreign Secretary, Douglas Hurd, was holding the optimistic view that sanctions and military pressures would cause the Iraqis to withdraw from Kuwait, the Prime Minister's reaction was a beacon of clarity. 'We will have to fight Saddam, you mark my words', she said.[10]

Convinced of this outcome of events, she devoted a huge amount of time and effort in her last four months of power to preparing Britain and its coalition partners for the conflict. 'I found myself reliving in an only slightly different form my experiences of the build-up to the battle for the Falklands', she recalled.[11] With a small group of ministers and service chiefs, she made almost daily decisions on selecting military targets, wording UN resolutions and questioning the military about the quality of their equipment. Her grilling of the directors of Vickers about the reliability of the Challenger tank became a legend in company folklore.

One of her last major decisions as Prime Minister was to double the British commitment to the Gulf War preparations to 30,000 men, an upgrade from a brigade to a division. It was ratified by the cabinet at their historic meeting on 22 November, the day when she announced her resignation as Prime Minister.

Such was the febrile state of parliamentary opinion on domestic issues in the autumn of 1990 that the Prime Minister's preparations for the defeat of Saddam Hussein were seen as a sideshow. But the fact that Britain, the United States and their coalition partners were so ready and so determined to restore the lawful government of Kuwait deserves to be recorded in history as another of Margaret Thatcher's finest hours, even though she was forced out of office five months before the eventual victory in the Gulf War.

THE POISON OF THE POLL TAX

The year 1990 was when the poll tax poisoned the relationship between Margaret Thatcher and her backbenchers. The month of March was the turning point. The rot started with a disastrous by-election in Mid Staffordshire on 22 March. When Conservative MPs saw a Tory majority of 14,654 converted into a Labour gain by 9,449, many of them were aghast; not only about their own electoral prospects, but even more about the root cause of the 21 per cent swing against the government – which they identified as the growing unpopularity of the new tax.[12]

On 31 March, the day before the introduction of the Community Charge in England and Wales, a demonstration at Trafalgar Square erupted into serious rioting, with 341 arrests and 331 police officers, plus eighty-six members of the public injured.[13] Although Margaret Thatcher rightly blamed the violence on left-wing militants, there was almost as much non-violent anger in the Tory shires when the first poll tax bills arrived. MPs' post-bags were full of furious letters demanding a U-turn.

Margaret Thatcher had executed many a discreet reversal of policy during her eleven years as Prime Minister, but this was a U-turn too far. The problem was that she had gone out on such a limb with her passionate advocacy for her flagship tax. This zeal was to prove her undoing. Unable to back down, she tried to alleviate the effects of the tax with a series of complicated emasculations. They included transitional relief measures, capping proposals, and a root and branch review carried out by the new Secretary of State for the Environment, Chris Patten. However, the most important of the changes required legislation, and it looked as though the mood on the back benches was so anti-poll tax that no measure except dropping the tax would pass through the House. It was stand-off time between the Prime Minister and her party in Parliament.

Meanwhile the political situation in the country continued to deteriorate. Opinion polls in April showed that Labour was enjoying a 24.5 per cent lead over the Conservatives. Margaret Thatcher's personal ratings plummeted to 23 per cent, even worse than her low point in 1981, when she had been deemed to be the most unpopular prime minister ever.[14]

On 4 May 1990 there were English local government elections that confirmed to the Prime Minister's critics that her unpopularity was increasing. The Tories lost control of another twelve councils and could only hold on to 32 per cent of the overall vote. However, there were some pleasant surprises amidst the general disaster. A handful of councils, which had been pursuing a strategy of Thatcherite expenditure cuts, demonstrated that their good housekeeping could result in low Community Charge figures and electoral popularity. These local authorities, which included Wandsworth, Westminster, Hastings, Thanet, Trafford and Southend, held on to their Conservative majorities. Margaret Thatcher seized on these scraps of good electoral news as evidence that 'the Community Charge is beginning to work. It will increasingly bring the profligate and inefficient to book'.[15]

Although she may well have been right about this, a growing number of Tory MPs were in no mood to give their leader time to work out solutions to the poll tax problems. An alarmist atmosphere began to take root at meetings of the 1922 Committee and other party committees. Late at night around the bars on the House of Commons terrace, a spirit of *sauve qui peut* emerged among the defeatist tendency of colleagues who had convinced themselves that they would lose their seats in two years time. A whispering campaign got under way with the message that both the poll tax and the Prime Minister should go.

This was by no means a one-way street. In the country, there was evidence to suggest that the tide was turning in Margaret Thatcher's direction. Opinion polls indicated that Labour's lead had been halved, and that the Prime Minister was well ahead of the opposition leader, Neil Kinnock, on the question of 'Who would you trust to run the country?' There was also a solid hard core of government loyalists at Westminster who grew increasingly angry at the whisperers and the trouble-stirrers associated with Michael Heseltine.

Amidst the growing tension, the loyalists were fond of quoting two lines from a previous era of Tory infighting: 'Steady the Buffs' and 'Pro bono publico, no bloody panico'. But in the volatile mood among at least a third of Conservative MPs in the summer of 1990, there was too little steadiness and too much 'panico'.*

---

* The first of these lines was the battle cry of the East Kent Regiment. The second came from Rear Admiral Sir Morgan Morgan-Giles, MP for Winchester, addressing the 1922 Committee in 1975.

The government did have one stroke of luck in the middle of the poll tax crisis. On the night of 13 June, the Prime Minister was working her way through her pile of red boxes when she came across a note from her private secretary, reporting on a telephone call received earlier in the evening from government lawyers. They advised, on the basis of a recent court judgment, that many local authorities could have their spending capped under the existing legislation, if the government set an early figure for what it deemed to be 'excessive' spending.[16]

Margaret Thatcher went into overdrive once this legal view was established as watertight. A cabinet committee decided to cap local authorities if their rate of spending resulted in a Community Charge above £379. This was an expensive solution requiring extra public expenditure of £3 billion. Yet it was a workable outcome, which would probably have allowed the new Community Charge to bed down and become established.[17] But the 'panico' faction among the fractious Tory back-benchers was in no mood to listen to compromise solutions. They wanted the poll tax scrapped – period. So the summer of discontent rumbled on, and Margaret Thatcher remained vulnerable.

HER LAST ROW ON EUROPE

Before Margaret Thatcher's last great row with Europe she made an important concession. She agreed to join the ERM. Her persuader in chief for this *volte-face* was John Major, who had become convinced of the case for entry by his Treasury officials and by the Bank of England. Coaxing the Prime Minister towards the view that the time was right was a difficult and sensitive enterprise. Douglas Hurd was also a strong advocate of it. As she listened to her two most senior ministers, Margaret Thatcher must have had at the back of her mind the realisation that she could not possibly afford to lose another Chancellor or another Foreign Secretary. Even though Major and Hurd were too gentlemanly to play this card, she was aware that the ace of trumps was up their sleeve. So she began to move.

According to her memoirs, her movement was reluctant. But this was revisionism. Her Chancellor John Major recalled:

> It is a myth to say that she was un-persuaded. She had come to realise that there was no other way of getting inflation down that was likely to be successful. When we were

approaching the decision to go in she actually brought forward the announcement by one week. She also advocated a higher and therefore more punitive sterling–Deutschmark exchange rate because she wanted to bear down on inflation even harder. These were not the actions of a prime minister being bullied into joining the ERM. The fact of the matter is that she was enthusiastic and committed on the day we joined. She changed her mind afterwards.[18]

The only obstacle to Margaret Thatcher's conversion to joining the ERM was her insistence that the announcement of entry should be accompanied by the announcement of an interest-rate cut. Although both the Treasury and the Bank of England opposed this linkage on economic grounds, the Prime Minister's view prevailed. She used the one point reduction in interest rates as her political fig leaf. When she made the announcement outside No. 10 with her Chancellor standing silently beside her, Margaret Thatcher made it sound as though the interest-rate cut and the ERM entry were two sides of the same coin, as she claimed, 'The fact that our policies are working and are seen to be working have made both these decisions possible'.[19]

The instant reaction by politicians of all parties and by the media bordered on the ecstatic. Neil Kinnock welcomed the ERM decision as 'momentous'. Many newspaper commentators used similar adjectives. The CBI and the TUC applauded. The stock market soared. But there were a few dissenting voices. William Keegan, Economics Editor of the *Observer*, predicted trouble because Britain had entered at too high a rate (DM2.95).[20] John Major's Parliamentary Private Secretary Tony Favell MP resigned in protest.[21] Teddy Taylor and other leaders of the Conservative European Reform Group demanded to know what our exit strategy was if ERM pressures became intolerable.

Margaret Thatcher listened with some sympathy to these Eurosceptic concerns, saying privately that we could easily realign. She would not favour using either significant reserves or higher interest rates to defend the exchange rate. Her off the record comments were a revealing indication of her lack of commitment to the policy she had announced a few days earlier. But she justified the decision to enter the ERM on the curious grounds that it would make it easier for her to continue to block moves toward European Monetary Union (EMU).

This last view was soon shown to be flawed. It was exposed by what became known as the 'Italian ambush' at a meeting of the European Council in Rome on 28 October. At this summit, contrary to all prior expectations and assurances, the Italians brought forward a firm timetable for implementing EMU. They suddenly proposed that the Delors Plan for stage two of monetary union should start on 1 January 1994, and that the single currency should begin in 2000. This zeal for announcing a fast track towards a monetary and political union that had not been agreed became infectious.

The leaders of eleven member states, headed by Chancellor Kohl and President Mitterrand, were all ready to sign up to the Italian timetable on the spot. Britain was isolated. The Prime Minister was shocked to be in this position, but had no qualms about standing alone. Asked what she felt about being the sole objector among twelve member states to the plan, her reply was: 'Sorry for the other eleven!'[22]

The way she said 'No' added insult to injury. At her press conference in Rome, she let fly. She attacked the Italians for managing the summit incompetently, declaring it to be 'a mess'.[23] She taunted the Commission for proposing firm timetables for implementing schemes for monetary and political union, but without receiving any agreement on the substance of these schemes. 'People who get on a train like that deserve to be taken for a ride', she declared, adding that the train appeared to be heading for 'cloud cuckoo land'.

These robustly expressed criticisms were right. The Italian ambush had been chaotic and procedurally absurd. The cart of Euro-dreams had been put before the horse of substantive negotiations on EMU, and before a number of far more pressing issues such as the GATT* round of negotiations and the crisis in the Gulf. Even the pro-European Foreign Secretary Douglas Hurd was shocked by the management of the summit and by the muddle of its declaratory outcome.

By the time the Prime Minister made a statement on the European Council to the House of Commons twenty-four hours after her return to London, she was riding on a high horse of righteous indignation. She was not merely smarting from the Italian ambush. She had decided in her mind that the outcome of the meeting marked what she called the beginning of 'the ultimate battle for the future of the Community'.[24] It was a battle she was determined not to lose.

---

* GATT: General Agreement on Tariffs and Trade, forerunner of the World Trade Organization (WTO).

Parliamentary statements on the outcome of European Council meetings are notorious for the tedium of their language and detail. Not this one. In my seventeen years as an MP I had never seen the House more electrified, except by the debate immediately after Argentina's seizure of the Falkland Islands. For, when answering questions, the Prime Minister threw caution to the winds. With eyes flashing, gestures flamboyant and vocal chords stretched to a timbre fit for sounding the last trumpet, she transformed herself into Queen Boadicea driving her chariot against the Roman invaders with a combination of passion and fury.

During the ninety minutes she blazed away from the despatch box that afternoon, she slaughtered one sacred Euro-cow after another. The single currency was dismissed as 'not the policy of this Government'. The alternative British proposal for a parallel currency, known as the hard ECU, fared little better, for she dismissed it with the withering comment: 'In my view, it would not become widely used . . . Many people would continue to prefer their own currency.'[25] Her Chancellor, John Major, who had spent months promoting the hard ECU, said he 'nearly fell off the bench'[26] in reaction to this surprise declaration, because he realised it would wreck all his recent efforts at economic diplomacy.

But Margaret Thatcher had by no means finished. At various stages in these exchanges she asserted that the Commission was 'striving to extinguish democracy' and planning to take us through 'the back door to a federal Europe'. She declared, 'We have surrendered enough' to the Community. For good measure, she added, 'It would be totally and utterly wrong' to agree to 'abolish the pound sterling, the greatest expression of sovereignty'. She fired her biggest guns at Jacques Delors, bombarding him with a salvo of triple negatives:

> The President of the Commission, M. Delors, said at a press conference the other day that he wanted the European Parliament to be the democratic body of the Community, he wanted the Commission to be the Executive and he wanted the Council of Ministers to be the Senate. *No. No. No.*[27]

The mounting crescendo with which she so passionately delivered those last three words was greeted by a chorus of cheers in all parts of the House. The Tory Eurosceptics were in ecstasy, for they sensed a conversion moment in the

Prime Minister, and perhaps within their own party. For it appeared from the tide of the exchanges that the Europhiles were in a minority and in retreat.

Those appearances were to prove deceptive in at least one important case. But at the time, there seemed to be a sea change in parliamentary opinion that was by no means confined to the government's side of the House. A good number of anti-Brussels Labour MPs were cheering. The Ulster Unionists, encouraged by Enoch Powell, were in a similarly exultant mood.

Perhaps the question that best caught the mood of the House came from the SDP Leader, David Owen. 'Is it not perfectly clear that what was being attempted at Rome was a bounce which led only one way – to a single federal united states of Europe? . . . Would not Britain be entitled and right to use the veto?'

'I totally agree with the right hon. Gentleman', replied the Prime Minister.[28]

As she left the chamber that afternoon to continuous 'hear, hear' and waving of order papers, Margaret Thatcher must have felt that she had routed her critics and redefined where she and her government stood on the issue of progress towards monetary and political union in Europe.

If there was any one single moment when EMU and its successors, the euro and the eurozone, were decisively rejected by the British political system, that afternoon in the House of Commons on 30 October 1990 was it.

The consequences of what happened in Parliament that day were to have profound implications for the future of Britain's long-term relationship with Europe. But in the short term there were even more momentous consequences for Margaret Thatcher. The impact on her immediate future came from the reactions of Sir Geoffrey Howe.

HOWE PREPARES TO STRIKE

Sir Geoffrey Howe had long been a believer in the need for Britain to be a full participant in European economic and political union. He supported the single currency. He gave the impression of approving the vague declaratory outcomes of the Italian summit. At the time when the Prime Minister was denouncing the possibility of a single currency in Rome, Howe spoke live on London Weekend Television to Brian Walden, saying that Britain was not opposed to the idea, and implying that Margaret Thatcher would probably be won round to it.[29] She characterised his intervention as 'either disloyal or remarkably stupid'.[30]

As a result of this clash over the airwaves, the Deputy Prime Minister and the Prime Minister were once again at loggerheads. Just before she rose to deliver her statement on the European Council, Neil Kinnock tried to expose their divisions during Prime Minister's Questions by asking whether Sir Geoffrey Howe enjoyed her full confidence. 'My right hon. and learned Friend the deputy Prime Minister is too big a man to need a little man like the right hon. Gentleman to stand up for him', she retorted.[31] It was hardly a ringing endorsement. Howe suspected that she was deliberately distancing herself from him in a manner she had used before when undercutting Nigel Lawson.

It was revealing to watch the Deputy Prime Minister's body language on 30 October, as he sat on the front bench alongside his boss when she opened fire on Jacques Delors and all his works. When she reached her explosive punch line of '*No. No. No*' Howe's normally sphinx-like imperturbability crumbled. His wincings of dismay were plain for all to see. The only Member of the House who seemed not to notice his discomfort was the Prime Minister.

The following day, Sir Geoffrey resolved to resign. His motives for this decision were the cause of much speculation. He himself pinned his reasons to the 30 October statement, citing his distaste for 'the increasingly nationalist crudity of the Prime Minister's whole tone'.[32]

Margaret Thatcher believed that her Deputy was shaken by the shift in opinion of Conservative MPs towards a much more Eurosceptic position. As she put it, 'Perhaps the enthusiastic – indeed uproarious – support I received from the backbenchers convinced him that he had to strike at once, or I would win round the Parliamentary Party to the platform I earlier set out in Bruges.'[33]

It is more probable that the reasons for Howe's exit from the government were a longer-term mixture of pent-up anger and political frustration. Ever since his removal from the job of Foreign Secretary, which he loved, growing bitterness had been fermenting within his soul. This rancour was largely created by Margaret Thatcher's style of man-management, which was both deplorable and unpleasant towards Sir Geoffrey. Yet he was not without fault in their relationship. Not only did he fail to confront or at least reason with her about her excesses of aggressive behaviour. He had a long history of shutting up in masochistic silence, but then putting up in public with coded attacks on the Prime Minister when she became a vulnerable target. Rather like a hunter-killer submarine, HMS *Howe* spent long periods lurking secretively below the surface until he suddenly launched his torpedoes at a moment when he could inflict maximum damage. His Walden interview on 29 October was an example of this deliberate yet unexpected style of clandestine counter-attack.

The vehemence of Margaret Thatcher's reaction to the Rome summit unsettled Geoffrey Howe for two reasons. Although he was clear minded enough to see that the Italian manoeuvres were unprofessional and unfair, he nevertheless believed that Britain should have given a measured and patient response by simply postponing the arguments on EMU until the next Intergovernmental Conference. When the Prime Minister came out of her corner with unconcealed rage, Sir Geoffrey's pro-European sensibilities were grievously offended.

A more serious blow was Howe's realisation that Margaret Thatcher's rejection of EMU and the Delors philosophy that accompanied it were surprisingly popular. As Leader of the House, he could read the parliamentary runes as well as anyone. The eruptions of cheering during the 30 October statement marked a watershed. Sir Geoffrey was a child of the Heath era, when most Conservatives intoned the mantra, 'We are the party of Europe'. Suddenly it was apparent that this ground was crumbling. The Eurosceptics had moved into the ascendant.

Everything that Howe had worked for as Foreign Secretary was being challenged by a populist Prime Minister who was showing a fierce determination to rally support for her cause, not only in the House but also in the country. This last fear loomed large in Sir Geoffrey's mind as he asked himself: 'Was she, I began to wonder, talking herself into the mode in which she intended, consciously or unconsciously, to fight the next election?'[34]

To heighten such worries, this anti-European populism, which the Prime Minister had unleashed in Parliament, was magnified by the media. 'Up Yours – Delors' was the headline in the *Sun* on 31 October. It was the most colourful example of a swelling chorus of support for the Prime Minister. To see this surge of public opinion erupting so passionately against Europe upset Sir Geoffrey even more. It was sweeping away whatever residual hopes he might still have harboured of succeeding Margaret Thatcher as Prime Minister. It was breaking his remaining moorings of loyalty and collective responsibility to her government. So it was for a variety of complex private emotions and public policy differences that Geoffrey Howe seized his moment and sat down to compose his letter of resignation.

The letter was a laborious production running to nearly 1,200 words, and taking two days to draft. When it was still incomplete, the Deputy Prime Minister attended his last cabinet meeting. He had little more than a walk-on part in the proceedings, but before he opened his mouth several colleagues picked up the vibrations of heightened Howe–Thatcher antagonism.

One perceptive observer of the scene, a Howe sympathiser, was John Major, who described Howe's final cabinet meeting, on the morning of his resignation, as the worst of all:

> Geoffrey and Margaret were sitting side by side, directly opposite me. They could barely bring themselves to look at one another. Geoffrey stared down at his papers, his lips pursed; Margaret had a disdainful air, her eyes glittering. When he looked down the long cabinet table, she looked up it. When she put her head down to read her notes, he looked straight up. The body language said it all. This treatment of a senior colleague was embarrassing for the whole cabinet.[35]

The treatment got worse. When the discussion turned to the legislative programme, which was due to be introduced at the opening of the new session of Parliament in a few days time, Geoffrey Howe as Leader of the House and Lord President of the Council made the anodyne comment that two or three departments had not yet finalised their bills. This was merely a polite prompt to the ministers concerned, which needed no further comment. The Prime Minister exploded like a headmistress delivering a rocket to an errant schoolboy. 'Why aren't their bills ready?' she demanded. 'Isn't it the Lord President's responsibility to see that this kind of thing has been done?' The rebuke flowed on for a couple of embarrassing minutes.

'What the hell? This is positively the last time', was Howe's unspoken thought as he suffered the insults in silence. He had already made up his mind to resign. As he later recalled the incident: 'So far from being the last straw, this final tantrum was for me the first confirmation that I had taken the right decision.'[36]

The Prime Minister and the Deputy Prime Minister met for the last time as cabinet colleagues at 6 p.m. later that day. Although she had been forewarned of his imminent resignation, she appeared to be shaken by it. 'Is there anything we can do that would cause you to change your mind?' she asked. The answer was a polite negative. Geoffrey Howe then produced his resignation letter. 'It's very generous', she commented as she reached the end of page one. 'Better wait till you've read it all', was his response. By the time she finished reading it her tone had changed. 'I can see now why we shouldn't be able to change your mind. You've obviously thought a lot about it.'[37]

They parted with the odd formality of their first-ever handshake. In the tension of the moment, both of them forgot the tradition that fellow Members of Parliament do not shake hands. It was a strange ending to what, at its best, had once been a strong political partnership.

The artificiality continued with the exchange of resignation letters. Howe's was too turgid to make much impact – at least in comparison with his resignation statement to the House of Commons two weeks later. He made the obvious point that he felt he must leave the government because he did not share the Prime Minister's views on Europe. But then he confused the issue by presenting a most opaque picture of his own views. He was not a Euro-idealist or federalist. He was against an *imposed* single currency, but believed that the risks of being left out of EMU were severe. On the other hand, he thought that, 'more than one form of EMU possible. The important thing is not to rule in or out any one particular solution absolutely.'[38] When these words of Delphic ambivalence were passed round late at night in the smoking room of the House of Commons, the Tory MP for Saddleworth, Geoffrey Dickens, created pantomime hilarity by booming out, 'Written by Mr Wishy-Washy!'[39]

The obscurity of Howe's prose style in his letter of resignation left it far from clear what exactly were his disagreements with the Prime Minister over Europe. This gave Margaret Thatcher the opportunity to blur their differences still further in her reply. Her line was that their policy disagreements were not nearly as great as he had suggested. She even had the chutzpah to claim that her statement on the Rome summit had demonstrated the unity of the Conservatives: 'We have always been the party of Europe and will continue to be so.'[40] Prime Ministerial correspondence at the time of resignations often falls into the category of what Dr Johnson called, 'in lapidary inscriptions a man is not upon oath'.[41] Parts of Margaret Thatcher's valedictory epistle to Sir Geoffrey Howe might well win first prize for lapidary fabrication.

Having completed her reply to his resignation letter, the Prime Minister faced the new political situation with gritty realism. 'It was a relief he had gone. But I had no doubt of the political damage it would do. All the talk of a leadership bid by Michael Heseltine would start again' was her assessment.[42] So her first moves were to try and shore up her crumbling authority with the necessary reshuffle – her fourth in less than a year. She made John McGregor the new Leader of the House; moved Kenneth Clarke into McGregor's job at Education; and brought William Waldegrave into the cabinet as Secretary of State for Health. Her first priority had been to persuade Norman Tebbit to come back into her first line of senior ministers, but he declined on the grounds that he had to look after his paralysed wife, Margaret. Another explanation voiced by some wag in Annie's Bar* was that 'Norman may have been a pilot, but he's not a kamikaze pilot'.[43]

Whatever the reasons at the time, Tebbit was remorseful about his decision in later life. Three days after the death of Margaret Thatcher he caustically told the House of Lords, 'I left her, I fear, at the mercy of her friends. That I do regret.'[44]

There was a widespread expectation at Westminster among both friends and foes that another leadership election would take place in the new session of Parliament, but no one knew who would stand in it, or who would win it. Michael Heseltine was the obvious contender, having been trailing his coat ever since his departure over the Westland crisis almost five years earlier. Yet he began by playing his hand badly. He published an open letter to his constituency chairman calling for the Conservative Party to chart a new course in Europe. But before the ink was dry, its author set off on a private visit to the Middle East. This absence was an error of judgement, which became a focal point for mockery by his critics. The noisiest of these was Bernard Ingham, who orchestrated a 'put up or shut up' stream of anti-Heseltine stories in the press. 'This was just lighting the blue touch paper and retiring to a safe distance – in this case to Amman', was Ingham's contribution to the furore from the Downing Street press office.[45]

With Heseltine hesitating in Arabia, and MPs enjoying a brief recess away from Westminster, there was an uneasy lull in the countdown to the anticipated outbreak of hostilities against the Prime Minister. For a week or so it looked as though the pressures on her might be receding. Then they were sharply increased

---

* Annie's Bar was a popular watering hole in the Palace of Westminster, frequented by MPs and Lobby correspondents.

by two dreadful by-election results, first in Bootle and then an even worse one in Bradford North, where the Tory candidate came bottom of the poll.[46] These humiliations had been preceded by a disastrous Tory defeat in Ian Gow's old stronghold of Eastbourne, where the Liberal Democrats captured the seat, with a swing of 21.1 per cent against the government.[47]

Despite the ill omens from the electorate, the new session of Parliament began well for Margaret Thatcher, as she wiped the floor with Neil Kinnock in her opening speech in the debate on the Loyal Address. In those exchanges the Prime Minister indulged in a sally of over-confidence, which had serious consequences for her with one of her listeners. Attempting to play down the seriousness of her quarrels with her recently departed Deputy, Margaret Thatcher declared

> If the Leader of the Opposition reads my right hon. and learned Friend's letter, he will be very pressed indeed to find any significant policy difference on Europe between my right hon. and learned Friend and the rest of us on this side.[48]

This was a factually correct statement, yet it contained a great untruth. Sir Geoffrey Howe's resignation letter had waffled negatively about 'the mood' the Prime Minister had struck after the Rome summit, but had omitted the specifics of their disagreements. Nevertheless, their divisions on Europe ran deep, as she well knew. Her attempt to minimise their differences on policy was a sophistry that infuriated Sir Geoffrey. From that moment he was determined not only to make a resignation statement, but to bring the Prime Minister down with it. At long last he prepared to strike.

REFLECTION

The final months of Margaret Thatcher's eleven years as Prime Minister were dominated by two contradictory features: her inability to listen to her political friends at home and her ability to make far-sightedly bold judgements on major international issues.

Longevity in high office often leads to arrogant remoteness. The nineteenth-century historian Lord Acton expressed this in his aphorism, 'Power tends to corrupt, and absolute power corrupts absolutely'.[49] There was nothing corrupt in the venal sense of the word about Margaret Thatcher. But in the decaying or decomposing meaning of the word, her political antennae were falling apart. She was looking tired. Her Defence Secretary, Tom King, noticed 'her worrying new tendency to yawn with exhaustion at cabinet meetings'.[50] Whether it was from tiredness or stubbornness, she was no longer a listening politician.

All sorts of friendly voices tried to warn her about the danger signals. Right up to the time of his assassination, Ian Gow kept begging her not to let her irritation with Geoffrey Howe fester into an irreparable rift. Tristan Garel-Jones, who had played a key role in minimising the Meyer vote in the 1989 leadership election, told her in the bluntest of terms that she could lose up to a hundred more votes to Heseltine in any future contest if she did not sort out the poll tax. George Younger urged her to tone down the aggression in her anti-European rhetoric because over half the party were still pro-Europe. These well-intentioned suggestions were made to the Prime Minister in late 1989, but she took no notice of any of them.

Perhaps the most balanced flow of advice came from the Executive of the 1922 Committee, who met her on a monthly basis. All shades of party opinion were represented at these small gatherings. The overwhelming majority of the Executive were supporters of the Prime Minister and wanted her to continue in office. But she ignored their suggestions with an ill-disguised contempt that was painfully reminiscent of Ted Heath's rudeness to the 1922 Committee fifteen years earlier.

One of Margaret Thatcher's keenest supporters on the back benches was Dame Jill Knight, whose popularity with her colleagues ensured her re-election as Vice-Chair of the 1922 Committee for over a decade. She became disappointed with the Prime Minister's intransigence, particularly on the poll tax. 'Sadly, Margaret got to the point where she just wouldn't listen to any of us', she recalled. 'She hunkered down in her Downing Street bunker with Charles Powell and Bernard Ingham, and preferred their opinions to those of us who knew what was going on in the country and in the House. It was terribly sad.'[51]

The sadness of her supporters was matched by the high spirits of her adversaries. Michael Heseltine sensed that the Prime Minister was on the skids, so he greased them with cunning and diligence. Support for him was growing since he was the obvious rallying point for discontent, even though he seemed cautious about actually raising the standard of rebellion. But even those who opposed Heseltine's policies, particularly towards Europe, saw him as a formidable challenger. One of the most vocal Eurosceptics, Tony Marlow, the MP for Northampton North, was gloomily predicting 'a new Prime Minister by Christmas' as early as mid-October.[52] To the listeners who agreed with this forecast, the PM in waiting was Hezza.

Yet for all her mistakes, her high handedness, and her poor party management, Margaret Thatcher remained a colossus who bestrode the world as well as the domestic stage. Her preparations for the coming conflict in the Gulf were applauded by the defence and foreign-policy specialists in the House. There was a feeling that if it came to hostilities over Kuwait, then Britain's experienced Prime Minister was indispensable as a war leader.

On Europe, opinions on Margaret Thatcher were more divided. Yet, as the dust began to settle after her 'No. No. No' denunciation of Delors, there was a growing feeling that she had been right to take a strong stand against European Monetary Union. The Tory party began shifting its ground in response to her strong leadership. It was moving towards the much more Eurosceptic-inclined policy it has embraced today. All this started to happen in the early days of November 1990. Like all huge policy upheavals, it was confusing at first. But few now would argue in the age of the eurozone crisis that Margaret Thatcher was wrong to sound the tocsin of battle about British opposition to monetary and political union in Europe.

Perhaps it was the realisation that Britain had arrived at a crossroads of European policy that encouraged Sir Geoffrey Howe to unsheathe his dagger, as he prepared what turned out to be the most dramatic resignation statement in parliamentary history.

36

End game

HOWE GOES FOR THE JUGULAR

The days leading up to Geoffrey Howe's resignation statement were packed with tension at Westminster. Margaret Thatcher was worried, although this was hard to discern from the carapace of calm with which she carried out her public duties at constituency events and at the Cenotaph on Remembrance Sunday. But she let the mask slip in her speech at the Lord Mayor's Banquet on Monday 12 November, where she gave way not to emotions of anxiety but to an excess of bravado. Using the imagery of cricket, she struck a high note of defiance:

> I am still at the crease, though the bowling has been pretty hostile of late. And in case anyone doubted it, can I assure you there will be no ducking bouncers, no stonewalling, no playing for time. The bowling's going to get hit all round the ground.[1]

Margaret Thatcher's sally into the unfamiliar language of Wisden not only revealed her ignorance of cricket* (bouncers usually should be ducked!); it acted as a further provocation to Sir Geoffrey Howe. As he sat in the pavilion composing his resignation speech, he seized the opportunity offered by her metaphor, proving himself to be no flannelled fool when it came to venomous spin. Yet almost no one, particularly the Prime Minister, believed he was capable of knocking out her middle stump.

A resignation speech from the departed Deputy Prime Minister was bound to be a significant event. Yet in the days before he delivered his bombshell there

---

* The sporting analogy was crafted by Charles Powell, whose duties as overseas affairs private secretary to the Prime Minister had by this time extended to domestic speechwriting. Unfortunately he knew nothing about cricket either.

was no expectation of an impending apocalypse. In the Commons, Howe was regarded as a capable but colourless speaker. Even if he decided to be severely critical of the Prime Minister, most MPs anticipated that she would survive it. On past form, Howe had been unimpressive when trying to wield the knife. It was 'rather like being savaged by a dead sheep' had been Denis Healey's disparaging description of Sir Geoffrey's best-known previous attempt at launching an *ad hominem* attack on an opponent.[2]* The taunt was much cited as the political world waited to hear what he had to say.

It may never be clear, perhaps even to himself, when precisely the worm turned in Geoffrey Howe and changed his instinct to be loyal into a determination to have revenge. Was there an accumulation of bitterness over Margaret Thatcher's numerous acts of rudeness to him, which finally boiled over? Or was there a sudden rush of anger caused by unpleasant surprises from 30 October onwards. Her '*No. No. No.*' denunciation of Jacques Delors; her effrontery in pretending that the differences between Prime Minister and Deputy Prime Minister were about style not substance; and her boastful assertion that she would hit his bowling all over the ground had been blows for Sir Geoffrey's pride. But did they add up to a *casus belli* for an all-out war? On past form, it seemed improbable.

Like Brutus in Julius Caesar, Howe struggled to be seen as an honourable man. He had hesitated, retreated and avoided confrontation for years, before aligning himself with the Cassiuses and Cascas of the Conservative Party who were plotting to bring about the political death of Margaret Thatcher. But once he finally decided to make his move, he delivered the unkindest cut of all.

At 3.30 p.m. on Tuesday 13 November, Sir Geoffrey Howe made far and away the most memorable and effective speech of his career. His purpose was to destroy the Prime Minister using a lethal blend of sarcastic humour mingled with personal poison. The House was spellbound, realising that history was being made.

Howe began with a joke about the claim that he had resigned over issues of style, not substance. 'If some of my former colleagues are to be believed,' he said, 'I must be the first Minister in history who has resigned because he was

---

* In 1978, Denis Healey was Labour Chancellor of the Exchequer and Geoffrey Howe was his opposite number on the Conservative front bench.

in full agreement with Government policy.'[3] Even the Prime Minister managed to simulate laughter at that one, but her smile soon vanished as her former Deputy moved into stiletto plunging mode, blaming her for damaging the government and its efforts to control inflation by delaying entry into the ERM.

Then he compared the European vision of Winston Churchill and Harold Macmillan with

> the nightmare image sometimes conjured up by my right hon. Friend, who seems sometimes to look out upon a continent that is positively teeming with ill-intentioned people scheming, in her words, to 'extinguish democracy', to 'dissolve our national identities', and to lead us 'through the back door into a federal Europe.' What kind of vision is that . . . ?

By now, there were perceptible shivers running down the Tory back benches, as Sir Geoffrey exposed raw nerve after raw nerve on the rift over European policy.

He accused the Prime Minister of sabotaging the efforts of the Chancellor of the Exchequer and the Governor of the Bank of England to put forward Britain's hard ECU proposal, by casually dismissing the very idea 'with such personalised incredulity'. How on earth, he asked, are the Chancellor and the Governor of the Bank of England 'to be taken as serious participants in the debate against that type of background noise?' Sharp intakes of breath from all parts of the House followed that phrase.

Worse reactions followed as Sir Geoffrey poured scorn on Margaret Thatcher's cricketing allusions, linking them with a better one of his own to her treatment of the Chancellor and Governor: 'It is rather like sending your opening batsmen to the crease only for them to find, the moment the first balls are bowled, that their bats have been broken before the game by the team captain.'[4]

By coincidence, I was sitting on the fourth bench below the gangway immediately behind Sir Geoffrey Howe as he delivered his resignation statement. This meant that I was 'doughnutted' in the television pictures of virtually every word he uttered. My agonised grimaces were thus captured for posterity and have been replayed many times since. They were also recorded in his diary by Alan Clark, who wrote of the moment of the broken bats analogy, 'Everyone gasped, and I looked round to catch Jonathan's eye. He had that special incredulous look he occasionally gets, mouth open.'[5]

However incredulous my expression, it was nothing to the waves of emotion that rippled through the House in various forms. Labour and a few members of the Howe–Heseltine fan club guffawed derisively. Thatcher loyalists reeled in horror, some with eyes closed as if to avert their gaze from the brutality of the killing. It was the equivalent of the cathartic moment in Shakespeare's play when Julius Caesar is struck down with the assassin's cry, 'Speak, hands, for me!'[6]

A few feet along the back benches, I saw Dame Elaine Kellett Bowman start to weep. Dame Jill Knight gripped the bench in front of her, seeming to writhe in pain as though she had been physically stabbed herself. As for the most important lady in the House, on whom all eyes were focused, she appeared as steady as a rock. But 'underneath the mask of composure, my emotions were turbulent', Margaret Thatcher recalled. 'I had not the slightest doubt that the speech was deeply damaging to me.'[7]

After the damage came a few mock turtle tears as Howe spoke of his 'sadness and dismay' over the 'very real tragedy that the Prime Minister's perceived attitude towards Europe is running increasingly serious risks for the future of our nation'. Then, in the last sentence of his statement, the ex-Chancellor, ex-Foreign Secretary, ex-Deputy Prime Minister put a deadly thrust into his ex-colleague the Prime Minister: 'The time has come for others to consider their own response to the tragic conflict of loyalties with which I have myself wrestled for perhaps too long.'[8]

Stunned silence was the immediate response of the House. There were no sounds of 'hear, hear', no groans of disapproval, and only a single muted rumble of 'Shame!' from Michael Carttiss, the MP for Great Yarmouth. But as the chamber emptied, the collective shock at having witnessed an assassination was replaced by a growing hubbub of speculation. For we all knew that the landscape of British politics had irreversibly changed. Howe's last twenty-six words were seen as a carefully calculated call to Michael Heseltine to unsheathe his sword and destroy the Prime Minister.

Depending on your point of view, Howe had either given an unpopular leader her deserved come-uppance, or he had committed an unforgivable act of malicious insurrection. Many Tory MPs were apoplectic at what some were calling co-ordinated treachery. This derived from the speech's implied invitation for Michael Heseltine to stand against Margaret Thatcher. Both Howe and Heseltine subsequently denied any collusion. Perhaps their remarkable collaboration happened by telepathy.

HESELTINE ENTERS THE RING

Scenes close to internecine mayhem exploded within the Tory Party during the hours after Geoffrey Howe's statement. It was reported that two colleagues came to blows in the tea room, but even without the fisticuffs the angry divisions were erupting, with colleagues ferociously arguing the toss on questions like: Was Howe a regicide or a hero? Had Elspeth written the most venomous parts of the speech? Was Heseltine a party to the plot? The most frequently repeated inquiry of the day was: 'What happens next?'

Cabals and conclaves were forming in the corridors, the bars and the smoking room with raised voices and jabbing fingers. The only people who looked happy were Michael Heseltine's camp followers, headed by William Powell, Michael Mates and Keith Hampson. They were in a frenzy of excitement. It did not take long for their hero to pick up the gauntlet so helpfully thrown at his feet. The following morning, Michael Heseltine formally announced his candidacy. The 1990 Tory leadership battle had begun, with the first ballot fixed for Tuesday 20 November.

There were two enormous surprises in the next few days. They were that both the challenger and the incumbent lost the election. This was only partly a product of the complex rules, which ordained that for either of them to win the contest outright without a second ballot, the victor had to achieve a simple majority plus 15 per cent – a total of 208 votes.

What stymied Margaret Thatcher and Michael Heseltine was not the artificial target of 208 votes. It was that they both carried too much baggage to reach this winning post, and that they both ran campaigns of considerable incompetence.

Michael Heseltine should have been an entirely credible candidate to become leader of the party and the next prime minister. He had the necessary ministerial experience. He was an outstanding speaker, blessed with the gift of political charisma. He had spent the past four years running a well-planned and handsomely financed campaign to become Margaret Thatcher's successor.

And yet when his hour came, in the most favourable circumstances imaginable, Heseltine failed. Why?

The answer lies in what is known as the 'ocean liner test' – an amusing analogy invented by Nye Bevan and embellished by Michael Foot. It compares a sojourn in the House of Commons to setting off on a long voyage with a collection of fellow passengers you might never have picked to be your companions. But by the time the ship has crossed the Bay of Biscay and passed through the Straits of Gibraltar, the changing seas and the shared experiences of shipboard life have made it possible for the leading figures on the boat to have their characters assessed with remarkable accuracy. These favourable and unfavourable judgements are the House of Commons equivalent of the separation of the sheep and the goats. In the context of the 1990 leadership election, all that needs to be said is that Michael Heseltine failed the ocean liner test.

Tarzan looked good from the outside, but among his own parliamentary colleagues he had never been able to muster anything like the required level of support. He was too much of a loner to be liked, and too much of an egoist to be trusted. His motives, his volatility and his vanity were considered highly suspect. 'He is so uninterested in meeting his fellow Members, he doesn't even know where the tea room is', grumbled Gerald Howarth.[9] Yet, for all these long-standing disadvantages, the extraordinary circumstances of the election gave him a better chance than he could ever previously have hoped for. Sir Geoffrey Howe had effectively endorsed his candidacy. Opinion polls suggested that with Heseltine as leader, the Conservatives would have their best chance of winning the next election. His strongest card was that he was promising an immediate review of the poll tax. This should have been the ace of trumps when it came to picking up new votes in the leadership election, because so many Tory MPs were convinced that they would lose their seats unless the poll tax was dropped.

Yet, even with these strong tides running in his favour, Heseltine could not build sufficient momentum to pull ahead of Margaret Thatcher. This was partly because his campaign was badly run. His principal lieutenants, Michael Mates, the MP for Petersfield, and Keith Hampson, the MP for Ripon, did not have sufficient organisational skills.

To counter the impression that he was leading a second eleven team, Hezza turned his strategy into a one-man band operation. The cat who walked by himself now had to canvass by himself. He did this rather embarrassingly, standing for hours at a stretch in the Members' Lobby, accosting colleagues as they went in and out of the chamber. 'How about coming my way?' he asked me on the steps of the stone-flagged corridor leading down from the lobby to the Members' Cloakroom. 'Your talents have been overlooked for far too long. We'd love to have you with us.'[10]

Variations on these lines were deployed to dozens of other colleagues. Some were flattered, while others were repelled by Hezza's synthetic smiles and ersatz charm at these forced encounters. Norman Lamont mocked Heseltine for canvassing 'like a child molester, hanging around the lavatories and waiting to pounce on people'.[11] Even for Michael Heseltine, a shy and sensitive man beneath the flashy surface, these advances must have felt almost as maladroit as they seemed to his targets.

Even worse than the awkward methodology of Hezza's canvassing were the results of it. For in the opening days of the campaign the number of polite (sometimes not so polite!) rebuffs to Heseltine were discouraging. If he was keeping any kind of reliable scorecard, he must have known that he was well behind Margaret Thatcher. She was clearly ahead of him, even if the size of her lead was unclear. So the election was hers to lose – and lose it she did.

PETER MORRISON'S COMPLACENCY

Margaret Thatcher badly misjudged her campaign to be re-elected as leader of the Conservative Party. The reasons were a combination of hubris, poor intelligence and complacency. She also made a bad decision to attend a non-essential Conference for Security and Co-operation in Europe (CSCE) in Paris on the day of the vote, which she should have devoted to corralling waverers and doubters. These failures were part of a wider picture of being out of touch with the MPs who were the lifeblood of her support.

The hubris was the product of her increasingly isolated life at No. 10 after eleven and a half years as Prime Minister. She had become a poor listener, unable to grasp the seriousness of the Howe–Heseltine threat to her position. Instead of realising that she needed to put up a strong personal fight, she decided to remain aloof from the battle and to rely on surrogates and subordinates, who performed far from competently.

Her first hubristic decision was not to do any canvassing. Her attitude was, 'Tory MPs know me, my record and my beliefs. If they were not already persuaded, there was not much left for me to persuade them with'.[12] This was a serious mistake, as she belatedly acknowledged in her memoirs. 'She's off her rocker', said Nicholas Budgen, who at the time was looking forward to his anticipated audience with the Prime Minister. 'I suppose I'll vote for her just the same, but I know at least a dozen colleagues who will be so offended by her refusal to see them that they'll take umbrage and abstain or vote for Heseltine just to teach her a lesson.'[13]

Budgen's comment reflected the fact of parliamentary life that many colleagues were expecting to be seen by their leader in the days before the election. This was the custom and practice of previous contests. To be snubbed by not being seen was a vote loser. More importantly, there is little doubt that in the run-up to the poll Margaret Thatcher could have won over a substantial number of waverers by meeting them in small groups and asking for their support. The power of prime ministerial incumbency can be magical, but Margaret Thatcher was too proud to use it. As a result, she forfeited anywhere between ten and thirty vital votes.

Her pride was buttressed by poor intelligence. She herself believed that it was unthinkable for a prime minister, in power with a large majority, to be thrown out between general elections as a result of a coup organised by her own MPs. This self-certainty was reinforced by unreliable forecasts of the votes she was confident of receiving. She had no help from the whips' office in calculating this total. Although she had previously referred to it as 'my office', it was no such thing. Under the new Chief Whip, Tim Renton (a close friend of Geoffrey Howe), it was decreed that the whips as a body would stay scrupulously neutral in the campaign, in order to reflect the divisions in the party. To many back-benchers, it seemed an odd decision that the government whips were not supporting the head of the government, as they had done in the leadership election a year earlier. Their neutrality was a symptom of the undisciplined malaise that had infected the parliamentary party.

With the whips' office neutralised, the task of counting, canvassing and organising Margaret Thatcher's supporters fell to her campaign team. But this was not a well-drilled or energetic unit. It was characterised by absenteeism, lack of commitment, laziness and incompetence. Why the leader herself failed to know this when half her party saw it all too clearly was a mystery.

Margaret Thatcher was nominated for the leadership by her Chancellor and Foreign Secretary, but neither John Major nor Douglas Hurd was asked to do any canvassing for their nominee. This task fell to her appointed campaign manager, George Younger, the Member for Ayr and a former Secretary of State for Scotland.

Although he had done a competent job in the role a year earlier, when given the much easier task of seeing off Sir Anthony Meyer, Younger was not the right man to deliver the defeat of Heseltine. He was too much of a Scottish gent, too remote from the new intake of English MPs preoccupied with the poll tax and too busy with his extensive business interests, which included being Chairman of the Royal Bank of Scotland.

If 'Gentleman George' was only a part-time member of the Prime Minister's campaign team, some of the others she invited to help in this task were even less committed. Michael Jopling, the former Chief Whip, bowed out. So did Norman Fowler, citing his friendship with Geoffrey Howe. John Moore was absent on a business trip to the United States for most of the campaigning period. Although some robust cheer-leading came from Norman Tebbit, who had the chutzpah to hold a press conference on the doorstep of Michael Heseltine's Wilton Crescent mansion, the team effort as a whole was noticeably lacklustre. The gaps in it had to be covered by Margaret Thatcher's recently appointed Parliamentary Private Secretary, Peter Morrison, who *de facto* became her acting campaign manager. He was a disaster.

I knew Peter Morrison as well as anyone in the House. We had been school friends. He was the best man at my wedding in St Margaret's, Westminster. We shared many private and political confidences. So I knew the immense pressures he was facing at the time when he was suddenly overwhelmed with the greatest new burden imaginable – running the Prime Minister's election campaign.

Sixteen years in the House of Commons had treated Peter badly. His health had deteriorated. He had an alcohol problem that made him ill, overweight and prone to take long afternoon naps. In the autumn of 1990 he became embroiled in a police investigation into aspects of his personal life. The allegations against him were never substantiated, and the inquiry was subsequently dropped. But at the time of the leadership election, Peter was worried, distracted and unable to concentrate. He covered up his difficulties by exuding an air of supreme confidence about the solidity of support for Margaret Thatcher. Not for him the tried and tested methods of probing voting intentions in this notoriously mendacious electorate. He blandly accepted every assurance he was given at face value, making little or no effort to check and double check them with the help of third parties. Unsurprisingly, this laid-back indolence produced false optimism and false figures.

One Thatcher supporter whose antennae detected the disintegration of the Prime Minister's campaign team was Alan Clark. The day before the poll, he was sufficiently worried to cancel his afternoon engagements at the Ministry of Defence. He went to the House of Commons to see if he could help pull in a few more votes.

Clark found Peter Morrison asleep in his room. When roused, the Prime Minister's Parliamentary Private Secretary dismissed his visitor's anxiety.

'Quite all right, old boy, relax.'

'What's the arithmetic look like?'

'Tightish, but OK . . . I've got Michael on 115. It could be 124, at the worst.'

'Look, Peter, I don't think people are being straight with you', said Alan Clark. 'Don't you think we should be out there twisting arms?'

'No point. In fact, it could be counter-productive. I've got a theory about this. I think some people may abstain on the first ballot in order to give Margaret a fight, then rally to her on the second.'

Clark thought this was 'balls'. He left the room in deep gloom, complaining in his diary, 'There is absolutely no oomph in her campaign *whatsoever*. Peter is useless, far worse than I thought . . . He's sozzled. There isn't a single person working for her who cuts any ice at all . . . And she's in Paris.'[14]

The decision to go to Paris instead of staying at Westminster to campaign was a fatal error of judgement. What was calling her to the other side of the Channel was the Conference for Security and Co-operation in Europe, a largely ceremonial event to celebrate the ending of the Cold War and to set up a new forum for discussing human rights and security issues in Eastern Europe. The heads of government attending the conference included Presidents Bush, Mitterrand, Gorbachev and Chancellor Kohl. They were all politicians capable of understanding Margaret Thatcher's need to be absent in order to fight a leadership election at home. But she had no such understanding herself. She wanted to be on the world stage, not grubbing around for votes at Westminster. It was another indication of her aloofness from domestic politics, which was making her unpopular with her own troops.

The final clincher of her decision to go to Paris was the report from her campaign team that she was home and dry. Margaret Thatcher held a supper at Chequers on the evening of Saturday 17 November for her core group of supporters and campaigners. The guests included Peter Morrison, Kenneth Baker, John Wakeham, Gerry Neale and Michael Neubert – MPs who had supposedly been assiduously working to re-elect the Prime Minister. All of them were supremely optimistic about her prospects. Peter Morrison reported that he was confident of 220 votes for Thatcher, 110 for Heseltine and with forty predicted abstentions. That gave the Prime Minister what she called 'an easy win'. However, she was also cautious enough to warn her listeners of what she called 'the lie factor'. She told Morrison, 'I remember Ted thought the same thing. Don't trust our figures – some people are on the books of both sides.'[15]

There was one other last-minute ingredient in the election that may have swung votes away from her. The only form of campaigning she engaged in was giving newspaper interviews. Her final salvo appeared in *The Times* on Monday 19 November. It was counter-productive. Interviewed by the paper's editor, Simon Jenkins, Margaret Thatcher launched an aggressive attack on Michael Heseltine, stabbing her heavily annotated copy of his book *Where There's a Will* as she declared that his policies of interventionism, corporatism, reducing the Community Charge and reducing taxation 'sounds just like the Labour party'. Her challenger, she claimed, would 'stop up the well-head of enterprise' and take the country back to the bad old days. To many readers, this sounded batty. Whatever could be said about Michael Heseltine, he was no socialist. As for his plans to cut the poll tax, this was just what many Tory MPs wanted if they were going to have any chance of retaining their seats. Some of them crossed over into the Heseltine camp after reading this interview.

Perhaps Margaret Thatcher may have intuitively sensed that her grip on her party was slipping. She had growing doubts about the upbeat Morrison vote predictions. Simon Jenkins felt he had spotted a moment of her personal vulnerability during his *Times* interview with her when Margaret lent forward in her chair to say: 'After three election victories, it really would be the cruellest thing.'[16]

Despite these forebodings, she ignored her electorate at Westminster in the vital forty-eight hours before the vote, and headed off to Paris.

A HARD DAY'S NIGHT IN PARIS

Election day dawned uneasily and lethargically for the headless Thatcher camp at Westminster. Not only was the candidate absent; her proposer, John Major, was in hospital having a wisdom tooth extracted and her seconder, Douglas Hurd, was accompanying the Prime Minister to Paris. Peter Morrison, in contrast to the Heselteenies, decided not to do any last-minute campaigning. Instead, on the morning of the poll he intermittently patrolled the corridor outside Committee Room 14 where MPs were trickling in throughout the day to cast their votes. 'Thank you for supporting the Prime Minister',[17] he kept intoning, like a bishop bestowing blessings on those he presumed were the faithful. If his assumptions had been correct she would have won by a landslide.

In Paris, Margaret Thatcher was having a busy forty-eight hours. She breakfasted with President Bush at the US Embassy, lunched with the other leaders at the Elysée Palace, spoke at the CSCE conference and had bilateral talks with several heads of government, including President Gorbachev. The conference ended at 4.30 p.m. with a final dinner at Versailles, scheduled for 8 p.m. Between the two engagements she returned to the British Embassy to await the result, which was due soon after 6 p.m.

At the appointed hour her inner circle assembled in her bedroom at the Embassy. Peter Morrison had flown over to be at her side for the result. Also present were Charles Powell, Bernard Ingham, Cynthia Crawford and the British Ambassador Sir Ewen Fergusson. The Chief Whip, Tim Renton, rang with the result at 6.20 p.m. It was already known to Charles Powell, who had ingeniously set up his own line to the House of Commons. So he got the bad news ten seconds earlier. He did not pass it on to the Prime Minister, but gave a thumbs-down sign behind her back.[18]

As the official channel of communication, Peter Morrison took down the figures from Renton and passed them to Margaret Thatcher, who was sitting calmly at the dressing table with her back to everyone else. 'Not, I am afraid, as good as we had hoped', was the verdict of her PPS as he handed her the result.[19] It showed: Thatcher 204; Heseltine 152; Abstentions or Void 16.

What to an outsider would have looked like a victory was immediately recognised by the insiders as a defeat. For by the tantalisingly narrow margin of four votes, she had just failed to avert a second ballot. This was a body blow, as Margaret Thatcher knew. Although her back was turned to everyone in the room as the news came through, Charles Powell was watching her reflection in the dressing-table mirror. 'I could see from the look that crossed her face that her immediate reaction was "That's it"', he recalled.[20]

If that was her real thought, she concealed it remarkably well. Maintaining her unbroken calm, she asked Powell to check that Hurd and Major would support her in round two. Powell found Hurd in the next room on the telephone to John Major so he got a quick answer. The Prime Minister was then able to stride out into the courtyard of the British Embassy to deliver her verdict on the result to the assembled media.

In a moment of pure pantomime, the Prime Minister headed for the wrong microphone. Instead of going to the press stand prepared for her by Bernard Ingham, she somehow, amidst much pushing and shoving between journalists and embassy staff, ended up seizing the microphone of the BBC's political correspondent John Sergeant. He was telling his viewers that Margaret Thatcher would not be coming out of the Embassy to make a comment. With comic confusion growing as the BBC's newsreader in London, Peter Sissons, shouted in his earpiece, 'She's behind you!' the heavily jostled Sergeant yielded his microphone to the Prime Minister, who robustly declared:

> Good evening gentlemen. I am naturally very pleased that I got more than half the Parliamentary Party and disappointed that it's not quite enough to win on the first ballot, so I confirm it is my intention to let my name go forward for the second ballot.[21]

The chaos of this scene in the British Embassy courtyard gave the immediate impression that the Prime Minister was losing her grip on power. Watching the live coverage – an unintended BBC exclusive – in the crowded MPs' viewing room at Westminster, opinions were divided as to whether her defiant courage would turn the tide in her favour for the second ballot, or whether she was done for. Confusion reigned, probably in Margaret Thatcher's mind also, for her evening in Paris continued with mood swings from the magnificent to the maudlin.

Her first action after going back inside the Embassy was to telephone Denis in London. According to Carol, he was marvellously supportive: '"Congratulations, Sweetie Pie, you've won; it's just the rules", he said, as the tears trickled down his face. He was crying for her, not for himself.' Although he listened sympathetically to her insistence that she would be fighting to win on the second ballot, he did not believe a word of it. For as he put down the phone, he said to the friend who was with him, 'We've had it. We're out.'[22]

Margaret Thatcher was far too intelligent a politician not to have concluded from the voting figures that her days as Prime Minister were likely to be coming to an end. But although she was down, she did not yet accept that she was out. She kept up the façade of an embattled warrior, repeating over and over again to Peter Morrison, 'We have got to fight and win the second ballot'.[23] Perhaps this mantra was intended to convince herself as well as her PPS.

In Paris she still had a job to do and she did it superbly. Her immediate obligation was to attend a ballet and a banquet at Versailles as the finale to the conference. Thanks to the events in London, her schedule was awry, so she sent a message to President Mitterrand saying that she would arrive late. But he wanted to honour her, as did the other assembled leaders, in her hour of travail. So the start of the ballet was delayed. Her belated entrance, gallantly escorted by President Mitterrand, was an emotional moment.

The presidents and prime ministers who applauded her were astonished by her plight, and deeply sympathetic. They found it hard to believe that in a modern democracy the elected head of government could be overthrown while out of the country by a minority faction in her own party. The word 'coup' was much used in Versailles that evening. To foreigners unversed in the 1922 Committee's arcane rules for leadership elections, the ousting of Margaret Thatcher seemed more like a putsch in central Asia than the democratic politics of central London. The process looked all the more incredible when contrasted with the stability and splendour of Versailles and the Prime Minister's own impeccable dignity and graceful demeanour throughout the marathon evening. As her Foreign Secretary, Douglas Hurd, recalled the scene:

She carried herself magnificently at the great dinner at Versailles that evening. All eyes were on her as dinner followed ballet, and course followed course at the immense table in the Galerie des Glaces. They looked on her as some wounded eagle, who had herself wounded many in the past, but whom no one wished to see brought down, unable to soar again. Thanks to her own style and courage, she was not humiliated . . . I never felt so admiring as on that last night in Paris in November 1990.[24]

The Foreign Secretary's admiration was widely shared by the foreign leaders. Presidents Bush, Mitterrand, Gorbachev and Chancellor Kohl all said their farewells to Margaret Thatcher in moving terms. Perhaps the most poignant parting words in Versailles came from Mikhail Gorbachev. He clasped both his hands around hers, and said in a choking voice, 'Да хранит Вас Бог!' The phrase was translated by the Soviet leader's interpreter, Pavel Palazchenko, as 'God bless you'.[25]

Margaret Thatcher's brave face to her fellow leaders at Versailles crumbled when she returned to the privacy of her room at the British Embassy just before midnight on 20 November. There she sat up until dawn talking to Crawfie, her closest confidante after Denis. As Cynthia Crawford recalled:

She wasn't all right, she wasn't going to sleep and we decided to have a drink, and then we just stayed up all night and talked about every aspect of her life – her childhood, her father, her mother, getting married to Denis, having the twins and her political career – and we just never went to bed, and then about half past six we just sort of got ready for the day.[26]

What the day or days ahead would bring, no one could know. Margaret Thatcher's heart was telling her that she must fight with every sinew to hold on to her power as Prime Minister. Yet at the same time her head must have told her that power was ebbing away from her, and might hacmorrhage so quickly that her political death would become inevitable. A night without sleep was not helpful in making the right calculations and judgements in such a situation. So, it was in a mixed up mood of tension, apprehension and confusion that the wounded leader returned to London from Paris.

REFLECTION

The sequence of end-game events that brought down Margaret Thatcher combined the worst frailties of politicians. Some of them were her own. Yet for most of the drama she was largely a passive participant. Indeed, for almost the only time in her career she was too passive, remaining aloof from a battle she should have been leading. Her great fault was that she had lost touch with her tribe of parliamentary supporters.

As a member of the tribe for the previous sixteen years I was appalled by the way so many of my colleagues lost their moral and political moorings. It was a time of collective madness. Even if you were a critic, as I was, of some of Margaret Thatcher's mistakes and high-handed behaviour, this was no justification for staging a coup against a sitting and three times elected prime minister.

We were eighteen months away from an election, plenty of time in which to modify the poll tax. The economy was improving. Our armed forces were on a war footing, poised for what became the successful eviction of Saddam Hussein from Kuwait. For all the above reasons, aided by the abysmal performance of Neil Kinnock in the campaign, the Conservatives won the 1992 general election. Who can be sure that this combination of events would not have given Margaret Thatcher her fourth victory as Prime Minister just as it helped John Major to his first? Even if she had gone down to defeat, it would have been an honourable decision by the people in a general election – infinitely preferable to a fearful, spiteful stab in the back by an aggrieved minority of plotting Conservative parliamentarians.

The Tory Party spent over a decade in the political wilderness because the public could not forgive or forget the coup against Margaret Thatcher. As a modest participant on the fringes of the drama, I can at least lay claim to have got it right when I said on BBC *Newsnight* on the evening of Geoffrey Howe's resignation statement: 'If we throw out Britain's most successful peacetime Prime Minister in a backstage party bloodbath, we will come to regret it as our darkest hour.'[27]

37

Exit

FIRST SOUNDINGS

'Don't go on, love', were the first words of advice Margaret Thatcher received as she returned to 10 Downing Street from Paris.[1] They came from Denis, who had worked out that her position was untenable. She had not yet reached the same conclusion, being determined to fight hard as long as there might be a chance of winning on the second ballot. During the next few hours she discovered, in a painful process, that there was no such chance.

It took a while before she was told the truth. After her talk with Denis in the flat, she met in her study with Peter Morrison, Norman Tebbit and John Wakeham. Soon afterwards she went down to the Cabinet Room where they were joined by Kenneth Baker, John MacGregor, Tim Renton, Cranley Onslow and John Moore. To Margaret Thatcher's dismay, the priority that emerged from the discussion was the importance of stopping Heseltine. Even her most ardent supporters seemed to be emphasising that this was the principal reason why she should go forward to the second ballot. The consensus was that she was the best bet as the candidate who could keep Tarzan at bay.[2]

This was hardly a flattering endorsement of her record as a Prime Minister who had won three elections. To make matters worse, the consensus about the bet was unclear. Tim Renton, the Chief Whip, reported on the basis of his soundings that she would be defeated by Heseltine. John MacGregor, who had been tasked with checking out the cabinet, held a similar view but he pulled his punches. He knew that a significant minority of his cabinet colleagues either wanted the Prime Minister to go or thought that she would not beat Heseltine in the run-off. However, MacGregor did not wish to pass on his findings in front of Renton, who was suspected of being a supporter of the Howe–Heseltine pincer movement. So Margaret Thatcher was kept in the dark about the extent to which her support was haemorrhaging among her most senior colleagues.

The position was further blurred by the Chairman of the 1922 Committee, Cranley Onslow, who decided to preserve the strict neutrality of the election umpire. So he offered no advice on how the currents of opinion were moving among back-benchers. However, he did say that the argument about European policy was fading as an issue. His view was that voting would turn the following week on whether or not something substantial could be done on the Community Charge. Margaret Thatcher told Onslow that she could not suddenly pull a rabbit out of a hat in the five days before the ballot.

Her staunchest supporter was Norman Tebbit. He did not minimise the effect that Michael Heseltine's promise to make a radical review of the poll tax was having on many MPs. But Tebbit was certain that if her senior ministers stood by her, then the Prime Minister could make up lost ground and win over enough votes to beat her challenger. This became Margaret Thatcher's strategy. She resolved to confirm her support base among her cabinet, and to woo her back-benchers in the way she had so conspicuously failed to do before the first ballot.

The duties of a Prime Minister had to take precedence over the task of being a candidate. In the early afternoon she made a statement on the CSCE summit in Paris. As she left Downing Street for the House of Commons, she called out to the throng of journalists, 'I fight on, I fight to win'. When she saw the coverage of her words on the evening news bulletins, she thought, 'I looked a great deal more confident than I felt'.[3]

The CSCE statement went well, but there was no meat in it for either side since it was largely about the uncontroversial goal of promoting democracy and human rights in Eastern Europe. The Prime Minister answered all questions authoritatively, giving no clues that she was planning to do anything other than remain in office. Immediately afterwards, she set off for the tea room accompanied by Norman Tebbit. This was such an unexpected move that she was greeted as if she was an apparition. 'Here's Banquo's ghost!',[4] called out one unfriendly voice. She pretended not to have heard the jibe, and sat down at a big oval table just beyond the cafeteria counter for tea, but not enough sympathy.

She moved round to four groups of colleagues. They were almost universally critical of her first-round campaign. 'Michael has asked me two or three times for my vote already. This is the first time we have seen you', was one reproach.[5] It came from a committed supporter, George Gardiner, who wanted to hear her assurance that she would from now on be fighting for every vote. He got it. By the time she arrived at the table where I was sitting, her tone was superficially upbeat. Teddy Taylor and I said we would canvass every single MP in our Conservative European Reform Group. We thought we could deliver at least forty votes from our fifty members, whose Eurosceptic sympathies were firmly with the Prime Minister. 'But will they all tell the truth?'[6] she asked, somewhat plaintively. It was a small sign that her confidence might be faltering.

Meanwhile, the confidence of her opponents was soaring. Michael Heseltine's long-serving lieutenant, Keith Hampson MP, was pirouetting gleefully in the corridor beside the tea room, saying to all and sundry, 'Yipee! Tee-hee! She's standing. We've made it. We can't lose now.'[7] A burly whip, David Lightbown, told him to shut up. Corridor conversations were getting even more acerbic than they had been on the afternoon of the Howe resignation statement. Vehemence in both directions seemed to be the order of the day.

'I shall stiffen my sinews to get her elected', announced Nicholas Budgen, sounding as though he was Henry V at the siege of Harfleur. 'What we need now is a unity candidate to stop all this nonsense' was the gloomy view of Robert Rhodes James, the Member for Cambridge.[8] Almost as he spoke, Margaret Thatcher was talking to the two most likely players of that role. She asked Douglas Hurd to propose her nomination in the second ballot. He reaffirmed his willingness to do this, even though he was aware that there was a groundswell of support already building for his own entry into the race.

With Hurd signed up, the Prime Minister telephoned John Major. He was convalescing at his home in Huntingdon from a wisdom-tooth extraction. Contrary to some later reports, this dental procedure, arranged two weeks earlier, was entirely genuine. When Margaret Thatcher got through to him she briskly asked him to second her nomination. 'There was a moment's silence. The hesitation was palpable', she thought.[9] John Major did indeed pause before replying, but his hesitation was not because he was thinking of his own chances. He was put off by the peremptory tone of her voice and her automatic assumption of his support. He thought her approach to him was a classic example of her high-handed management style. He would have liked to be consulted, not bossed about. But he swallowed his doubts and answered, 'If that is what you want, I will'.[10]

With her two nominators in place, the Prime Minister set about organising her campaign team. She was not going to leave her destiny in the hands of Peter Morrison for a second time. She turned, through John Wakeham, to two of the most effective campaigners who had delivered a good result for her in the 1989 contest – Tristan Garel-Jones and Richard Ryder. They both refused to help. As the former was an avid Europhile, she was not unduly disappointed by his refusal to serve. But the defection of Richard Ryder was a blow that hurt. He had been her political secretary from 1975 to 1981, and was married to her closest aide and diary secretary, Caroline Stephens. Margaret Thatcher regarded Ryder almost as family. She had given him fast-track promotion after he became an MP in June 1983. It was a grim sign for her survival prospects that he was deserting.

Although the shadows were closing in on her, Margaret Thatcher had not yet lost her self-belief. On that fateful evening of Wednesday 21 November, she had an audience with the Queen, who was informed that the Prime Minister intended to stand in the second ballot. On returning to the House of Commons, she started a series of one-on-one appointments with her senior cabinet ministers. This was where her re-election prospects finally came unstuck.

THE CABINET DEFECTS

The cabinet killed Margaret Thatcher's chances of survival. Their motives were mixed. Some wanted her out because they had come to dislike her. Others thought they were giving her the only realistic advice in the light of faltering support. A few reckoned that once she was gone they had a much better chance of stopping Heseltine and holding on to their jobs under Douglas Hurd or John Major. Only a handful stayed loyal to the Prime Minister who had made their careers.

The momentum to ditch rather than follow the leader had been building steadily within the cabinet for the past twenty-four hours. Soon after the first-ballot result was announced, a group of ten ministers, five of them in the cabinet, met at the Westminster home of Tristan Garel-Jones. Margaret Thatcher was spoken of almost entirely in the past tense, apart from a brief tribute from William Waldegrave. Her departure was regarded as a *fait accompli*. So the conversation focused on who was the best candidate to beat Heseltine. At this early stage, the consensus chez Garel-Jones was that this candidate would be Douglas Hurd. Malcolm Rifkind, Chris Patten, Tony Newton and William Waldegrave all seemed to be leaning this way. Others, like Norman Lamont, kept their own counsel. But not a single minister advocated putting up a fight to keep Margaret Thatcher.

Similar if smaller groups were talking together all through Tuesday evening and Wednesday. So by the time Margaret Thatcher began seeing her cabinet individually, the die was cast. They had made up their minds not to support her, and many of them had even collectively rehearsed their speeches of regret.

Between 7 and 9 p.m. on Wednesday 21 November, fifteen ministers, twelve of them from the cabinet, called one by one on the Prime Minister. This procedure, recommended by John Wakeham, was a tactical mistake. Margaret Thatcher might have done better if she had brought them all together, and in the presence of her proposer and seconder had simply asked each minister how they would vote and whether they would go out and campaign for her. In such a collegiate atmosphere the ranks might have closed behind her. Certainly, the level of her support would have been much higher.

Even under the one-on-one arrangement, only three cabinet ministers had the guts to tell Margaret Thatcher that she should go. They were Kenneth Clarke, Malcolm Rifkind and Chris Patten. The most brutal of these was Kenneth Clarke, who advised her that if she stood she would 'lose big', and that the crown would go to Michael Heseltine, who would split the party.[11]

Seven members of the cabinet used what was clearly a previously agreed 'line to take' in their interviews. They all told the Prime Minister they would support her in the second ballot, but that she could not win it. So in varying tones of regret that ranged from the embarrassment of a candid friend to the tearfulness of a bereaved mourner, they advised her to quit now. 'Almost to a man,' she sourly complained, 'they used the same formula . . . I felt I could almost join in the chorus.'[12]

The chorus line included Peter Lilley, John Gummer, William Waldegrave, John MacGregor, Tony Newton and Norman Lamont. Margaret Thatcher was retrospectively harsh in her criticism of the messengers who dressed up their message in this way. 'What grieved me', she wrote in her memoirs, 'was the desertion of those I had always considered friends and allies, and the weasel words whereby they had transmuted their betrayal into frank advice and concern for my fate.'[13] Later, she characterised their behaviour as 'Treachery with a smile on its face'.[14]

Those cabinet colleagues she acquitted of the charge of treachery were Cecil Parkinson, John Wakeham, Peter Brooke, David Waddington, Michael Howard and Tom King. But even some of those loyalists expressed their doubts. King came up with a suggestion that she should offer to stand down at the conclusion of the Gulf War. She rejected it on the grounds that she had no wish to stay on as a lame-duck Prime Minister.

By the end of her cabinet interviews, she knew it was all over. But she was not admitting it. The nearest she came to this was when, amidst all the comings and goings of her senior colleagues, Alan Clark was allowed access 'for a split second' by Peter Morrison. 'She looked calm, almost beautiful', said Clark, who proceeded to tell her that she 'was wonderful', heroic, but that the party would let her down.

'I am a fighter', she replied.

'Fight, then. Fight right to the end, a third ballot if you need to. But you lose.'

There was a pause. Then came a most telling response.

'It'd be so terrible if Michael won', she said. 'He would undo everything I have fought for.'[15]

A day after this exchange, Alan Clark told me that when he heard her say these words, he knew he had accomplished his mission. He venerated Margaret Thatcher, but desperately wanted to find a way of persuading her to leave the battlefield with honour. In the role of 'a gallant friend' (her description of him)[16] singing her praises, he may have nudged her towards the exit more effectively than any hostile member of her cabinet.

The fear of Heseltine was a surprising infection, and now it had gripped her. The reality was that no one knew what sort of a prime minister he would make if he reached this pinnacle. The idea that he would destroy the achievements of Margaret Thatcher over the past decade was fanciful. Indeed, when announcing his candidacy he had proclaimed himself 'to be have been at the leading edge of Thatcherism'.[17] But because he was mistrusted so much and had communicated so little, many people at the top of the party had exaggerated anxieties about the Heseltine destabilisation factor. Would he purge the cabinet? Make radical changes in policy? Split the party? Destroy the Prime Minister's legacy? All this was unlikely, but as the barbarian drew close to the gates of

No. 10, irrational rumours spread. Stop him at all costs became the cry, and in the end even Margaret Thatcher joined the chorus.

After the cabinet ministers and Alan Clark had said their pieces, Margaret Thatcher was visited by a smattering of uber-loyal ministers and MPs. The first one in was Michael Portillo, the thirty-seven-year old Minister of State at the Department of the Environment with responsibility for the poll tax. He was followed by a delegation from the right-of-centre 92 Group.* Their message was the polar opposite of the doom and gloom purveyed by the cabinet. These young and impassioned Thatcherite MPs told the Prime Minister that she was being misled by her senior ministers, and that with an energetic fight she could still triumph on the second ballot. Their heroine was touched. 'With even a drop of this spirit in higher places, it might indeed have been possible',[18] she wrote later. But at the time, she weighed the optimism of youth against the pessimism of the reports she was getting from her campaign manager, John Wakeham, and others close to her. The pessimists produced grim estimates to suggest that her vote had now fallen below 150, a figure that would have given Heseltine a seventy-plus majority. With growing sadness, Margaret Thatcher returned to No. 10.

Denis was waiting for her. He had been dining at Mark's club with Carol and Alistair McAlpine. Thatcher *père et fille* had put on a brave face during the meal, but as they walked across Horse Guards Parade they broke down in tears. 'Oh, it's just the *disloyalty* of it all', said Denis. It was the only time Carol had ever seen her father cry.[19]

Despite his tears, Denis wanted his wife to depart with dignity and not to be hustled out in humiliation. He had seen the outcome more clearly than she did from the moment the first-ballot result came through. So he comforted her and with his special brand of loving, down-to-earth practicality, he guided her to the inevitable decision.

She had work to do before any announcement of her resignation could be made. At the height of the Tory traumas Labour had tabled an opportunistic motion of no confidence, which was to be debated on the afternoon of Thursday 22 November. Knowing that she would have announced her

---

* The 92 Group was so called because members used to meet at 92 Cheyne Walk, the home of their first Chairman, Patrick Wall MP.

resignation by then, it would have been easy to ask another senior minister, probably the Leader of the House, John MacGregor, to reply to the debate on behalf of the government. But this thought did not occur to her.

Instead, at around 11 p.m. she knuckled down to the task of writing her last speech as Prime Minister, calling in Charles Powell, Tim Bell, Gordon Reece and John Gummer for help. The drafting was briefly interrupted by Michael Portillo, accompanied by Michael Forsyth and Michael Fallon, who made one final appeal to her to fight on. It was an emotional moment, but after wiping away a tear she refused to be swayed by these 'last-ditchers', as she called them.[20]

At about 3 a.m. she went to bed, insisting that she would follow her usual practice of sleeping on important decisions. The short night's rest did not change her mind. At 7.30 on the morning of Thursday 22 November, she telephoned down to her Principal Private Secretary, Andrew Turnbull, to say that she had finally resolved to resign. He implemented a prepared plan for the day ahead, which included a briefing for Prime Minister's Questions, a statement to the cabinet and an audience with the Queen.

The cabinet met at 9 a.m. that morning, ninety minutes earlier than usual, not because of the leadership drama but because several ministers planned to attend the Westminster Abbey memorial service for Lady Home of the Hirsel.* The atmosphere in the anteroom resembled a gathering of mourners assembling in church before a funeral. Margaret Thatcher, red-eyed and in a black suit, noticed how her colleagues 'stood with their backs against the wall, looking in every direction except mine'.[21]

She began by saying that before the formal business of the cabinet she wanted to make her position known. She started to read from a paper in front of her, but after the first five words, 'Having consulted widely among colleagues . . .' she broke down and was unable to continue.[22] 'For God's sake, you read it, James', said Cecil Parkinson to the Lord Chancellor, Lord Mackay.

The Prime Minister shook her head, blew her nose, and unsuccessfully tried to start again. Her distress moved several ministers to tears of their own, some real, some crocodile. Eventually she got it all out:

---

* Lady Home (1909–1990), wife of Lord Home of the Hirsel who as Sir Alec Douglas-Home was Conservative Prime Minister, 1963–1964.

Having consulted widely among colleagues, I have concluded that the unity of the party and the prospects of victory in a General Election will be better served if I stood down to enable colleagues to enter the ballot for the Leadership. I should like to thank all those in Cabinet and outside who have given me such dedicated support.[23]

Lord Mackay then read out a tribute on behalf of the cabinet to which Kenneth Baker and Douglas Hurd added their own words of appreciation. Margaret Thatcher found the sympathy almost unbearable, so she intervened with some practical politics. Her line was that the cabinet must unite to defeat Heseltine, otherwise all the things she had stood for during the past eleven years would be lost. How many of her colleagues agreed with this final imperative command was unclear.

After a short coffee break, during which the news of her impending resignation was released, the cabinet resumed its normal business. The most important decision was to increase British forces in the Gulf by sending a second armoured brigade. Margaret Thatcher handled the agenda with subdued aplomb, although she was again close to tears towards the end.

Her last cabinet ended at 10.15 a.m. She invited its members to stay on for an informal political discussion. The officials melted away. Among the politicians sitting round the table, the talk immediately turned to the leadership election. Again, there was much emphasis on the importance of stopping Heseltine. In a heated moment, one colleague declared, 'We're going to pin regicide on him'. Margaret Thatcher looked perplexed for a moment, and then made a devastating reply. 'Oh no, it wasn't Heseltine, it was the Cabinet', she said.[24] The way she delivered the line, without a trace of rancour, gave the impression of a history teacher correcting an error of fact in a pupil's essay. Of course, she was right.

Her last tasks of the morning were to send messages to Presidents Bush and Gorbachev, and to European heads of government. Then she went to Buckingham Palace for an audience with the Queen. After that, she went back to work on the draft of her speech for the no confidence debate. Curiously, this lifted her spirits. For the realisation struck home that now she had announced her resignation, the Tory Party would be totally united behind her. Even the opposition might be sympathetic. So she began to anticipate a good reception in the House. She guessed it would be 'roses, roses, all the way'.[25] Again, she was right.

A BRAVURA FAREWELL PERFORMANCE

Margaret Thatcher's last speech to the House of Commons as Prime Minister was a triumph. After a morning in tears, she had an afternoon of glory. It was as though a diva was singing her last and greatest ever role, hitting all the high notes at her final appearance. To do this on the day of her resignation was a miracle of political confidence and courage. Those who were present in the chamber will never forget it.

Many MPs thought she would not come to Parliament that day. They expected her to be traumatised by the speed and brutality of her fall. But the Iron Lady knew that she had been presented with a great theatrical opportunity. She seized it, fortified by a vitamin B6 booster injection and by the mood of the parliamentary audience, which was in overdrive with excitement at the high drama it was about to witness.

As usual, Neil Kinnock helped her. Even allowing for the fact that his fox had been shot before the debate began, he managed to deliver an opening speech which was not just mediocre; it was abysmal. So she hit a soft target when in her opening sentences she attacked him for his 'windy rhetoric . . . just a lot of disjointed opaque, words'.[26]

She was the opposite of opaque. When preparing the final draft of her speech with the help of Charles Powell, she said she wanted it to be 'my testament at the bar of History'.[27] Her delivery was too rough-hewn to fulfil the elegiac nature of this aspiration. But as a robust and often spontaneous defence of her record it was a thrilling performance, vintage Margaret Thatcher with the bark off. It was, as Morley said of Gladstone, 'the character breathing through the sentences that counted'.[28]

She was at her best when dealing with interventions. She chided Labour for not saying where they stood on the central issues of Europe's future. 'Do they want a single currency? The right hon. Gentleman does not even know what it means, so how can he know?'[29]

Neil Kinnock feebly interjected, 'It is a hypothetical question'. 'Absolute nonsense. It is appalling', she thundered back, hammering on the despatch box. 'It will not be a hypothetical question. Someone must go to Europe and argue knowing what it means.'[30]

The Deputy Leader of the Liberal Party, Alan Beith, intervened to ask, 'Will the Prime Minister tell us whether she intends to continue her personal fight against a single currency and an independent central bank when she leaves office?'

Before she had time to reply, Dennis Skinner, the Labour MP for Bolsover, bellowed from a sedentary position on the first bench below the gangway, 'No. She is going to be the governor.'

Margaret Thatcher rode on the wave of laughter and joined in the knockabout.

'What a good idea!' she retorted. 'I had not thought of that.' Then she turned the humour to her advantage.

But if I were, there would be no European central bank accountable to no one, least of all national Parliaments. The point of that kind of Europe with a central bank is no democracy, taking away powers from every single Parliament, and having a single currency, a monetary policy and interest rates which take all political power away from us . . . a single currency is about the politics of Europe, it is about a federal Europe by the back door. So I shall consider the proposal of the Hon. Member for Bolsover. Now, where were we? I am enjoying this.[31]

The House of Commons was enjoying it too. Amidst the cheering, the Tory MP for Great Yarmouth, Michael Carttiss, shouted, 'Cancel it. You can wipe the floor with these people.'

'Yes, indeed', beamed Margaret Thatcher.[32]

There was little doubt in anyone's mind that she was wiping away the impact of Geoffrey Howe's resignation statement. For she was counter-attacking his ideas so forcefully. Moreover, she was winning both the argument and the presentation. It was game, set and match to Thatcher. An important legacy of this speech was that it killed the chances of Britain ever signing up to EMU, or to the euro.

Moving to the higher ground of international statecraft, she claimed credit for helping Eastern Europe to escape from totalitarian rule, and for ending the Cold War. 'These immense changes did not come about by chance. They have been achieved by strength and resolution in defence, and by a refusal ever to be intimidated.'[33]

The theme of intimidation brought her to a powerful peroration focused on the past conflict in the South Atlantic, and the coming conflict in the Gulf.

Twice in my time as Prime Minister we have had to send our forces across the world to defend a small country against ruthless aggression: first to our own people in the Falklands, and now to the borders of Kuwait. To those who have never had to take such decisions, I say that they are taken with a heavy heart and in the knowledge of the manifold dangers, but with tremendous pride in the professionalism and courage of our armed forces.[34]

Roars of 'hear, hear' rang out again, but then the House fell to a hush, perhaps sensing that as Britain was again on the brink of a war, the former war leader might have an important message in her closing sentences. She did not disappoint. Dropping her voice low before soaring upwards to the climax of her speech, she said:

There is something else which one feels. That is a sense of this country's destiny: the centuries of history and experience which ensure that, when principles have to be defended, when good has to be upheld and when evil has to be overcome, Britain will take up arms. It is because we on this side have never flinched from difficult decisions that this House and this country can have confidence in this Government today.[35]

The cheers rang to the welkin of the chamber, and not just from her own side. By any standards it had been one of the most remarkable House of Commons speeches in living memory. The supreme irony was that many of those cheering loudest and waving their order papers most vigorously were those who had just voted her out. Hypocrisy *in excelsis*! Behind the applause one could hear the sound of consciences pricking. If the leadership ballot could have been reinstated and held that afternoon, she would have won by a landslide.

In the tea room afterwards I sat at a table with Michael Carttiss, the rough and ready Norfolk MP who had made the 'You can wipe the floor with these people' interjection in the Prime Minister's speech. He was in a state of utter despair. 'What have we done? What have we done?' he kept asking. He was not alone in his anguish.

The fact of the matter was that back-bench opinion on Margaret Thatcher was extremely volatile. Her fans and her foes remained more or less constant. But the fickle middle of the party lurched from being for her or against her depending on whether they had spent the weekend in their constituencies (where local support for the Prime Minister was generally strong), or whether they had been listening to Geoffrey Howe or courted by Michael Heseltine, or now whether they had seen and heard Margaret Thatcher on her finest form as a leader.

In the aftermath of her final speech as Prime Minister, guilt stalked the corridors of Conservative Westminster. The *Daily Mail* caught the spectre of this shame with its headline, 'Too Damn Good for the Lot of Them'.[36] That was the perfect epitaph for her on the day when her stature had soared stratospherically above the MPs and cabinet ministers who had abandoned her.

THE ELECTION OF A NEW LEADER

It was an extraordinary irony that Margaret Thatcher put in much more hard work to secure the election of John Major on the second ballot than she had to support her own position on the first. He suddenly became her chosen successor, although this process required some degree of self-delusion. Faced with choosing between the three candidates, she did not hesitate. Michael Heseltine was anathema to her. She respected Douglas Hurd, but thought him too much of an old school consensualist. As she told Woodrow Wyatt:

> It may be inverted snobbishness but I don't want old style, old Etonian Tories of the old school to succeed me and to go back to the old complacent consensus ways. John Major is someone who has fought his way up from the bottom and is far more in tune with the skilled and ambitious and worthwhile working classes than Douglas Hurd is.[37]

Even so, to anoint John Major with enthusiasm she needed to believe that he was a right-winger, a Eurosceptic and a Thatcherite. None of these three labels rang true. But she convinced herself otherwise. This was superficially possible because, having been Foreign Secretary for only three months and Chancellor for only a year, John Major carried little baggage. Ideologically, he was the unknown candidate, even to the Prime Minister who now wanted him to be her successor.

Major had the best campaign team, led by Norman Lamont. Hurd was a half-hearted starter. As Willie Whitelaw shrewdly observed of him, 'The trouble with Douglas is the same with me in 1975. He doesn't really want the job.'[38]

As for Heseltine, he again was handicapped by having weak campaign managers. Yet even so, some momentum started to build for him for the first couple of days after the resignation. Ironically, this new but fleeting support came mostly from furious Thatcherites. They were so angry at the assassination of their heroine that they wanted to have nothing to do with those they thought had betrayed her. So, to punish Norman Lamont, Richard Ryder and Peter Lilley, who had by now become the leaders of John Major's campaign, some hotheads of the Thatcher fan club declared they would vote for Heseltine. Another tranche of pledges came from MPs who felt that the colourful Tarzan was a future election winner, while 'the grey men in suits' (Hurd and Major) were not.

Margaret Thatcher did a valuable service to the Major camp by reversing this flow of support for Heseltine. She telephoned a number of her loyalists to urge them to vote for her chosen successor. Her advocacy of the reasons why Heseltine must be stopped was powerful. By the time she deployed these arguments, many a Tory MP was feeling guilty about the deposition of a leader who, for all her faults, had just put on a firework display of her leadership skills in the no confidence debate.

One way or another, her enthusiastic backing for Major was an important factor in swinging the contest his way. However, it was not as important as a MORI opinion poll, which suggested that John Major would be even more successful as a vote-getter with the electorate than Michael Heseltine.[39] Once the febrile party started to believe that Tarzan's alleged powers of election winning might be surpassed by the least known prime ministerial candidate, the Heseltine bandwagon juddered to a halt, and the uncommitted votes rolled Major's way.

Margaret Thatcher was active but not over-active in the five days of second-ballot leadership campaigning. She was too busy with the mundane but essential task of moving out. Packing up her flat after eleven and a half years in residence at No. 10 proved a wearisome task. Fortunately, unlike some previous prime ministers who lost office unexpectedly, she had somewhere to move to.

Three years earlier, Denis had presciently said, 'Look, we should never be homeless. You don't know with politics; we might have to move in a hurry and we must have somewhere to go.'[40] As a result, the Thatchers had bought a house on a new estate overlooking the golf course at Dulwich. So their accumulated possessions were transported there in a shuttle service operated mainly by Denis's Ford Cortina and Carol's Mini-Metro.

With the help of Crawfie, Carla Powell and Joy Robilliard (her constituency secretary), Margaret Thatcher supervised the moving operations, padding around in her stockinged feet as she filled tea chests and mobile wardrobes. No longer occupied with the decisions of government, she spent her time deciding 'whether to wrap knick-knacks in two layers of paper, or whether one would do'.[41]

Her last weekend as Prime Minister was spent at Chequers. It was a house she had come to love, so parting from it was an emotional wrench. On her final Sunday there she went to church, gave a drinks party for the Chequers staff and then, in the late afternoon, had a farewell stroll round the main rooms as the winter light was fading. She and Denis were in tears as they walked hand in hand along the gallery that overlooked the great hall.

Returning to No. 10, it was clear to her and other insiders that the momentum in the leadership election was moving heavily towards John Major. But she did make one or two last canvassing phone calls on his behalf, only to find that these alleged waverers had already become his supporters.

Her only outside public engagement on Monday was to go and say a farewell thank you to the staff at Central Office. This caused the sole glitch in her post-resignation appearances, when she told them that she would be 'a very good back seat driver'.

The remark was immediately misinterpreted, not least in the Major campaign headquarters in Gayfere Street, where I heard an explosion of expletives in reaction to it. This was an error of judgement. For Margaret Thatcher was not signalling her intention of exercising influence on her successor.

It was clear from the context that she was not referring to John Major, but to President George Bush. She told the Central Office staffers that she had been 'very, very thrilled' to receive a phone call from the President soon after her resignation announcement. She went on to say that they had discussed the military situation in the Gulf, where 'He won't falter, and I won't falter. It's just that I won't be pulling the levers there. But I shall be a very good back seat driver.'[42]

Two last outings as a front-seat driver took place at a party for the staff of 10 Downing Street and at her final appearance at Prime Minister's Questions. The farewell staff party attended by cleaners, drivers, police officers and telephonists, as well as by her private office, was described by Ronnie Millar as a 'triumphant' occasion. She expressed her farewell thanks with great verve, standing on a chair to be cheered. Her last line, 'Life begins at sixty-five', brought the house down. She was presented with a first edition of Kipling's poems and a high-frequency portable radio. Her Private Secretary, Andrew Turnbull, said that the gift had been chosen 'So wherever you are in the world, you can continue to be cross with the BBC'.[43]

On Tuesday 27 November, her last full day in office, she cast her own vote in the leadership election and then answered her 698th session of Prime Minister's Questions. It was more of an occasion for congratulations than interrogation. But she did get in one Parthian shot when the Liberal MP, Rosie Barnes, asked her about electoral reform of the national voting system. 'I am sure that the hon. Lady will understand that I am all for first past the post', replied Margaret Thatcher.[44] The laughter among Tory MPs included many pangs of regret that such a system had not been in place for her leadership election.

Soon after 6 p.m., the results of the ballot were announced. John Major topped the poll with 185 votes to Heseltine's 131 and Hurd's 56. Although this left Major technically short of two votes for the absolute majority required under the rules, this was academic since Heseltine and Hurd immediately withdrew. So the crown went to John Major, although as Margaret Thatcher observed to her family, he was elected by nineteen fewer votes than she had received a week earlier.

As soon as Michael Heseltine and Douglas Hurd had delivered their withdrawal statements, the outgoing Prime Minister went through the connecting door to No. 11 and congratulated her successor. 'Well done, John, well done', she said, shaking his hand.[45] She was more effusive to Norma Major, giving her a hug and a kiss, saying, 'It's everything I've dreamt of for such a long time. The future is assured.'[46]

With the media massing in Downing Street, it was time for John Major to emerge with a victory statement. Margaret Thatcher wanted to make it a joint appearance. 'I'll come out', she said. But Norman Lamont, sensitive to the 'back-seat driver' controversy of the previous day, dissuaded her with the request, 'Please let him have his moment'.[47] She complied, and watched him from an upstairs window, peeping sadly from behind a curtain. It made a poignant photograph symbolising the passing of her era.

Her last night at No. 10 consisted of more hard labour filling up the last of the packing cases, followed by a quiet supper with Denis, Mark and Carol.

In the morning, she was down in the front hallway just after 9 a.m., where the entire No. 10 staff were lined up, some of them weeping. They burst into applause as she appeared. She shook hands with her private office team and many others. At first, she tried to suppress her own tears at these farewells, but soon was unable to stem the flow. By the time she had gone down the line of well-wishers her eyes were red and her mascara was smudged. Crawfie had to step in with a handkerchief to do some emergency make-up repairs.

With composure recovered, the front door opened. She stepped out to a bank of microphones, and said:

> Ladies and Gentlemen. We're leaving Downing Street for the last time after eleven and a half wonderful years, and we're very happy that we leave the United Kingdom in a very, very much better state than when we came eleven and a half years ago.

After reiterating her gratitude to her staff and to the people who had sent her flowers and letters, she ended:

> Now it's time for a new chapter to open, and I wish John Major all the luck in the world. He'll be splendidly served and he has the makings of being a great Prime Minister, which I am sure he will be in a very short time. Thank you very much. Goodbye.[48]

She and Denis got into the waiting car. As it moved away, she turned in her seat for a sideways look at the throng of media. The photographers caught an affecting picture of her face crumpling in sadness. It was a reminder of Enoch Powell's adage, 'All political careers end in tears'.[49]

REFLECTION

Politics is a rough trade, but the fall of Margaret Thatcher will go down as the most unpleasant and unattractive destruction of a prime minister in modern history. It brought out the worst aspects of the Tory Party – panic, disloyalty, deviousness, score settling and a cavalier disregard for the rights of the electorate.

The big question remains: should a serving prime minister ever be removed by a faction of MPs within their own party? In Margaret Thatcher's case, the issue was particularly acute because she was a leader of such outstanding stature, who had been confirmed as Prime Minister by three substantial election victories. If she was going to be overthrown, it should have been done by the voters, in a general election.

It is true that Margaret Thatcher brought many of her troubles on herself. She stopped listening to her party, and even to the most loyal of her colleagues. Her man-management became deplorable. Hubris and arrogance grew within her. The way she handled her leadership election challenge from Michael Heseltine was downright sloppy – an adjective which could not be applied to any other episode in her political career. These were grave mistakes, but did they amount to a charge sheet that justified her political execution? 'No! No! No!', to echo the words she memorably used in an earlier context.

She was ousted because a section of the Conservative Party in Parliament, and particularly about half the members of the cabinet, worked themselves up into a mid-term panic. The woes of the poll tax and a clutch of bad by-election results meant that a swathe of MPs, particularly in the North West, were convinced that they were going to lose their seats. Experience suggests that by the time a general election came round in 1992 these fears would have significantly abated. The poll tax was in the process of being amended and alleviated. Other issues such as the improvement in the economy and success in the Gulf War would have had more impact in an election.

A Kinnock versus Thatcher head-to-head contest at the polls would have broken all precedents if the result had been a knockout victory for the challenger. If these probabilities of political life had been explained by reassuring voices from the cabinet, the chances are that the back-bench hysteria would have been contained.

Unfortunately, several cabinet ministers were themselves in a state of panic. All of them liked and respected Geoffrey Howe. They were aghast at the harshness of his treatment by the Prime Minister and at the havoc unleashed by his resignation statement.

Michael Heseltine would never have challenged Margaret Thatcher as a sitting Prime Minister had it not been for the invitation to do so issued at the end of Howe's resignation statement. The collusion between these two enemies of their leader, whether plotted or telepathic, caused chaos. Most of the cabinet were not expecting it. They reacted with irrational fear. Had they closed ranks and strongly supported the Prime Minister, the chances of her defeating him by a simple majority (as the second-ballot rules required) would have risen to at least 50–50. But instead of giving her that steadfast support, the cabinet's loyalty disintegrated.

The charge of treachery by the cabinet, which Margaret Thatcher herself made in her post-resignation years, is difficult to sustain, at least in the extreme form that involves plotting and backstabbing. What happened was that the cabinet took its lead from the back-benchers. Usually in politics it is the other way round. But this cabinet lacked ministers willing to go into battle for their leader. They were feeble turncoats rather than resolute traitors. In retrospect, they look like weak politicians who lost their bearings in a crisis. Some may have been treacherous, but most of them defected because they had no stomach for the fight.

Three members of the cabinet (Kenneth Clarke, Malcolm Rifkind and Chris Patten) told her to her face that they would not vote for her. Most of the rest genuinely believed that her support among the back-benchers was collapsing. But they made no concerted attempt to claw back the votes that were slipping away from the Prime Minister. Instead, they became paralysed at the prospect of Heseltine arriving at No. 10, a fear that turned into a stampede of cabinet ministers running with the herd of alarmed Tory back-benchers.

As a back-bencher with a ringside seat at this debacle, I was amazed and ashamed by it. I thought Margaret Thatcher's achievements and virtues far outweighed her misjudgements and failings. Overthrowing her because of the poll tax on the eve of the Gulf War and in the middle of a strategic struggle over the future direction of Europe seemed a myopic and tragic mistake.

Sadly, the Conservative parliamentary party had changed its nature too much to recognise its mistake. Long-term loyalty to the nationally elected leader was at a discount. Short-term fixes to the problems of the Community Charge were at a premium. The Prime Minister worked on longer horizons and bigger visions. Saving our seats was to her a mere parochial imperative compared to saving our country, which had been her mission since the day she came to power in 1979. Winning the Gulf War, defeating inflation and preventing Britain from sliding into the single currency and European federalism were her priorities in the autumn of 1990. Because she took her stand on them so forcefully to the exclusion of most other considerations, she fell – but over much smaller issues and at the hands of much lesser men.

Perhaps the British public would have supported her view of the bigger issues when asked to back her or sack her at a mid-1992 general election, which I and many others believe she would have won. But if it had been the latter decision, at least her rejection would have been at the hands of the national electorate rather than by a party faction. That would have been a better departure for her. Instead, she left in a mind-set of emotionally charged bitterness that was to make life difficult for herself, her successor and her party for many years to come.

38

The agony after the fall

TRAUMA AND TANTRUMS

The first weeks after the fall were traumatic. Margaret Thatcher was in a black mood that combined shocked emotions of bereavement, betrayal and blind fury.

Immediately after leaving No. 10, she and Denis were driven to their new home in Dulwich. So troubled were her feelings that she did not speak a single word to her husband on her fifty-minute journey, according to her driver.[1] Soon she was facing some uncomfortable domestic realities. After eleven years at the apex of power, she was unable to cope with many of life's simplest practicalities. She did not know how to dial a telephone number,* how to send a fax or how to operate the washing and drying machines in her basement. Her Special Branch protection team, who had installed themselves in the garage, helped her over these hurdles. One of the first outside calls she made, on a police line, was to Crawfie. 'This is Margaret. From the garage',[2] was her poignant opening to the conversation.

Seven hours after leaving Whitehall she returned to it in order to attend a party in the Cabinet Office organised in her honour by Sir Robin Butler. Proposing her health to the carefully chosen gathering of her favourite Permanent Secretaries and senior officials, he said, 'When we are old the one thing our children and grandchildren will be most interested in is that we worked for Margaret Thatcher'.[3]

The guest of honour liked this prediction. But she visibly disliked Butler's maladroit presentation to her of a Cabinet Office pass giving her full access as

---

* New codes and push buttons had been introduced by the privatised British Telecom.

an ex-Prime Minister to government buildings. Even more did she dislike his next move of Whitehall housekeeping. This consisted of sending her the standard Cabinet Secretary's letter to former Prime Ministers asking for the return of all government documents in her possession. She refused in a tirade that was extreme even by her standards.

Her parliamentary colleagues also had to get used to her lashings out and eruptions in this dark period. The whips were berated for not immediately finding her an office within the Palace of Westminster. Alastair McAlpine, the Conservative Party Treasurer, came to the rescue by lending her his house in Great College Street. She used it as a base for her secretariat and for receiving visitors in a poky first-floor sitting room.

One cold January evening in 1991 I was walking along Great College Street towards my home in Lord North Street when Peter Morrison popped his head out of the door and said, 'Can you spare a moment, old boy? Margaret could do with some company'.

In the hallway he explained that the recently deposed Prime Minister was 'like a bear with a sore head. She can't stand the sight of the swine who had stabbed her in the back. But she knows you were a last ditcher. So do her a favour and come in and have a nightcap'.[4] He made the invitation sound like an SOS message. In a way it was, for I soon discovered that Margaret Thatcher's state of aggression was elephantine as well as ursine on the Richter scale of rampages.

For well over an hour I listened to what could only be called a hysterical rant. If the former Prime Minister had been equipped with tusks she would have tossed and gored half the Conservative parliamentary party. Her angriest thrusts were directed against her most recently promoted ministers, who she now vilified as 'spineless, gutless Judases'. She set off down what she called 'My list of turncoats and traitors'. The intensity of her rage was increased by the liberal glasses of Famous Grouse Whisky being dispensed by the understandably tired Peter Morrison. He rolled his eyes to the ceiling once or twice as to indicate that he had heard this litany of denunciation many times before. It was a painful, embarrassing and apparently recurring scene. At the time I felt heartbroken for Margaret Thatcher as this dreadful session wore on. Nearly a quarter of a century later, I know it is fairer to draw a veil over these depths of her agony.

The evening ended, however, with a contrastingly brisk decision on her part. Making one effort to distract her from her hymns of hate against her assassins,

I tried to turn the conversation, or to be more accurate her monologue, towards the subject of writing her memoirs. My attempt failed at first instance. Her only response was to fulminate with longer diatribes about betrayals. Making a second try to divert the flow, I talked about the White House aides who had betrayed Richard Nixon. 'How do you know all that?' she asked.

'Originally, because I was staying at San Clemente when Nixon was writing the Watergate chapter of his memoirs. I talked a lot to him and to the researchers who worked on the draft. I think you were once interviewed by one of them – Diane Sawyer of CBS.'

'Diane Sawyer – are you sure?'

'Absolutely certain', I replied, going on to describe how my American friends Frank Gannon and Diane Sawyer had borne the brunt of the research work on the massive Nixon memoirs.

'Well, that's interesting', said Margaret Thatcher. 'Let's have another discussion about how exactly President Nixon wrote his book – but not now. It's time to get back to Dulwich.'[5]

About ten days later I did have a well-focused discussion with Margaret Thatcher about how the memoirs of the 43rd President of the United States had been researched and written. By this time I had done my homework and knew exactly which sections, on issues as diverse as the vice presidency, the opening to China and Watergate, had been worked on by which researcher.

Margaret Thatcher was intrigued. At one point I told her that Nixon had grilled Diane Sawyer for hours at a stretch of intense questioning about her draft pages on Watergate. 'The longest of these lasted six and a half hours without even a bathroom break', I said. This detail got a human reaction from the former Prime Minister.

'Without even a bathroom break!' she exclaimed. 'Poor girl! How inconsiderate of Mr Nixon. One must be considerate to one's staff.'

The final consideration that was discussed in our talk about Nixon's memoirs was time. She asked how long she would need to write her memoirs. The subject must have been on her mind, since the press were reporting that there was a bidding war between Robert Maxwell and Rupert Murdoch for the worldwide rights to her autobiography.

'President Nixon took two and a half years to write his book', I said.

The Iron Lady became the impatient Lady.

'Two and a half years!' she said, her voice rising. That's half the time it took to win the Second World War! And this Parliament may last another two and a half years. There's work for me to do in the House!'

I was too polite to say so at the time, but I thought this was one of the silliest statements I had ever heard from her lips. The notion that she should be sitting around in the House of Commons as an ex-Prime Minister looking for work to do was a certain recipe for increasing her frustration. This was indeed the pattern for her last eighteen months as a back-bencher. Far from simmering down in the slower pace of life after high office, she boiled over with increasingly venomous anger about the way she had been treated. She vented her spleen not just in private conversations but also in public interviews. She repeatedly referred to herself as 'The only undefeated Prime Minister'.

As she complained to *Vanity Fair* in March 1991: 'I have never been defeated in an election. I have never been defeated in a vote of confidence in Parliament . . . I have never been defeated by the people.' In the same interview she described with emotional imagery how 'The pattern of my life was fractured . . . It's like throwing a pane of glass with a complicated map upon it on the floor . . . You threw it on the floor and it shattered.'[6]

The pain of her shattering resulted in many outbursts and tantrums. Denis bore the worst of these storms but not always stoically. He too could become angry. The unsuitability of the house in Dulwich was one bone of contention. This difficulty was solved by Kathleen Ford, the widow of Henry Ford, who lent the Thatchers her twelve-room duplex apartment in 93 Eaton Square for over a year in 1990–1991 until they acquired a lease on a five-storey house two minutes walk away at 73 Chester Square.

Being comfortably housed was not the real problem. The root cause of Margaret Thatcher's restlessness was that she retained a hunger and a capacity for power but had no field in which to exercise it. She found it impossible to fill this gap in her life since she had no interests beyond the arena of politics. As Charles Powell said after her death, 'She never had a happy day after being ousted from office'.[7]

TRAVELLING, SPEECH-MAKING AND WRITING

The first break in the clouds that were causing her gloom came when she started to travel the world earning huge fees from speech-making. The first of these excursions was to Texas, where Mark's contacts in Dallas clubbed together to provide a speaker's honorarium of $250,000 for the ex-Prime Minister. 'It gave my mother an enormous boost of confidence at a time when she was feeling very uncertain about her future', said Mark.[8]

The engagement opened the door to a relationship with the prestigious Washington Speakers Bureau who for several years arranged lectures for her at a fee of $50,000 a time. As always, she felt at home in the United States, having made ten visits there in 1991–1992. They included not only set-piece speeches to paying audiences but also public events at which she was honoured for her historic achievements. These included receiving the Congressional Medal of Freedom from George H.W. Bush at a lavish ceremony in the White House; and attending Ronald Reagan's eightieth birthday party in California.

Her travels soon became global. In August 1992 she set off to Taiwan and Hong Kong. The first of these assignments required a speech of careful diplomatic balance. The second was an even harder balancing act for she had to decide whether to oppose or support what were called the 'Patten reforms' for the colony in its last years before the handover. This was not an easy judgement. She had been 'distinctly sniffy'[9] about Chris Patten's appointment as Governor. However, against the urgings of her former adviser, Sir Percy Cradock, she sided, not entirely successfully, with Patten's attempts to introduce democratic freedom into the governance of Hong Kong. But, because of the immense respect accorded her by the leadership in Beijing, behind the scenes she was a helpful influence on various difficult issues in the run up to China's absorption of the colony.

From Hong Kong, she flew by a BP corporate jet to Baku, Azerbaijan, whose President Abulfaz Elchibey would not agree a major oil contract with the company unless Margaret Thatcher was present at the signing ceremony. Her presence was requested by the president to give a 'free of corruption' seal of approval to the deal. She was delighted to be 'batting for Britain' again in this way. She refused all offers of payment for her speeches and appearances in Taiwan, Hong Kong and Baku, even though she had prepared for them with a thoroughness almost as intense as for a prime ministerial tour.

After she returned from this Far East–Central Asia series of engagements, the newly appointed head of her office, Julian Seymour, thought that the contribution she felt she had made to Britain's national interests gave her a fresh sense of purpose. 'From then on she was much more focused. She had found a way of exerting influence again.'[10]

One other dimension of her speech-making after leaving office deserves to be highlighted. She enjoyed influencing the minds of the young. She accepted, always without taking a fee, many invitations from universities and colleges. She became Chancellor of William and Mary College in Virginia where she gave lectures and participated in Charter Day activities.

In Britain she was more selective in speaking to academic audiences, but in different ways she was supportive of Buckingham University, Churchill College, Cambridge and the Saïd Business School at Oxford. She never quite got over the hostility of the Oxford dons who had voted against awarding her an honorary degree. But for old friends such as Wafic Saïd and Robin Butler she made an exception to her anti-Oxford bias.

It was an invitation from her former private secretary, now Lord Butler of Brockwell and Master of University College, Oxford, which produced a rare example of Margaret Thatcher being outflanked by a sharp questioner. The scene of this uncomfortable exchange came when she addressed the students of University College at a private gathering organised by Robin Butler.

In her brief opening remarks the former Prime Minister said she would like her listeners from the rising generation to reflect on just two points:

'First, about the world; you should remember that during the 20th century, my century, more people died of tyranny than died in war. So you must always be ready to fight for freedom.

'Secondly, about Britain; the problems facing your generation will not be economic problems. They have been solved', she announced, modestly refraining from saying who she thought had solved them.

'But I think you will have to face a severe social problem which could better be described as a behavioural problem', she continued. 'When I was growing up, even during the war, five per cent of children were born illegitimate. Today thirty-two per cent of births are illegitimate, and the number is rising. I don't know what the consequences of this will be, but it worries me.'

During the Q & A session a student challenged her views on this issue: 'Lady Thatcher, don't you think it's a little unfair to describe a child as illegitimate throughout its life when it has had no influence over the circumstances of its own birth?'

'Well, what would you call it?' she retorted. 'I can think of another word to use. But I prefer not to use it in this company.'[11]

There was a stunned silence. But after an uneasy pause, the questioning resumed on other topics. Then there was chapel, dinner at high table and a nightcap in the Master's lodgings.

Over a whisky with Denis and Robin Butler, Margaret Thatcher suddenly said: 'Robin, that young man who asked the question about the word illegitimate – he had a point didn't he?'[12]

The episode highlighted three aspects of Margaret Thatcher's personality. First, her sometimes insensitive forthrightness. Second, her reluctance to yield, let alone apologise for, a bad point. Third, her willingness to learn from a mistake.

'I will wager she never used the word illegitimate again', said Robin Butler.[13]

The written word became a major preoccupation to Margaret Thatcher after she signed a £3.5 million deal with Rupert Murdoch's publishing house, HarperCollins, for the world rights to her memoirs. The first volume, *The Downing Street Years*, took only eighteen months to write. Completing the gargantuan task of covering her entire premiership in such a short time meant that she had to rely too heavily on her team of ghost writers, who included Robin Harris, a former director of the Conservative Research Department; John O'Sullivan of the *Daily Telegraph*; and Christopher Collins, a young Oxford academic. But parts of this somewhat stilted autobiography bear the unmistakable stance of her personality and style. In particular, the Falklands chapters are such a vivid account of the conflict that they could only have been written by herself.

Margaret Thatcher did not enjoy the literary process. She was at best a reluctant author. However, she well understood the importance of setting down her testament of history, and as a result her book shows many traces of self-serving revisionism – a common weakness among writers of political memoirs!

By the time she got round to the second volume, *The Path to Power*, the failings of stiltedness and an excess of amanuenses were even more apparent. Charles Moore, her official biographer, perceptively noted that the two volumes of her memoirs 'could never quite overcome the problem that they were the autobiography of someone who did not think autobiographically'.[14]

Such a mind-set leaves all the more scope for her biographers. But she was not thinking of them either at the time when she was working on her memoirs. For she was a woman who infinitely preferred action to authorship. She wanted to stay in the arena where her passions and prejudices were focused. As a result, she stirred up a lot of action and argument on the stage of contemporary politics throughout the years 1990–1997, much to the chagrin of her party and her successor as prime minister.

LAST MONTHS AS A MEMBER OF PARLIAMENT

Even when she was working on her memoirs, Margaret Thatcher was determined to fulfil her duties as an elected Member of the House of Commons. The readjustment process from the life of a prime minister to the life of a back-bencher was not easy.

The problem of not having a Commons office was solved by Archie Hamilton vacating his far from spacious junior minister's room. It was the first of his many acts of kindness towards her. Over the next few years, Ann and Archie Hamilton regularly invited Denis and Margaret to stay for long weekends, Easters and Christmases at Rhyll Manor, their country house in Devon. Their kindness was a major boon to both Thatchers, as was the similar hospitality they received from another parliamentary couple, Michael and Susan Forsyth.

Peter Morrison was fading in health and diligence as a notional PPS. Margaret Thatcher let him down gently. She never criticised him publicly or privately for his disastrous handling of her leadership election campaign. He never reproached himself for it either. They were both in denial. Although the blame gaming of her betrayers became tedious, her loyalty to Morrison was exemplary. Fidelity to old friends was one of her most admirable qualities.

New friends came into her parliamentary life. There were two identifiable Thatcher followings among Tory back-benchers. They were the Eurosceptics, particularly the Conservative European Reform Group run by Teddy Taylor, and the right-of-centre No Turning Back group run by Gerald Howarth.

Margaret Thatcher seemed to be suffering not only from withdrawal symptoms over her loss of power but from guilt feelings about her failure not to have recognised early enough that the Delors vision of the EEC was posing a growing threat to Britain's economic and political well-being. So, in her last months as an MP she spent much time in receiving briefings from two back-benchers whom many of their colleagues described as 'completely mad' about Europe – Teddy Taylor and Bill Cash. Both were obsessive masters of detail on the creeping federalism of EEC directives. Margaret Thatcher was their most willing pupil, sitting for hours with them (separately) in her small office as she immersed herself in their tutorials. Her absorption was amazing for its humility and its capacity to tolerate the boredom of the minutiae of EU documents.

A glimpse of her commitment to the Eurosceptic cause and its rebel leaders came in 1991 when Teddy Taylor was awarded a knighthood after thirty-three years of parliamentary service. I hosted a drinks party in my home to celebrate this event. Margaret Thatcher accepted the invitation and inevitably became the star guest of the evening. She made a ringing speech lauding Teddy to the skies 'for keeping the torch of freedom aloft for so many years'.[15] She was also charming to the Taylors' two teenage sons, George and John, singing their father's praises to them. To one or two cynical observers it seemed remarkable that the former Prime Minister had taken so long to recognise the virtues of a colleague who had been in her shadow cabinet as early as 1976 but who she had passed over for any kind of promotion or recognition in the intervening years.

The MP who did her the greatest service in the period after the fall was Gerald Howarth, the Member for Cannock and Burntwood. He worshipped Margaret Thatcher. One of his first moves, immediately after her overthrow, was to organise the delivery to Dulwich of a gargantuan bouquet of flowers from the No Turning Back group of Thatcherites. On the day when she was feeling catastrophically unloved, being bunched by a group of admiring young backbenchers counted with her.

Gerald Howarth was a shrewd operator. He knew how to handle both the political instincts and the feminine instincts of Margaret Thatcher. As her appointed PPS, he used both skills to bring her into contact with younger MPs she barely knew.

Politically, she was like a great ship without an anchor as she navigated the unfamiliar waters of the back benches in 1991–1992. She knew the course she wanted to steer – as far as possible away from Brussels without demanding withdrawal from the EEC – but she had little or no idea of how to impose discipline on herself or on her new crew. The result was unhappy chaos, as almost any discontented Tory MP was welcomed on board as a 'Thatcherite'. This label, which had once meant a principled belief in free markets, strict control of public expenditure, upholding the rule of law and firm moral values, began to look like the skull and crossbones flag of rebellious right-wing malcontents.

As individuals, they proclaimed fealty to their wounded queen over the water. However, as Tory MPs, it was far from clear how much distance they and she wanted to keep from the government headed by her chosen successor.

Her speeches in the House of Commons as a back-bencher were rare but high-voltage events. She declared outward support for John Major, describing him as 'a leader of vision',[16] but created the impression that she would be much more robust than he was likely to be in keeping Britain out of the single currency and preserving national sovereignty. These confusing signals narrowly managed to keep within the boundaries of political propriety and loyalty.

With a general election looming in the spring of 1992, the potential Thatcherite splinter group of the Conservative parliamentary party closed ranks with the Major government. The only issue where the splintering continued to hurt concerned the question of whether or not to hold a referendum before the forthcoming Maastricht Treaty was approved.

In the spring of 1992, making an unprecedented move for an ex-prime minister, Margaret Thatcher actively encouraged and supported the Private Member's Bill of Richard Shepherd, designed to require certain treaties to be ratified by a national referendum.

Richard Shepherd was one of the Eurosceptic back-benchers who found themselves admired by Margaret Thatcher after her fall, even though they had been ignored by her while she was in power. So he approached her to see if she would be willing to support his bill. He was trying to make it compulsory for the government to hold a national referendum before future international treaties involving changes to the British constitution could be ratified. This was a thinly veiled pre-emptive strike against the impending Maastricht Treaty.

Thirteen months after her defenestration from Downing Street, the former Prime Minister was feeling guilty about not having done enough to halt the momentum towards full European union. So she asked to be sent an advance copy of Richard Shepherd's bill and invited him to come and discuss it with her. He recalled:

> I went to see her in the room she had been allocated in the House. I was shocked to discover how badly a former Prime Minister was being treated. Her office was on the lower ministerial corridor. It was smaller than a small bathroom, cramped and uncomfortable. The sole sign that she had been head of the government for eleven years was a policeman perched on a chair outside the door. When I went in, the only space to sit

down was on a small sofa that I shared with her. She was holding a copy of my bill which she had annotated in detail.

Huddled together on the sofa with the lucky winner of the Private Member's ballot, the former Prime Minister said she very much approved of his bill but had detailed questions about the drafting of certain sections. 'I remember her saying about one particular clause that it was far too open', recalled Richard Shepherd. 'She urged me to get it tightened up saying, "You can't trust anybody".'[17]

The bill had no chance of reaching the statute book because it was too controversial and had arrived too late in the truncated session shortly before Parliament was to be prorogued for the impending general election. Nevertheless it was debated for five hours. Margaret Thatcher sat in her new place below the gangway listening to the entire proceedings which ended in a vote. Because the bill could not proceed further, the division was a purely symbolic rebellion, attended on a quiet Friday afternoon only by friends of Richard Shepherd and fans of the referendum he was championing.

As I fell into both categories, I was in the rebel lobby, along with a mere forty-three colleagues. Margaret Thatcher was the most prominent supporter of this bill, whose purposes were the opposite of the government's. It was the last vote she ever cast in the House of Commons. This made it, in a small way, an historic occasion. More ominously, it was a warning sign that she might be about to become an outright saboteur of John Major's government and its policies.

SABOTAGING HER SUCCESSOR

The referendum question was the first of many issues on which Margaret Thatcher became a thorn in the flesh of her successor, John Major.

Supporting Richard Shepherd's bill was an early pinprick. A worse one came when she publicly condemned the Prime Minister for being 'arrogant'[18] in his refusal to declare his backing to a pre-Maastricht referendum. This was ironic for two reasons. First, because her use of language sounded ridiculous, attacking the mild-mannered Major for the offence of political hubris, of which she had been the worst of sinners. Second, because her intervention torpedoed the prospects for a referendum, which the new Prime Minister would otherwise have supported.

As John Major recalled in an interview for this biography:

'From the early 1990s I wanted to make a public commitment to hold a referendum if any future government wanted to join the Euro,' said John Major. But I faced problems with this: several Members of the Cabinet were deeply opposed to a referendum as a matter of principle. That had once been Margaret's position. Now, her fierce opposition to the Euro made her favour such a move. But – ironically – her advocacy provoked strong opposition in the Cabinet, thus making agreement to a referendum even more difficult. This was not a unique problem: her strident views on Europe made decisions about a number of other European policy issues infinitely more difficult.[19]

The difficulties became worse because of the style as well as the substance of her attacks on her successor. Egged on by sycophants in the press and in her new parliamentary fan club, she became recklessly indiscreet. I recall a dinner in the home of John Aspinall in late 1991 when she openly mocked John Major as 'A puir wee bairn' and 'the boy from Coldharbour Lane'. She accused him of 'having no courage and no backbone'. He was 'hell-bent on destroying the legacy I left him'.[20] Many such derisive sneerings found their way into the press.

It was clear that some of this criticism was close to irrational. For example, she fulminated against the compassionate but minor policy of paying compensation to haemophiliacs who had been infected with HIV as a result of contaminated blood transfusions supplied by the NHS. On a larger canvas, she was furious that Michael Heseltine was brought back into the cabinet. She even railed against the inevitable decision to halt the poll tax and revert to a much more equitable version of the Community Charge. But her two greatest battles of overt opposition to the government were over Bosnia and Maastricht.

As the ethnic violence in the republics of former Yugoslavia worsened, Margaret Thatcher championed the cause of Western military intervention to oppose the Serbian excesses and atrocities, particularly in Bosnia. The Major government – and for a long while the Clinton administration – rejected her advice on the grounds that the West should avoid getting dragged into a Balkan civil war. But in the end, Margaret Thatcher's view was largely vindicated. The Serbs only stopped their horrific practice of ethnic cleansing because the deployment of US military power brought them to the negotiating table and the Dayton Agreement in 1995.

The anger unleashed in her by Bosnia was exceeded by the passion with which she opposed the Maastricht Treaty. To widespread surprise, John Major achieved a considerable success in securing an opt-out for Britain from joining the single currency, and an exemption from signing up to the Social Chapter. Had Margaret Thatcher still been at the helm, the probability is that she would have been delighted at these results, which saved the pound sterling and guaranteed its independence from the euro. But by this time, nothing that Major did was right in her eyes. So she worked overtime to undermine him. She came perilously close to succeeding.

The votes on Maastricht in the House of Commons were a cliff-hanger. Margaret Thatcher, who had kept silent about the proposed treaty during the 1992 general election, became an outright opponent of its ratification. Elevated to the House of Lords as Baroness Thatcher of Kesteven, she worked vigorously to corral her coterie of Eurosceptic Tory MPs into opposing the enabling legislation of Maastricht. From her new base in the upper house, she ran a campaign of persuading potential rebels from the Commons to vote against or at least abstain in the most crucial division of all – on the so-called 'paving' amendment. She was at her most manipulative: charming some waverers, flattering others and giving one or two of them brutal handbaggings. Her former political secretary, John Whittingdale, the newly elected MP for Colchester, broke down in tears after she told him: 'The trouble with you, John, is that your spine does not reach your brain.'[21] He abstained.

It was without precedent to have a former Conservative Prime Minister fighting at one end of the corridors of the Palace of Westminster to incite Conservative back-benchers into rebellion against her successor's most important legislation. Her campaigning, aided and abetted by her fellow new peer Lord Tebbit, came within a hair's breath of blocking the treaty. For the tightest division on the 'paving' amendment was carried by the government by only three votes. Right up to the last minute, Margaret Thatcher had been doing her utmost to get the government defeated. Had she succeeded, the consequences for John Major would have been catastrophic.

Although Margaret Thatcher's opposition to the Maastricht Treaty marked her most determined efforts to derail the new Conservative government, she continued her sabotage activities in numerous other ways. Because of her enduring agony at losing office, she could not control her tongue or her emotions. She began to half-believe in extraordinary conspiracy theories, of which the silliest was the notion that John Major had feigned his wisdom-tooth operation in order to be absent from the campaign for her re-election as Conservative leader in November 1990.

This was nonsense, and her rational mind knew it. But her irrational, wounded side could spread poison, or at least pejorative propaganda, among the many acquaintances she saw privately. As her new circle included many journalists, from press barons to political reporters, her hostility towards the Prime Minister did not stay private for long. Instead of the loyalty he had hoped to receive from his predecessor, John Major was constantly having to handle a barrage of negativity from her, which steadily made his life impossible.

As he recalled:

> Leading the Conservative Party at this time was like sitting on a volcano about to erupt. I don't think I lived through a single day without worrying whether the party was going to split into two. If I had chosen to be as fierce in my own views as she was in hers, I think that fear might have become a reality. But I was forever trying to knit things together, and prepared to do a great deal to stop it splitting. As a result, I had to keep silent in the face of a great deal of provocation.[22]

The silence was one sided. Margaret Thatcher could not find the self-discipline to stop her complaining and carping. Because her wounds had not healed, they festered. She encouraged denigration of the Prime Minister, and legitimised the internal opposition towards him. She openly mocked several of his Cabinet Ministers. One amusing example of this occurred when she came to a drinks party at the home of Alan Duncan MP in 1997. There she saw Michael Portillo, the new Defence Secretary who told her that he had put out many invitations to tender since he assumed his office.

'Invitations to tender!' snorted the former Prime Minister in tones of ringing scorn. 'You'll never win a war Michael with invitations to tender! I know about these things. You'll have to do far better than talking about invitations to tender.'

As she stalked off to another part of Alan Duncan's drawing room she muttered to her host 'I know I mustn't! I know I mustn't'!'[23]

The fierceness and the frequency of her grumblings against the Major government took their toll. They had a huge knock on effect in spreading discontent, particularly on Europe. Although the Conservative Party did not actually split, it looked and behaved as though it was a house bitterly divided against itself. This was the darkest side of Margaret Thatcher's legacy.

REFLECTION

In the 1970s, it was said that no Conservative Party leader had ever behaved as badly towards their successor as Ted Heath did with his sulks, snubs and unhelpful behaviour towards Margaret Thatcher.

In the 1990s, this view had to be revised. For Margaret Thatcher's political behaviour towards John Major was infinitely worse and far more destructive.

There were both human and political explanations for Margaret Thatcher's malevolence. On the human side, she had every justification for fury at the internal coup that had brought about her fall. Her anger and her sickness of heart were so profound that she could not overcome them. This was her personal tragedy.

On the political front, she was entitled to hold passionate views about both Bosnia and Europe. Freed from the constraints of office, she could use wilder words and take up more extreme stances. Since she was broadly right about both issues, her principled beliefs deserve respect.

Unfortunately for her reputation, the human bitterness began to damage the political respect. She abandoned some of the qualities that had stood her in good stead in her early years as Prime Minister, such as self-discipline, caution and an acceptance of the norms of political conduct. She no longer listened enough to objective, let along critical, advice. Instead, she was misled towards further furies by voices who pandered to her worst fears and prejudices. Her denigration of John Major was a bad blot on her record.

Internationally, the picture was much more positive. On her global travels she did the state some service, built up her finances, and enhanced her reputation as an icon of historic achievements. Yet, even so, this chapter of her life was a sad one. Her agony after the fall did not enable her to go gently into the twilight of retirement.

39

Snapshots of her retirement years

STRATEGIC IDEAS AND PERSONAL CONVERSATIONS

The newly ennobled Baroness Thatcher of Kesteven did not settle comfortably into the House of Lords. Her early speeches on Maastricht were listened to politely but voted against by overwhelming majorities. She tended to misjudge the mood of the upper house, particularly on 14 July 1993 when she launched an emotional attack against further erosions of sovereignty to Brussels unless sanctioned by a national referendum.[1] The motion she supported was defeated by 445 votes to 146. Such speeches, aggravated by her continuing snipings against John Major, began to irritate not only the Tory establishment but also the party rank and file, who gave her noticeably shorter ovations when she appeared at party conferences.

None of these fluctuations in her domestic popularity worried her in the slightest. The contrast between the acclaim she was receiving on her international speaking tours and the anxiety she caused by her interventions in domestic politics could have been an echo of the biblical line 'a prophet is without honour in his own country'.[2]

On the world stage some of her speeches deserved the adjective prophetic. In March 1996 at Fulton, Missouri (where Winston Churchill had given his great 'Iron Curtain' address in 1945), she coined another memorable phrase by warning of the threat posed by 'rogue states'. She specified in this category 'Syria, Iraq and Gaddafi's Libya' and highlighted 'the danger from the proliferation of weapons of mass destruction'.[3]

Despite Margaret Thatcher's vast experience of geopolitical issues, her hostility towards John Major meant that he and his government had ceased to consult her on foreign policy. However, there was no ban on ministers taking advice from the former Prime Minister. So a few weeks after my appointment as Minister of State for Defence I went to see her. Despite some handwringing from my officials ('Are you sure it would be wise, minister?') I felt I would benefit from her advice over the biggest decisions on my desk involving potential orders for missiles, torpedoes and aircraft. The rationale for them ultimately centred on a strategic question: Was there or was there not likely to be a future military threat to the UK from Russia now that the Soviet Union had collapsed?

I asked Margaret Thatcher if I could come and talk to her on this issue. She had unrivalled experience of making geopolitical judgements and an unequalled range of contacts in both Washington and Moscow. So for over an hour we had a deep and detailed discussion about the various factors that might cause a Russian resurgence as an aggressive military power.

She was still at the top of her game, well understanding why a new Defence minister might want to ask her advice on questions that could decide whether certain kinds of procurement orders should be confirmed or cancelled. After a conversation that ranged across both strategic and specific considerations, it emerged that she was a cautious optimist about Russian intentions. 'The Bear may get hungry and angry towards its neighbours, but not for a generation or two.'[4] I agreed, and told her that as a result of her advice I would shortly be cancelling the £1 billion Spearfish torpedo programme.*

At the end of this talk I said I would like to mention something rather personal. Taking a deep breath I began:

> We were last on our own together nearly thirteen years ago, and I have often thought that if we ever found ourselves in a one-on-one situation again then I would like to apologise to you. You see, I think I handled the break-up with Carol terribly badly. I am on good terms with her again, but I know I made such a mess of things that I upset you too as her mother. So I just wanted you to know that I am very sorry for that.[5]

Margaret Thatcher looked totally stunned. There was an awkward silence in which she seemed to be choking up. I understood this, knowing how difficult

---

* Spearfish was a highly sophisticated £1.2 billion torpedo system designed to destroy Russian submarines. Its cancellation caused the First Sea Lord to resign in protest. After this story hit the headlines Margaret Thatcher said to me: 'Don't worry about the brass hats. They always want their toys.'

she found any kind of personal or family matters. So I took my leave quickly, wondering whether I had made a mistake in reopening a painful memory.

However, a week or two later Denis Thatcher came over to me at a large cocktail party and said, as we shook hands: 'Thank you for what you said to Margaret the other day. She appreciated it a lot and so did I.'[6]

From that moment onwards, my communications with Margaret Thatcher got better and better. I was a regular guest at her drinks and dinner parties, and she came to some of mine. She particularly enjoyed arguing over a meal with visiting foreign statesmen such as Henry Kissinger, Ghazi al Gosaibi of Saudi Arabia and HM the Sultan of Oman.

On one occasion her arguing went completely over the top. Margaret and Denis came down to Sandwich Bay to stay the weekend with Julian and Diana Seymour. As their near neighbour I invited the Thatchers and the Seymours over for lunch. It was a disaster.

Margaret had read a story in the Sunday papers about the deteriorating situation in Bosnia. So she arrived with her dander up to press the argument for immediate British military intervention. By this time I was in the cabinet as Chief Secretary to the Treasury. So I parroted the Treasury line that such a commitment could lead to an unpredictably high cost to public expenditure. I might just as well have lit the blue touch paper to a barrel of gunpowder.

In the explosions that followed, the table of Sunday lunch guests fell into cowed silence as Margaret denounced the 'cowardice and the shame' of our policy of non-intervention. One of her milder rhetorical questions was: 'Are you ministers so weak that you are going to twiddle your thumbs while the Serbs inflict genocide?' It did not help the temperature of the discussion when my Serbian-born wife, Lolicia, observed that most Serbs did not agree with genocide. More gunpowder exploded.

Although I had caught glimpses of Margaret Thatcher in this kind of a mood back in her Leader of the Opposition days, I was startled by the ferocity of her anger. It was eventually curtailed by Denis taking advantage of a pause in the explosions to issue the quiet command, 'Cut it out girl!' Amazingly she did, making on abrupt and barely polite exit a few minutes later. 'It's not cricket to behave like that', observed one of our guests, E.W. 'Jim' Swanton, whose opinion carried some authority since he had been the chief cricket correspondent of the *Daily Telegraph* for many years.[7]

The outburst had an unexpected sequel. Perhaps realising that she had over-reacted, Margaret asked to see me in the House of Lords a few days later. Apologies were not her style but she went out of her way to be gracious and charming on a most unexpected subject – the choice of her official biographer. She said that she was considering the possibilities. Julian Seymour had recommended me for the job.

She stressed that she would not be making up her mind quickly, but was I interested? Naturally I was. So I sent her an inscribed copy of my 670-page biography of Richard Nixon and hoped for the best.

Meanwhile, I learned that the field of authors under consideration had narrowed down to four runners – Simon Heffer, Antony Beevor, Charles Moore and myself. Some months went by. Then Margaret said to me, 'I'm afraid I have decided not to ask you to be my official biographer because' – and nothing could possibly have prepared me for the next four words – 'you're too old'.

For a moment I thought I must be mishearing her. But in the next few sentences she explained she was going to make it a pre-condition that her official biography should not be published until after her death. I was left to draw the conclusion that she expected to outlive me. This seemed an optimistic assumption on her part since at the time (1996) I was fifty-four to her seventy. Perhaps she had other reasons. Whatever they may have been, she made a wise choice in appointing the excellent Charles Moore to be her official biographer.

One of the oddities of conversations with Margaret Thatcher in her retirement was that they sometimes contained an ambush of eccentric unpredictability. Two subjects on which she showed this side of her personality concerned the dangers (as she saw them) of a reunited Germany and the opportunities created by the collapse of the Soviet Union.

On the first subject she often lurched into embarrassing tirades against Helmut Kohl and his German reunification policies. On one occasion in 1997 she was giving a drink to a group of Eurosceptic Tory MPs who included Iain Duncan Smith, Bernard Jenkin, Bill Cash and Richard Shepherd. They were gathered in the Chesham Place offices of the Thatcher Foundation which overlooked the German Embassy in the same street. As the former Prime Minister's denunciations of the Bundestag and the Berlin government became particularly vehement, Richard Shepherd gestured towards the Embassy and joked, 'Careful

Margaret, they'll hear you!' Raising her voice and shaking her fist at the gates of the German Embassy she shouted across to the other side of Chesham Place, 'Oh I do hope so!'[8]

A more endearing example of her spontaneous reaction to a foreign-policy issue occurred later the same year when she went to visit Sir James Goldsmith at Montjeu, his country house in France. Escorted by her host and accompanied by her fellow house guests, Bill and Biddy Cash, she and Denis went for a walk on the estate. To her surprise they came across, in a woodland grove, a huge bronze statue of Lenin. Margaret Thatcher insisted on posing for a photograph in front of this monument to the founding father of communism saying, 'I just want to show him we won!'[9]

Winning battles remained on her agenda in the late 1990s. On the whole they were not political. She made occasional speeches in the constituencies of MPs she wanted to help, including a fiery one for me in South Thanet in which she all but called for Britain's withdrawal from the EU. But because she was so alienated from the official Conservative policy towards Europe she was a major contributor to the rift in the party which intensified the size of the government's defeat in the 1997 election.

Before that debacle took place she was always keen to do her bit for some cause in Britain's interest where she felt she could make a difference. British exports generally and defence exports in particular received considerable help from her as she travelled across the world, well briefed by the Foreign Office to put right words into the ears of the heads of state or government she was visiting. As the following story shows, she could be at her best in the Gulf.

STILL BATTING FOR BRITAIN

Margaret Thatcher has remained a heroine in the Gulf for the part she played in the war to liberate Kuwait. Because of this, she seemed the best person to help with a different sort of rescue operation in that country. This was a crisis over a vital Kuwaiti export order for armoured cars made by GKN in Birmingham.

As the Minister for Defence exports, I had been supporting GKN's efforts to secure this contract. The company's bid succeeded. The government of Kuwait publicly announced that it would be ordering £1 billion worth of GKN's Warrior armoured cars as part of its armed forces re-equipment programme.

But just before the contract was due to be signed, a US defence manufacturer put in a counter-bid. Under the conventions among NATO countries and under normal business practices in Kuwait, such an opportunistic move would never normally have been considered. But this particular American counter-bid broke all the rules. It was accompanied by an extraordinary level of political lobbying from Washington, which climaxed in a telephone call to the Crown Prince from the US Vice President Al Gore and a personal letter to the Emir from President Bill Clinton.

Faced with the prospect of a British export triumph turning into a last-minute defeat, I did my ministerial best to organise some high-level counter-lobbying from London. Knowing that Margaret Thatcher, like the British government, had been personally assured by the Kuwait ruling family that this contract was coming to Britain, I went round to her house in Chester Square to see if she could help.

The action of the next forty minutes was a marvellous demonstration of Thatcher power at its fiercest, funniest and most effective. As I recounted the sequence of events in the contract battle so far, my narrative was punctuated by a succession of explosive epithets from Margaret Thatcher: 'Outrageous!' 'Appalling!' 'Disgraceful!' and finally, 'I will not allow this!' Having started the adrenalin flowing at warlike levels in the former Prime Minister, my next challenge was to persuade her to charge at the right target. No such persuasion was required. The lady was for phoning. 'Do you have the Crown Prince of Kuwait's home telephone number?' she demanded. Fortunately I had, and dialled it. Amazingly, Sheikh Jabr Al Sabah answered the line himself. 'Your Highness, I am in Margaret Thatcher's house. She is right beside me, and would like to speak to you about an urgent matter', I began. 'Jonathan, you must be joking', the bemused heir apparent said. Before I could explain that jokes were not on the evening's agenda, Margaret Thatcher seized the receiver. In tones of rising passion she reminded the Crown Prince of the part Britain had played in the liberation of Kuwait and of his pledge that Britain would get its fair share of the armed forces re-equipment programme. She also reminded him that debts of honour were debts of honour, and that only a month or so ago he had personally assured her that Britain had won the armoured vehicle competition.

'Now what I want to know is: do Kuwaitis keep their promises?'

The answer was apparently less than satisfactory. 'Your Highness, I do not like what I am hearing. Let me ask you again. Do Kuwaitis keep their promises? Are you going to keep your word or break your word?'

'I'm beginning to feel a bit sorry for this chappie', observed Sir Denis *sotto voce* as he sipped his gin and tonic. His sympathy was evidently not shared by his spouse. Her decibels rose as she enlarged on her strong feelings to the Crown Prince. 'So what exactly are you going to do at your cabinet meeting tomorrow?' she crescendoed. 'You are not going to run away from your responsibilities, are you?'

I was beginning to wonder whether my bright idea would provoke a major diplomatic incident in Anglo-Kuwaiti relations when sweetness and light broke out. 'Thank you so much, Your Highness. I knew you would be a man of your word', I heard Margaret Thatcher coo in dulcet tones.

'He was wobbly, but he'll be all right', she declared as she put down the receiver. 'Now I must sort out the Americans. Let's get Al Gore on the line.' I confessed that my skills as an impromptu switchboard operator did not include carrying around the telephone number of the Vice President of the United States. 'Well then, get Robin Renwick. He'll know it.' The number of the British Ambassador in Washington was not at my fingertips either.

Margaret Thatcher was in no mood to be thwarted by these pettifogging obstructions. 'Then I must speak to Ray Seitz at once. He must be made to order the Clinton administration to stop their dirty tricks immediately.' With some difficulty I tracked down the Ambassador of the United States to the Court of St James, only to be told by the butler at the US Embassy Residence in Regent's Park that His Excellency was unavailable to come to the telephone because he was having a shower. For the second time Margaret Thatcher seized the receiver from me. 'This is Margaret Thatcher. Please tell Ambassador Seitz that I will hold on until he comes out of the shower.'

The butler did not argue with these orders, and apparently delivered them to the ambassador's bathroom, for a couple of minutes later a presumably wet and dripping Raymond Seitz came to the telephone to receive a broadside, from which he escaped only by promising to pass on a 'back off' message to Washington immediately.

Justifiably pleased though she was by her evening's work, Margaret Thatcher had not quite finished. 'Now, our last task tonight is to tell the Prime Minister exactly what's been happening. I'd like him to know that I can still bat for Britain.' I said I would tell John Major about all the boundaries his predecessor had scored in the morning. That was not good enough. 'A prime minister likes to know these things at once. Do it now!' was the command. With some trepidation, I rang No. 10 and was relieved to be told that the Prime Minister could not be disturbed. 'And perhaps it might be wiser not to disturb him at all on this one', murmured the well-trained private secretary. 'Let's take stock in the morning.' I agreed with alacrity to this proposition, with wise nods coming from Denis and Julian Seymour.

By the time we got round to taking stock the following morning in Whitehall, the cabinet in Kuwait had approved the final details of the armoured vehicle contract, and authorised the Defence Minister to sign it in the British Embassy. GKN got its £1 billion order, and the Warrior subsequently performed superbly both in the snows of Bosnia and in the sands of Kuwait. Britain had achieved a great export success – but we would never have done it without Margaret Thatcher.[10]

A BREAK IN THE HIGHLANDS

Margaret Thatcher was not an easy holiday guest. She did not take naturally to the theory or practice of leisure. The month of August was always a challenging time for her. In the years of retirement, when no red boxes were emanating from No. 10 to distract her from the burdens of relaxation, the challenge was even greater.

In August 1996 Margaret and Denis travelled to the Highlands of Scotland to spend a few days as the guests of Lord Pearson of Rannoch. His Perthshire estate is one of the most windswept and inaccessible wildernesses in the United Kingdom. Its terrain is character building. The same could be said of a sojourn at Rannoch Barracks under the imperious direction of the laird. Amusing and lovable to his friends, Malcolm Pearson on the hill or on the port can be an acquired taste for newcomers who do not share his passions for militant Euroscepticism, deer stalking and political incorrectness.

Margaret Thatcher had great respect and affection for her host. Their friendship went back to the mid-1970s when the Pearson chequebook funded telex machines in Central Office and, more daringly, *samizdat* newsletters behind the

Iron Curtain. She admired his subversive support for anti-Soviet dissidents and his pioneering friendship with Aleksandr Solzhenitsyn whose sons became his wards. For such good works, Margaret Thatcher made Malcolm Pearson a working Conservative life peer in 1990.

The newly ennobled Pearson worked assiduously in the House of Lords, but not always in the Conservative Party's interest. He was too wild a stag to be constrained by the dictates of the whips. So he bolted to the UK Independence Party, eventually becoming Leader of UKIP in 2008. Although this defection troubled traditional Tories, it was of no concern to their former leader, whose views on the EU had by this time become closely allied to UKIP's. So her visit to Rannoch was as much an opportunity for recharging her Eurosceptic batteries with 'one of us' as it was for savouring the beauty of the Scottish scenery.

Margaret Thatcher was an enjoyable guest but not an entirely peaceful one. First clash with the laird came over the timing of breakfast which she wanted to be at 7 a.m. The rest of the household preferred 9.30 a.m. After some discussion she agreed to what she called 'a compromise' – 7.15 a.m.

The second argument came over suitable attire for hill climbing. 'I can see you're not a country girl', said her host when he observed her black suede Ferragamo bootees topped with ribbons. 'I have several excellent pairs of gumboots, so I can lend you one in your size.' She declined his offer.

The journey from the house to the hill was a royal procession, at least by the standards of Rannoch Moor. Two estate Land Rovers; one Scotland Yard Range Rover; two trucks towing Argo-Cats (mountain-climbing vehicles with rubber tracks); two back-up cars for the guests; one back-up car for the police; one lorry for assorted stalkers, gillies, lunch carriers and teenage boys.

This caravan managed to get about half the way up the paths towards the destination of 'The Craggie', the highest peak on the estate. The last 1,000 feet or so could only be climbed on foot or navigated by Argo – which for most of the ascent was the guest of honour's preferred mode of travel. But after an hour of bumping and twisting through the heather clumps and peat hags, she was still quite a trek from the summit, with the Argos juddering on sluggishly. 'Oh I'll walk the last bit', declared Baroness Thatcher leaping into a bog completely unsuitable for her black bootees. Tightening her headscarf she strode onwards and upwards. It must have been one of the coldest and longest walks of her life. Determined not to be defeated by the elements, she struggled all the way to the top. On arrival at The Craggie, the Laird handed out soup to the frozen, observing that the panorama had been Solzhenitsyn's favourite view. 'He must have felt at home here after all those years in Siberia', muttered Denis.[11]

Hill walking would not by itself have constituted a sufficient holiday pastime for Margaret Thatcher. So her host invited suitable conversationalists to keep her entertained. 'She likes to talk a lot about Europe these days', he said.[12]

The three front-line respondents for this task were Christopher Booker, author of *The Great Deception* and other writings on the evils of the EU; Malcolm Pearson, deliverer of innumerable pro-UKIP speeches in the Lords; and myself, a poor third, but qualifying as a Eurosceptic parliamentarian of early vintage. Between us, we engaged with the great lady from dawn to dusk on matters of detail and principle relating to Europe. She had lost little of her prime ministerial fire on the subject, except perhaps in the evening when the generous whiskies led to some repetition.

Two other glimpses of Margaret Thatcher at Rannoch linger in the memory. The first was her sweetness and light towards Malcolm's Down's Syndrome daughter Marina. How she and the former Prime Minister managed to communicate so energetically for long periods of dialogue was a mystery, but it happened.

A second example of Margaret's rapport with the young came when Malcolm broke up the flow of adult conversation one evening with the command 'Time for Prime Minister's Questions'. This meant putting her metaphorically back at the despatch box responding to well over ninety minutes' worth of questions from the four teenage boys staying in the house – Christopher Booker's sons Alex and Nick; Edward Rose, the nephew of Lady Pearson; and my son William.

The session bore more than a passing resemblance to the House of Commons on a rowdy afternoon. Some of the questions were bright, and the replies were often passionate. Heckling was encouraged. The adult audience cheered. At one point Denis said proudly, 'If we'd ever gone broke she could have earned her living as a bloody good teacher'.[13]

Some of her best sallies were about Europe. 'If God had intended us to be a member of the EU he would not have put the Channel where it is', was one.

Seventeen-year-old Nicholas Booker followed up by asking her: 'Lady Thatcher, do you think we should leave the European Union?'

She replied: 'There are five reasons why we should leave it.' Then she soared away on the wings of her oratory, ticking the arguments off on the fingers of her right hand. When she drew breath some fifteen minutes later, Nicholas said: 'Lady Thatcher, you've only given us four reasons. What is the fifth?'

'You're quite right', she said, holding up her little finger. 'The fifth reason why we should leave' – dramatic pause – 'is that THEY STOLE OUR FISH!'[14]

The last question was about achieving greatness. She gave a splendid answer, whose last line was, 'And if you follow my advice, you four will have great lives as great politicians and great servants of our country'. 'Hear, hear!' boomed Denis. 'And now I'm taking you off to bed.'[15]

It made a memorable evening. Yet there was poignancy too. For below the surface it was clear that she was a restless soul, utterly unfulfilled by retirement. As I wrote in my diary, paraphrasing Dean Acheson: 'Margaret has lost an empire but not yet found a role.'[16]

SEVENTIETH BIRTHDAY

Her seventieth birthday was marked by events and celebrations designed to suggest that she might be moving into more senior and peaceful waters. She had other ideas.

Her memoirs *The Downing Street Years* received a good reception in terms of both sales and critics. The only discordant note came when she told the book buyers in Hatchards that she should have titled the book *Undefeated!*

Despite his predecessor's tendency to express unhelpful views on his premiership, John Major graciously hosted a birthday dinner in her honour at No. 10. She, with rather less grace, paused on the doorstep to say that she still thought of this address as home; that Gladstone had formed his fourth administration when he was over eighty; and that if anyone thought that it was fine for her to relax and give the other side a chance, the answer was 'No! No! No!'[17] The humour was uncertain but the message was clear. In her own irrepressible way, she was going on and on.

She reinforced this theme at a second seventieth birthday dinner for around eighty friends held at Claridge's. She had arranged the seating plan for her guests with special care. One charming touch was that she put Jack Profumo at the top table on her right and on the Queen's left – a beautiful touch of kindness agreed by both great ladies.

Her health was elegantly and humorously proposed by Bill Deedes, who in his own gentle way seemed to be suggesting that even ex-prime ministers may need to slow down. To drop this hint he quoted (though without attribution) from Psalm 90: 'The days of our age are three score years and ten, and though some be so strong that they come to four score years, then is their strength only labour and sorrow . . .'

Apparently thinking that these sentiments were from Bill rather than the Bible, when the guest of honour came to respond she gave Deedes a good handbagging in her speech along the lines of, 'What's all this stuff and nonsense about labour and sorrow after three score years and ten?' Later in the evening when she was mingling with her guests, I asked if she realised that the stuff and nonsense was a quotation. 'Who wrote it?' she demanded. 'King David – in the Psalms', was my answer. Margaret Thatcher, on the crest of her seventieth-birthday wave, could have been back at the despatch box at Prime Minister's Questions: 'Well, he got a lot of things wrong', she retorted, 'as kings in the Middle East still do!'[18]

FINDING HER SPIRITUAL HOME

Faith was always important to Margaret Thatcher. Ever since her strict Methodist upbringing in Grantham she had been an assiduous attender of services, a thoughtful critic of the sermons she heard, and an occasional stirrer of public controversies against the Church of England.

She did a great deal of Bible reading, even in her busiest years at No. 10. She liked to discuss faith issues with a handful of trusted interlocutors. The most regular of these were two evangelical Christians who were Downing Street insiders during the 1980s – Michael Alison, her PPS in her second term, and Brian Griffiths, the Head of her Policy Unit. She also had a high regard for the teachings and writings of the Chief Rabbi Immanuel Jakobovits, whom she elevated to the House of Lords in 1988. His greatest influence was to help her understand, through Judaism, that the rule of law had its roots in religious as well as secular principles.

After she fell from power and entered a mindset of personal bitterness, Michael Alison tried to reach out to her on a spiritual level. His well-meaning seeds fell on stony ground. After listening to one of her many diatribes against her betrayers in the cabinet, he suggested that she should try to forgive them. He also offered to pray with her. 'That's not for me', she replied.

Alison urged her to 'find a good church', suggesting that she would be warmly welcome at Holy Trinity Brompton in Knightsbridge, where he was the church warden. It was a proposal she considered, at least to the extent of reading some printed sermons by its vicar, The Revd Sandy Millar. As she approved of them she thought of going to his church one Sunday until she read in the newspapers that it was practising the Toronto Blessing, a form of Spirit-filled swooning in the aisles. 'What exactly is this about Michael?' she asked Alison, flourishing a picture of HTB worshippers prostrating themselves on the church floor. His explanations failed to convince her. 'Denis couldn't stand it', she declared. 'We like to reflect on religion privately. Not too much enthusiasm, y'know.'[19]

The phrase about enthusiasm may have come from the recesses of the Methodist memories of Margaret Roberts. In the eighteenth and nineteenth centuries, the followers of John Wesley were dismissed as 'enthusiasts' by the established church. The pejorative code word survived into the twentieth century, usually in the context of one Methodist chapel looking down on the other on grounds of 'too much enthusiasm'. Alfred Roberts would certainly have been familiar with the description. His daughter quietly dropped her Methodism a year or two after Oxford. Possibly under the influence of Denis, a wartime C of E who addressed every vicar as 'padre', she joined the Church Reticent wing of Anglicanism. There she uneasily remained despite many rumblings and grumblings about the qualities of its bishops.

The church where she worshipped most frequently was St Margaret's, Westminster. Situated in the precincts of the Abbey, it is a favourite venue for politicians' memorial services. These are run with heavy formality and emphasis on split-second timings for the entrances of dignitaries such as royal representatives, ambassadors, party leaders and, of course, the prime minister.

During her years in power, Margaret Thatcher regularly threw these meticulous schedules into disarray by arriving too early. The Rector, The Revd Canon Dr Donald Gray, politely raised the problem with No. 10. It made no difference.

So, on one of the next occasions when she entered St Margaret's at a premature 11.45 a.m. for a 12 noon memorial service, he dropped her a hint.

'Good morning, Prime Minister. Early again, I see.'

'Yes, Canon Gray, I like to be here in good time – to say my prayers', was the icy response.

The Rector knew when he was beaten.[20]

For the first three years after she ceased being Prime Minister, the Thatchers were regular attendees at St Margaret's, Westminster for the 11 a.m. Sunday service. But they were slightly uncomfortable with its sung Eucharist and Abbey liturgy. So they discreetly went 'church shopping'. Their first port of call was St Michael's, Chester Square, which had the advantage of being less than 200 yards from the front door of no. 73, the four-storey house they bought in 1991.

Brian Griffiths was a leading member of the congregation at St Michael's whose vicar was Charles Marnham. He had founded the Alpha Course when a curate at Holy Trinity Brompton. With such a pedigree, his services were bound to be evangelical, although moderately so by HTB standards, but their repetitive guitar choruses were a step too far for Denis.

After some trial excursions to the Guards Chapel and the Chapel Royal, the Thatchers agreed that their preferred place of worship should be at the Royal Hospital Chelsea. Its historic seventeeth-century chapel appealed to Margaret because of its traditional English Matins and Hymnody. She also liked to engage with which she called its 'sound common sense preaching'.[21]

The Chaplain, The Revd Dick Whittington, recalled:

I could usually see Lady Thatcher leaning forward in her seat, listening to my sermons with extraordinary concentration. Often, she would like to have a conversation afterwards on some aspect of it. Almost always, she was highly perceptive and supportive. But once, when I had preached on Martha and Mary, emphasising how Mary had listened so carefully to Our Lord while her sister was doing the household chores, Lady Thatcher struck a critical note. 'We mustn't underestimate the value of the Marthas who knuckle down and get the work done', she told me.[22]

The chaplain, a no-nonsense combat soldier before taking holy orders, gradually entered into a close pastoral relationship with the two most famous members of his congregation. When Denis died of pancreatic cancer in the nearby Lister Hospital in 2003, The Revd Dick Whittington was present at the moment of his death, leading Margaret Thatcher in prayer as she knelt at her husband's bedside, holding his hand.

Denis departed in peace with a traditional funeral service, which included his favourite hymn, 'Immortal Invisible', and prayers he had chosen from the South African Prayer Book and the Book of Common Prayer.

On the day of the service Margaret was confused as well as distressed. She did not seem to know whose coffin the pallbearers were carrying in and out of the chapel. Yet, on both good and bad days she always felt at home in the Royal Hospital, continuing for the final years of her life to enjoy the company of its colourfully attired Chelsea Pensioners, and to be a regular attender at its chapel services. She was delighted when the governing body decided to name its new £27 million hospital facility as the Margaret Thatcher Infirmary.

A few yards outside the main entrance to the infirmary, still within the confines of the Royal Hospital, stands a tranquil lawn. The ashes of Denis were interred there in 2003. Ten years later Margaret's last remains were laid to rest alongside him. Perhaps for the first time since she was ousted from power, she was at peace.

Epilogue

DECLINE

There are many stories about Margaret Thatcher's kindness to people in trouble. This one happened to involve me. It is historically interesting for a different reason: it marked the beginning of her downward spiral into ill health, memory loss and dementia that cast such a difficult cloud over the last years of her life.

In January 2000 I was released from prison after serving seven months of an eighteen-month sentence for perjury. Forty-eight hours after beginning to breathe the air of freedom my telephone rang. 'Denis Thatcher here', said the unexpected voice on the line. 'Would you do me the honour of joining me for lunch at my club one day next week?'

For a moment I thought I was having my leg pulled by an impostor. But it was the real Denis. He gave me a superb four-hour lunch at the East India Club. The warmth of his hospitality and cheerfulness of his conversation performed wonders for my battered morale. As we tottered out into St James's Square he said: 'Margaret's been concerned about you. She'd like to see you on the quiet sometime. I'll be in touch.'

Before anything happened on this front, other members of the Thatcher family made contact. Mark, whom I did not know well, also took me out to lunch. Gauche in manner, he overflowed with generosity. He offered me financial support; an all-expenses paid holiday at his house in Constantia near Cape Town; and the loan of office space and a secretary. He came back to see me to repeat his urgings to accept this help.

As I was about to become a mature student at Oxford, Mark's offers were not taken up but they were greatly appreciated. I was touched by his genuine compassion. I learned from this good experience of him that Mark Thatcher can be the kindest and most caring of friends to someone going through a difficult patch.

Also in the weeks after my release I often saw Carol. In her different way she too was a rock of loving support and friendship.

As is her habit, Carol may well have been acting entirely independently of other members of her family. But instinctively I felt that Denis and Mark would not have approached me so warmly and so generously without the encouragement, perhaps even the orchestration, of Margaret.

A further indication of her kindness towards me came a few weeks later. She asked her former PPS, Michael Alison, to organise a supper party at his home in Chelsea, saying 'I'd like to talk to Jonathan'. When it took place, in early June 2000, the gathering consisted only of Margaret and Denis Thatcher, Michael and Sylvia Mary Alison, General Sir Michael Rose (an Alison cousin) and myself.

It was a delightfully relaxed evening. Talking one-on-one Margaret wanted to know every detail about prison life, saying at one point: 'I really should have done something to shake up this part of the criminal justice system. I listened too much to Willie and his stuff about what he called "the glasshouse".'

Around the table there was some interesting conversation about church life. Denis described himself as a 'middle stump Anglican'; and Michael Alison (a churchwarden) defended the stumps while Margaret bowled fast at them. She denounced the 'general wetness' of the Church of England, saying: 'It's so difficult to hear a good strong teaching sermon these days. I'd like to listen to a preacher tackling a challenging text like "the Fear of the Lord is the beginning of wisdom" for twenty-five fiery minutes.'

'You'd put the fear of God into any padre if he went on for more than ten minutes', observed Denis.

Because Michael Rose had recently been in command of the UN Protection Force in Bosnia, his brains were well and truly picked about the latest developments in the Balkans. Margaret Thatcher was characteristically on top of the details of the genocides, war crimes, atrocities and refugee movements of the region. Her moral fervour was passionate. 'How I wish you were still Prime Minister', declared Sylvia Mary Alison.

'I'd sort these problems out with whatever force was necessary and stop the evil', replied the guest of honour.

Two days later Margaret and Carol had a rare mother and daughter lunch in the coffee shop of the Mandarin Oriental Hotel, overlooking Hyde Park. I had described the Alisons' dinner party in some detail to Carol, so one of her first questions to her mother was about General Sir Michael Rose. Carol recalled:

> I fully expected her to give me lengthy chapter and verse on Bosnia and sat back waiting for a characteristic monologue. But she soon became confused and a few sentences later discussion of Bosnia had moved to the Falklands as she muddled up the Falklands and that of the Yugoslav wars. You could have knocked me down off my chair. Watching her struggle with her words and her memory I simply couldn't believe it. She was in her seventy-fifth year but I had always thought of her as ageless, timeless and one hundred per cent damage proof.[1]

Carol was so upset by those sudden signs of her mother's memory loss that she questioned me closely about the Alison supper later that evening. It soon became evident that the situation was rather worse. For Margaret, who as Carol put it 'always had a memory like a website',[2] had clearly been in a horrendous muddle about who had been present and what had been discussed. 'Houston, we have a problem', said Carol gloomily.[3]

The problem may have surfaced briefly in Hong Kong a few months earlier when Crawfie and Julian Seymour thought that Lady Thatcher had been temporarily confused at a reception. But on that occasion the seriousness of it had been missed. Now the difficulties needed a proper medical diagnosis.

This was not easy because the patient's health fluctuated – sometimes for the better, but occasionally for the sharply worse. She had a serious stroke when on holiday in Madeira in 2001. She made a good recovery from it, but from then on she had to draw on all her reserves of determination and will-power to cover up the failings in her memory.

When she saw her doctors she put on a virtuoso performance of not only being on the ball but of hitting every medical question for six. But good diagnosticians are not easily fooled, even by formidable ex-prime ministers. It took years to happen, but slowly and inexorably the shutters of her mind were closing down.

Margaret Thatcher was never diagnosed with Alzheimer's. But there are at least forty-eight different types of dementia and related illnesses. She held them intermittently at bay for the next three years by a combination of personal strength and carefully balanced medication. But her inner circle knew the worst, for she grew increasingly forgetful, distressingly repetitious, unpredictably volatile, frail in body and unsteady on her feet.

The unsteadiness was caused by her insistence on wearing high-heeled shoes, not, as was sometimes rumoured, by too many whiskies. Although she drank more in retirement than in power she was usually a careful watcher of her intake. 'How many units of alcohol is that dear?' she asked me in 2007 when I was refilling her glass of claret over dinner in our home. This form of measurement (unheard of by Denis) had been introduced to her by an American doctor. She heeded his advice but not to the letter. At that same dinner party she was easily persuaded to have one last nightcap of champagne on the grounds that 'it's weaker than whisky they tell me'. Then as if to ease her units of alcohol conscience still further she added a few moments later, 'Winston used to say that he was often the better for a glass of Pol Roger – but never the worse'.

Having Margaret Thatcher to dinner in her old age was rather like entertaining an antique lighthouse. At first you would not be entirely sure if the lights were working. But gradually the electricity began to flicker at recognition of old landmarks. My wife and I kept our dinners for Margaret to six or eight people, most of whom were familiar faces to her.

On one evening her first PPS, Sir Clive Bossom, by then in his nineties, had an amusing argument with her about whether they had travelled together by train or by no. 11 bus when going to inspect the kitchens at his father's house, No. 5 Carlton Gardens, shortly before she and Denis held their wedding reception there in 1951.

At another dinner Sir Edward du Cann reminded her (not entirely to her satisfaction!) about the loyalty of the 1922 Committee to her at the time of the 1981 Budget. Amusing reminiscences of how the Thatcher family had cruised around the Mediterranean on the yacht *Melita* in 1975 were shared with Lady Brinckman, the daughter of Sir Robert Grant Ferris MP, who had owned and skippered it. Gloria, Countess Bathurst, brought out sparkles from the guest of honour as they both remembered hilarious details of a 1980s Conservative Party rally held at Cirencester Park, the Bathursts' house in Gloucestershire.

Like many elderly people Lady Thatcher was better at ancient memories than current topics. Sometimes the lighthouse would fall dark for disconcerting periods. Then suddenly it would shine a beam that illuminated the whole table, as when she told Norman Lamont that entry to the ERM had been 'a disastrous folly . . . thank goodness you got us out of it!'

At another moment she came to life with an anthem of praise for Sir Keith Joseph whom she described as 'the most original intellect I ever met . . . he completely changed my mind on the moral issue of encouraging the free market'.

On a topical theme she congratulated Iain Duncan Smith for his pioneering work 'fighting the good fight to reduce the dependency culture. We'll never get Britain right until we do that'.

As these fragments from our dinner parties show, Margaret Thatcher's conversation came in flashes of light out of a background of darkness. She knew what she wanted to say but had to struggle to make herself understood.

In her early eighties, she was often lonely and in need of company. She liked the buzz of going out in the evenings, as always beautifully dressed and coiffured. She had conversational defence mechanisms which sometimes resulted in non sequiturs. 'Would you like some more gravy, Lady Thatcher?' was met by the response, 'I always say the most important thing in life is to make up your mind and then to stick to it'.

Jokes were usually not her forte but there was one she adored. It concerned a London taxi driver picking up a German tourist after a trip on the London Eye.

The visitor had been mightily impressed. He was loud in his compliments for the view, the engineering and the experience. 'Vot a great vheel! Wunderbar!' he kept saying.

The cabbie was in a mickey-taking mood.

'Well, you've seen the wheel', he quipped, 'but wait till you've seen the 'amster.'

This Cockney humour left the German tourist totally baffled. But when Margaret Thatcher heard it she blew up with laughter. She enjoyed the East End wordplay on wheels and hamsters. Even more did she enjoy the Teutonic incomprehension. It became her favourite funny story which Julian Seymour had to repeat over and over again to her.

Although making the lighthouse laugh was a rare achievement, her enjoyment of a dinner with comfortable friends was pleasantly apparent. She ate and drank heartily. She always made a point of popping into the kitchen to thank the cook. Even when she dropped out of the conversation for a while she seemed relaxed in her private world.

At the end of one evening when I was escorting her out of our front door she became disconcertingly critical, saying: 'Why does Jonathan give us Belgian chocolates? What's wrong with English chocolates? Why doesn't he have good old Terry's English chocolates?'

I promised to do better next time but she thought I was someone else. 'You won't tell Jonathan I said that about the chocolates will you?' was her parting murmur to me as her detectives helped her into the car.

It was easier to feel love and sympathy for Margaret Thatcher when she was vulnerable than when she was powerful. By the time she was eighty-five she only felt able to go out on the rarest of occasions, and even those exeats were sometimes due to other people's manipulations. From 2010 onwards she lived in an increasingly circumscribed world of shrinking horizons and darkening twilight.

FADING OUT WITH DIGNITY

Her final years were more contented than they looked from the outside. The public, when they glimpsed her, saw the Iron Lady reduced to a frail shipwreck, tottering in and out of Gordon Brown's No. 10 Downing Street, snapped on a bench in the gardens of Chester Square, or attending with emptiness in her eyes a drinks party organised by Liam Fox MP.

Such excursions did not seem to bring her much joy. But thanks to the medication she was generally calm and peaceful. She did become upset when Carol spoke publicly about the medical details of her dementia. A far worse blow came when Mark got into trouble after being embroiled in an alleged plot to organise a coup in Equatorial New Guinea. Although his mother was not well enough to understand the details she grasped the size of the problem when she had to put up the £100,000 of bail money to get him released from police custody in South Africa and help with the payment of his £265,000 fine.

Although she loved her son through thick and thin, this and other episodes caused some disillusionment with him in old age. The only outward sign of this was her decision not to appoint him as an executor of her will, and giving the final rights of decision-making about her funeral arrangements to Julian Seymour.

One blessing of her decline was that she stayed comfortable and well looked after. She had no money worries so could afford excellent carers supervised by an outstanding team of doctors headed by Dr Christopher Powell-Brett of the Basil Street practice and Dr Michael Pelly of the Chelsea and Westminster Hospital. Her afflictions included a succession of transient ischemic attacks (mini-strokes); polymyalgia rheumatica (muscle pains); continuing episodes of dementia; growing deafness; and a malignant tumour of the bladder which required surgery at Christmas 2012.

After this operation she could no longer manage the stairs at her home in Chester Square, a house without a lift. So she convalesced at the Ritz Hotel whose owners, the Barclay brothers, allocated a suite of rooms to her at a generously low rate.

Sir David and Sir Frederick Barclay were part of a network of friends, former colleagues and admirers who in their different ways wanted to pay continuing homage to the former Prime Minister. It would be invidious to name them or describe their attentiveness. But Mark Worthington played an exceptionally kind and caring role as her last private secretary well aided by Conor Burns MP. Julian Seymour, who had become head of her private office in 1991 and later handled all her legal, financial and administrative arrangements, deserves the palm for faithful and efficient stewardship of her affairs. She showed her absolute trust in him by appointing him as the principal executor of her will, a simple testament which divided her estate into three equal parts – one to Mark, one to Carol and one to her grandchildren.

Heading a regiment of supportive friends, Charles Powell was extraordinary in his devotion to her. Throughout the twenty-two years that elapsed between her departure from Downing Street and her death, he saw her two or three times each month, often taking her out to meals and always being available for telephone calls and wise counsel, even from the furthest corners of his peripatetic world. 'Charles was unquestionably the greatest hero of her declining years', was the judgement of Julian Seymour.

It was consistent with Charles Powell's loyalty that he should have been her last visitor at the Ritz. On the evening of Sunday 7 April, the day before she died, he made one of his regular calls. He was with her for over an hour. He thought that his former boss was weary, but her spirits seemed good. Her heart was strong and she had come through the bladder-cancer operation and its general anaesthetic with amazing resilience. There was no reason why she should not have lived on into her nineties. But it was not to be.

On the morning of Monday 8 April, sitting in an armchair in her suite while reading a picture book, Margaret Thatcher suffered another stroke. This one ended her life. Within fifteen minutes of the attack her heartbeat stopped. It was an easeful and mercifully sudden death.

FAREWELL

The public arrangements for her funeral had been meticulously planned – largely by Margaret Thatcher herself. As early as 2006, discussions began with the Cabinet Office during Tony Blair's premiership. Before Gordon Brown left Downing Street in 2010 the detailed preparations for what was fairly called 'a state funeral in all but name'[4] had been approved in the format used on the day in 2013.

The key figure in this process was Sir Malcolm Ross, a former royal courtier who had organised the funerals of Diana, Princess of Wales, and the Queen Mother. The Thatcher family paid him fees and costs in excess of £100,000 for these well-rehearsed arrangements, which were made in coordination with the Dean of St Paul's Cathedral, the Ministry of Defence and the Metropolitan Police.

The announcement of Margaret Thatcher's death was accompanied by an avalanche of tributes, obituaries and assessments across the world. Internationally the surprise was the enormous scale of the appreciation. Domestically the coverage was even larger but with a more astringent mixture of praise and criticism.

On the critical side of the balance sheet the most overworked adjective to describe Margaret Thatcher was 'divisive'. It appeared to be used mainly by commentators who had forgotten how deeply divided Britain had been during the 'winter of discontent' before she was elected Prime Minister.

Another manifestation of the divisiveness was a handful of demonstrations supported mainly by students. Most of them had not been born by the time Margaret Thatcher left office, so their explanations to the media on why they were demonstrating seemed as thin as their limited numbers of fellow protesters.

The most exotic yet idiotic protest took the form of organising a downloading campaign to ensure that the BBC were required to play on their Top 40 chart show 'Ding Dong! the Witch is Dead'. This seventy-year-old number from the film *The Wizard of Oz* was temporarily manoeuvred into number two in the charts. The embarrassed BBC gave it seven seconds' airtime on Radio 1. In the middle of the tabloid headlines about this incident I found myself on the breakfast TV programme *Daybreak* sharing the sofa with the downloader-in-chief of 'Ding Dong'. He was so inarticulate and ineffective that I felt more like saying 'Please do continue' instead of attacking his protest.

By the day of the funeral the national mood had changed. Student japes and 'Ding Dongs' evaporated. Even among the millions who disagreed with Margaret Thatcher's politics there was an atmosphere of respect for her personal achievements. This was reflected by the attitudes in the crowds lining the streets on the processional route. Expressions of hostility were minimal. Not a single arrest was made all day. Immediately around St Paul's the popular reactions to the sight of her cortège were positive and surprising.*

Inside the cathedral, the quintessential Englishness of the order of service produced a near perfect mixture of history and holiness, high ceremonial and human touches. What made it so special was that Margaret Thatcher had chosen all the key ingredients herself. She blended resounding hymns from Denis's service ten years earlier with the 1662 Book of Common Prayer liturgy used at Sir Winston Churchill's state funeral at St Paul's in 1965.

Few concessions were made to the temporal world. Faith, hope and the message of the Resurrection were the spiritual signals. In her youth Margaret Thatcher had been a devout Methodist. As an Oxford student she preached sermons before she delivered her first speeches. She knew her King James Bible, Charles Wesley's hymns and Cardinal Newman's prayers. All were included, ringing out to the 3,000 strong congregation just as she had wanted, with the most powerful reading (Ephesians 6:10–18) coming from her nineteen-year-old Dallas-born granddaughter, Amanda Thatcher.

There were highlights in the panoply of beauty at St Paul's that morning which moved me and perhaps many others to tears. One was the finest funeral address I have ever heard. It was delivered by Margaret Thatcher's favourite prelate, the Right Reverend Richard Chartres, Bishop of London, clad in a magnificent black cope designed for and last used at Churchill's funeral. He began in his episcopal *basso profundo*:

> After the storm of a life lived in the heat of political controversy there is a great calm. The storm of conflicting opinions centres on the Mrs Thatcher who became a symbolic figure, even an 'ism'. Today the remains of the real Margaret Hilda Thatcher are here at her funeral service. Lying here she is one of us, subject to the common destiny of all human beings.

---

* See Prologue.

The Bishop had cleverly incorporated the phrase Margaret Thatcher used to describe her praetorian guard of true believers – 'one of us' – into what was ostensibly a non-political address. Stirring passages in it were as politically effective as Mark Antony's oration over the grave of Julius Caesar.

Perhaps the unfairest calumny ever used by the left to attack the political philosophy of Margaret Thatcher was the wrenching out of context of her words 'There is no such thing as society'. The Bishop skilfully set this part of her record straight by quoting from a sermon she had preached at St Lawrence Jewry before becoming Prime Minister. In it she referred to the Christian doctrine

> that we are all members of one another, expressed in the concept of the Church on earth as the Body of Christ. From this we learn our interdependence and the great truth that we do not achieve happiness or salvation in isolation from each other but as members of society.

British society, revolutionised and restored to confidence by Margaret Thatcher, will continue to argue over her for generations to come. Already there have been a plethora of books, movies, plays, TV series and even an opera about her, but this is just the beginning. She is one of those seminal personalities whose charisma in her lifetime will continue to generate curiosity into the far horizons of history.

Although she was endearingly disinterested in books and biographies about herself during her life time, it is possible that she had a presentiment of her legacy's longevity when she was selecting the readings for her funeral. For the first words printed on its service sheet were from T.S. Eliot's *Four Quartets*:

> What we call the beginning is often the end
> And to make an end is to make a beginning
> The end is where we start from.

As Margaret Thatcher's funeral came to an end with the choir singing *Nunc Dimittis* as the military pallbearers carried her coffin out of St Paul's, there was a completely unexpected new beginning marked by the crowd erupting into applause.

This book began and now concludes at this same moment. After the applause comes the appraisal: 'The end is where we start from.'

Bibliography

BOOKS

Aitken, Jonathan, *Nixon: A Life*, Weidenfeld & Nicolson, 1993.

Aitken, Jonathan, *Heroes and Contemporaries*, Continuum, 2007.

Aldous, Richard, *Reagan and Thatcher: The Difficult Relationship*, Hutchinson, 2012.

Allen, Jim, *The Grantham Connection*, Grantham Book Centre, 1986.

Annan, Noel, *Our Age: The Generation that Made Post-War Britain*, Fortuna, 1991.

Baker, Kenneth, *The Turbulent Years: My Life in Politics*, Faber and Faber, 1993.

Bawden, Nina, *In My Time*, Virago, 1995.

Benn, Tony, *The Benn Diaries 1940–1990*, Arrow Books, 1996.

Berlinski, Claire, *There is No Alternative: Why Margaret Thatcher Matters*, Basic Civitas Books, 2008.

Blair, David, *The History of the Oxford University Conservative Association*, OUCA, 1995.

Blake, Robert, *Disraeli*, Faber and Faber, 2010.

Boswell, James, *The Life of Samuel Johnson* (edited by George Birbeck Hill), Clarendon Press, 1971.

Boyd-Carpenter, John, *Way of Life*, Sidgwick & Jackson, 1980.

Bush, George and Brent Scowcroft, *A World Transformed*, Alfred A. Knopf, 1998.

Butler, David and Dennis Kavanagh, *The British General Election of 1979*, Macmillan, 1980.

Butler, David and Dennis Kavanagh, *The British General Election of 1987*, Macmillan, 1988.

Campbell, John, *Margaret Thatcher, Volume One: The Grocer's Daughter*, Vintage Books, 2007.

Campbell, John, *Margaret Thatcher Volume Two: The Iron Lady*, Vintage Books, 2008.

Campbell, John, *Pistols at Dawn*, Vintage, 2010.

Carrington, Lord, *Reflect on Things Past*, Collins, 1988.

Carter, Jimmy, *Keeping Faith: Memoirs of a President*, University of Arkansas Press, 1995.

Castle, Barbara, *The Castle Diaries, 1974–1976*, Weidenfeld & Nicolson, 1980.

Clark, Alan, *Diaries: Into Politics*, Weidenfeld & Nicholson, 1993.

Cockerell, Michael, *Live from Number 10: The Inside Story of Prime Ministers and Television*, Faber and Faber, 1988.

Cosgrave, Patrick, *Thatcher: The First Term*, Bodley Head, 1990.

Cox, David (ed.), *The Walden Interviews*, LWT Boxtree, 1990.

Cradock, Sir Percy, *Experiences in China*, John Murray, 1994.

Cradock, Sir Percy, *In Pursuit of British Interests*, John Murray, 1994.

Creighton, Louise, *Life and Letters of Mandell Creighton*, Vol. I, Longmans, Green, 1904.

Crick, Michael, *Scargill and the Miners*, Penguin, 1985.

Critchley, Julian, *Palace of Varieties: An Insider's View of Westminster*, John Murray, 1989.

Crozier, Brian, *Free Agent*, HarperCollins, 1993.

Dale, Iain (ed.), *Memories of Maggie: A Portrait of Margaret Thatcher*, Politico's, 2000.

Dale, Iain (ed.), *Margaret Thatcher: In Her Own Words*, Biteback, 2010.

Dally, Ann, *A Doctor's Story*, Macmillan, 1990.

Devonshire, Deborah, *Wait for Me! Memoirs of the Youngest Mitford Sister*, John Murray, 2010.

du Cann, Edward, *The Political and Business Careers of Edward Du Cann*, Images, 1995.

Fallon, Ivan, *The Brothers: The Rise and Rise of Saatchi and Saatchi*, Hutchinson, 1998.

Freedman, Lawrence, *The Official History of the Falklands Campaign*, 2 vols, Routledge, 2005.

Gardiner, George, *Margaret Thatcher: From Childhood to Leadership*, William Kimber, 1975.

Giles, Frank, *Sunday Times*, John Murray, 1986.

Gilmour, Ian, *Dancing with Dogma: Britain under Thatcherism*, Simon & Schuster, 1992.

Gorbachev, Mikhail, *Memoirs*, Bantam, 1997.

Halcrow, Morrison, *Keith Joseph: A Single Mind*, Macmillan, 1989.

Hallam, Margaret, *The Life and Times of Huntingtower C.P. School*, Grantham, n.d.

Harris, Robert, *A Good and Faithful Servant: The Unauthorised Biography of Bernard Ingham*, Faber, 1990.

Harris, Robert, *Talleyrand: Betrayer and Saviour of France*, John Murray, 2007.

Harris, Robin, *Not for Turning: The Life of Margaret Thatcher*, Bantam Press, 2013.

Hastings, Max and Simon Jenkins, *The Battle for the Falklands*, Michael Joseph, 1983.

Healey, Denis, *The Time of My Life*, Michael Joseph, 1989.

Heath, Edward, *The Course of My Life*, Hodder & Stoughton, 1998.

Henderson, Nicholas, *Mandarin: The Diaries of an Ambassador 1969–1982*, Weidenfeld & Nicolson, 1995.

Hennessy, Peter, *The Prime Minister: The Office and its Holders since 1945*, Allen Lane, 2000.

Hollingsworth, Mark, *The Ultimate Spin Doctor: The Life and Fast Times of Tim Bell*, Hodder & Stoughton, 1997.

Honeybone, Michael, *The Book of Grantham: the History of a Market and Manufacturing Town*, Barracuda Books 1980.

Hoskyns, John, *Just in Time: Inside the Thatcher Revolution*, Aurum Press, 2000.

Howe, Geoffrey, *Conflict of Loyalty*, Macmillan, 1994.

Hunt, Rex, *My Falkland Days*, David & Charles, 1992.

Ingham, Bernard, *Kill the Messenger*, HarperCollins, 1994.

Jenkins, Roy, *European Diary, 1977–1981*, Collins, 1989.

Junor, John, *Listening for a Midnight Tram: Memoirs*, Chapmans, 1990.

Junor, Penny, *Margaret Thatcher: Wife, Mother, Politician*, Sidgwick & Jackson, 1983.

Junor, Penny, *John Major: From Brixton to Downing Street*, Penguin, 1996.

Kesteven and Grantham Girls' School and Amy C. Old, *The History of Kesteven and Grantham Girls' School, 1910–1987*, Kesteven and Grantham Girls' School, 1987.

King, Cecil, *Strictly Personal*, Weidenfeld & Nicolson, 1969.

King, Cecil, *The Cecil King Diary 1970–74*, Jonathan Cape, 1975.

Laban, Matthew, *Mr Speaker: The Office and the Individuals*, Biteback, 2013.

Laing, Margaret, *Edward Heath: Prime Minister*, Sidgwick & Jackson, 1972.

Lamont, Norman, *In Office*, Little, Brown, 1999.

Lawson, Nigel, *The View from No. 11: Memoirs of a Tory Radical*, Bantam Press, 1992.

Lewis, Russell, *Margaret Thatcher: A Personal and Political Biography*, Routledge & Kegan Paul, 1975.

Longford, Elizabeth, *Wellington: Pillar of State*, Weidenfeld & Nicolson, 1972.

Maddox, Brenda, *Maggie: The First Lady*, Hodder & Stoughton, 2003.

Major, John, *The Autobiography*, HarperCollins, 1999.

Marsh, David, *The Euro: The Battle for the New Global Currency*, Yale University Press, 2011.

Millar, Ronald, *A View from the Wings: West End, West Coast, Westminster*, Weidenfeld & Nicolson, 1993.

Money, Ernle, *Margaret Thatcher: First Lady of the House*, Leslie Frewin, 1975.

Moore, Charles, *Margaret Thatcher: The Authorized Biography, Volume One: Not for Turning*, Allen Lane, 2013.

Morley, John, *The Life of William Ewart Gladstone*, 3 vols, Macmillan, 1903.

Mount, Ferdinand, *Cold Cream: My Early Life and Other Mistakes*, Bloomsbury, 2008.

Murray, Tricia, *Margaret Thatcher*, W.H. Allen, 1979.

Nott, John, *Here Today and Gone Tomorrow: Memoirs of an Errant Politician*, Politico's Publishing, 2002.

Parkinson, Cecil, *Right at the Centre*, Weidenfeld & Nicolson, 1992.

Parris, Matthew, *Chance Witness: An Outsider's Life in Politics*, Viking, 2002.

Prior, James, *A Balance of Power*, Hamish Hamilton, 1986.

Ramsden, John, *Winds of Change: Macmillan to Heath, 1957–1975*, Longman, 1996.

Ranelagh, John, *Thatcher's People: An Insider's Account of the Politics, the Power and the Personalities*, HarperCollins, 1991.

Rawlinson, Peter, *A Price Too High*, Weidenfeld & Nicolson, 1989.

Reagan, Ronald, *An American Life*, Arrow Books, 1991.

Reagan, Ronald and Douglas Brinkley (ed.), *The Reagan Diaries*, HarperCollins, 2007.

Rees-Mogg, William, *Memoirs*, HarperCollins, 2011.

Renwick, Robin, *A Journey with Margaret Thatcher: Foreign Policy under the Iron Lady*, Biteback Publishing, 2013.

Riddell, Peter, *The Thatcher Era and its Legacy*, Blackwell, 1991.

Ridley, Nicholas, '*My Style of Government*': *The Thatcher Years*, Hutchinson, 1991.

Schlutz, George P., *Turmoil and Triumph: My Years as Secretary of State*, Scribner's, 1993.

Sergeant, John, *Maggie: Her Fatal Legacy*, Pan Books, 2005.

Shepherd, Robert, *Iain Macleod*, Hutchinson, 1994.

Simpson, John, *Strange Places, Questionable People*, Macmillan, 1998.

Sked, Alan and Chris Cook, *Post-War Britain: A Political History, 1945–1992*, 4th edn, Penguin, 1993.

Smith, Geoffrey, *Reagan and Thatcher*, Bodley Head, 1990.

Spicer, Michael, *The Spicer Diaries*, Biteback Publishing, 2012.

Strachey, Lytton, *Queen Victoria*, Chatto & Windus, 1951.

Taylor, Peter, *Provos: The IRA and Sinn Fein*, Bloomsbury, 1998.

Tebbit, Norman, *Upwardly Mobile*, Weidenfeld & Nicholson, 1988.

Thatcher, Carol, *Below the Parapet: The Biography of Denis Thatcher*, HarperCollins, 1996.

Thatcher, Carol, *Memoir: A Swim-On Part in the Goldfish Bowl*, Headline, 2010.

Thatcher, Margaret, *The Path to Power*, HarperCollins, 1995.

Thatcher, Margaret, *The Downing Street Years*, Harper Press, 2011.

Thomson, Andrew, *Margaret Thatcher: The Woman Within*, Allen Lane, 1989.

Urban, George R., *Diplomacy and Disillusion at the Court of Margaret Thatcher: An Insider's View*, I.B.Tauris, 1996.

Voltaire, *Candide*, Arcturus, 2009.

Walker, Peter, *Staying Power: An Autobiography*, Bloomsbury, 1991.

Wall, Stephen, *A Stranger in Europe: Britain and the EU from Thatcher to Blair*, Oxford University Press, 2008.

Walden, George, *Lucky George: Memoirs of an Anti-Politician*, Penguin, 2000.

Walters, Dennis, *Not Always with the Pack*, Constable, 1989.

Wapshott, Nicholas and George Brock, *Thatcher*, Macdonald, 1983.

Watkins, Alan, *A Conservative Coup: The Fall of Margaret Thatcher*, Duckworth, 1992.

Weinberger, Caspar, *Fighting for Peace: Seven Critical Years in the Pentagon*, Michael Joseph, 1990.

Whitehead, Phillip, *The Writing on the Wall: Britain in the Seventies*, Channel 4/Michael Joseph, 1985.

Whitelaw, William, *The Whitelaw Memoirs*, Aurum Press, 1989.

Woodward, Sandy, *One Hundred Days: The Memoirs of the Falklands Battle Group Commander*, HarperCollins, 1992.

Wyatt, Woodrow, *The Journals of Woodrow Wyatt*, edited by Sarah Curtis, 3 vols, Macmillan, 1998–2000.

Young, Hugo, *One of Us: A Biography of Margaret Thatcher*, Macmillan, 1991.

Young, Hugo and Anne Sloman, *The Thatcher Phenomenon*, BBC, 1986.

Young, Lord, *The Enterprise Years: A Businessman in the Cabinet*, Headline, 1990.

Ziegler, Philip, *Edward Heath: The Authorised Biography*, Harper Press 2010.

ARTICLES

Bridgman, Joan, 'At School with Margaret Thatcher', *Contemporary Review*, September 2004.

Moore, Charles, 'The Invincible Mrs. Thatcher', *Vanity Fair*, December 2011.

Orth, Maureen, 'Maggie's Big Problem', *Vanity Fair*, June 1991.

Powell, Charles, 'Differences Were in the Detail', *The Tablet*, 19 April 2012.

Scott-Smith, Giles, ' "Her Rather Ambitious Washington Programme": Margaret Thatcher's International Visitor Program Visit to the United States in 1967', *British Contemporary History*, vol. 17, no. 4, Winter 2003.

Sheehy, Gail, 'The Blooming of Margaret Thatcher', *Vanity Fair*, June 1989.

Touhy, Denis, 'Iron and Velvet', *The Tablet*, 11 February 2012.

Principal sources

THE AITKEN COLLECTION OF PERSONAL PAPERS, RECOLLECTIONS AND INTERVIEWS

This is the author's personal collection of diary entries, journal notes, records of conversations, meeting notes and personal recollections. Many of these have been donated to the Churchill Archive Centre, Churchill College, Cambridge. Others, still in the author's possession, will go here in due course.

The interviews tape-recorded for this book will also be donated to the Churchill Archives Centre.

UNIVERSITIES AND LIBRARIES

Margaret Thatcher Foundation: www.margaretthatcher.org
Churchill Archives Centre, Cambridge: The Thatcher Papers; British Diplomatic
    Oral History Programme; Papers of Lord Hailsham; Papers of Sir Alan Walters
Templeman Library, University of Kent, Canterbury: Bernard Weatherill Papers
British Library
British Library Newspaper Library

UNPUBLISHED MANUSCRIPTS

Aitken, Jonathan, personal diary
Hart, David, personal diary
Huntingtower Road Council School *Log Book*

PRIMARY SOURCES

Falkland Islands Review: Report of a Committee of Privy Counsellors, Chairman:
    The Rt. Hon the Lord Franks, OM, GCMG, KCB, CBE. Presented to Parliament
    by the Prime Minister by Command of Her Majesty, January 1983, London

Parliamentary Debates (Hansard), *House of Commons*, 1940–1990
Parliamentary Debates (Hansard), *House of Lords*, Official Report, Death of
   a Member: Baroness Thatcher: *Tributes*, 10 April 2013
Who's Who, A.C. Black, 2013

INTERVIEWS

Sir Antony Acland; Lord Armstrong of Ilminster; Lord Baker of Dorking; Lord Bell of Belgravia; Sir Clive Bossom; Sheira, Lady Brinckman; Lord Brittan of Spennithorne; Sir Nigel Broomfield; Lord Brownlow; Lord Burns of Hetton-le-Hole; Lord Butler of Brockwell; Lord Carrington; Sir Bryan Cartledge; Professor John Casey; Mr. Bill Cash; Major-General Peter Currie; Mr. Eric Deakins; Lord Donoughue of Ashton; Sir Edward du Cann; Mr. Alan Duncan; Sir Richard Evans; Lord Garel-Jones of Watford; Sir Anthony Garner; Mr. Mikhail Gorbachev; The Rev Canon Dr. Donald Gray; Sir Ronald Grierson; Lord Griffiths of Fforestfach; Dr. Keith Hampson; Professor Pauline Harrison; Mrs John Henderson; Mrs. Diana Honeybone; Mr. Michael Honeybone; Sir John Hoskyns; Sir Gerald Howarth; Baroness Howe of Idlicote; Lord Howell of Guildford; Mrs. Tony Hunter-Tilney; Sir Bernard Ingham; Lord Jenkin of Roding; Lord King of Bridgwater; Dr. Henry Kissinger; Mr. Malcolm Knapp; Dame Jill Knight; Mr. Denis Lambley; Lord Lamont of Lerwick; Mrs. Betty Langan; Lord Lawson of Blaby; Sir John Major; Mr. William Mullins; Sir John Nott; Hazel O'Leary; Mr. Derek Owens; Mr. Pavel Palazchenko; Mr. Michael Palmer; Lord Parkinson of Carnforth; Lady Pearson of Rannoch; Lord Pearson of Rannoch; Major-General Jeremy Phipps; Mrs. J. Enoch Powell; Lord Powell of Bayswater; Lord Ryder of Wensum; Lord Sacks of Aldgate; Mr. Wafic Saïd; Lord St. John of Fawsley; Sir Michael Scholar; Professor Roger Scruton; Sir Richard Shepherd; Sir Stephen Sherbourne; Mr. Julian Seymour; Sir Kenneth Stowe; Lord Tanlaw; Sir Teddy Taylor; Lord Tebbit of Chingford; Sir Mark Thatcher; Lord Thomas of Swynnerton; Lord Turnbull of Enfield; Dame Jane Whiteley; The Rev Dick Whittington; Lord Wilson of Tillyorn; Mr. Mark Worthington; Lord Young of Graffham; and others who preferred to remain anonymous.

NEWSPAPERS AND MAGAZINES

Daily Express, Daily Mail, Daily Mirror, Daily Telegraph, Dartford Chronicle, Erith Observer & Kentish Times, Evening News, Evening Post, Evening Standard, Finchley Press, Grantham Journal, Guardian, Gravesend and Dartford Reporter, Independent, Kommersant Vlast (Moscow), *Observer, Sleaford Gazette, Sunday Express, Sunday Graphic, Sunday People, Sunday Pictorial, Sunday Telegraph, Sunday Times, The Economist, The Spectator, The Tablet, The Times, Vanity Fair*

BROADCAST SOURCES

The Woman at Number Ten, De Wolfe Productions, 1983
Woman to Woman, Yorkshire Television, 1985
Thatcher: The Downing Street Years, BBC, 1993
Maggie: The First Lady, Brook Lapping, 2003
A Parliamentary Coup, BBC Parliament, 4 May 2009

Notes describing sources

ABBREVIATIONS

AC: The Aitken Collection of Personal Papers, Recollections and Interviews
CAC: Churchill Archives Centre, Cambridge
DOHP: British Diplomatic Oral History Programme
KGGS: Kesteven and Grantham Girls' School
MTF: Margaret Thatcher Foundation
OUCA: Oxford University Conservative Association
THCR: The Thatcher Papers
TNA: The National Archives, Kew

1 THE EARLY YEARS

1 Gail Sheehy, 'The Blooming of Margaret Thatcher', *Vanity Fair*, June 1989.
2 Ibid.
3 *Woman to Woman*, Interview by Miriam Stoppard, Yorkshire Television, 19 November 1985.
4 AC: Interview with Malcolm Knapp.
5 Margaret Thatcher, *The Path to Power*, HarperCollins, 1995, p. 4.
6 Ibid., p. 5.
7 AC: Conversation with Ted Heath, 1973.
8 *Grantham Journal*, 6 July 1945.
9 *Daily Mail*, 26 February 1975.
10 AC: Interview with Betty Langan (née Morley).
11 *Grantham Journal*, 17 October 1925.
12 Hugo Young and Anne Sloman, *The Thatcher Phenomenon*, BBC, 1986, p. 16.
13 Charles Moore, *Margaret Thatcher: The Authorized Biography, Volume One: Not for Turning*, Allen Lane, 2013, p. 9.
14 Margaret Thatcher, *Talking Politics* (BBC Radio 4), 31 August 1974. www.bbc.co.uk/archive/thatcher.
15 *Daily Express*, 17 April 1961.

16   Sheehy, *Vanity Fair*, June 1989.
17   AC: Interview with Betty Langan.
18   Tricia Murray, *Margaret Thatcher*, W.H. Allen, 1979, p. 17.
19   *Woman to Woman*, 19 November 1985.
20   Thatcher, *The Path to Power*, p. 15.
21   Ernle Money, *Margaret Thatcher*, Leslie Frewin, 1975, p. 38.
22   AC: Interview with Betty Langan.
23   *Woman to Woman*, 19 November 1985.
24   Ibid.
25   Thatcher, *The Path to Power*, p. 12.
26   Ibid., p. 11.
27   Murray, *Margaret Thatcher*, p. 25.
28   Ibid.
29   Thatcher, *The Path to Power*, p. 10.
30   Joan Bridgman, 'At School with Margaret Thatcher', *Contemporary Review*, September 2004.
31   Ibid.
32   Hansard, HC Deb 19 April 1983.
33   *Daily Mirror*, 26 February 1975.
34   MTF: Margaret Thatcher to Gerald Tuppin, 7 July 1980.
35   Huntingtower Road Council School, *Log Book*, p. 225.
36   Ibid., p. 229.
37   George Gardiner, *Margaret Thatcher*, William Kimber, 1975, p. 23.
38   MTF: Remarks on becoming Prime Minister, 4 May 1979.
39   Thatcher, *The Path to Power*, p. 6.
40   Ibid.
41   John Campbell, *Margaret Thatcher, Volume One: The Grocer's Daughter*, Vintage Books, 2007, p. 33.
42   Murray, *Margaret Thatcher*, p. 17.
43   AC: Interview with Denhys Lambley.
44   Thatcher, *The Path to Power*, p. 5.
45   CAC: The Thatcher Papers, THCR 1/9/8, Sermon notes prepared by Alfred Roberts, 1 January 1941.
46   Ibid.
47   AC: Interview with Denhys Lambley.
48   Thatcher, *The Path to Power*, p. 6.
49   AC: Conversation with Margaret Thatcher, 1976.
50   *Daily Mail*, 13 February 1975.
51   Interview with Lady Thatcher, cited in Moore, *Margaret Thatcher, Vol. 1*, p. 17.

52 Thatcher, *The Path to Power*, p. 6.
53 *Evening Standard*, 15 April 1983.

2 THE WAR, GRAMMAR SCHOOL AND FIGHTING HER HEADMISTRESS

1 Thatcher, *The Path to Power*, p. 26.
2 Interview with Lady Thatcher, cited in Moore, *Margaret Thatcher, Vol. 1*, p. 20.
3 Edith Mühlbauer's story, *Sunday Times*, 28 May 1998.
4 AC: Conversation with Margaret Thatcher at the unveiling of the statue of Air Marshal Sir Arthur Harris, May 1992.
5 *Grantham Journal*, 16 July 1945.
6 Moore, *Margaret Thatcher, Vol. 1*, p. xv.
7 Moore, *Margaret Thatcher, Vol. 1*, pp. 22–28.
8 Thatcher, *The Path to Power*, p. 31.
9 AC: Interview with Betty Langan.
10 Campbell, *Margaret Thatcher, Volume Two: The Iron Lady*, Vintage Books, 2008, p. 372.
11 Young and Slowman, *The Thatcher Phenomenon*, p. 14.
12 Sheehy, *Vanity Fair*, June 1989.
13 CAC: THCR 1/9/8, Alfred Roberts notebooks.
14 Thatcher, *The Path to Power*, p. 19.
15 Ibid., p. 8.
16 Penny Junor, *Margaret Thatcher: Wife, Mother, Politician*, Sidgwick & Jackson, 1983, p. 10.
17 AC: Interview with Betty Langan.
18 *Daily Mirror*, 26 February 1975.
19 Kesteven and Grantham Girls' School and Amy C. Old, *The History of KGGS*, KGGS, 1987, p. 7.
20 *The Gospel of St Matthew*, Chapter 7, verse 9.
21 AC: Conversation with Lady Thatcher, Lamberhurst Church, Kent, January 1979.
22 AC: Interview with Catherine Henderson (née Barford).
23 KGGS and Old, *The History of KGGS*, p. 18.
24 *Daily Mirror*, 26 February 1975.
25 Russell Lewis, *Margaret Thatcher: A Personal and Political Biography*, Routledge & Kegan Paul, 1975 , p. 12.
26 AC: Interview with Malcolm Knapp.
27 MTF: School days in Grantham, 1942.
28 Campbell, *The Grocer's Daughter*, pp. 42–43.

29 Young and Sloman, *The Thatcher Phenomenon*, p. 14.
30 AC: Interview with Betty Langan.
31 Thatcher, *The Path to Power*, p. 34.
32 Ibid.
33 Campbell, *The Grocer's Daughter*, p. 43.
34 'Margaret Thatcher: A Tribute, Return to Grantham', *Grantham Journal*, 8 April 2013. Accessed online www.granthamjournal.co.uk

3 OXFORD, BOYFRIENDS AND POLITICAL AMBITION

1   Thatcher, *The Path to Power*, p. 35.
2   Margaret Wickstead (née Goodrich) interviewed on *Maggie: The First Lady*, Brook Lapping, 2003.
3   AC: Interview with Pauline Harrison (née Cowan).
4   Murray, *Margaret Thatcher*, p. 41.
5   Thatcher, *The Path to Power*, p. 37.
6   Nicholas Wapshott and George Brock, *Thatcher*, Macdonald, 1983, p. 49.
7   Campbell, *The Grocer's Daughter*, p. 62.
8   Ibid.
9   Ibid.
10 Campbell, *The Grocer's Daughter*, p. 47.
11 The Gospel of St Matthew, Chapter 6, verse 33.
12 Campbell, *The Grocer's Daughter*, p. 48.
13 Interview with Betty Robbins (née Spice), cited in Moore, *Margaret Thatcher, Vol. 1*, p. 43.
14 AC: Interview with Pauline Harrison.
15 Junor, *Margaret Thatcher*, p. 20.
16 AC: Interview with Lord Tanlaw.
17 Margaret to Muriel, September 1944, cited in Moore, *Margaret Thatcher, Vol. 1*, p. 41.
18 Margaret to Muriel, 25 March 1945, ibid., pp. 62–63.
19 Ibid., p. 62.
20 AC: Interview with Pauline Harrison.
21 Nina Bawden: *In My Time*, Virago, 1995, p. 76.
22 Thatcher, *The Path to Power*, p. 33.
23 Campbell, *The Grocer's Daughter*, p. 62.
24 *Grantham Journal*, 6 July 1945.
25 *Sleaford Gazette*, 29 June 1945.
26 MTF: OUCA Policy Sub-Committee Report, 1 December 1945.

27 AC: Conversation with Mrs Stella Gatehouse.
28 AC: Author in conversation with Margaret Thatcher in 1977.
29 *Daily Express*, 17 April 1961.
30 Sheehy, *Vanity Fair*, June 1989.
31 Campbell, *The Grocer's Daughter*, p. 65.
32 AC: Interview with Sir Stephen Sherbourne.

4 FIRST STEPS IN POLITICS

1   Thatcher, *The Path to Power*, p. 61.
2   Junor, *Margaret Thatcher*, p. 28.
3   Money, *Margaret Thatcher*, p. 45.
4   Wapshott and Brock, *Thatcher*, pp. 51–52.
5   AC: Conversation with Lady Thatcher and Sir Clive Bossom at dinner in the author's home, 20 April 2009.
6   AC: Interview with Sir Clive Bossom.
7   Ibid.
8   Ibid.
9   Thatcher, *The Path to Power*, p. 63.
10 Ibid.
11 Ibid., p. 62.
12 Ibid., p. 63.
13 Carol Thatcher, *Below the Parapet: The Biography of Denis Thatcher*, Harper-Collins, 1996, p. 58.
14 Campbell, *The Grocer's Daughter*, p. 72.
15 Ibid., p. 73.
16 *Erith Observer & Kentish Times*, 4 March 1949.
17 Ibid.
18 Carol Thatcher, *Below the Parapet*, p. 58.
19 Interview with Sir Denis Thatcher, cited in Moore, *Margaret Thatcher, Vol. 1*, p. 82.
20 Margaret to Muriel, 17 March, 1949, Ibid., p. 81.
21 Carol Thatcher, *Below the Parapet*, p. 59.
22 Margaret to Muriel, 23 March 1949, cited in Moore, *Margaret Thatcher, Vol. 1*, p. 89.
23 Margaret to Muriel, 21 July 1949, ibid., p. 91.
24 Margaret to Muriel, October 1950 (undated), ibid., p. 106.
25 Carol Thatcher, *Below the Parapet*, p. 61.
26 *Dartford Chronicle*, 10 February 1950.

27 Carol Thatcher, *Below the Parapet*, p. 61.
28 *Daily Mail*, 28 June 1949.
29 *Sunday People*, 12 February 1950.
30 *Gravesend and Dartford Reporter*, 28 January 1950.
31 Ibid.
32 Murray, *Margaret Thatcher*, p. 47.
33 Campbell, *The Grocer's Daughter*, p. 83.
34 MTF: *Evening Post*, 17 January 1950.
35 Thatcher, *The Path to Power*, p. 68.
36 AC: Interview with Sir Edward du Cann.
37 Thatcher, *The Path to Power*, p. 75.
38 AC: Interview with Sir Clive Bossom.
39 Margaret to Muriel, March 1950 (undated), cited in Moore, *Margaret Thatcher, Vol. 1*, p. 100.
40 Margaret to Muriel, May 1950 (undated), ibid., p. 101.
41 Margaret to Muriel, 28 May 1951, ibid., p. 105.
42 Alfred Roberts to Muriel, 25 September 1951, ibid., p. 105.
43 Carol Thatcher, *Below the Parapet*, p. 63.
44 Ibid., p. 51.
45 Alfred Roberts to Muriel, 25 September 1951, cited in Moore, *Margaret Thatcher, Vol. 1*, p. 105.
46 Carol Thatcher, *Below the Parapet*, p. 64.
47 MTF: Beryl Cook to Conservative Central Office, Report on Miss M. Roberts, 19 November 1951.

5 MARRIAGE, MOTHERHOOD AND FINCHLEY

1   Carol Thatcher, *Below the Parapet*, p. 64.
2   AC: Interview with Sir Clive Bossom.
3   Carol Thatcher, *Below the Parapet*, p. 65.
4   Thatcher, *The Path to Power*, p. 77.
5   *Sunday Graphic*, 17 February 1952.
6   MTF: Beryl Cook to John Hare, 12 June 1952.
7   Campbell, *The Grocer's Daughter*, p. 97.
8   Ann Dally, *A Doctor's Story*, Macmillan, 1990, pp. 9–10.
9   Thatcher, *The Path to Power*, p. 80.
10 Ibid., pp. 80–81.
11 Wapshott and Brock, *Thatcher*, p. 60.
12 Carol Thatcher, *Below the Parapet*, p. 71.

13 Ibid.

14 Gardiner, *Margaret Thatcher*, p. 54.

15 Margaret to Muriel, 20 January 1954, cited in Moore, *Margaret Thatcher, Vol. 1*, p. 126.

16 Interview with Sir Frederick Lawton, ibid., p. 126.

17 Carol Thatcher, *Below the Parapet*, p. 73.

18 Gardiner, *Margaret Thatcher*, p. 53.

19 Thatcher, *The Path to Power*, p. 94.

20 AC: Conversation with Bill Henderson, 1985.

21 MTF: Entwisle to Donald Kaberry, 18 March 1958.

22 Ibid.

23 Dennis Walters, *Not Always with the Pack*, Constable, 1989, pp. 103–104.

24 Campbell, *The Grocer's Daughter*, pp. 112–113.

25 *Finchley Press*, 18 July 1958.

26 MTF: Miss Harris to Donald Kaberry, 15 July 1958.

27 *Evening Standard*, 15 July 1958.

28 Carol Thatcher, *Below the Parapet*, p. 78.

29 Campbell, *The Grocer's Daughter*, p. 114.

30 Ibid.

31 *Finchley Press*, 8 August 1958.

32 Thatcher, *The Path to Power*, p. 98.

33 MTF: Margaret Thatcher to Donald Kaberry, 18 August 1958.

34 Thatcher, *The Path to Power*, p. 98.

35 *Finchley Press*, 27 February 1959.

36 Thatcher, *The Path to Power*, p. 92.

37 AC: Interview with Eric Deakins.

38 Ibid.

39 Ibid.

40 Ibid.

41 MTF: Report on Mrs Thatcher, Central Office Area Agent Finchley, 1 November 1959.

42 AC: Conversation with Lord Spicer, 2013. See also Michael Spicer, *The Spicer Diaries*, Biteback Publishing, 2012, p. 498.

6 FIRST YEARS IN PARLIAMENT

1 AC: Conversation with Baroness Hornsby-Smith, 1976.

2 Thatcher, *The Path to Power*, p. 110.

3 Money, *Margaret Thatcher*, p. 57.

4 MTF: Admission of the Press Adjournment Debate, 1 February 1960, Memo by C.J. Pearce, 29 January 1960.

5 Thatcher, *The Path to Power*, p. 111.
6 Ibid., p. 122.
7 *Independent*, 23 November 1994.
8 MTF: Admission of the Press Bill, Dame Evelyn Sharp to the Parliamentary Secretary, 11 January 1960.
9 Ibid.
10 *Independent*, 23 November 1994.
11 *The Times*, 14 April 1960.
12 *Daily Express*, 6 February 1960.
13 *Sunday Dispatch*, 7 February 1960.
14 *Daily Telegraph*, 6 February 1960.
15 AC: Conversation with Sir William Aitken, circa 1963.
16 AC: Conversation with Lady Aitken, circa 1975.
17 *Sunday Dispatch*, 7 February 1960.
18 Julian Critchley, *Palace of Varieties: An Insider's View of Westminster*, John Murray, 1989, p. 122.
19 *Sunday Pictorial*, 23 April 1961.
20 Alfred Roberts to Muriel Cullen, 27 September 1960, cited in Moore, *Margaret Thatcher, Vol. 1*, p. 154.
21 Hansard, HC Deb 19 April 1961.
22 Ibid.
23 AC: Rt Hon. Selwyn Lloyd, conversation with author, 1961.
24 Ibid.: Interview with Sir Clive Bossom.
25 Thatcher, *The Path to Power*, p. 117.
26 AC: Conversation with Margaret Thatcher, 1976.
27 Ibid.: Conversation with James Ramsden, 1978.
28 Young and Slowman, *The Thatcher Phenomenon*, p. 23.
29 *The Times*, 11 October 1961.
30 Thatcher, *The Path to Power*, p. 119.
31 Campbell, *The Grocer's Daughter*, p. 145.
32 John Boyd-Carpenter, *Way of Life*, Sidgwick & Jackson, 1980, p. 133.
33 AC: Interview with Sir Clive Bossom.
34 Ibid.
35 Thatcher, *The Path to Power*, p. 123.
36 Ibid., p. 124.
37 Boyd-Carpenter, *Way of Life*, p. 133.
38 MTF: Address by Lady Thatcher, Memorial Service for Lord Boyd-Carpenter, St Margaret's Westminster, 3 November 1998.
39 Hansard, HC Deb 16 July 1962.
40 AC: Interview with Derek Owens.

41 Ibid.: Interview with Chief Rabbi Lord Sacks.

42 Ibid.

43 Ibid.

44 AC: Interview with Prince Naif bin Abdul Aziz Al Saud, 1975.

45 *Daily Express,* 17 April 1961.

46 Margaret Thatcher to Muriel Cullen, late 1960 (undated), cited in Moore, *Margaret Thatcher, Vol. 1,* p. 154.

47 *Evening News,* 25 February 1960.

48 AC: Interview with Sir Edward du Cann.

49 Carol Thatcher, *Below the Parapet,* p. 90.

50 Ibid., p. 88.

51 Ibid., p. 91.

52 Ibid., pp. 91–92.

7 FRONT-BENCH OPPOSITION

1 Thatcher, *The Path to Power,* p. 133.

2 Ibid., p. 136.

3 Ibid., p. 137.

4 AC: Meriden 1966.

5 AC: Margaret Thatcher to the author, March 1966.

6 AC: Meriden 1966.

7 Ibid.: Meriden Campaign Diary, March 1966.

8 Thatcher, *The Path to Power,* p. 134.

9 James Prior, *A Balance of Power,* Hamish Hamilton, 1986, p. 42.

10 Hansard, HC Deb 5 May 1966.

11 Ibid.

12 Robert Shepherd, *Iain Macleod,* Hutchinson, 1994, p. 429.

13 *Daily Mail,* 10 May 1966.

14 MTF: Speech to Party Conference, Blackpool, 12 October 1966.

15 Ibid.

16 AC: Mrs Stella Gatehouse, speaking lessons, OUCA 1961.

17 *Daily Mail,* 18 October 1966.

18 *Sun,* 13 October 1966.

19 *Sunday Express,* 30 June 1968.

20 Sir Peter Rawlinson, *A Price Too High,* Weidenfeld & Nicholson, 1989, p. 247.

21 AC: Interview with Lord Carrington.

22 Thatcher, *The Path to Power,* p. 143.

23 Ibid., p. 146.

24 Ibid., p. 147.

25 Ibid., p. 143.
26 MTF: 'What's Wrong with Politics', CPC Lecture, Blackpool, 11 October 1968.
27 Ibid.
28 MTF: Giles Scott-Smith interview with Dean B. Mahin. Giles Scott-Smith, 'Margaret Thatcher's International Visitor Programme to the United States', *British Contemporary History*, vol. 17, no. 4, Winter, 2003, pp. 13–14.
29 Moore, *Margaret Thatcher*, Vol. 1, p. 199.
30 Thatcher, *The Path to Power*, p. 155.
31 AC: Interview with Sir Edward du Cann.
32 'Spot the Prime Minister', *Sunday Times*, 5 March 1967.
33 AC: Interview with Michael Palmer.
34 *Daily Express*, 7 February 1970.
35 MTF: Shadow Cabinet Conference, 1 February 1970.
36 Ibid.
37 Alfred Roberts to Muriel Cullen, 4 December 1969, cited in Moore, *Margaret Thatcher, Vol. 1*, p. 206.
38 Wapshott and Brock, *Thatcher*, p. 63.
39 Thatcher, *The Path to Power*, p. 162.
40 Carol Thatcher, *Below the Parapet*, p. 97.
41 Talleyrand, January 1809, cited in Robin Harris, *Talleyrand: Betrayer and Saviour of France*, John Murray, 2007, p. 199.
42 Thatcher, *The Path to Power*, p. 163.

8 SECRETARY OF STATE FOR EDUCATION

1 AC: Interview with Lord St John of Fawsley.
2 Thatcher, *The Path to Power*, p. 169.
3 Hansard, HC Deb 8 July 1970.
4 Ibid.
5 Ibid.
6 Cabinet Secretary's notebooks, 23 June 1970, cited in Moore, *Margaret Thatcher, Vol. 1*, p. 221.
7 Ibid., p. 207.
8 *Third Way*, vol. 18, no. 6, July 1995, p. 8.
9 AC: Conversation with Iain Macleod 1968.
10 Campbell, *The Grocer's Daughter*, p. 229.
11 MTF: Speech to the Conservative Party Conference 12 October 1972.
12 AC: Interview with Lord St John of Fawsley.
13 Ibid.
14 Ibid.

15 Ibid.
16 *Daily Mirror*, 6 October 1971.
17 *Guardian*, 28 October 1970.
18 *Sun*, 25 November 1971.
19 Thatcher, *The Path to Power*, p. 181.
20 Hansard, HC Deb 18 November 1971.
21 Ibid., 5 November 1971.
22 Ibid., 18 November 1971.
23 Campbell, *The Grocer's Daughter*, p. 233.
24 AC: Interview with Lord St. John of Fawsley.
25 Campbell, *The Grocer's Daughter*, p. 232.
26 Carol Thatcher, *Below the Parapet*, pp. 98–99.
27 Gardiner, *Margaret Thatcher*, pp. 114–115.
28 AC: Conversation with Ted Heath, 1981.
29 Hansard, HC Deb 3 February 1972.
30 *Sunday Telegraph*, 9 April 1972.
31 Thatcher, *The Path to Power*, p. 190.
32 *The Times*, 20 June 1972.
33 Thatcher, *The Path to Power*, p. 191.
34 *Guardian*, 7 December 1972.
35 AC: Interview with Dr Henry Kissinger.
36 MTF: AmEmbassy to Department of State, 25 June 1973.
37 *Observer*, 2 December 1973.
38 *Finchley Press*, 13 and 20 August 1971.
39 Hansard, HC Deb 28 January 1974.
40 *Finchley Press*, 23 November 1973.
41 Ibid., 1 February 1974.
42 Thatcher, *The Path to Power*, p. 233.
43 AC: Interview with Sir Edward du Cann.
44 Thatcher, *The Path to Power*, p. 239.
45 Philip Ziegler, *Edward Heath: The Authorised Biography*, Harper Press, 2011, p. 440.
46 Campbell, *The Grocer's Daughter*, p. 255.
47 *A Chance to Meet*, BBC1, 21 March 1971, cited in Moore, *Margaret Thatcher*, *Vol. 1*, p. 222.
48 AC: Interview with Lord St John of Fawsley.

9 HEATH ON THE ROPES

1 Margaret Laing, *Edward Heath: Prime Minister*, Sidgwick & Jackson, 1972, p. 205.
2 AC: Conversations with Ted Heath and Teddy Denman, Summer 1972.

3 Ibid., 5 March 1974.
4 Thatcher, *The Path to Power*, p. 246.
5 *Evening Standard*, 28 August 1974.
6 BBC Radio 4, 8 July 1990, cited in John Ranelagh, *Thatcher's People: An Insider's Account of the Politics, the Power and the Personalities*, HarperCollins, 1991, p. 192.
7 John Junor, *Listening for a Midnight Tram: Memoirs*, Chapmans, 1990, p. 227.
8 Peter Walker, *Staying Power: An Autobiography*, Bloomsbury, 1991, p. 126.
9 AC: August 1974.
10 Thatcher, *The Path to Power*, p. 255.
11 *The Times*, 6 September 1974.
12 *Daily Mirror*, 28 September 1974.
13 *Sun*, 28 September 1974.
14 *Finchley Press*, 4 October 1974.
15 Campbell, *The Grocer's Daughter*, p. 279.
16 AC: 1922 Committee Meeting, 31 October 1974.
17 Ibid.: Dinner party hosted by Hugh Fraser, 2 December 1974.
18 *The Times*, 16 October 1974.
19 Ibid.
20 John Campbell, *Pistols at Dawn*, Vintage, 2010, p. 316.
21 CAC: Hailsham Papers, Diary, 12 November 1974.
22 Interview with Lady Thatcher, cited in Moore, *Margaret Thatcher, Vol. 1*, p. 256.
23 Interview with Sir Alfred Sherman, cited in Moore, *Margaret Thatcher, Vol. 1*, p. 254.
24 Joseph, Keith, *Reversing the Trend*, Barry Rose, 1975, p. 4.
25 Thatcher, *The Path to Power*, p. 261.
26 Ibid., p. 263.
27 *Evening Standard*, 19 October 1974.
28 *Guardian* 21 October 1974.
29 Thatcher, *The Path to Power*, p. 263.

10 WINNING THE LEADERSHIP

1 Hansard, HC Deb 14 November 1974.
2 Ibid.
3 Ibid.
4 Thatcher, *The Path to Power*, p. 266.
5 Ibid.
6 Ibid.
7 Interview with Sir Denis Thatcher, cited in Moore: *Margaret Thatcher, Vol. 1*, p. 275.

8   AC: Peter Morrison, 28 October 1974.
9   Ibid., Peter Morrison, 29 October 1974.
10 Moore, *Margaret Thatcher, Vol. 1*, p. 283.
11 AC: Interview with Sir John Nott.
12 Ibid.
13 Ibid.: Peter Rees, January 1975.
14 CAC: Hailsham Papers, Diary, 12 November 1974.
15 AC: Interview with Sir Edward du Cann.
16 Ibid.
17 Ibid.
18 Ibid.: Commander John Kerans RN to author, 1975.
19 Ibid.: Interview with Lord Tebbit.
20 Ibid.: Interview with Sir Edward du Cann.
21 Ibid.
22 *The Times*, 28 November 1974.
23 *Daily Telegraph*, 12 October 2005.
24 Thatcher, *The Path to Power*, p. 269.
25 AC: Author's conversations, 1975.
26 Ibid.: Author's recollection, anecdote frequently retold in 1974.
27 Thatcher, *The Path to Power*, p. 272.
28 AC: Conversation with Edward Heath, 17 December 1974.
29 Hansard, HC Deb 21 January 1975.
30 Ibid., 22 January 1975.
31 Ibid.
32 Ibid.
33 *The Times*, 28 January 1975.
34 Ziegler, *Edward Heath*, p. 485.
35 AC: Interview with Lord Tebbit.
36 Ibid.: Author's recollection, January 1975.
37 Ibid.: Conversations with Sir John Rodgers, 1975.
38 AC: Interview with Lord Lamont.
39 Thatcher, *The Path to Power*, p. 277.
40 AC: Author's recollection, House of Commons, 5 February 1975.

11 LEADER OF THE OPPOSITION: A FRAGILE BEGINNING

1   AC: Author's recollection, 9 February 1975.
2   *Sun*, 12 February 1975.
3   AC: Author's recollection, 11 February 1975.
4   Ibid.

5   Hansard, HC Deb, Standing Committee A (Finance Bill), 11 February 1975.
6   Carol Thatcher, *Below the Parapet*, p. 11.
7   Money, *Margaret Thatcher*, p. 95.
8   *Private Eye*, 4 April 1979.
9   AC: Author's meeting with Margaret Thatcher, 10 March 1975.
10 Ibid.: Conversation with Nicholas Budgen, 1976.
11 Thatcher, *The Path to Power*, p. 295.
12 *Sunday Times*, 25 May 1975.
13 AC: Author's recollection, 1975.
14 *The Times*, 7 March 1975.
15 AC: Off-the-record interview.
16 Ibid.: Lady Tilney to Lady Aitken, the author's mother, 1975.
17 *The Times*, 21 September 1978.
18 AC: Interview with Lord Donoughue.
19 Ibid.: Author's recollection, 1976.
20 Ibid.: Interview with Sir Mark Thatcher for Aitken, *Heroes and Contemporaries*,
    p. 135.
21 Ibid.: Author's recollection, 4 April 1977.
22 Ibid.: Author's recollection of conversation with Councillor Harry Anish,
    1 January 1979.
23 Barbara Castle, *The Castle Diaries, 1974–1976*, Weidenfeld & Nicolson, 1980,
    5 August 1975, p. 487.
24 AC: Interview with Sir John Nott.
25 Matthew Parris, *Chance Witness: An Outsider's Life in Politics*, Viking, 2002, p. 189.

12 THREE FRUSTRATING YEARS

1   MTF: Speech to the Conservative Party Conference, Blackpool, 10 October 1975.
2   Ibid.
3   *Daily Mail*, 11 October 1975.
4   Thatcher, *The Path to Power*, p. 307.
5   AC: Interview with Sir Stephen Sherbourne, October 1975.
6   Ronald Millar, *A View from the Wings, West End, West Coast, Westminster*,
    Weidenfeld & Nicolson, 1993, p. 236.
7   Ibid., p. 240.
8   Ibid.
9   AC: Interview with Dr Henry Kissinger.
10 Ibid.
11 President Gerald Ford and Dr Henry Kissinger, Memorandum of Conversation,
    9 May 1974, cited in Moore, *Margaret Thatcher, Vol. 1*, p. 313.

12 Hansard, HC Deb 8 June 1976.
13 Ibid., 29 June 1976.
14 Frank Giles, *Sunday Times*, John Murray, 1986, p. 226.
15 AC: Remarks made by David Crouch, 23 March 1977.
16 Ibid.
17 AC: Interview with Sir Edward du Cann.
18 Thatcher, *The Path to Power*, p. 319.
19 Deborah Devonshire, *Wait for Me! Memoirs of the Youngest Mitford Sister*, John Murray, 2010, p. 258.
20 MTF: Interview for *World in Action*, Granada TV, 30 January 1978.
21 Thatcher, *The Path to Power*, p. 408.
22 MTF: Speech at Kensington Town Hall, 19 January 1976.
23 Thatcher, *The Path to Power*, p. 362.
24 Ibid.
25 Phillip Whitehead, *The Writing on the Wall: Britain in the Seventies*, Channel 4/Michael Joseph, 1985, p. 336.
26 Prior, *A Balance of Power*, p. 108.
27 *Evening Standard*, 27 June 1985.
28 AC: Interview with Sir John Hoskyns.
29 Thatcher, *The Path to Power*, p. 317.
30 Ranelagh, *Thatcher's People*, p. 28.
31 AC: Meeting with Airey Neave, May 1975.
32 Ibid.: Interview with Professor John Casey, 1975.
33 Ibid.
34 Ranelagh, *Thatcher's People*, p. ix.
35 Campbell, *The Grocer's Daughter*, p. 372.

13 LAST LAP TO THE ELECTION

1 Hansard, HC Deb 25 July 1978.
2 Ibid.
3 *Financial Times*, 26 July 1978.
4 AC: Interview with Lord St John of Fawsley.
5 Hansard, HC Deb 25 July 1978.
6 Ibid.
7 AC: Conversation with Nicholas Fairbairn, 1978.
8 Ibid.: Interview with Lord Bell.
9 Ibid.
10 Ibid.
11 MTF: Interview for Central TV, 7 September 1978.

12   AC: Interview with Lord Donoughue.
13   Ibid.: Interview with Lord Bell.
14   Ibid.
15   Ibid.
16   Ibid.
17   Ibid.
18   *The Times*, 26 October 1978.
19   *Daily Express*, 10 November 1978.
20   Norman Tebbit, *Upwardly Mobile*, Futura, 1989, p. 199.
21   Thatcher, *The Path to Power*, p. 419.
22   *Sun*, 11 January 1979.
23   Millar, *A View from the Wings*, pp. 247–248.
24   MTF: Conservative Party Political Broadcast by Margaret Thatcher, 17 January 1979.
25   Ibid.
26   Millar, *A View from the Wings*, p. 249.
27   AC: Conversation with Margaret Thatcher, 18 January 1979.
28   Ibid.: Interview with Lord Bell.
29   *Daily Express*, 6 February 1979.
30   Hansard, HC Deb 7 May 1940.
31   Thatcher, *The Path to Power*, p. 431.
32   Thomas Babington Macaulay, '*Horatius*', *Lays of Ancient Rome*, Longman, 1849.
33   Hansard, HC Deb 28 March 1979.
34   Ibid.
35   Ibid.
36   AC: Author's recollection, 28 March 1979.
37   Hansard, HC Deb 28 March 1979.
38   AC: Author's recollection, 28 March 1979.
39   Ibid.: Carol Thatcher to the author, 1 April 1979.
40   AC: Interview with Lord Bell.

14   THE FINAL ASCENT TO NO. 10

1   Ipsos MORI, 3–5 March 1979.
2   Thatcher, *The Path to Power*, p. 434.
3   Millar, *A View from the Wings*, p. 251.
4   *Daily Express*, 31 March 1979.
5   Millar, *A View from the Wings*, p. 253.
6   Ibid., p. 255.
7   Ibid.

 8 AC: Interview with Sir Kenneth Stowe.
 9 Ibid.
10 Ibid.
11 *Observer*, 15 April 1979.
12 Thatcher, *The Path to Power*, p. 451.
13 Millar, *A View from the Wings*, p. 262.
14 Ibid.
15 UK Polling Report, 1974–1979.
16 Millar, *A View from the Wings*, p. 262.
17 *Guardian*, 5 May 1979.
18 *Daily Mail*, 19 April 1979.
19 AC: Conversation with Gordon Reece, circa 1983.
20 Denis Tuohy, 'Iron and Velvet', *The Tablet*, 11 February 2012.
21 *Daily Mail*, 30 April 1979.
22 Millar, *A View from the Wings*, p. 261.
23 MTF: Conservative Party Election Broadcast, 30 April 1979.
24 AC: Author's recollection, 30 April 1979.
25 Ibid.: April 1979.
26 Ibid.: April 1977.
27 *Observer*, 25 February 1979.
28 AC: Author's unpublished diary, 28–29 April 1979.
29 Ibid.: Interview with Lord St John of Fawsley.
30 Jonathan Aitken, *Nixon: A Life*, Weidenfeld & Nicolson, 1993, p. 546.
31 The Prayer of the Most Distinguished Order of St Michael and St George (1818).
32 AC: Denis Thatcher to author, Spring 1979.
33 Noel Annan, *Our Age: The Generation that Made Post-War Britain*, Fortuna, 1991, p. 585.
34 AC: Interview with Lord Donoughue.
35 Ibid.
36 *Daily Mirror*, 4 May 1979.
37 *Sun*, 3 May 1979.
38 *Daily Express*, 4 May 1979.
39 MTF: BBC Radio News Report at 07.00, 4 May 1979.
40 This prayer, attributed to St Francis of Assisi, was written by an unknown nineteenth-century author.
41 Millar, *A View from the Wings*, p. 266.
42 David Butler and Dennis Kavanagh, *The British General Election of 1979*, Macmillan, 1980, pp. 199 and 395.
43 AC: Interview with Lord Bell.
44 Millar, *A View from the Wings*, p. 267.

45 Ibid., p. 268.
46 Ibid., p. 269.
47 AC: Interview with Sir Teddy Taylor.
48 Iain Dale (ed.), *Margaret Thatcher: In Her Own Words*, Biteback, 2010, p. 110.
49 AC: Interview with Lord Bell.
50 MTF: Speech at Cardiff, 16 April 1979.
51 Butler and Kavanagh, *The British General Election of 1979*, p. 343.

15 FIRST MOVES AS PRIME MINISTER

1   AC: Interview with Sir Kenneth Stowe.
2   Edward Heath, *The Course of My Life*, Hodder & Stoughton 1998, p. 574.
3   AC: Interview with Sir Kenneth Stowe.
4   *Guardian*, 7 May 1979.
5   Edmund Burke, Speech to the Electors of Bristol, 3 November 1774.
6   Hansard, HC Deb 15 May 1979.
7   AC: Author's recollection, 15 May 1979.
8   Ibid.: 15 May 1979.
9   Tony Benn, *The Benn Diaries, 1940–1990*, Arrow Books, 1996, 15 May 1979, p. 476.
10 Margaret Thatcher, *The Downing Street Years*, Harper Press, 2011, p. 42.
11 Ibid., p. 43.
12 *The Times*, 16 November 1979.
13 AC: Enoch Powell to the author, December 1979.
14 Ibid.: Interview with Lord Howell.
15 Ibid.: Interview with Lord Lamont.
16 Patrick Cosgrave, *Thatcher: The First Term*, Bodley Head, 1985, p. 105.
17 AC: Interview with Lord Baker.
18 Ibid.: Interview with Lord Howell.
19 Ibid.: Interview with Lord St John of Fawsley.
20 Ibid.: Interview with Lord Jenkin.
21 Ibid.
22 Ibid.: Peter Morrison to the author, November 1979.
23 Thatcher, *The Downing Street Years*, p. 48.
24 AC: Interview with Lord Carrington.
25 Thatcher, *The Downing Street Years*, p. 48.
26 Prior, *A Balance of Power*, p. 136.
27 AC: Interview with Lord Armstrong.
28 Ibid.: Interview with Lord Parkinson.
29 Ibid.: Interview with Lord Armstrong.

16 THE LEARNING CURVE

1   AC: Interview with Sir Kenneth Stowe.
2   Ibid.: Interview with Lord Armstrong.
3   Ibid.
4   CAC: DOHP/115, Sir Bryan Cartledge, pp. 37 and 40.
5   Young, *One of Us*, p. 158.
6   AC: Interview with Lord Burns.
7   Ibid.: Interview with Sir John Hoskyns.
8   CAC: DOHP/115, Sir Bryan Cartledge, pp. 38–39.
9   *Daily Telegraph*, 30 December 2011.
10 AC: Conversation with Ian Gow, December 1979.
11 Ibid.: Interview with Sir Bernard Ingham.
12 Ibid.
13 AC: Interview with Lord Howell.
14 Ibid.: Interview with Sir Bernard Ingham.
15 Ibid.: Conversations with Ian Gow, 1980–1981.
16 Ibid.: Conversation with Peter Bauer, December 1979.
17 Ibid.: Interview with Lord Thomas.
18 Ibid.
19 Ibid.: Interview with Lord Armstrong.
20 Ibid.: Interview with Sir Kenneth Stowe.
21 Ibid.: Conversation with Arthur Martin of MI5, 1980.
22 Howe, *Conflict of Loyalty*, pp. 347–348.
23 AC: Interview with Lord Lawson; see also Nigel Lawson, *The View from No. 11: Memoirs of a Tory Radical*, Bantam, 1993, p. 314.
24 MTF: B. Ingham to the Prime Minister, 5 January 1981, enc. Note for the Record: Lunch with Rupert Murdoch.
25 TNA: Fair Trading Act 1973 c. 41, S58 (3)(a).
26 MTF: E(81) 4th Meeting, Cabinet, Ministerial Committee on Economic Strategy, Minutes, 26 January 1981.
27 Ibid.: The Secretary of State for Trade, 26 January 1981.
28 AC: Conversation with John Biffen, 27 January 1981.
29 *The Journals of Woodrow Wyatt*, edited by Sarah Curtis, Macmillan, 2000, Vol. 3, 1 December 1985, p. 582.
30 AC: Interview with Lord Butler.
31 Ibid.: Conversation with John Biffen, 1980.
32 AC: Interview with Lord Armstrong.
33 Ibid.. Private Information: Special Branch source.
34 Ibid.: Conversation with Peter Morrison, summer 1979.

35 Ibid.
36 Ibid.
37 AC: Interview with Lord Carrington.
38 John Hoskyns, *Just in Time: Inside the Thatcher Revolution*, Aurum Press, 2000, p. 108.
39 Ibid., p. 107.
40 AC: Interviews with Lord Armstrong and Lord Butler.
41 Ibid.: Conversation with David Gore-Booth, 1980.

17 FIRST STEPS IN FOREIGN AFFAIRS

1   AC: Interview, source off-the-record.
2   Thatcher, *The Downing Street Years*, p. 158.
3   AC: Interview with Lord Carrington.
4   Ibid.
5   Ibid.
6   Thatcher, *The Downing Street Years*, p. 66.
7   AC: Interview with Lord Carrington.
8   CAC: DOHP/115, Sir Bryan Cartledge, p. 39.
9   AC: Interview with Lord Carrington.
10 Ibid.
11 Ibid.
12 Thatcher, *The Downing Street Years*, p. 74.
13 Young, *One of Us*, p. 180
14 John Simpson, *Strange Places, Questionable People*, Macmillan, 1998, p. 243.
15 Millar, *A View from the Wings*, p. 320.
16 Young, *One of Us*, p. 180.
17 AC: Interview with Lord Carrington.
18 Andrew Thomson, Margaret Thatcher, *The Woman Within*, Allen Lane, 1989, p. 33.
19 AC: Interview with Lord Carrington.
20 Ibid.
21 Lord Carrington interviewed for *The Thatcher Factor*, Channel 4, 1989, quoted in Campbell, *The Iron Lady*, p. 62.
22 Thatcher, *The Downing Street Years*, p. 64.
23 Ibid., p. 79.
24 Ibid., p. 82
25 AC: Interview with Lord Carrington.
26 Roy Jenkins, *European Diary, 1977–1981*, Collins, 1989, p. 529.
27 Ibid., pp. 529–30.

28 Sir Crispin Tickell interviewed for *The Last Europeans*, Channel 4, 1995, quoted in Campbell, *The Iron Lady*, pp. 63–64.
29 AC: Margaret Thatcher at a dinner for Sir Teddy Taylor, 6 June 1996.
30 Young, *One of Us*, p. 189.
31 Ibid.
32 Ian Gilmour, *Dancing with Dogma: Britain under Thatcherism*, Simon & Schuster, 1992, p. 238.
33 Stephen Wall, *A Stranger in Europe: Britain and the EU from Thatcher to Blair*, Oxford University Press, 2008, p. 7.
34 MTF: CIA Memorandum, *Changing Power Relations Among OECD States*, 22 October 1979.
35 Ibid.
36 MTF: White House Memorandum, Zbigniew Brzezinski to President Carter, NSC Weekly Report #96, 12 May 1979.
37 Jimmy Carter, *Keeping Faith: Memoirs of a President*, University of Arkansas Press, 1995, p. 113.
38 MTF: Speech on the White House Lawn, 17 December 1979.
39 MTF: Telephone conversation Margaret Thatcher and President Carter, 28 December 1979.
40 AC: Interview with Lord Carrington.
41 Ibid.: Interview with Lord Armstrong.

18 STORM CLOUDS ON THE ECONOMY AND IN THE CABINET

1 Thatcher, *The Downing Street Years*, p. 122.
2 AC: Interview with Lord Carrington.
3 Young, *One of Us*, p. 203.
4 Thatcher, *The Downing Street Years*, p. 126.
5 Ibid., p. 97.
6 Denis Healey, *The Time of My Life*, Michael Joseph, 1989, p. 491.
7 AC: Author's recollection, April 1981.
8 Prior, *A Balance of Power*, p. 114.
9 Thatcher, *The Downing Street Years*, p. 104.
10 Prior, *A Balance of Power*, p. 138.
11 AC: Conversation with Lord Rawlinson, 2002.
12 Lord Prior interviewed for *The Thatcher Factor*, Channel 4, 1989, quoted in Campbell, *The Iron Lady*, p. 92.
13 Voltaire, *Candide*, Arcturus, 2009, p. 99.

14   Prior, *A Balance of Power*, p. 134.
15   Ibid.
16   CAC: Professor Sir Alan Walters, (unpublished) diary, 14 July 1981.
17   Prior, *A Balance of Power*, p. 134.
18   Geoffrey Howe, *Conflict of Loyalty*, Macmillan, 1994, p. 195.
19   AC: Interview with Lord Griffiths.
20   CAC: Walters, diary, 6 January 1981.
21   Ibid., 22 March 1981.
22   Howe, *Conflict of Loyalty*, p. 202.
23   AC: Interview with Sir John Hoskyns.
24   Thatcher, *The Downing Street Years*, p. 136.
25   Ibid.
26   Young, *One of Us*, p. 215.
27   Prior, *A Balance of Power*, p. 140.
28   Howe, *Conflict of Loyalty*, p. 207.
29   CAC: Walters, diary, 10 March 1981.
30   Howe, *Conflict of Loyalty*, p. 208.
31   *The Times*, 30 March 1981.
32   Young, *One of Us*, p. 217.
33   MTF: Speech to Conservative Central Council, Bournemouth, 28 March 1981.
34   AC: Interview with Sir John Hoskyns.
35   Young, *One of Us*, p. 239.
36   *The Times*, 10 July 1981.
37   CAC: Walters, diary, 25 August 1981.
38   Thatcher, *The Downing Street Years*, p. 148.
39   Ibid., p. 149.
40   Young, *One of Us*, p. 219.
41   AC: Interview with Lord Bell.
42   Ibid., Interview with Sir Michael Scholar.
43   John Hoskyns, *Just in Time: Inside the Thatcher Revolution*, Aurum Press, 2000, p. 301.
44   Ibid., p. 326.
45   'Your Political Survival,' memorandum in possession of Sir John Hoskyns, cited in Moore, *Margaret Thatcher, Vol. 1*, pp. 641–642.
46   AC: Interview with Sir John Hoskyns.
47   CAC: Walters, diary, 26 and 27 August 1981.
48   *The Times*, 15 September 1981.
49   Thatcher, *The Downing Street Years*, p. 151.
50   Ibid., p. 149.
51   AC: Interview with Sir Michael Scholar.

19 THE FALKLANDS WAR I: THE PRELUDE

1 AC: Interview with Lord Carrington.
2 Ibid.
3 Ibid.
4 Carrington to Prime Minister, 20 September 1979, cited in Moore, *Margaret Thatcher, Vol. 1*, p. 658.
5 AC: Interview with Lord Carrington.
6 Ibid.
7 Lawrence Freedman, *The Official History of the Falklands Campaign,* 2 vols, Routledge, 2005, *Vol. I: The Origins of the Falklands War*, p. 127.
8 Sir Robert Armstrong, Cabinet Secretary's notebooks, 7 November 1980, cited in Moore, *Margaret Thatcher, Vol. 1*, p. 659.
9 AC: Conversation with Ian Gow, 1 December 1980.
10 Ibid.: Conversation with Julian Amery, 2 December 1980.
11 Ibid.
12 Freedman, *The Official History of the Falklands Campaign, Vol. I*, p. 144.
13 Richard Luce, private memoir, cited in Moore, *Margaret Thatcher, Vol. 1*, p. 661.
14 MTF: UK Embassy Buenos Aires to FCO, 3 March 1982.
15 Thatcher, *The Downing Street Years*, p. 179.
16 AC: Interview with Sir Antony Acland.
17 Thatcher, *The Downing Street Years*, p. 179.
18 AC: Interview with Sir John Nott.
19 Ibid.
20 William Waldegrave, Old Etonian Association lecture, 28 February 2012.
21 AC: The lone voice, as the Chief Whip, Michael Jopling, often reminded me, was mine, 3 April 1982.
22 Campbell, *The Grocer's Daughter*, p. 133.
23 Robin Harris, *Not for Turning: The Life of Margaret Thatcher*, Bantam Press, 2013, p. 207. Harris was an eyewitness to Howe's comment.
24 AC: Conversation with John Biffen, 3 April 1982.
25 Harris, *Not for Turning*, p. 208.
26 Hansard, HC Debate, 3 April 1982.
27 Ibid.
28 Ibid.
29 Ibid.
30 Ibid.
31 AC: Alec Woodall to the author, 3 April 1982.
32 Ibid.: Conversation with Nicholas Ridley, 3 April 1982.

33 John Nott, *Here Today and Gone Tomorrow: Recollections of an Errant Politician*, Politico's Publishing, 2002, p. 267.

34 Alan Clark, *Diaries: Into Politics*, Weidenfeld & Nicolson, 1993, 15 January 1984, p. 64.

35 Thatcher, *The Downing Street Years*, p. 185.

36 AC: Interview with Lord Carrington.

37 Ibid.: Interview with Sir Antony Acland.

38 Ibid.: Interview with Lord Carrington.

39 Thatcher, *The Downing Street Years*, p. 306.

40 Winston Churchill comment during the Suez Crisis, 1956.

41 MTF: Government Chief Whip to Foreign Secretary, 6 April 1982.

42 Thatcher, *The Downing Street Years*, p. 143.

43 MTF: Jim Rentschler's Falklands diary, Thursday 1 April 1982.

44 Max Hastings and Simon Jenkins, *The Battle for the Falklands*, Michael Joseph, 1983, p. 128.

45 Thatcher, *The Downing Street Years*, p. 180.

46 Interview with Jim Rentschler, cited in Moore, *Margaret Thatcher, Vol. 1*, pp. 685–686.

47 Ibid., p. 686.

48 MTF: Jim Rentschler's Falklands diary, Thursday 8 April 1982.

49 Ibid.: Monday 12 April 1982.

50 Thatcher, *The Downing Street Years*, p. 198.

51 Ibid., p. 207.

52 Ibid.

53 Nicholas Henderson, *Mandarin: The Diaries of an Ambassador 1969–1982*, Weidenfeld & Nicolson, 1995, p. 446.

54 Thatcher, *The Downing Street Years*, p. 211.

55 Freedman, *The Official History of the Falklands Campaign, Vol. II, War and Diplomacy*, p. 177.

56 Campbell, *The Iron Lady*, p. 142.

57 MTF: Ronald Reagan, interview with the press, 30 April 1982.

58 John F. Lehman Jr., Keynote Address 'The Falklands War Thirty Years On', 19–20 May 2012, National Museum of the Royal Navy, Portsmouth.

59 Thatcher, *The Downing Street Years*, p. 211.

60 Ronald Reagan, *The Reagan Diaries*, edited by David Brinkley, HarperCollins, 2007, Monday 19 April 1982, p. 80.

61 Thatcher, *The Downing Street Years*, p. 219.

62 Cecil Parkinson, *Right at the Centre*, Weidenfeld & Nicholson, 1992, p. 201.

63 *Falkland Islands Review*, January 1983, HMSO, p. 98.

64 Hastings and Jenkins, *The Battle for the Falklands*, p. 424.

20 THE FALKLANDS WAR II: INTO THE FIGHTING

1 Peter Hennessy, *The Prime Minister: The Office and its Holders since 1945*, Allen Lane, 2000, p. 104.
2 Thatcher, *The Downing Street Years*, pp. 188–189.
3 *Daily Telegraph*, 31 March 2002.
4 Ian Gow to Margaret Thatcher, 8 April 1982, cited in Moore, *Margaret Thatcher, Vol. 1*, p. 697.
5 Thatcher, *The Downing Street Years*, p. 205.
6 Ibid., pp. 208–209.
7 Sandy Woodward, *One Hundred Days: The Memoirs of the Falklands Battle Group Commander*, HarperCollins, 1992, p. 148.
8 CAC: DOHP/57, Sir Antony Acland, p. 32.
9 Thatcher, *The Downing Street Years*, p. 216.
10 Hansard, HC Deb 4 May 1982.
11 AC: Interview with Mrs. Pamela Powell, reading from diary entry, 5 May 1982.
12 Carol Thatcher, *Below the Parapet*, p. 196.
13 AC: Interview with Sir Mark Thatcher.
14 Thatcher, *The Downing Street Years*, p. 217.
15 MTF: Margaret Thatcher to President Reagan, 5 May 1982, in Margaret Thatcher's personal papers, released 21 March 2013.
16 Ibid.
17 Freedman, *The Official History of the Falkland Islands, Vol. II, War and Diplomacy*, p. 328.
18 AC: Interview with Lord Thomas.
19 Ibid.
20 Thatcher, *The Downing Street Years*, p. 217.
21 Hansard, HC Deb 6 May 1982.
22 Ibid., 7 May 1982.
23 Thatcher, *The Downing Street Years*, p. 221.
24 Reagan, *The Reagan Diaries*, 13 May 1982, p. 84.
25 Henderson, *Mandarin*, p. 463.
26 Nott, *Here Today and Gone Tomorrow*, pp. 293–294.
27 Hastings and Jenkins, *The Battle for the Falklands*, p. 216.
28 CAC: DOHP/57, Sir Antony Acland, pp. 33–34.
29 AC: Interview, off-the-record.
30 Hansard, HC Deb 13 May 1982.
31 AC: Ian Gow to the author and others, 13 May 1982.
32 Ibid.: Ian Gow to the author, May 1982.

33 MTF: Speech to the Scottish Conservative Party Conference, Perth, 14 May 1982.
34 Hansard, HC Deb 20 May 1982.

21 THE FALKLANDS WAR III: VICTORY

1   AC: Interview with Lord Armstrong.
2   Carol Thatcher, *Below the Parapet*, p. 197.
3   Thomson, *The Woman Within*, pp. 174–178.
4   *The Times*, 22 May 1982.
5   Thatcher, *The Downing Street Years*, p. 226.
6   Carol Thatcher, *Below the Parapet*, p. 198.
7   Interview with Sir Denis Thatcher, cited in Moore, *Margaret Thatcher, Vol. 1*, p. 735.
8   AC: Interview with Sir Mark Thatcher quoting from the poem 'Heritage' by Rudyard Kipling.
9   Hastings and Jenkins, *The Battle for the Falklands*, p. 320; off-the-record interview with a member of the War Cabinet.
10 AC: Interview with Sir John Nott.
11 Interview with Lord Armstrong, cited in Moore, *Margaret Thatcher, Vol. 1*, p. 742.
12 Geoffrey Smith, *Reagan and Thatcher*, Bodley Head, 1990, p. 26.
13 Telephone call Ronald Reagan and Margaret Thatcher, 31 May 1982, excerpts published in the *Sunday Times*, 8 March 1992.
14 MTF: Rentschler's Falklands diary, 3 June 1982.
15 AC: Interview with Lord Armstrong.
16 Henderson, *Mandarin*, p. 466.
17 Ibid., p. 470.
18 MTF: Margaret Thatcher draft telegram to General Galtieri, 2 June 1982.
19 Hastings and Jenkins, *The Battle for the Falklands*, p. 328.
20 Thatcher, *The Downing Street Years*, p. 232.
21 Ibid., p. 234.
22 Nott, *Here Today and Gone Tomorrow*, p. 314.
23 Hansard, HC Deb 14 June 1982.
24 Ibid.
25 AC: Author's personal recollection, 14 June 1982.
26 CAC: DOHP/57, Sir Antony Acland, p. 33.
27 Elizabeth Longford, *Wellington: Pillar of State*, Weidenfeld & Nicolson, 1972, p. 7.
28 AC: Interview with Sir John Nott.
29 Ibid.: Interview with Lord Parkinson.

22 AFTER THE FALKLANDS

1 *Daily Express*, 26 July 1982.
2 Hansard, HC Deb 17 June 1982.
3 Marines land at Plymouth, BBC TV, 13 July 1982.
4 MTF: Speech to Conservative Rally, Cheltenham, 2 July 1982.
5 *The Times*, 25 August 1982.
6 *Daily Telegraph*, 15 November 1982.
7 Rex Hunt, *My Falkland Days*, David & Charles, 1992, p. 377.
8 Carol Thatcher, *Below the Parapet*, p. 201.
9 MTF: *The Woman at Number Ten*, interviewed by Sir Laurens van der Post, ITV, 29 March 1983.
10 AC: William Whitelaw to author and other Tory backbenchers, House of Commons, 10 July 1982.
11 Thatcher, *The Downing Street Years*, p. 112.
12 AC: Interview with Lord Young.
13 Nigel Lawson, *The View from No. 11*, p. 303.
14 Young, *One of Us*, p. 301.
15 *The Economist*, 18 September 1982.
16 Young, *One of Us*, p. 301.
17 AC: Interview with Sir Michael Scholar.
18 Young, *One of Us*, p. 301.
19 AC: Interview with Sir Kenneth Stowe.
20 Ibid.
21 MTF: Speech to the Conservative Party Conference, Brighton, 8 October 1982.
22 Peter Riddell, *The Thatcher Era and Its Legacy*, Blackwell, 1991, p. 88.
23 AC: Interview with Lord Jenkin.
24 Ibid.
25 Lawson, *The View from No. 11*, p. 217.
26 MTF: Speech, Brighton, 8 October 1982.
27 Ibid.
28 Ibid.
29 Thatcher, *The Downing Street Years*, p. 247.
30 Hansard, HC Deb 21 January 1982.
31 MTF: Press Conference with Chancellor Kohl, London, 4 February 1983.
32 Robert Blake, *Disraeli*, Faber and Faber, 2010, p. 279.
33 *The Times*, 23 April 1983.
34 Spicer, *The Spicer Diaries*, 7 April 1983, p. 62.
35 Parkinson, *Right at the Centre*, p. 224.

36 Ferdinand Mount, *Cold Cream: My Early Life and Other Mistakes*, Bloomsbury, 2008, p. 335.
37 Michael Cockerell, *Live From Number 10: Prime Ministers and Television*, Faber & Faber, 1988, p. 283.
38 Thatcher, *The Downing Street Years*, p. 301.
39 *Guardian*, 7 June 1983.
40 Ibid., 3 June 1983.
41 Ibid., 8 June 1983.
42 Thatcher, *The Downing Street Years*, p. 284.
43 Ibid., p. 287.
44 MTF: Speech at the Metropole Hotel, Birmingham, 3 June 1983.
45 Ibid.: Speech at City Hall, Cardiff, 23 May 1983.
46 Ibid.
47 *Daily Mirror*, 7 June 1983.
48 *The Times*, 5 May 1980.

23 STUMBLING INTO THE SECOND TERM

1 AC: Interview with Lord Parkinson.
2 Ibid.
3 Ibid.
4 Thatcher, *The Downing Street Years*, p. 310.
5 AC: Interview with Lord Parkinson.
6 Ibid.
7 Ibid.
8 Matthew Laban, *Mr Speaker: The Office and the Individuals*, Biteback, 2013, p. 45.
9 AC: Bernard Weatherill to the author, 18 June 1983.
10 Laban, *Mr Speaker*, p. 150.
11 Ibid.
12 *Sunday Telegraph*, 22 May 1988.
13 MTF: Interview for *Weekend World*, LWT, 8 May 1988.
14 Laban, *Mr Speaker*, p. 159.
15 AC: Interview with Lord Carrington.
16 *The Times*, 14 July 1983.
17 Prior, *A Balance of Power*, p. 229.
18 *The Times*, 21 July 1983.
19 AC: Dinner with Margaret Thatcher, July 1983.
20 Ibid.
21 Ibid.
22 *The Times*, 16 October 1981.

23 AC: Interview with Lord Young.
24 Ibid.
25 Ibid.
26 Thatcher, *The Downing Street Years*, p. 646.
27 Ibid., p. 309.
28 MTF: Interview for Glyn Mathias, ITN, 28 July 1983.
29 Hansard, HC Deb 31 January 1984.
30 Nigel Lawson, *The View from No. 11*, p. 357.
31 AC: Interview with Lord Jenkin.
32 Thatcher, *The Downing Street Years*, p. 676.
33 MTF: Speech to the Conservative Party Conference, Blackpool, 13 October 1989.
34 William Congreve, *The Mourning Bride* (1687), Act III, Scene viii.
35 AC: Interview with Lord Butler.
36 Sir Anthony Parsons interviewed for *Thatcher: The Downing Street Years*, BBC, 1993.
37 AC: interview with Lord Butler.

24 TERRORISM, IRELAND AND HONG KONG

1   Thatcher, *The Path to Power*, p. 434.
2   *Daily Express*, 28 August 1979.
3   Ibid., 30 August 1979.
4   AC: Conversation with Harry West, September 1979.
5   *Guardian*, 24 July 2002.
6   AC: Interview with former SAS officers.
7   Thatcher, *The Downing Street Years*, p. 90.
8   AC: Interview, with former SAS officers.
9   MTF: Press conference Dublin, 8 December 1980.
10 BBC, 28 May 1981, cited in Campbell, *The Iron Lady*, p. 425.
11 Peter Taylor, *Provos, The IRA and Sinn Fein*, Bloomsbury, 1998, p. 237.
12 BBC News, *On This Day*, 20 July 1982.
13 Thatcher, *The Downing Street Years*, p. 397.
14 Carol Thatcher, *Below the Parapet*, p. 219.
15 AC: Interview with Lord Butler.
16 Carol Thatcher, Below the Parapet, p. 220.
17 Millar, *A View from the Wings*, p. 301.
18 AC: Conversation with Michael Alison, 1997.
19 Ibid.
20 Iain Dale (ed.), *Memories of Maggie*, Politico's, 2000, p. 107.

21 Thatcher, *The Downing Street Years*, p. 380.
22 Ibid., p. 381.
23 AC: Interview with Lord Butler.
24 Ibid.
25 Thatcher, *The Downing Street Years*, p. 382.
26 AC: Conversation with Denis Thatcher, March 2000.
27 *Daily Express,* 15 October 1984.
28 Carol Thatcher, *Below the Parapet*, p. 219.
29 Ibid.
30 Ibid.
31 MTF: 25th anniversary as MP, speech at Finchley, 20 October 1984.
32 *The Times*, 10 December 1980.
33 AC: Interview with Sir Kenneth Stowe.
34 AC: Conversation with Ian Gow, December 1980.
35 Ibid.: Interview with Sir Kenneth Stowe.
36 CAC: DOHP/47, Sir Robert Wade-Gery, p. 84.
37 Ibid., p. 85.
38 AC: Interview with Lord Armstrong.
39 Thatcher, *The Downing Street Years*, p. 399.
40 MTF: Press conference, 19 November 1984.
41 *Guardian*, 26 November 1984.
42 *The Times* 16 November 1985.
43 AC: Interview with Lord King.
44 Ibid.
45 *The Times*, 25 November 1985.
46 Hansard, HC Deb 18 November 1985.
47 Ibid., 14 November 1985.
48 AC: Conversation with Margaret Thatcher at Ian Gow's funeral at Eastbourne, 8 August 1990.
49 Thatcher, *The Downing Street Years*, p. 415.
50 Howe, *Conflict of Interest*, p. 361.
51 Ibid., p. 363.
52 Sir Percy Cradock, *Experiences in China*, John Murray, 1994, p. 125.
53 Ibid., pp. 175–176.
54 Ibid., p. 179.
55 Ibid., p. 186.
56 AC: Interview with Lord Wilson.
57 Ibid.
58 AC: Interview with Lord Powell.
59 Thatcher, *The Downing Street Years*, p. 492.

25 BATTING FOR BRITAIN IN SAUDI ARABIA

1 AC: Interview with Sir Richard Evans, confirmed by author's earlier conversations in Saudi Arabia with Princes Sultan bin Abdul Aziz, Fahd bin Salman, Mohamed bin Fahd and others.
2 Ibid.: Interview with Wafic Saïd.
3 Ibid.
4 Ibid.
5 Ibid.: Interview with Sir Richard Evans and conversations with Prince Bandar bin Sultan.
6 Ibid.: Interview with Sir Richard Evans.
7 Ibid.
8 Ibid.: Interview with Wafic Saïd.
9 Ibid.
10 Ibid.: see note 1.
11 Ibid.: Interview with Sir Richard Evans.
12 Ibid.
13 Ibid.
14 Tornado Project – Commercial Negotiations, Confidential telegram, Sir Patrick Wright (Riyadh) to Ministry of Defense 6 January 1986, copied to Private Secretary, Prime Minister.
15 AC: Interview with Sir Richard Evans.

26 UNIONS AND MINERS

1 AC: Interview with Lord Carrington.
2 Ibid.: Interview with Sir John Hoskyns.
3 Ibid.
4 Ibid.
5 MTF: Interview for Brian Walden, *Weekend World*, LWT, 6 January 1980.
6 Hansard, HC Deb 22 January 1980.
7 AC: Interview with Lord Howell.
8 *The Times*, 5 July 1983.
9 Thatcher, *The Downing Street Years*, p. 341.
10 AC: Author's recollection, January 1984.
11 Ibid., February 1984.
12 *Daily Mirror*, 30 March 1983.
13 AC: Sir Ian MacGregor speaking to the Conservative Philosophy Group, May 1984.
14 *The Miner*, March 1983, quoted in Michael Crick, *Scargill and the Miners*, Penguin, 1985, p. 96.

15 AC: Interview with Lord Turnbull.
16 Ibid.
17 Ibid.
18 *The Times*, 30 May 1984.
19 MTF: Speech to farmers at Banbury Cattle Market, 30 May 1984.
20 AC: David Hart, June 1984.
21 David Hart, (unpublished) diaries, 26 October 1984.
22 AC: Interview with Sir Stephen Sherbourne.
23 Millar, *A View from the Wings*, p. 299.
24 Thatcher, *The Downing Street Years*, p. 365.
25 *Daily Express*, 2 October 1984.
26 *Sunday Times*, 28 October and 4 November 1984.
27 AC: Interview with Sir Stephen Sherbourne.
28 Mount, *Cold Cream*, p. 330.
29 AC: David Hart, June 1985.
30 Thatcher, The *Downing Street Years*, p. 365.
31 Ibid., p. 358.
32 Margaret Thatcher interviewed for *Thatcher: The Downing Street Years*, BBC, 1993.
33 AC: Interviews with Lord Bell.
34 MTF: Interview for *TV Eye*, Thames TV, 24 January 1985.
35 *The Times*, 26 January 1985.
36 Thatcher, *The Downing Street Years*, p. 375.
37 AC: Margaret Thatcher to the author, April 1985.
38 Thatcher, *The Downing Street Years*, p. 378.
39 Hansard, HC Deb 31 January 1985.
40 *The Times*, 20 July 1984.

27 STRENGTHENING THE SPECIAL RELATIONSHIP WITH RONALD REAGAN

1 AC: interview with Lord Carrington.
2 Ibid.
3 Charles Powell, 'Differences Were in the Detail', *The Tablet*, 19 April 2012.
4 Ronald Reagan, *An American Life*, Arrow Books, 1991, p. 204.
5 *Viewpoint*, Ronald Reagan Pre-Presidential Radio Broadcast, April 1975, cited in Moore, *Margaret Thatcher, Vol. 1*, p. 314.
6 Thatcher, *The Path to Power*, p. 372.
7 AC: Interview with Lord Carrington.

8   MTF: Exchange of toasts at the British Embassy dinner, 27 February 1981.
9   Reagan, *The Reagan Diaries*, 27 February 1981, p. 5.
10 MTF: Personal letter from Margaret Thatcher to Sir Nicholas Henderson, 5 March 1981.
11 Reagan, *The Reagan Diaries*, 27 February 1981, p. 5.
12 Young and Sloman, *The Thatcher Phenomenon*, p. 108.
13 George Shultz, *Turmoil and Triumph: My Years as Secretary of State*, Macmillan, 1993, p. 152.
14 Smith, *Reagan and Thatcher*, p. 224.
15 Aldous, *Reagan and Thatcher*, p. 148.
16 Reagan, *The Reagan Diaries*, 24 October 1983, p. 190.
17 Thatcher, *The Downing Street Years*, p. 331.
18 Hansard, HC Deb 25 October 1983.
19 Thatcher, *The Downing Street Years*, p. 332.
20 MTF: Telephone call from Reagan to Thatcher, 26 October 1983.
21 Ibid.
22 Aldous, *Reagan and Thatcher*, p. 151.
23 MTF: Telephone call from Reagan to Thatcher, 26 October 1983.
24 Brian Crozier, *Free Agent*, HarperCollins, 1993, p. 264.
25 Campbell, *The Iron Lady*, p. 278.
26 *The Economist*, 10 March 1984.
27 Ibid., 3 March 1984.
28 Aldous, *Reagan and Thatcher*, p. 163.
29 *The Times*, 11 June 1984.
30 Reagan, *An American Life,* p. 354.
31 MTF: Fred F. Fielding Memo to President Reagan, 25 July 1984.
32 AC: Conversation with Margaret Thatcher, 15 April 1984; see also Aitken, *Heroes and Contemporaries*, p. 142.
33 Powell, *The Tablet*, 19 April 2012.
34 Thatcher, *The Downing Street Years*, p. 447.
35 Kenneth Baker, *The Turbulent Years: My Life in Politics*, Faber and Faber, 1993, pp. 268–269.
36 Aldous, *Reagan and Thatcher*, p. 213.
37 Hansard, HC Deb 15 April 1986.
38 AC: Edward Heath to the author, 16 April 1986.
39 Reagan, *The Reagan Diaries*, 17 April 1986, p. 406.
40 *New York Times*, 26 April 1986.
41 'Reagan Urges Senate Action on U.S.–British Terrorism Treaty', *AP News Archive*, 31 May 1986.
42 Reagan, *The Reagan Diaries*, 17 June 1986. p. 425.

28 STARTING TO WIN THE COLD WAR

1   AC: Conversation with Richard Nixon in 1982.
2   Ibid.
3   Thatcher, *The Downing Street Years,* p. 451.
4   MTF: Sir Julian Bullard, Chequers Soviet Seminar, 8 September 1983.
5   Ibid.
6   Howe, *Conflict of Loyalty,* p. 317.
7   AC: Interview with Lord Powell.
8   Ibid.
9   Sir Percy Cradock, *In Pursuit of British Interests,* John Murray, 1994, p. 14.
10   Thatcher, *The Downing Street Years,* p. 456.
11   Aldous, *Reagan and Thatcher,* p. 160.
12   AC: Interview with Sir Nigel Broomfield.
13   Leonid Zamyatin, interview for *Kommersant Vlast,* Moscow, 4 May 2005.
14   AC: Interview with Sir Nigel Broomfield.
15   Ibid.
16   AC: Interview with Mikhail Gorbachev.
17   Ibid.: Interview with Lord Powell.
18   Ibid.: Interview with Sir Bernard Ingham.
19   Ibid.
20   Ibid.: Interview with Mikhail Gorbachev.
21   Thatcher, *The Downing Street Years,* p. 460.
22   AC: Interview with Mikhail Gorbachev.
23   Ibid.
24   Ibid.
25   Ibid.
26   Ibid.
27   Ibid.
28   Ibid.
29   Ibid.
30   Ibid.
31   Smith, *Reagan and Thatcher,* p. 149.
32   AC: Interview with Lord Powell.
33   President Reagan, 'Evil Empire' speech, Address to the National Association of Evangelicals, Orlando, Florida, 3 March 1983.
34   Thatcher, *The Downing Street Years,* p. 463.
35   AC: Interview with Sir Bernard Ingham.
36   MTF: Statement by Margaret Thatcher after her meeting with Mikhail Gorbachev, BBC News, 17 December 1984.

37 AC: Interview with Mikhail Gorbachev.

38 Smith, *Reagan and Thatcher*, pp. 150–151.

39 Bernard Ingham, *Kill the Messenger*, HarperCollins, 1994, p. 260.

40 Thatcher, *The Downing Street Years*, p. 466.

41 Powell, *The Tablet*, 19 April 2012.

42 MTF: Margaret Thatcher visit to Camp David, 22 December 1984.

43 Ibid.

44 Reagan, *The Reagan Diaries*, 22 December 1984, p. 289.

45 James Baker interviewed for *Thatcher: The Downing Street Years*, BBC, 1993.

46 AC: Conversation with Al Regnery Jr., 1987.

47 Claire Berlinski, *'There Is No Alternative': Why Margaret Thatcher Matters*, Basic Books, 2008, p. 289.

48 Thatcher, *The Downing Street Years*, p. 463.

49 MTF: Speech to Joint US Houses of Congress, 20 February 1985.

50 Campbell, *The Iron Lady*, p. 291.

51 Howe, *Conflict of Loyalty*, p. 392.

52 Aldous, *Reagan and Thatcher*, p. 194.

53 Smith, *Reagan and Thatcher*, p. 167.

54 Ibid.

55 Aldous, *Reagan and Thatcher*, p. 195.

56 Campbell, *The Iron Lady*, p. 293.

57 Thatcher, *The Downing Street Years*, p. 471.

58 Dale, *Memories of Maggie*, p. 144.

59 Margaret Thatcher interviewed for *Thatcher: The Downing Street Years*, BBC, 1993.

60 MTF: Press Conference at the British Embassy, Washington, DC, 15 November 1986.

61 *Sunday Times* 16 November 1986.

62 Thatcher, *The Downing Street Years*, p. 471.

63 AC: Interview with Mikhail Gorbachev.

64 Thatcher, *The Downing Street Years*, p. 479.

65 CAC: DOHP/115: Sir Bryan Cartledge, p. 56.

66 AC: Conversation with Carol Thatcher, 2000.

67 CAC: DOHP/115: Sir Bryan Cartledge, p. 56.

68 AC: Interview with Mikhail Gorbachev.

69 Ibid.

70 CAC: DOHP/115: Sir Bryan Cartledge, p. 56.

71 Mikhail Gorbachev, *Memoirs*, Bantam Books, 1997, p. 706.

72 Zamyatin, *Kommersant Vlast*, 4 May 2005.

73 Reagan, *The Reagan Diaries*, 7 December 1987, p. 555.

29 RUMBLINGS OF DISCONTENT

1　Margaret Thatcher interviewed for *Thatcher: The Downing Street Years*, BBC, 1993.
2　AC: Interview with Lord Carrington.
3　Ibid.: Interview with Lord Lamont.
4　Ibid.: Conversation with John Biffen, March 1986.
5　Thatcher and the Vegetables, Spitting Image, 1984–1996; see also *Guardian*, 10 April 2013.
6　*The Times*, 13 May 1986.
7　AC: Interview with Lord Butler.
8　William Waldegrave, Old Etonian Association Lecture, 28 February 2012.
9　Campbell, *The Iron Lady*, p. 445.
10　*Observer*, 17 February 1985.
11　Nigel Lawson, *The View from No. 11*, p. 674.
12　*Sunday Times*, 13 October 1985.
13　*New York Times*, 20 December 1985.
14　Thatcher, *The Downing Street Years*, p. 430.
15　AC: Interview with Lord Brittan.
16　Interview with Michael Pattison, cited in Moore, *Margaret Thatcher, Vol. 1*, p. 429.
17　AC: Interview with Lord Powell.
18　Ibid.
19　*The Times*, 4 January 1986.
20　Ibid., 3 January 1986.
21　Ibid., 7 January 1986.
22　*Sun*, 7 January 1986.
23　*The Times*, 7 January 1986.
24　Hansard, HC Deb 23 January 1986.
25　AC: Interview with Lord Brittan.
26　Ibid.
27　Hansard, HC Deb 29 October 1986.
28　Howe, *Conflict of Loyalty*, p. 467.
29　AC: Interview with Lord Brittan.
30　Lawson, *The View from No. 11*, p. 678.
31　*The Times*, 10 January 1986.
32　Young, *One of Us*, p. 452.
33　Clark, *Diaries*, 24 January 1986, p. 133.
34　Hansard, HC Deb 23 January 1986.
35　AC: Sir Bernard Braine to the author, 23 January 1986.
36　Ibid.: Interview with Lord Brittan.

37 Howe, *Conflict of Loyalty*, p. 471.
38 Ibid., p. 472.
39 AC: Interview with Lord Armstrong.
40 Hansard, HC Deb 27 January 1986.
41 AC: Interview with Winston Churchill in 1986.
42 Ibid.: Margaret Thatcher to the author, January 1987.
43 Ibid.
44 Ibid.
45 MTF: Interview with David Frost, TV-AM, 9 June 1985.
46 Voltaire, *Candide*, p. 7.
47 Daily Mail, 7 April 1986.
48 Hansard, HC Deb 23 January 1986.
49 Young, *One of Us*, p. 443.

30 INTO THE THIRD TERM

1   Thatcher, *The Downing Street Years*, p. 560.
2   *The Times*, 10 October 1986.
3   MTF: Speech to Conservative Party Conference, Bournemouth, 10 October 1986.
4   Ibid.
5   AC: Interview with Sir Bryan Cartledge.
6   Thatcher, *The Downing Street Years*, p. 576.
7   David Butler and Dennis Kavanagh, *The British General Election of 1987*, Macmillan, 1988, p. 154.
8   Carol Thatcher, *Below the Parapet*, p. 244.
9   AC: Interview with Lord Young.
10 Ibid.
11 Tebbit, *Upwardly Mobile*, p. 333.
12 Michael Dobbs interviewed for *Thatcher: The Downing Street Years*, BBC, 1993.
13 Thatcher, *The Downing Street Years*, p. 584.
14 Ibid., p. 585.
15 Mark Hollingsworth, *The Ultimate Spin Doctor: The Life and Fast Times of Tim Bell*, Hodder & Stoughton, 1997, p. 175.
16 Dale, *Memories of Maggie*, p. 172.
17 AC: Interview with Lord Young.
18 Ibid.
19 AC: Conversation with Robert Carvel, 6 June 1987.
20 UK Polling Report, 1983–1987: www.ukpollingreport.co.uk.
21 *Daily Telegraph*, 21 May 1987.

22 AC: Willie Whitelaw to author, Paul Channon, Julian Amery and others, Bucks Club, 18 June 1987.
23 Carol Thatcher, *Below the Parapet*, p. 246.
24 MTF: Speech to Party Conference, Blackpool, 9 October 1987.
25 Lord Shawcross, Obituary, *Daily Telegraph*, 11 July 2003.
26 Hansard, HC Deb 25 June 1987.
27 Clark, *Diaries*, 19 July 1987, p. 168.
28 AC: Interview with Lord Baker.
29 Millar, *A View from the Wings*, p. 319.
30 Baker, *The Turbulent Years*, p. 275.
31 AC: Interview with Lord Powell.
32 Ibid.: Willie Whitelaw at Bucks Club, 18 June 1987.
33 Ibid.: Conversations with Willie Whitelaw.
34 Clark, *Diaries*, 26 January 1990, p. 276.
35 AC: Conversation with Nick Budgen, 28 June 1987.

31 TROUBLE WITH NIGEL LAWSON

1 AC: Interview with Lord Lawson.
2 Lawson, *The View from No. 11*, p. 382.
3 Ibid.
4 Ibid., p. 697.
5 Ibid., p. 499.
6 Ibid., p. 500.
7 AC: Interview with Lord Burns.
8 Lawson, *The View from No. 11*, p. 501.
9 Ridley, '*My Style of Government*', p. 201.
10 Thatcher, *The Downing Street Years*, p. 701.
11 Lawson, *The View from No. 11*, p. 789.
12 AC: Interviews with Lord Butler and Lord Griffiths.
13 Ibid.: Interview with Lord Lawson.
14 Lawson, *The View from No. 11*, p. 788.
15 Ibid., p. 794.
16 Ibid., p. 795.
17 AC: Interview with Sir Richard Evans.
18 Thatcher, *The Downing Street Years*, p. 705.
19 Hansard, HC Deb 10 March 1988.
20 Lawson, *The View from No. 11*, p. 799.
21 Ibid., p. 814.
22 MTF: Speech to Conservative Central Council, Buxton, 19 March 1988.

23 Lawson, *The View from No. 11*, p. 799.
24 Hansard, HC Deb 12 May 1988.
25 Ibid., 17 May 1988.
26 Lawson, *The View from No. 11*, p. 845.
27 AC: Conversation with Peter Morrison, December 1988.
28 David Hart, (unpublished) diaries, 26 October 1989.
29 Lawson, *The View from No. 11*, p. 850.
30 AC: Conversation with Nicholas Budgen, July 1988.
31 Howe, *Conflict of Loyalty*, p. 575; Thatcher, *The Downing Street Years*, p. 704.
32 Howe, Conflict of Loyalty, p. 575.
33 Ibid., p. 576.
34 Ibid.
35 Ibid.
36 Thatcher, *The Downing Street Years*, p. 704.
37 Lytton Strachey, *Queen Victoria*, Chatto & Windus, 1951, p. 185.
38 Lawson, *The View from No. 11*, p. 307.
39 AC: Interview with Lord Burns.

32 SWINGING TOWARDS EUROSCEPTICISM

1 HC Deb, 30 October 1990.
2 *Sun*, 28 April 1975.
3 Interview with Lord Ryder of Wensum, cited in Moore, *Margaret Thatcher*, *Vol. 1*, p. 306.
4 Howe, *Conflict of Loyalty*, p. 538.
5 AC: Conversation Margaret Thatcher, Teddy Taylor and author, 26 June 1986.
6 Thatcher, *The Downing Street Years*, p. 741.
7 AC: Interview with Sir Ronald Grierson.
8 Margaret Thatcher interviewed for *The Poisoned Chalice*, BBC2, 1996, quoted in Campbell, *The Iron Lady*, p. 311.
9 AC: Interview with Lord Powell.
10 *Guardian*, 7 July 1988.
11 MTF: Interview for *The Jimmy Young Programme*, BBC Radio 2, 27 July 1988.
12 AC: off-the-record interview.
13 Thatcher, *The Downing Street Years*, p. 712.
14 Robin Renwick, *A Journey with Margaret Thatcher: Foreign Policy under the Iron Lady*, Biteback Publishing, 2013, p. 100.
15 AC: Off-the-record interview with senior FCO official.
16 Ibid.
17 AC: Interview with Bill Cash.

18   AC: Off-the-record interview with senior FCO official.

19   AC: November 1988.

20   Ibid.

21   AC: Conversation with John Biffen, 1980.

22   *Independent*, 9 June 1993.

23   AC: AC: Interview with Baroness Howe of Idlicote.

24   MTF: Speech to the College of Europe, Bruges, 20 September 1988.

25   Sir Michael Butler interviewed for *The Poisoned Chalice*, quoted in Campbell, *The Iron Lady*, p. 605.

26   Howe, *Conflict of Loyalty*, p. 538.

27   MTF: Speech to the Conservative Party Conference, Brighton, 14 October 1988.

28   AC: Conversation with Carol Mather, November 1986.

33   BOILING OVER ON EUROPE

1   Howe, *Conflict of Loyalty*, p. 538.

2   MTF: Speech to the College of Europe, Bruges, 20 September 1988.

3   Lawson, *The View from No. 11*, p. 917.

4   Ibid., p. 918.

5   Thatcher, *The Downing Street Years*, p. 749.

6   Lawson, *The View from No. 11*, p. 921.

7   MTF: Speech to European Election Rally, Nottingham, 12 June 1989.

8   *The Times*, 20 June 1989.

9   Ibid.

10   Thatcher, *The Downing Street Years*, p. 710.

11   Howe, *Conflict of Loyalty*, p. 579; Lawson, *The View from No. 11,* p. 931.

12   Thatcher, *The Downing Street Years*, p. 712.

13   Lawson, *The View from No. 11*, p. 933.

14   Thatcher, *The Downing Street Years*, p. 712.

15   Ibid.

16   AC: Interview with Lord Powell.

17   Ibid.

18   Howe, *Conflict of Loyalty*, p. 582.

19   Thatcher, *The Downing Street Years*, p. 750.

20   Howe, *Conflict of Loyalty*, p. 582.

21   AC: Interview with Boris Johnson.

22   Thatcher, *The Downing Street* Years, p. 713.

23   Howe, *Conflict of Loyalty*, p. 583.

24   Ibid., p. 586.

25 Ibid., p. 587.
26 Ibid., p. 590.
27 AC: Interview with Sir Bernard Ingham.
28 *Sun*, 26 July 1989.
29 AC: Comments by MPs, 31 July 1989.

34 EXIT THE CHANCELLOR, ENTER THE STALKING HORSE

1   Thatcher, *The Downing Street Years*, p. 755.
2   *Daily Express*, 30 October 1989.
3   Thatcher, *The Downing Street Years*, p. 714.
4   Ibid., p. 715.
5   Hansard, HC Debate 24 October 1989.
6   Ibid.
7   Thatcher, *The Downing Street Years*, p. 716.
8   Lawson, *The View from No. 11*, p. 961.
9   Ibid., p. 969.
10 David Cox (ed.), *The Walden Interviews*, LWT Boxtree, 1990, pp. 32–33.
11 Ibid., Margaret Thatcher, *The Walden Interview*, 29 October 1989, pp. 36–37.
12 AC: Winston Churchill to author, 13 November 1989.
13 Ibid.: Interview with Keith Hampson.
14 Ibid.: Ian Gow to the author, November 1989. See also 1 Samuel 22:2.
15 AC: Interview with Lord Garel-Jones.
16 Ibid.
17 Ibid.
18 Thatcher, *The Downing Street Years*, pp. 761–762.
19 *Financial Times*, 13 April 1913. See also David Marsh, *The Euro: The Battle for the New Global Currency*, Yale University Press, 2011, p. 216.
20 George R. Urban, *Diplomacy and Disillusion at the Court of Margaret Thatcher: An Insider's View*, I.B. Tauris, 1996, p. 104.
21 AC: Interview with Lord Thomas.
22 Urban, *Diplomacy and Disillusion*, p. 128.
23 *Financial Times* magazine, Simon Kuper on 'Thatcher Abroad', 13 April 2013.
24 Thatcher, *The Downing Street Years*, p. 791.
25 *The Spectator*, 14 July 1990.
26 Thatcher, *The Downing Street Years*, p. 312.
27 AC: Margaret Thatcher to the author at Ian Gow's funeral, 8 August 1990.
28 William Shakespeare, *Hamlet*, Act III, Scene I.

35 COUNTDOWN TO THE COUP

1 George W. Bush and Brent Scowcroft, *A World Transformed*, Alfred A. Knopf, 1998, p. 352.
2 Thatcher, *The Downing Street Years*, p. 820.
3 Ibid., p. 823.
4 Ibid., p. 826.
5 Hansard, HC Deb 7 September 1990.
6 Thatcher, *The Downing Street Years*, pp. 825–826.
7 Ibid., p. 824.
8 AC: Interview with Lord King.
9 Ibid.: King Fahd bin Abdul Aziz Al Saud to the author, February 1992.
10 AC: Conversation with Margaret Thatcher, 8 August 1990.
11 Thatcher, *The Downing Street Years*, p. 826.
12 *The Times*, 23 March 1990.
13 Ibid., 2 April 1990.
14 Ibid., 6 April 1990.
15 Ibid., 5 May 1990.
16 Thatcher, *The Downing Street Years*, p. 665.
17 Ibid., p. 666.
18 AC: Interview with Sir John Major.
19 MTF: Press conference in Downing Street, 5 October 1990.
20 *Observer*, 7 October 1990.
21 *The Times*, 17 October 1990.
22 AC: Interview with Lord Powell.
23 *Financial Times*, 29 October 1990.
24 Thatcher, *The Downing Street Years*, p. 767.
25 Hansard, HC Deb 30 October 1990.
26 John Major, *The Autobiography*, HarperCollins, 1999, p. 176.
27 Hansard, HC Deb 30 October 1990.
28 Ibid.
29 Geoffrey Howe, interview by Brian Walden, *Weekend World*, LWT, 3 September 1989.
30 Thatcher, *The Downing Street Years*, p. 833.
31 Hansard, HC Deb 30 October 1990.
32 Howe, *Conflict of Loyalty*, p. 645.
33 Thatcher, *The Downing Street Years*, p. 833.
34 Howe, *Conflict of Loyalty*, p. 645.
35 Major, *The Autobiography*, p. 177.
36 Howe, *Conflict of Loyalty*, p. 647.

37 Ibid., p. 648.

38 *The Times*, 2 November 1990.

39 AC: Geoffrey Dickens, 1 November 1990.

40 Howe, *Conflict of Loyalty*, p. 651.

41 James Boswell, *The Life of Samuel Johnson* (edited by George Birbeck Hill), Claren-
    don Press, 1971, p. 407.

42 Thatcher, *The Downing Street Years*, p. 834.

43 AC: Author's recollection, 1 November 1990.

44 Hansard, House of Lords, Official Report, 10 April 2013. Death of a Member:
    Baroness Thatcher, *Tributes*.

45 Ingham, *Kill the Messenger*, p. 379.

46 *The Times*, 9 November 1990.

47 Ibid., 19 October 1990.

48 Hansard, 7 November 1990, vol. 180, col. 29.

49 Letter from Lord Acton, 1887, cited in Louise Creighton, *Life and Letters of
    Mandell Creighton*, Vol. 1, Longmans, Green, 1904, p. 372.

50 AC: interview with Lord King.

51 Ibid.: Interview with Dame Jill Knight.

52 Major, *The Autobiography*, p. 179.

36 END GAME

1   Thatcher, *The Downing Street Years*, p. 838.

2   Hansard, HC Deb 14 June 1978.

3   Ibid., 13 November 1990.

4   Ibid.

5   Clark, *Diaries*, 13 November 1990, p. 347.

6   William Shakespeare, *Julius Caesar*, Act III, Scene I.

7   Thatcher, *The Downing Street Years*, p. 839.

8   Hansard, HC Deb 13 November 1990.

9   AC: Interview with Gerald Howarth.

10 Ibid.: Michael Heseltine to the author, November 1990.

11 Wyatt, *Journals*, vol. 2, 20 November 1990, p. 394.

12 Thatcher, *The Downing Street Years*, p. 836.

13 AC: Remarks by Nicholas Budgen, 13 November 1990.

14 Clark, *Diaries*, 19 November 1990, pp. 354–355.

15 Thatcher, *The Downing Street Years*, p. 841.

16 *The Times*, 19 November 1990.

17 AC: Remarks by Peter Morrison, 21 November 1990.

18 Ibid.: Interview with Lord Powell.
19 Ibid.: Conversation with Peter Morrison, 22 November 1990.
20 Ibid.: Interview with Lord Powell.
21 Ibid.: Conversation with John Sergeant in Broadcasting House, 8 April. 2013; MTF: Margaret Thatcher remarks outside British Embassy Paris, 20 November 1990.
22 Carol Thatcher, *Below the Parapet*, pp. 263–264.
23 AC: 30 November 1990.
24 *The Spectator*, 6 November 1993.
25 AC: Interview with Mikhail Gorbachev and his interpreter, Pavel Palazchenko.
26 Cynthia Crawford interview, *Maggie: The First Lady*, Brook Lapping, 2003.
27 The author on *Newsnight*, BBC2, 13 November 1990.

37 EXIT

1 Thatcher, *The Downing Street Years*, p. 846.
2 Ibid., p. 847
3 Ibid., p. 849.
4 AC: Remarks to Margaret Thatcher on 21 November 1990.
5 Thatcher, *The Downing Street Years*, p. 850.
6 AC: Remarks to Margaret Thatcher on 21 November 1990.
7 Alan Clark, *Diaries*, 21 November 1990, p. 366.
8 AC: Remarks to Margaret Thatcher on 21 November 1990.
9 Thatcher, *The Downing Street Years*, p. 850.
10 Major, *The Autobiography*, p. 187.
11 Thatcher, *The Downing Street Years*, p. 852.
12 Ibid., p. 851.
13 Ibid., p. 855.
14 Margaret Thatcher for *Thatcher: The Downing Street Years*, Part 1, BBC, 1993.
15 Alan Clark, *Diaries*, 21 November 1990, p. 366.
16 Thatcher, *The Downing Street Years*, p. 853.
17 Alan Sked and Chris Cook, *Post-War Britain: A Political History, 1945–1992*, (4th edn) Penguin, 1993, p. 550.
18 Thatcher, *The Downing Street Years*, p. 855.
19 Carol Thatcher, *Below the Parapet*, p. 266.
20 Thatcher, *The Downing Street Years*, p. 856.
21 Ibid.
22 Baker, *The Turbulent Years*, pp. 409–410.
23 MTF: Speaking to her cabinet, 22 November 1990.

24 Parkinson, *Right at the Centre*, p. 4.
25 Thatcher, *The Downing Street Years*, p. 858.
26 Hansard, HC Deb 22 November 1990.
27 Thatcher, *The Downing Street Years*, p. 859.
28 John Morley, The *Life of William Ewart Gladstone*, 3 vols, Macmillan, 1903, p. 357.
29 Hansard, HC Deb 22 November 1990.
30 Ibid.
31 Ibid.
32 Ibid.
33 Ibid.
34 Ibid.
35 Ibid.
36 *Daily Mail*, 23 November 1990.
37 Wyatt, *Journals*, Vol. 2, 23 November 1990, pp. 401–402.
38 Baker, *The Turbulent Years*, p. 395.
39 *The Times*, 28 November 1990.
40 Carol Thatcher, *Below the Parapet*, p. 272.
41 Ibid., p. 271.
42 MTF: Speech to Conservative Central Office, 26 November 1990.
43 Millar, *A View from the Wings*, p. 362.
44 Hansard, HC Deb 27 November 1990.
45 Major, *The Autobiography*, p. 199.
46 Penny Junor, *John Major: From Brixton to Downing Street*, Penguin, 1996, p. 205.
47 Major, *The Autobiography*, p. 199.
48 MTF: Remarks departing Downing Street, 28 November 1990.
49 Enoch Powell, *Third Way*, October 2006.

38 THE AGONY AFTER THE FALL

1 Interview with Denis Oliver, BBC Radio 4, 11 April 2013.
2 Brenda Maddox, *Maggie: The First Lady*, Hodder & Stoughton, 2003, p. 219.
3 AC: Interview with Lord Butler.
4 AC: Peter Morrison to the author, January 1991.
5 Ibid.: Conversation with Margaret Thatcher, January 1991.
6 Margaret Orth, 'Maggie's Big Problem', *Vanity Fair*, June 1991.
7 BBC Radio 4, 10 April 1913.
8 Aitken, *Heroes and Contemporaries*, p. 147.

9   AC: Private information.

10   AC: Interview with Julian Seymour.

11   AC: Interview with Lord Butler.

12   Ibid.

13   Ibid.

14   Moore, *Margaret Thatcher, Vol. 1.*, p. xii.

15   AC: Author's party for Sir Teddy Taylor, 26 November 1991.

16   Hansard, HC Deb 26 June 1991.

17   AC: Interview with Sir Richard Shepherd.

18   Margaret Thatcher interview, ITN, 22 November 1991.

19   AC: Interview with Sir John Major.

20   AC: Conversation with Margaret Thatcher, December 1991.

21   *The Times*, 26 November 1992.

22   AC: Interview with Sir John Major.

23   AC: Interview with Alan Duncan MP.

39 SNAPSHOTS OF HER RETIREMENT YEARS

1   Hansard, House of Lords, 14 July 1993, vol. 548, cols. 281–6.

2   Gospel of St. Matthew, chapter 13, verse 32.

3   Speech in Fulton, Missouri, 9 March 1996.

4   AC: Conversation with Margaret Thatcher, June 1992.

5   Ibid.

6   Ibid.

7   AC: Lunch at Sandwich Bay, June 1996.

8   Ibid: Interview with Sir Richard Shepherd.

9   Ibid: Interview with Bill Cash.

10   Aitken, *Heroes and Contemporaries*, pp. 149–151.

11   AC: Denis Thatcher, Rannoch, 16 August 1996.

12   Ibid: Malcolm Pearson, Rannoch, 17 August 1996.

13   Ibid: Denis Thatcher, Rannoch, 16 August 1996.

14   Ibid. Margaret Thatcher, Rannoch, 18 August 1996. See also *Sunday Telegraph*, 14 April 2013.

15   AC: Denis Thatcher, Rannoch, 16 August 1996.

16   Ibid: Jonathan Aitken (unpublished) diary, 20 August 1996.

17   MTF: Lady Thatcher, remarks on the doorstep of 10 Downing Street, 26 September 1995.

18   AC: Conversation with Michael Alison.

19   Ibid.

20 Ibid: Interview with The Rev Dick Whittington.
21 Ibid.
22 Ibid.

EPIOLGUE

1 Carol Thatcher, *A Swim-on Part in the Goldfish Bowl*, Headline Review, 2008, p. 25.
2 Ibid., p. 260.
3 AC: Conversation with Carol Thatcher, June 2000.
4 *The Times*, 11 April 2013.

Index